I0817979

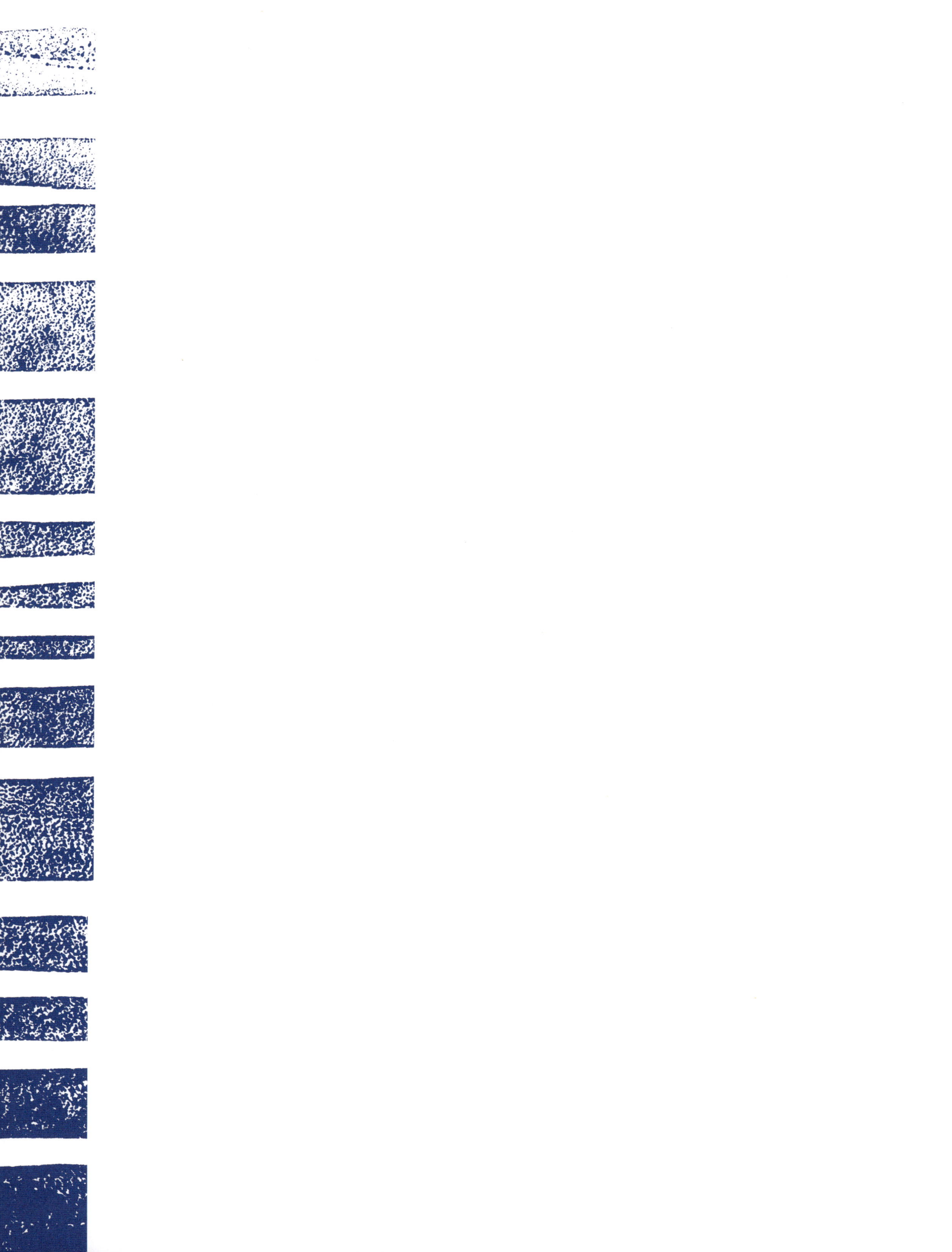

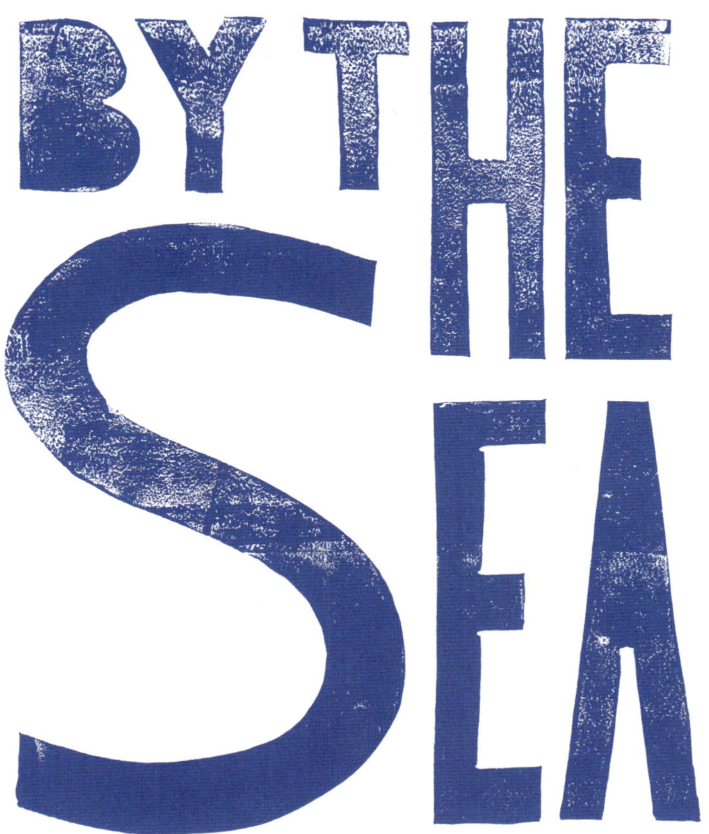
BY THE SEA

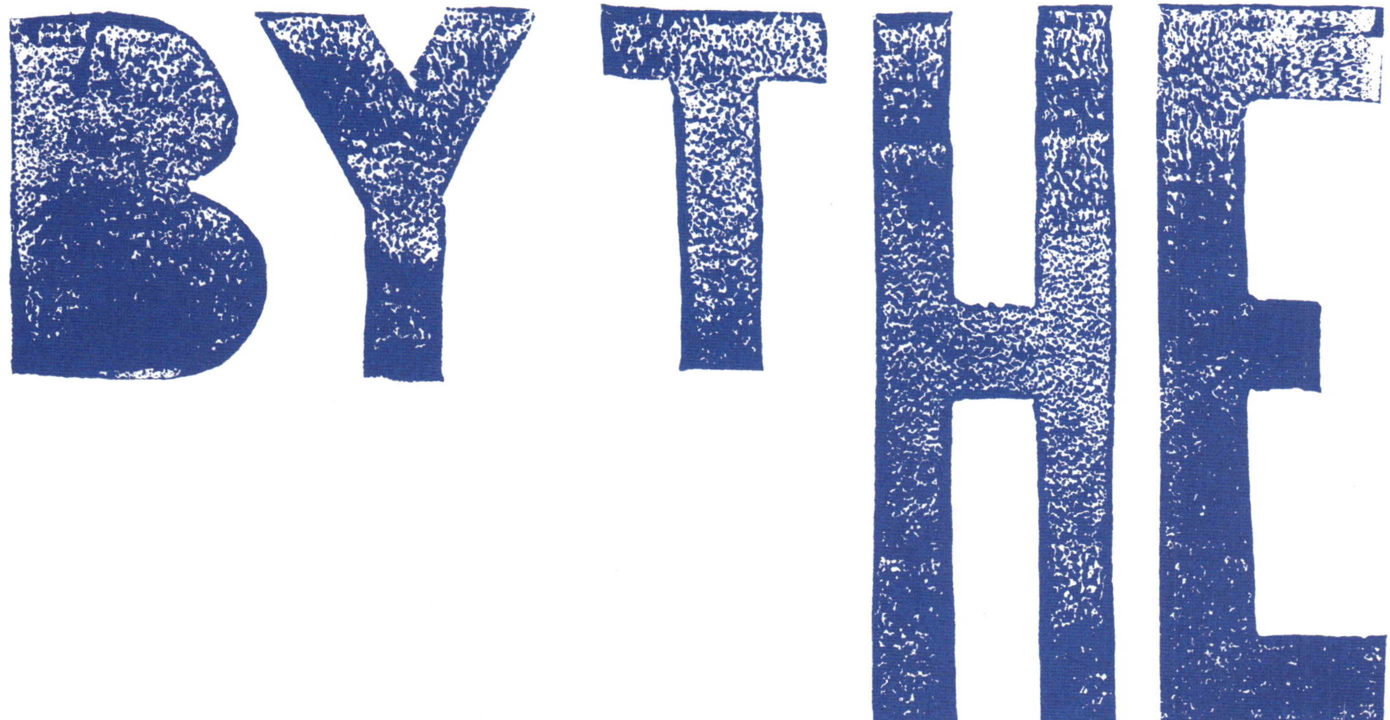
BY THE

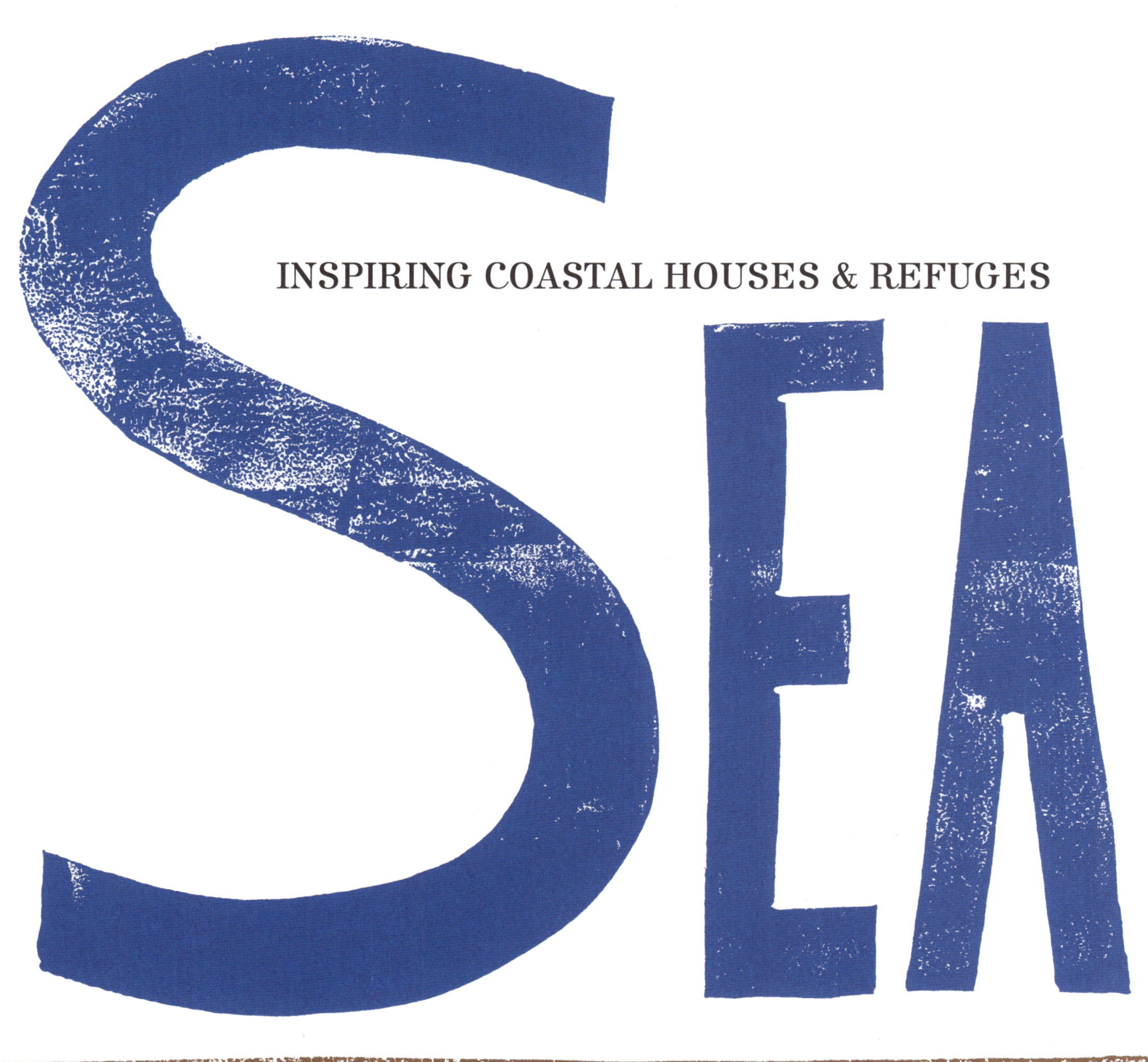

SEA

INSPIRING COASTAL HOUSES & REFUGES

MIRJAM BLEEKER & FRANK VISSER

LUSTER

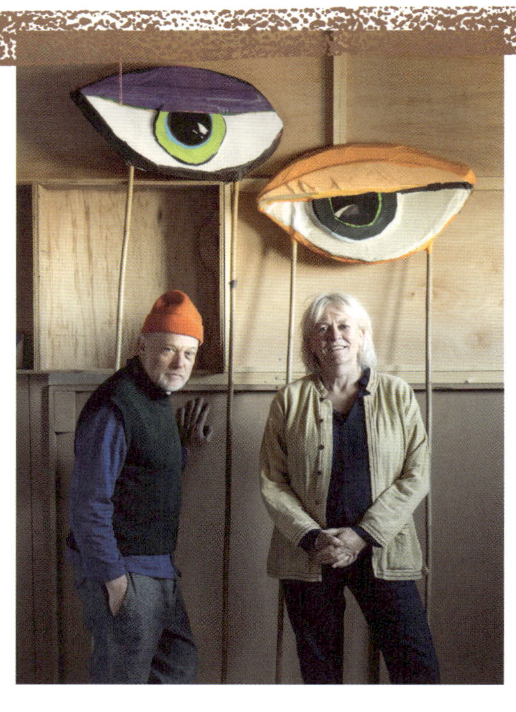

THE STORY

Mirjam Bleeker --- Frank Visser

About thirty years ago, Frank Visser and Mirjam Bleeker's shared desire for freedom and adventure led them to the colourful island of Curaçao, where they captured inspiring homes and places on film. This marked the start of a long-standing collaboration and friendship, culminating in countless interior and travel features, which have since been published worldwide in leading magazines. In 2014, they wrote their first book together, 'At the Ocean', later followed by 'Close to Nature' and 'South Africa, A Roadtrip'.

What sets Mirjam and Frank's work apart from others is how it originated: not on commission, but on their own initiative. When they end up somewhere, it is because they are curious to explore this place. When they choose to stay, it is because they feel inspired and creative there. That's their secret, and it's palpable and visible in everything they have done to date. Rather than being spectators who solely come to record something, Mirjam and Frank seek to connect with a place and with the people who live there. In their features, they reveal their own personalities, as well as those of the people whose houses they photograph. Their personal input is crucial to their photos, as is the sense of freedom they both value so highly.

On the one hand, little has changed since that first trip to Curaçao: Mirjam and Frank still travel freely, and they still find it important to leave room for chance when venturing out to work on travel and interior features. On the other hand, they and their work have of course evolved. Over the years, Frank has started to create more himself. Increasingly, he packs his suitcase with textiles, colours and objects from his studio in the Netherlands, bringing them with him to the next destination in order to let his creativity flow on location and to make art in dialogue with the environment. He is especially inspired by places along the coast: how the water makes the light vibrate, the power of the waves, and the vast horizon.

For Mirjam, travelling has taken on another, deeper dimension since the arrival of her son Boaz. She now wants to share the places she cherishes with her family. Boaz came along to Lamu and Uruguay, when Mirjam went there to take the photos featured in this book. While there may be a little less margin for adventure, exploring new places as a family paves the way for even more connection. At any rate, Mirjam has already instilled her love for life by the sea in the next generation.

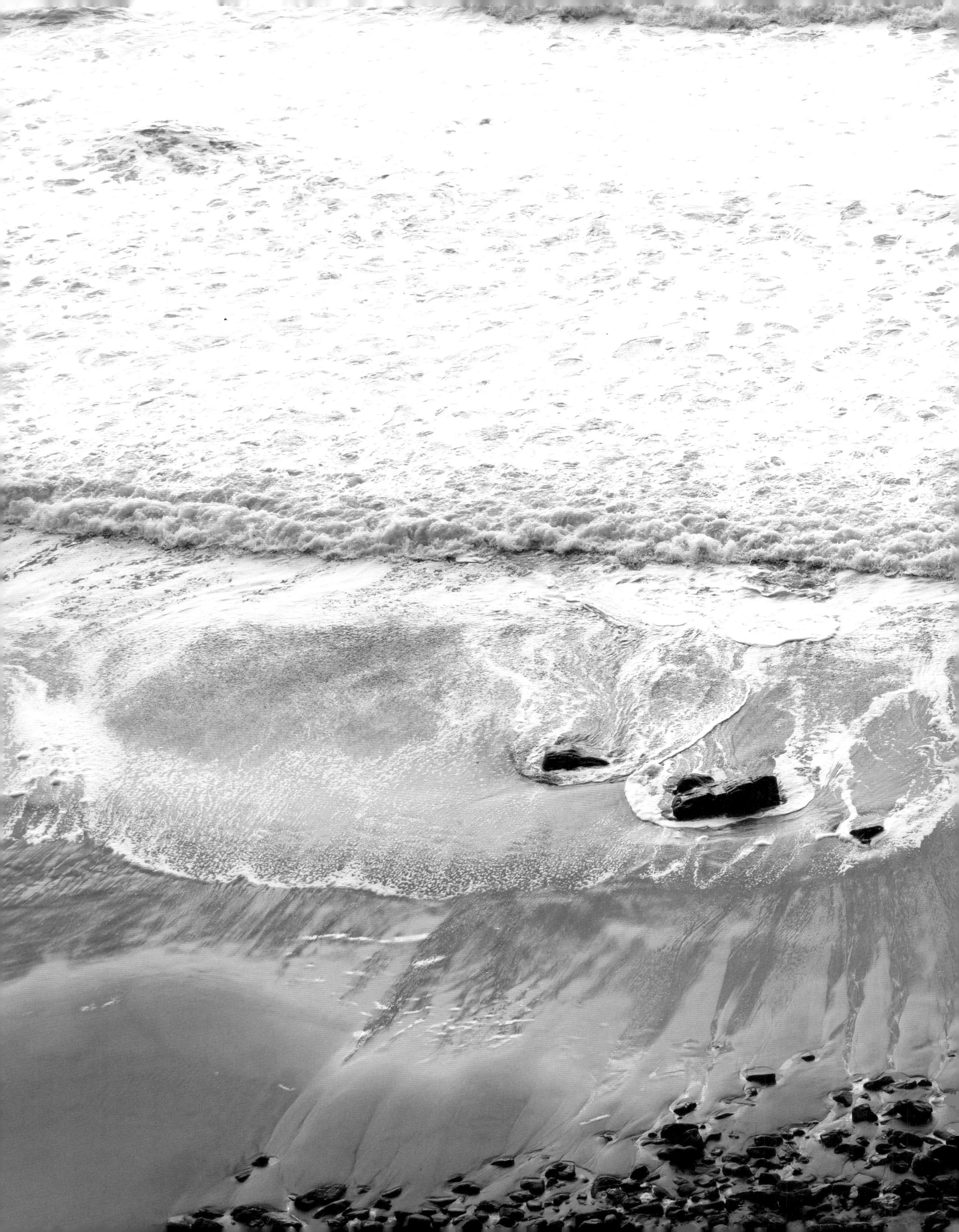

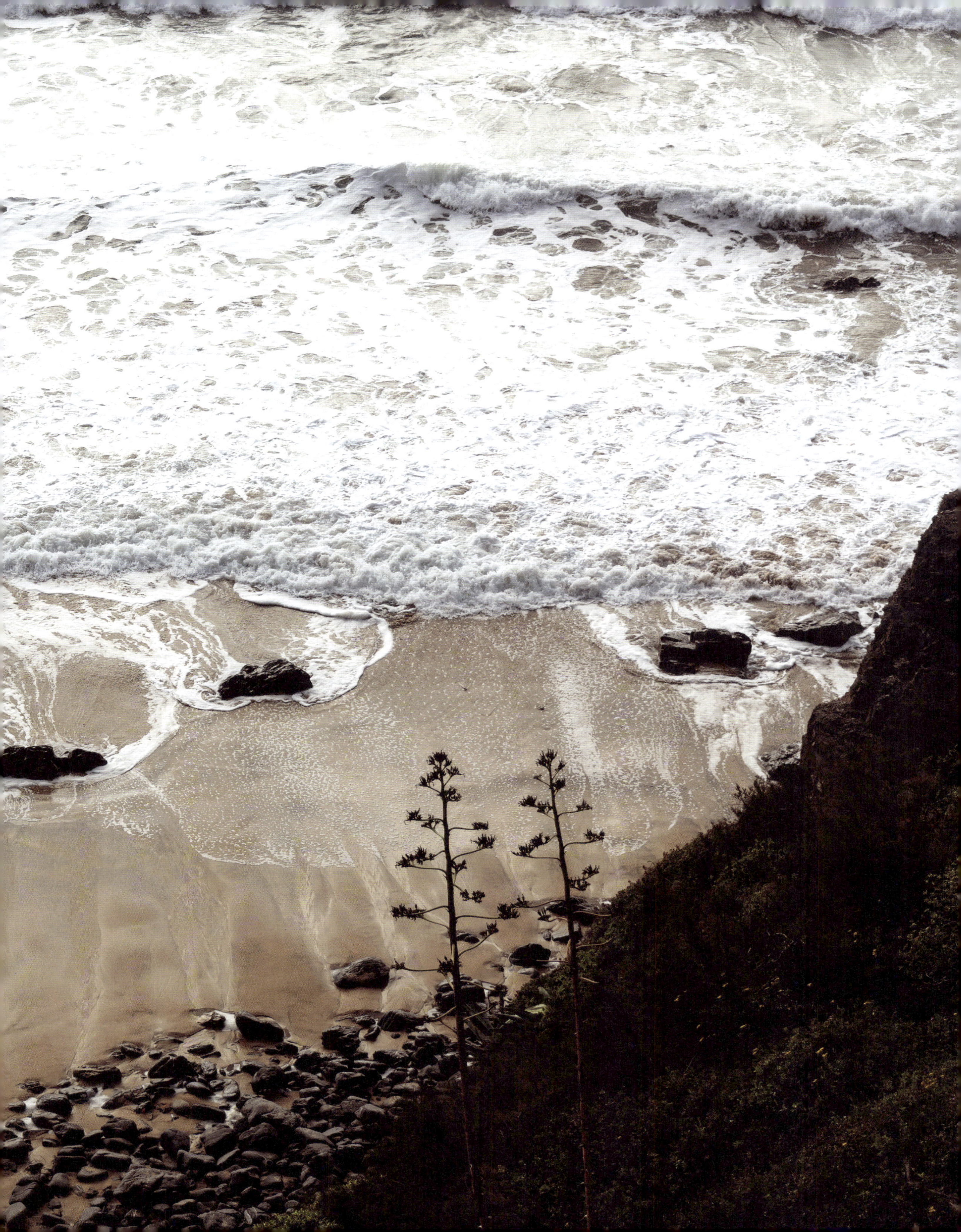

MALLORCA

Balearic Islands
Spain

Behind the Mediterranean Sea coast,
in unspoilt rural Mallorca, in the south of the island, lies the country estate of the family of Spanish architect Mariana de Delás. Her family has owned this land for over five hundred years, which was formerly cultivated by farmers and shepherds. In the 1920s, Mariana's great-grandfather built several small cottages and refuges on the site, so these men would have a place to sleep, seek shelter and store their equipment.

A few years ago, one of these traditional stone shelters became the favourite refuge of Mariana and her young family. Mariana runs her architectural firm from Madrid, Barcelona and Mallorca. The combination of the excitement of fast-paced city life and the peace and quiet of the countryside is something she has known all her life, and that's the way she likes it.

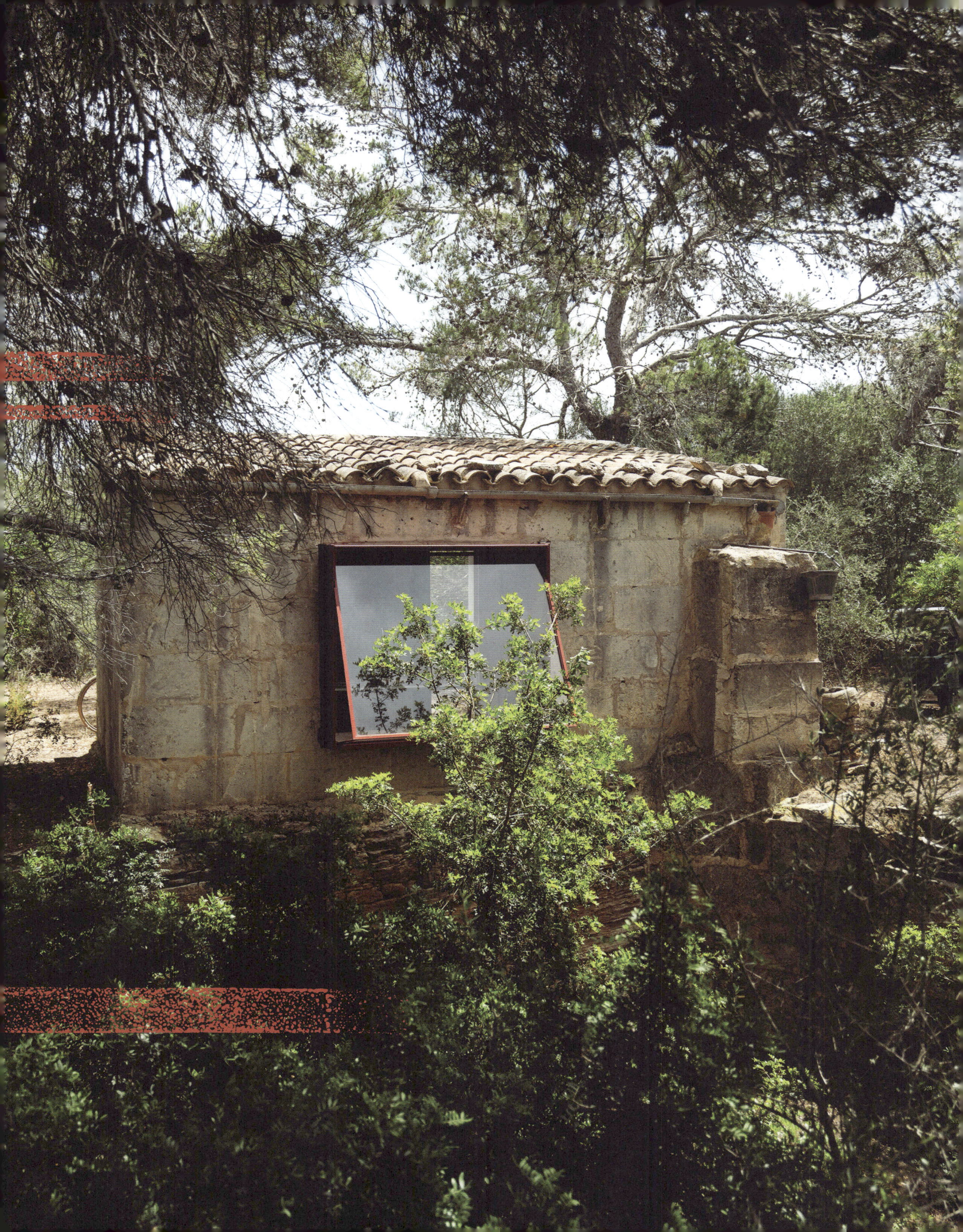

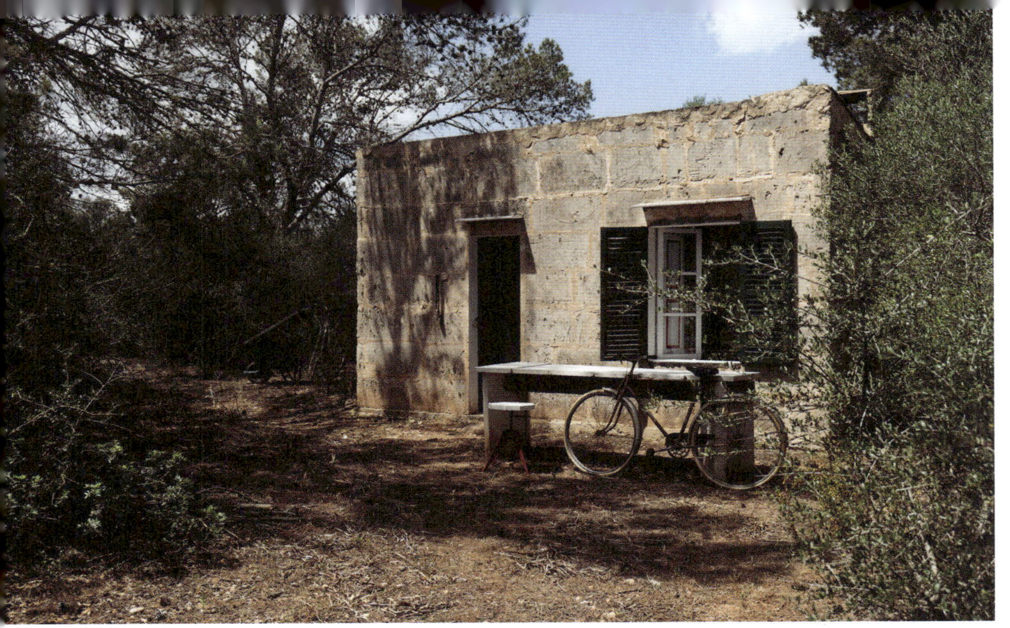

Mariana has largely rebuilt and renovated her home base on Mallorca herself, and named it 12 Volt Retreat. The main architectural intervention consists of the addition of a bright red bow window that opens into the old quarry. It frames the landscape, establishing a connection between the interior and the exterior that was missing. It also serves as a seating element inside, generating cross ventilation when open. The custom built-in daybed, benches, tables and stools are made with marés stone, erasing the lines between the inside and outside worlds even more. The bed is upholstered with traditional Ikat Mallorcan textiles, and the art by artists and friends was collected during the years that Mariana and her friends ran a gallery in Madrid.

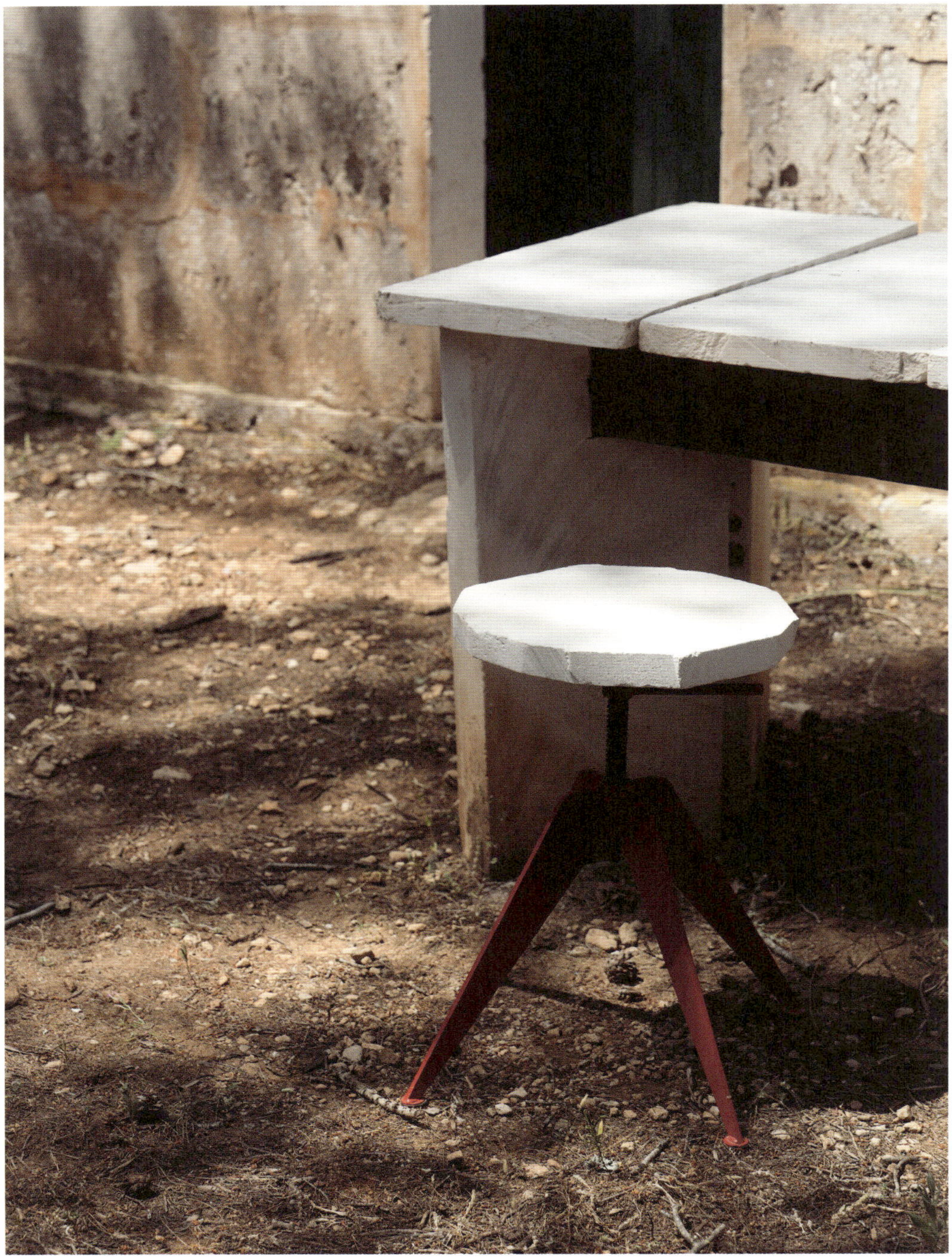

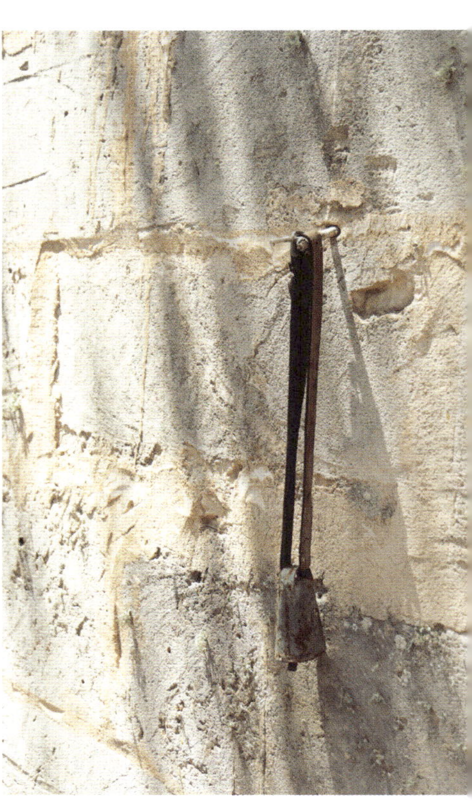

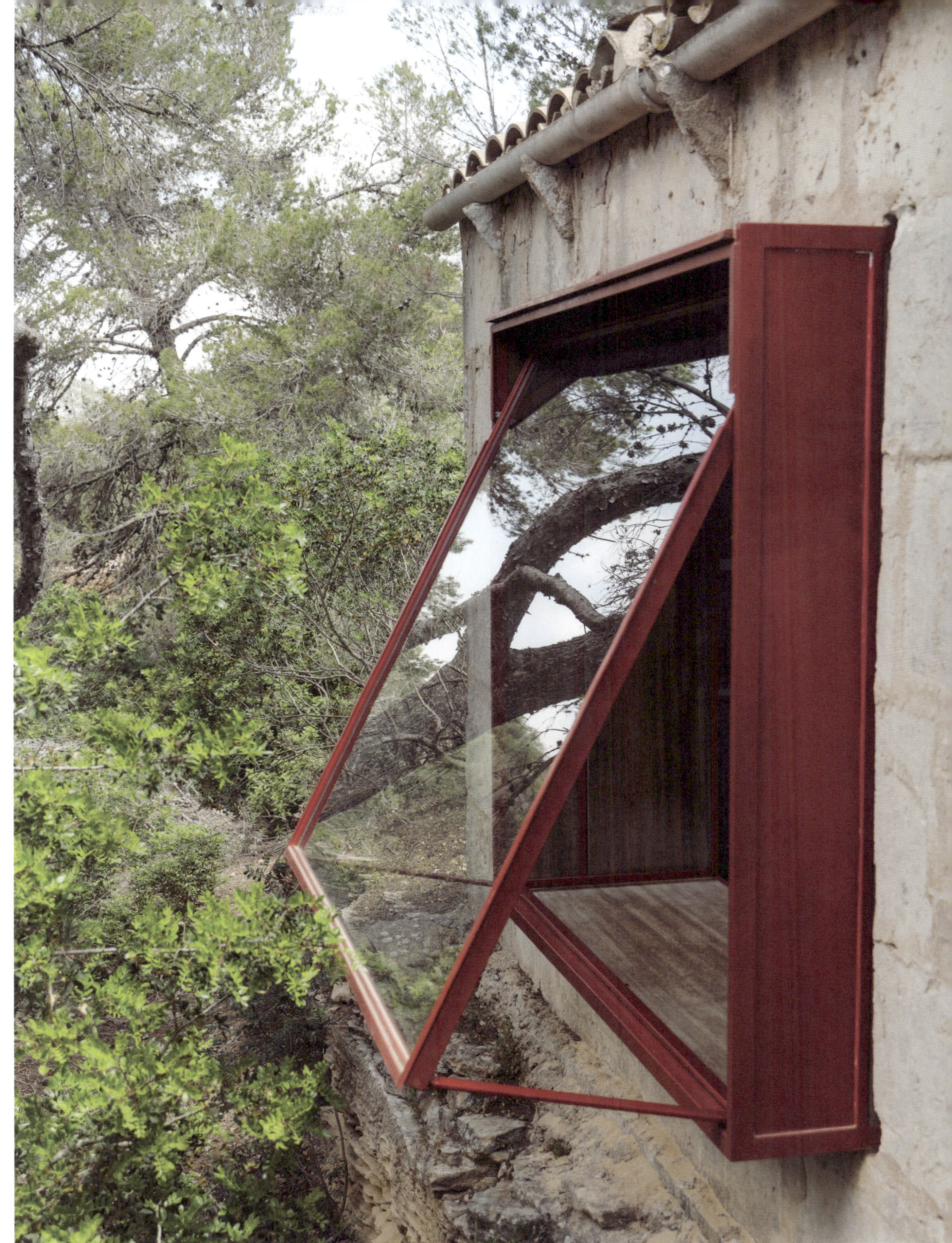

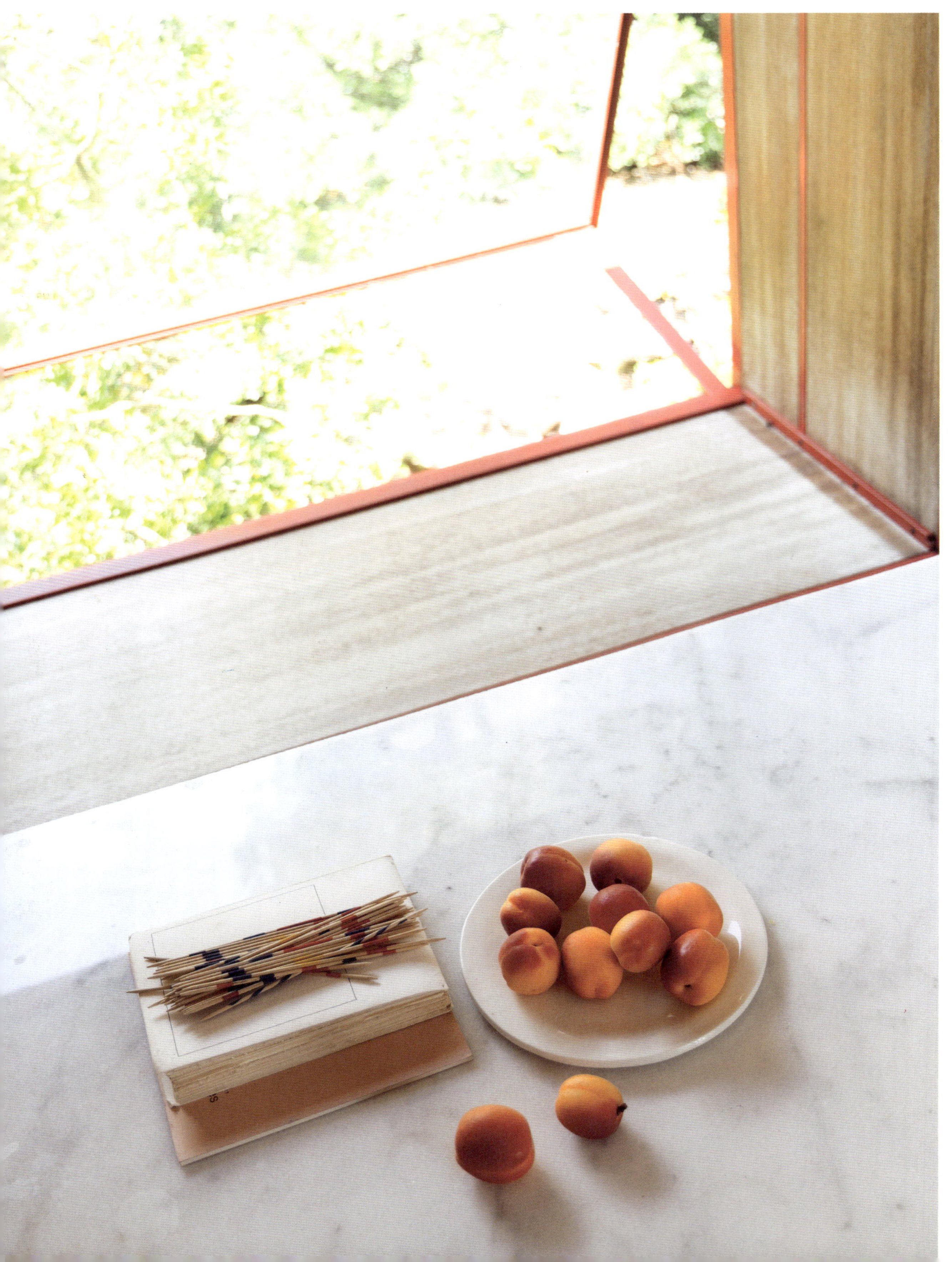

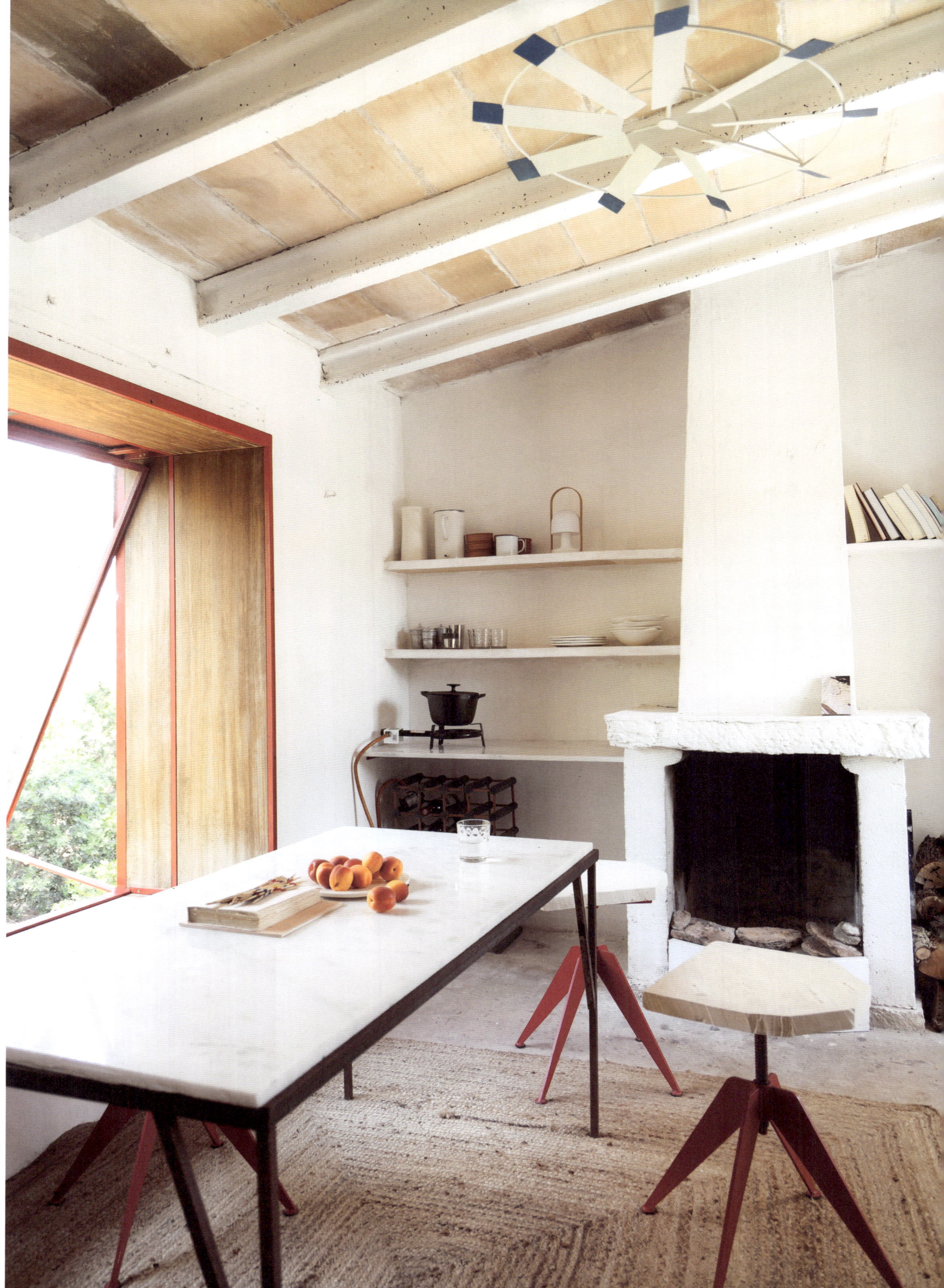

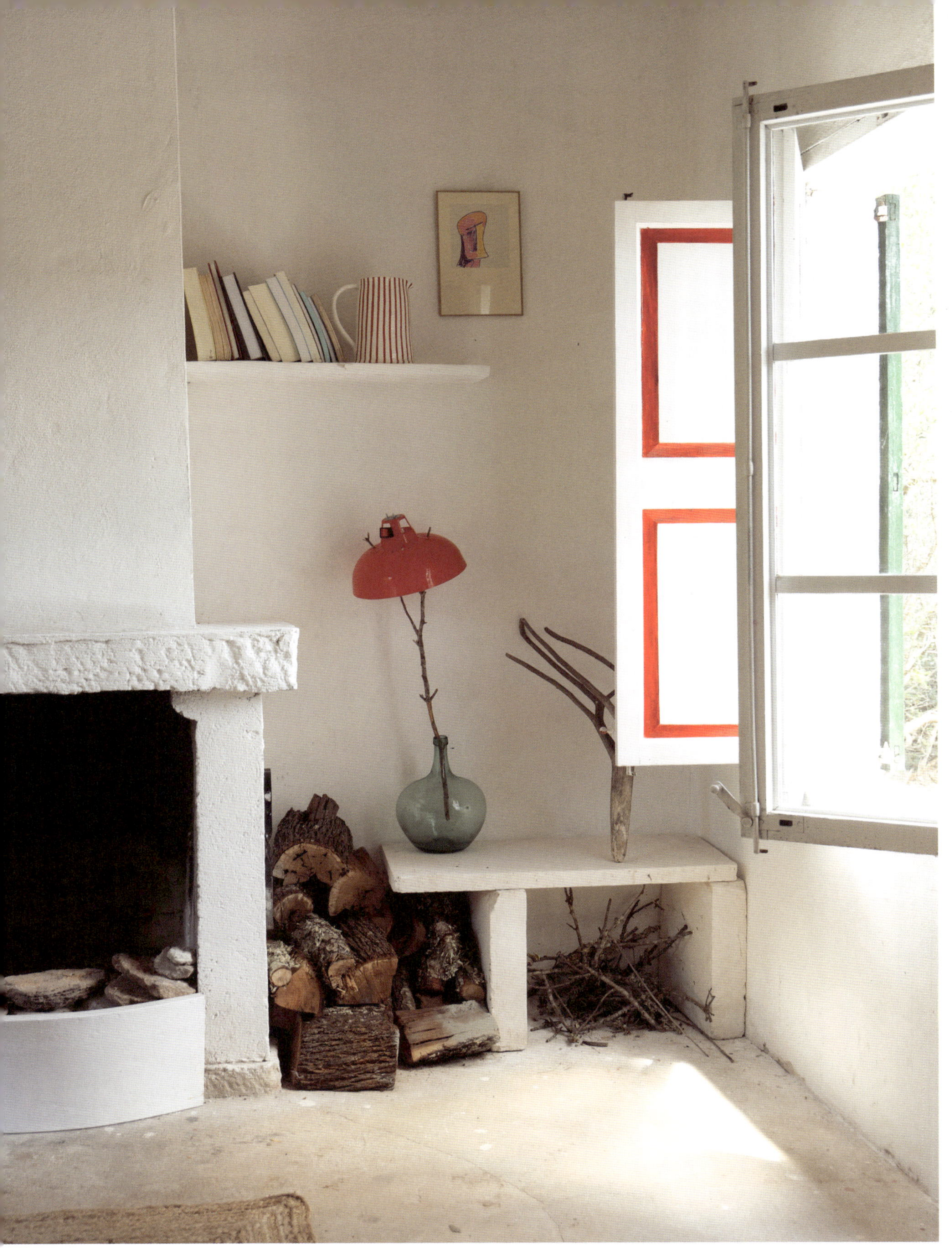

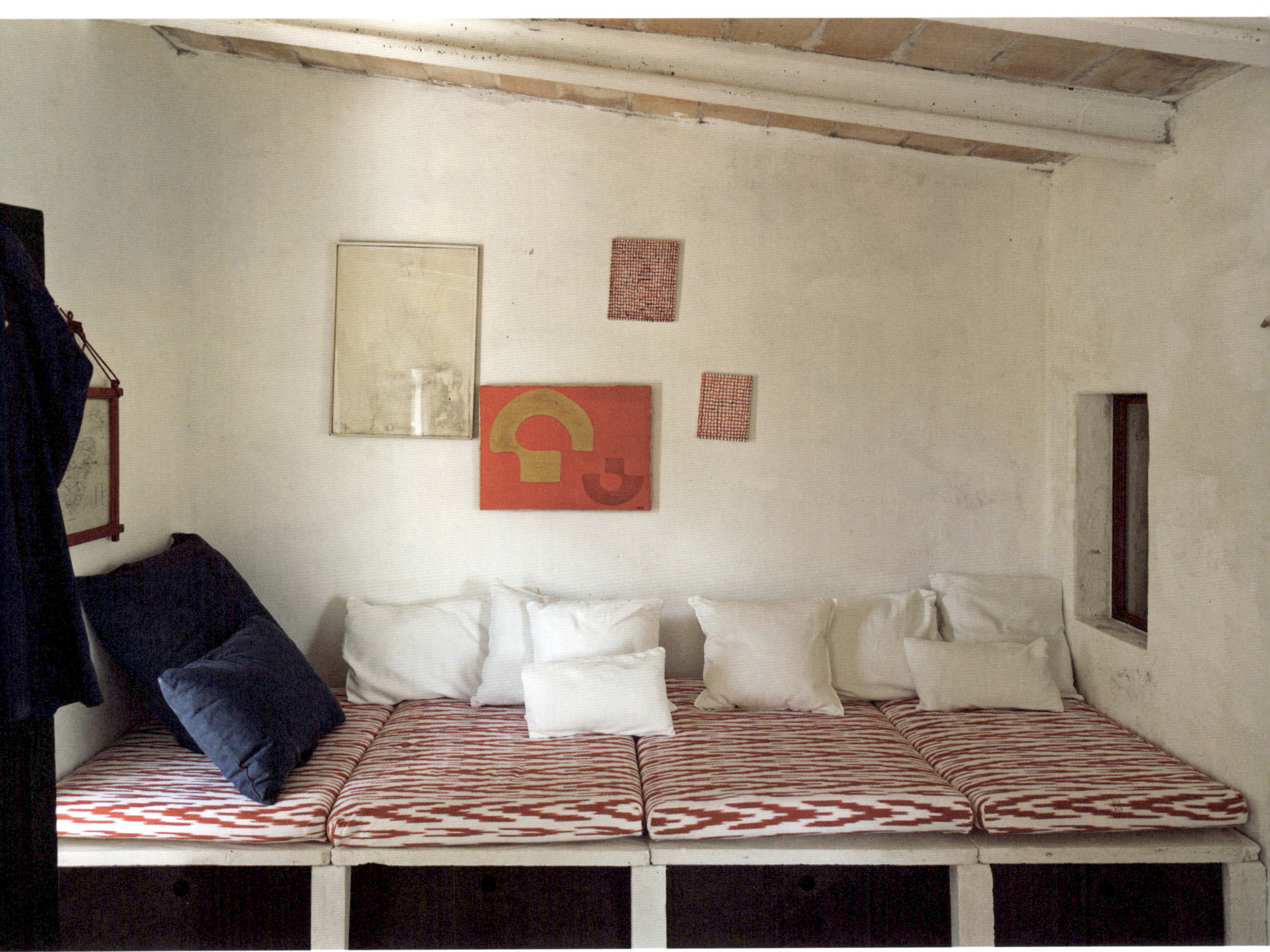

12 Volt Retreat is a pilot project: in the long run, Mariana hopes to give all the abandoned shelters on the family property a new lease of life for use by guests and artists or for workshops in the future. They will become part of a super sustainable, off-the-grid retreat where the emphasis is on organic farming and care for life in and around the sea. The proximity of the water makes this location even more special: as you doze off, you can hear the Aeolian sound of the rigging of the sailboats in the wind in the distance. You feel as if you are being lulled to sleep by the waves during a siesta on a wonderfully peaceful summer's day.

Living off the grid comes with its own challenges, which Mariana has embraced with a mix of curiosity and delight. She likes to experiment with new building techniques and devise new inventions, which may or may not work. The ceiling fan is a prototype inspired by the mills in the area and created by her studio. To compensate for the shortage of sunlight - the shelter sits in pineland - Mariana came up with The Solar Roller. This wheelbarrow with solar panels can be used to roll power banks and rechargeable batteries to a sunny spot where they can charge quickly.

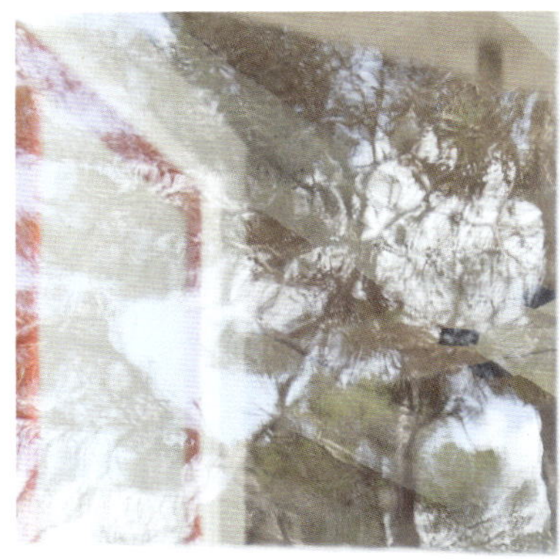

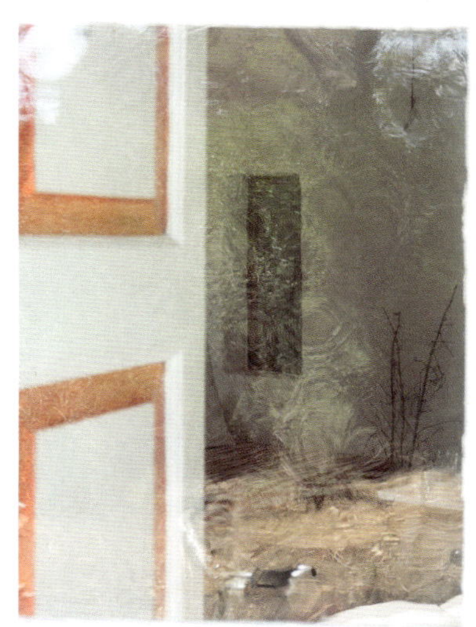

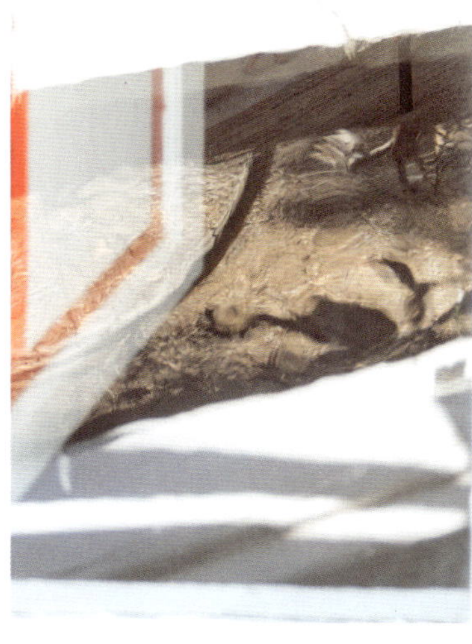

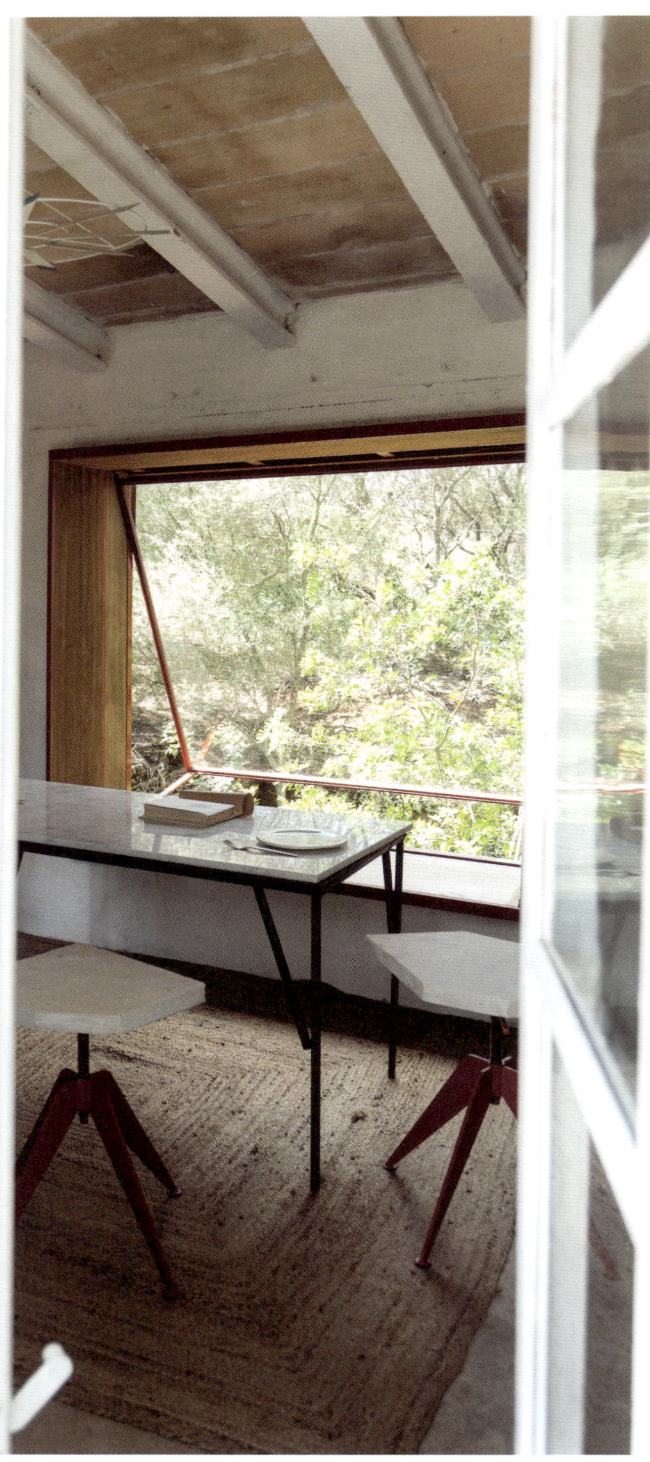

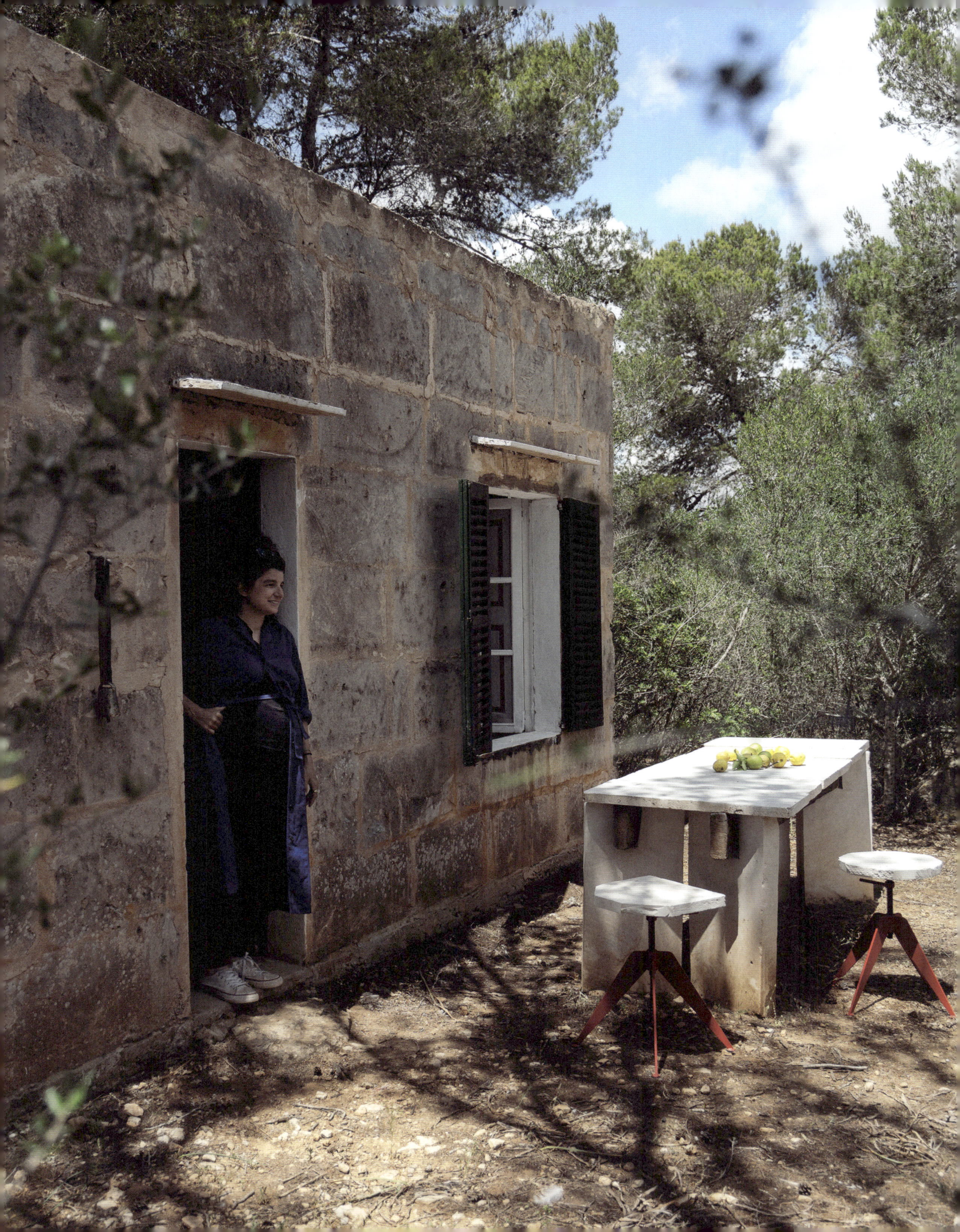

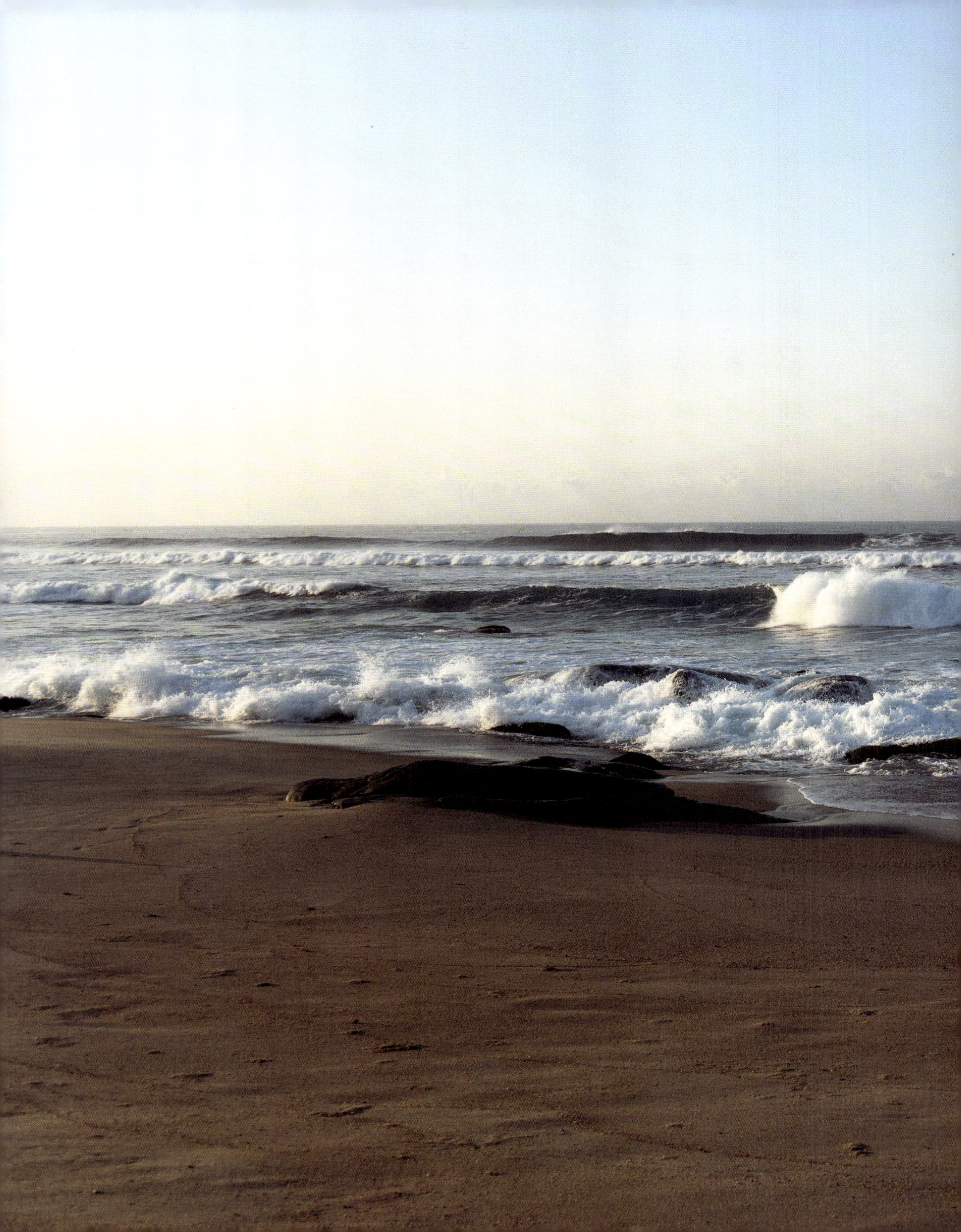

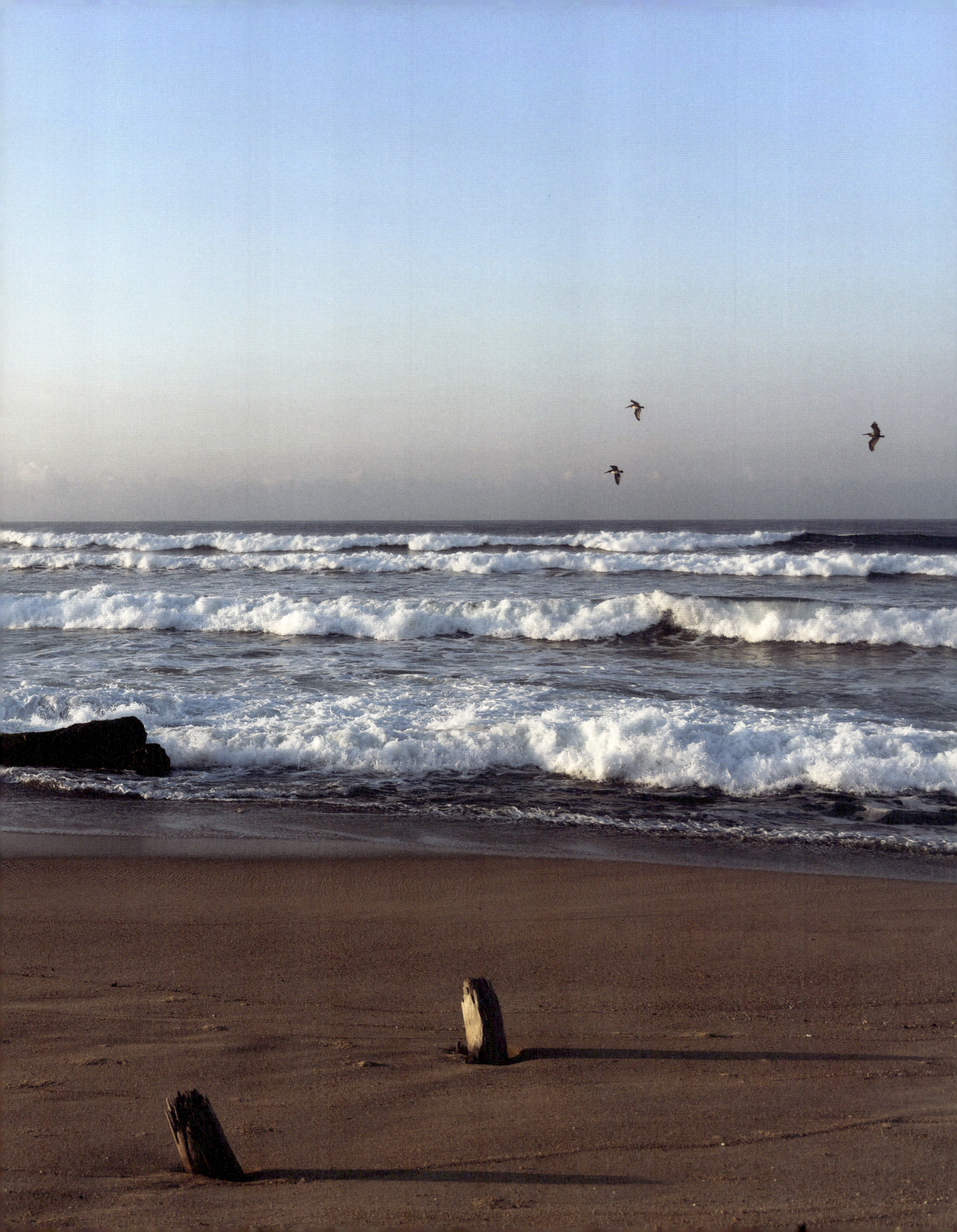

Living close to the Pacific Ocean feels like being in the presence of a powerful force of nature. To Mexican architect Alberto Ventosa, this is both a humbling and invigorating experience. Alberto lives in Mazul, a residential project located near Puerto Escondido, on one of the most paradisiacal beaches of the Pacific Coast in the state of Oaxaca, Mexico. Unlike the Caribbean, this coastline offers a tranquil escape, with vast stretches of empty beaches and the occasional spectacle of whales gracing the waters – a constant reminder of nature's grandeur.

PUERTO ESCONDIDO

Oaxaca
Mexico

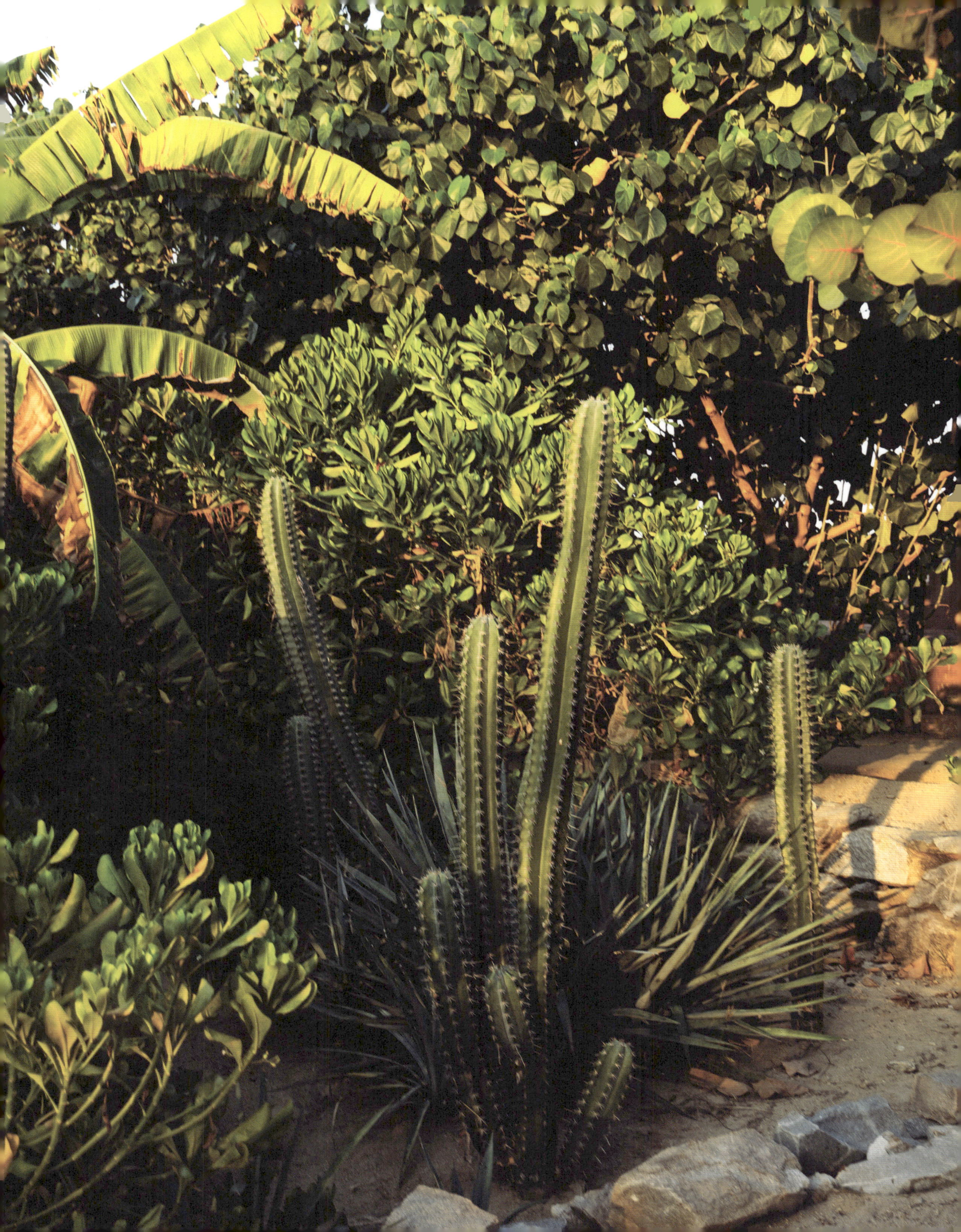

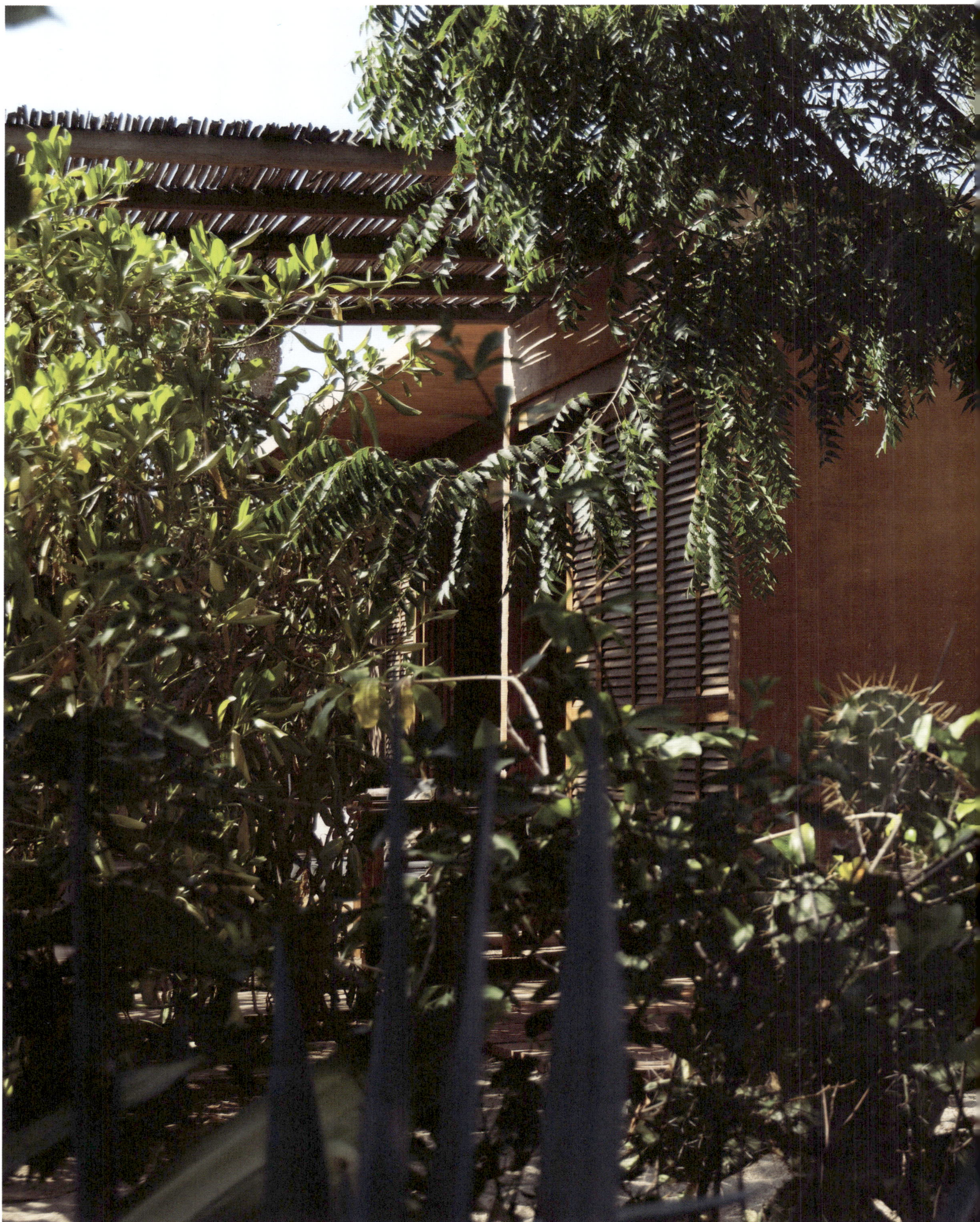

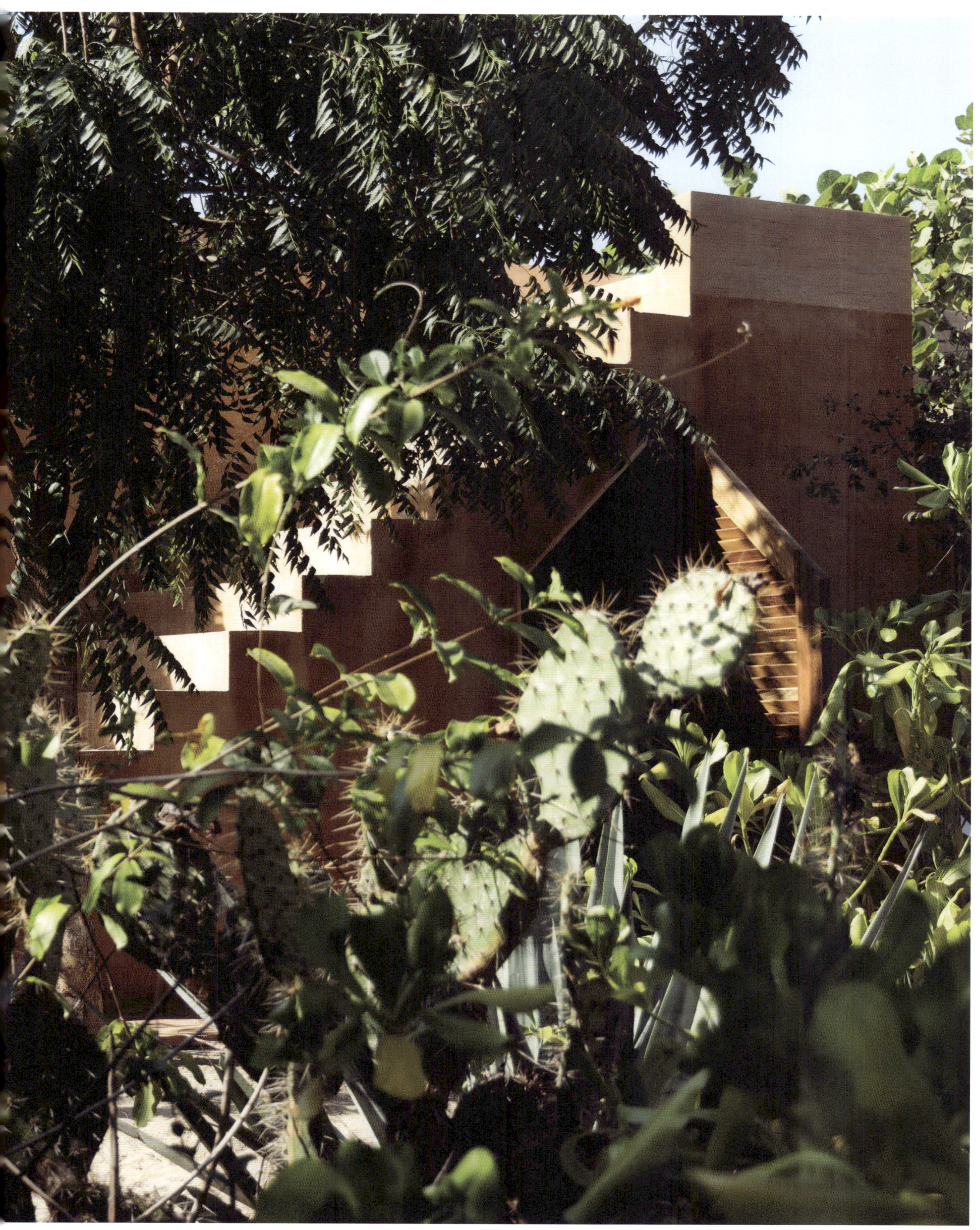

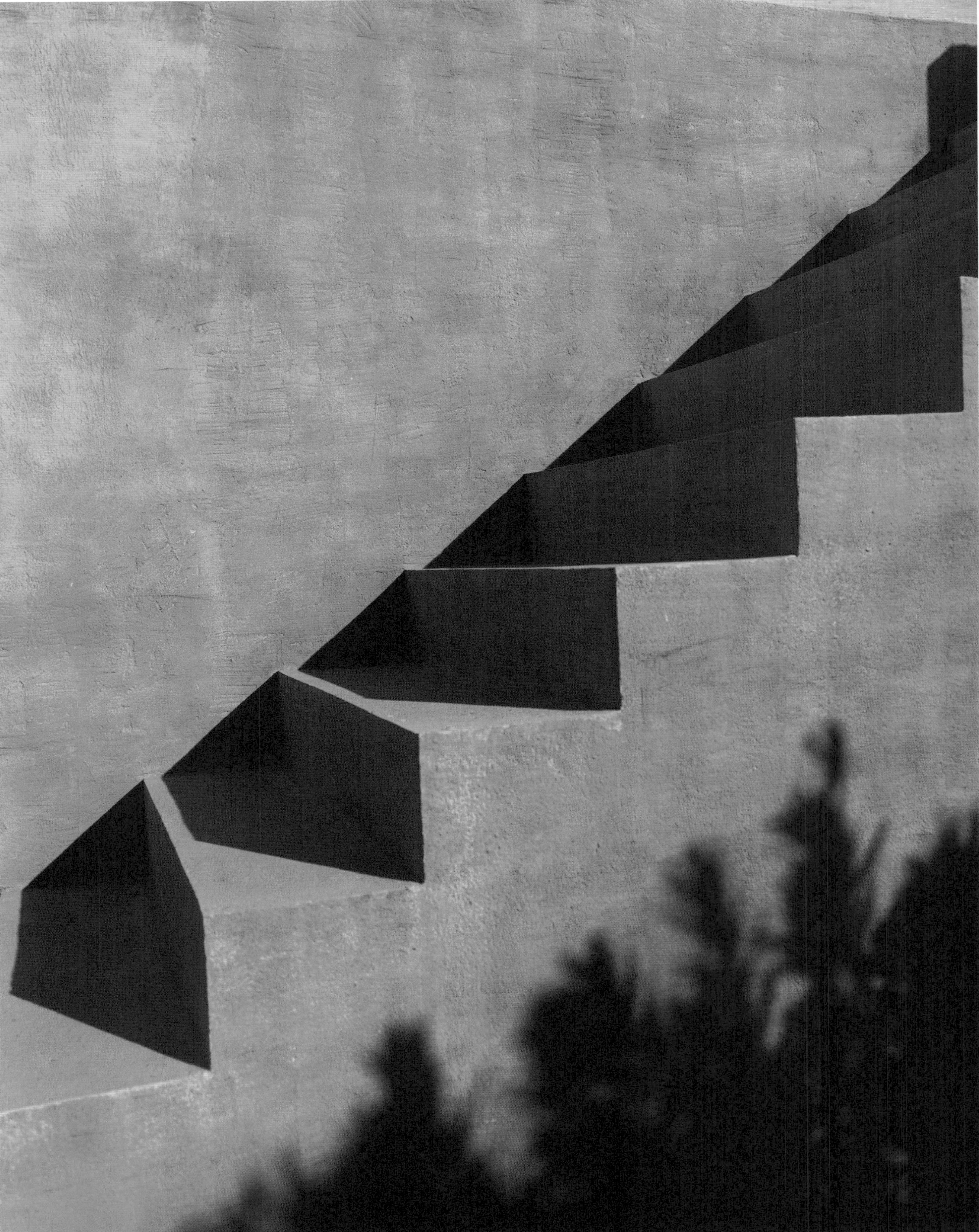

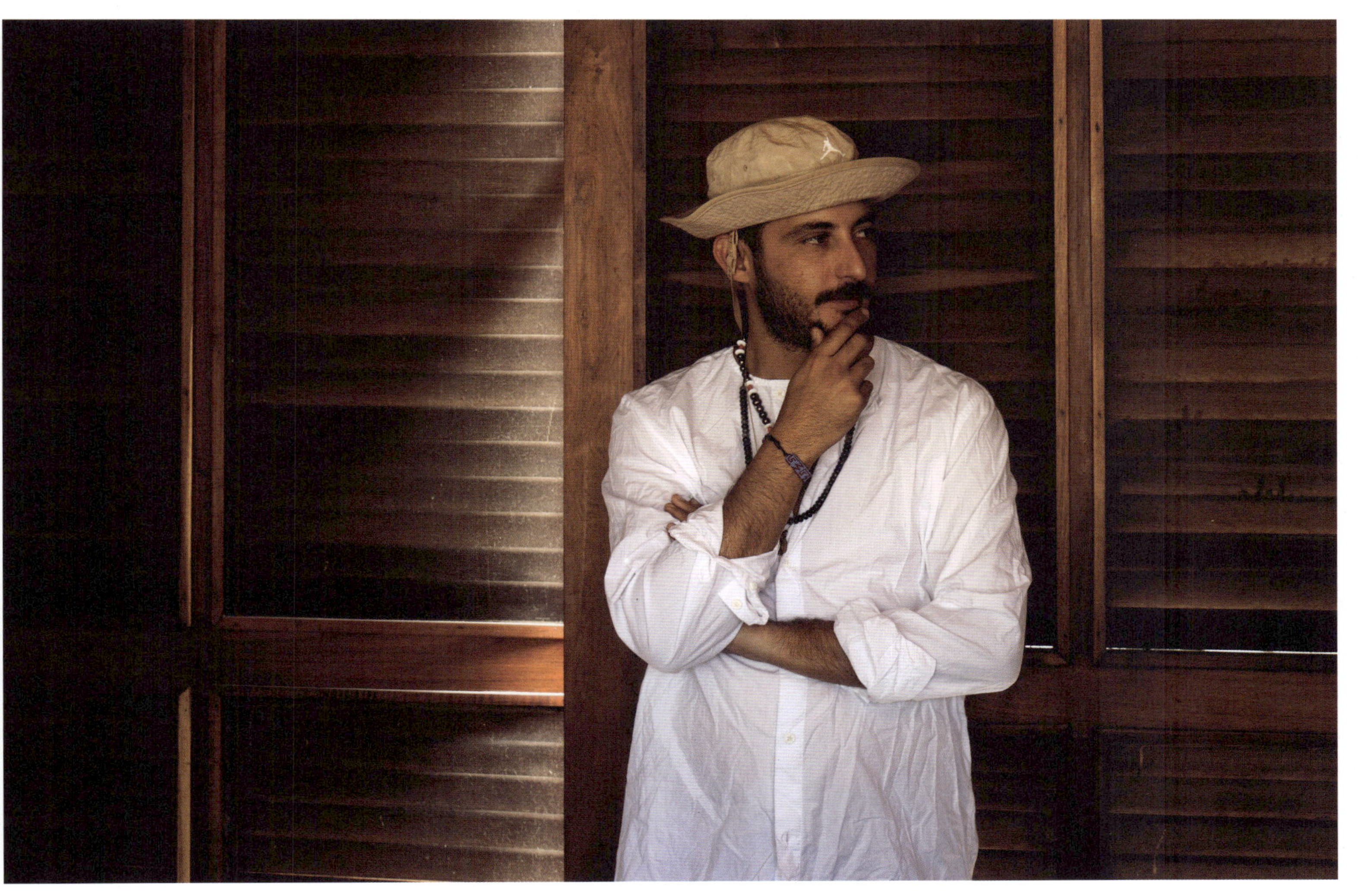

The ocean's rhythm guides Alberto's life. In his free time, he finds joy in activities such as surfing, horseback riding, motorcycling, painting, sculpture, and photography. They allow him to feel a connection with nature, the elements, and the stunning beauty of Mazul's seaside surroundings. Most of the time, he is accompanied by his two loyal dogs, Juju and Nova, who are as much a part of Mazul as the sea itself and are well-known and loved within the community.

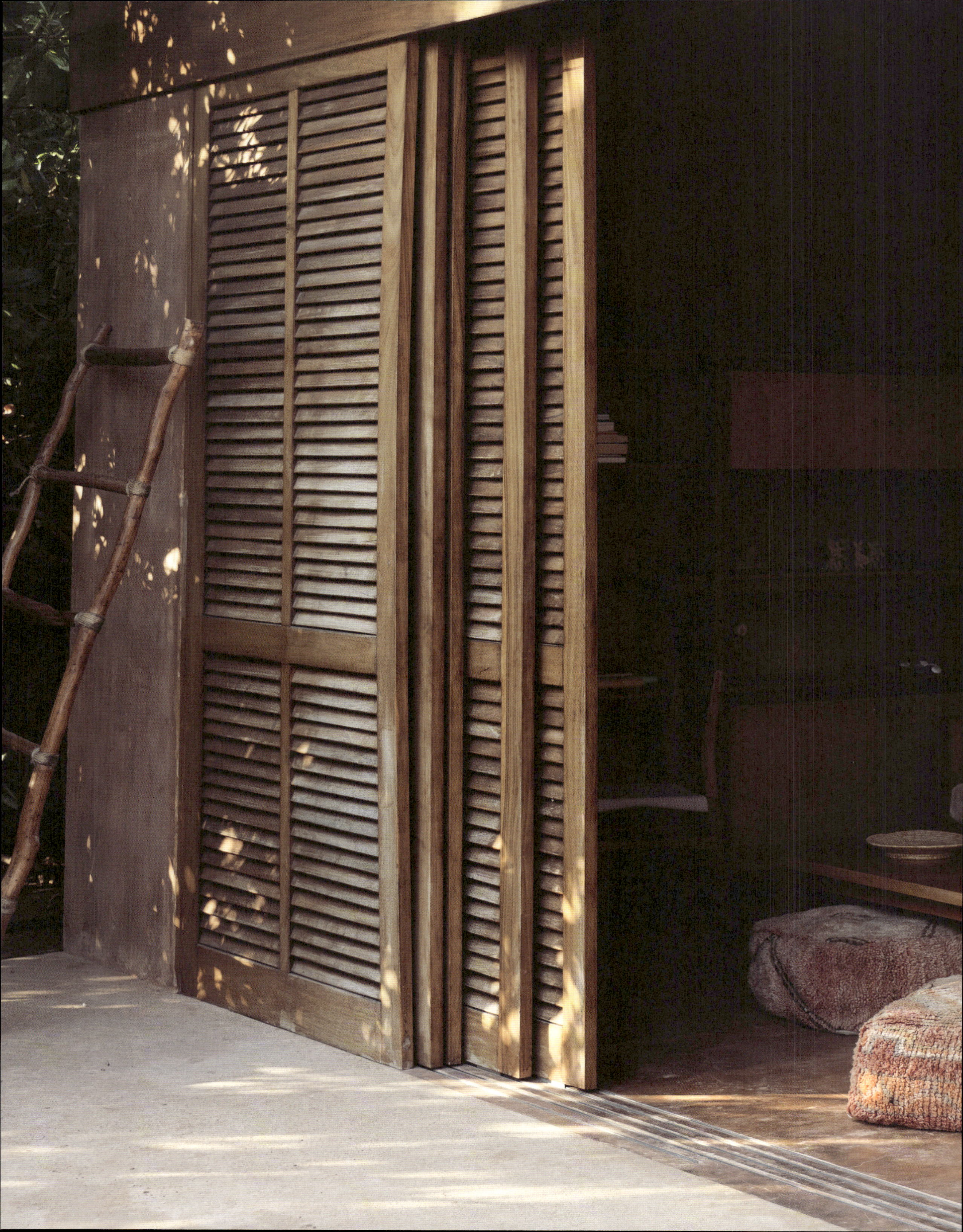

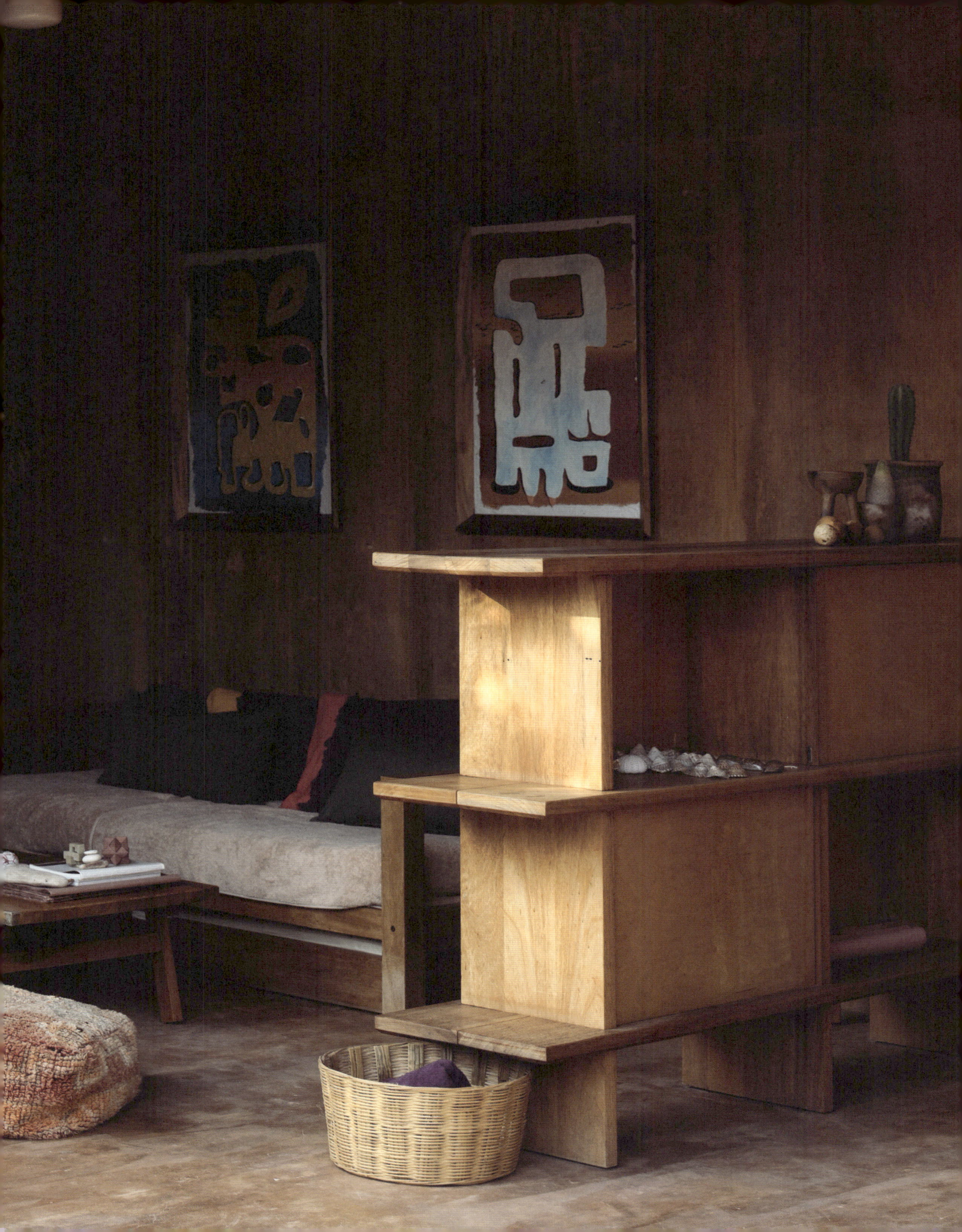

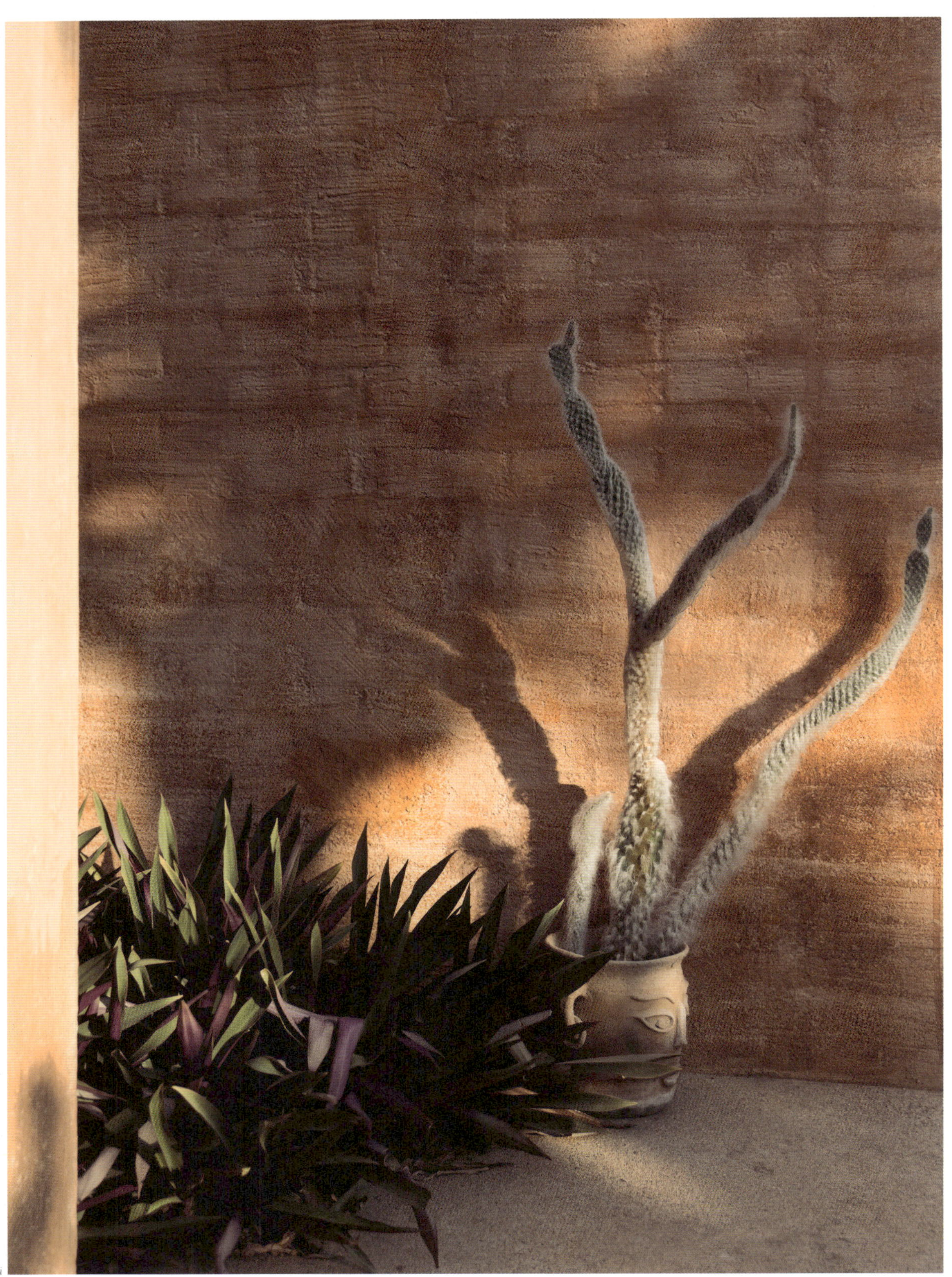

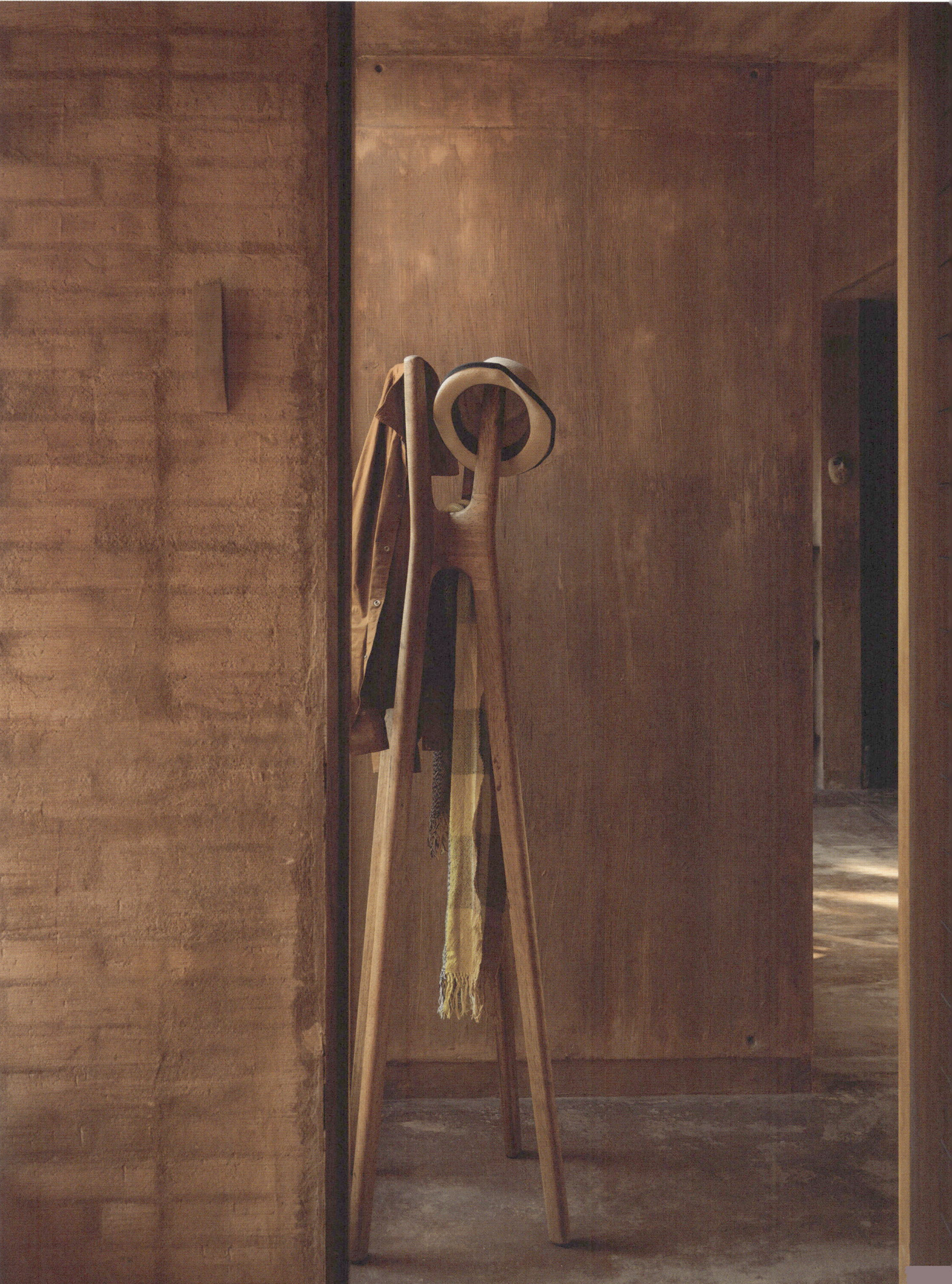

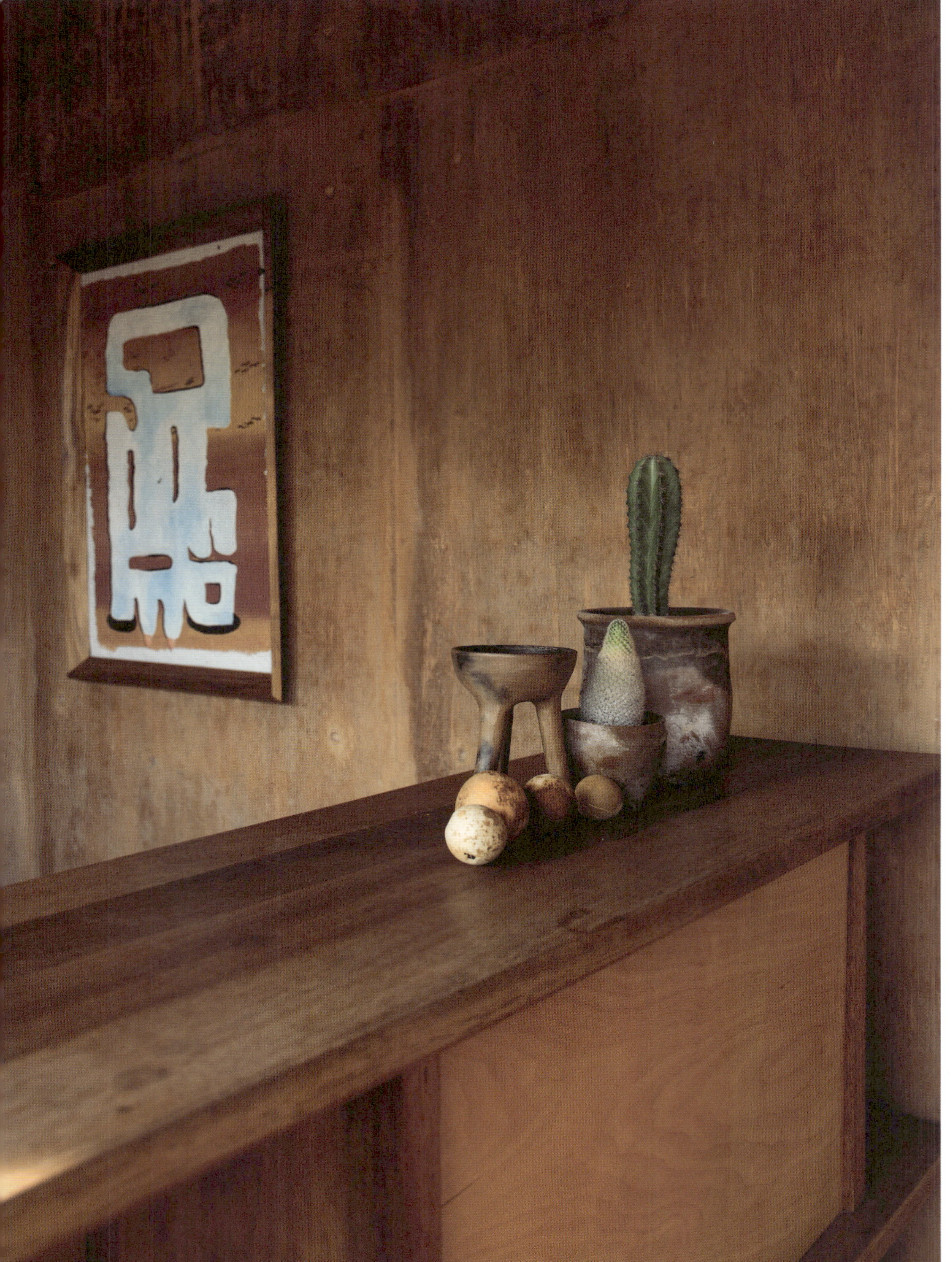

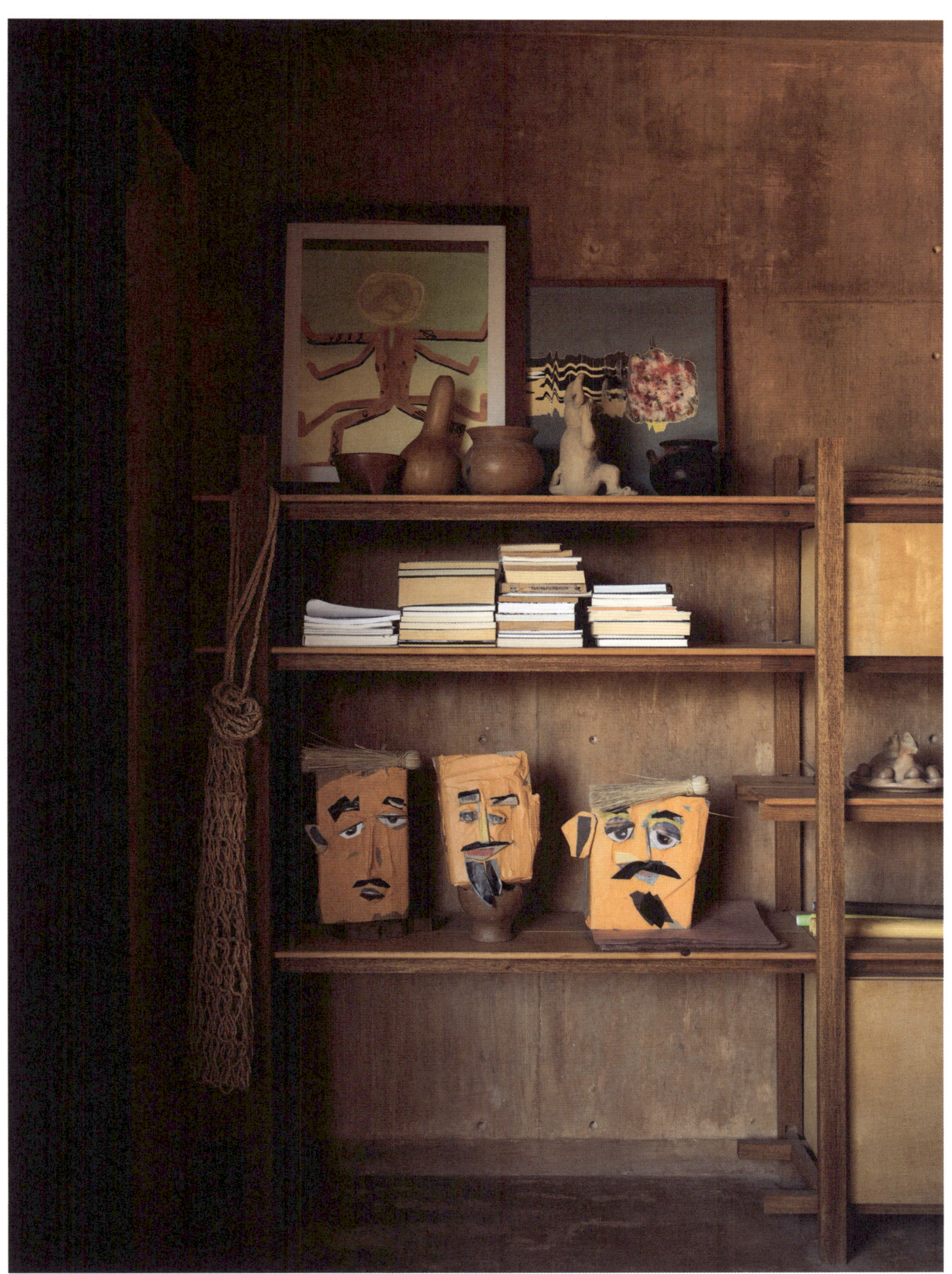

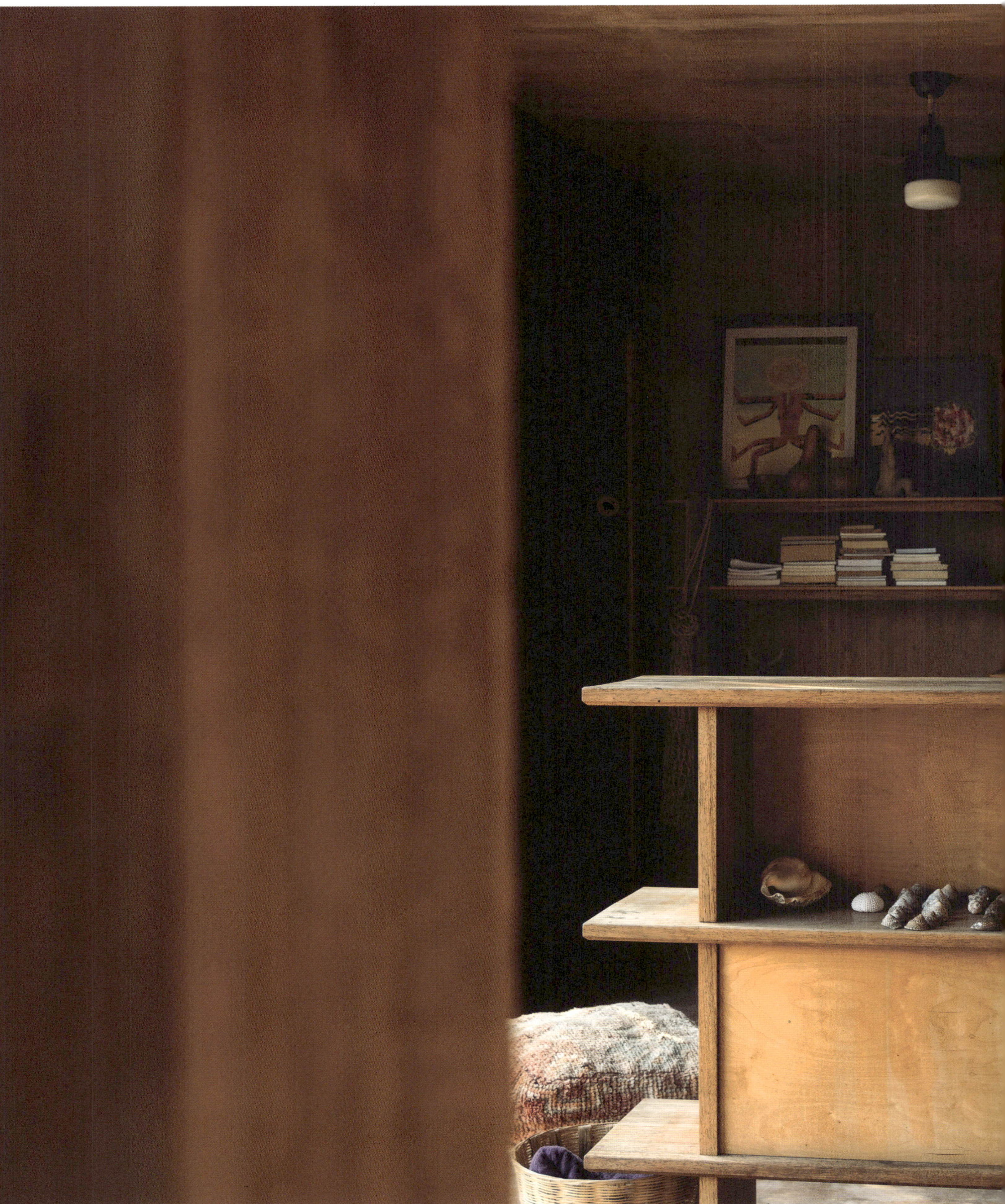

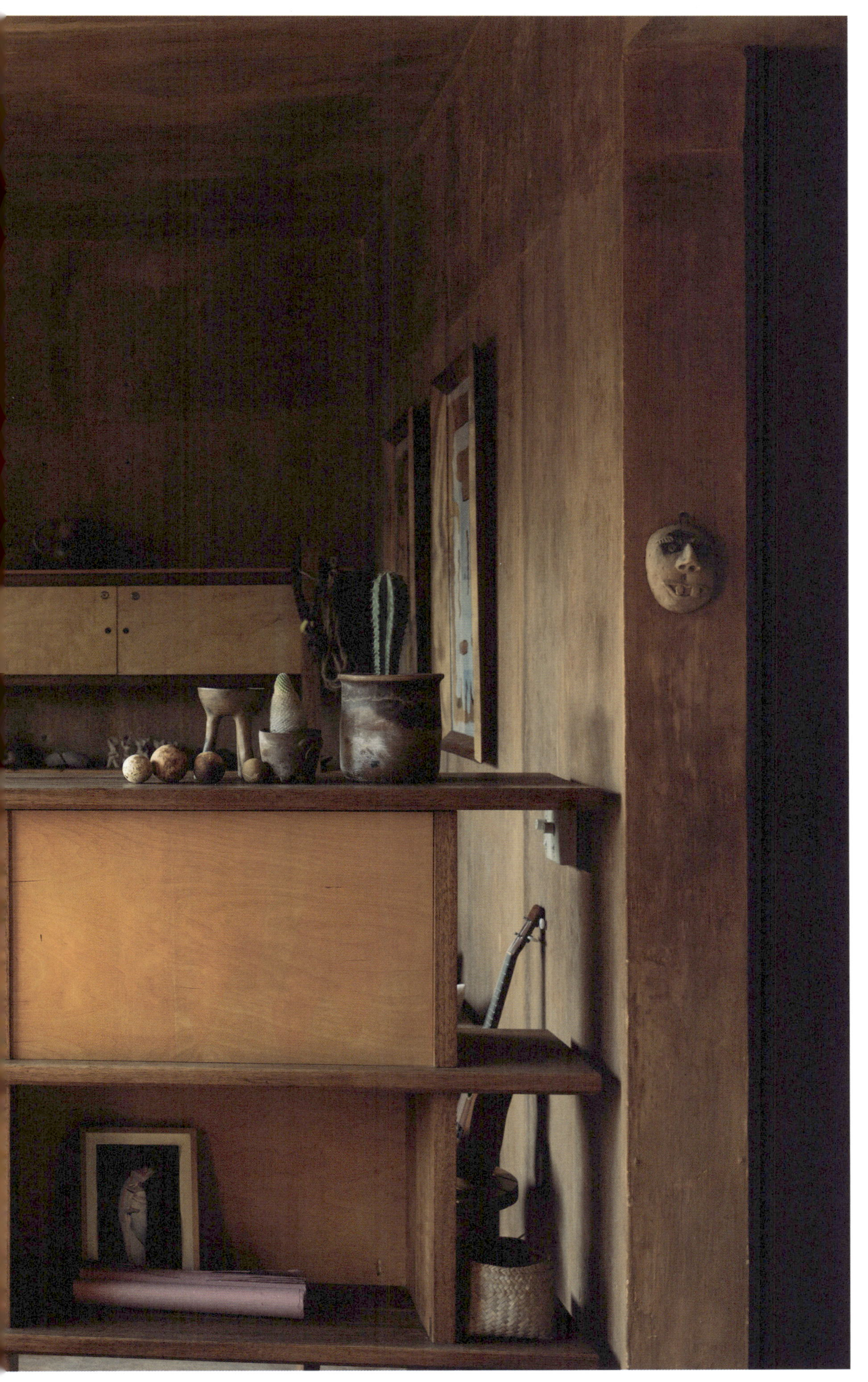

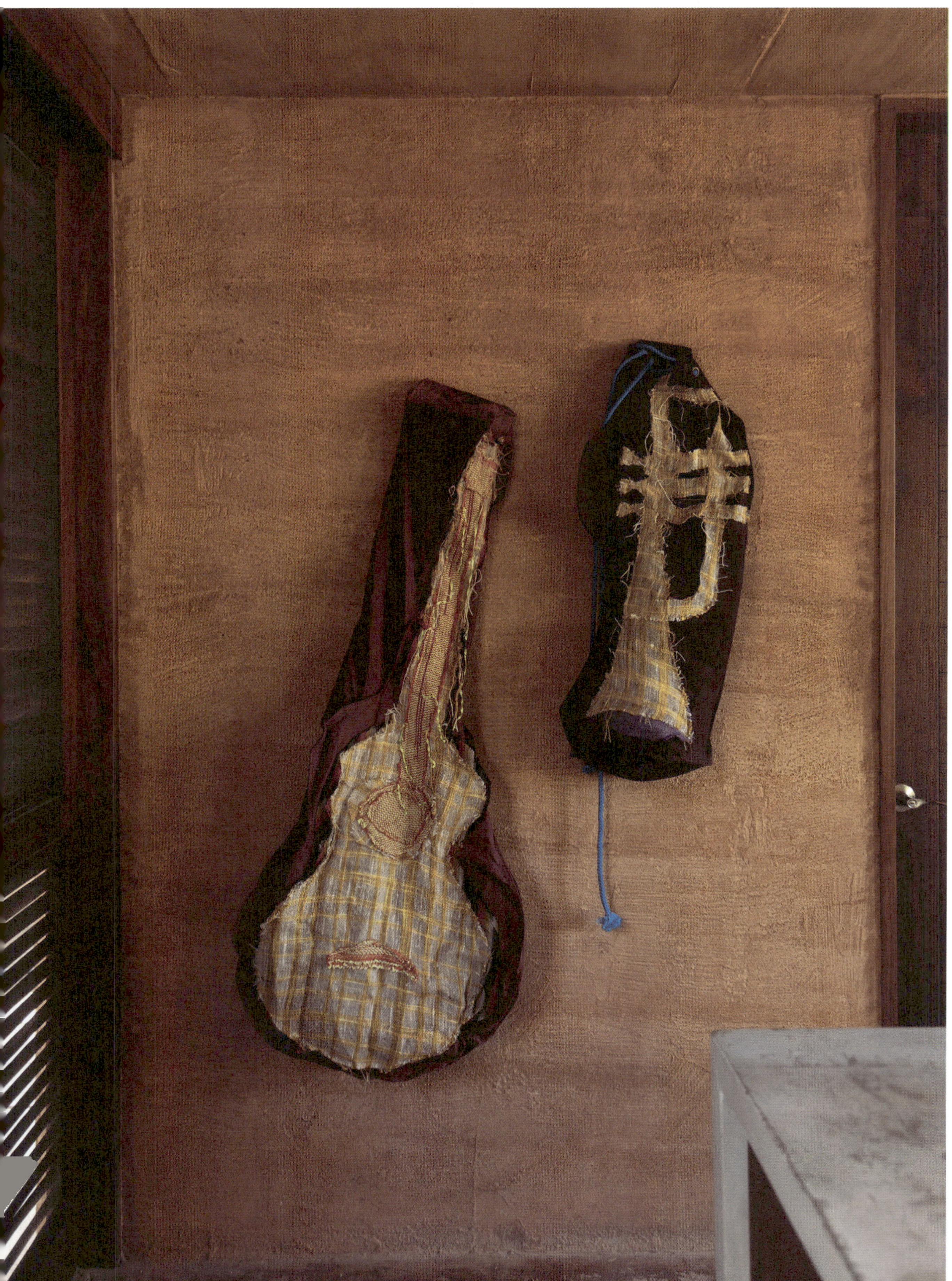

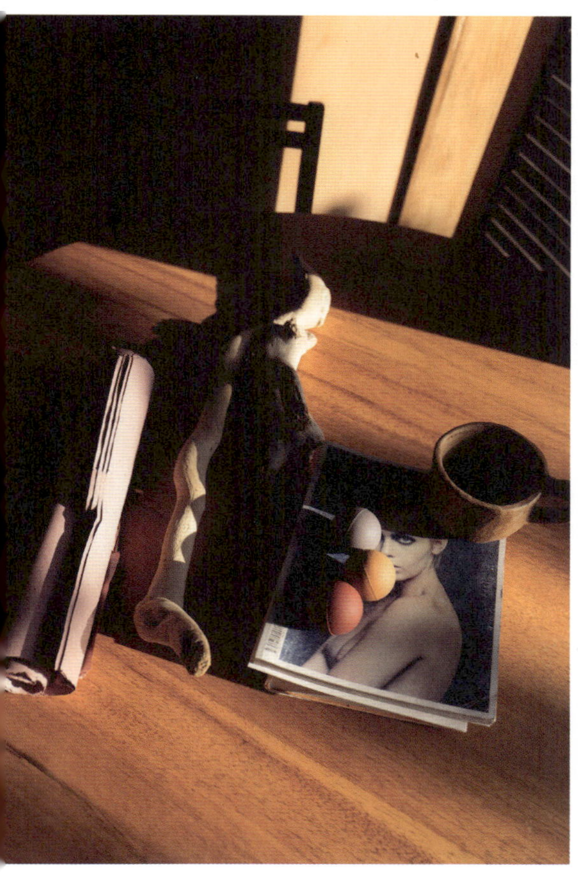

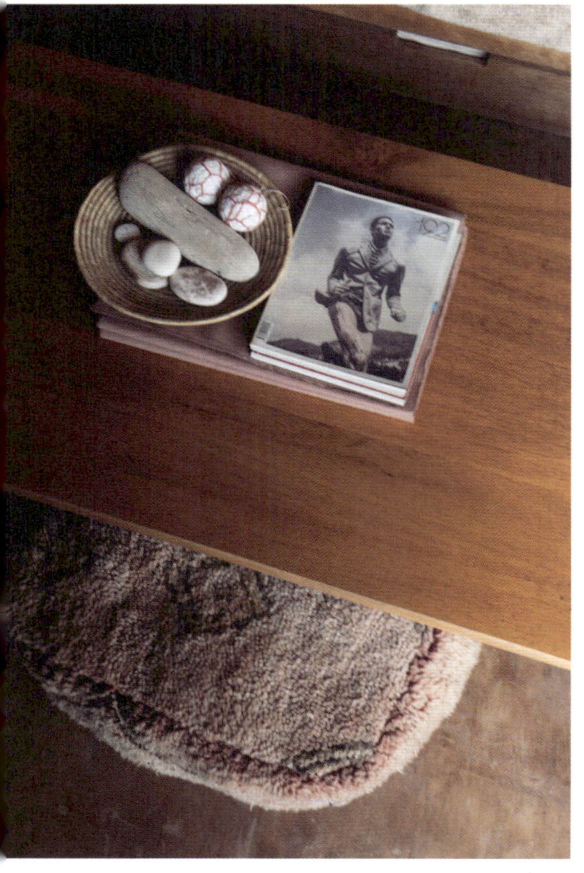

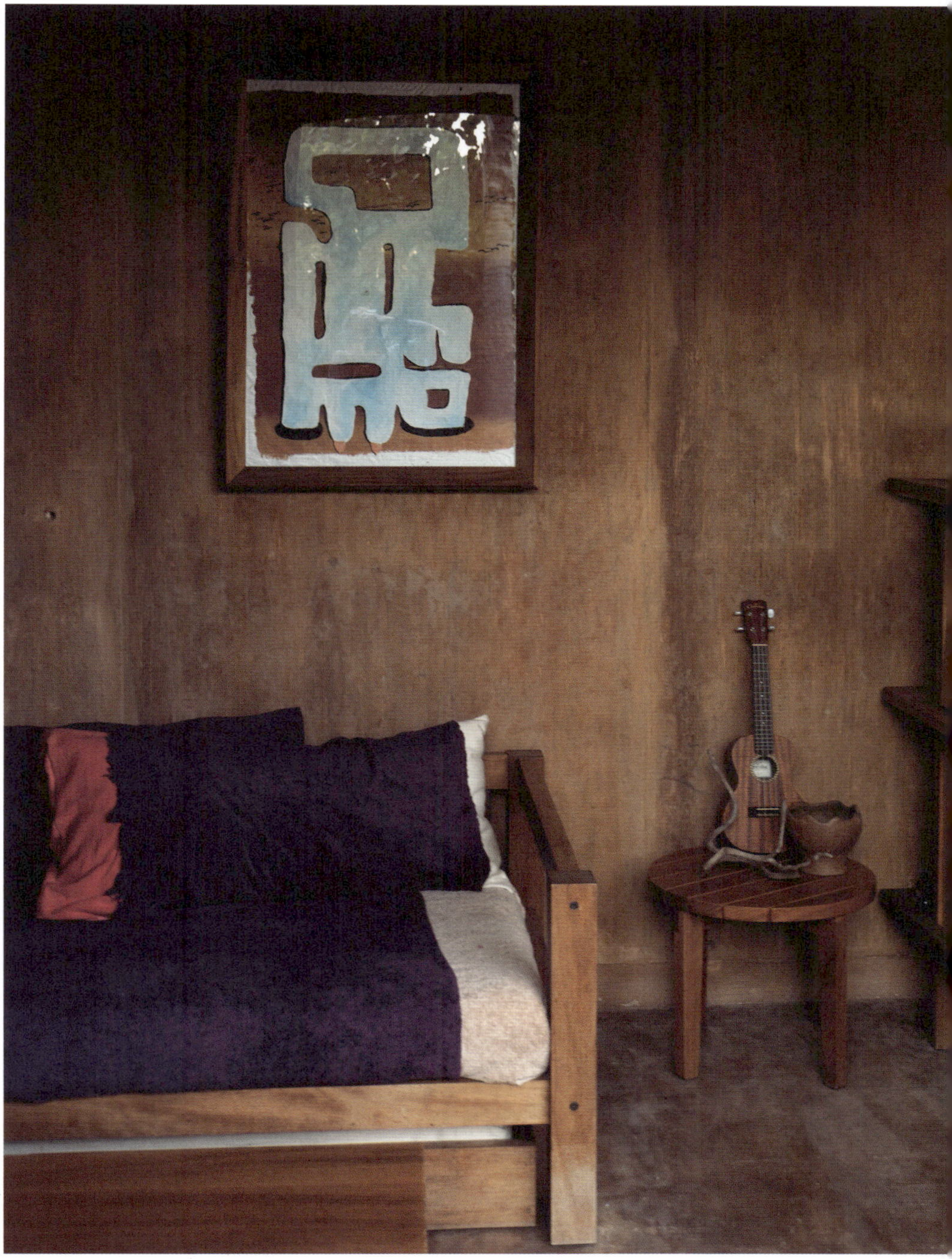

As an architect, Alberto is driven by the dream of creating developments along various burgeoning beachfronts like Mazul. The architectural concept of the homes here, including Alberto's, is rooted in the idea of seamless integration with the environment. His house showcases how modern aesthetics can be blended with the raw beauty of the surroundings: the concrete walls that are painted to mimic wood are an excellent example.

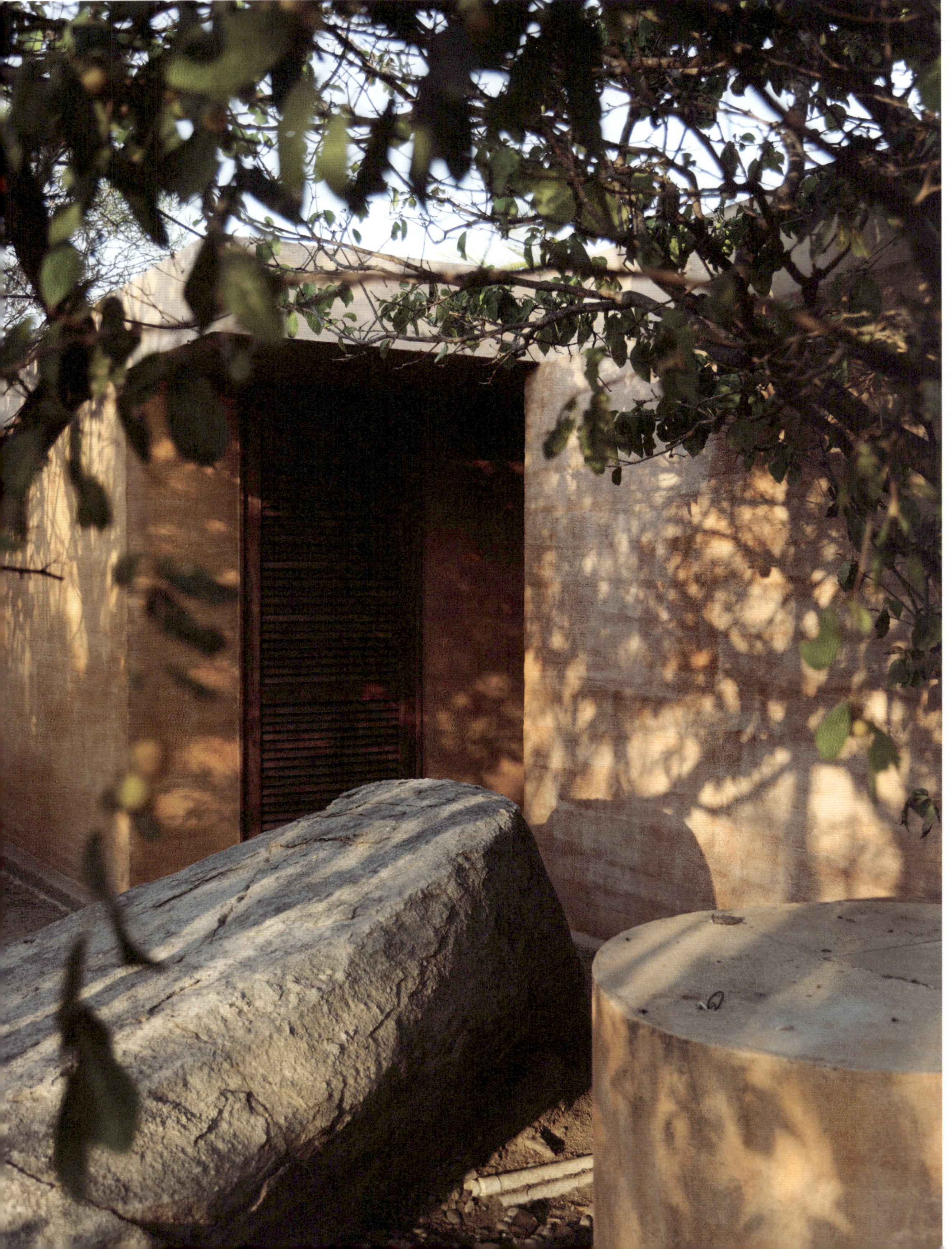

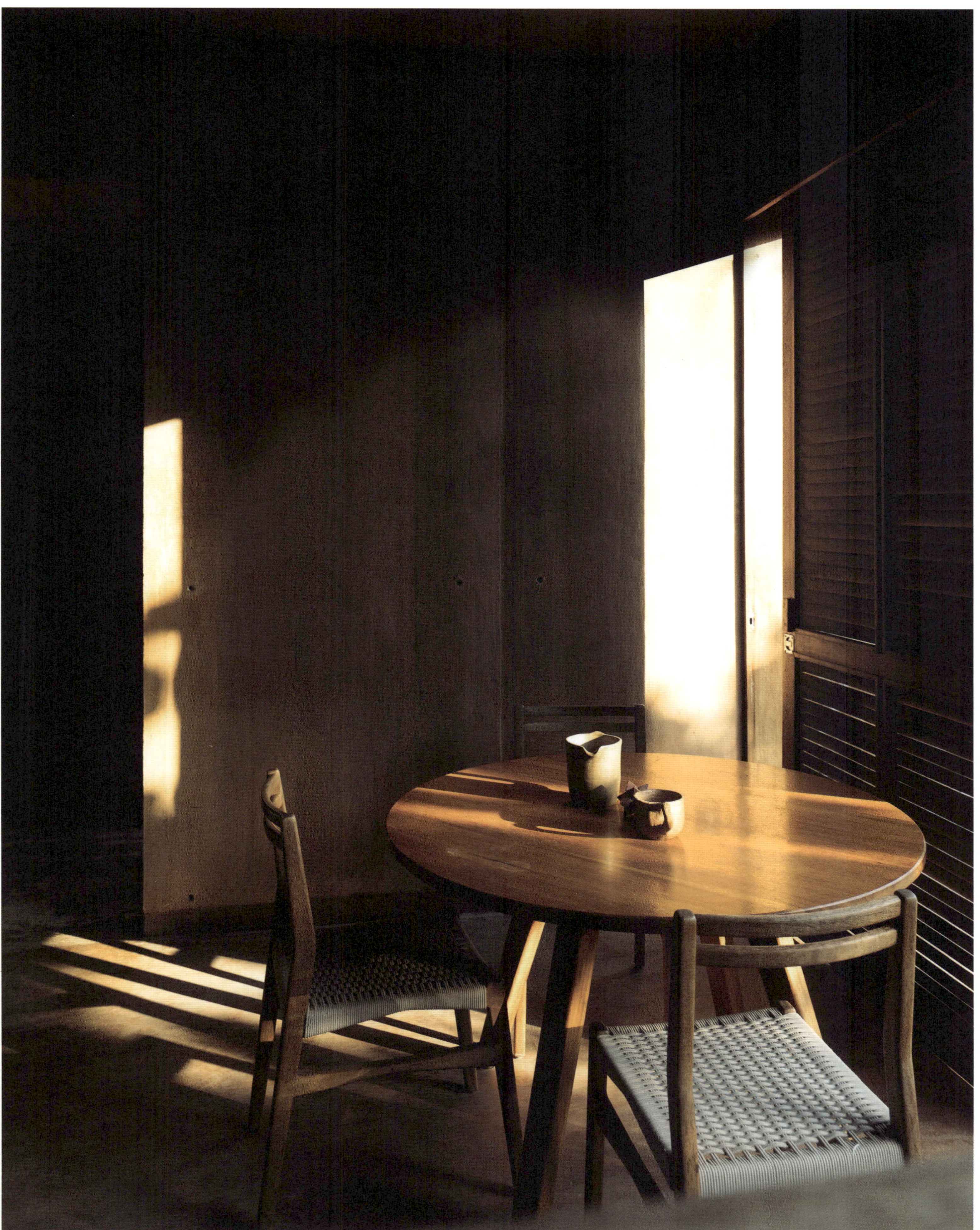

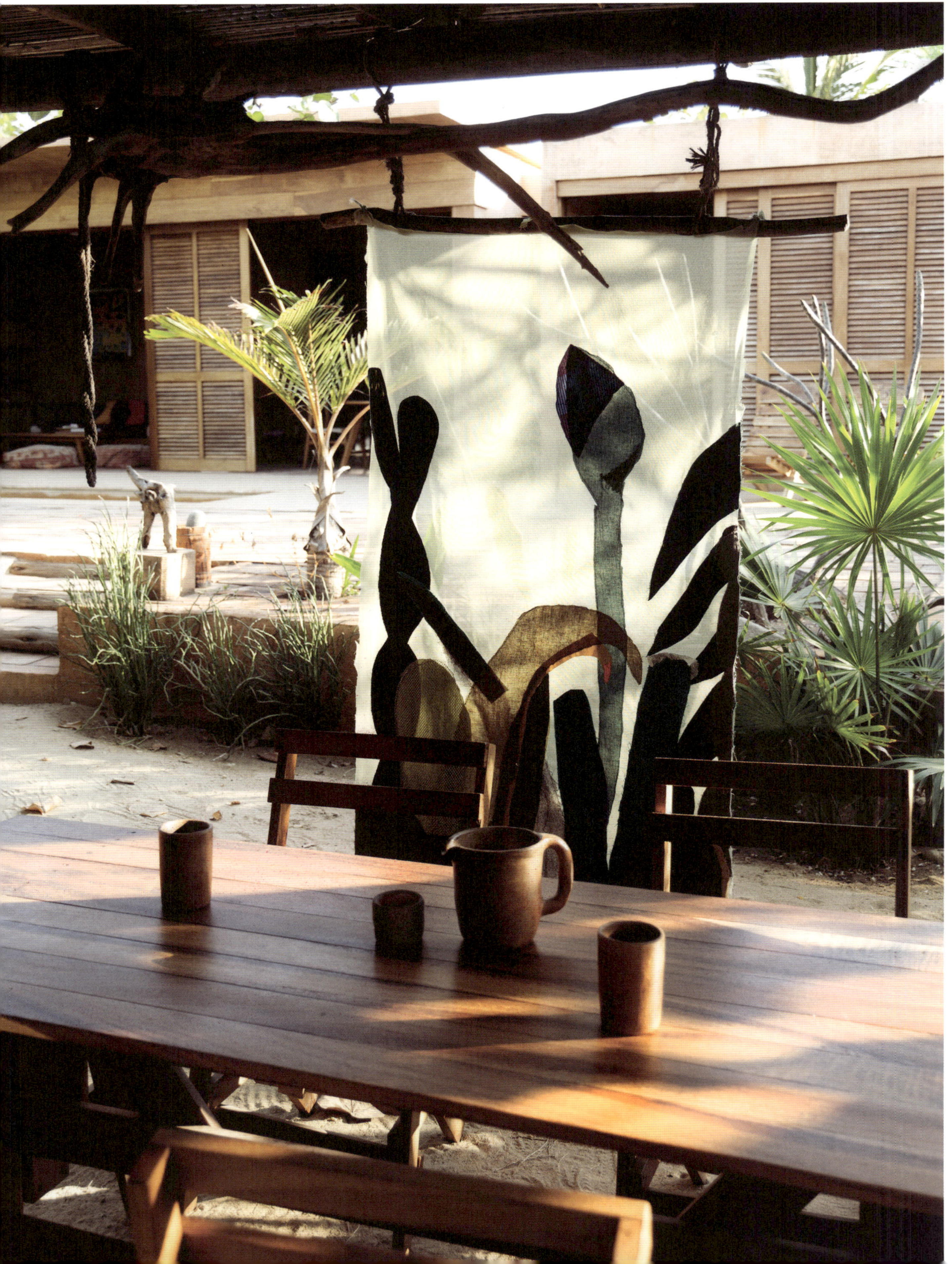

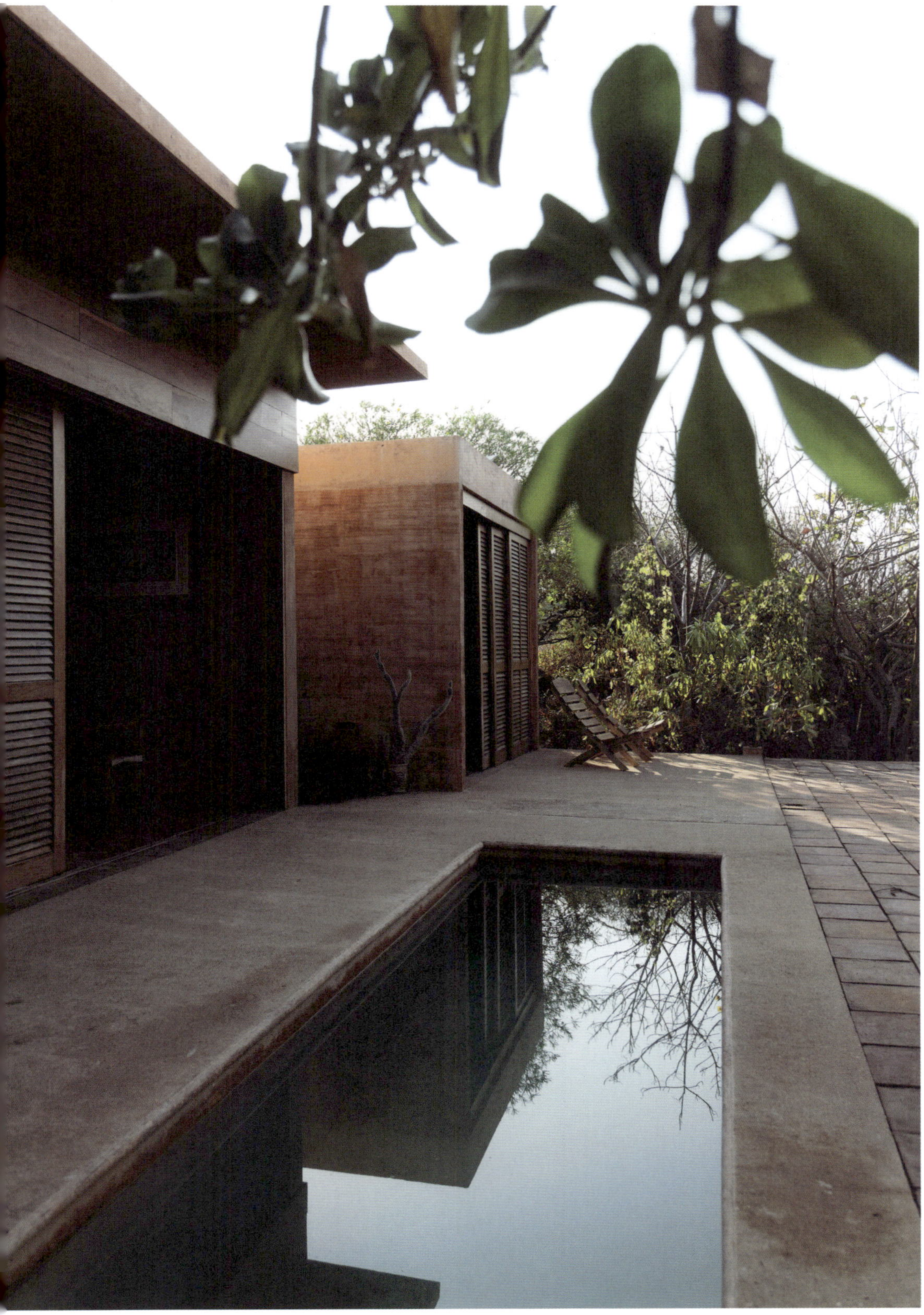

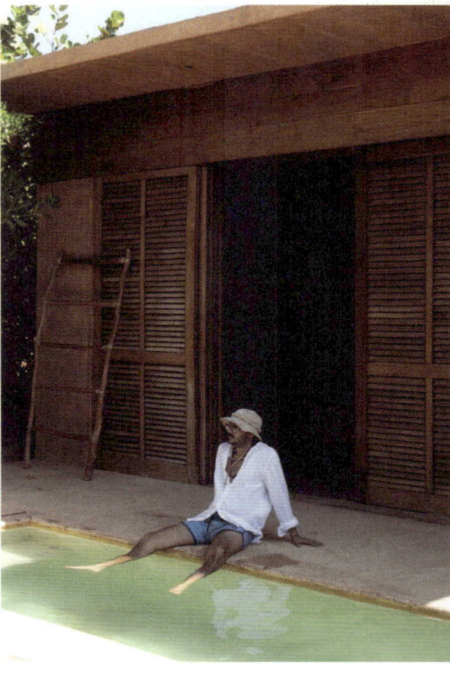

The architecture and interior of Alberto's house reflect his own personal taste but are also consistent with those of the other homes on the site, designed by friends and family. Mazul is a collective endeavour created by like-minded people who are guided by a shared ethos. Alberto's job is to oversee the different projects, ensuring that every detail aligns with the shared vision of harmony between architecture and nature.

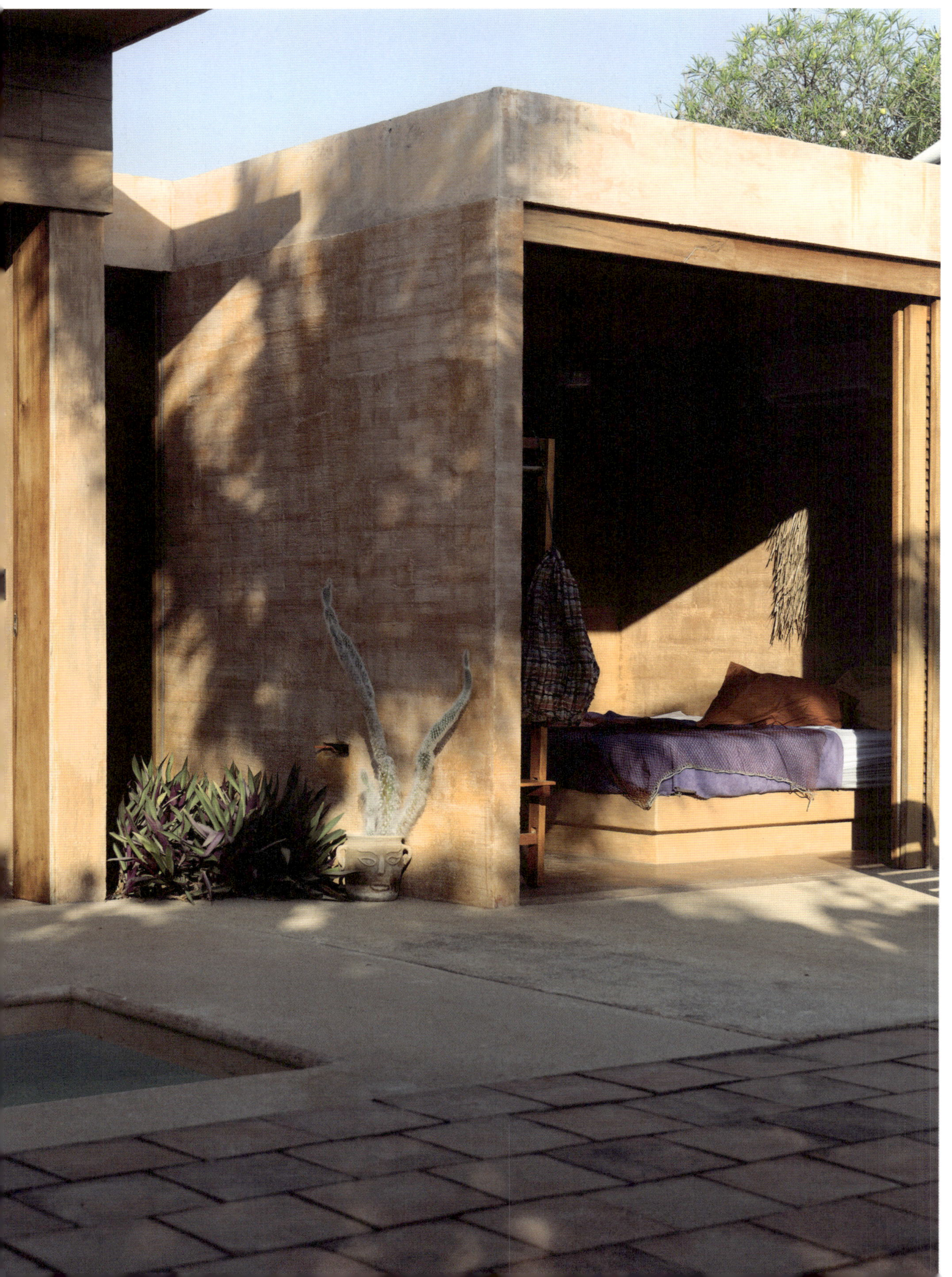

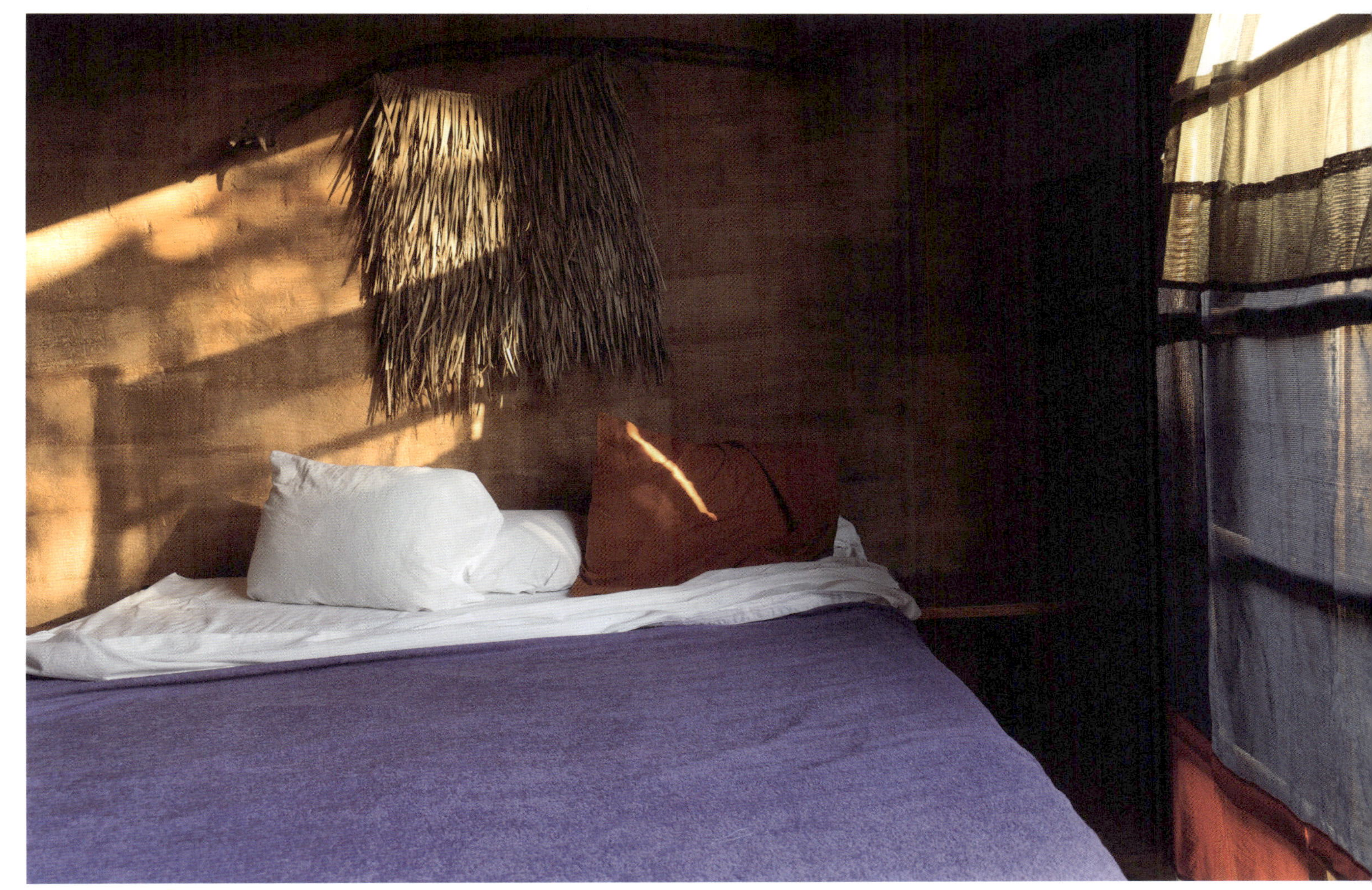

Living in Mazul feels like capturing the essence of life by the ocean. The blend of design and nature the project offers is hard to find elsewhere. Alberto hopes to foster more communities like it, resonating with a shared love for innovative architecture, the untouched beauty of nature, sports, and a nurturing family environment.

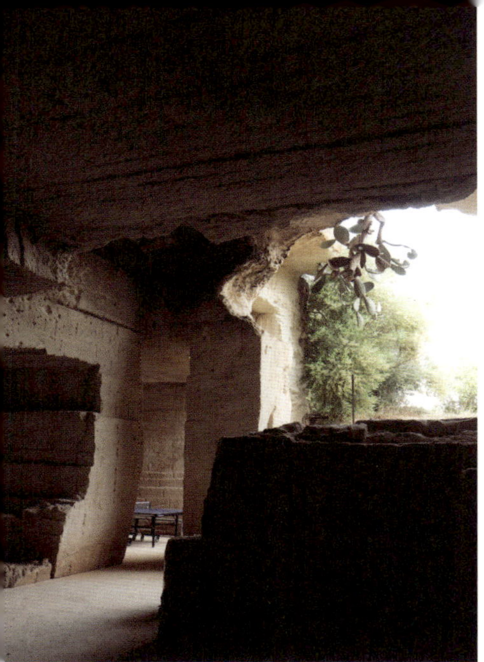

Balearic Islands
Spain

MENORCA

The Iberian Sea is part of the Mediterranean Sea, separating the Balearic Islands from the Iberian peninsula. Menorca is the second largest island in this sea – its name derives from its size and the Latin 'insula minor', meaning 'smaller island', compared to Mallorca. Menorca is a fairly rocky island: the sea has formed many caves along its coastline with gorges, caverns and shrubs contributing to the unpolished appearance of the rugged landscape.

During a holiday on the island, Antón García-Abril and Débora Mesa, who are both architects, became intrigued when they spotted a property for sale with what looked like a series of caves on its fringe. Instead of caves, however, they discovered a small abandoned quarry for marés stone, a sandstone from which nearly all the preindustrial – and some more recent – buildings on Menorca have been built. Once inside the quarry, they found that it had been partitioned into rooms, and there even was a kitchen.

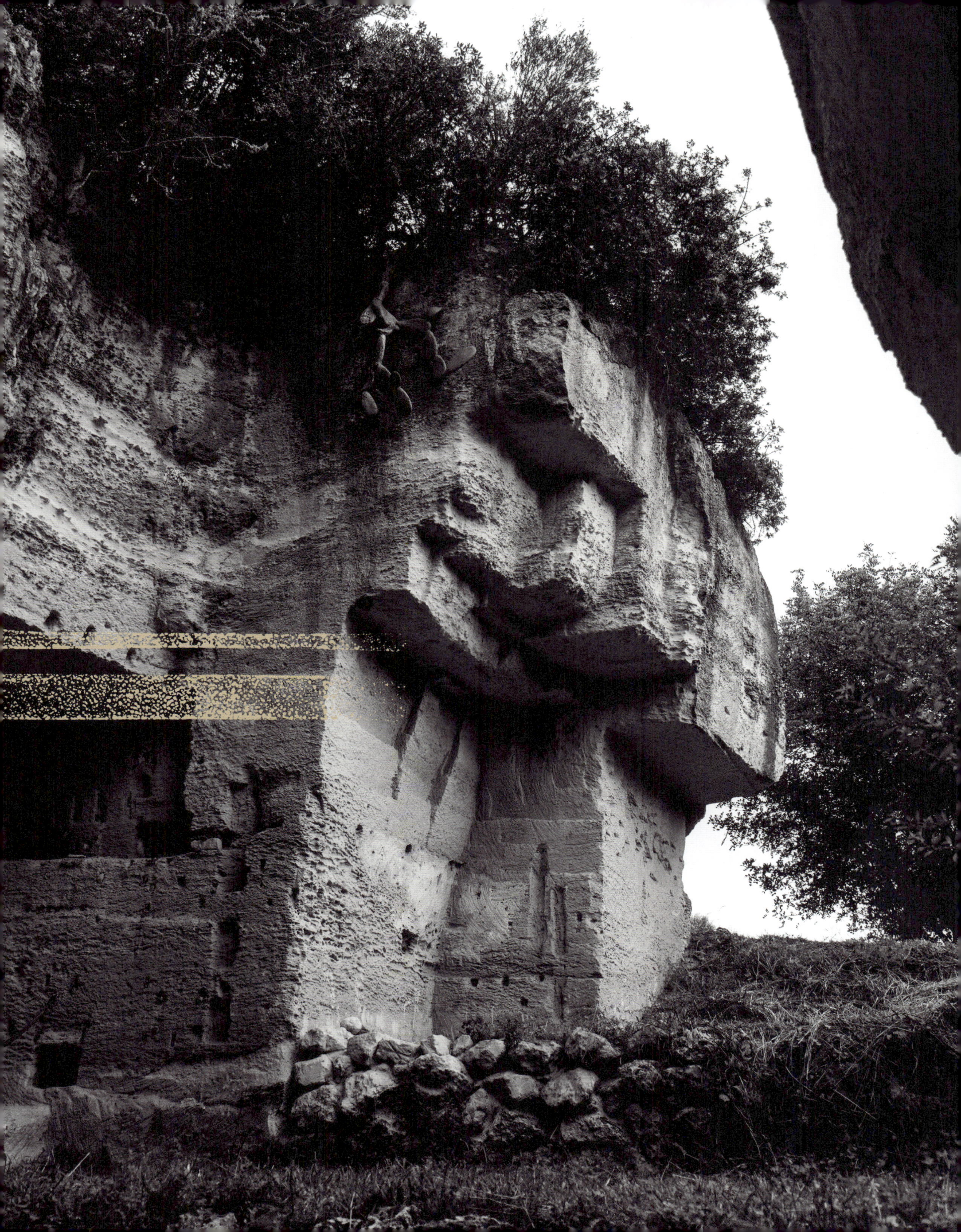

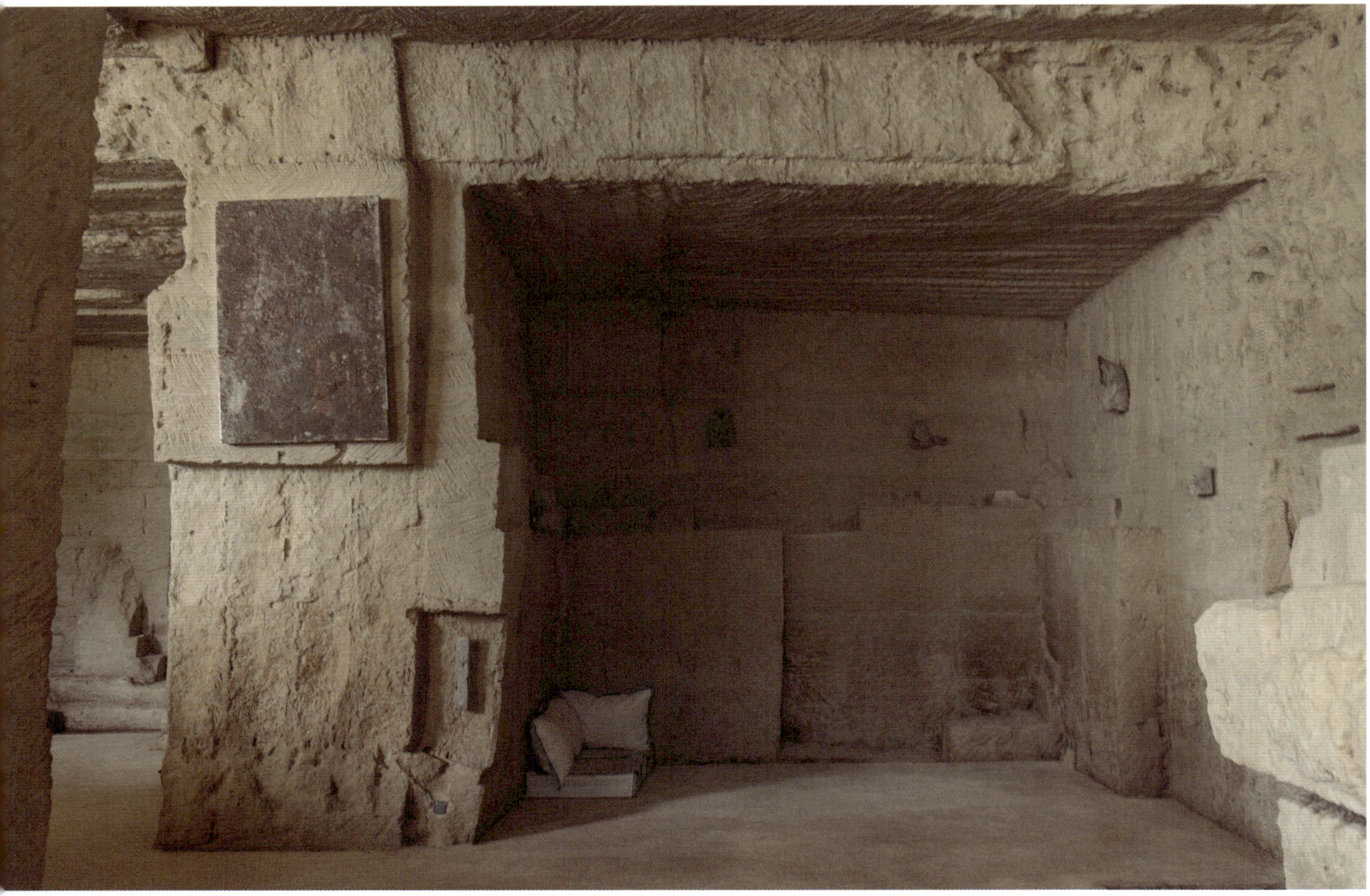

They later discovered that the space had been used by the military as an ammunition dump during and after the Spanish Civil War. Antón and Débora realised that the structure had an industrial logic, artistic potential, and architectural qualities and set about saving it from abandonment. They decided to find a way to inhabit this architecture but had no desire to impose the kind of programme you would expect in a conventional building. After clearing out the debris, they added concrete floors in the spaces closest to the exterior and carved out three skylights in the darkest corners to bring natural light and ventilation.

They named their ambitious and experimental project Ca'n Terra, meaning 'House of the Earth' in Catalan, but 'house' doesn't quite cover it. Entering this excavated space in the Earth is unlike anything else. It feels really primitive and raw because of the powdery marés stone all around, but modern and minimalistic at the same time, partly thanks to the translucent plastic sheets used to create intimacy and to define the spaces. They also prevent dust and animals from entering.

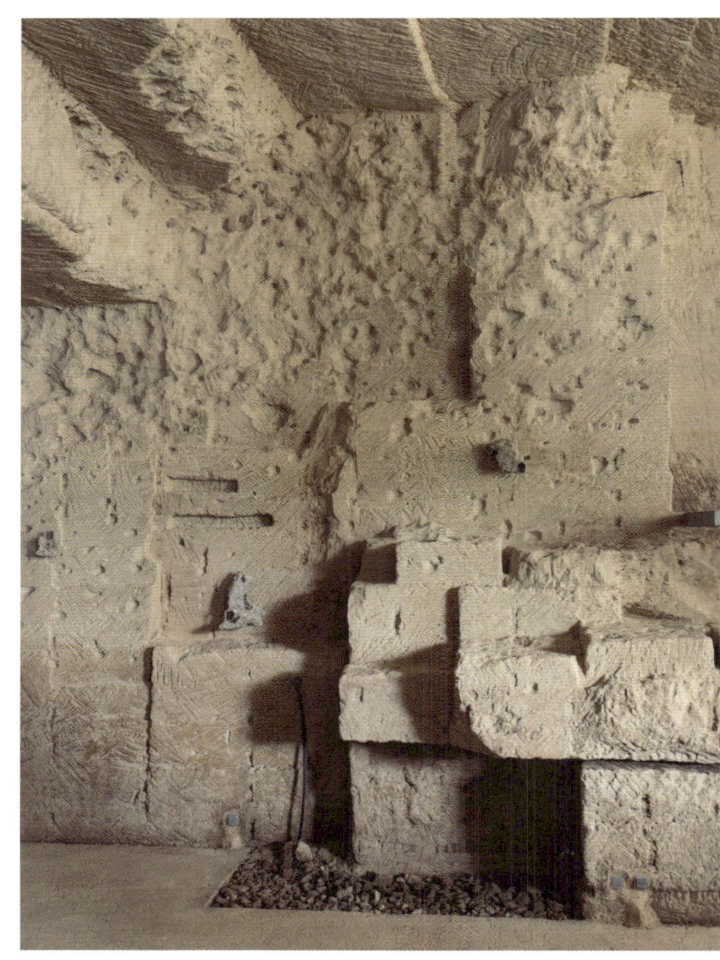

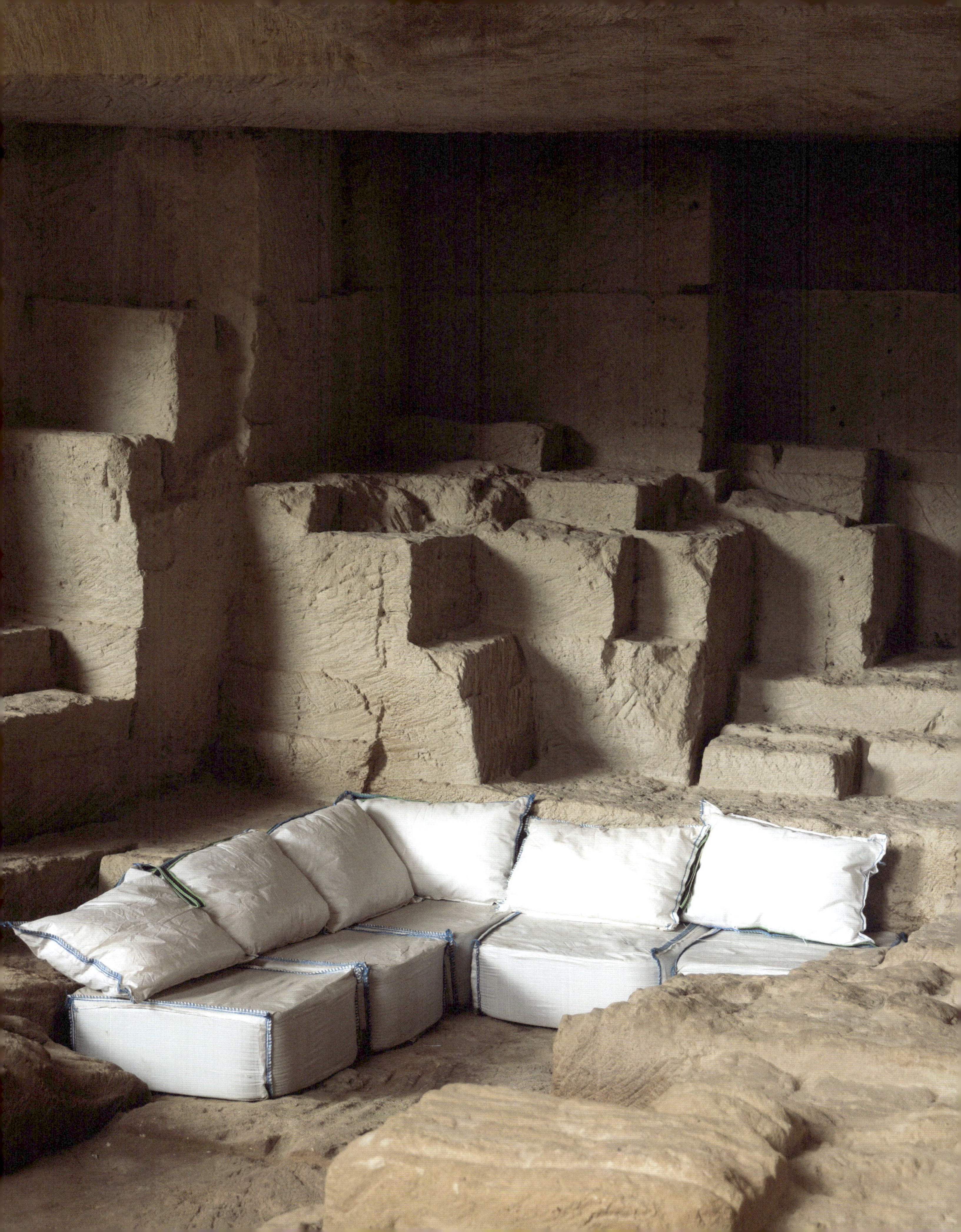

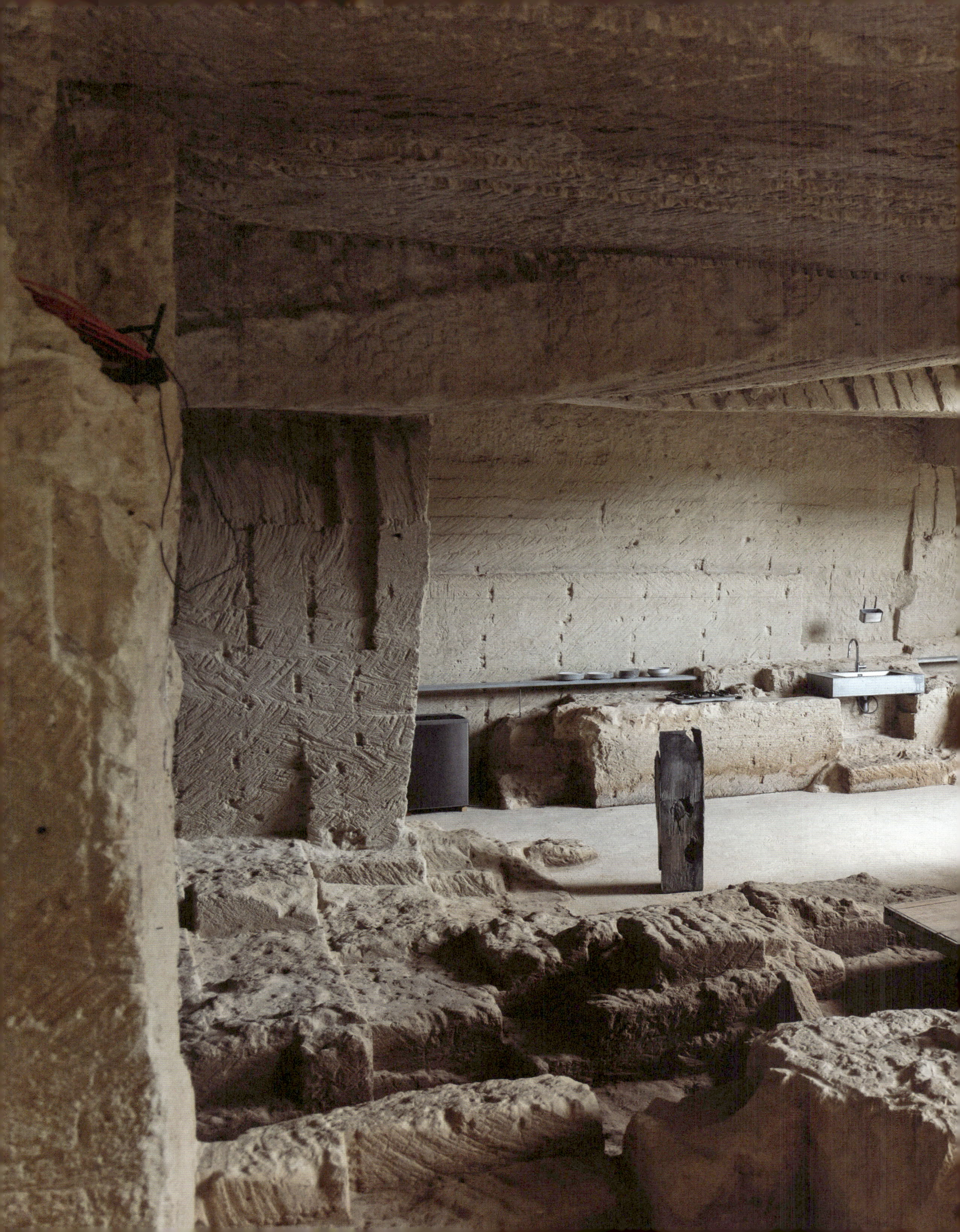

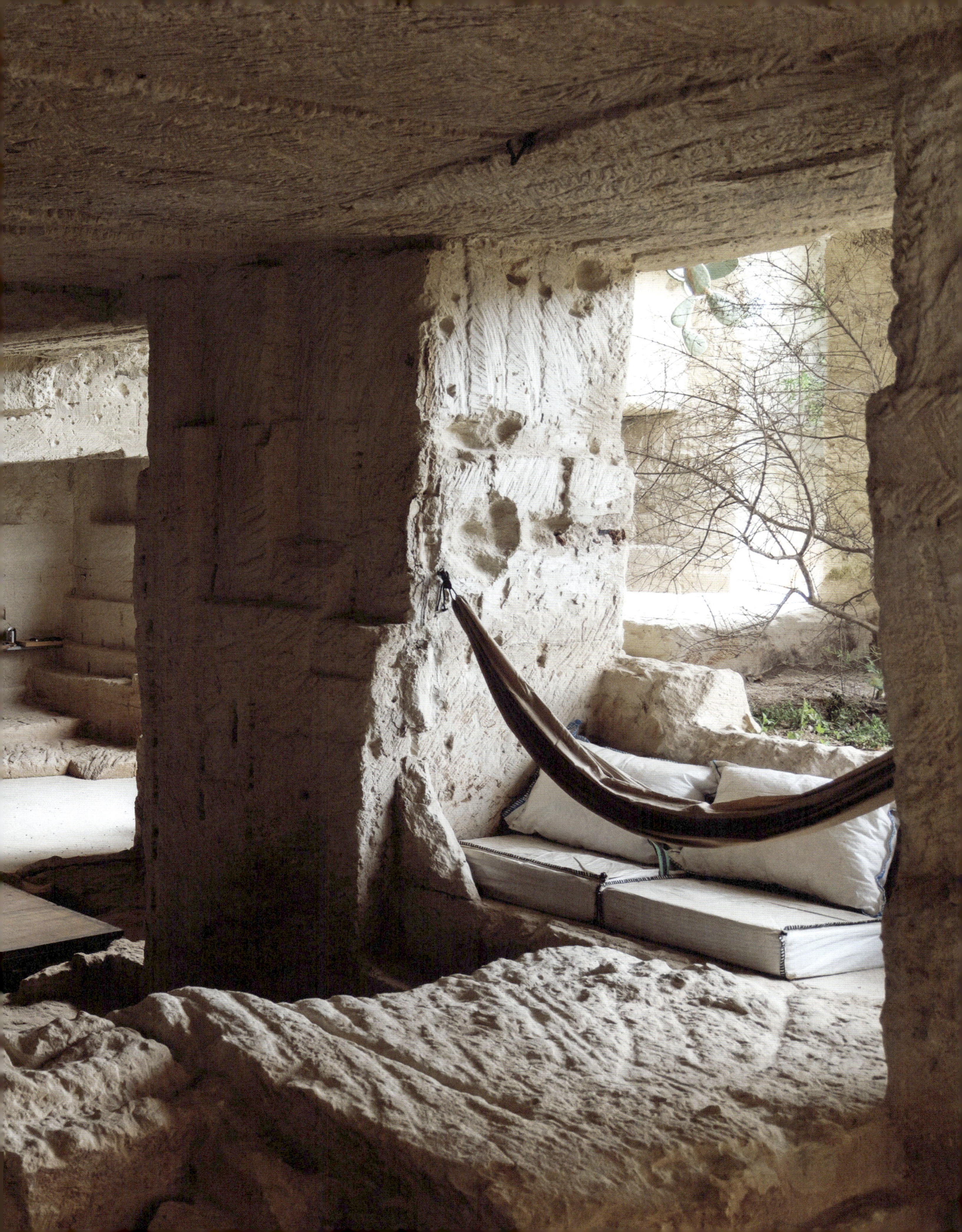

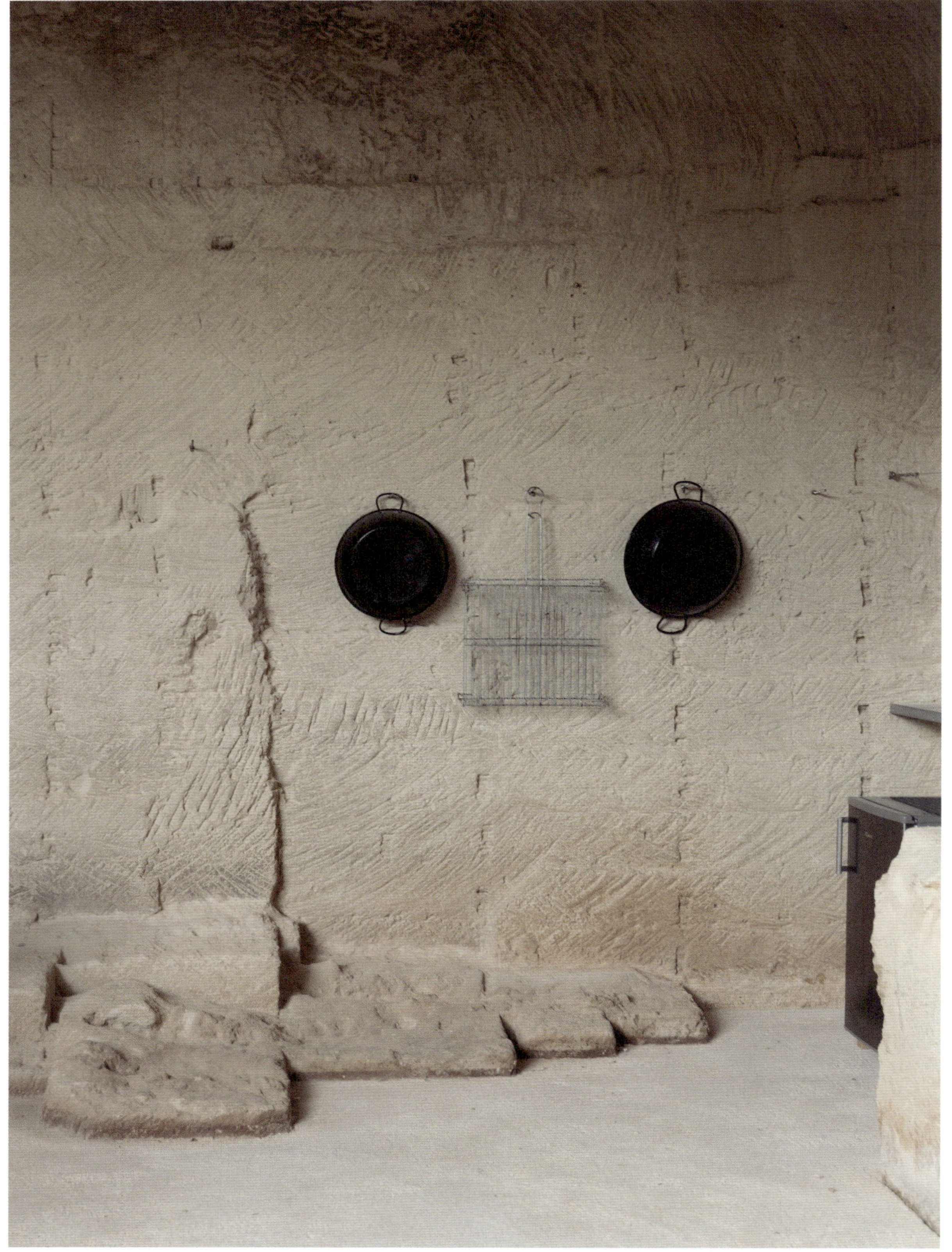

Ca'n Terra is a place of wonder. Its chambers extend as far as 150 feet deep into the rock, one after another, with an area of around 300 feet stretching out across the front. A new, jaw-dropping space awaits at every turn, including bathrooms and a kitchen. The surprising highlight is the house's bright blue swimming pool, creating an unearthly, stunning contrast with the marés stone all around it. Should the outside world ever feel unsafe, this would be the ideal hideaway: here it truly feels as if the past and the present, architecture and nature, man and Earth, have all become one.

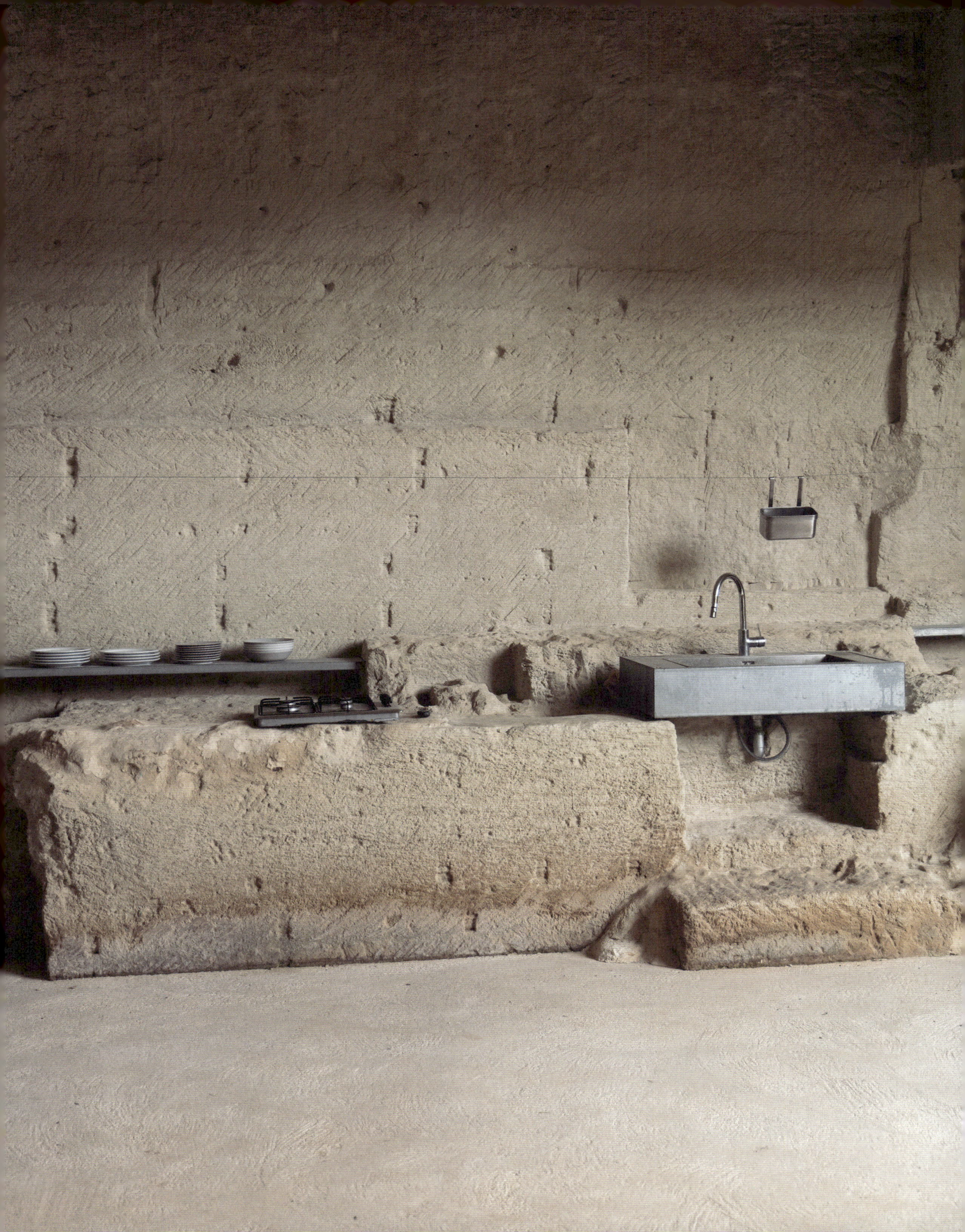

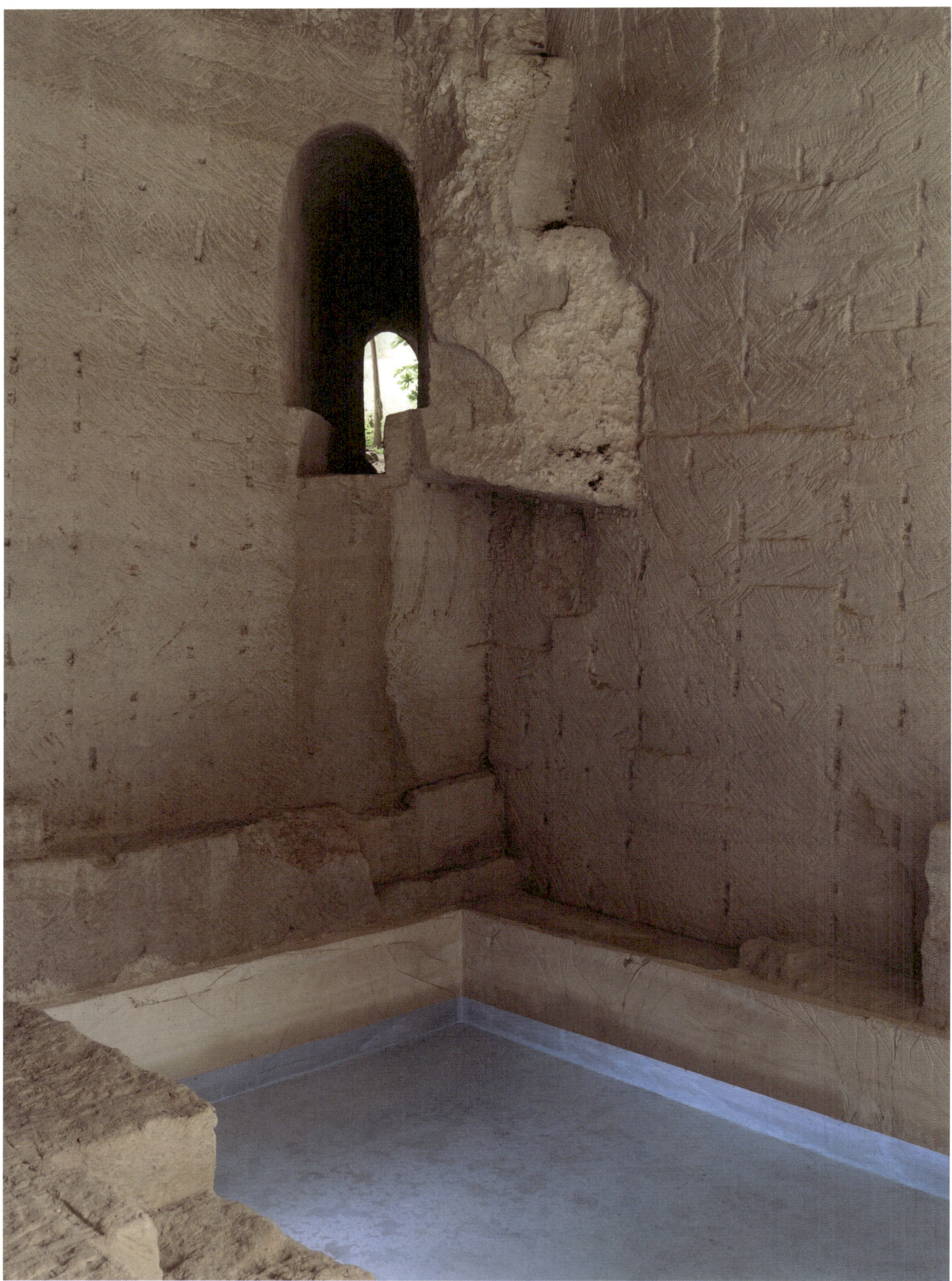

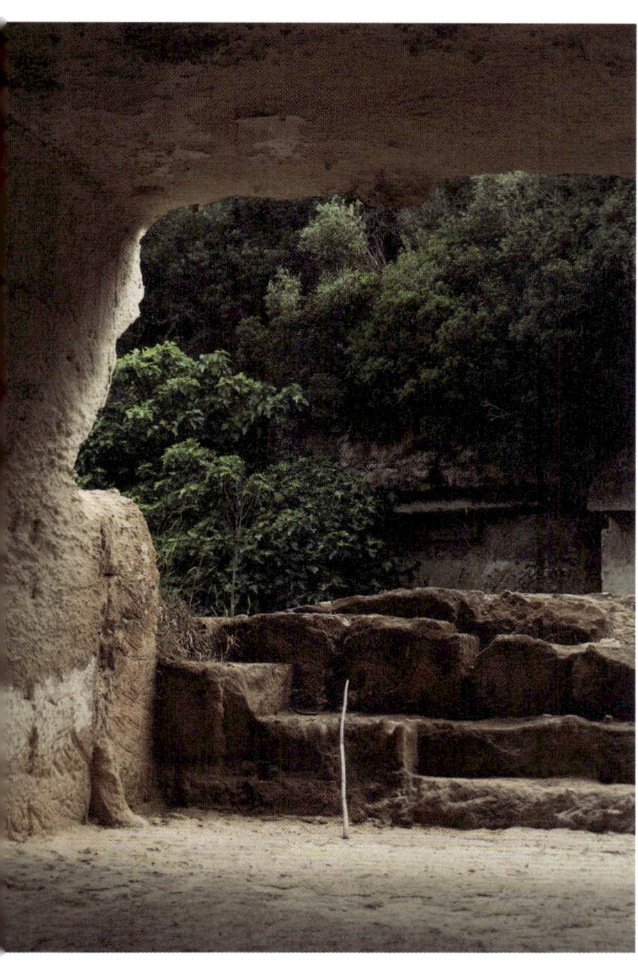

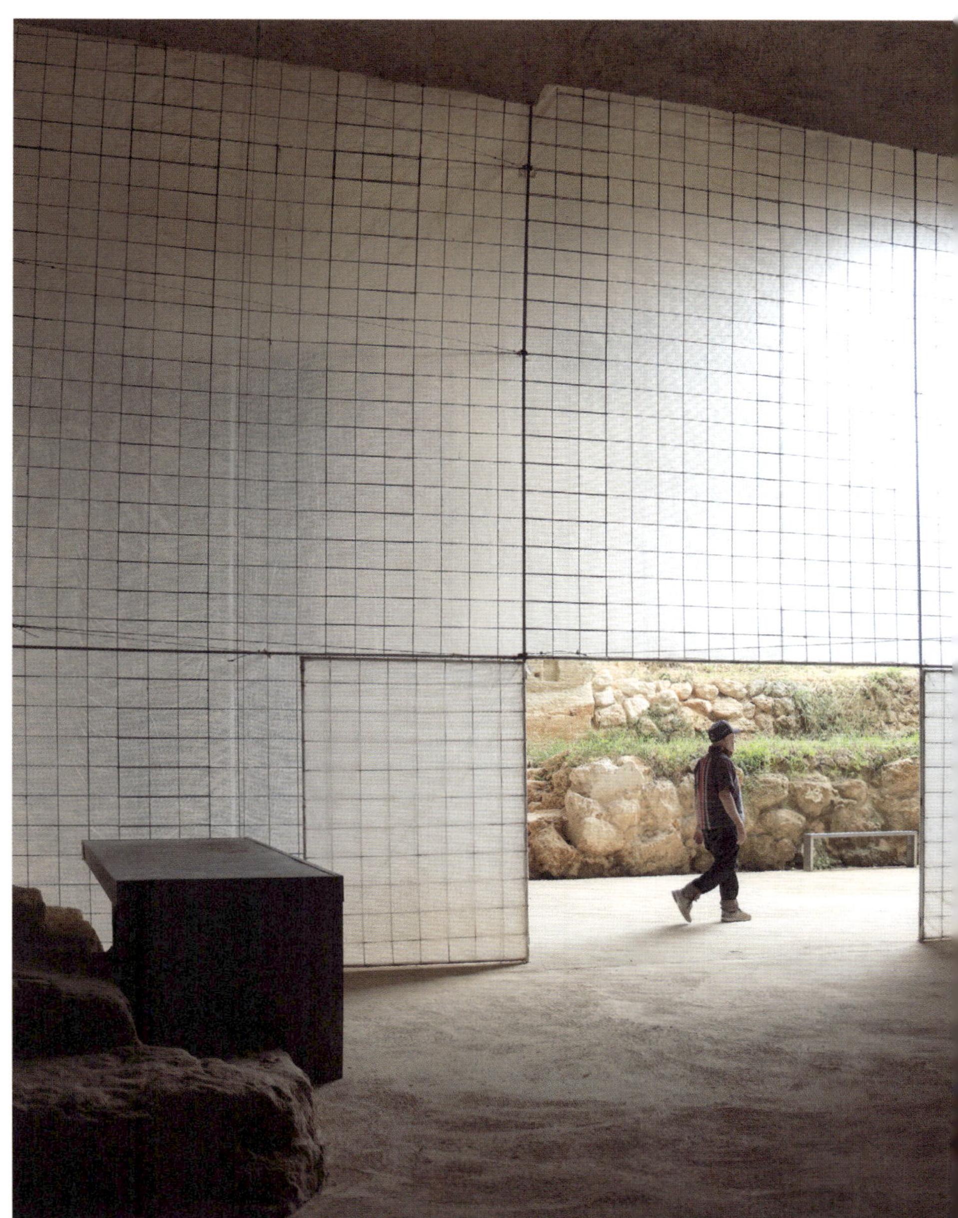

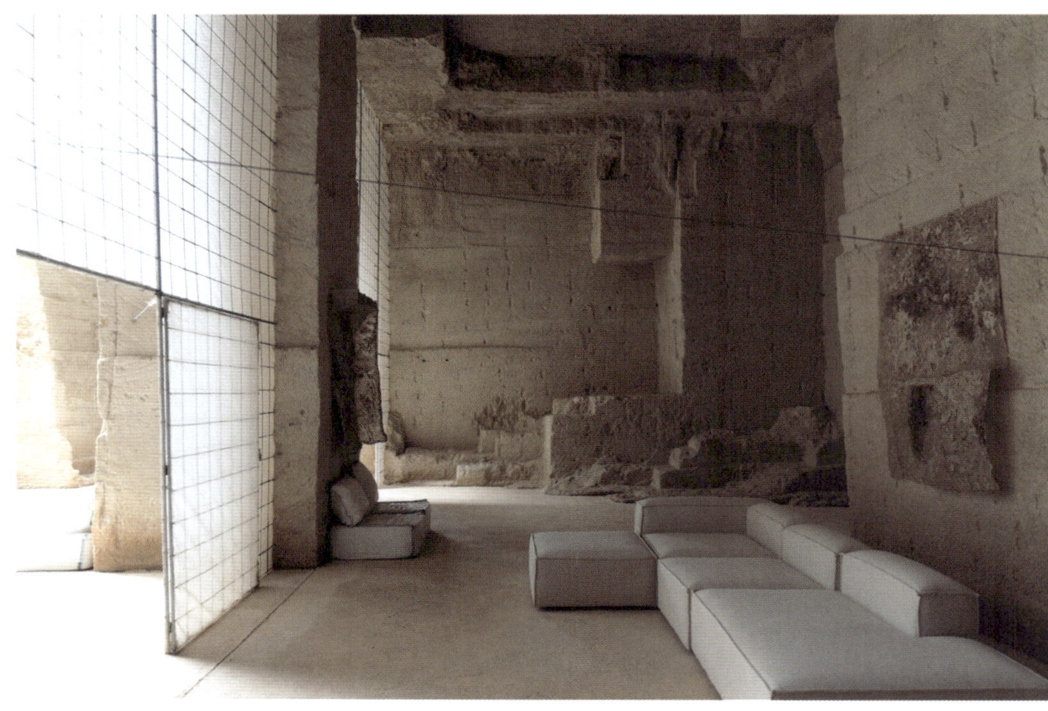

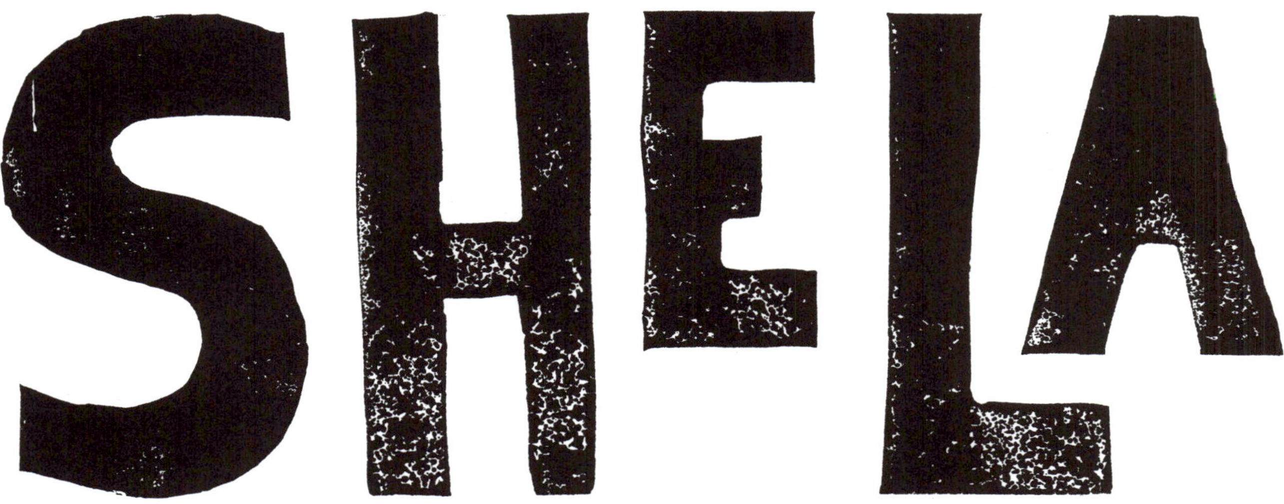

Lamu Island
Kenya

Surrounded by the waters of the Indian Ocean, off the eastern coast of Kenya, lies Lamu Island. One of the islands of the Lamu Archipelago, it can only be reached by boat. There are no cars on the island, and motorised vehicles are not allowed, adding to its undisputed charm. This is one of a dwindling number of pristine places on Earth where life is governed by the ocean. The people who live there plan their day according to the tides and the moon's phases, depending on fishing boats and donkeys for supplies.

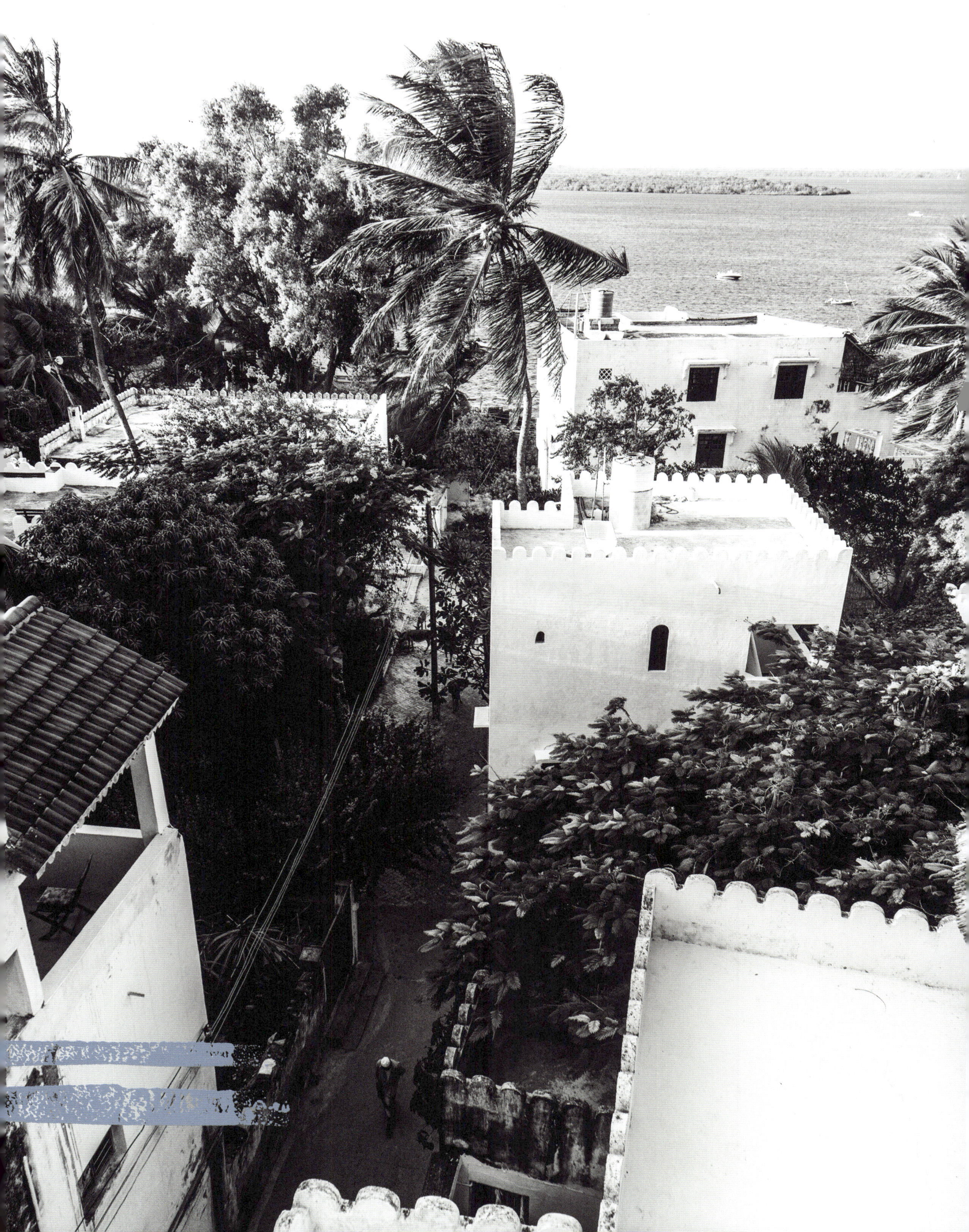

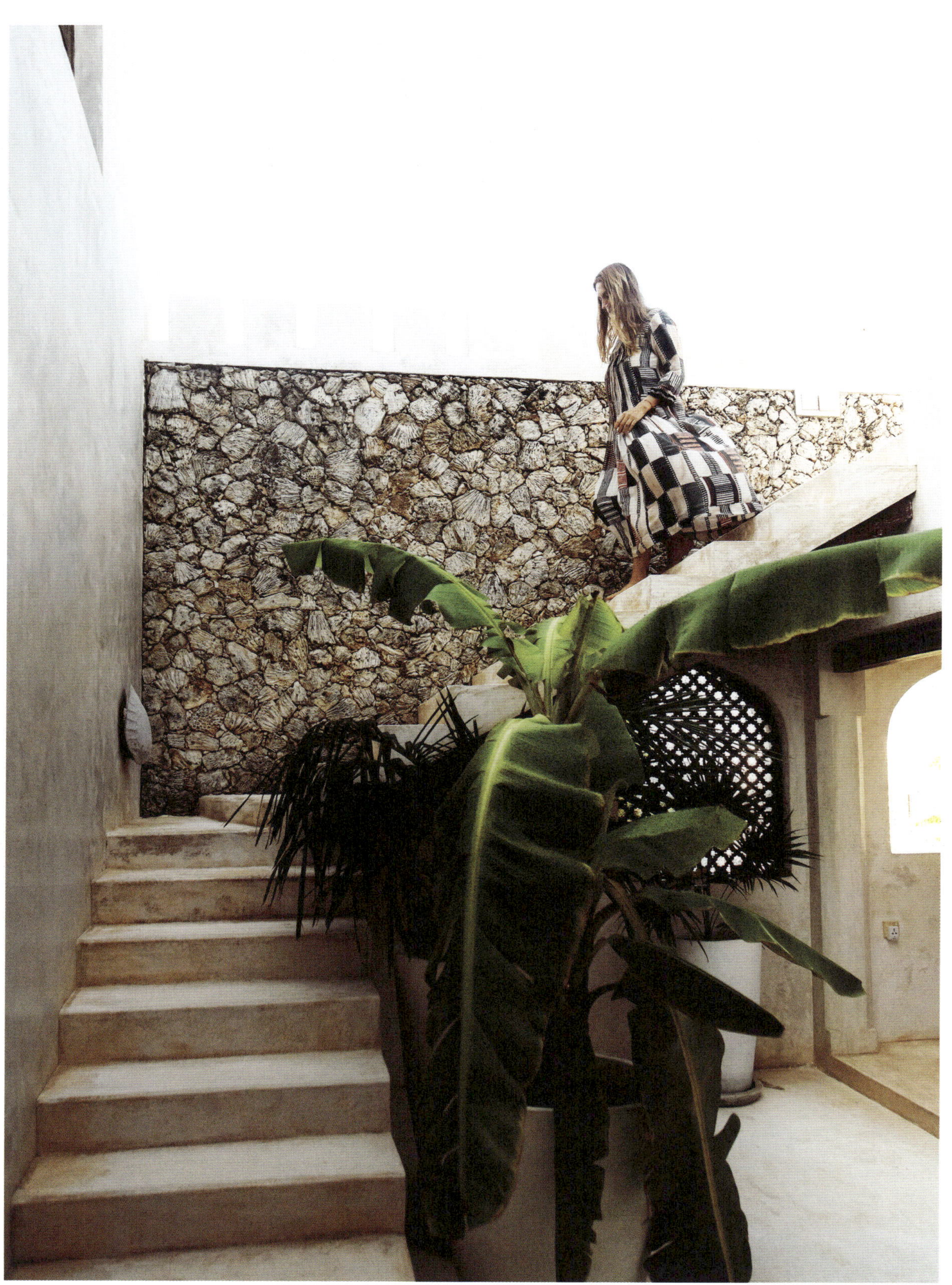

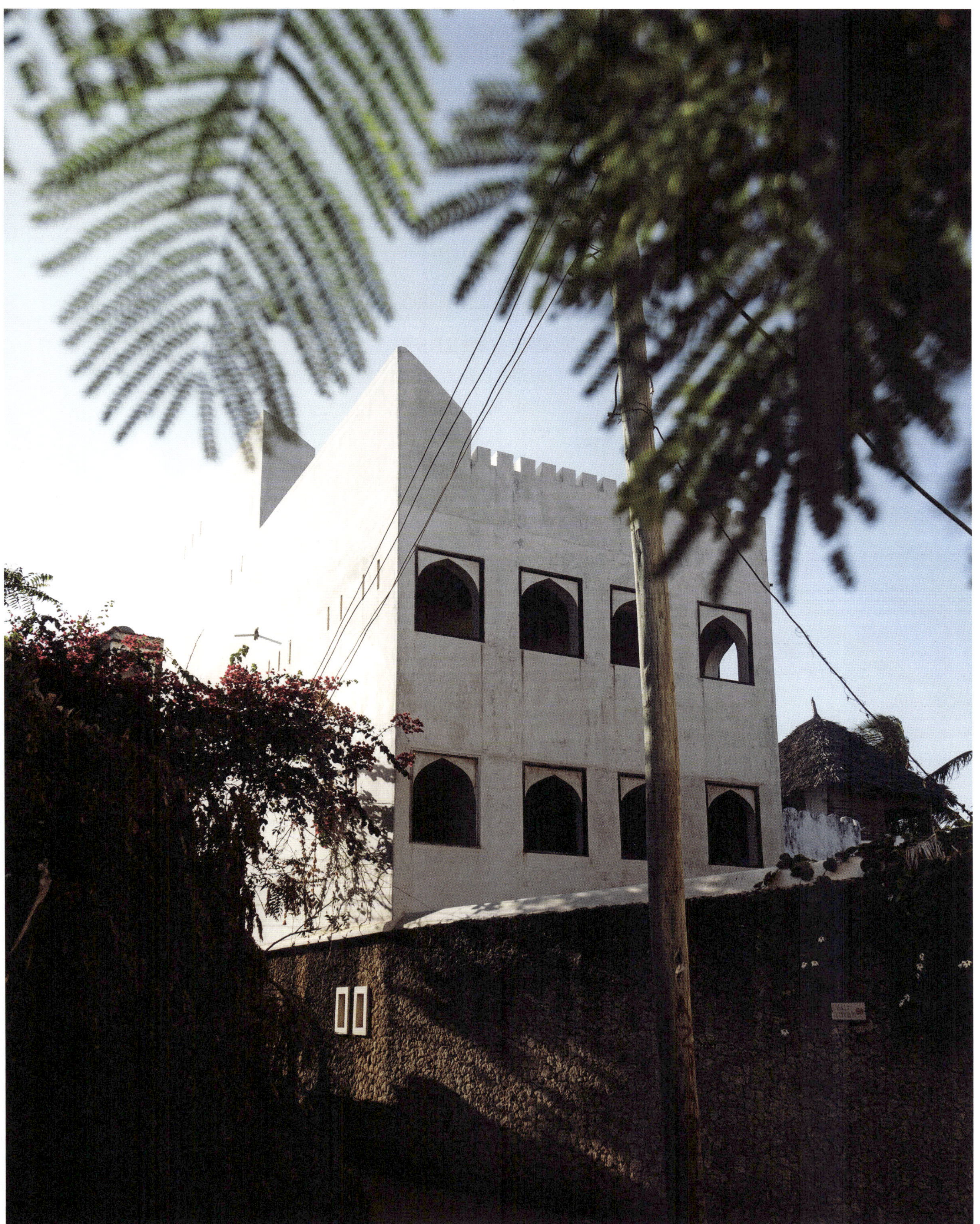

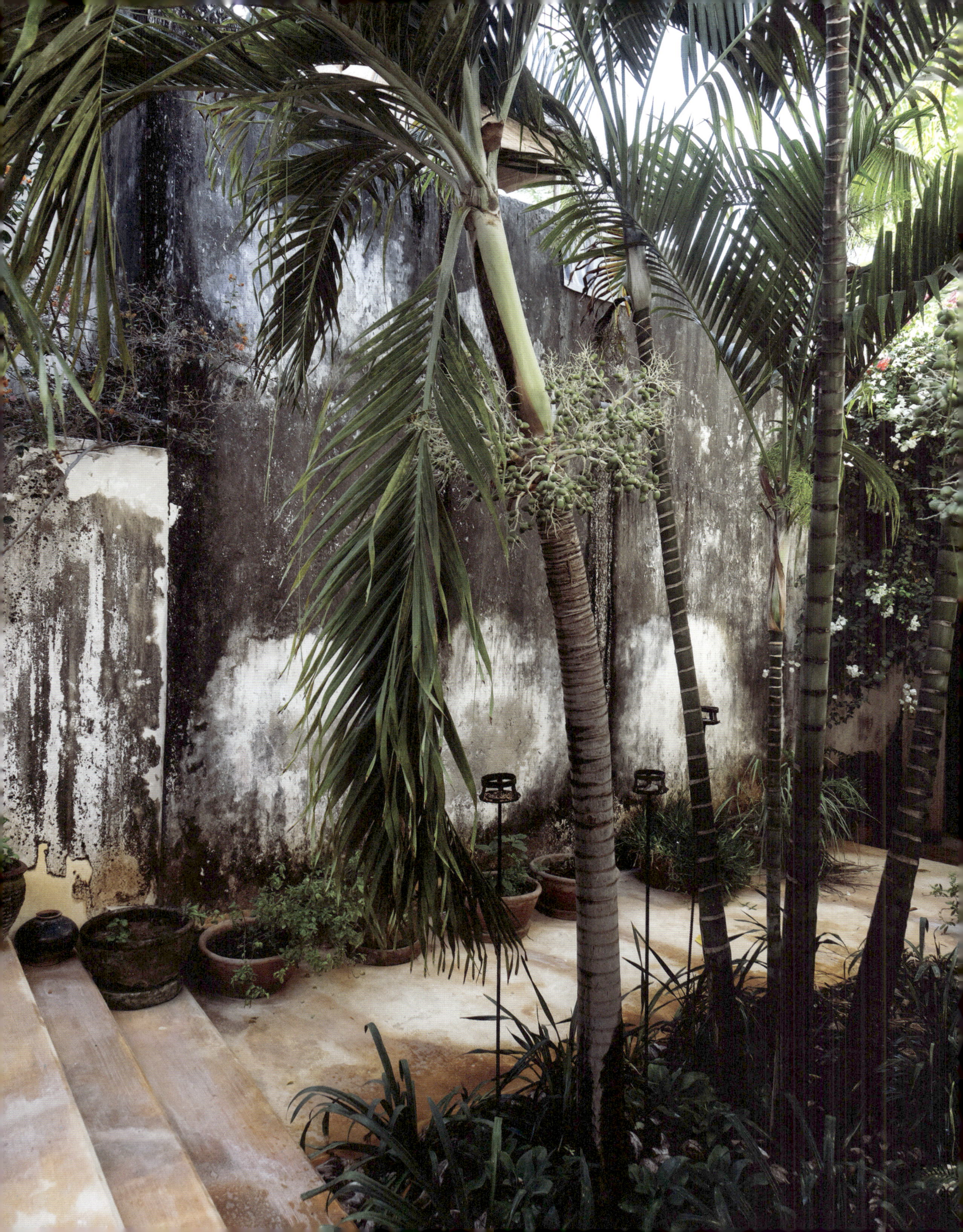

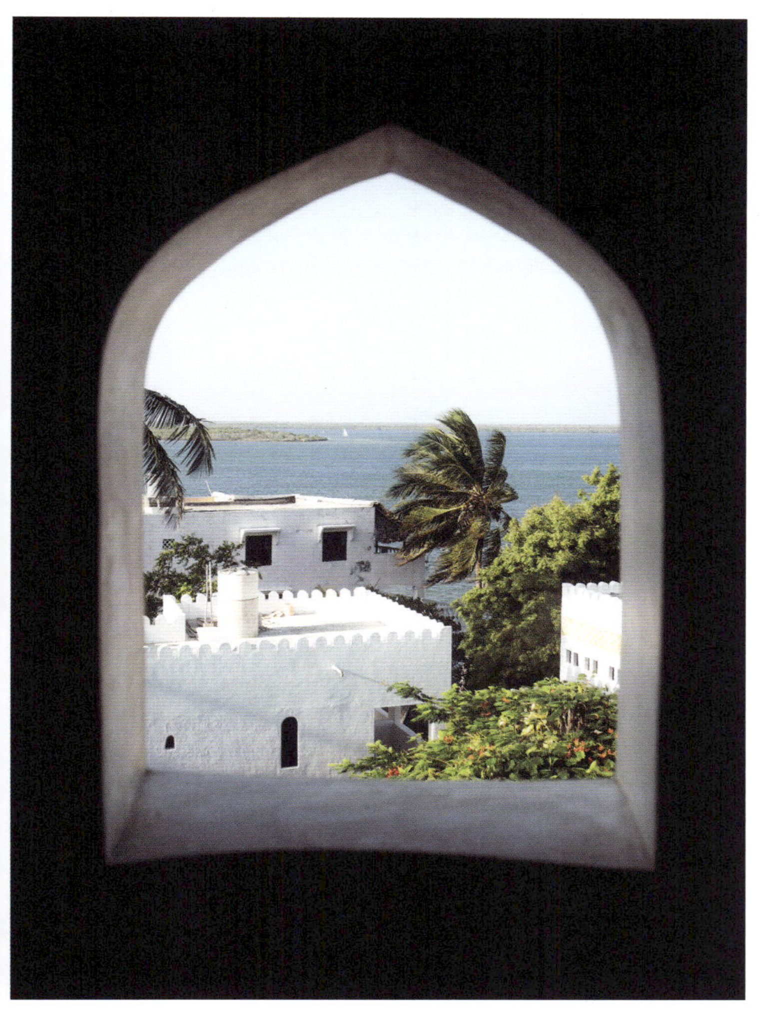

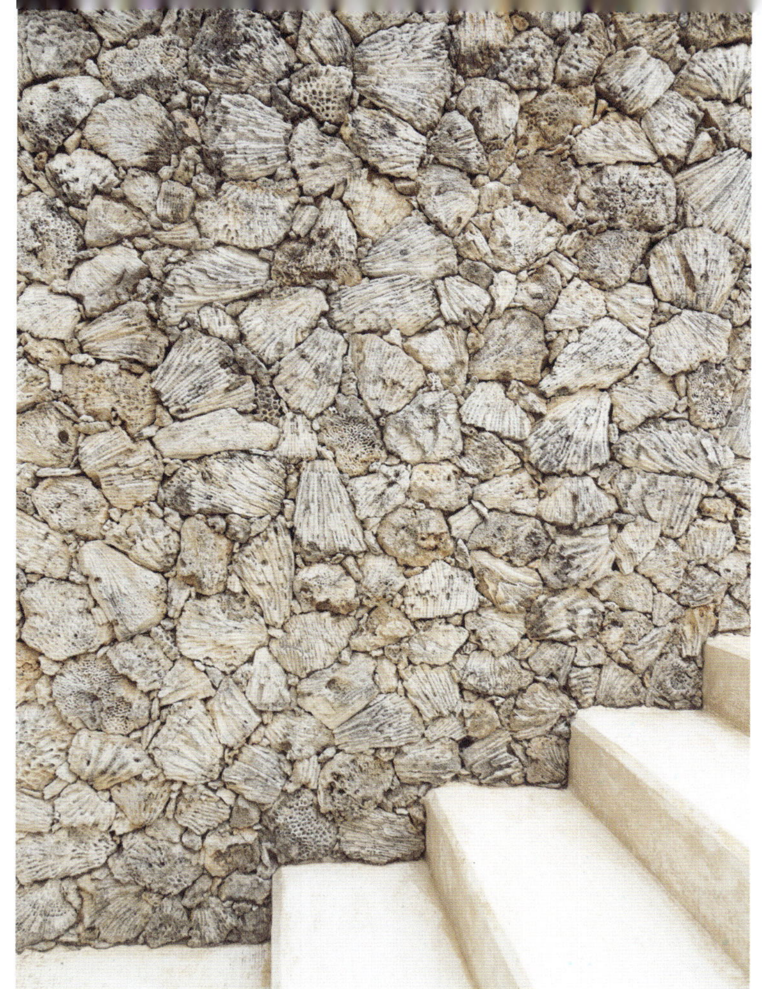

Lamu Island is not the first destination that comes to mind for many tourists, but creative souls in search of freedom and beauty know how to find their way there. It's the nature that draws them to this island, as well as the simple, unhurried pace of life and the unforgettable sunsets. Anyone who ends up there more often than not is tempted to stay for a while and, in some cases, even for good. One of these washashores is Sandy Bornman. Born and raised in South Africa, she grew up close to nature with vast open spaces. Later on in life, Sandy moved to Zambia, where she started a family. Twenty-five years ago, she and her two young daughters, Jemima and Ruby, visited Lamu Island for a holiday, and they never left.

These days, Sandy runs a womenswear, menswear and homeware brand called Aman & Ikeno. She is based in Shela, one of two villages/towns on Lamu Island where tide permitting, she prefers to start her days with a wild swim in the mangroves at 6:30 am, after which she gets to work with the tailors and managers. A typical evening on Lamu Island ends with a walk on the beach or a sunset sail on one of the traditional boats called 'dhows' as the sun dips below the horizon.

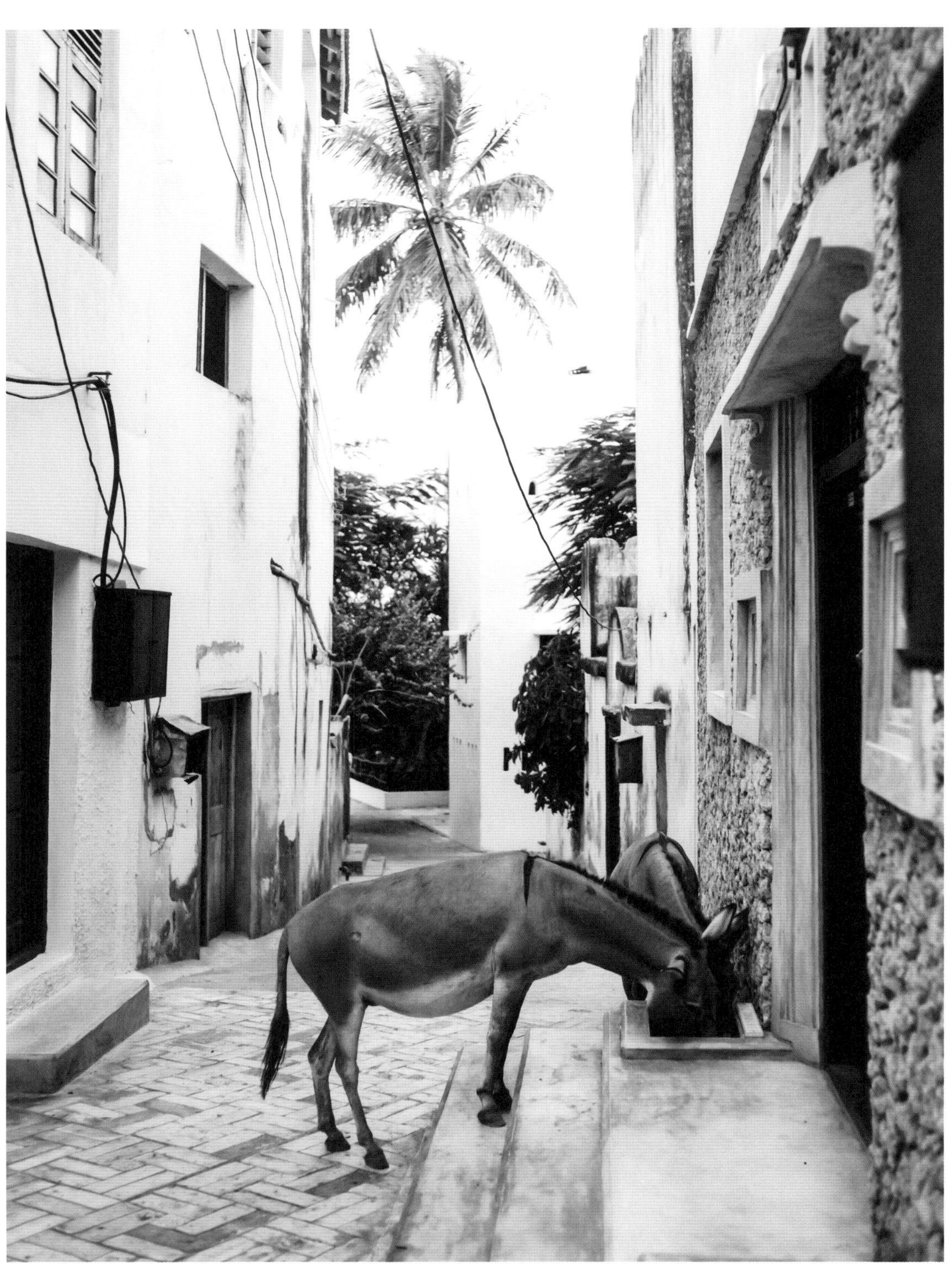

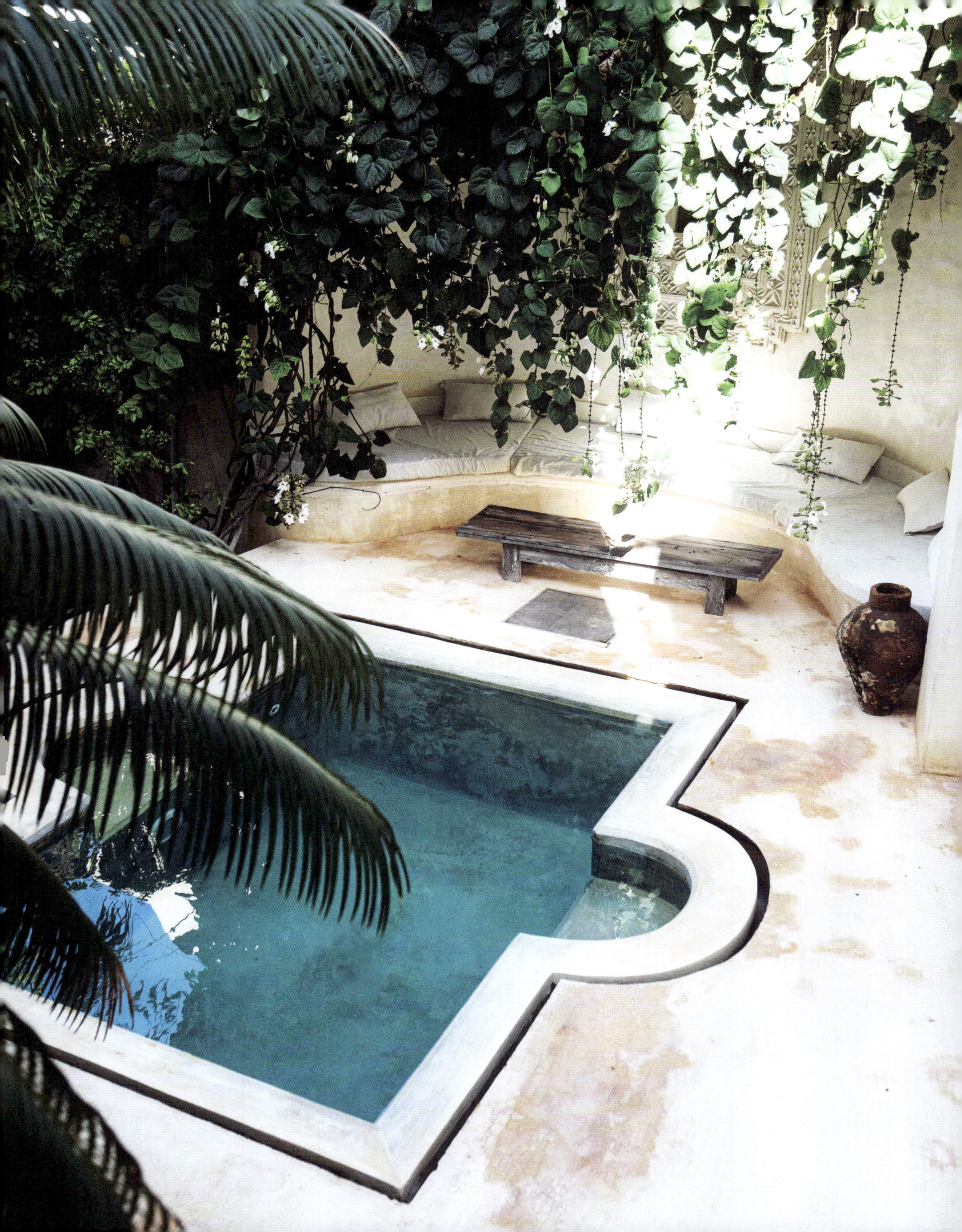

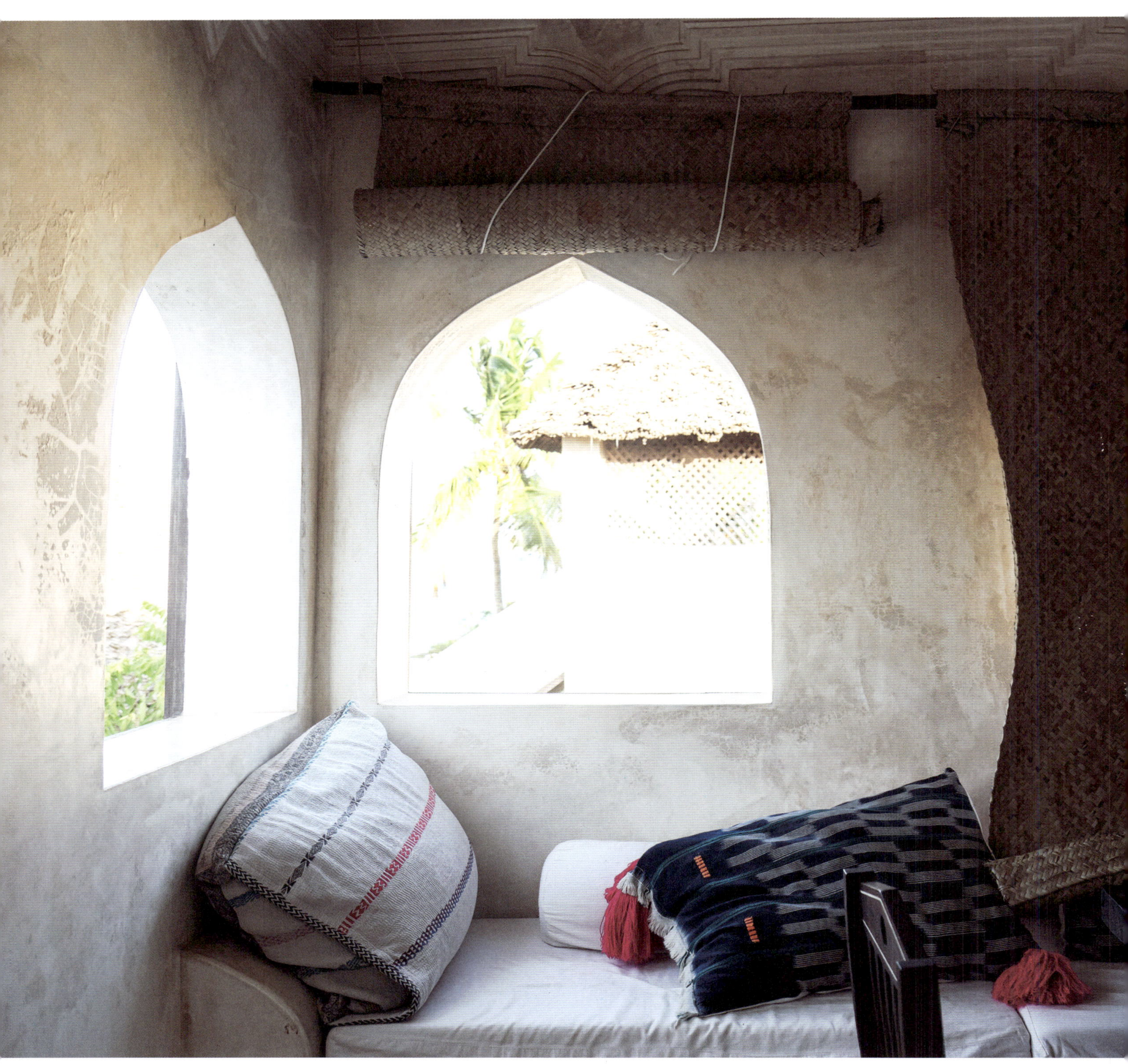

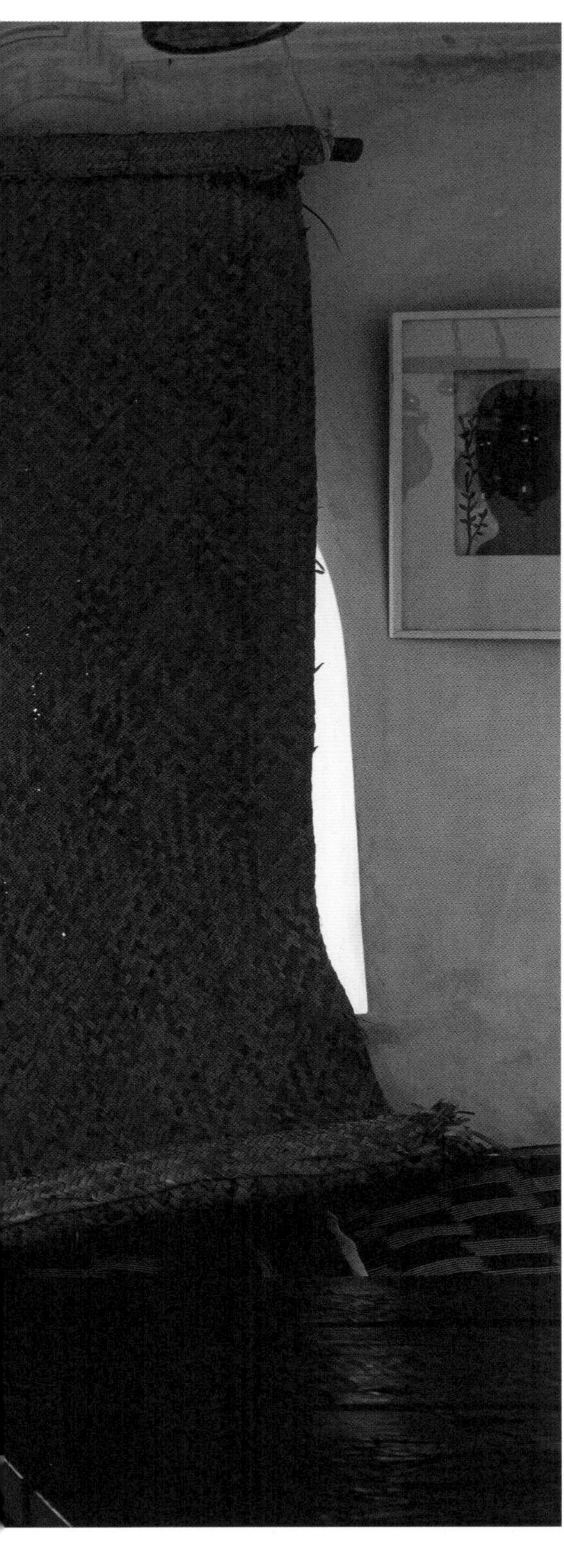

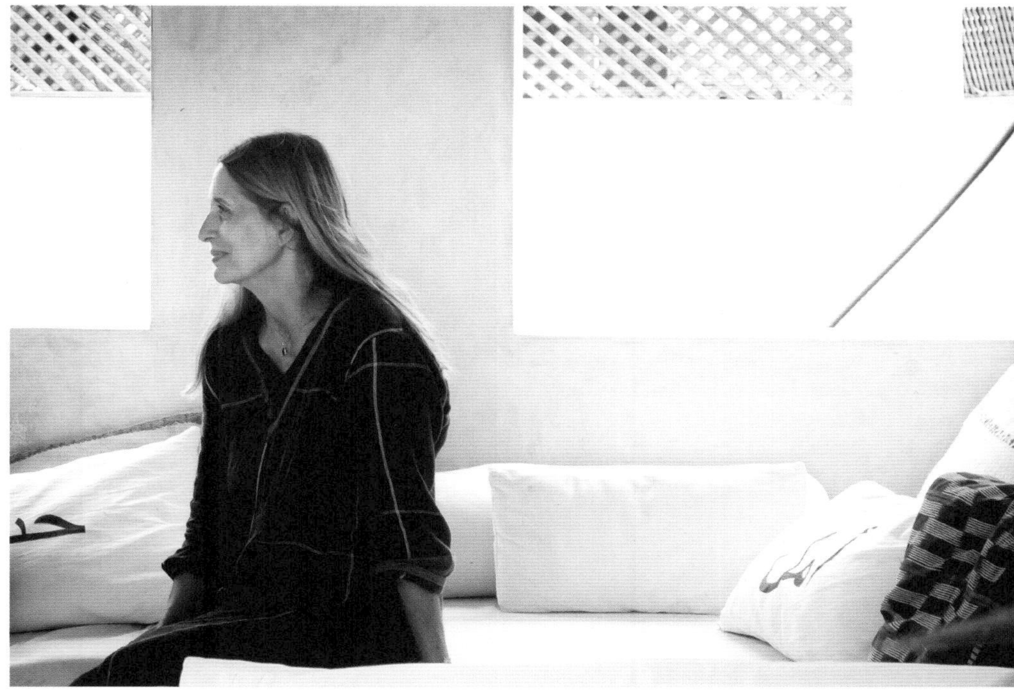

Sandy's home is a reflection of her own pure taste as well as Lamu's traditional architecture. Many of the houses on the island are built out of coral stone and limestone because they are tough, durable materials, but also because they are cooler than cement. The low houses are situated behind the dunes, making them barely visible from the beach. A lime and cement plaster or 'neru' is used to achieve a smooth finish. Influenced by a fusion of Swahili, Arabic, Persian and Indian styles, houses in Lamu typically have balconies, arches, courtyards and carved wooden doors.

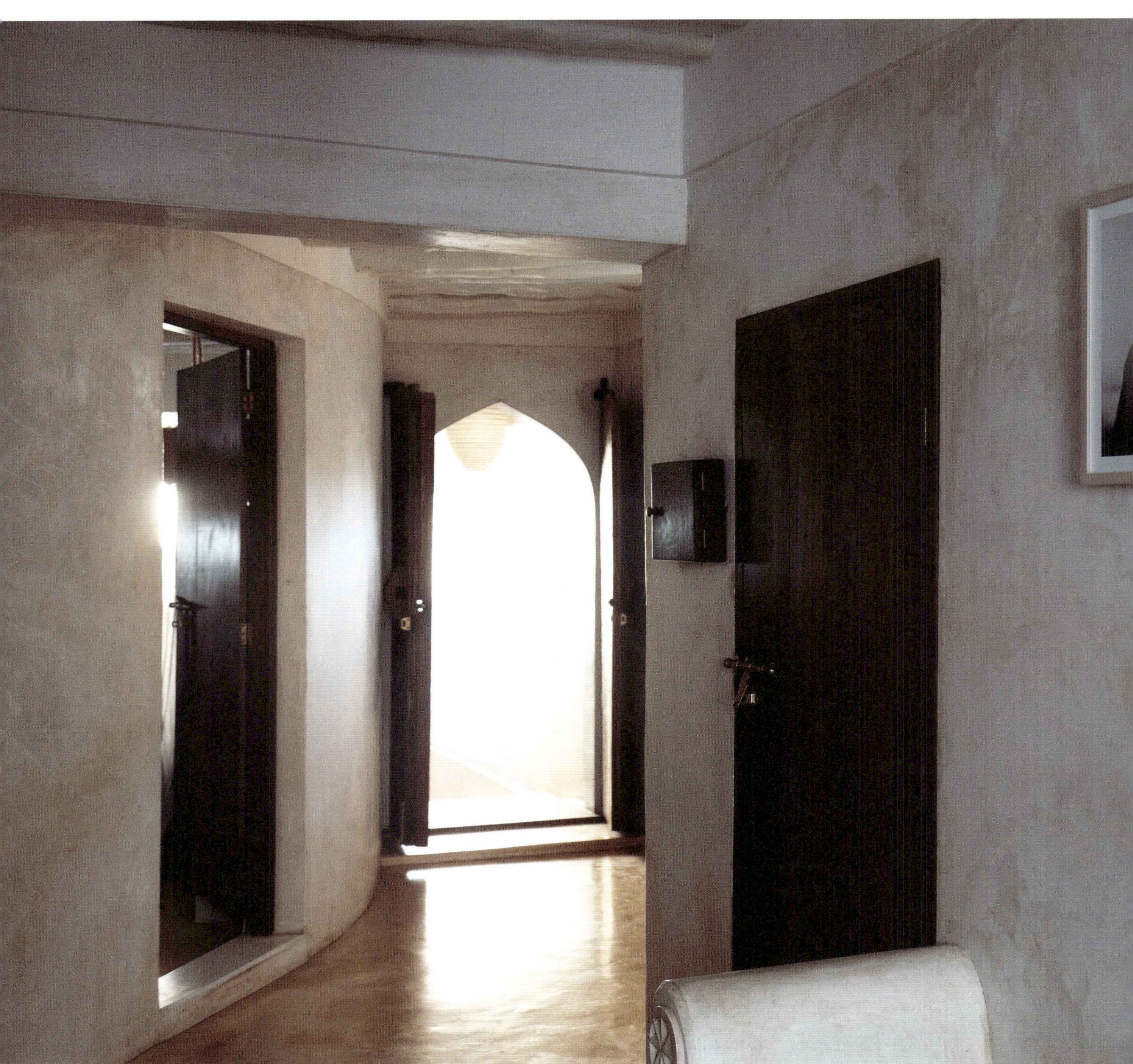

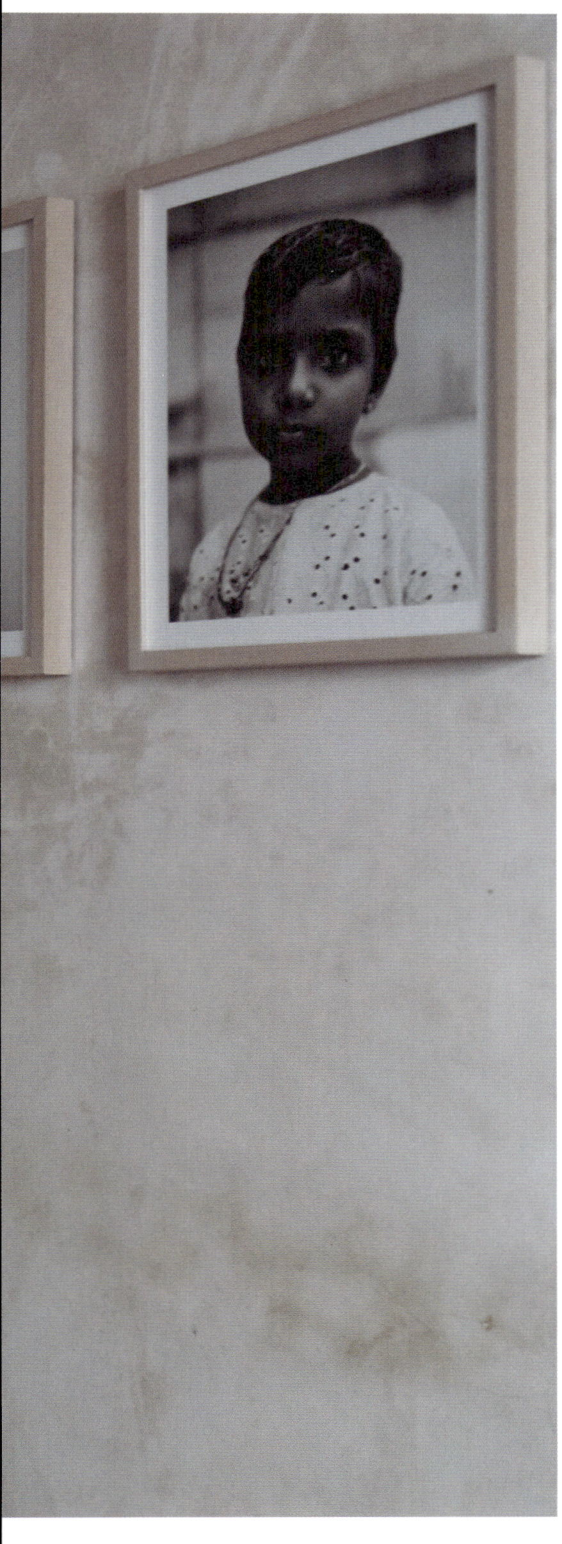

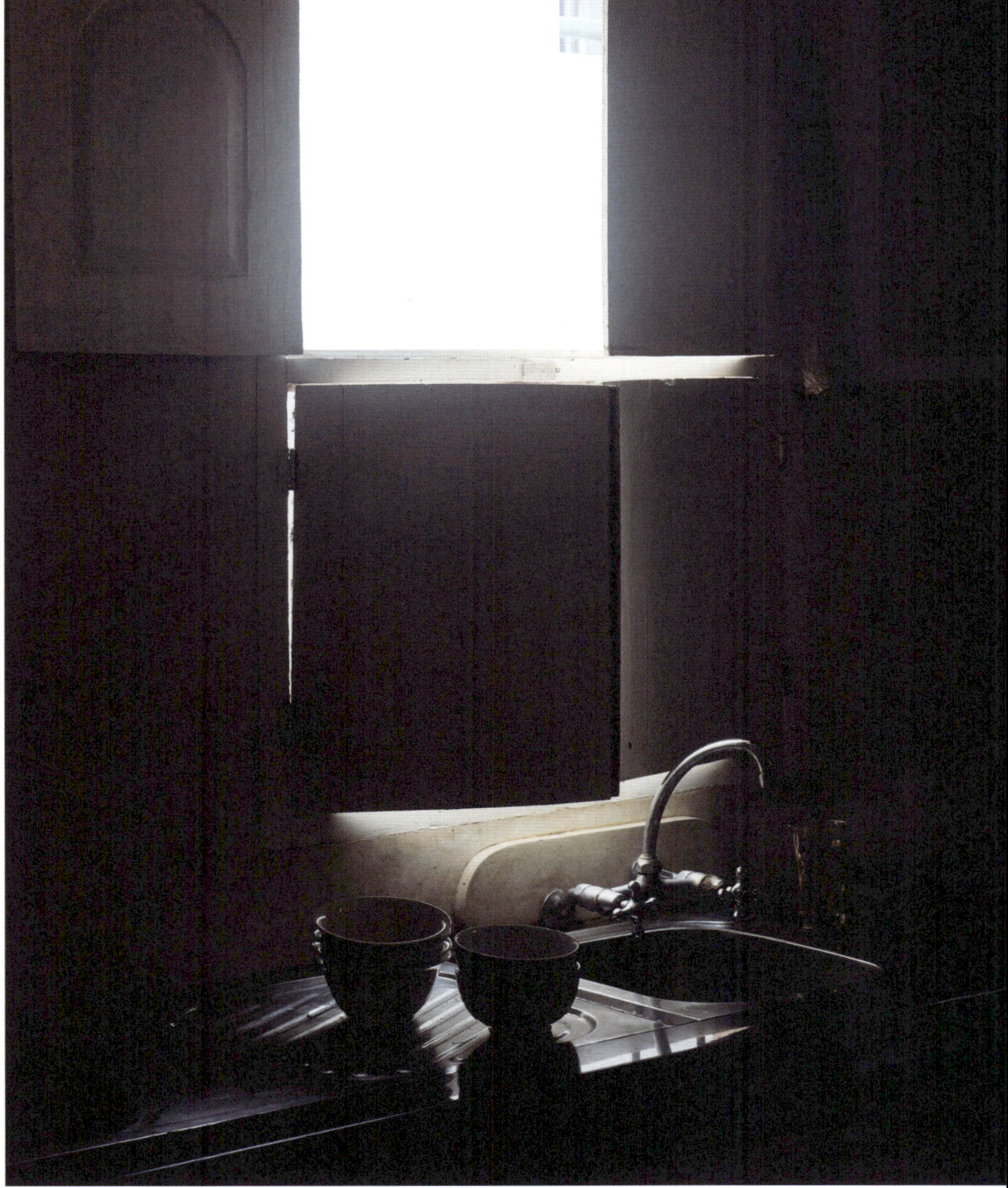

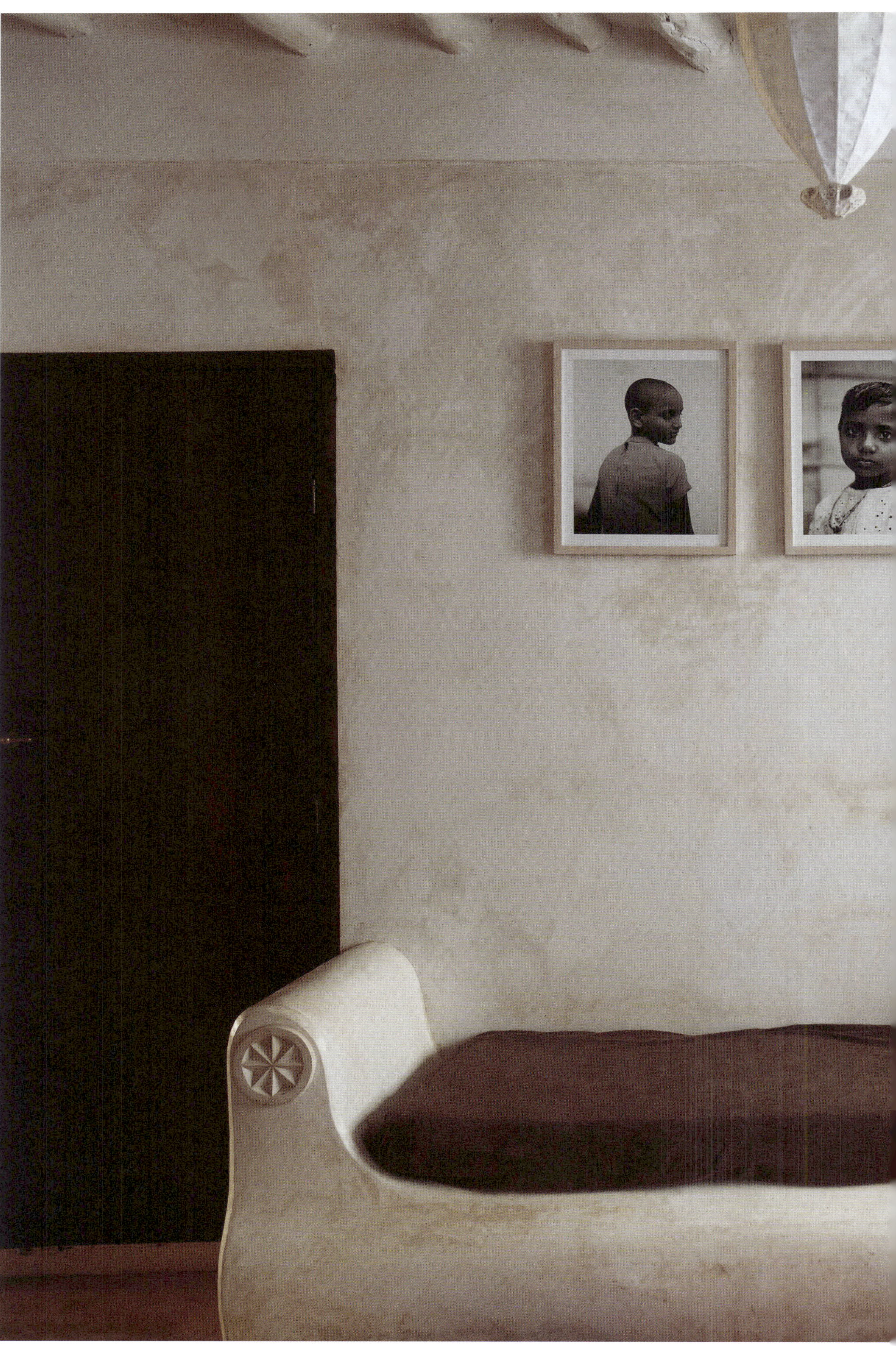

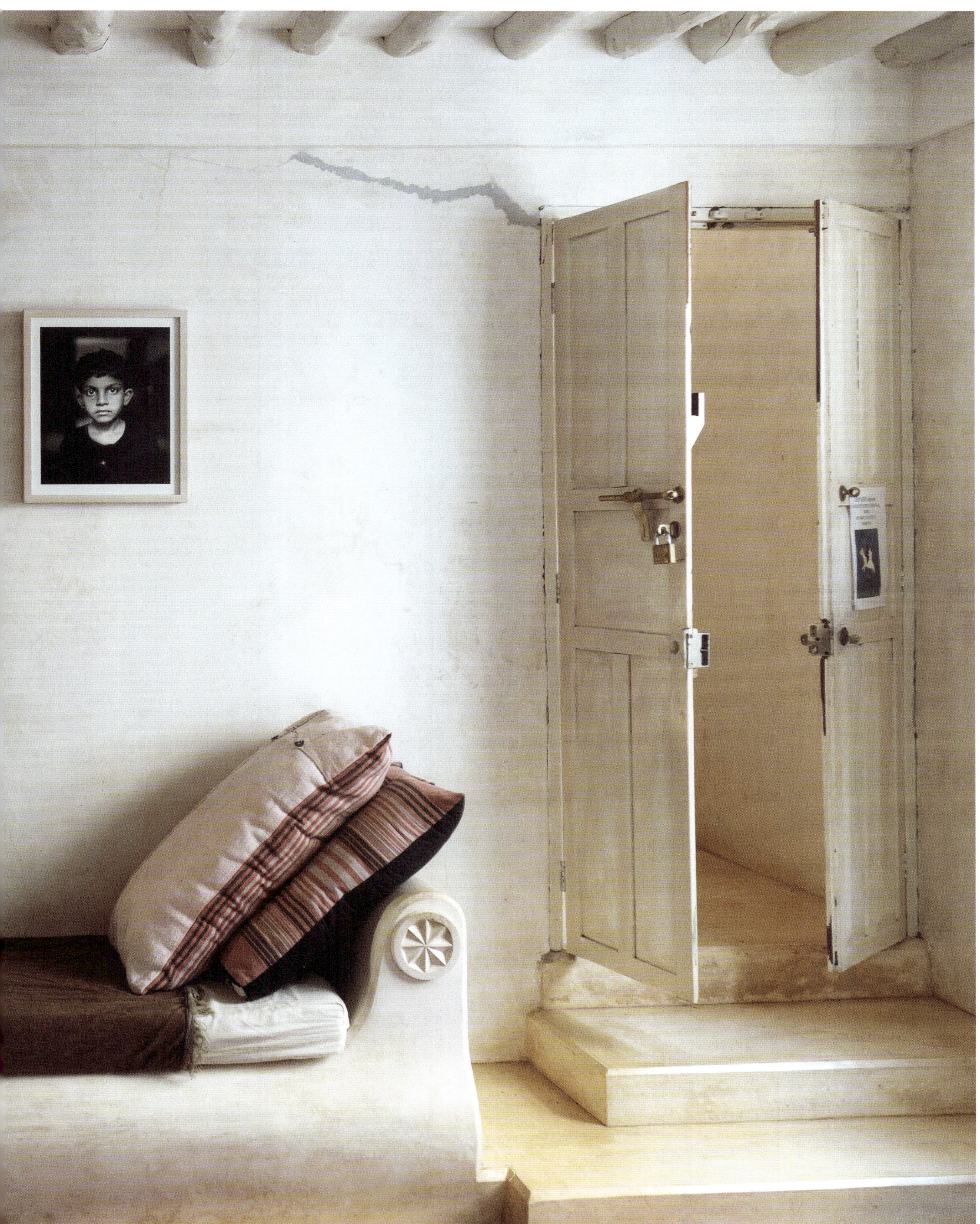

The house belongs to Majid Sheikh, a majestic man whose family originally came from Afghanistan. It was renovated by his son. Like so many houses in Lamu, it has a built-in seating area or 'baraza', beds and cupboards. The spaces have been kept simple, which only serves to accentuate their beauty. All are designed in function of the house's most important feature, its breathtaking views. The arches, open courtyard, and balconies all face the ocean, allowing the scent of ylang-ylang and frangipani to waft in on the sea breeze. This is a place that captivates the senses and soothes the soul.

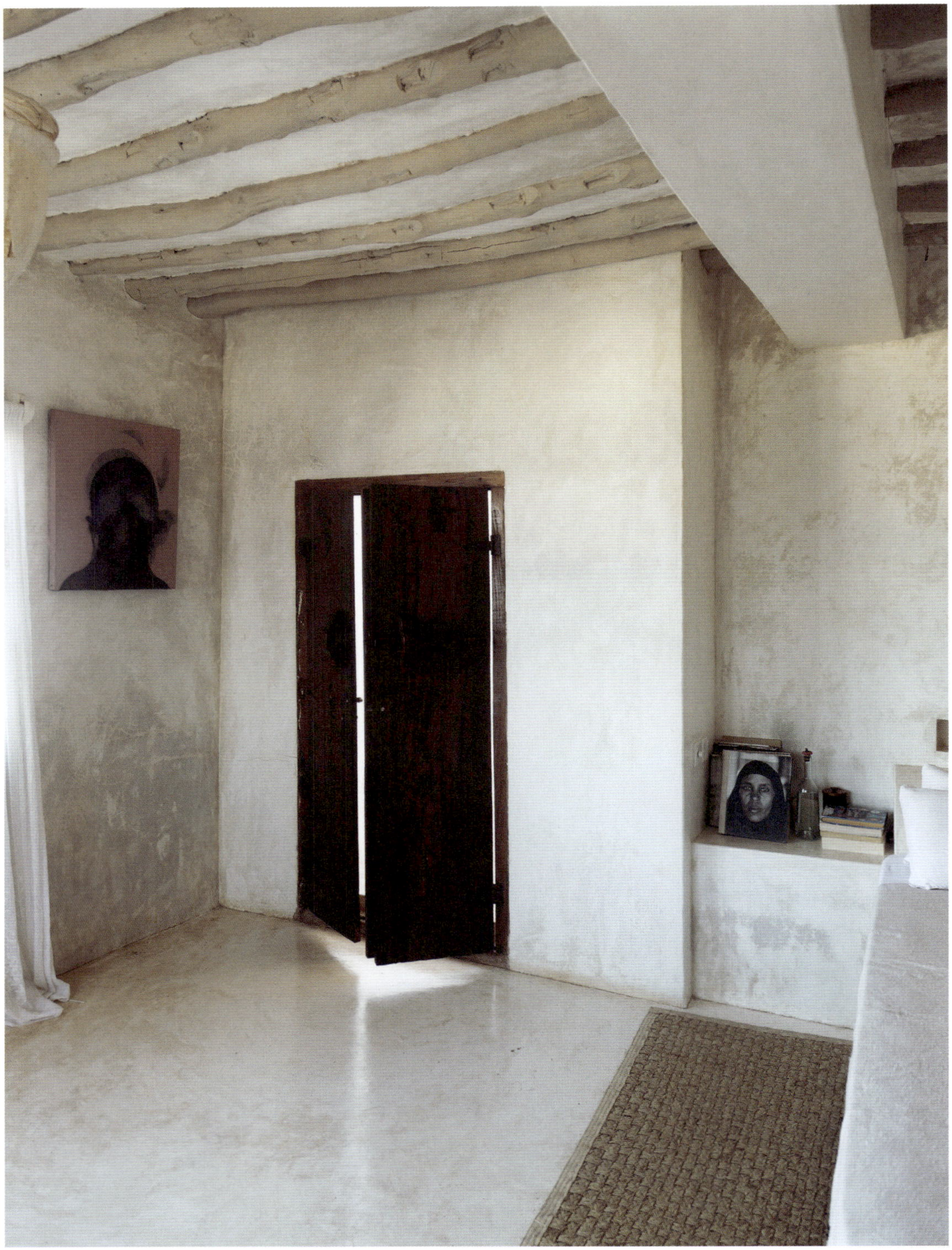

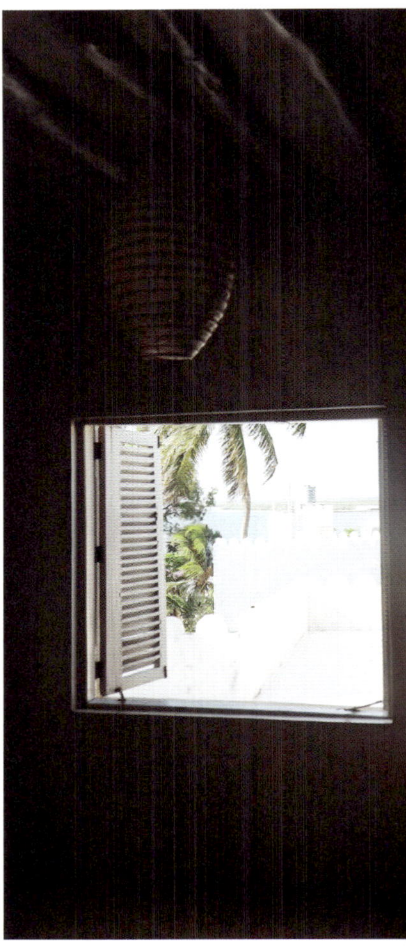

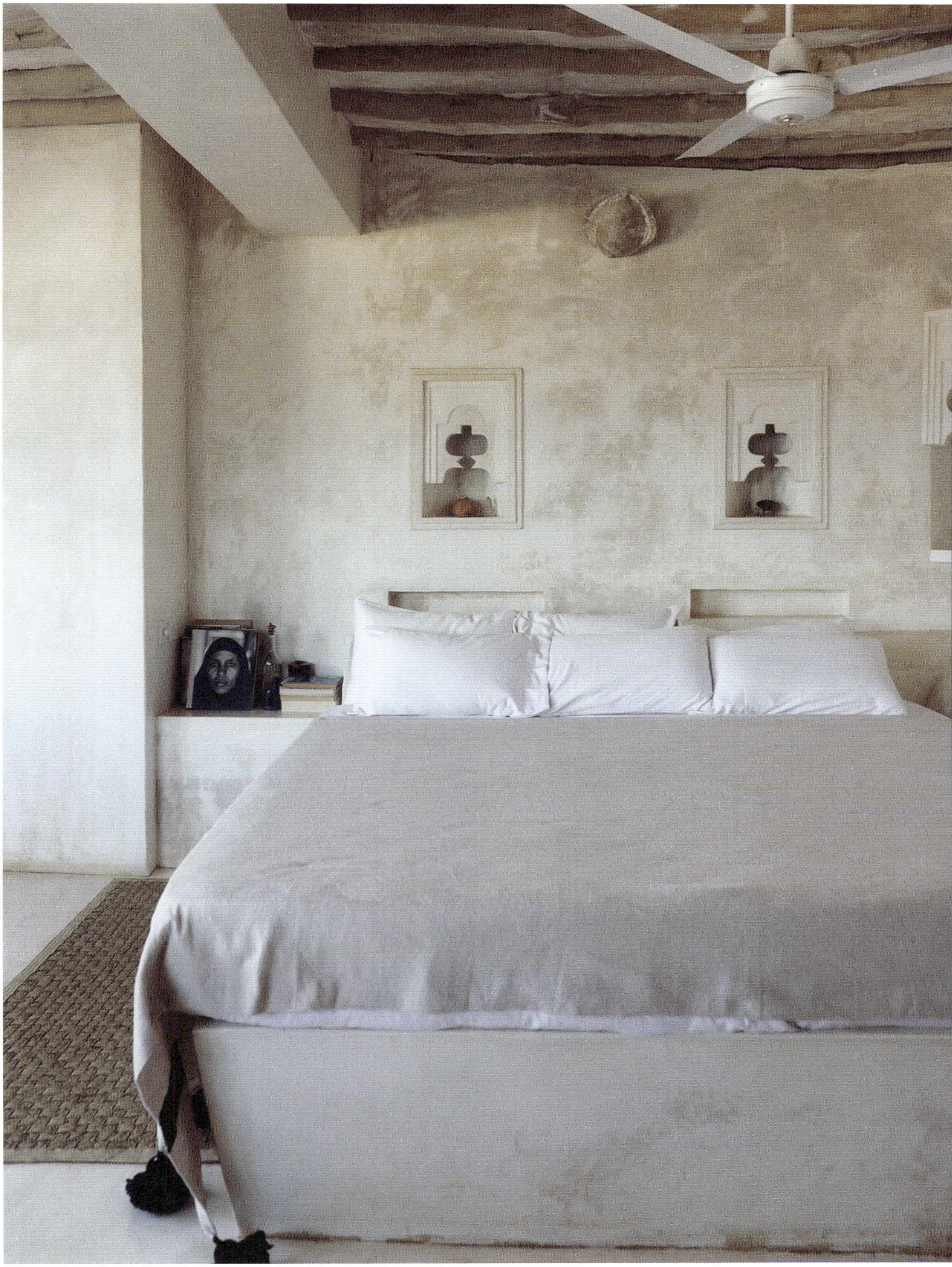

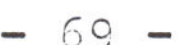

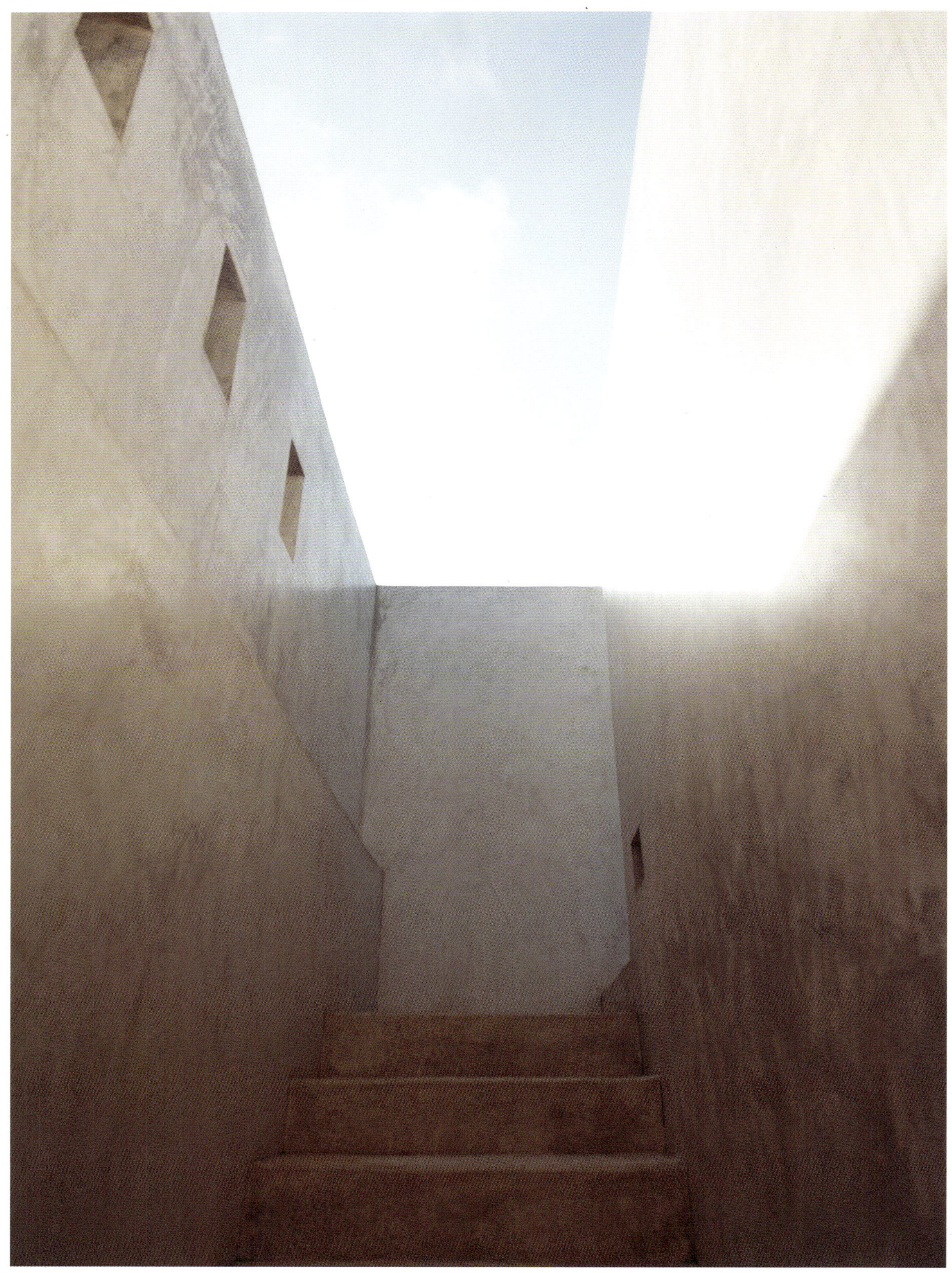

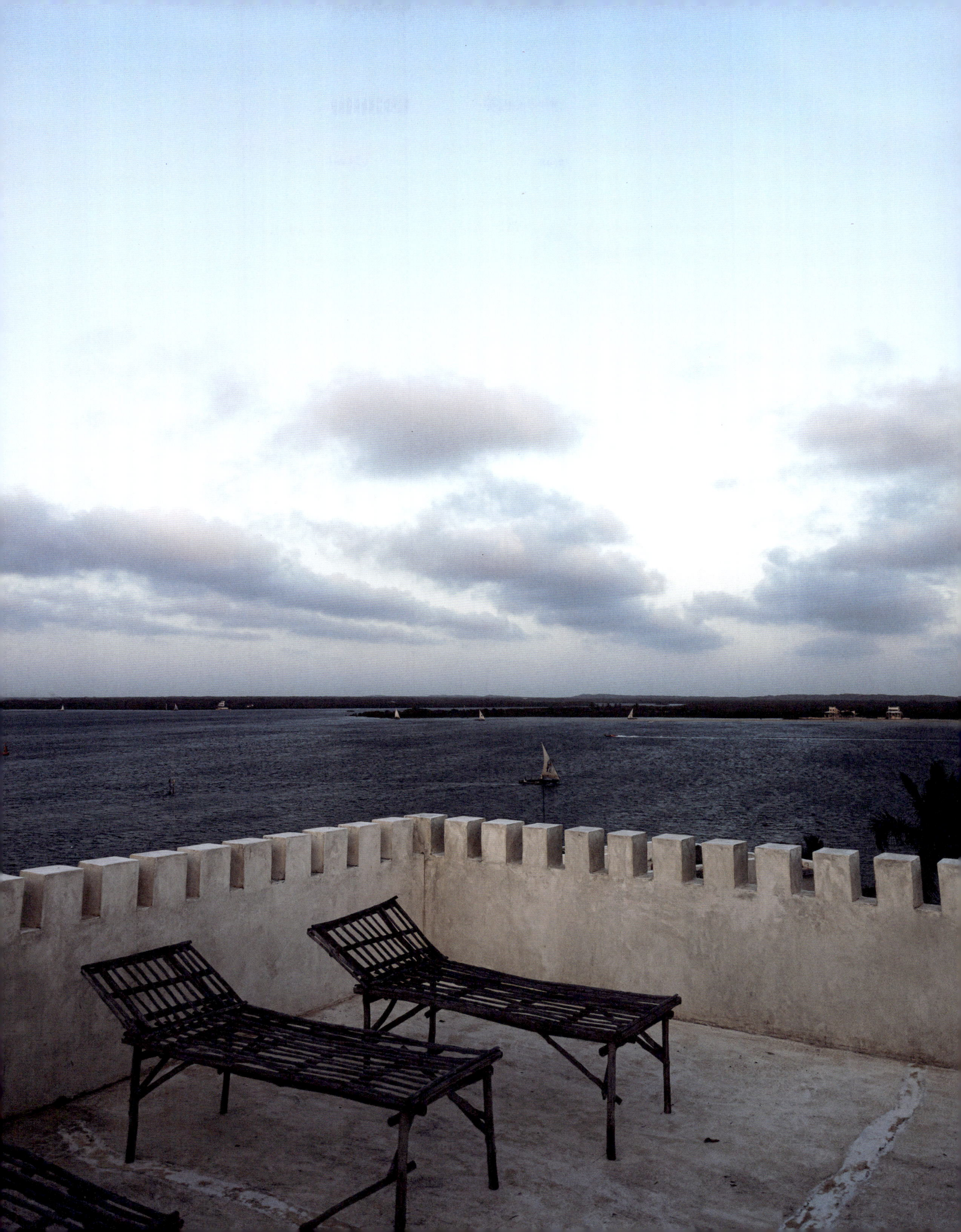

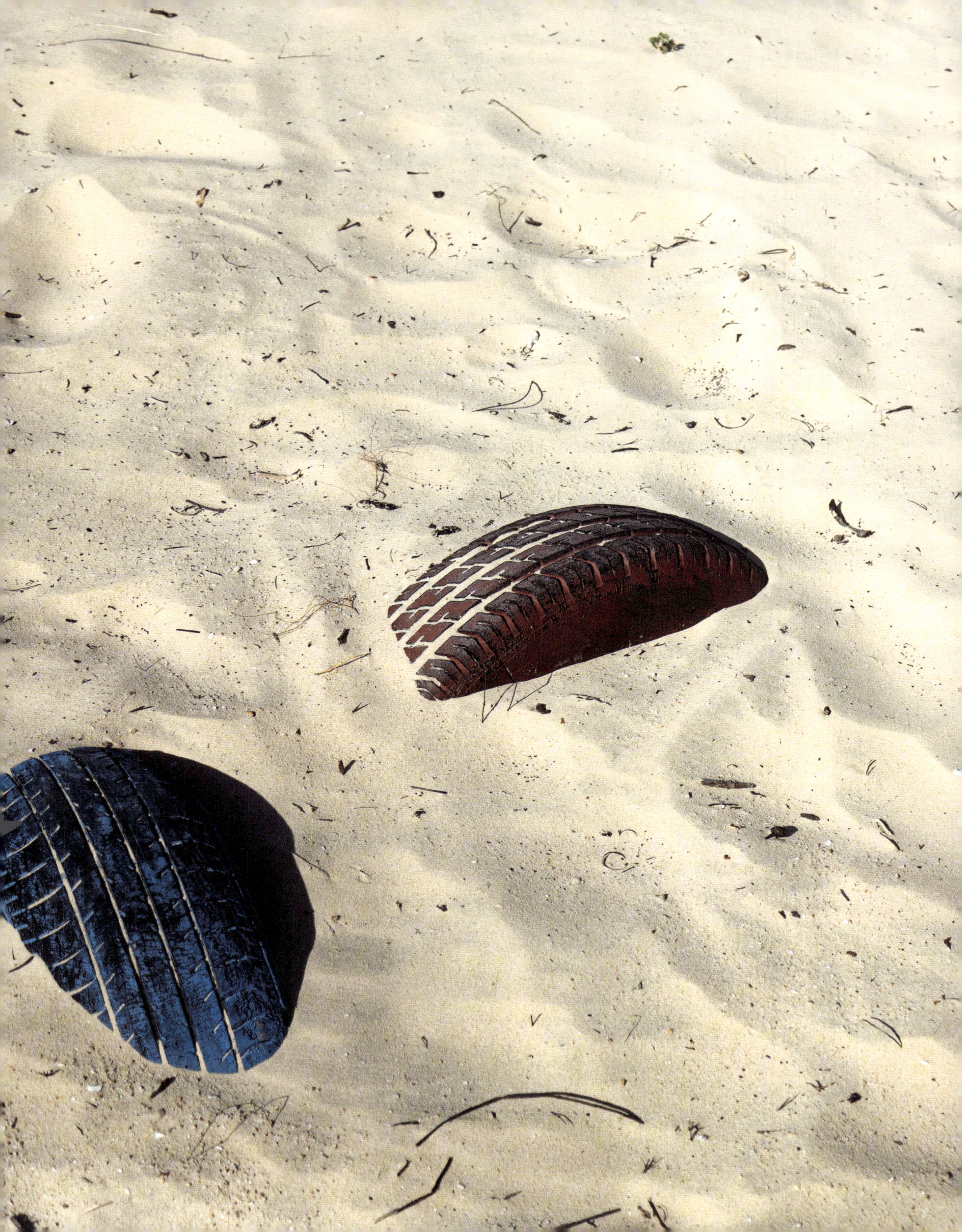

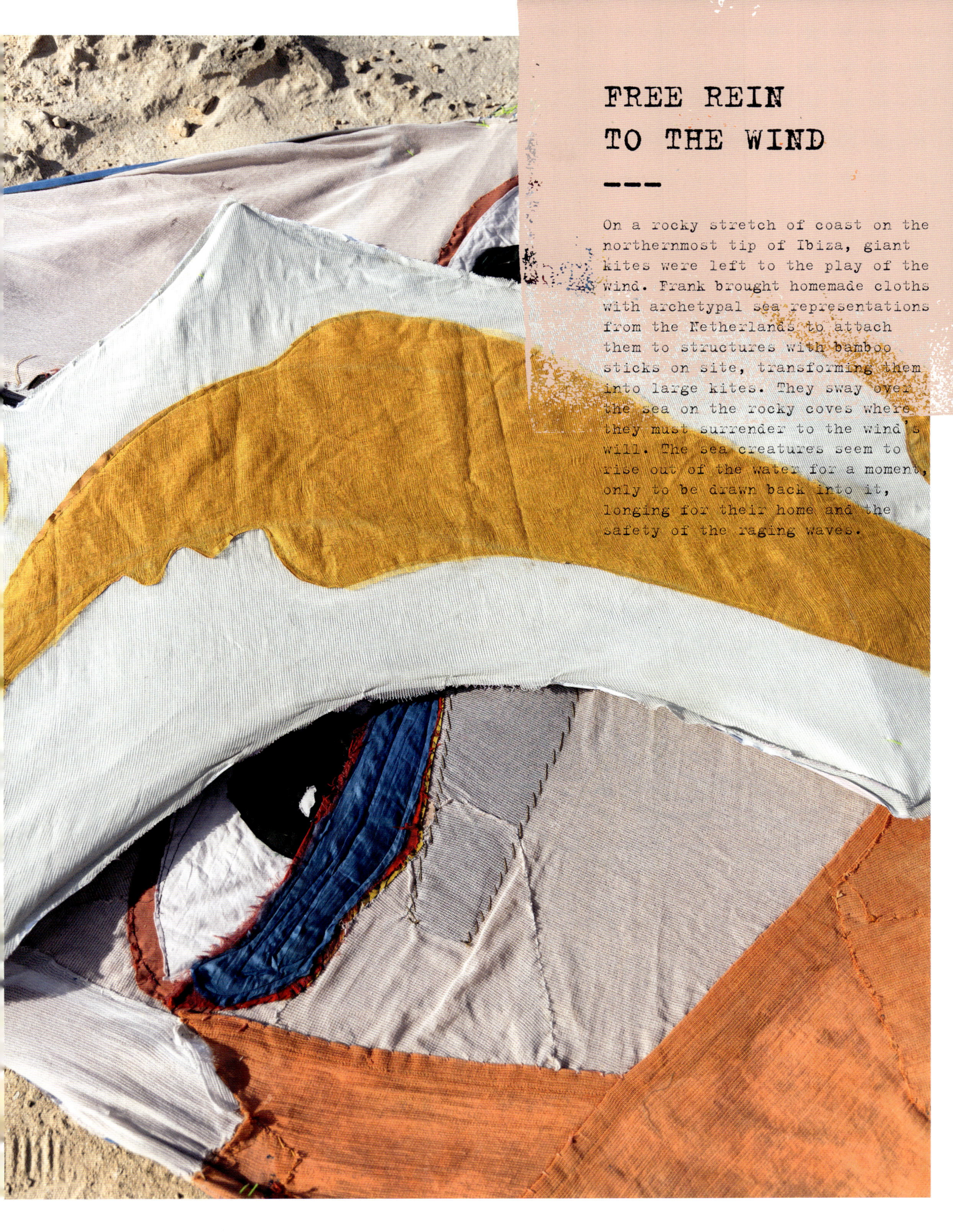

FREE REIN TO THE WIND

On a rocky stretch of coast on the northernmost tip of Ibiza, giant kites were left to the play of the wind. Frank brought homemade cloths with archetypal sea representations from the Netherlands to attach them to structures with bamboo sticks on site, transforming them into large kites. They sway over the sea on the rocky coves where they must surrender to the wind's will. The sea creatures seem to rise out of the water for a moment, only to be drawn back into it, longing for their home and the safety of the raging waves.

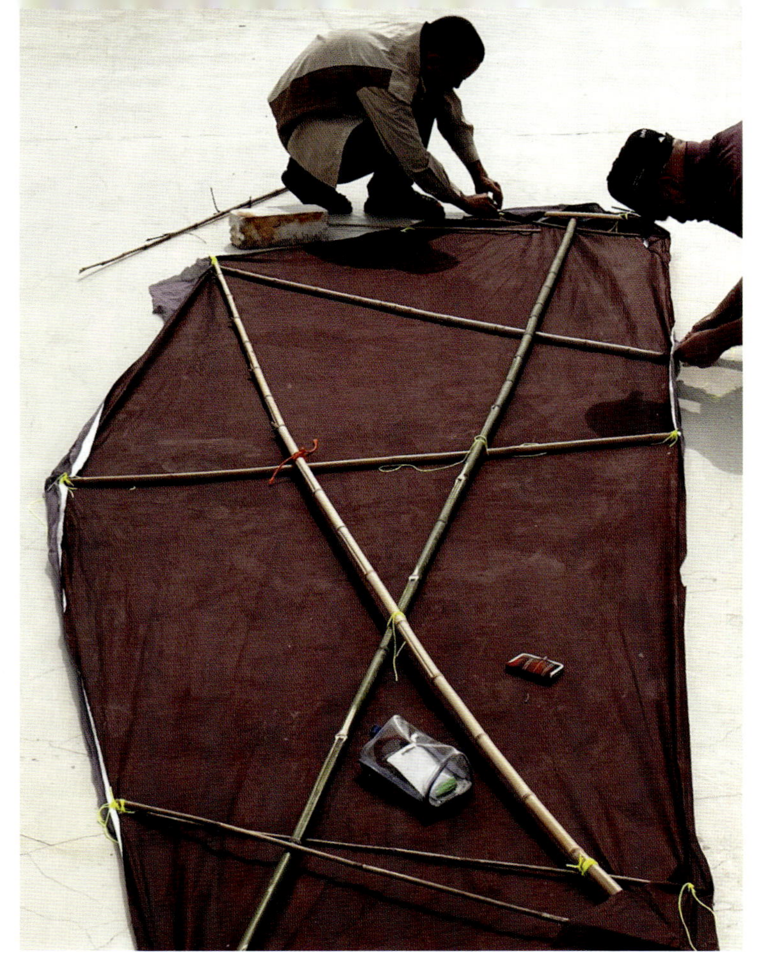

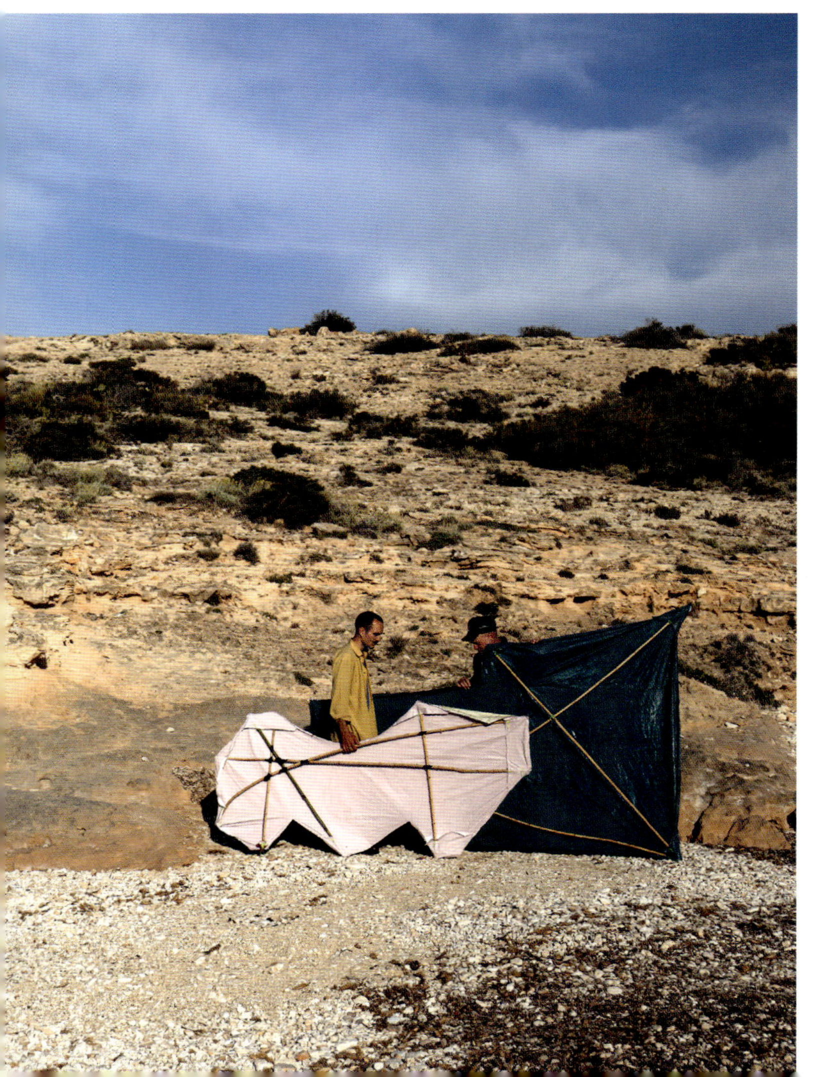

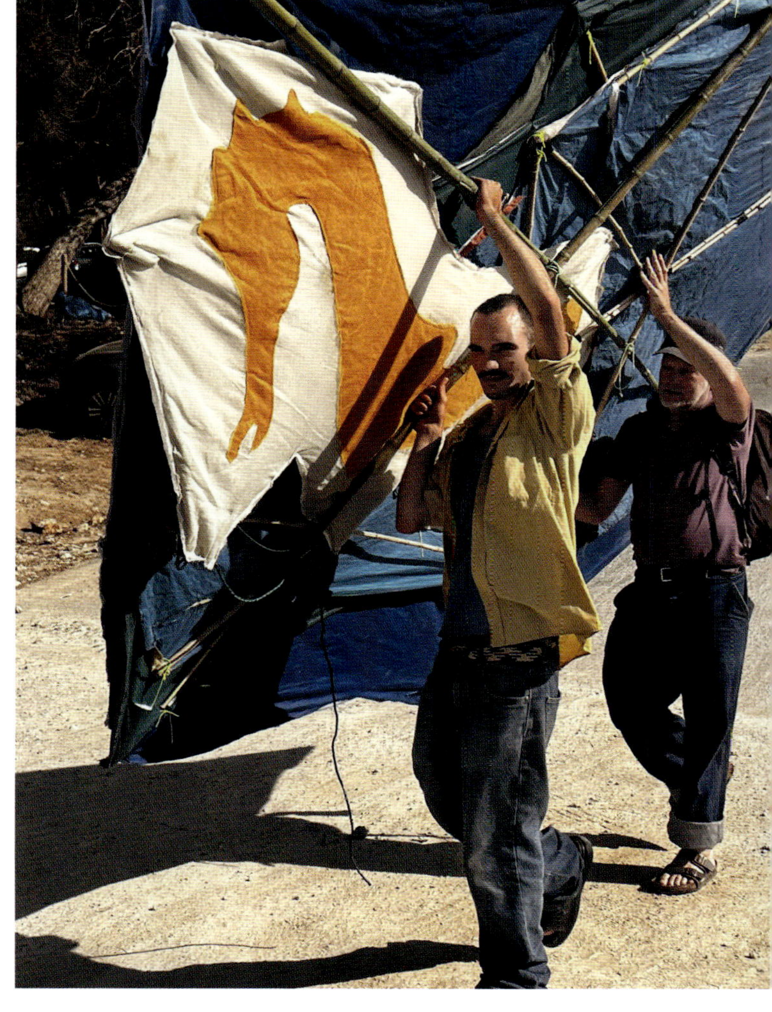

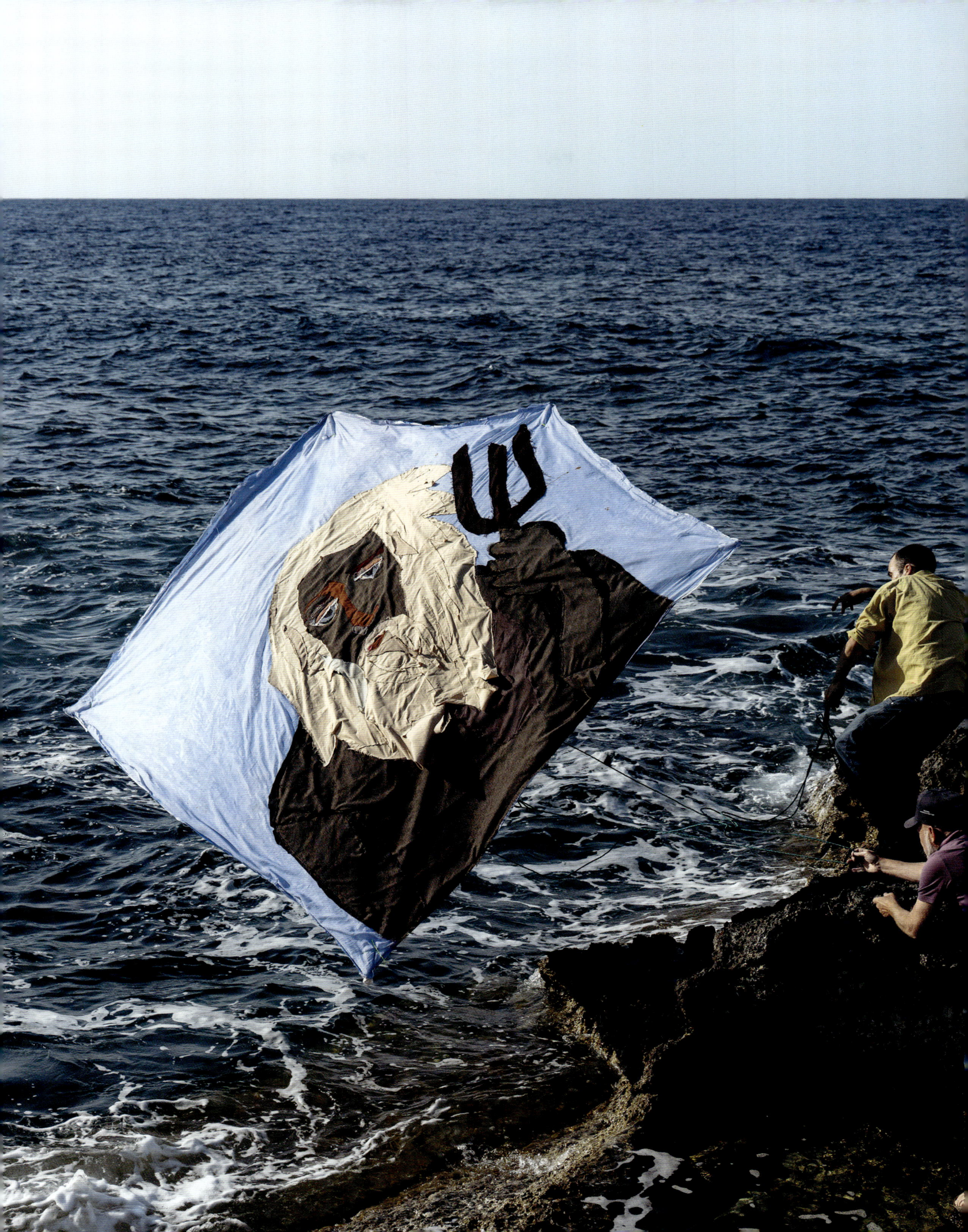

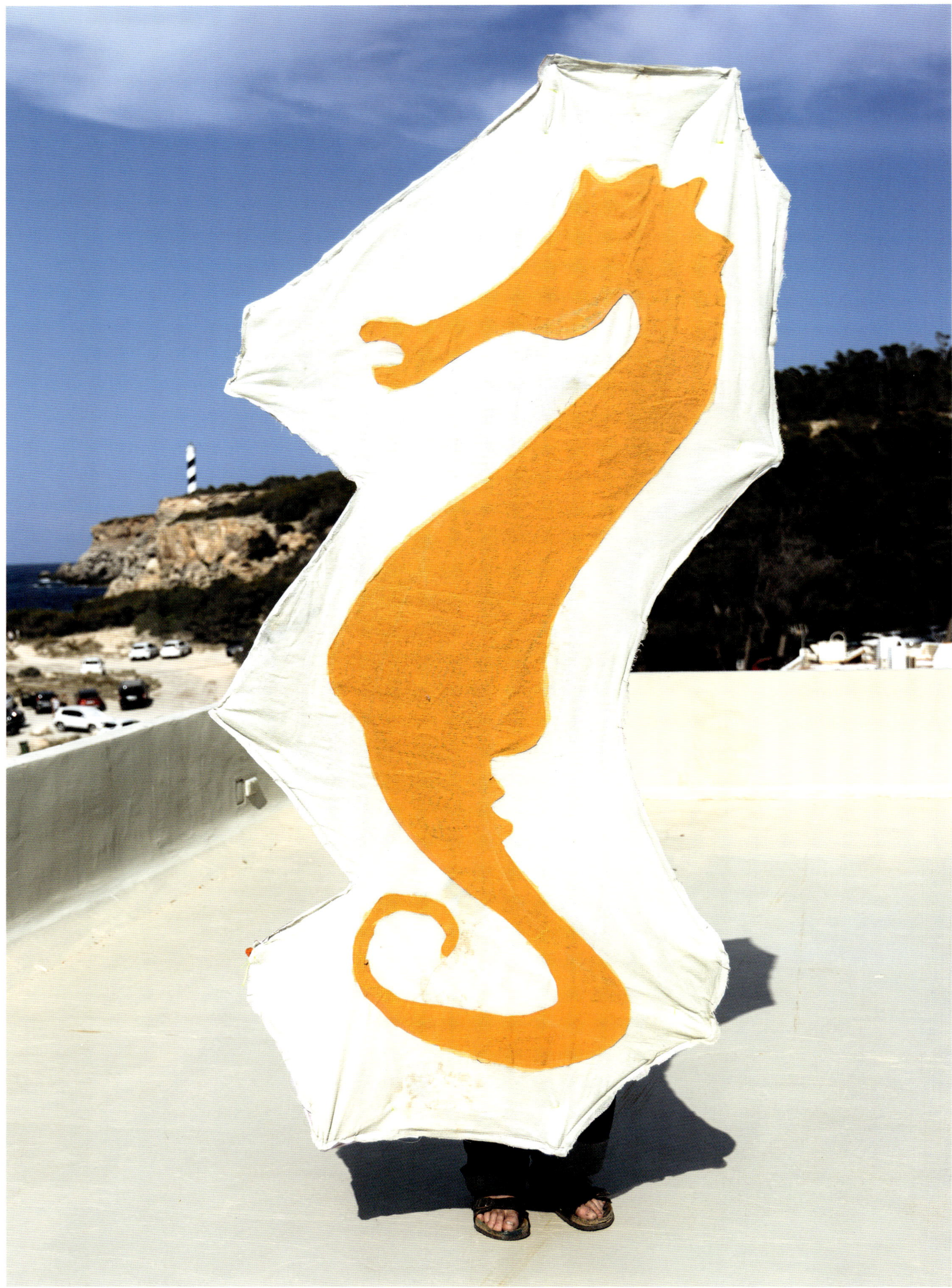

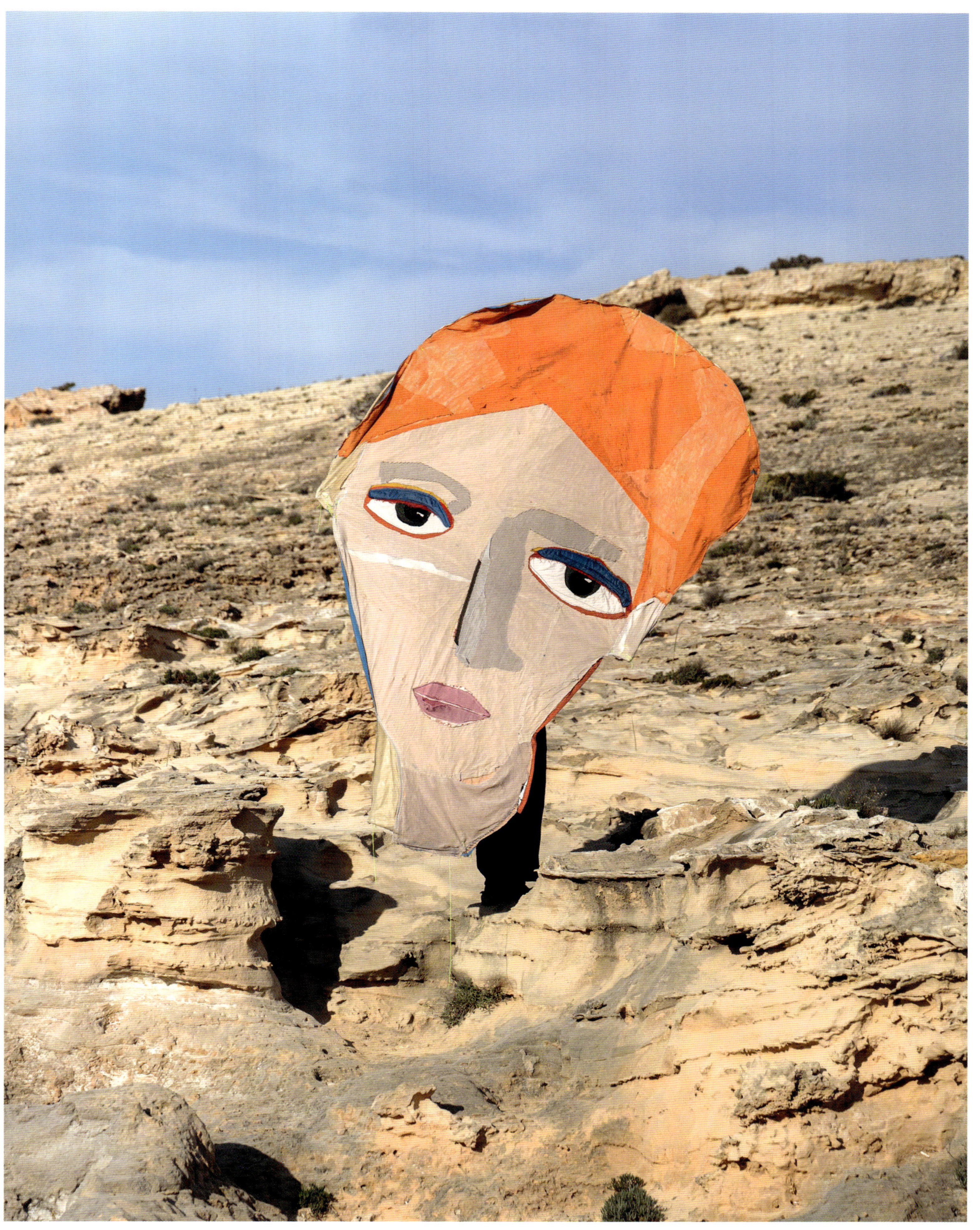

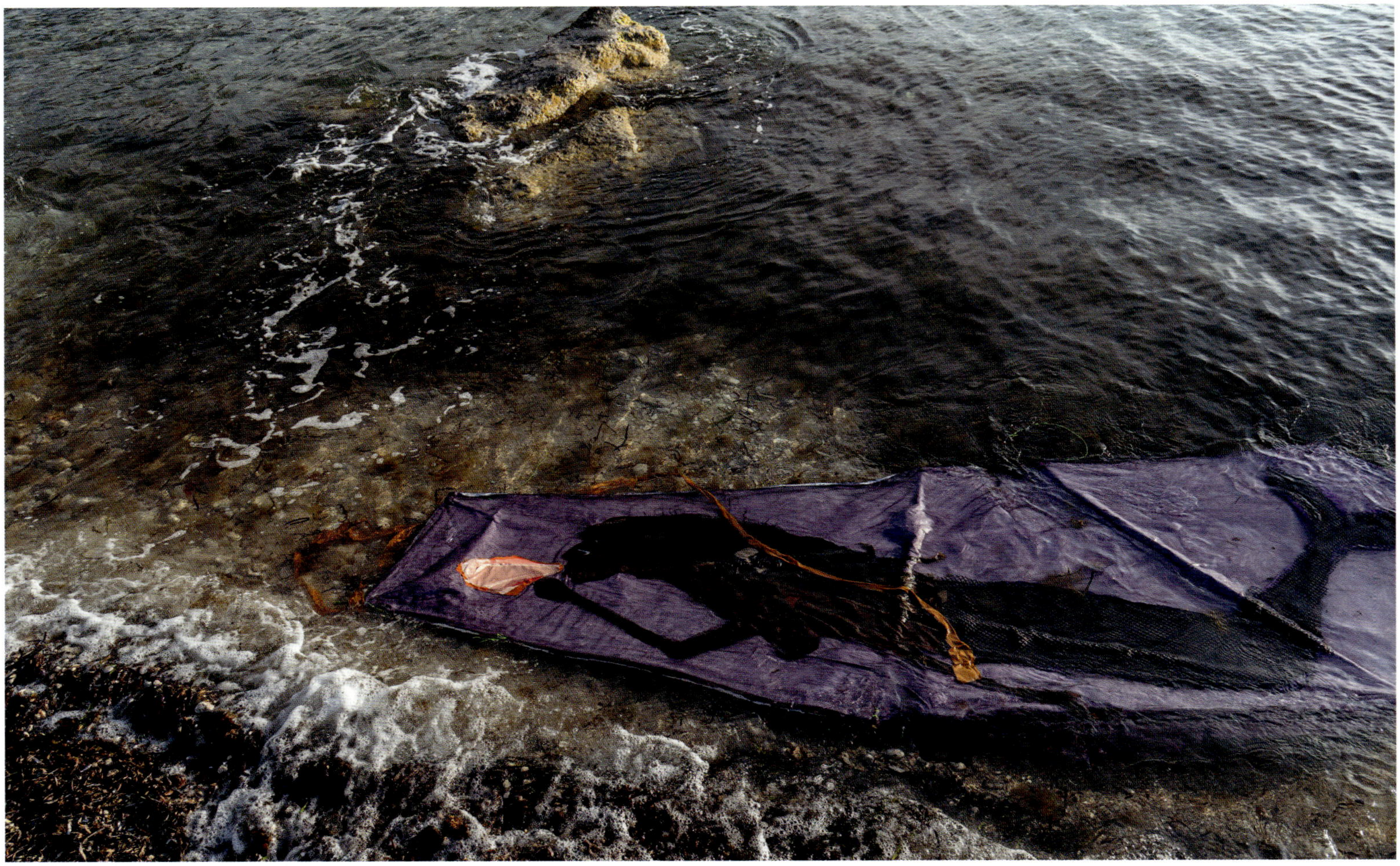

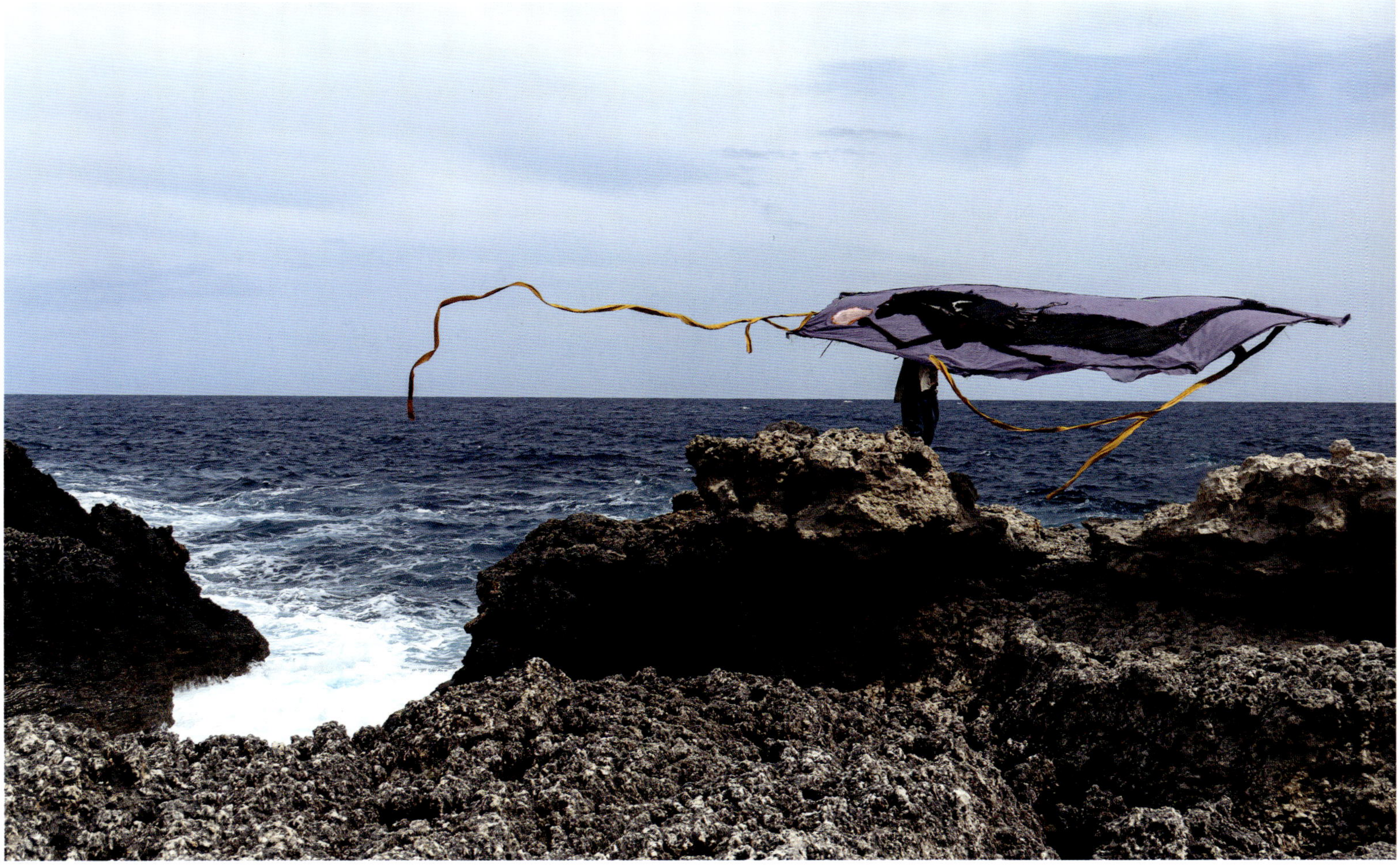

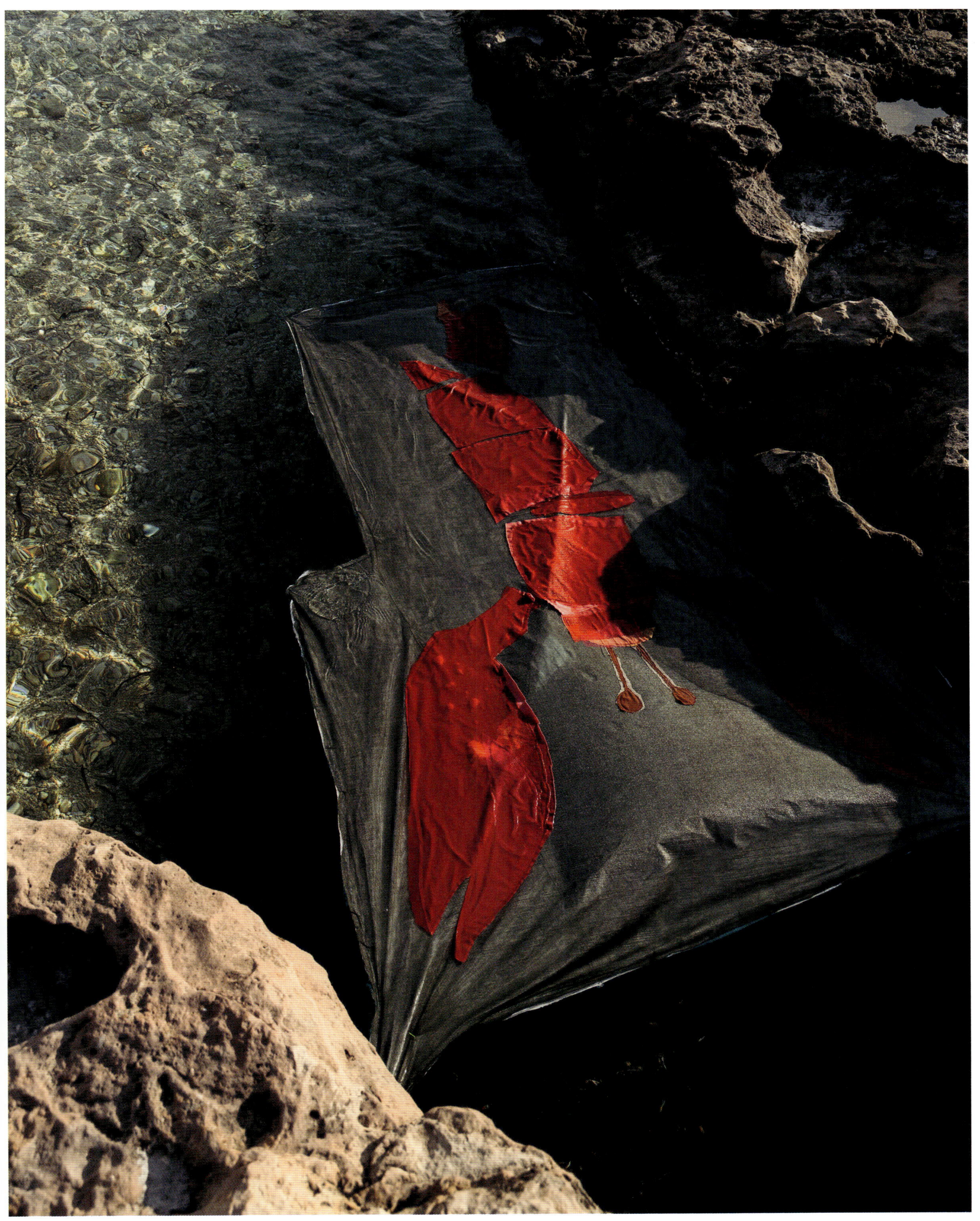

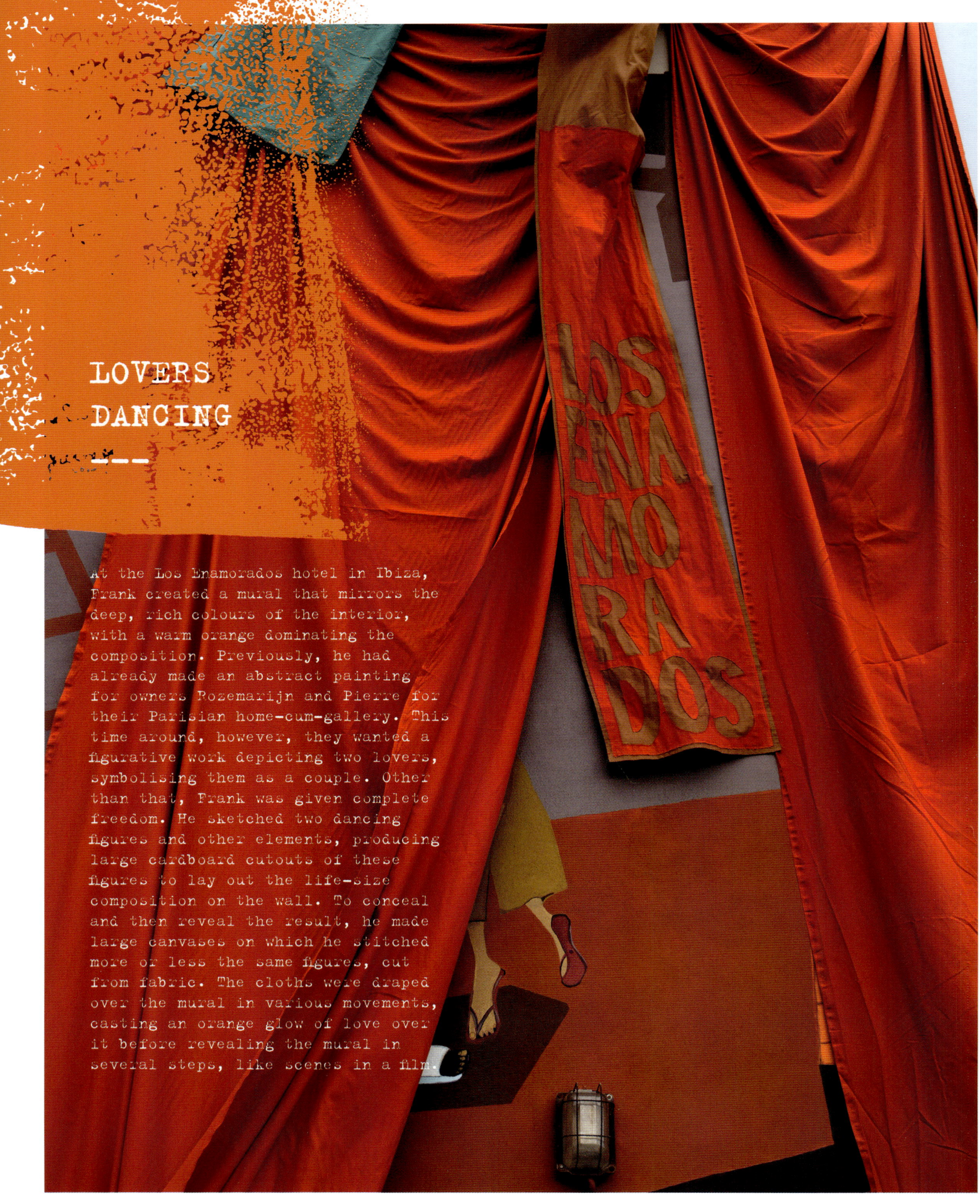

LOVERS DANCING

At the Los Enamorados hotel in Ibiza, Frank created a mural that mirrors the deep, rich colours of the interior, with a warm orange dominating the composition. Previously, he had already made an abstract painting for owners Rozemarijn and Pierre for their Parisian home-cum-gallery. This time around, however, they wanted a figurative work depicting two lovers, symbolising them as a couple. Other than that, Frank was given complete freedom. He sketched two dancing figures and other elements, producing large cardboard cutouts of these figures to lay out the life-size composition on the wall. To conceal and then reveal the result, he made large canvases on which he stitched more or less the same figures, cut from fabric. The cloths were draped over the mural in various movements, casting an orange glow of love over it before revealing the mural in several steps, like scenes in a film.

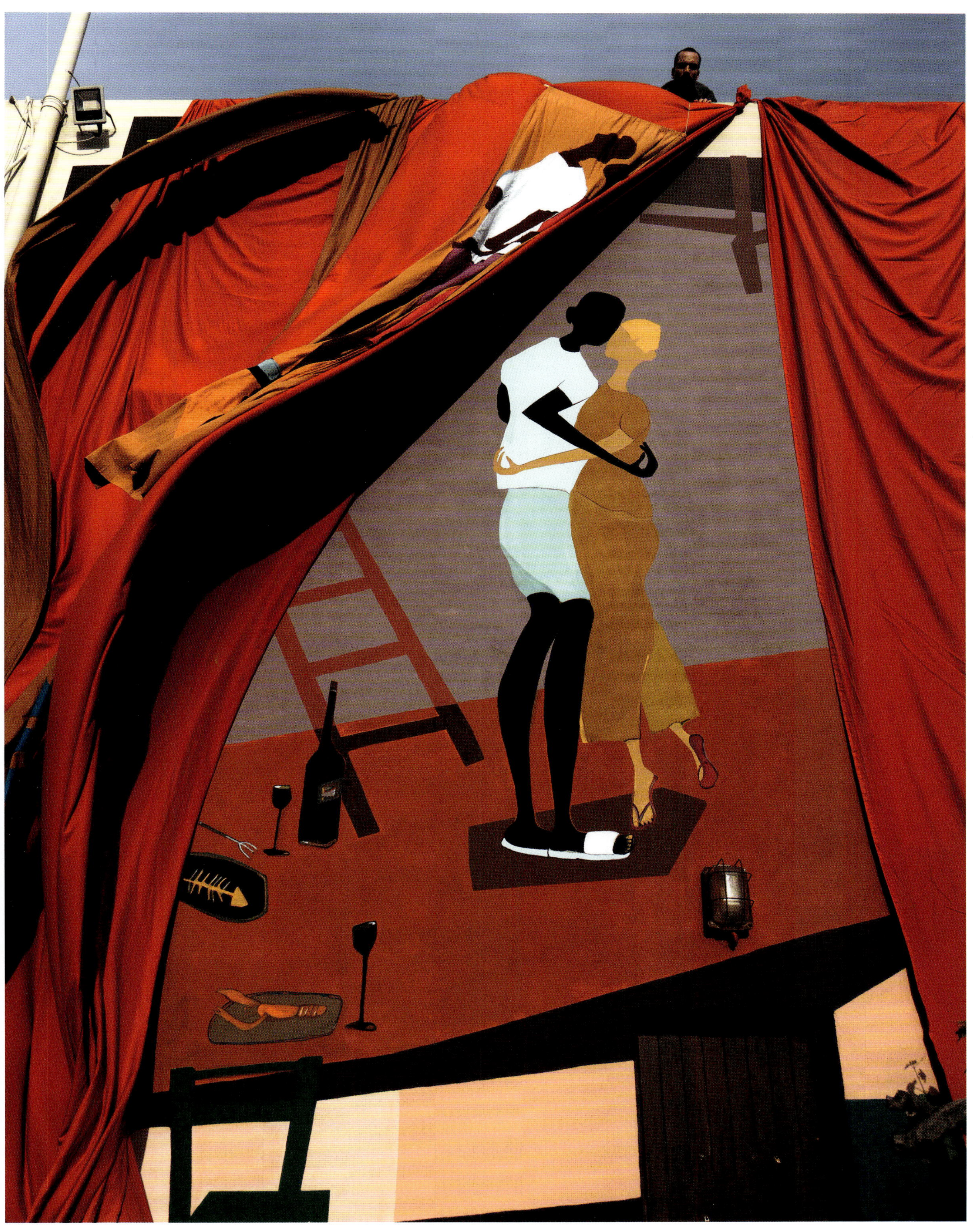

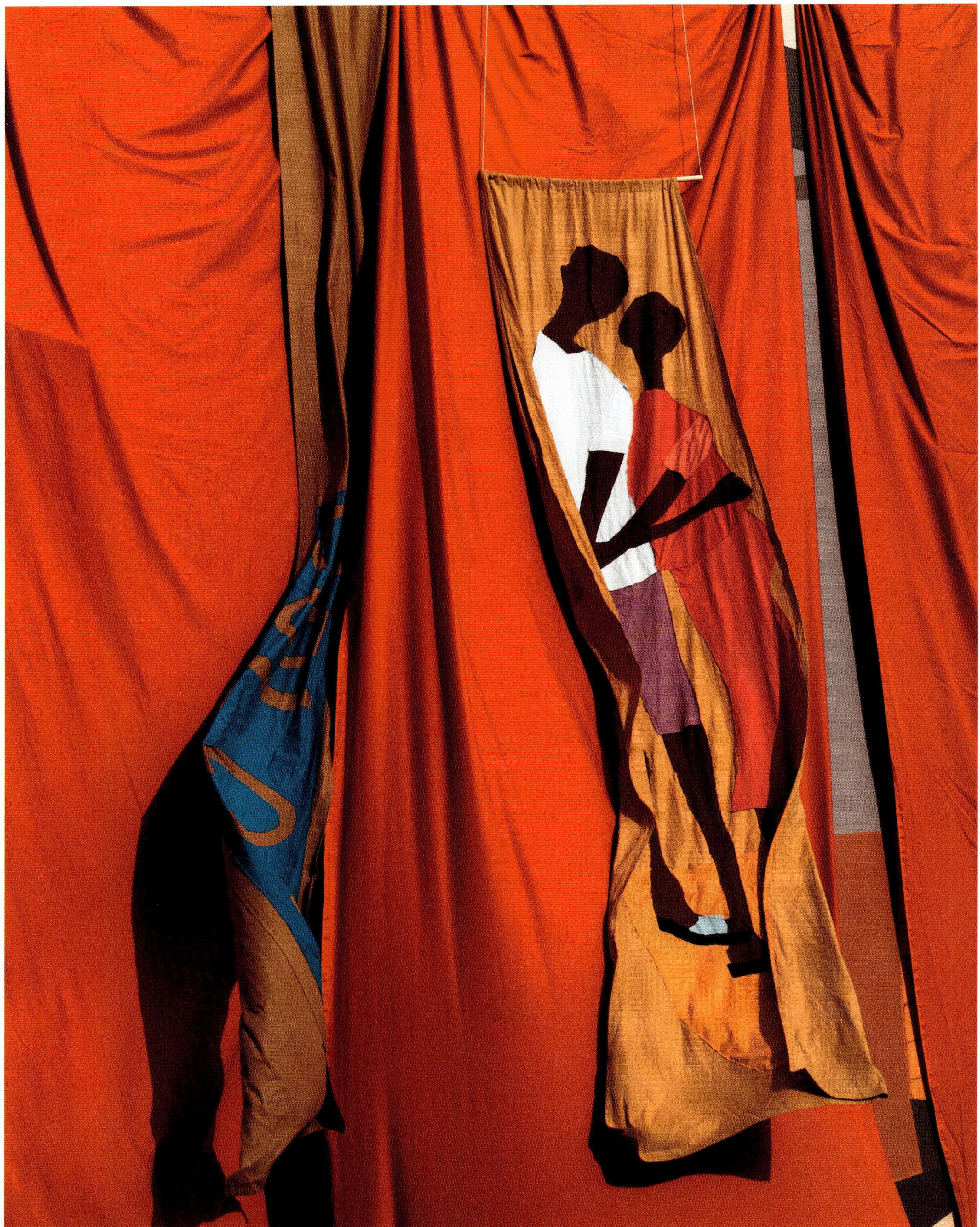

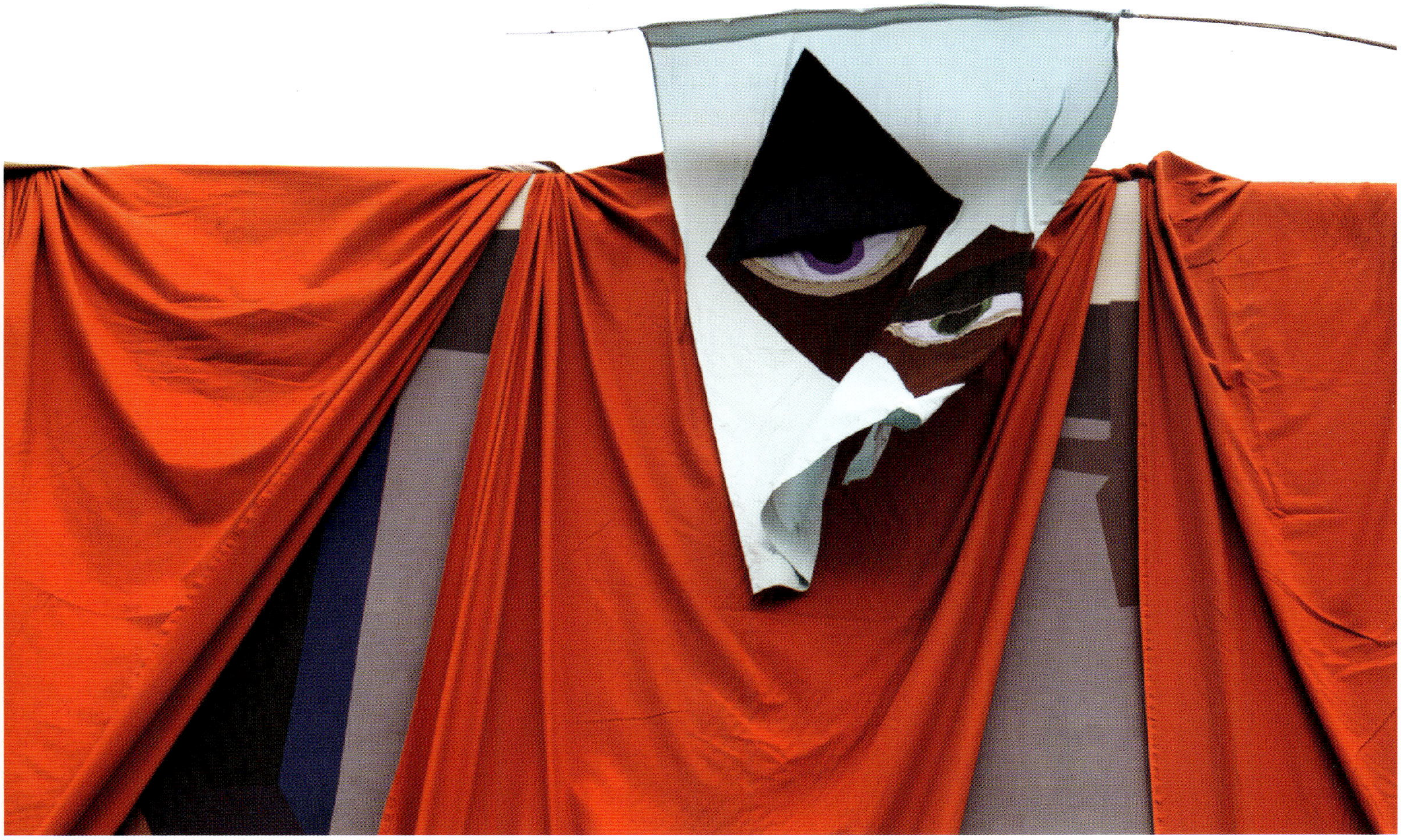

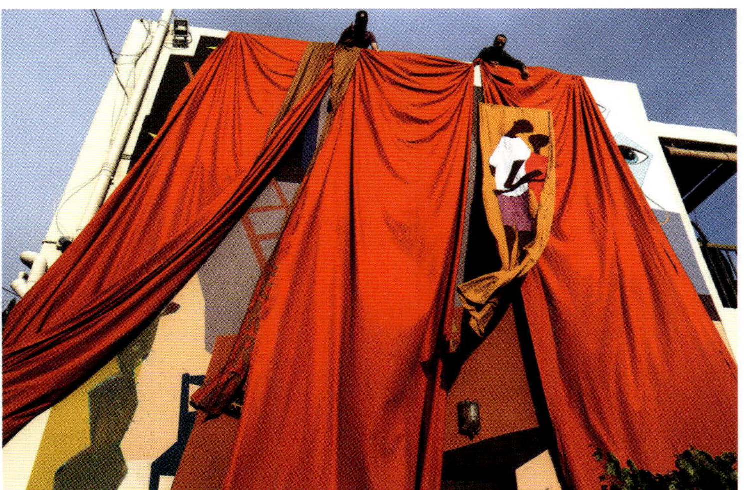

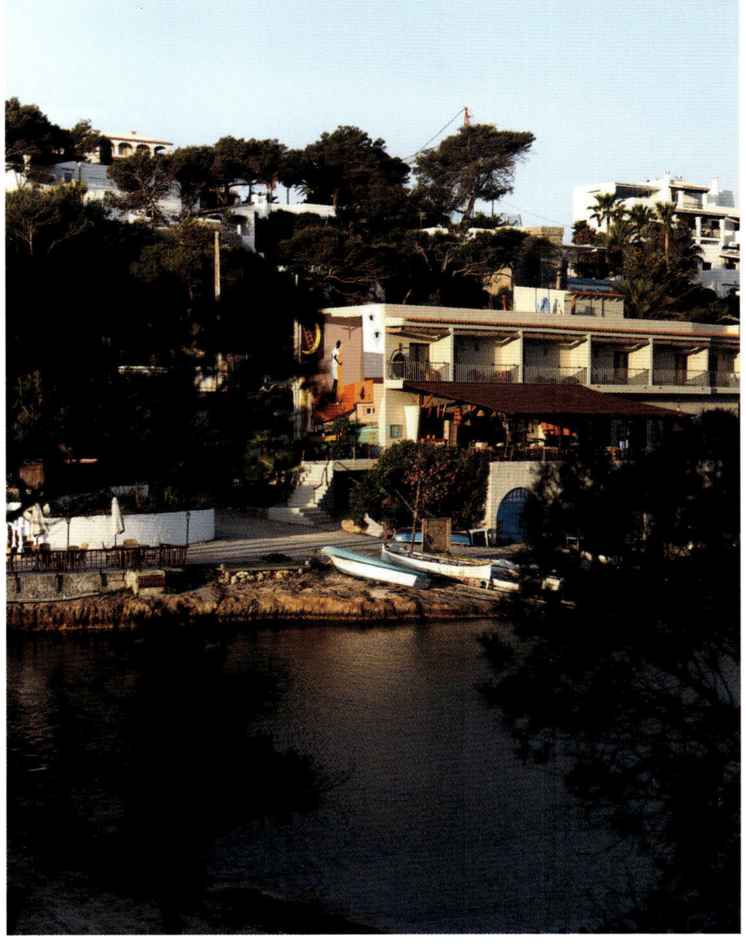

BOHEMIAN GLOW

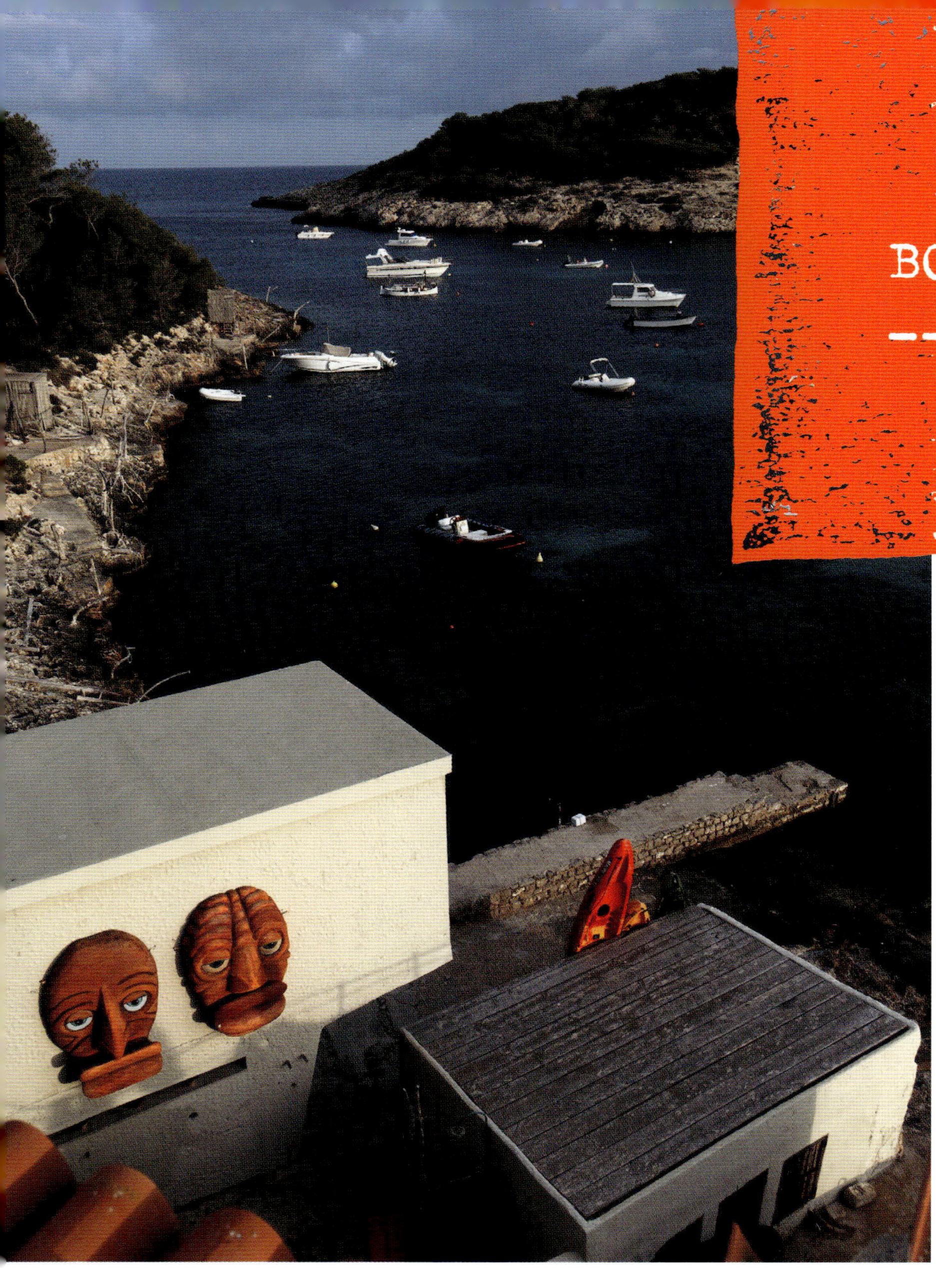

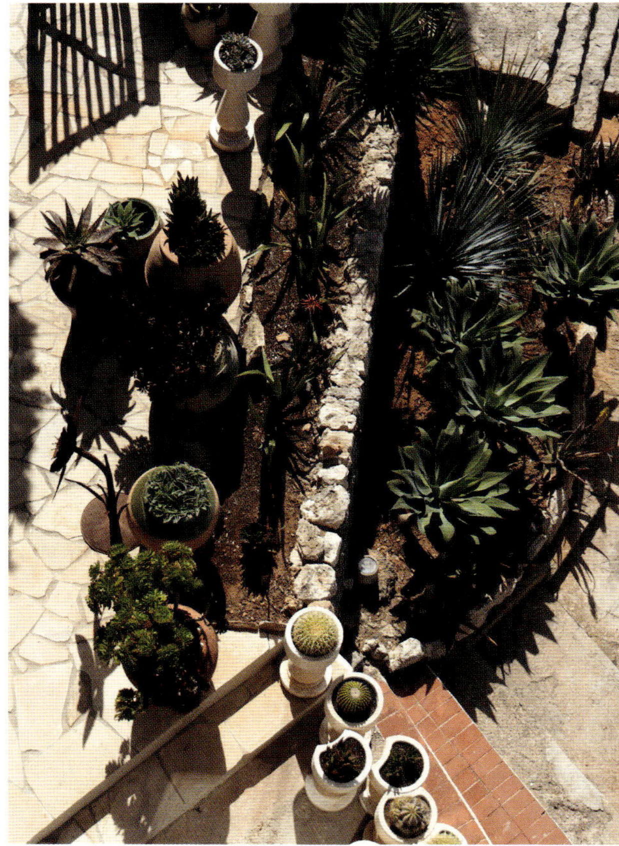

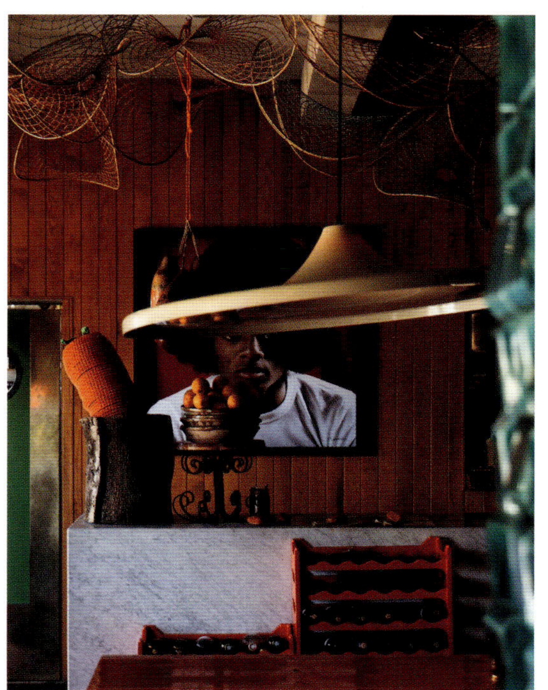

The clichéd maritime blue-and-white colour scheme that you encounter in so many seaside resorts is nowhere to be seen at Los Enamorados. On the contrary even, warm seventies hues such as beige, brown and orange are everywhere you look in this slice of paradise in Ibiza. Rugged yet elegant hand-crafted decorative objects and furniture lend the interior an artistic laidback chic vibe, imbuing everything with a relaxed feel and warmth and making you feel right at home.

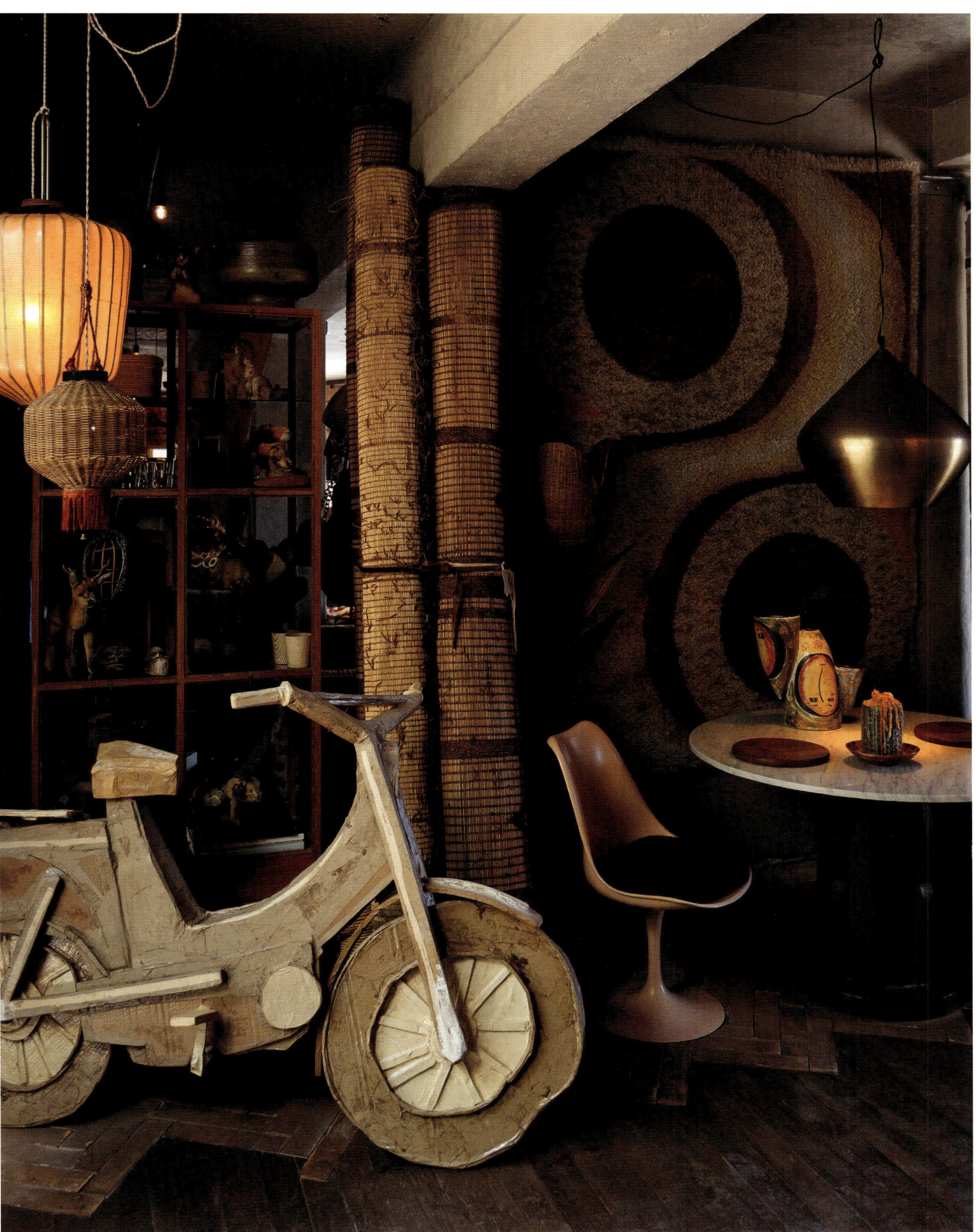

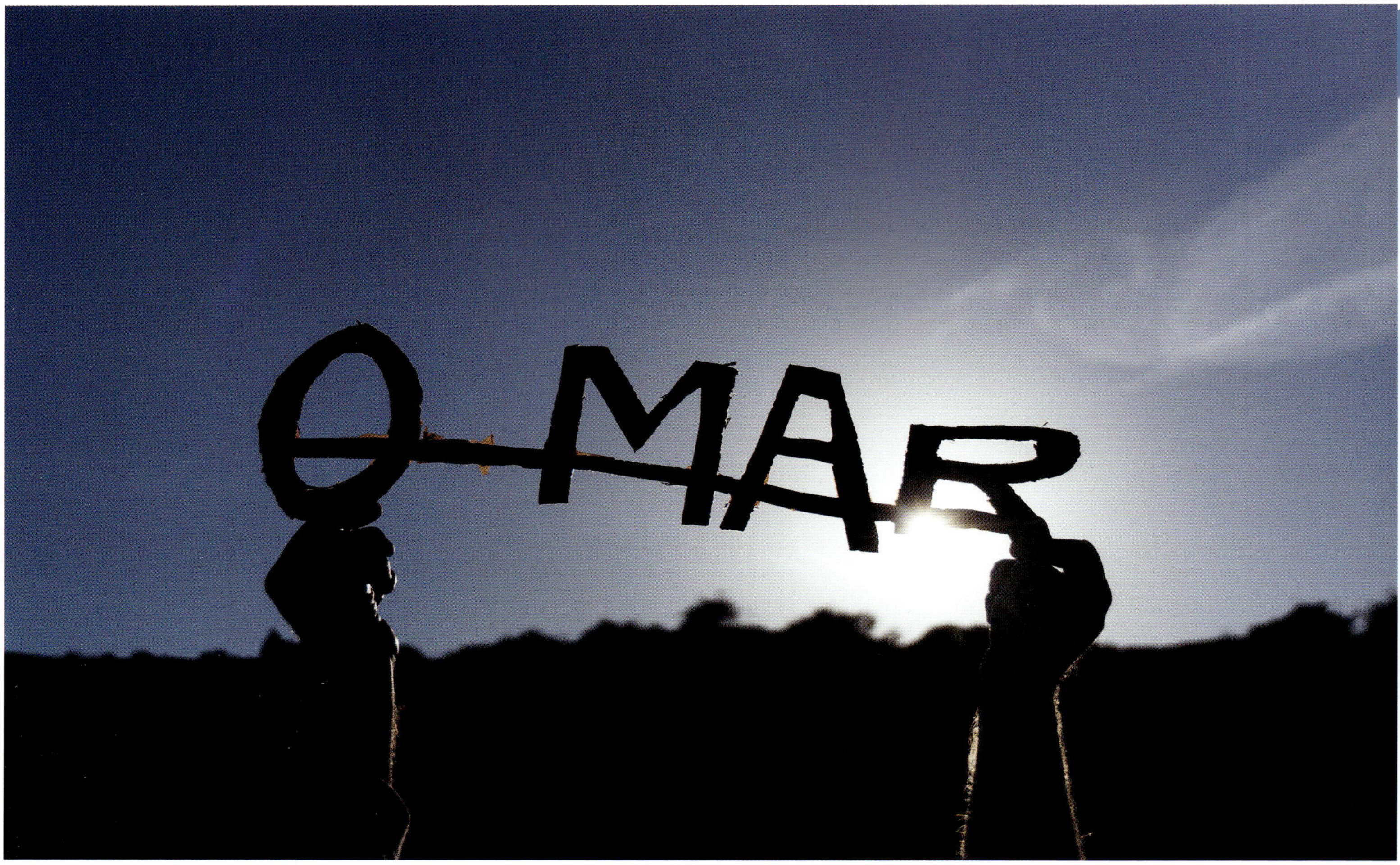

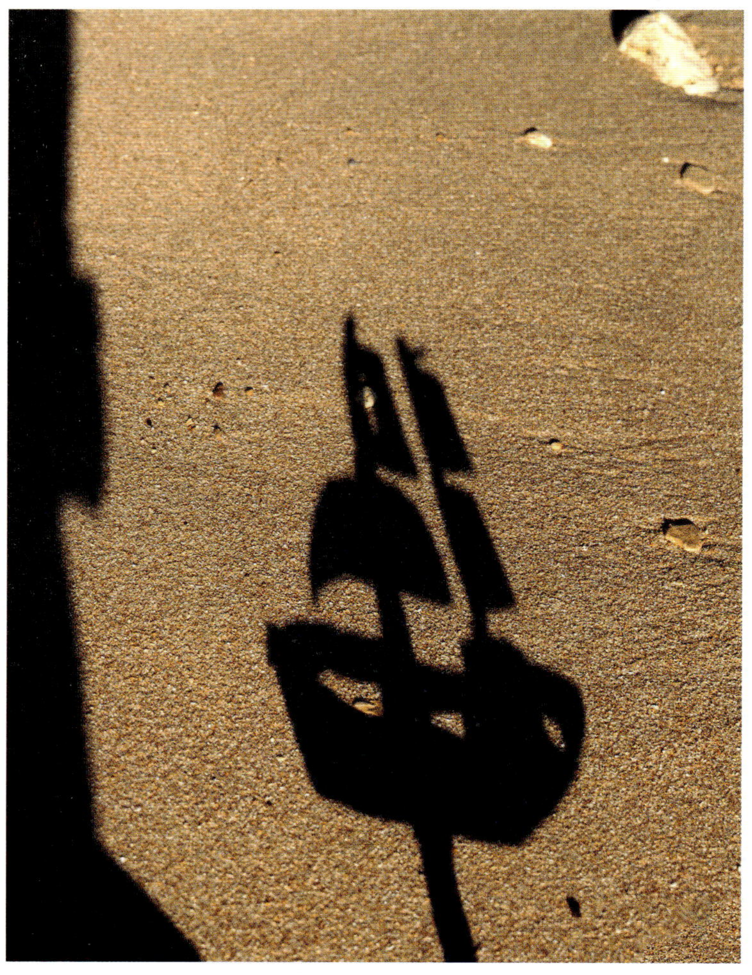

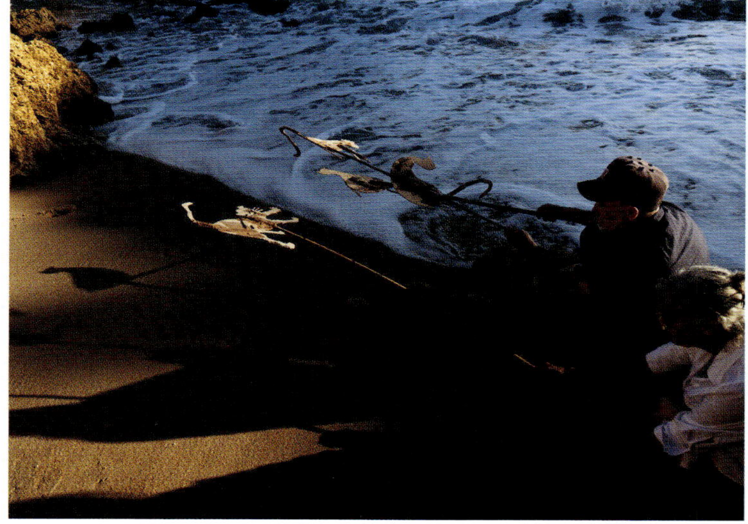

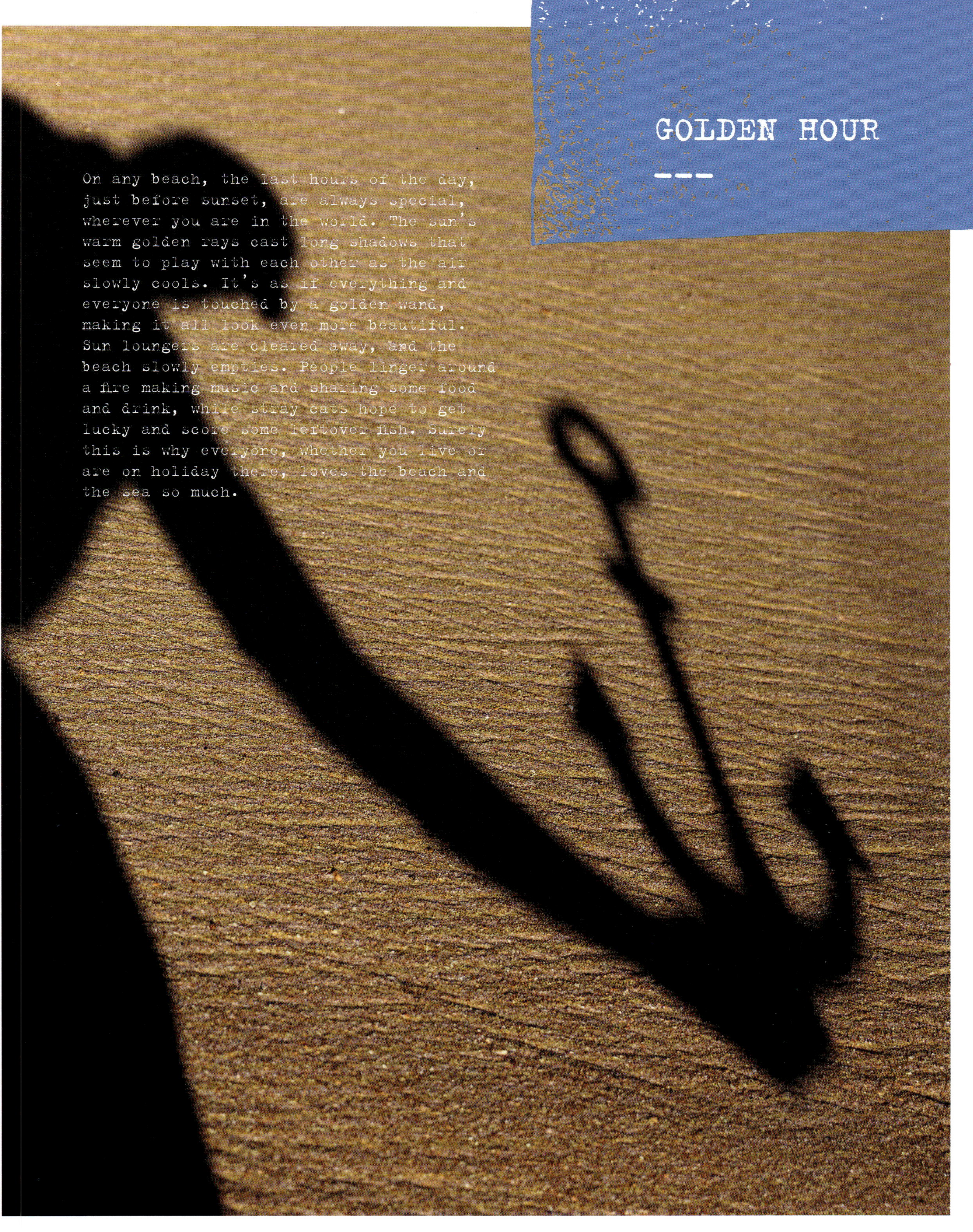

GOLDEN HOUR

On any beach, the last hours of the day, just before sunset, are always special, wherever you are in the world. The sun's warm golden rays cast long shadows that seem to play with each other as the air slowly cools. It's as if everything and everyone is touched by a golden wand, making it all look even more beautiful. Sun loungers are cleared away, and the beach slowly empties. People linger around a fire making music and sharing some food and drink, while stray cats hope to get lucky and score some leftover fish. Surely this is why everyone, whether you live or are on holiday there, loves the beach and the sea so much.

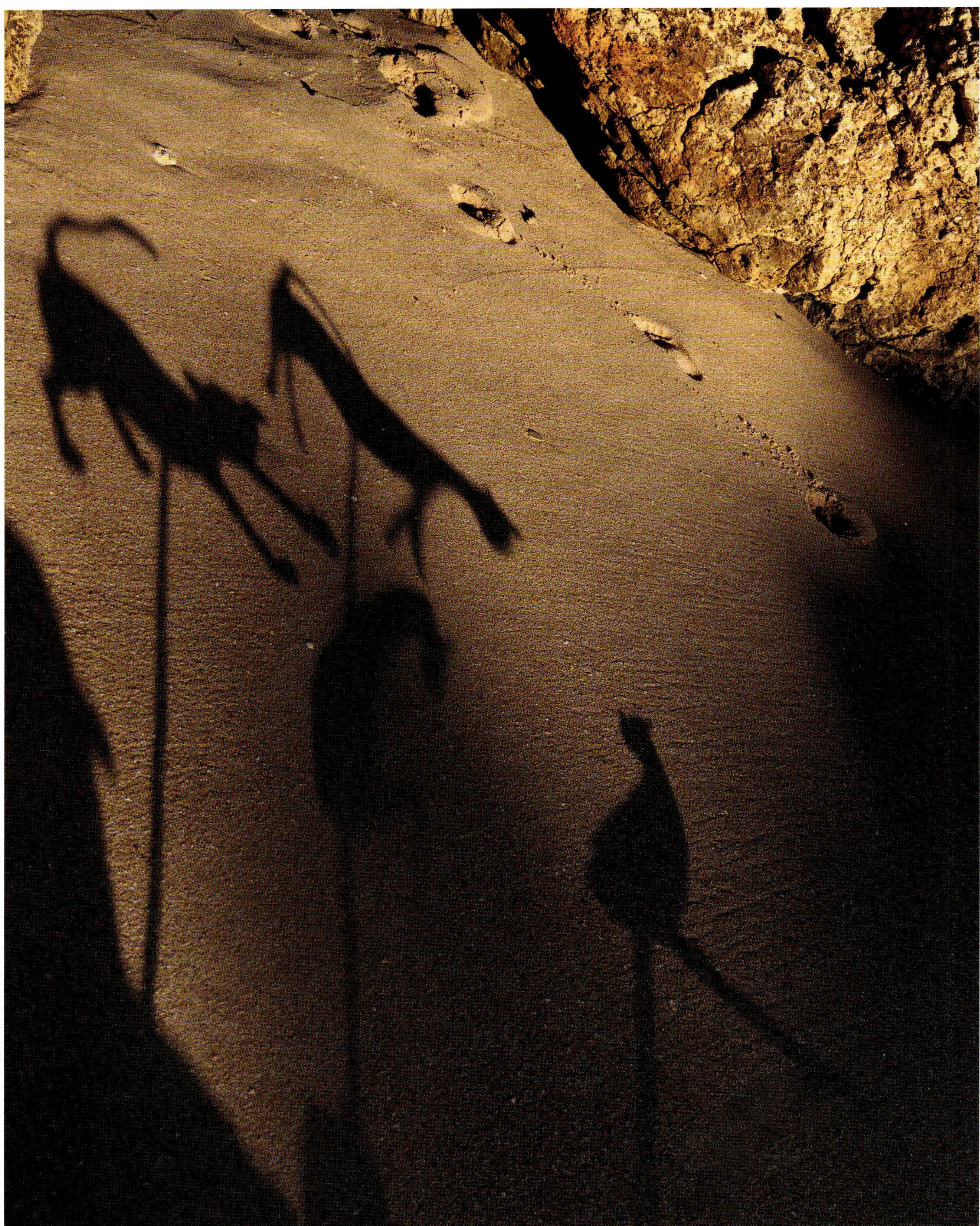

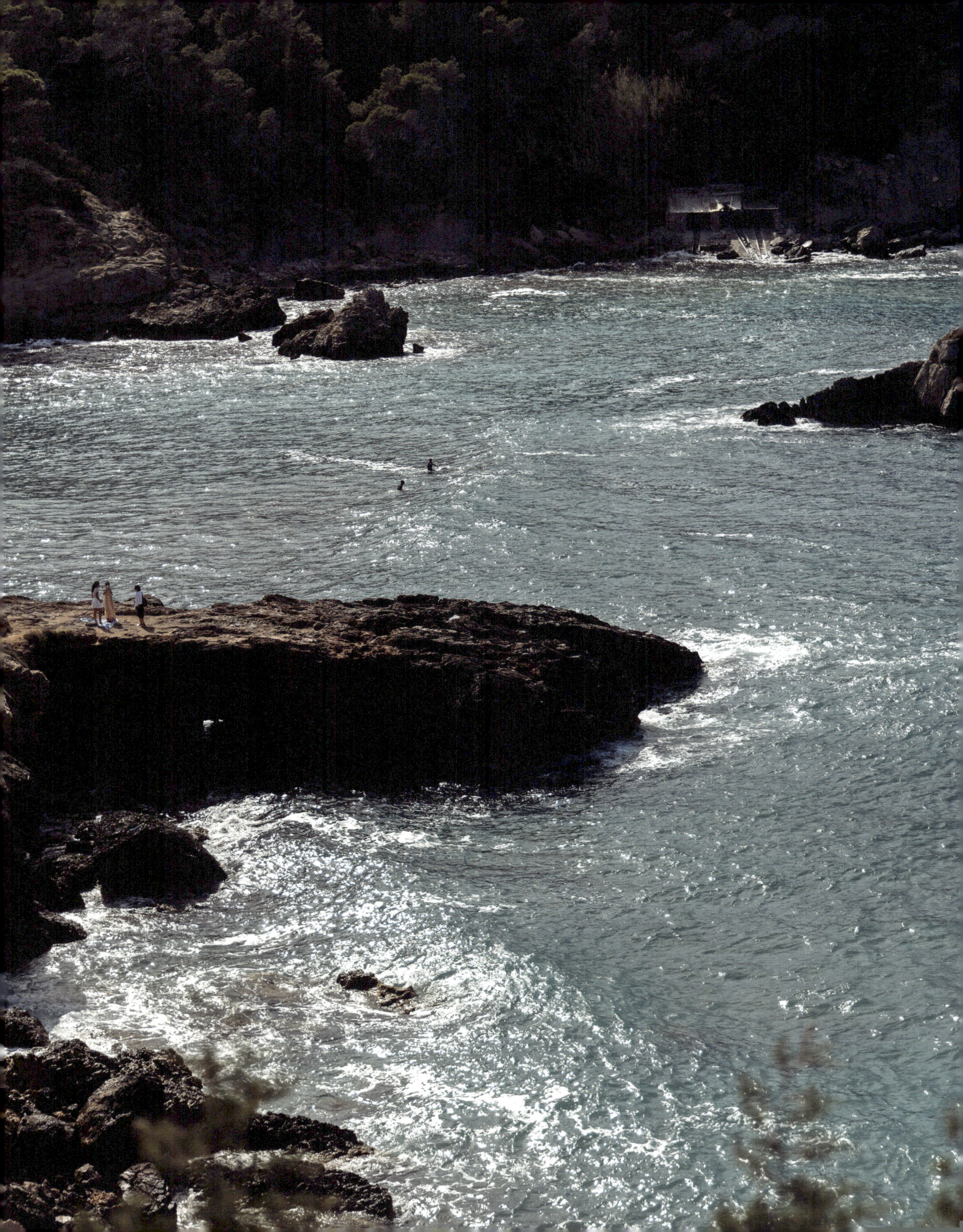

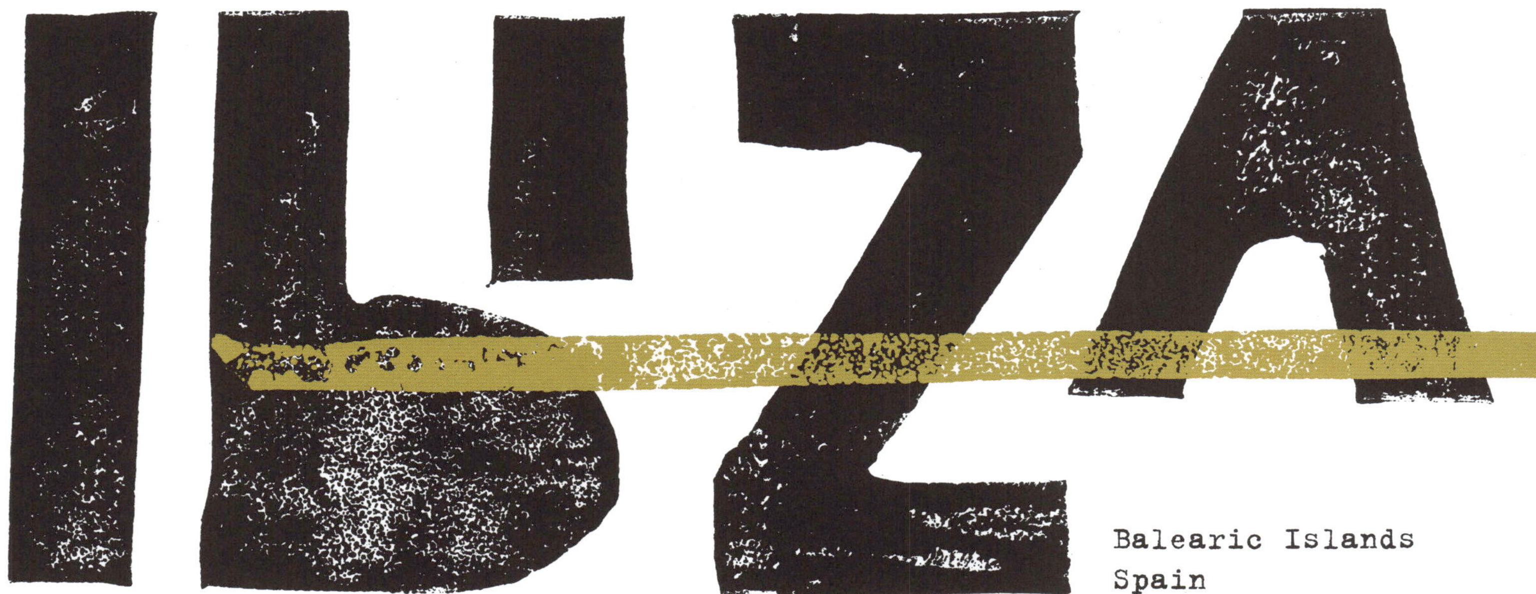

Balearic Islands
Spain

Their location in the middle of the Iberian Sea makes the Balearic Islands a popular holiday destination. Together they form an autonomous region of Spain, although each of the four inhabited islands has its unique character and image. Ibiza has two images actually: it's famous for its nightlife but is also a serene sanctuary. The northern part of the island, in particular, is very tranquil, with dreamy landscapes, small idyllic bays and cliffs, and unique views of the blue sea.

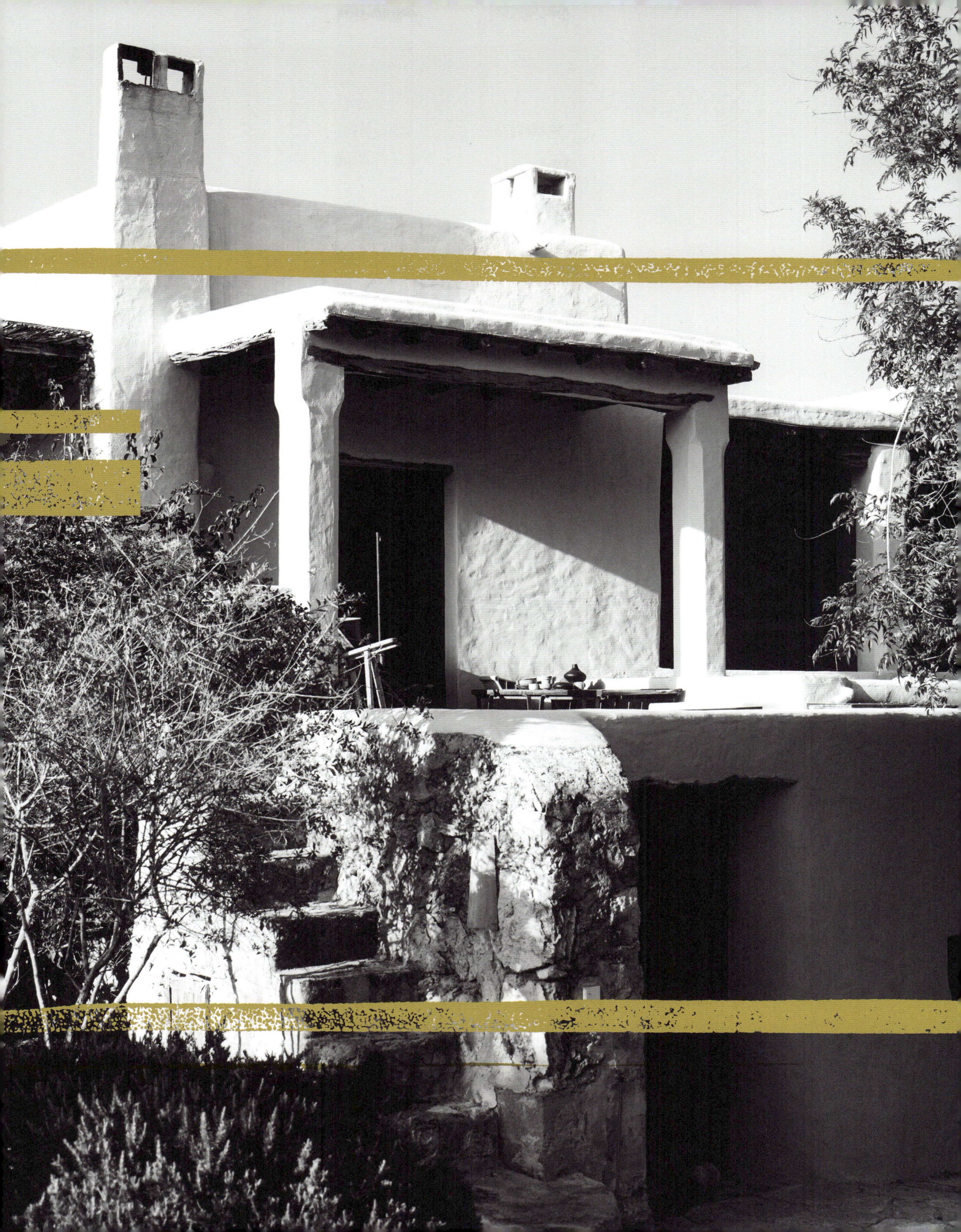

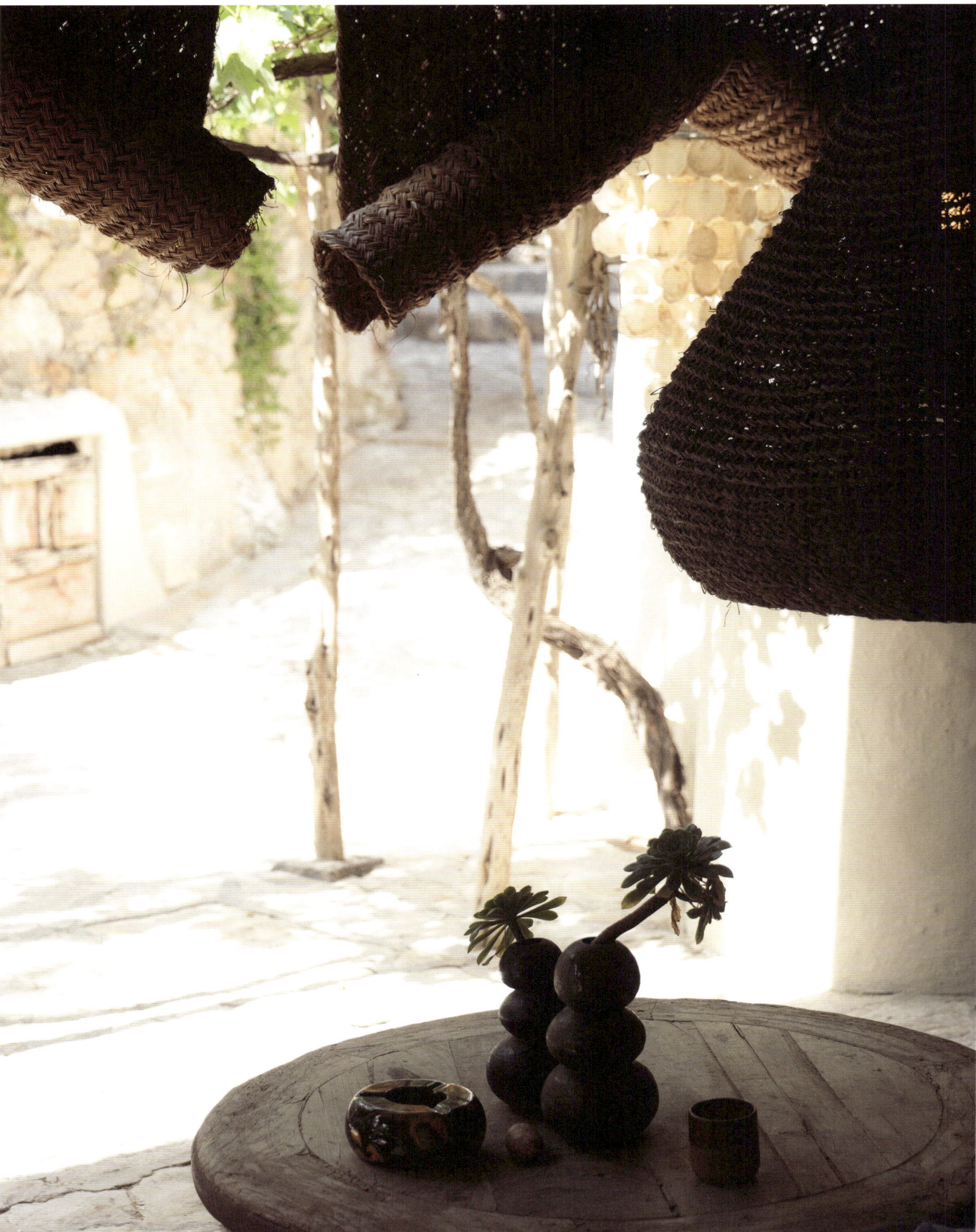

It is here that Rozemarijn de Witte, who is Dutch, and her husband Pierre, who hails from Paris, found their own little waterfront paradise tucked away on the northernmost tip of the island. They had been looking for a place in the sun and were drawn to that 'island feeling' which is so hard to describe: being surrounded by water makes them feel protected as if they're still part of the world, but in a secluded way. On the island, problems feel further away.

After looking at several houses, Rozemarijn and Pierre fell in love with this deeply romantic and authentic finca. Nowadays, many similar fincas in Ibiza have been heavily renovated and modernised. Still, Rozemarijn and Pierre deliberately chose to preserve their house as much as possible. In their eyes, the unusual layout and rustic atmosphere were its selling point. They have done little more than add cupboards and shelves in the island's traditional architectural style.

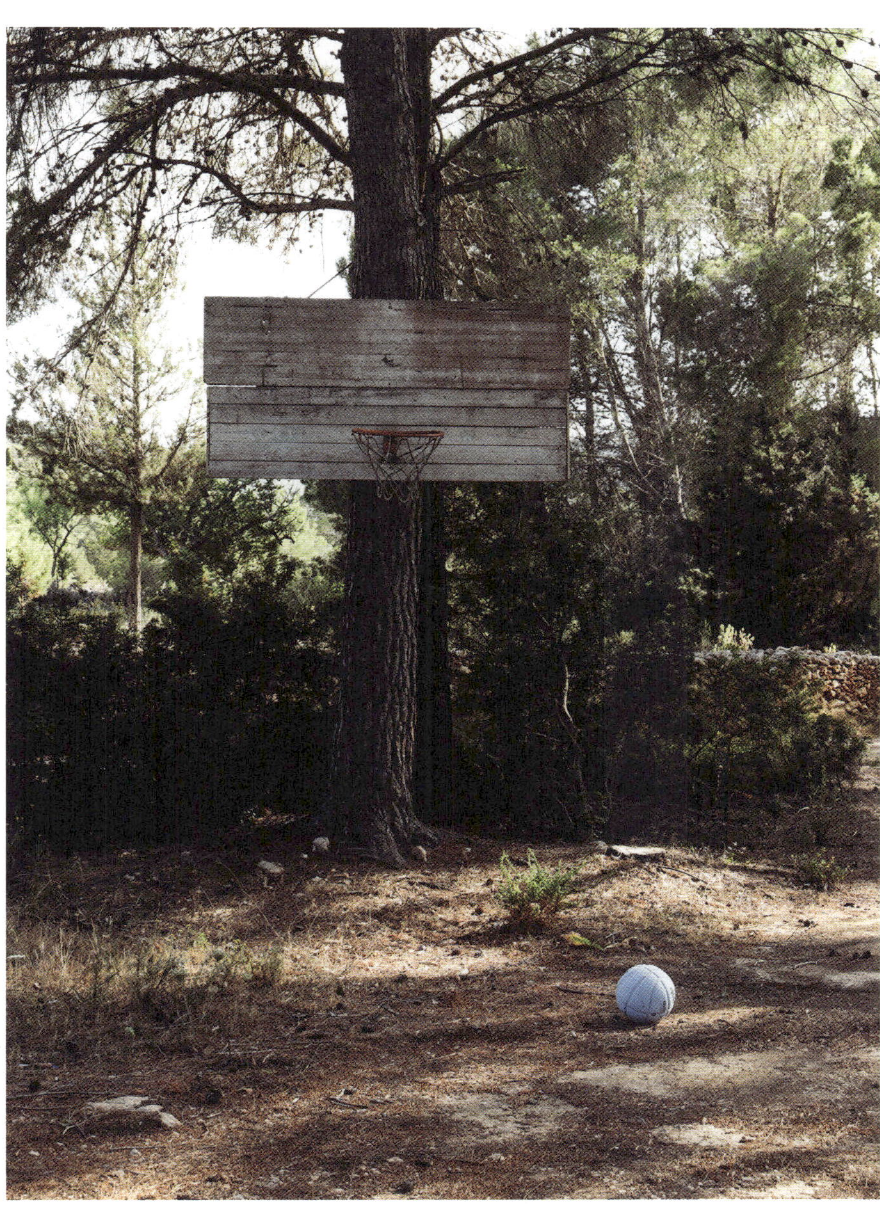

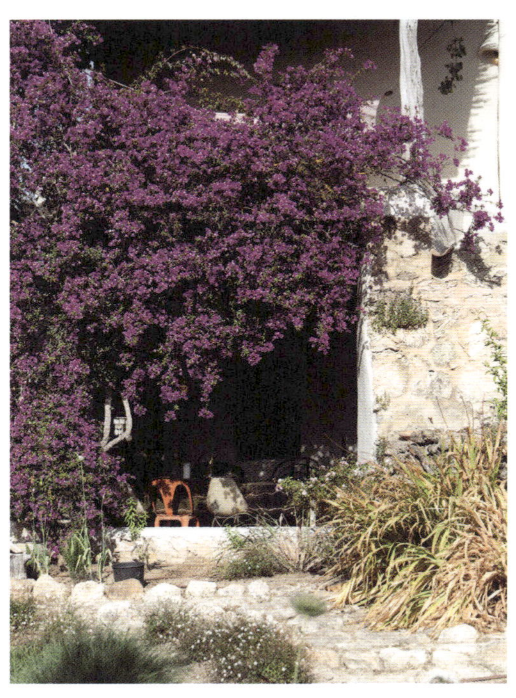

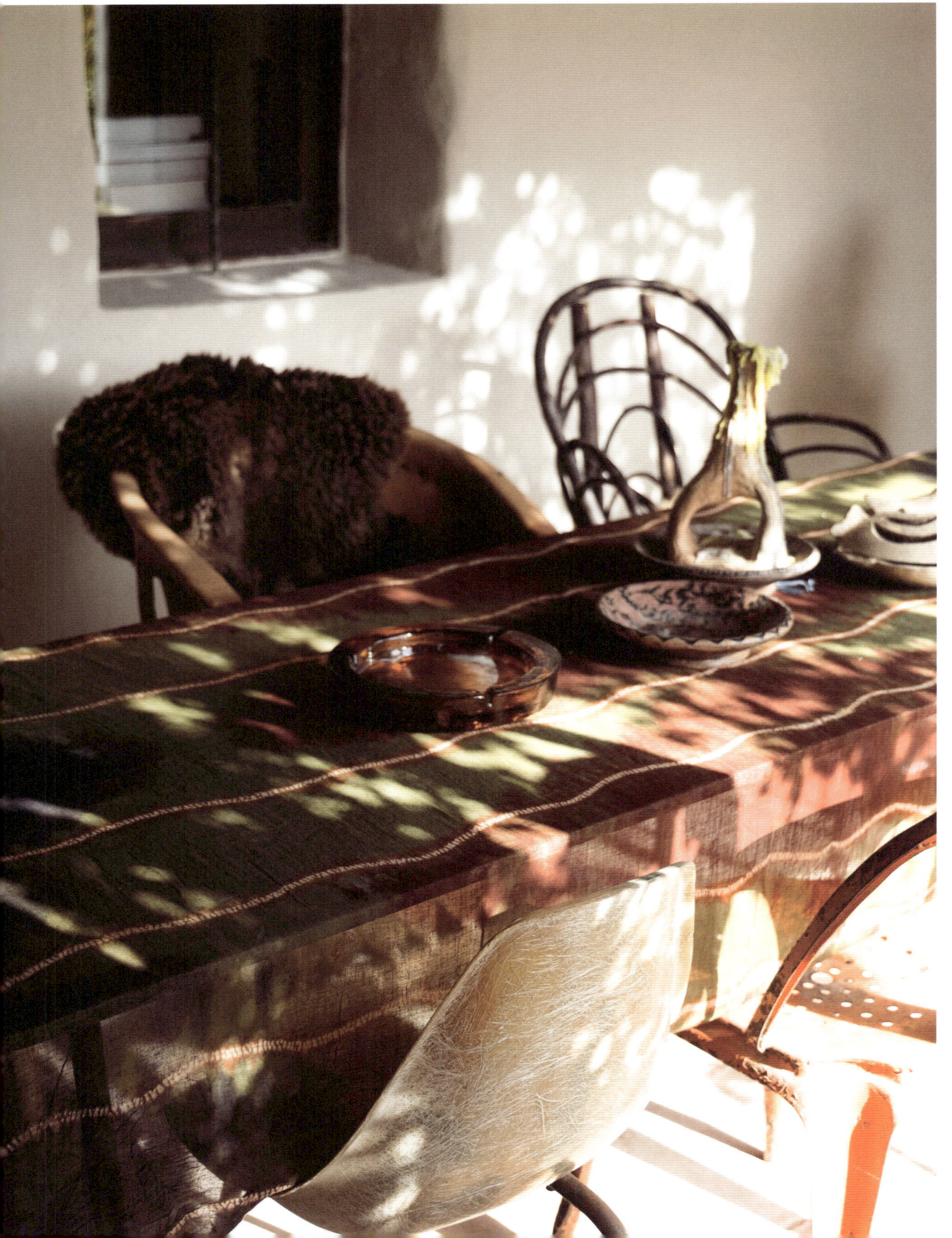

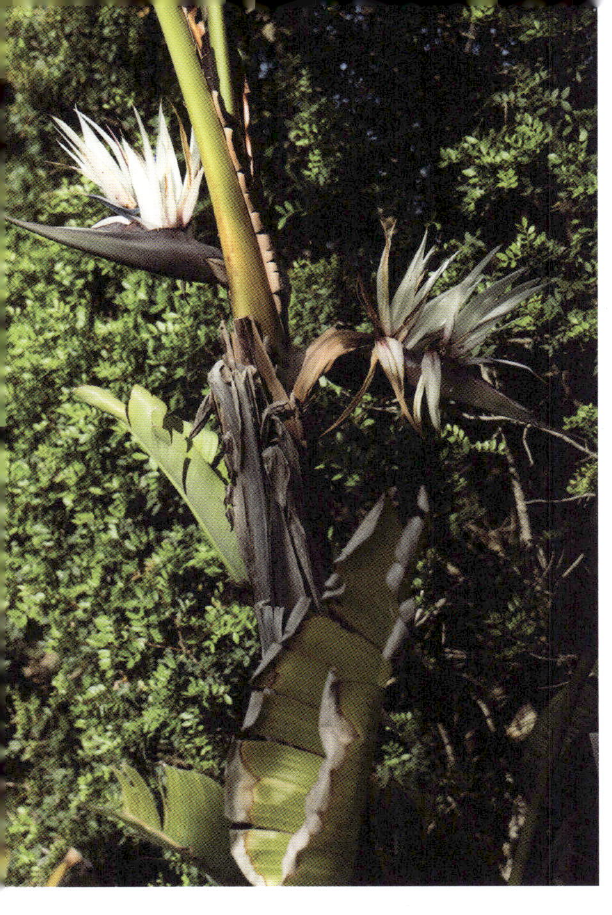

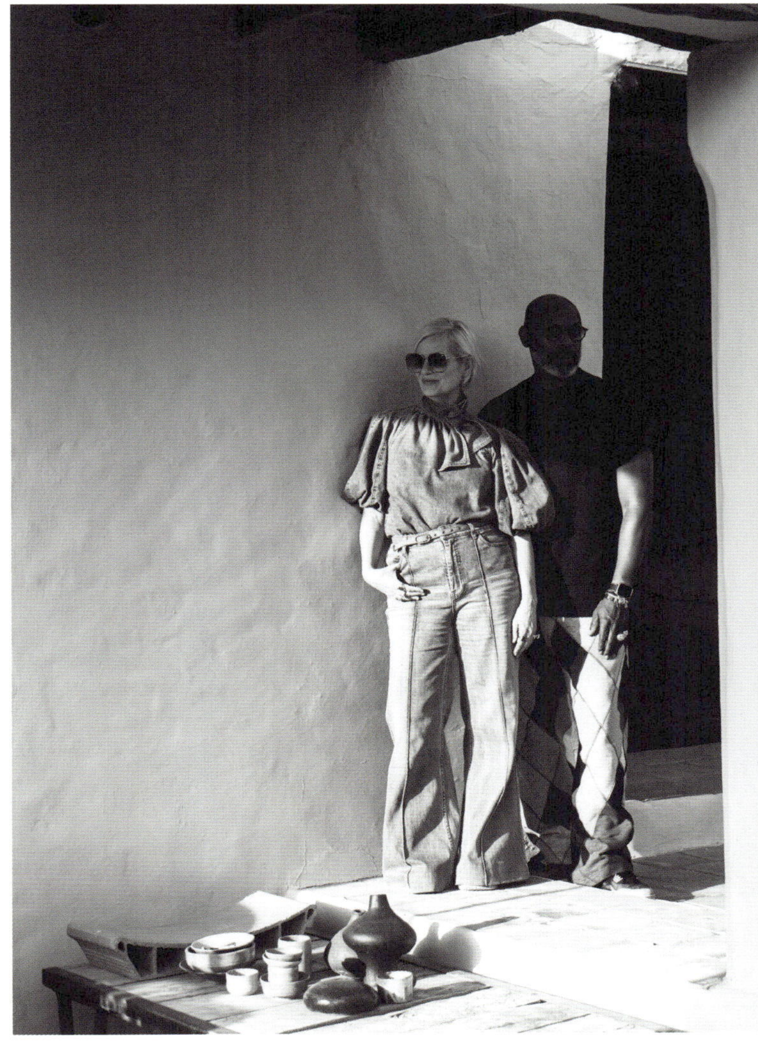

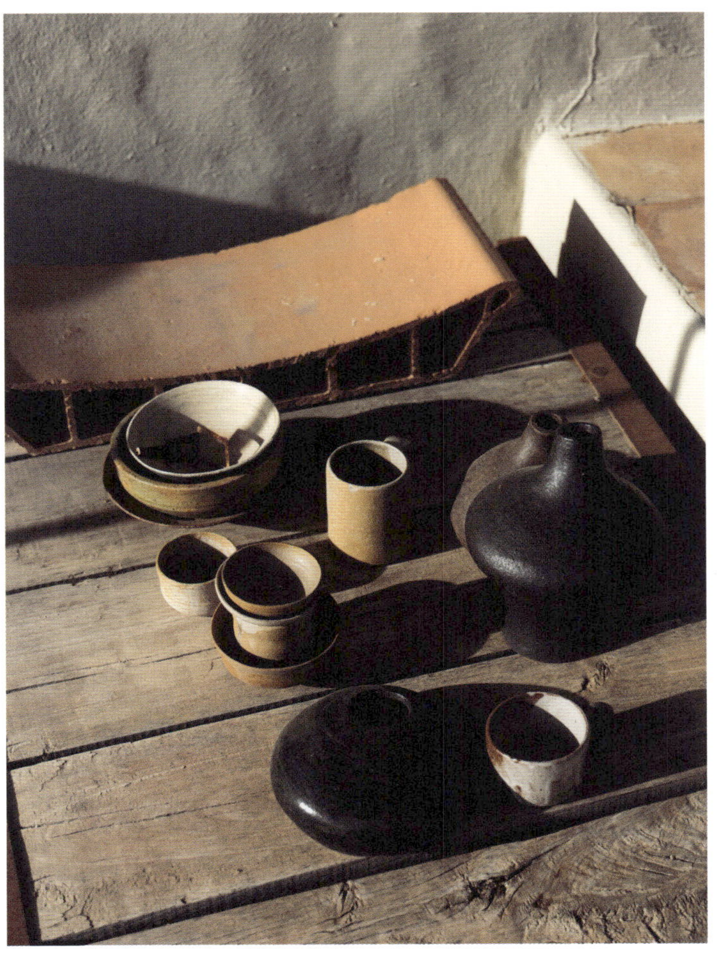

Today, Rozemarijn and Pierre divide their time between Ibiza, Amsterdam - where Rozemarijn built a career as the editor-in-chief of leading magazines - and Paris, where they run a gallery. While Rozemarijn loves the cultural scene in Paris, she is also always happy to return home to Ibiza. When she's on the island, the first thing Rozemarijn does after waking up every day is go for a swim. From her house, she walks down to the beach when there's still no one there. These early morning swims are everything to her. Each time again, she is reminded of the power of the sea: the water can be very violent and strong but very calming and healing too. Watching the sunset over the ocean, or just the horizon, is also so meditative: it makes you stronger and wiser.

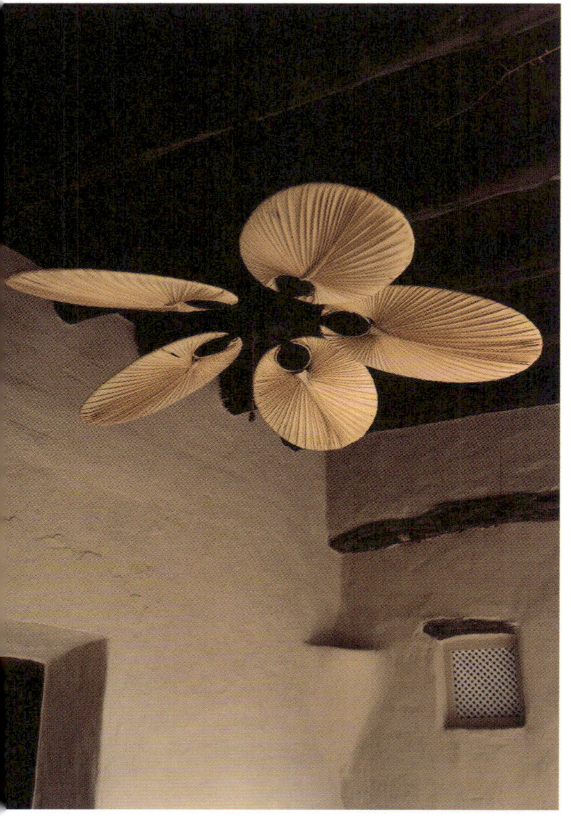

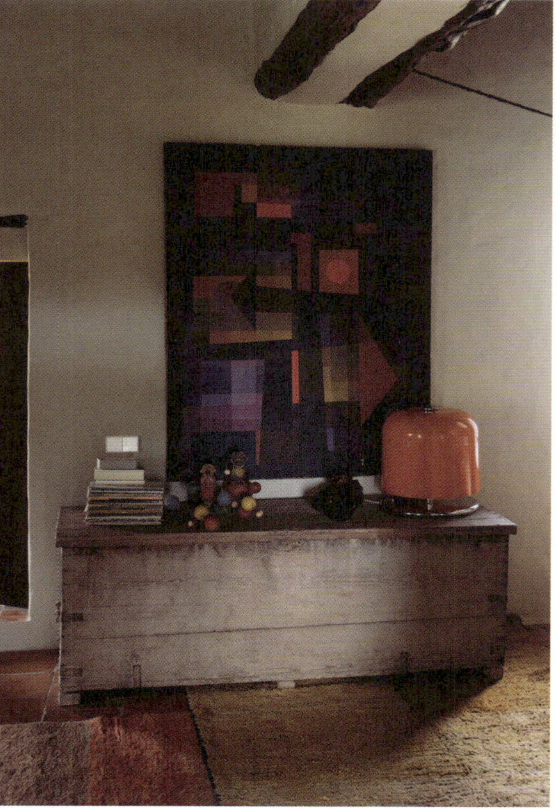

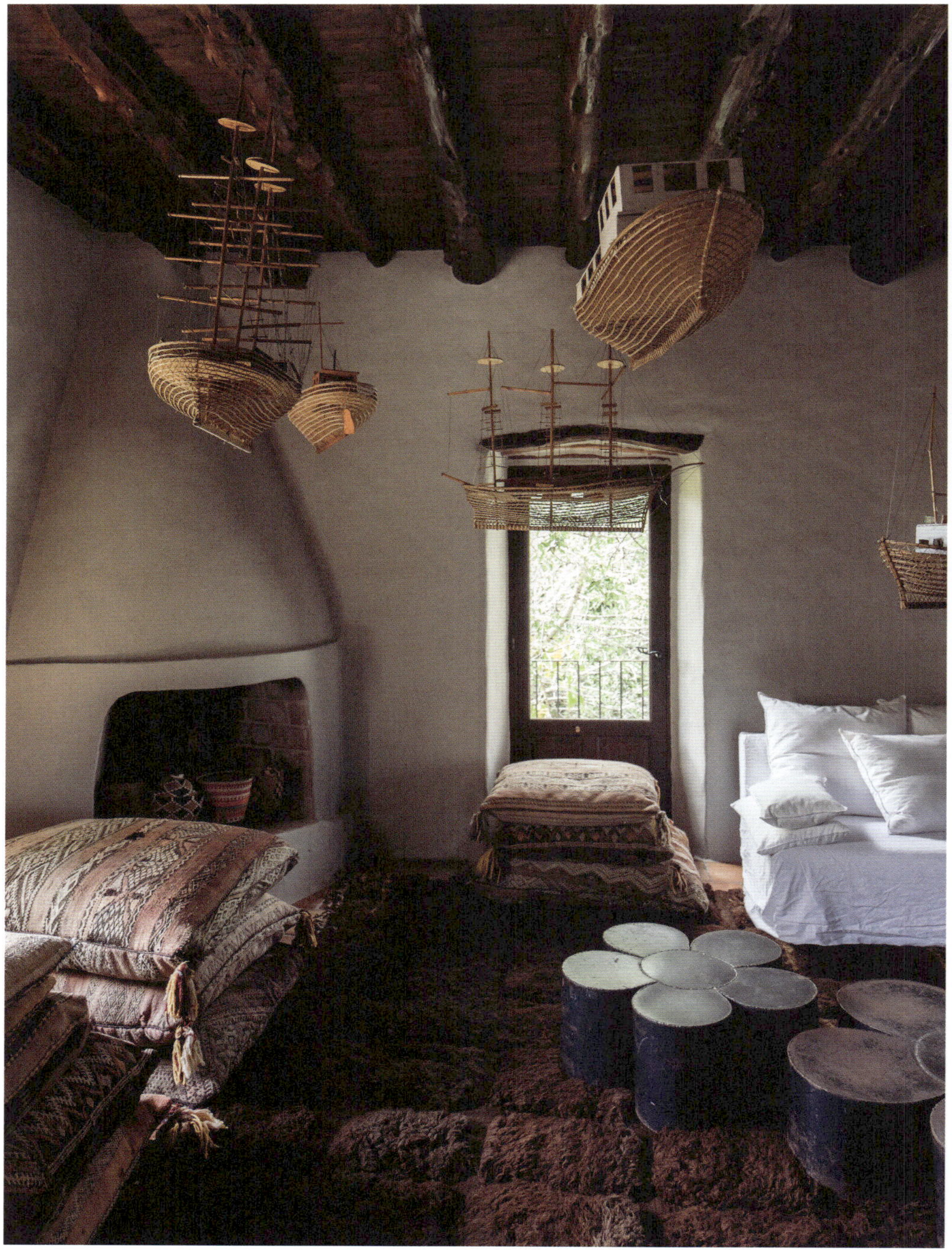

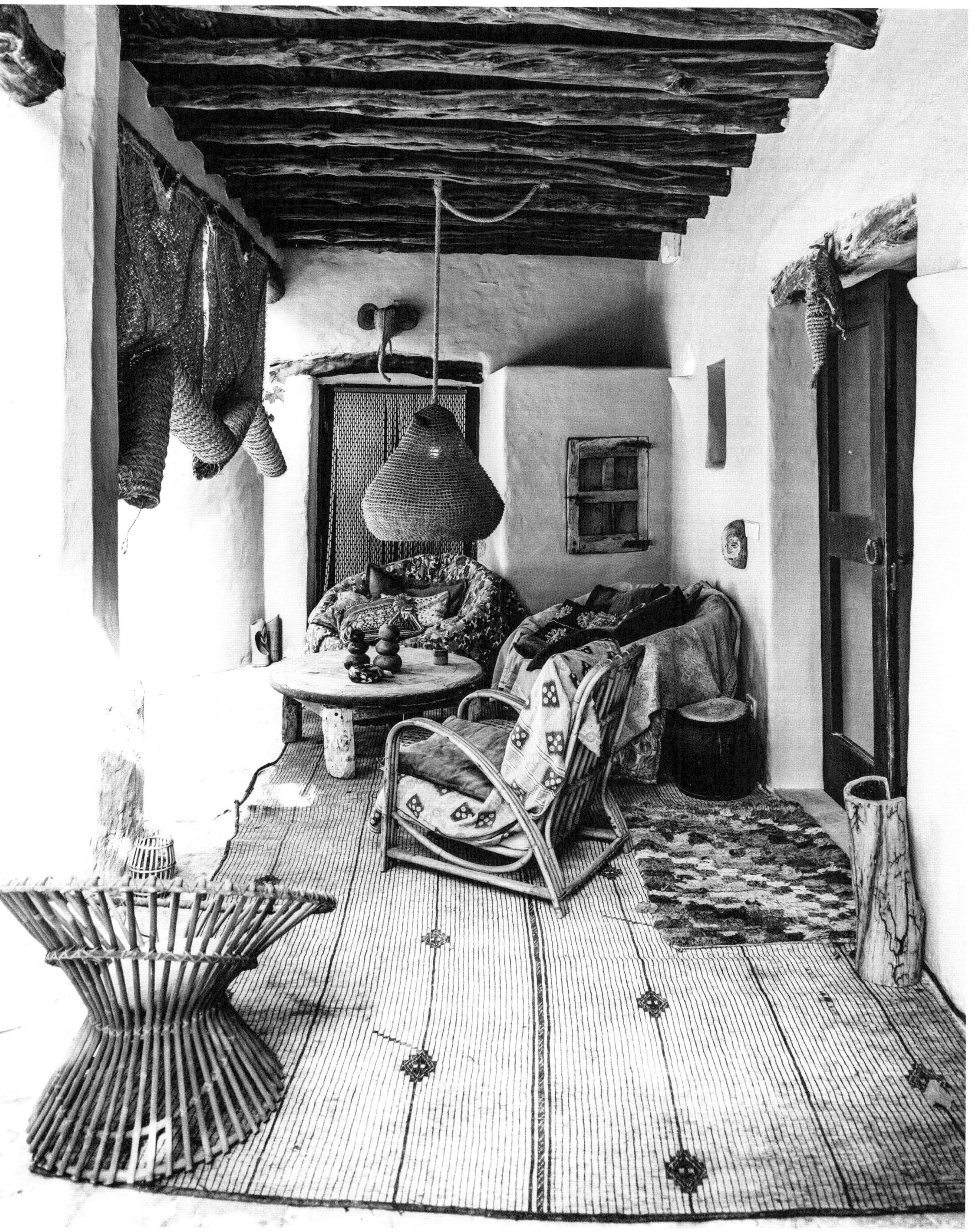

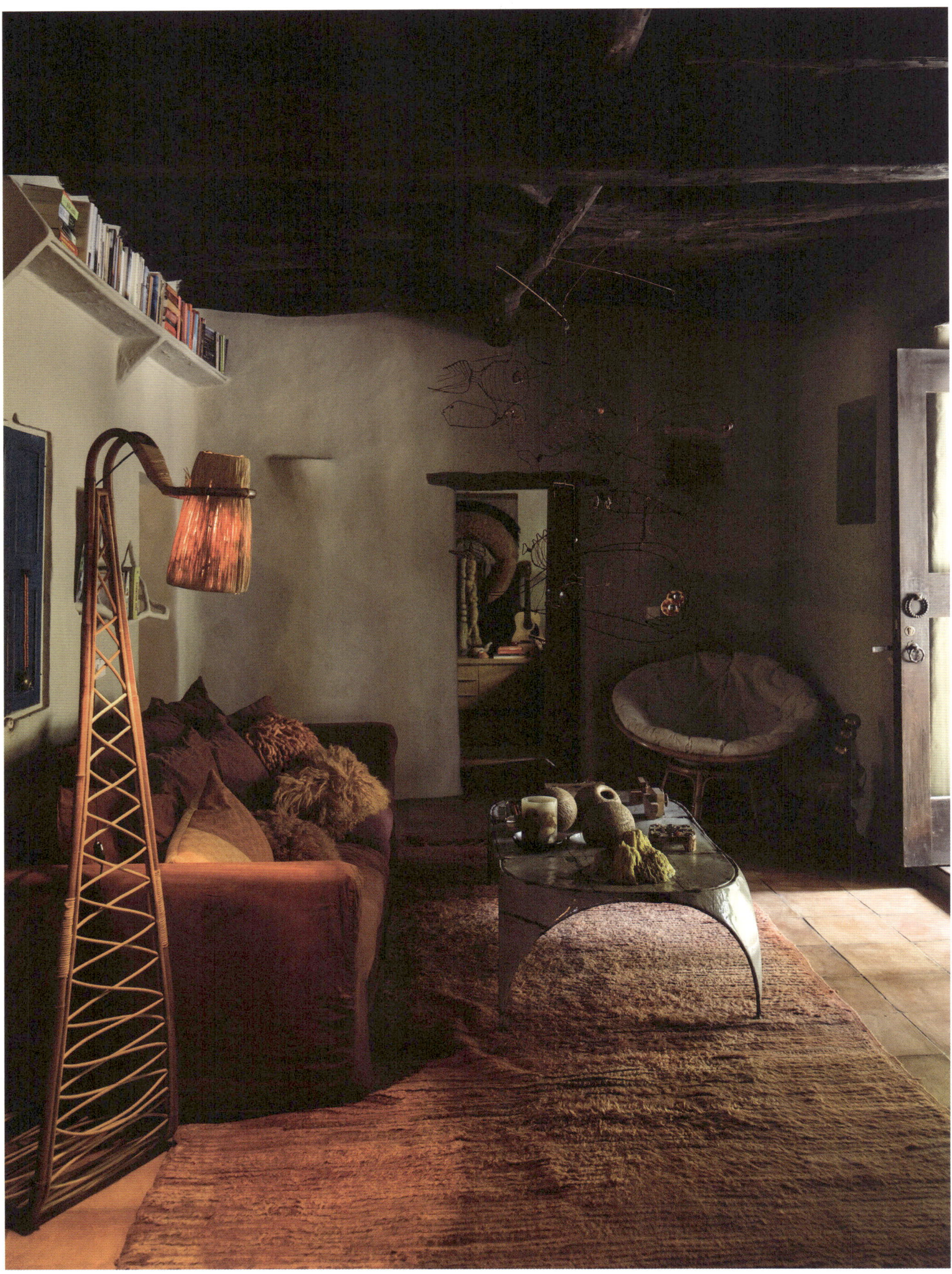

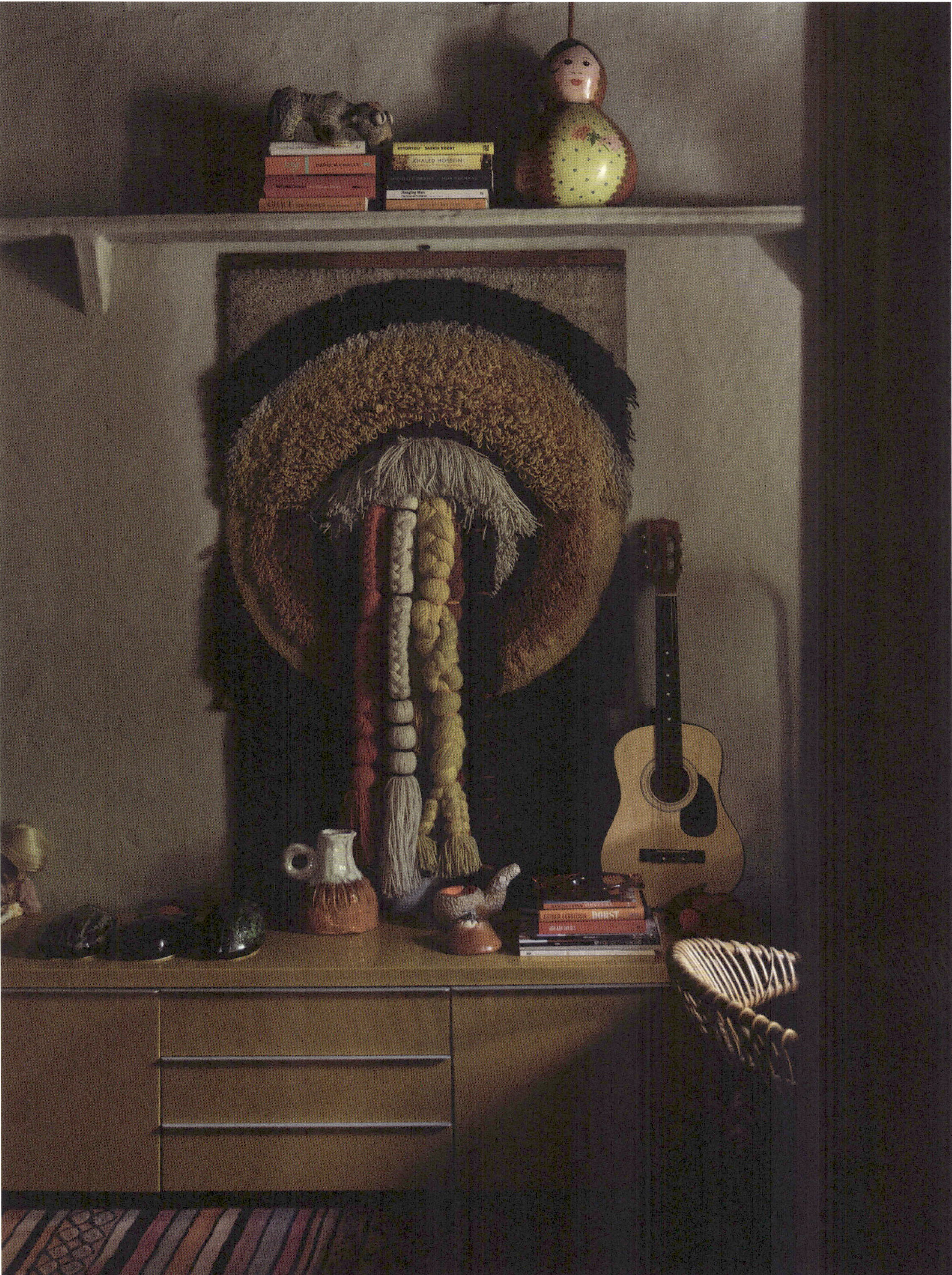
STROMBOLI SASKIA NOORT
KHALED HOSSEINI
DAVID NICHOLLS
GRACE
DORST
ADRIAAN VAN DIS

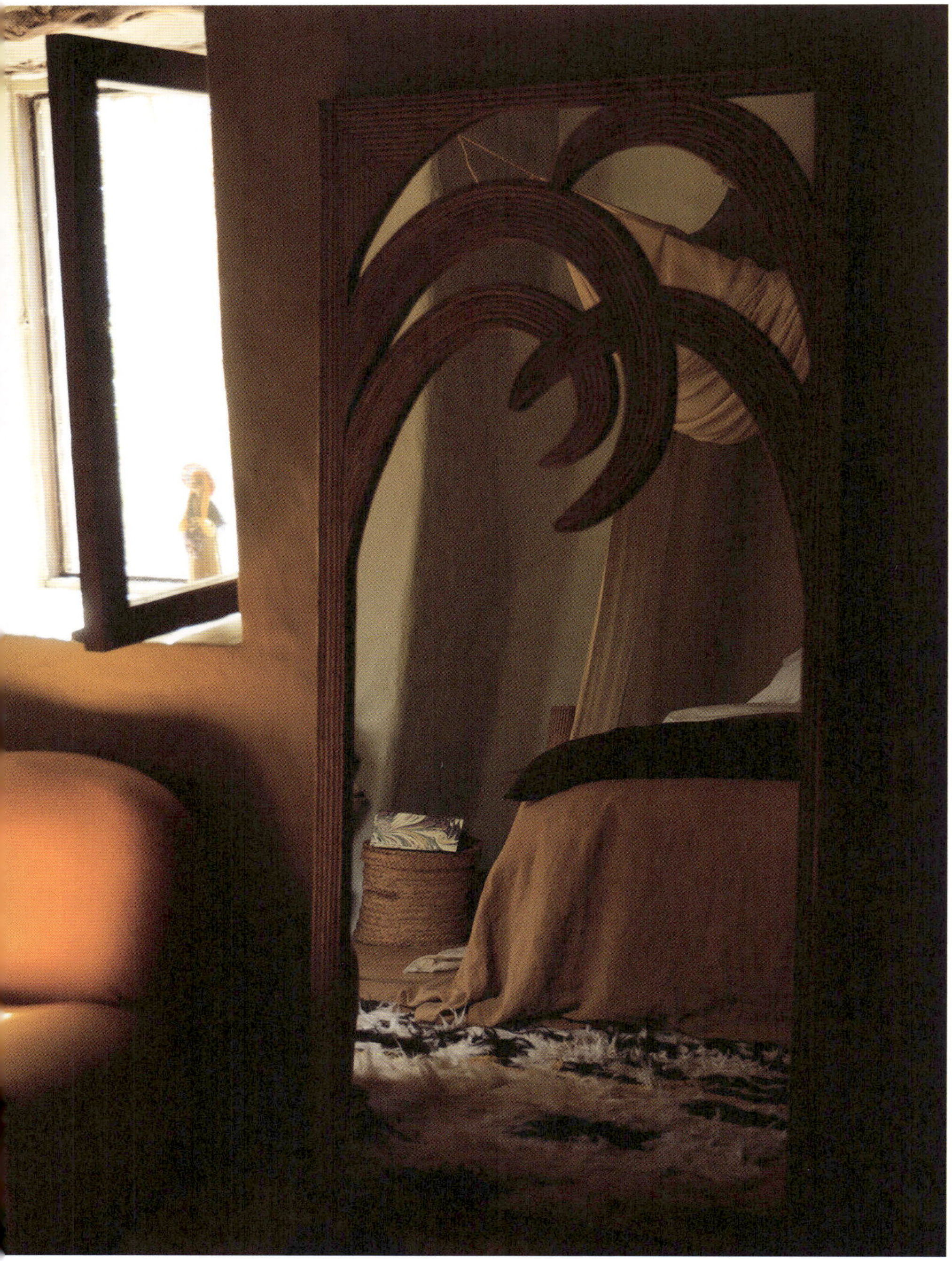

Rozemarijn and Pierre like to share the island experience with others, and have been welcoming guests at their house ever since they moved in. Then one day they found themselves opening a boutique hotel nearby. Becoming hoteliers was never the plan, but the hotel found them, more than the other way around. It was standing there alone and abandoned, right on the waterfront, next to the island's tallest lighthouse. It's hard to imagine a more beautiful location – you can enjoy both the sunrise and sunset there – and it felt like such a waste to leave the building standing empty. These days the hotel, called Los Enamorados, is brimming with energy and creativity. It's quite small, with just nine rooms, a restaurant, and a shop, and it has a wonderfully inspiring but unpretentious bohemian décor.

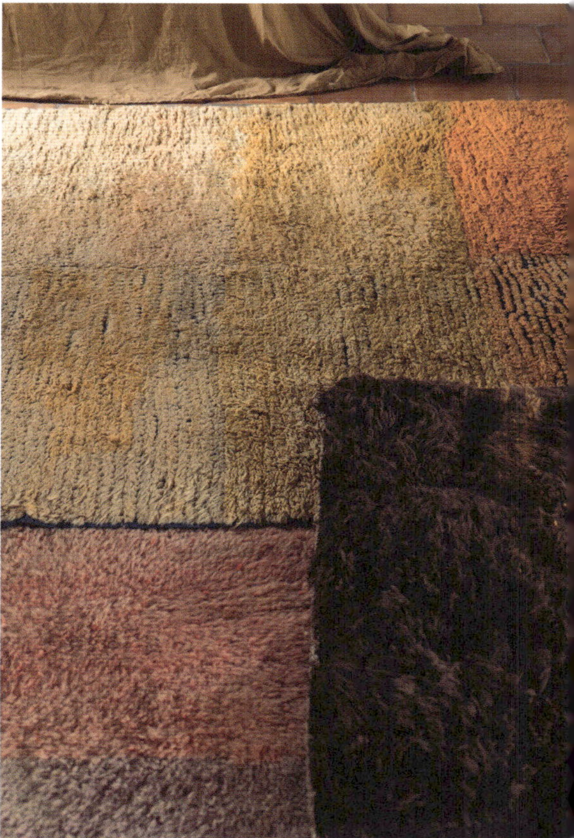

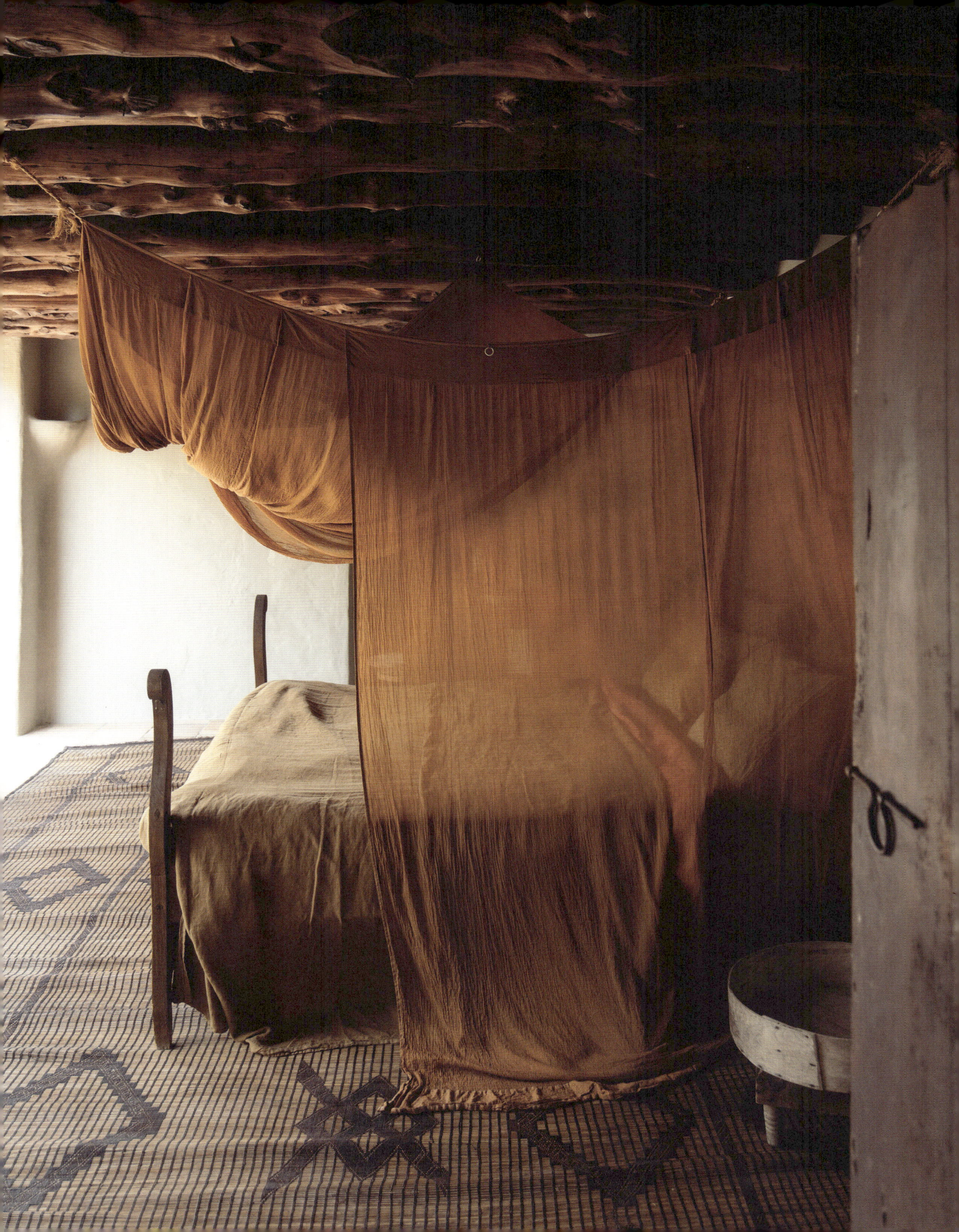

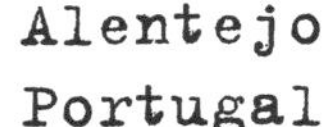

MILFONTES

The Atlantic
is everything in Olivia Piana's life. She lives next to and also on the water as much as possible: a professional windsurfer and Stand Up Paddle athlete, she has since ventured into the world of wing foiling. Sports play a significant role in her life, as a way of experiencing intense emotions and stepping out of your comfort zone. She finds it fulfilling to share these experiences with others. But Olivia's deep connection with nature is even more important to her. She lives in a camper van in the dunes on the southwest coast of Portugal and loves the simplicity and freedom that come with a nomadic lifestyle. Olivia's home is where the waves are.

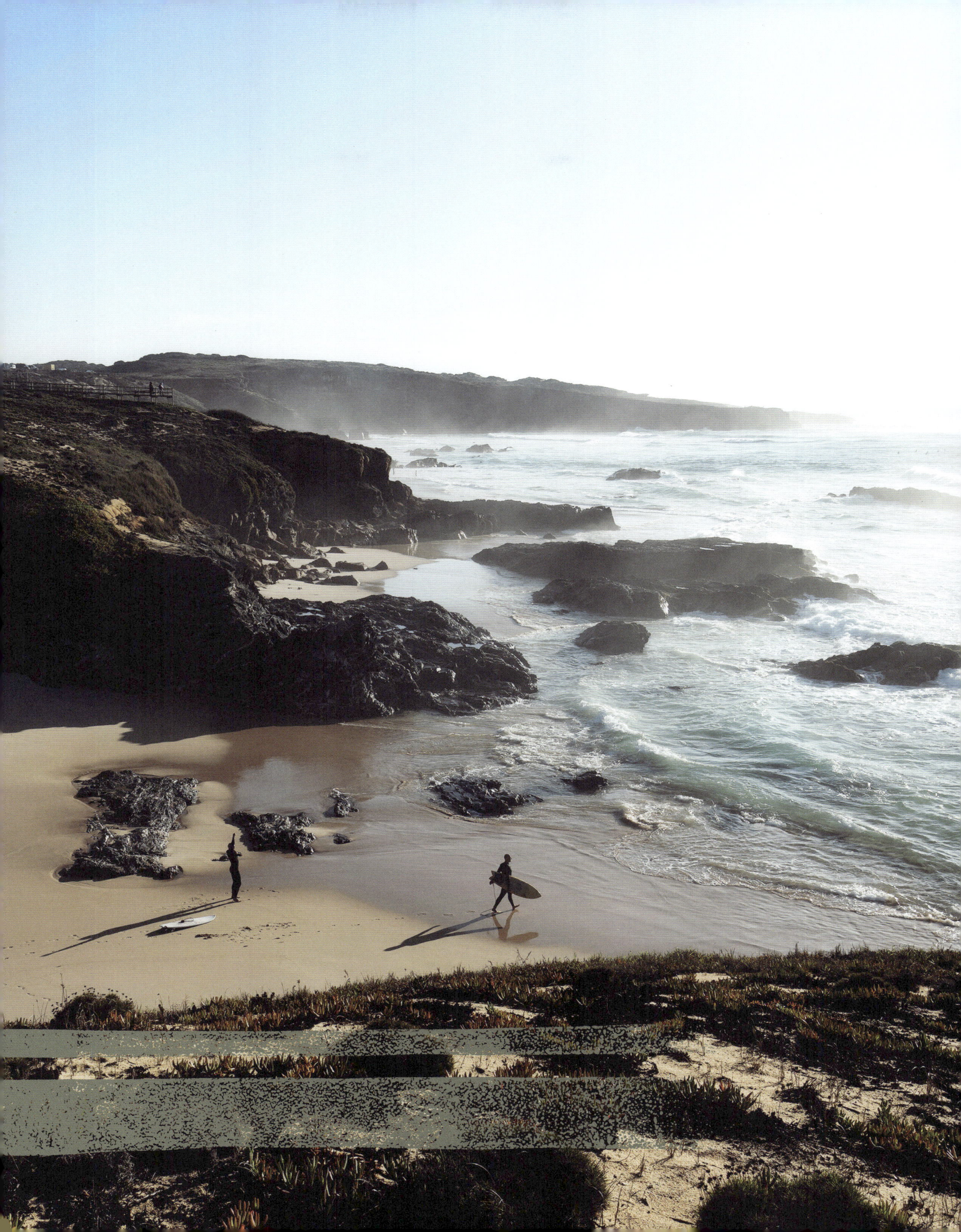

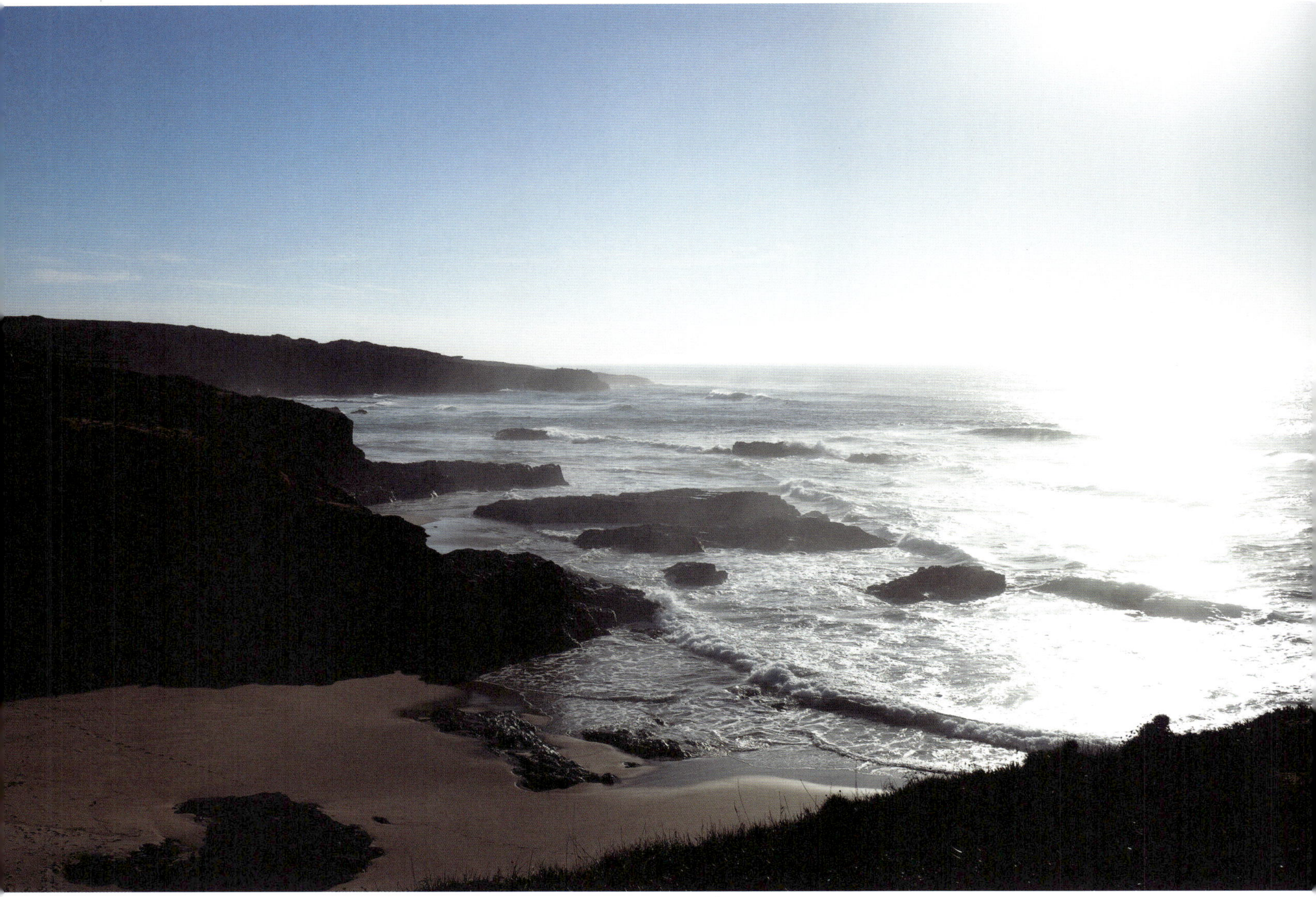

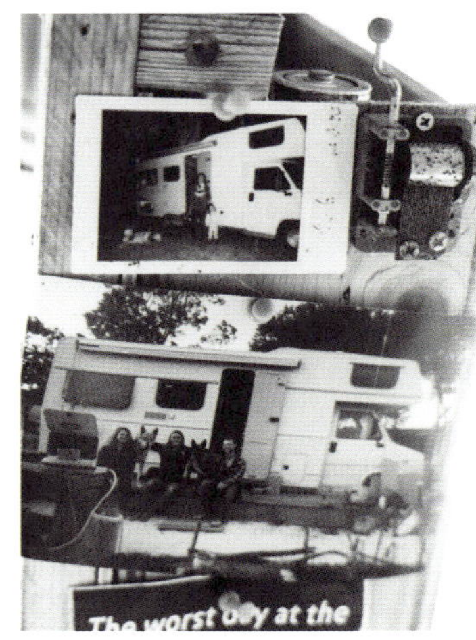
The worst day at the

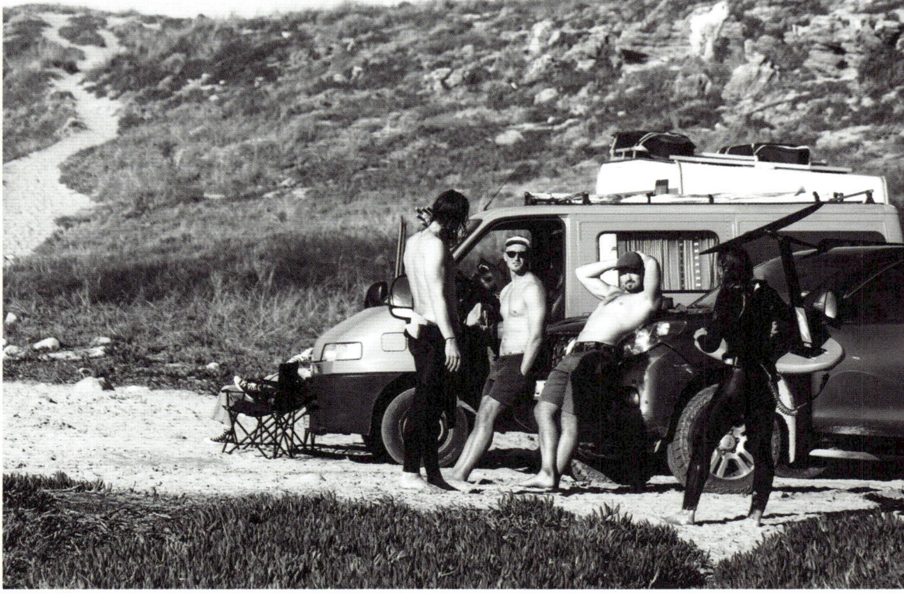

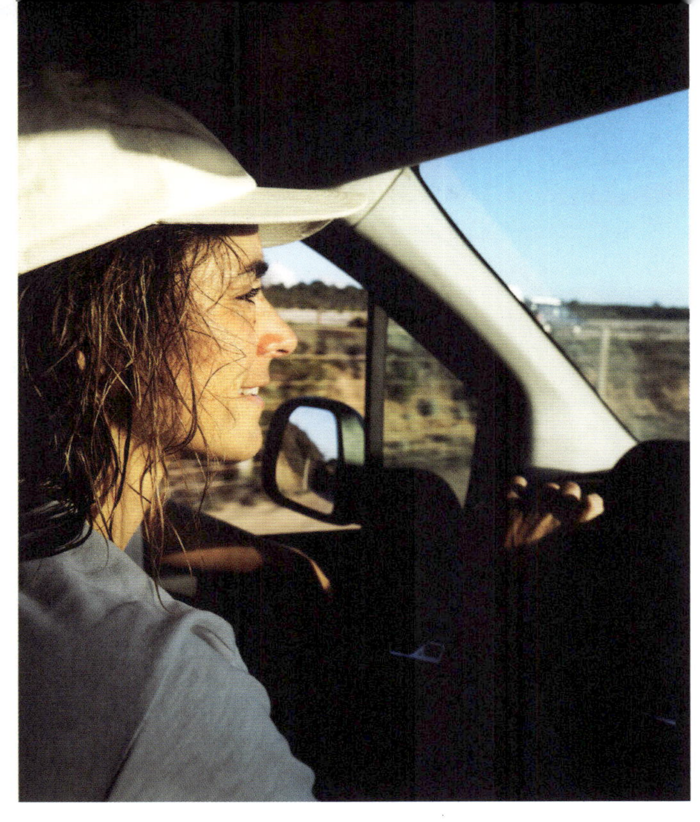

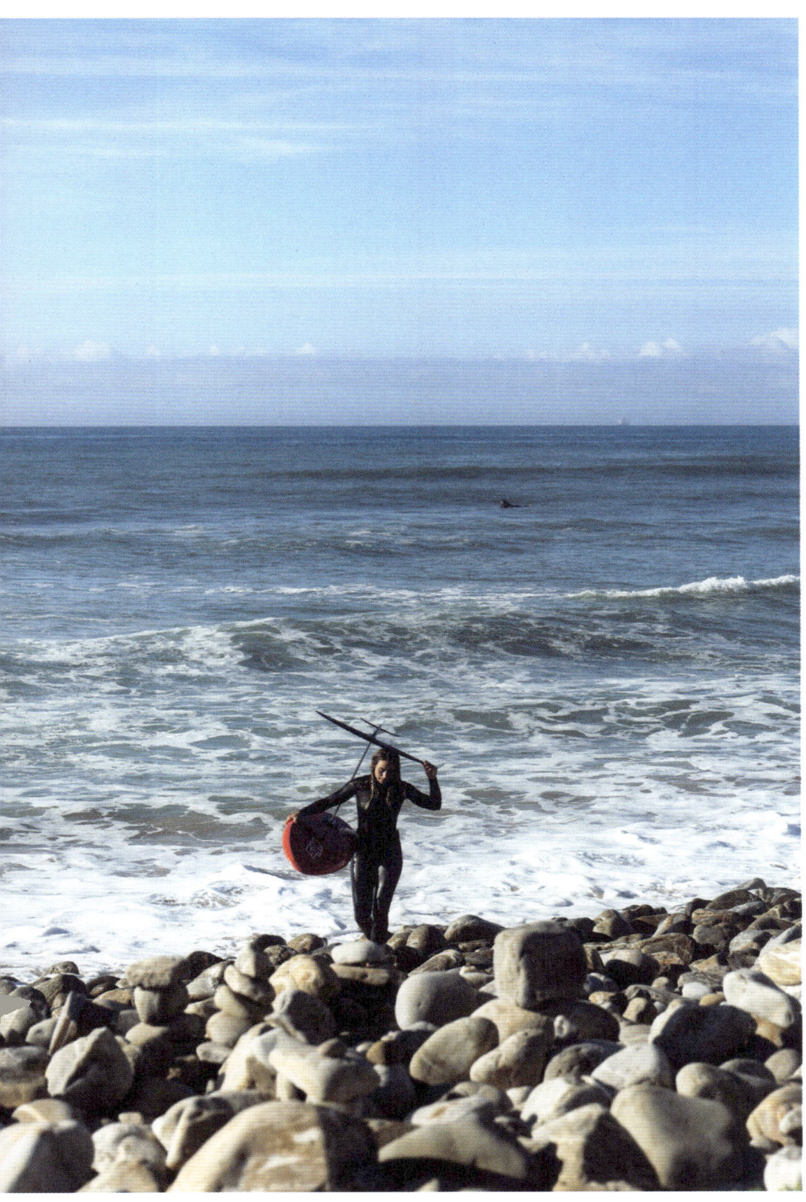

Olivia grew up in the south-east of France, close to the Alps and the Mediterranean Sea. She fell in love with the ocean when she started windsurfing with her mother at the age of twelve. Since then, she has spent most of her time on the water. Training in the south-west of Portugal took Olivia's performance as an athlete to the next level because she became so deeply enamoured with the beach spots where she trained. The region offers a wide variety of conditions, with the waves, the wind and the current changing as you move from place to place.

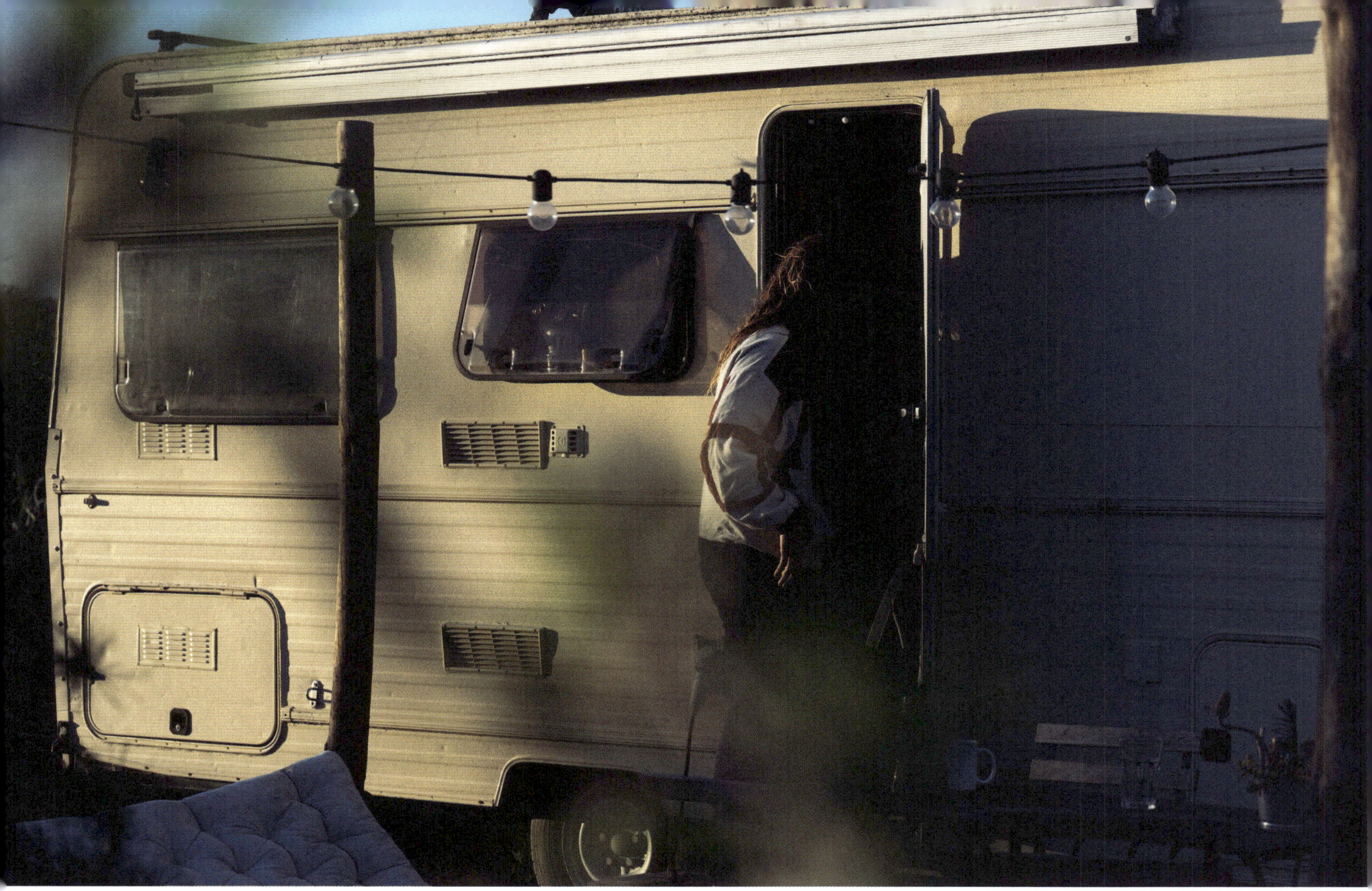

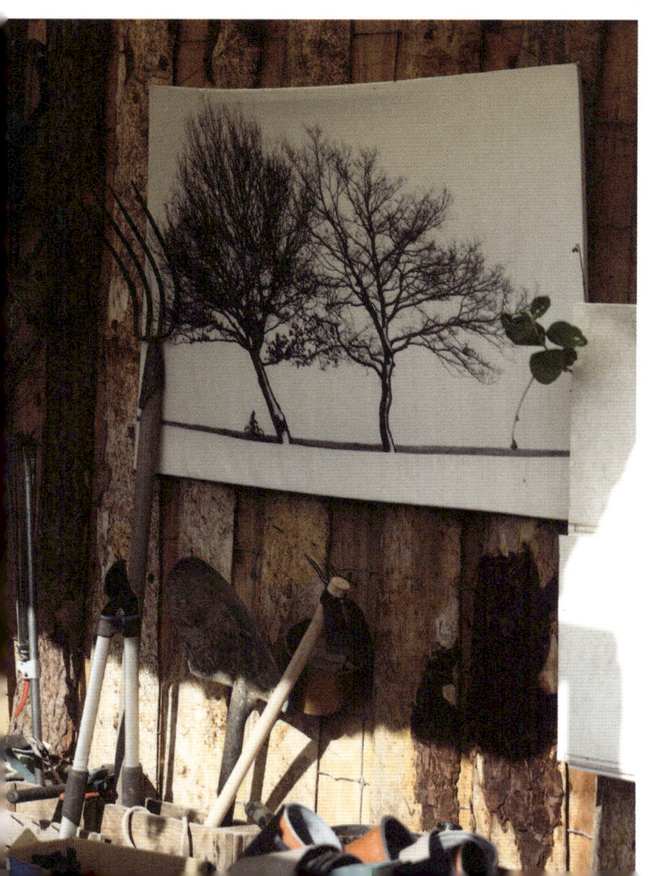

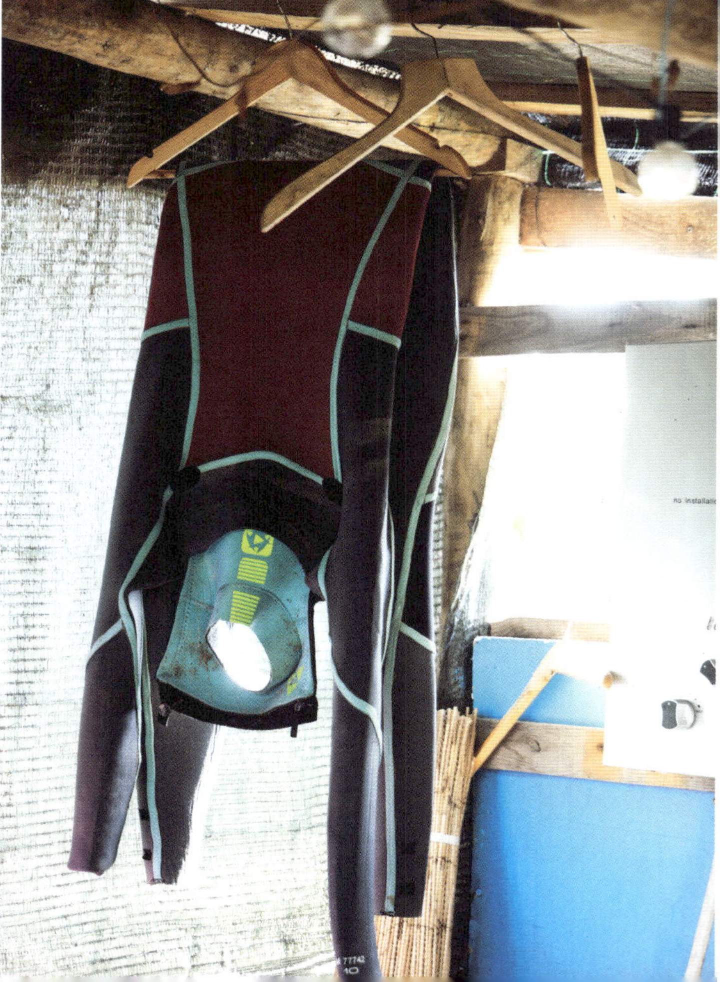

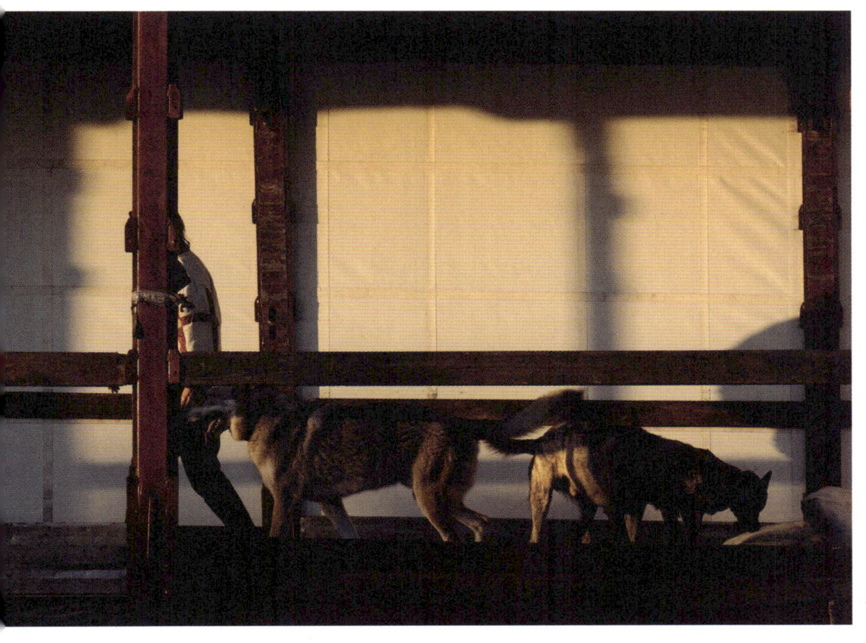
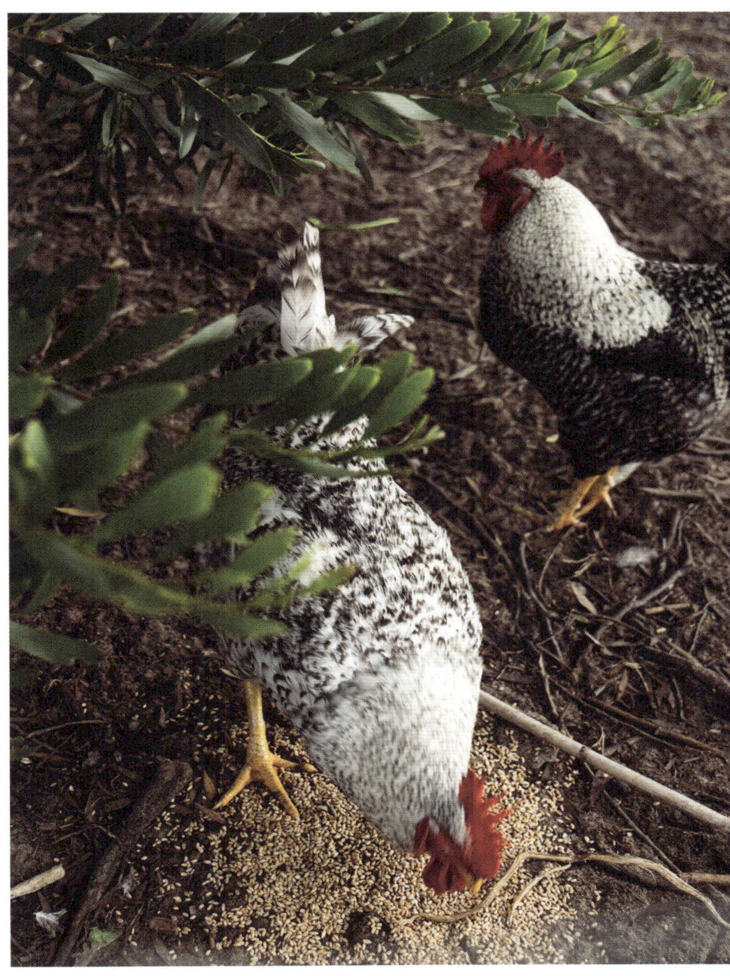
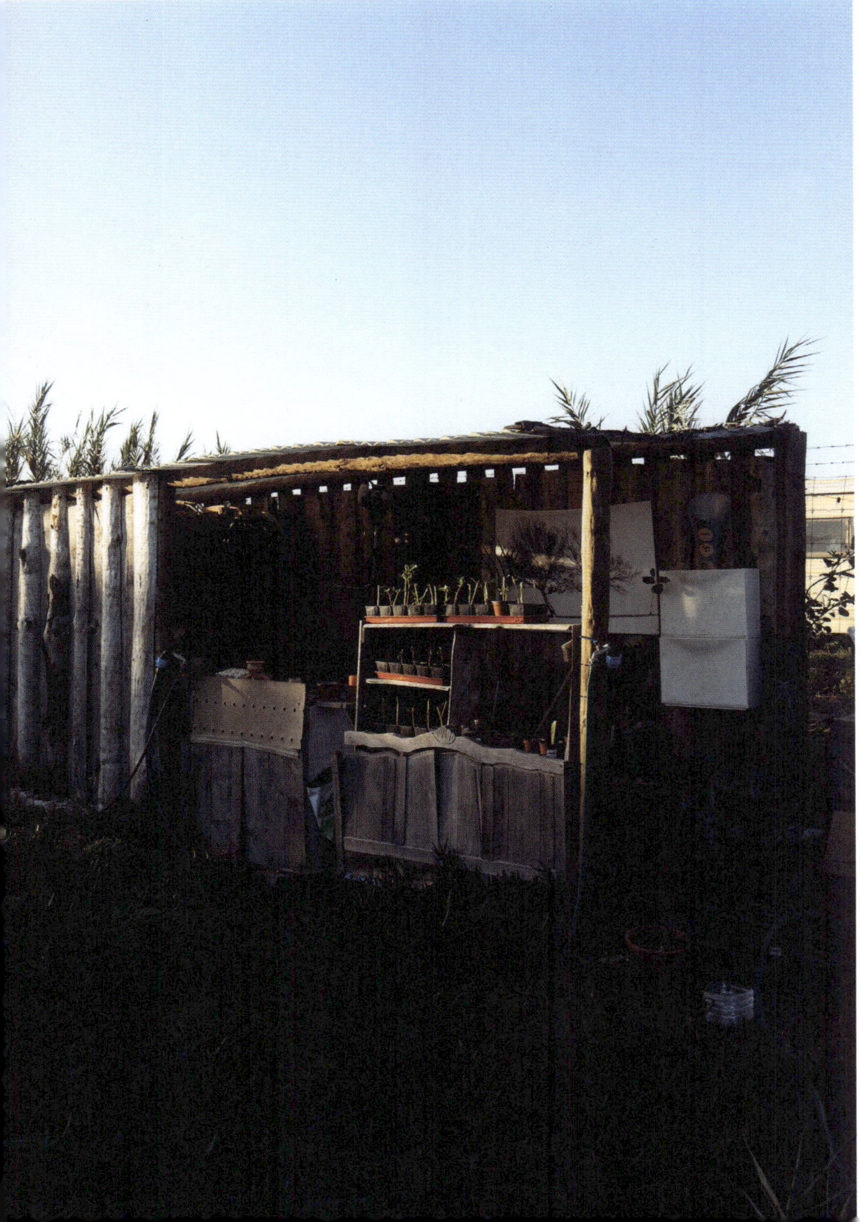

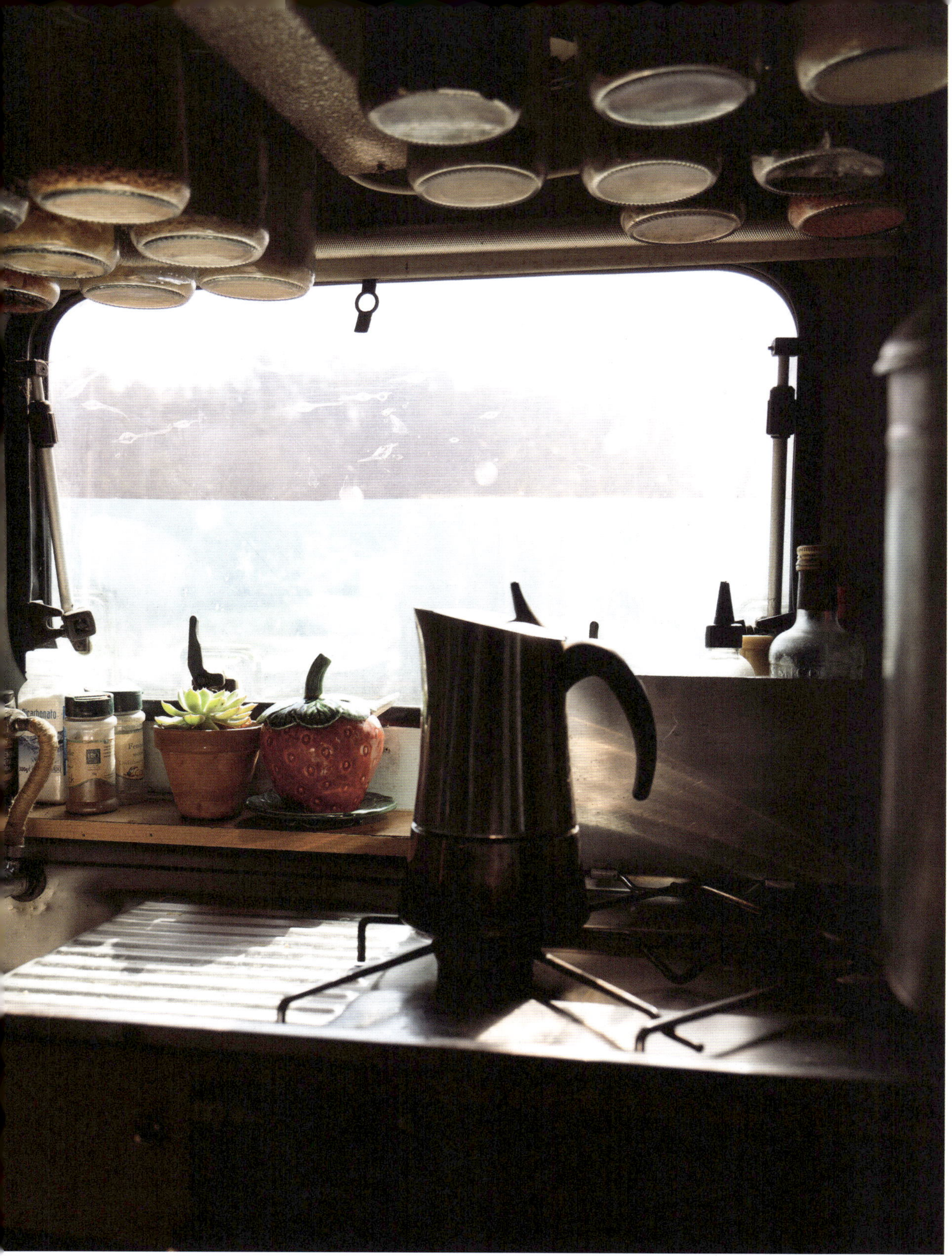

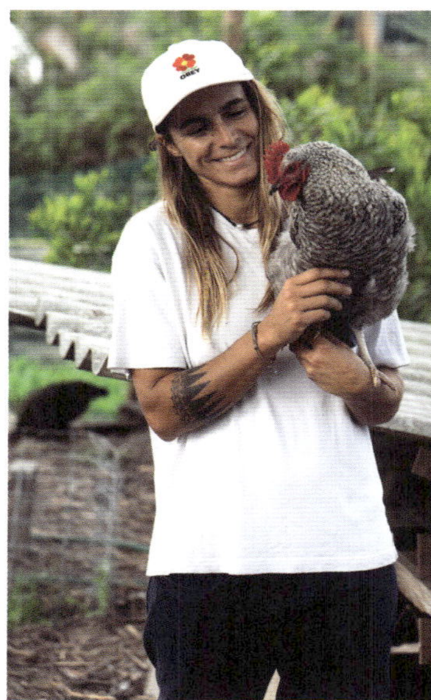

She still remembers the first time she ventured out into the ocean in southern Portugal, how the scent and light there instantly felt special. She was lucky enough to find a perfect plot of land for her camper along the Alentejo coastline; there she created what feels like a wonderfully chaotic and freespirited mini-universe in the dunes, with sofas to relax outside, a garden shed made from driftwood, and even a small permaculture garden. Caring for living things is something Olivia cherishes, whether it's gardening, watching the trees grow, or walking along the dune trails with her dogs. It's her second form of meditation, right after spending time on the water.

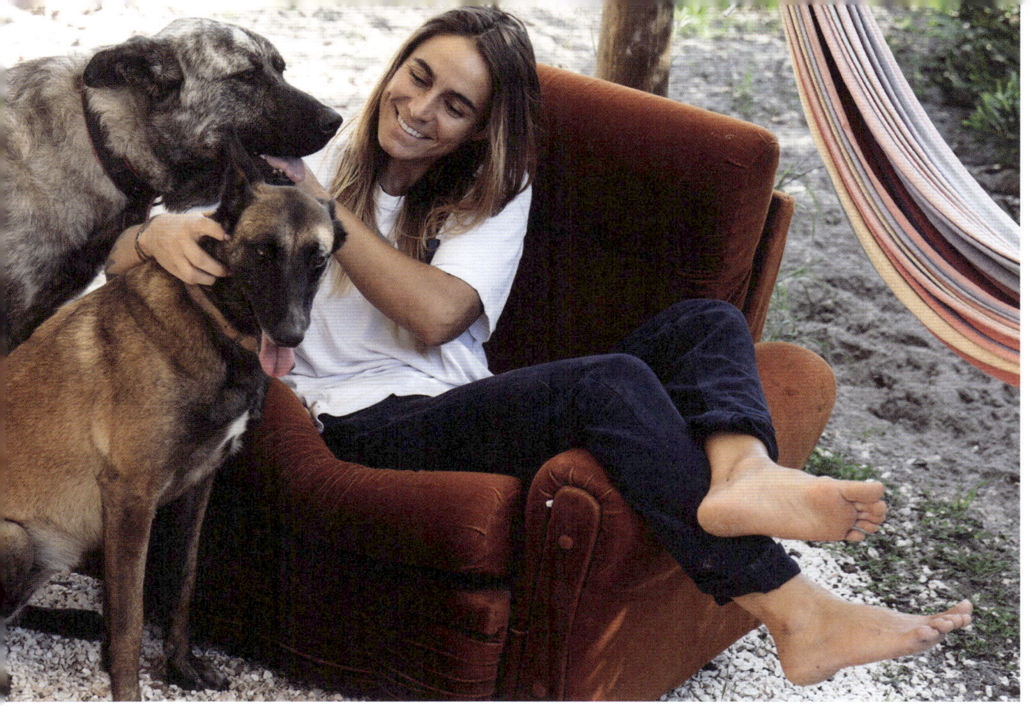

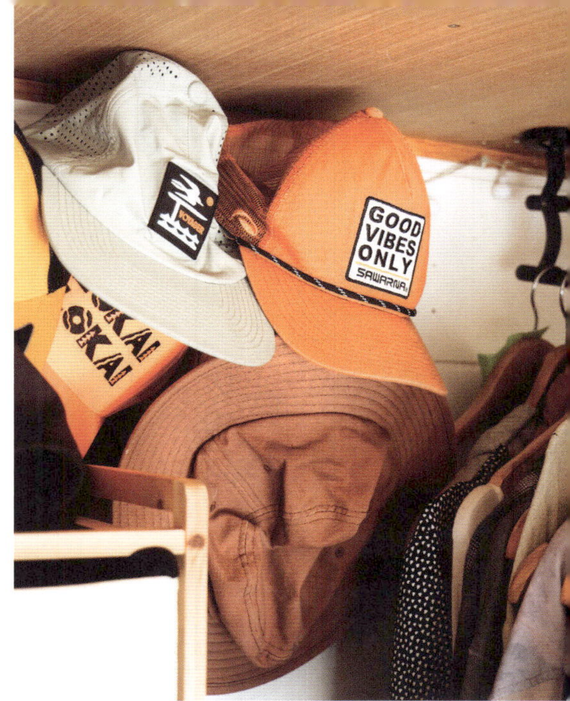

GOOD
VIBES
ONLY

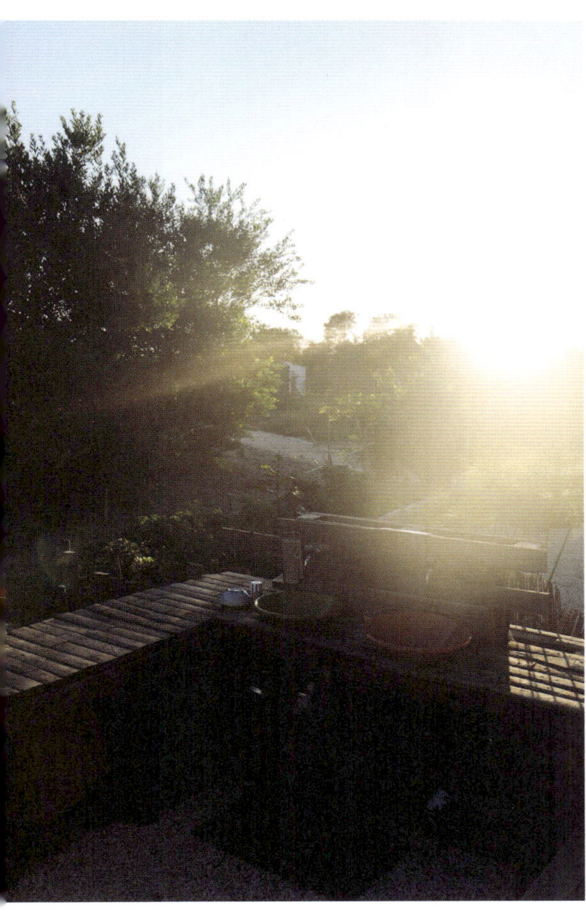

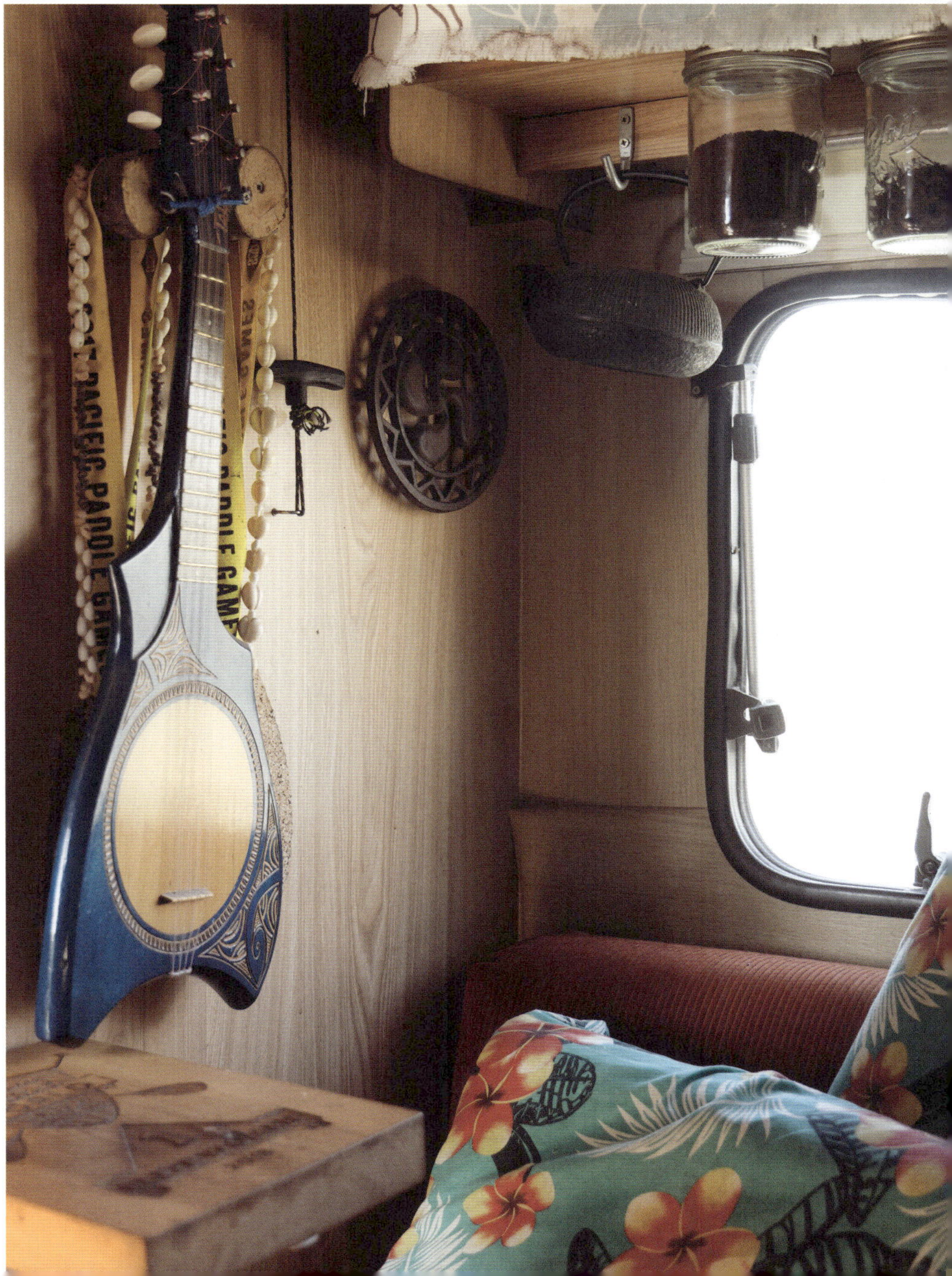

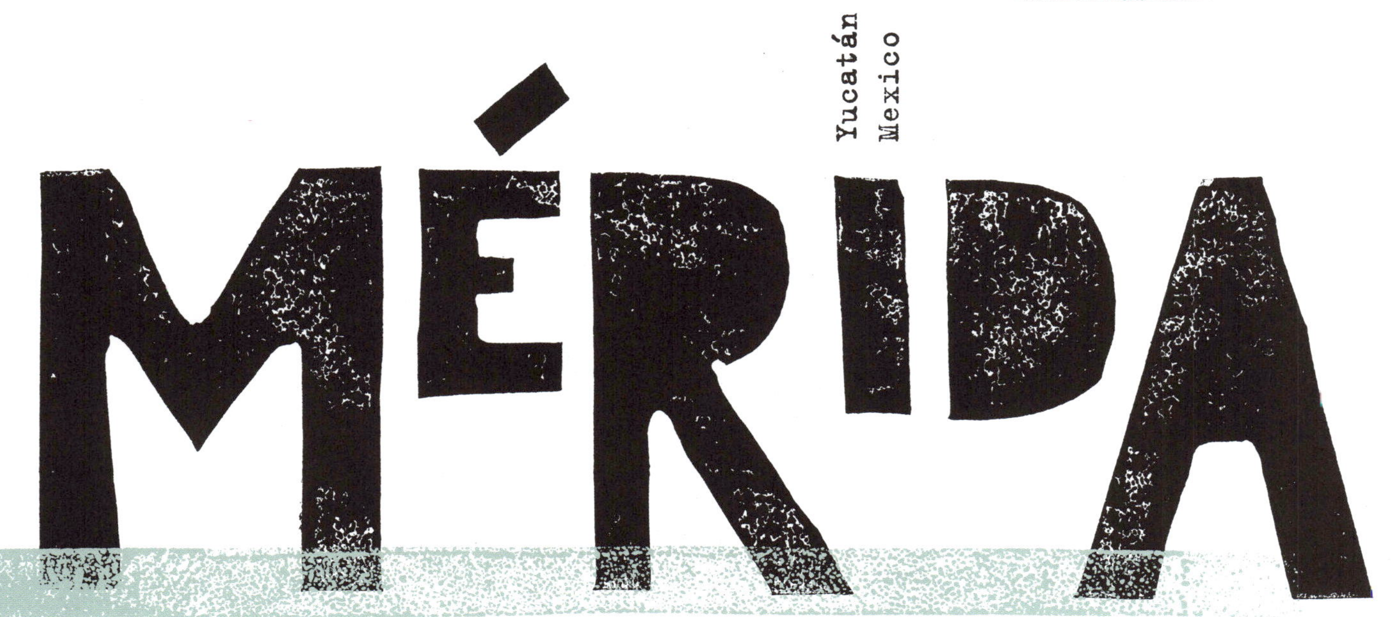

The coastline of the Gulf of Mexico, near the fishing village of Progreso, is a second home to many of the residents of the city of Mérida. The city itself is located slightly inland, offering the best of both worlds. The enchanting, authentic capital is the cultural heartland of the Yucatán peninsula, but the sea and the beach play an important part in the daily lives of the locals. During the day, the old boulevards lined with beautiful colonial homes are an excellent place for a stroll. In the evening, you can enjoy the magical sunsets over the water as you go kite surfing.

This balance between life in the city and by the sea has always been a given in the lives of interior designer Gina Góngora and architect Fernando Gomez Vivas. Although they were both born and raised in Mérida and thus had access to everything the city has to offer, they cherish the childhood memories of weekends and holidays in their families' country houses by the sea. And that is how the seeds were sown for their love for Yucatán's magnificent culture and rich history, as well as for the region's traditional artefacts. Both Gina and Fer are continually inspired by the imperfections of these objects, whose origins are rooted in the peninsula's culture.

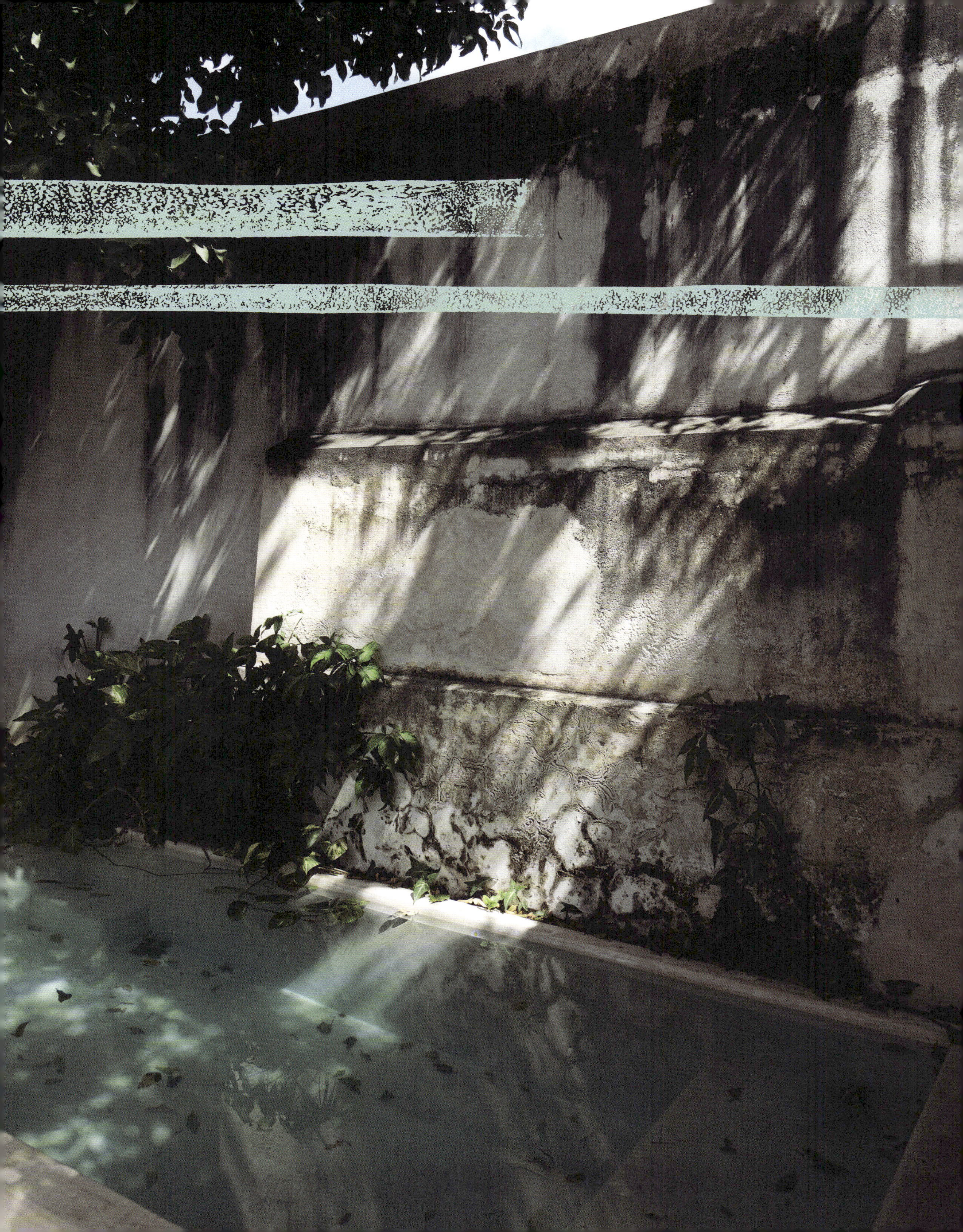

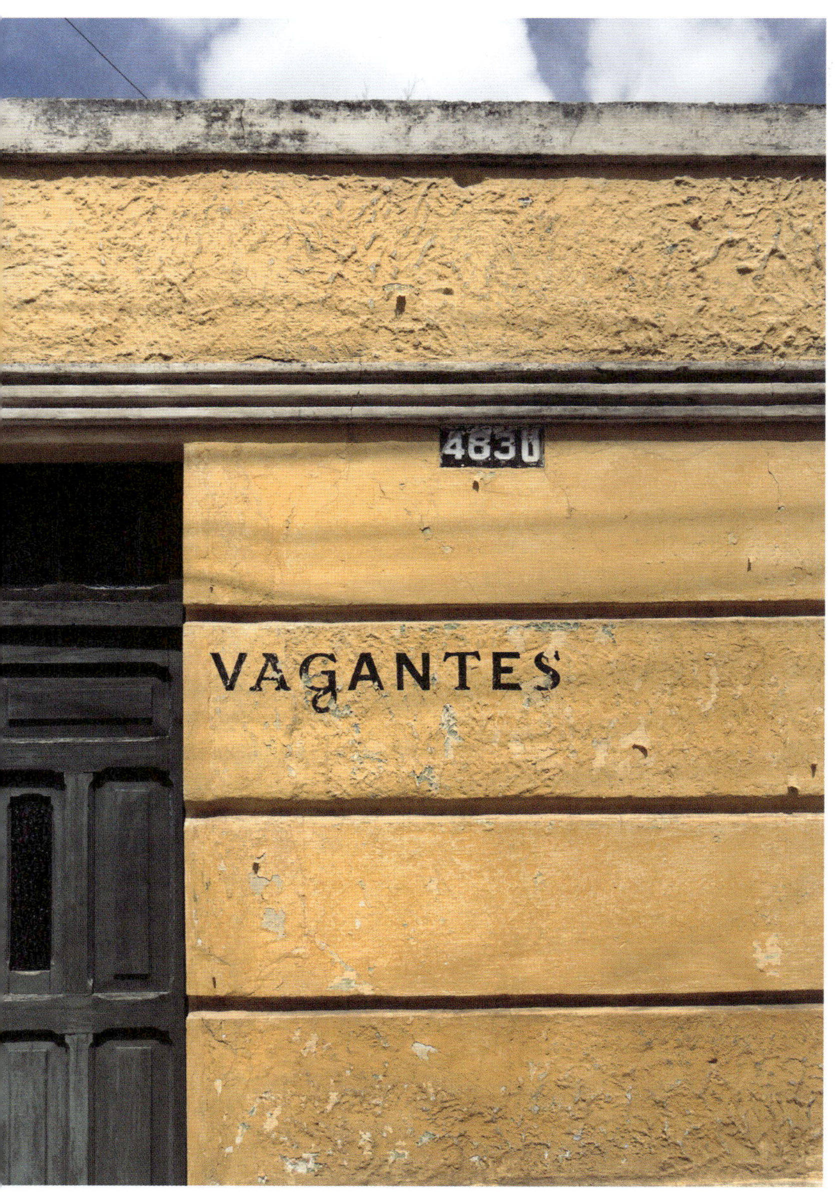

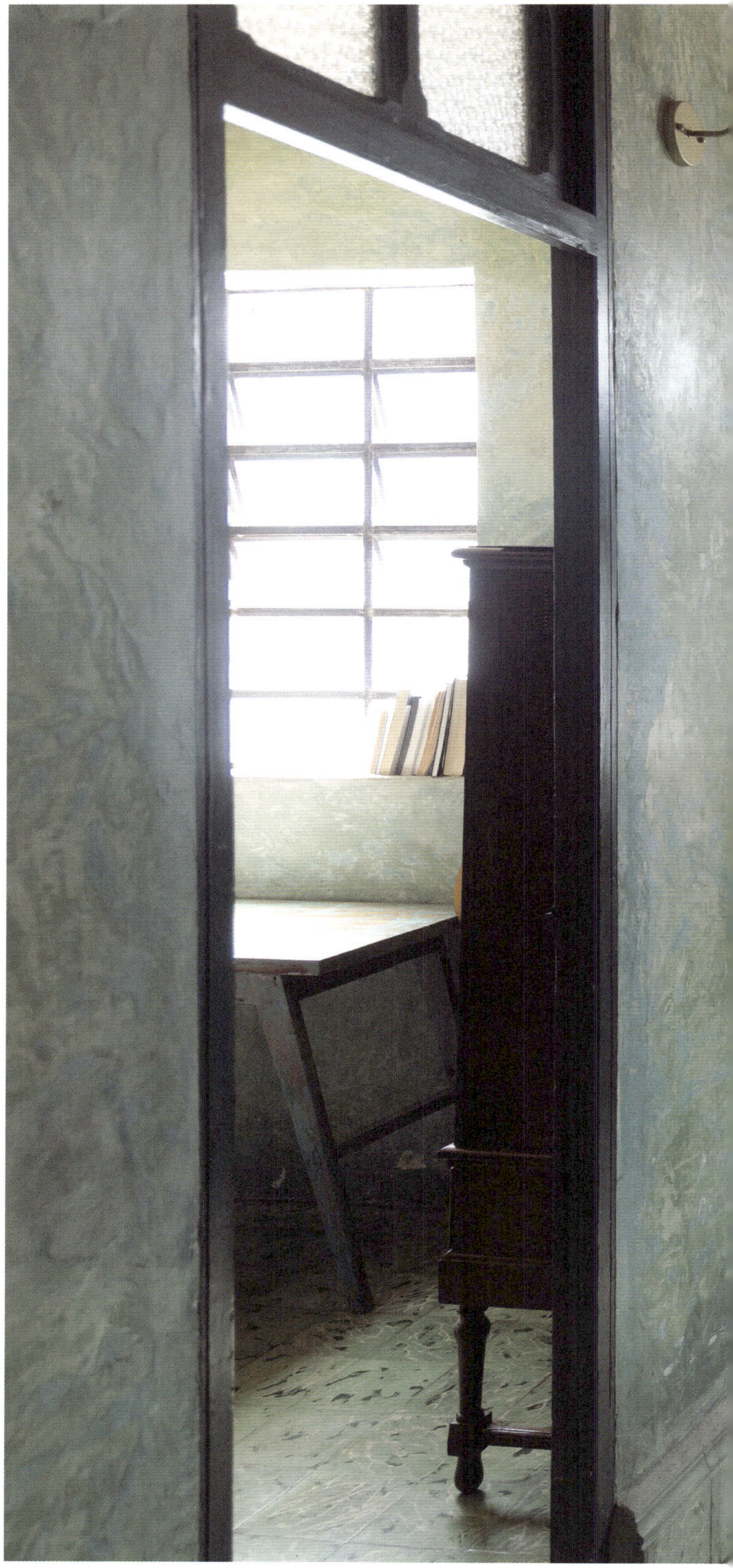

Gina and Fernando met at school and dreamed of one day buying a house in Mérida Centro, the lively historic district where their grandparents lived. They fell in love with this simple house just off Paseo Montejo, an iconic boulevard that crosses the city from north to south and where all the important periods of Mexican architectural history are represented. The house ticked all their boxes, but unfortunately, it had already been sold. A few months later, however, they got a call from the seller, who informed them that it was back on the market. Some things are meant to be...

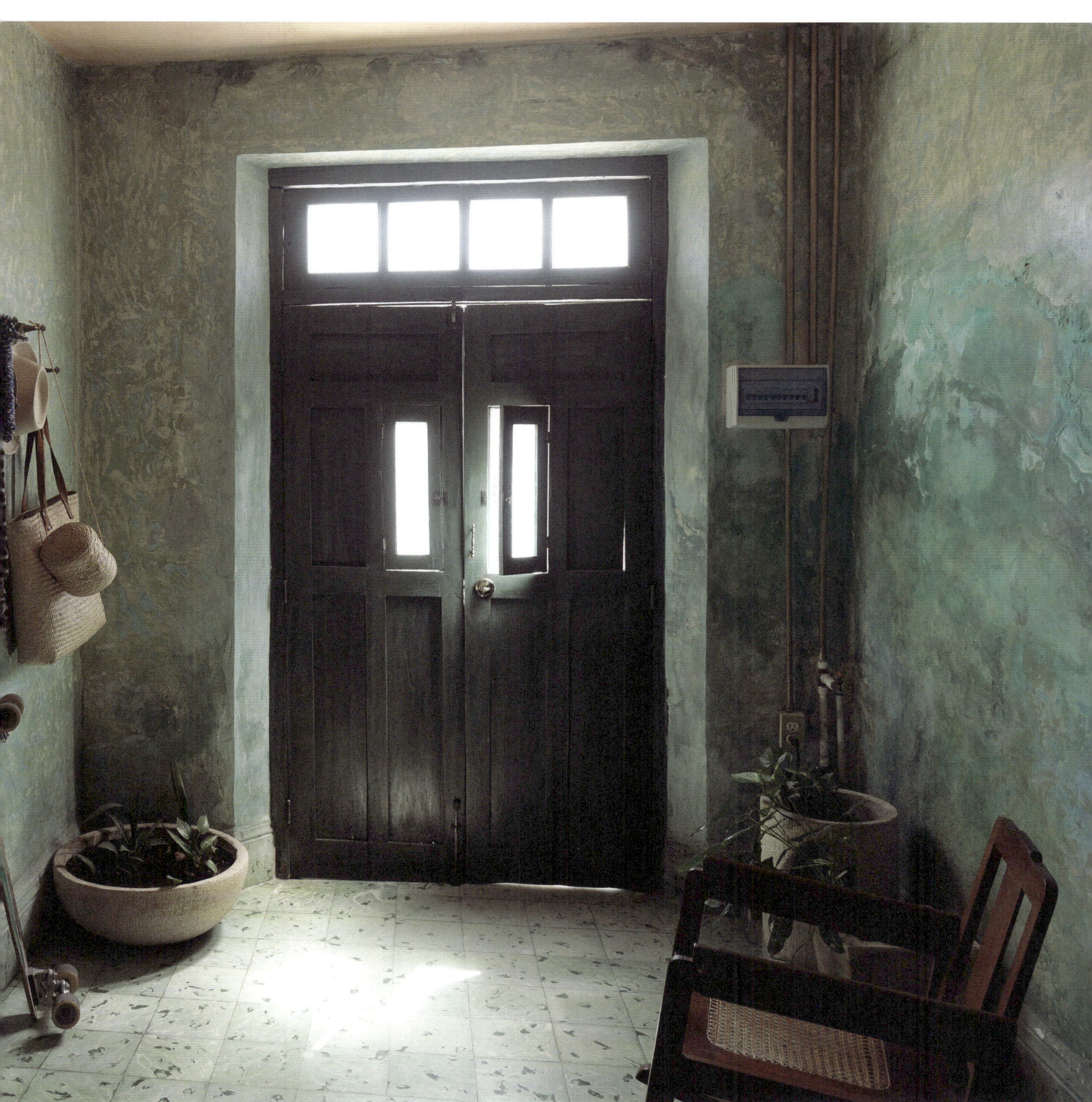

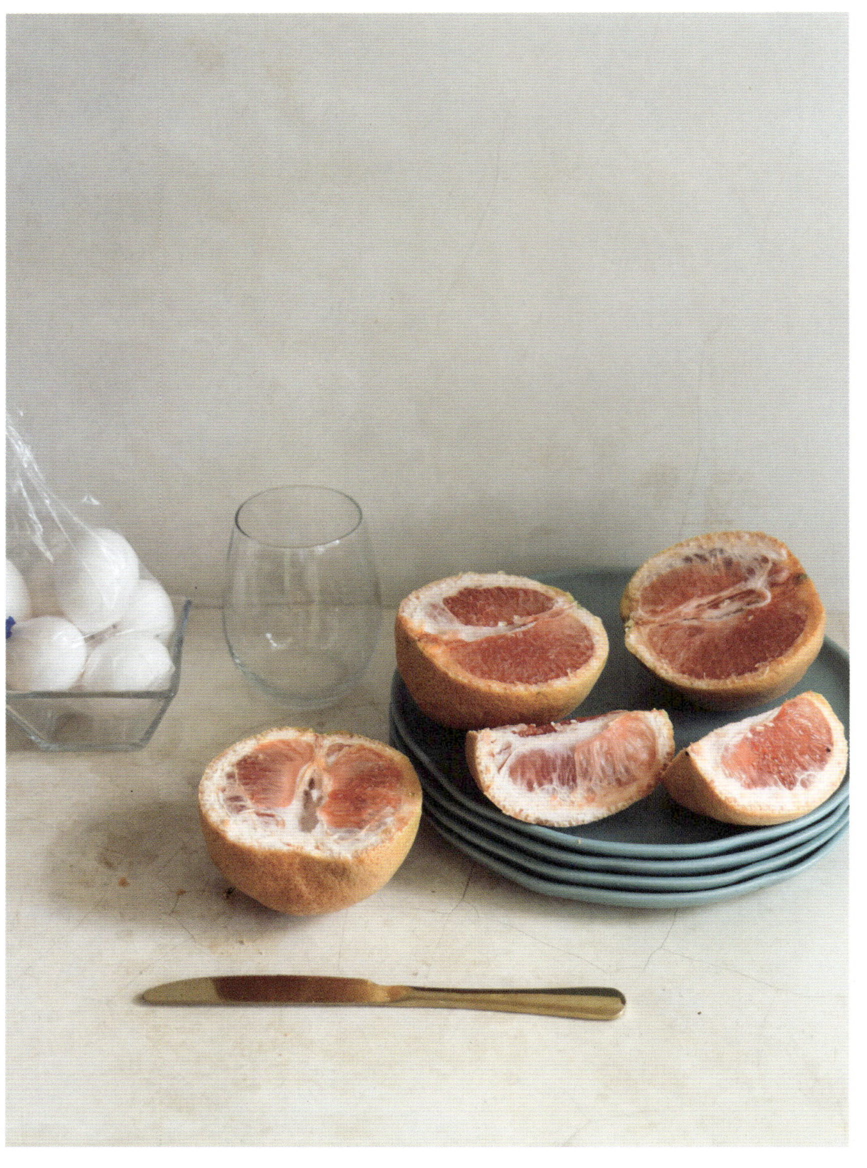

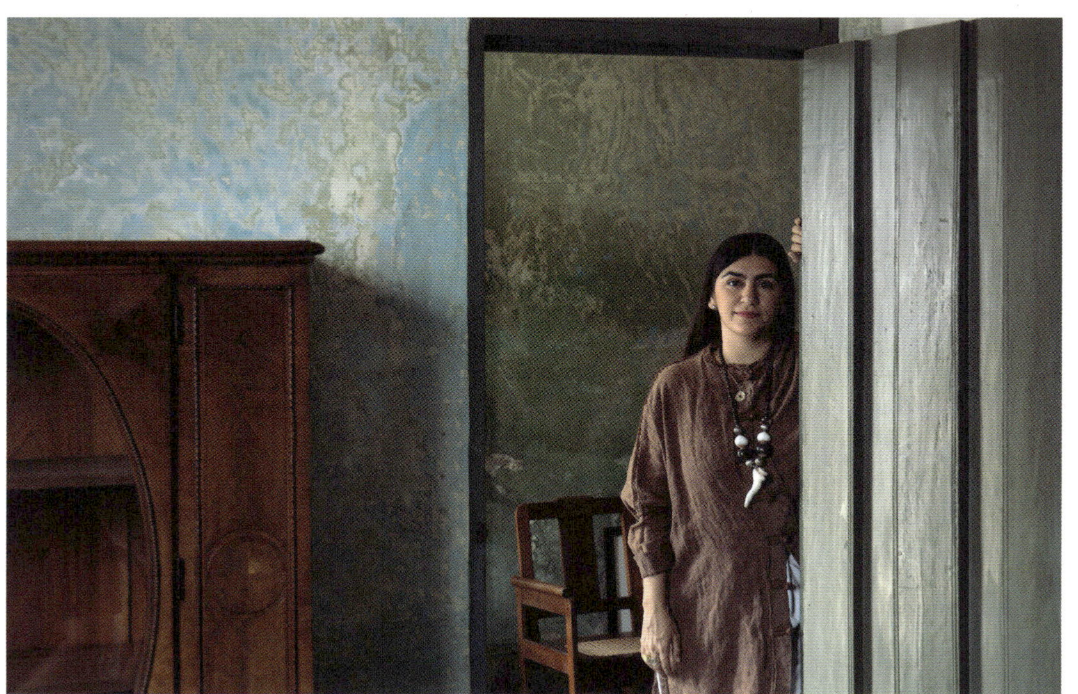

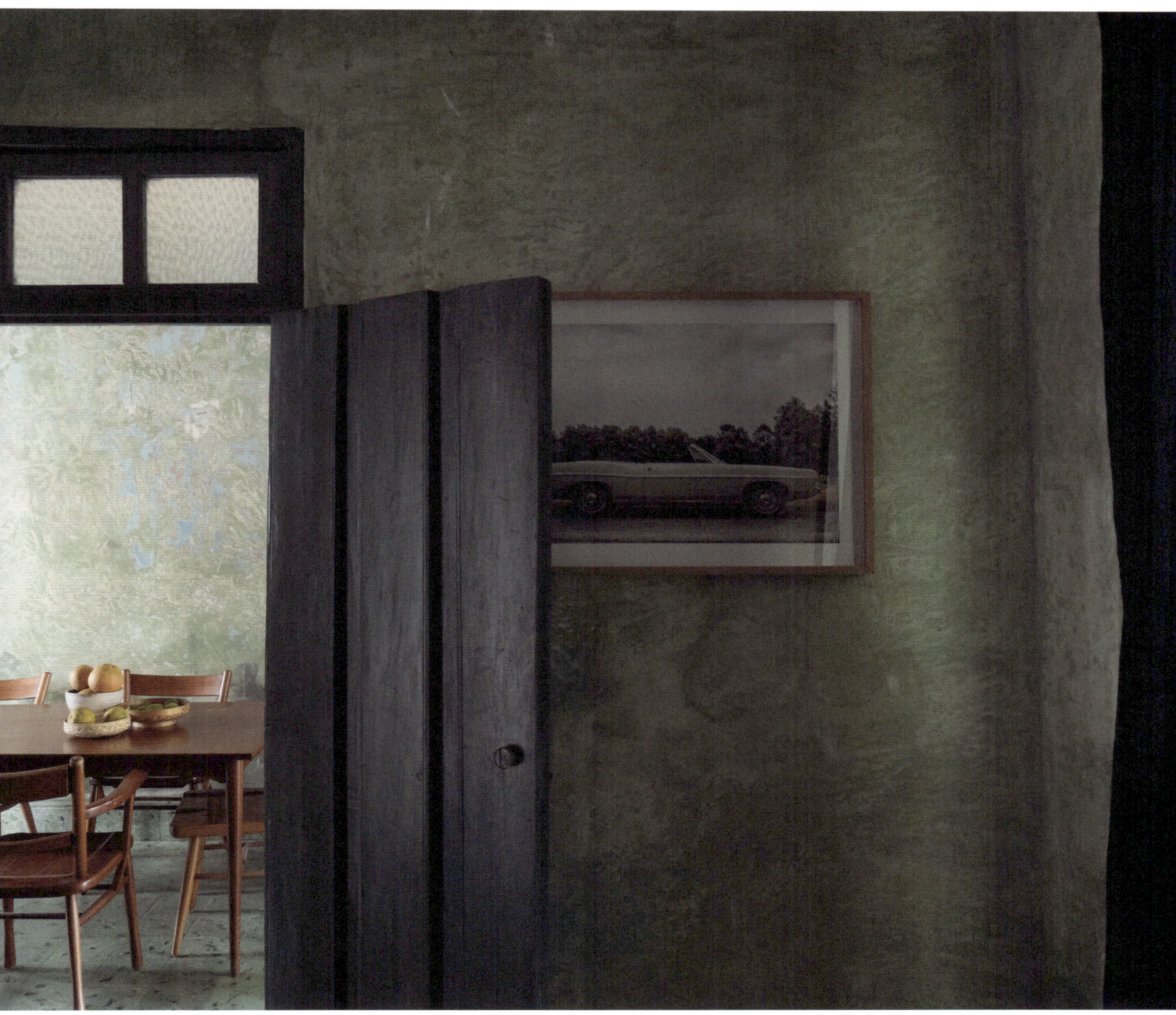

The renovation ushered in the next chapter in Gina and Fernando's life and career. Fernando left the architectural firm where he was a partner to start his own business, while Gina reinvented herself as an interior designer. The first project the couple tackled together was their own house, which also served as a calling card for their new brand, Vagantes. It also meant they were able to use their own taste and preferences as a guideline, showcasing the way of life that Vagantes epitomises.

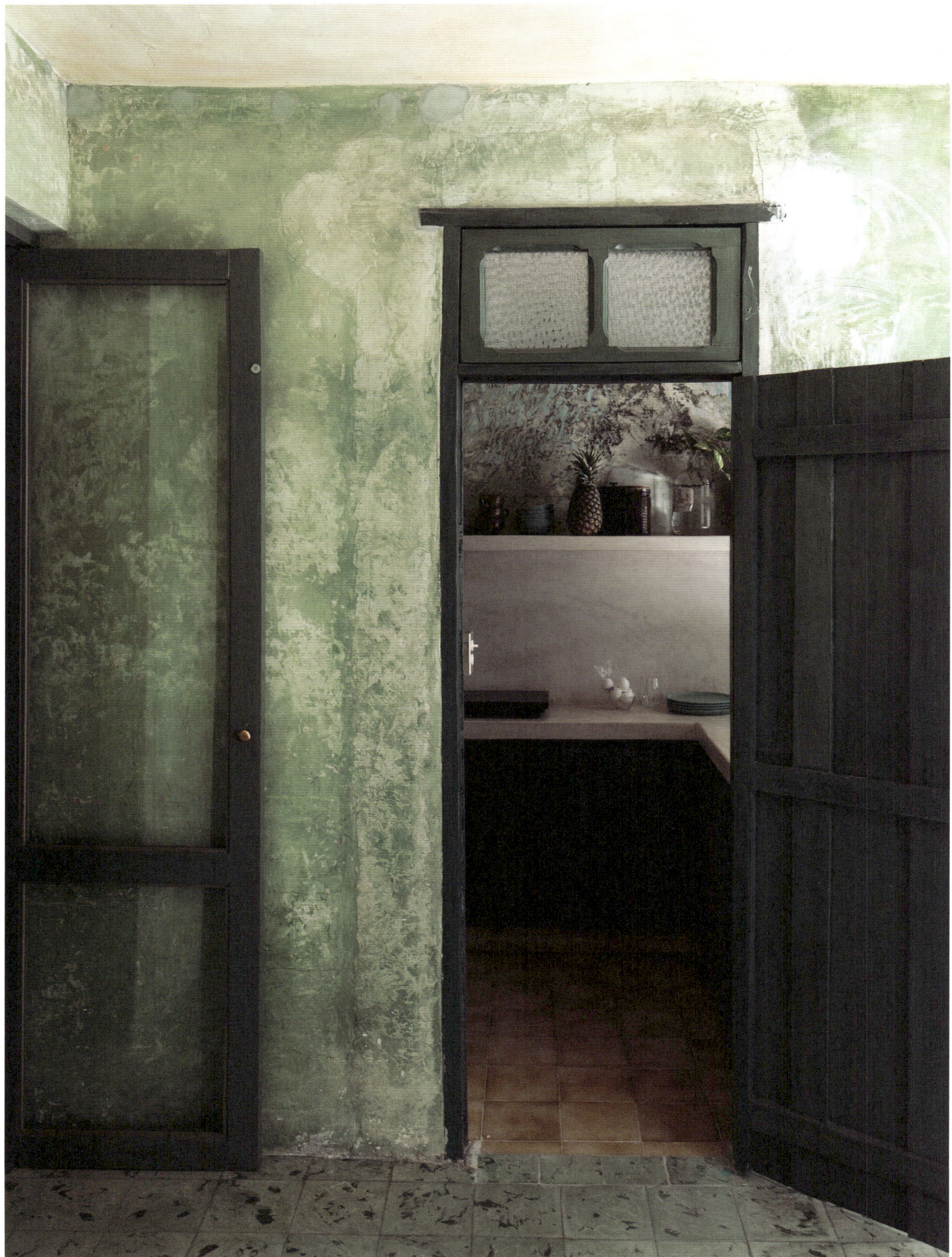

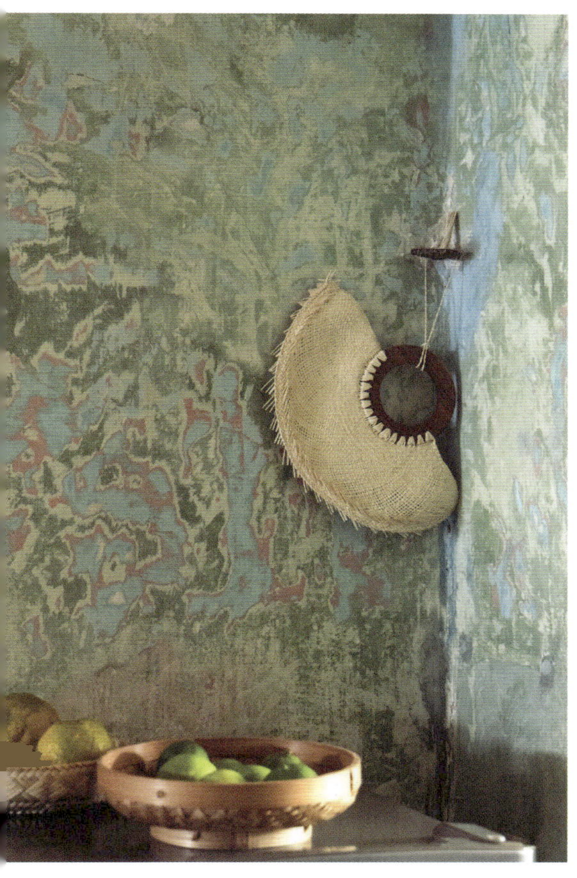

Gina and Fer are passionate about respecting houses as they find them. They feel that every (historical) dwelling has its own inherent value and that this should be preserved as is. Instead of embarking on a renovation, they prefer to be guided by the house, which, in some instances, dictates what should be done. The walls of their first Vagantes home are an excellent example of this approach. Originally painted white, the paint had broken down in places due to the humidity, revealing some blue, lots of green and even pink beneath it. The couple love that you can distil a house's history from these layers, the transformations it has undergone, and the personalities of previous occupants. To Gina and Fer, these decaying colours are quite romantic and highly unique and part of the house's personality, doing away with the need for lots of furniture or decoration.

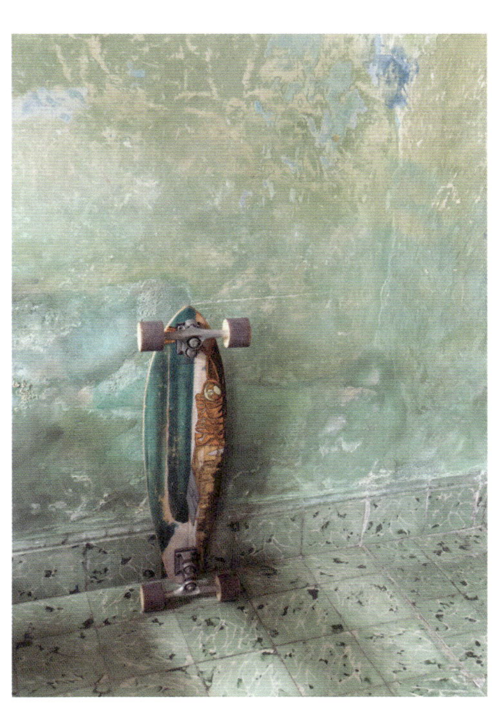

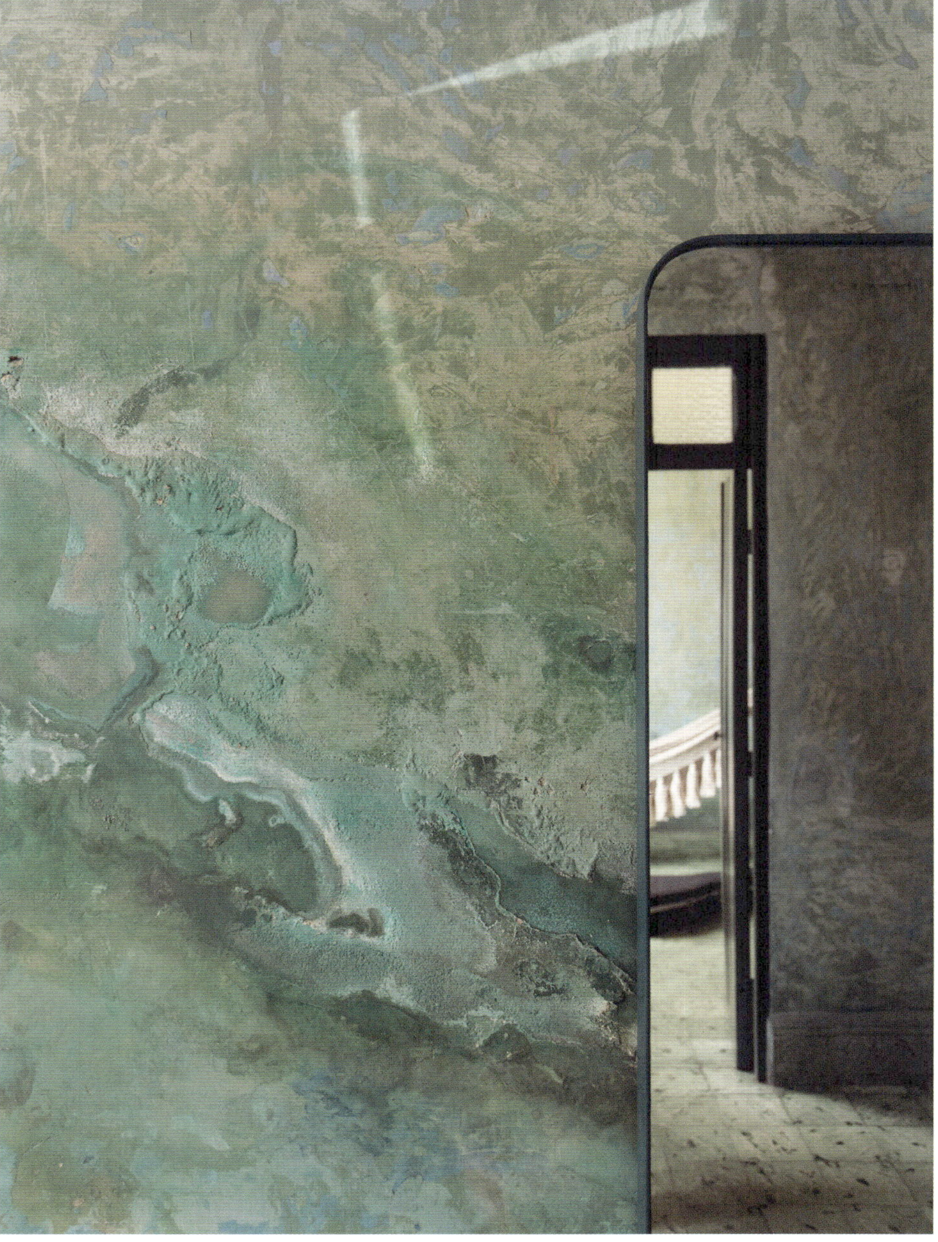

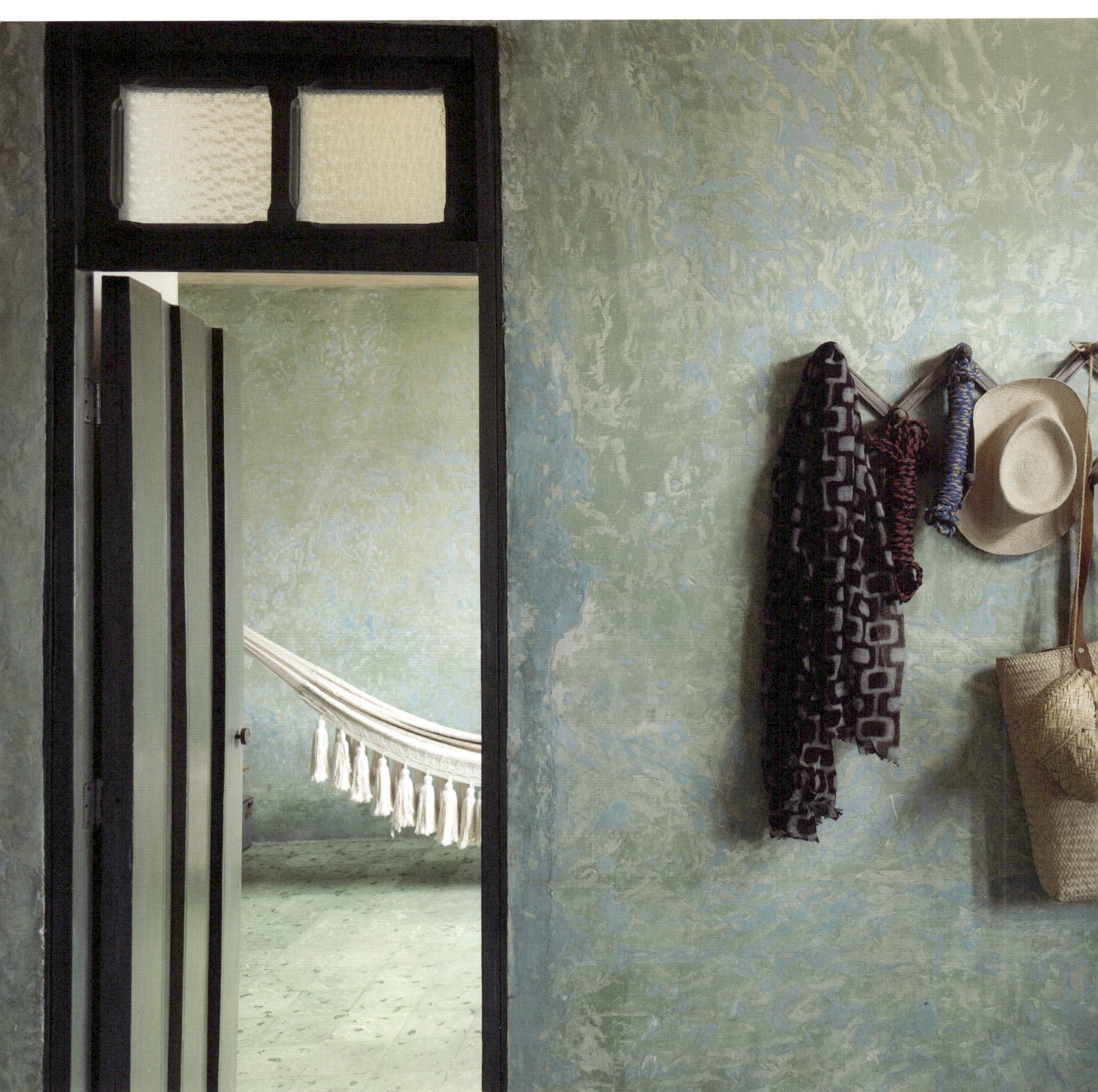

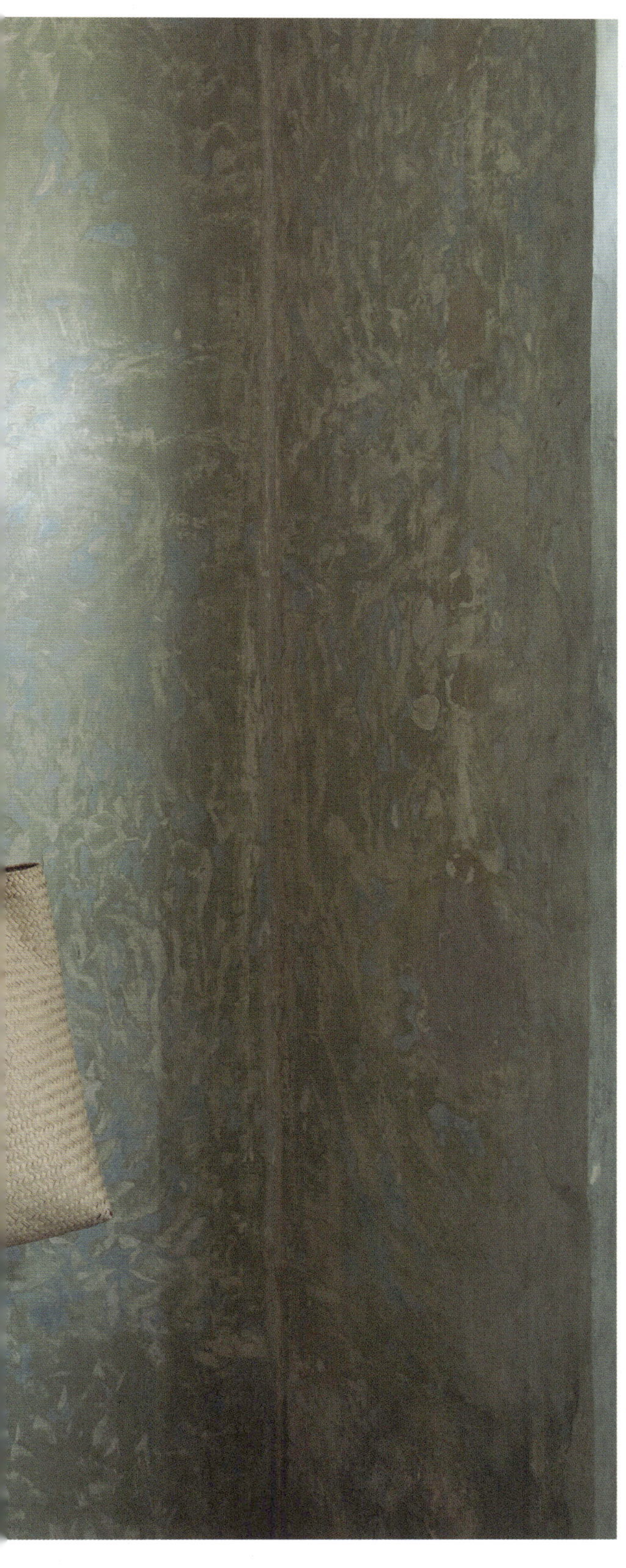
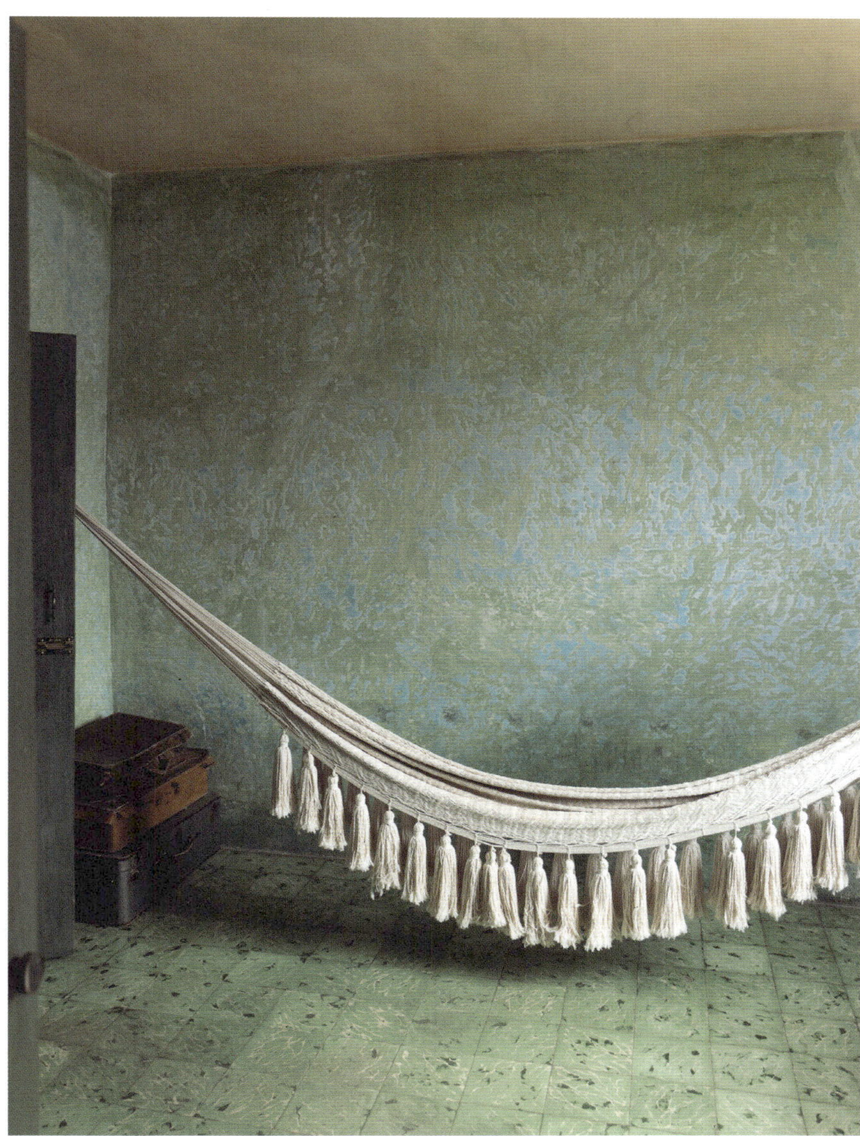
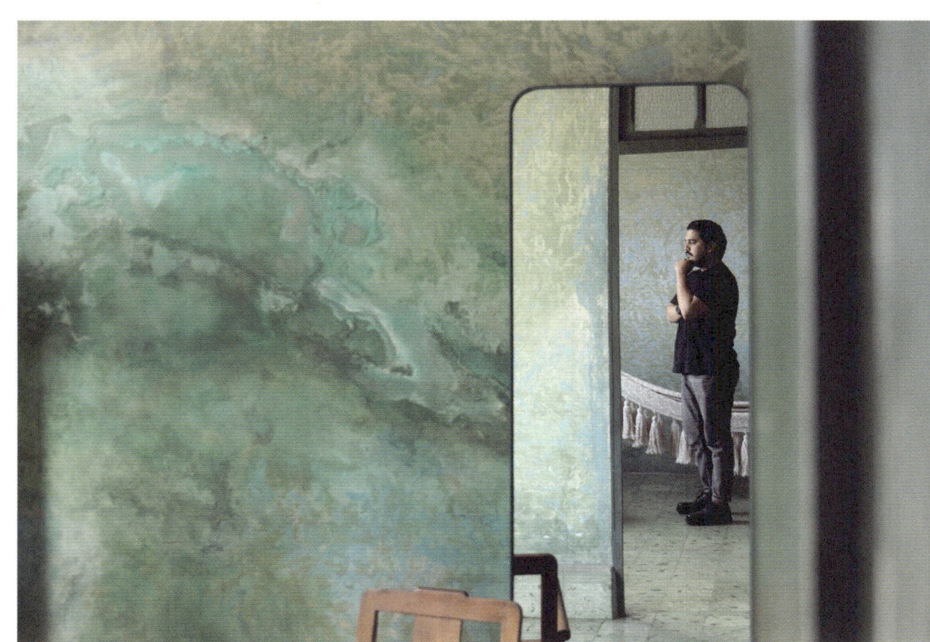

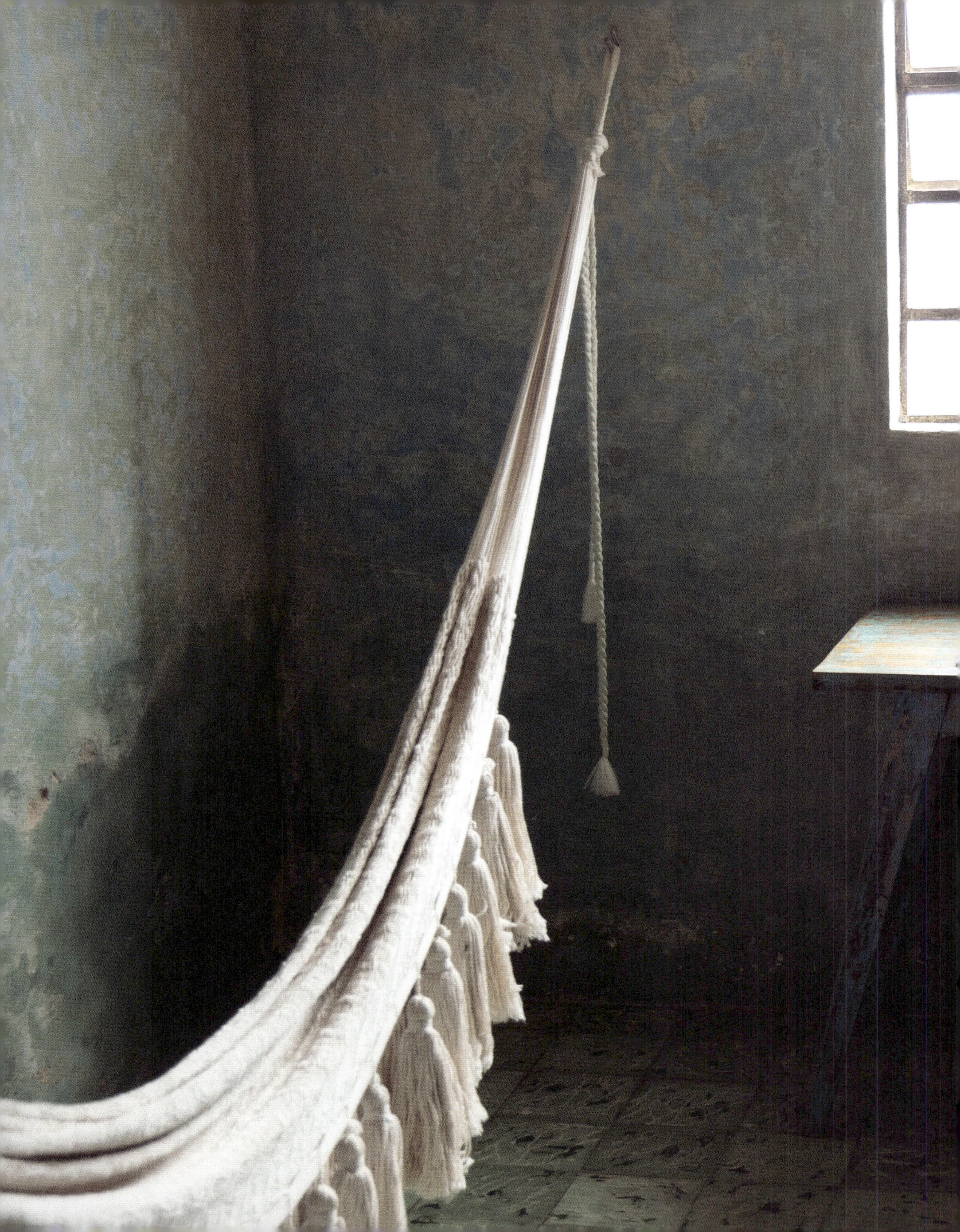

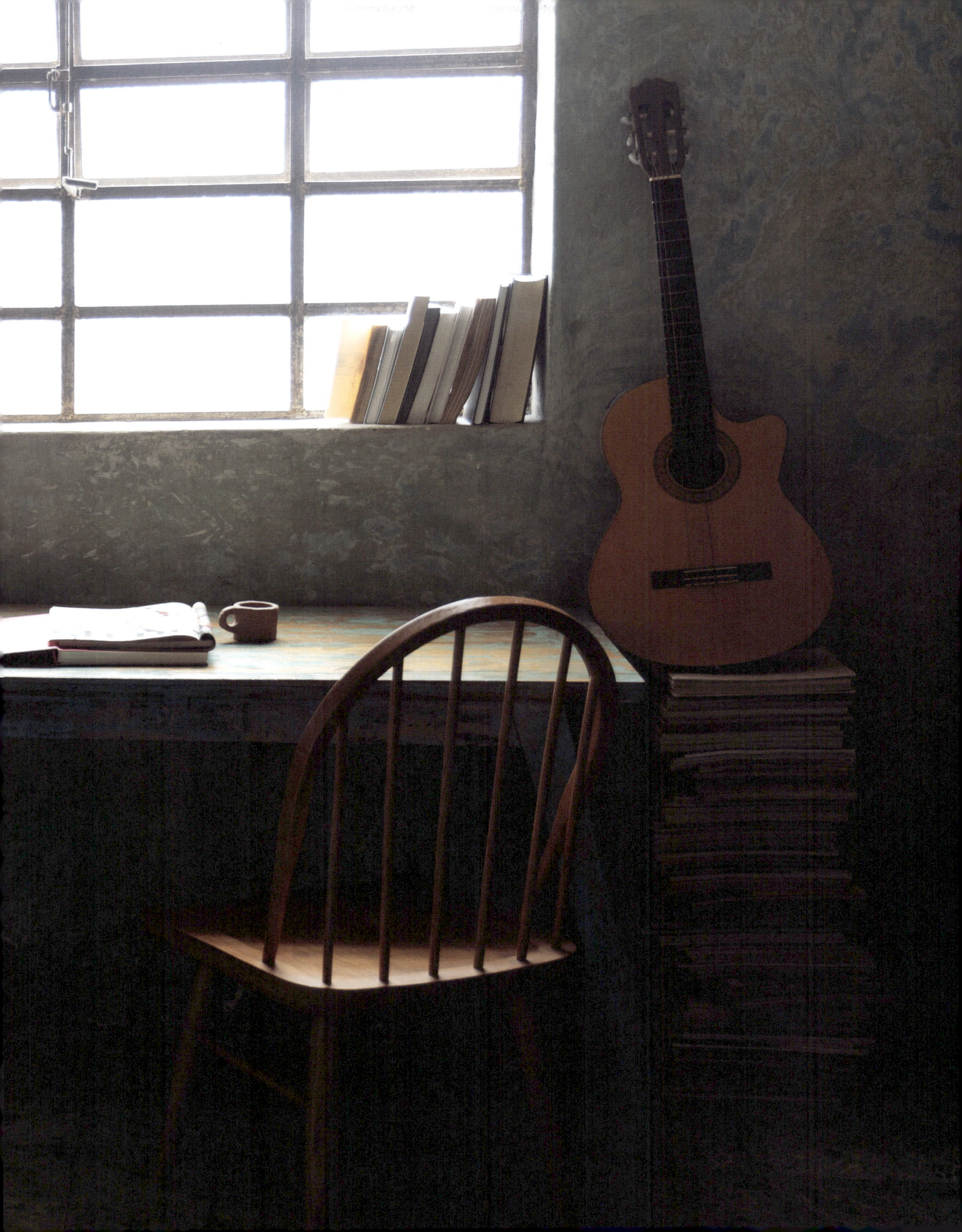

The Atlantic Ocean
makes up Uruguay's coast, acting as its eastern border. This is where you will find the family holiday home of writer Violeta Sticotti. It is just a five-minute walk from the beach, near the tiny seaside village of La Pedrera in the Rocha department of Uruguay. Violeta's father, the Argentinean architect Alejandro Sticotti, built this house for his family, tailoring its design to its enchanting surroundings. The ocean's power is palpable everywhere around you, borne on the salty air that wafts into the house and the breathtaking vistas around it.

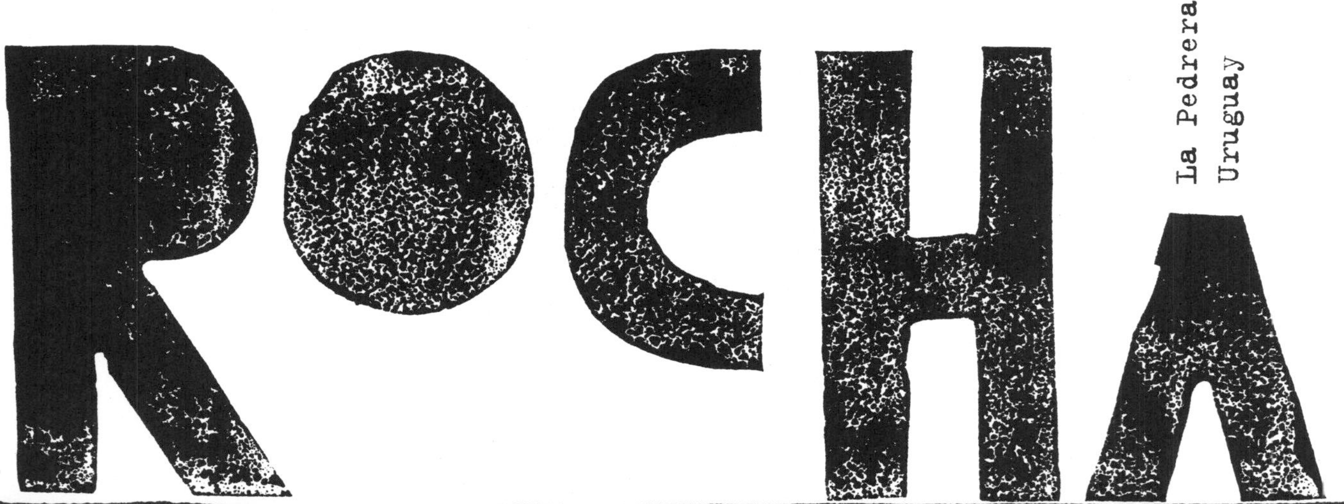

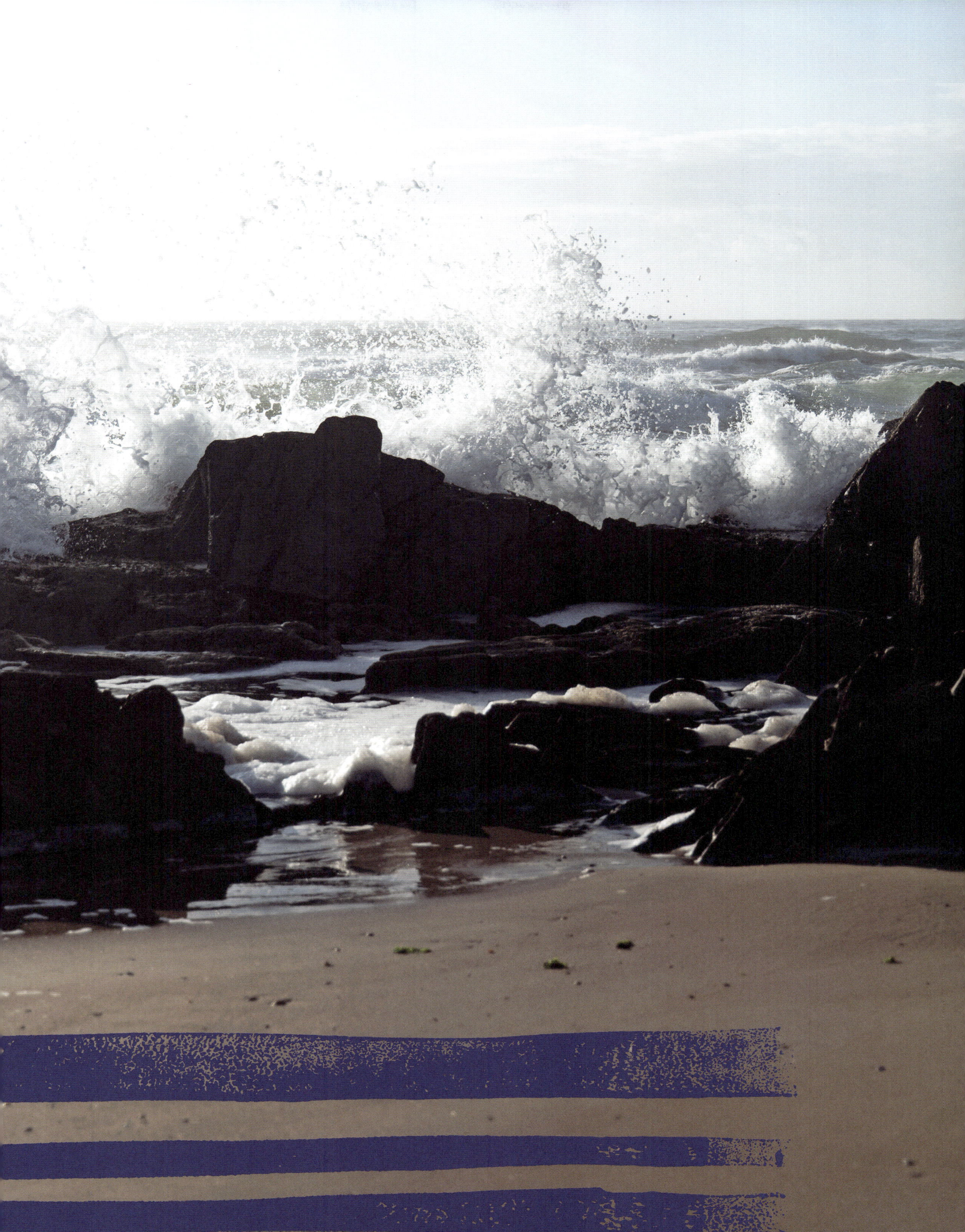

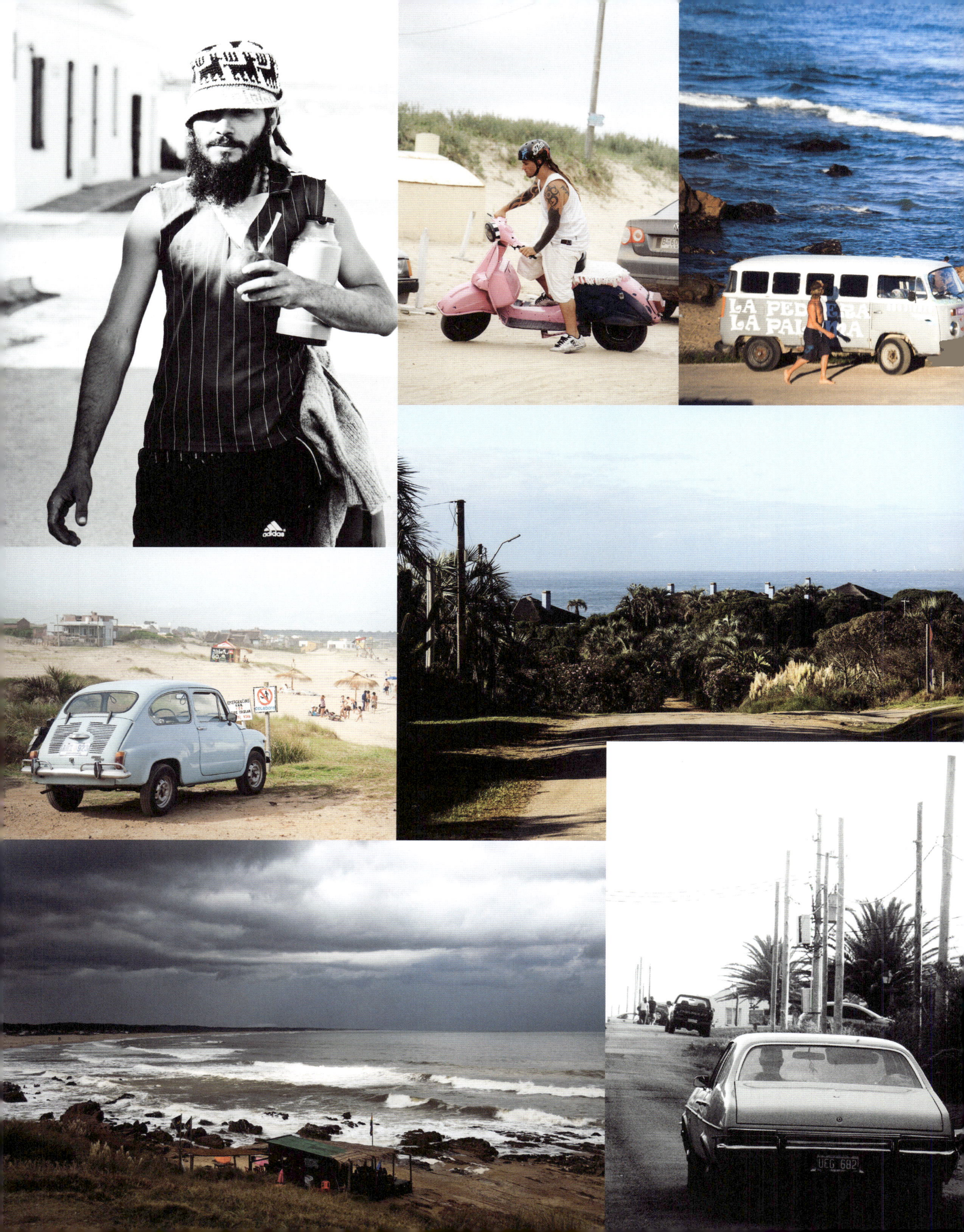
adidas
UEG 682

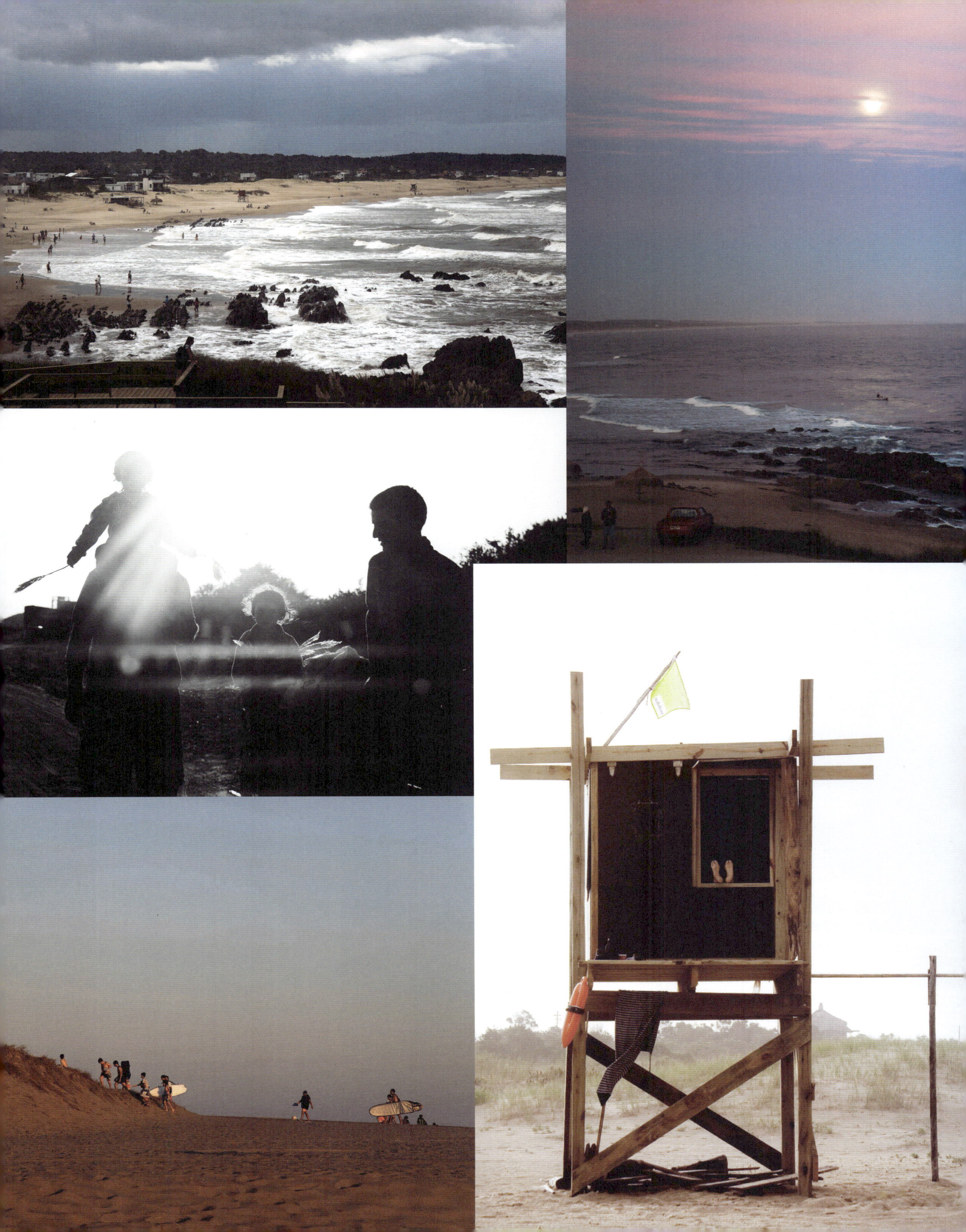

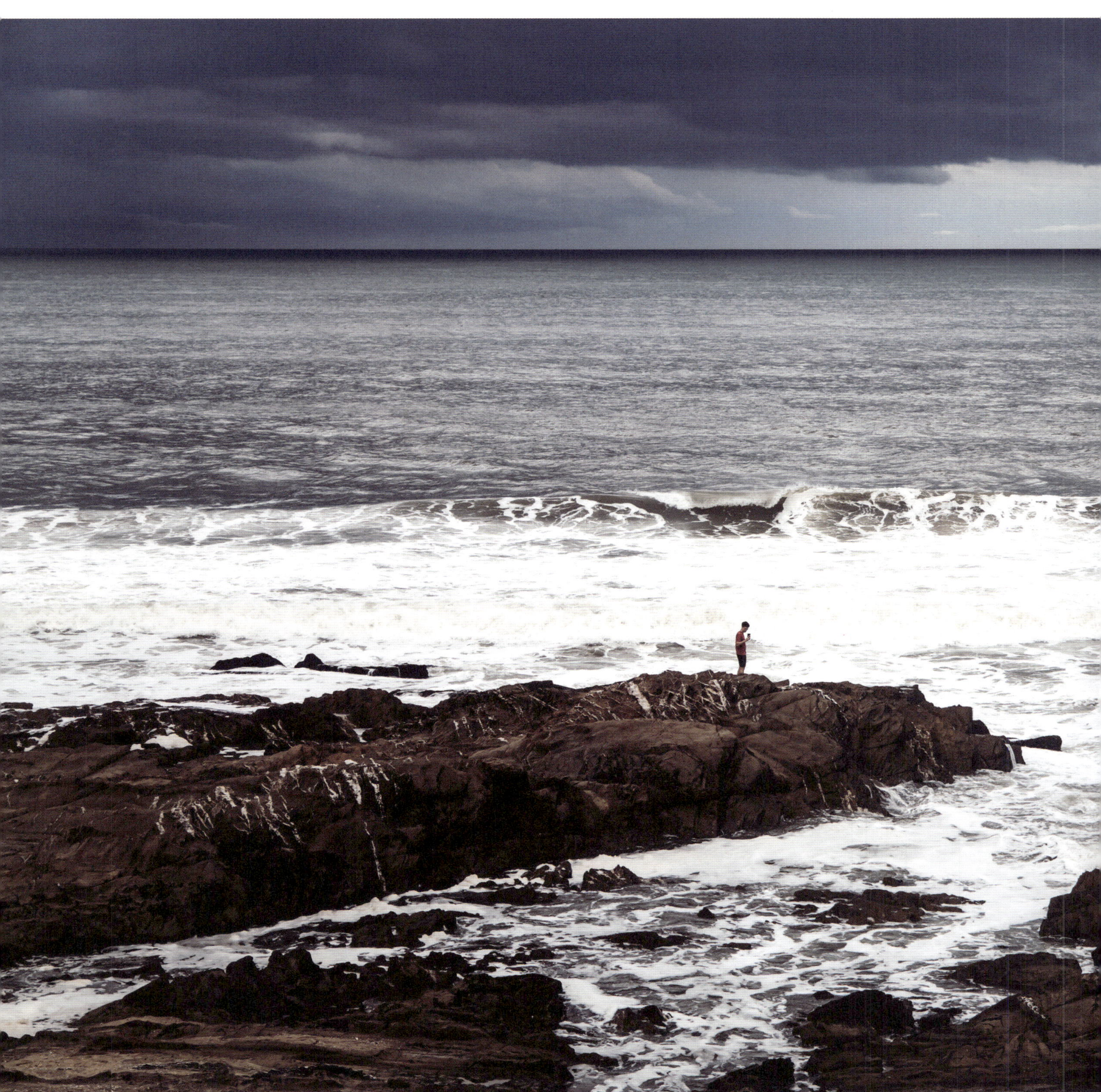

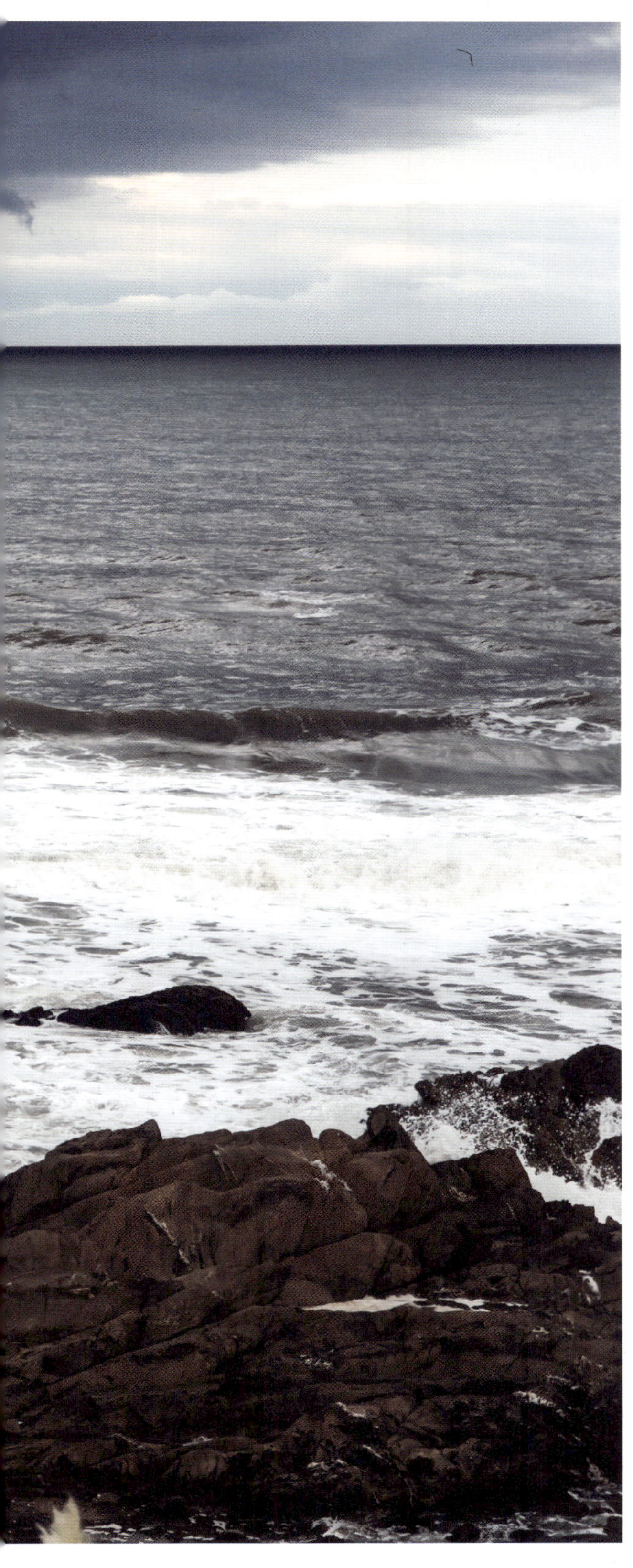

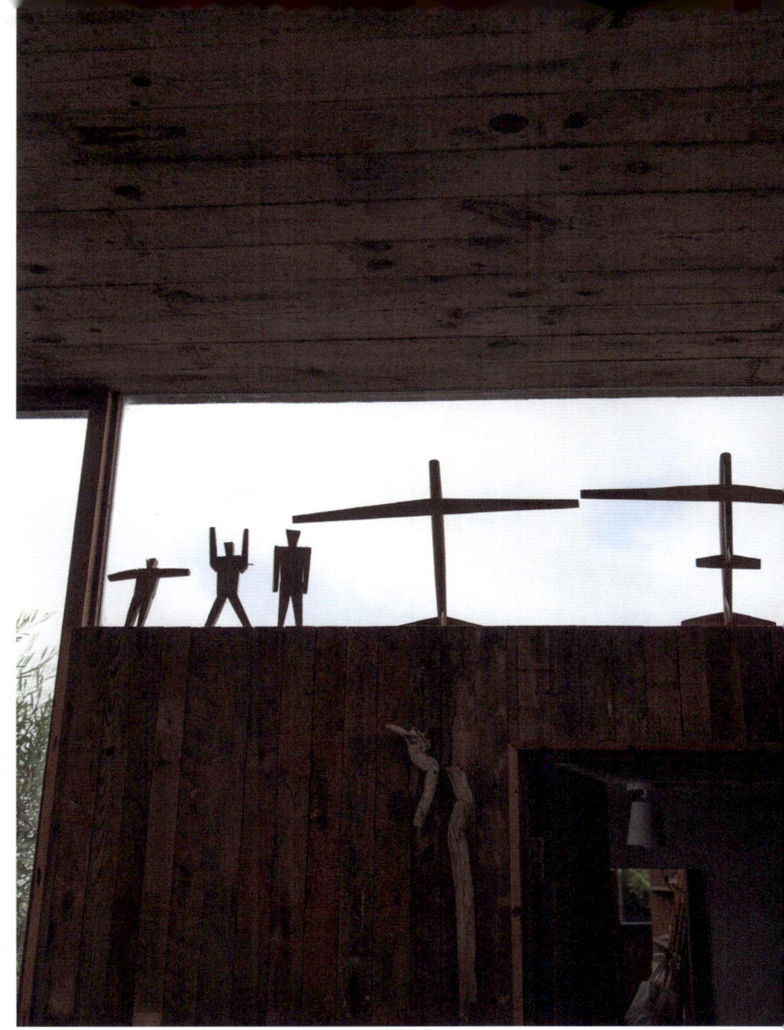

For Violeta, the family's holiday home evokes a unique feeling, epitomising everything her father and his work stood for: warmth and cosiness blend in with the unspoilt nature around the house. The ocean's proximity is both humbling and healing: the water and the wind clear your mind, offering you a perspective on issues that might feel suffocating in the city.

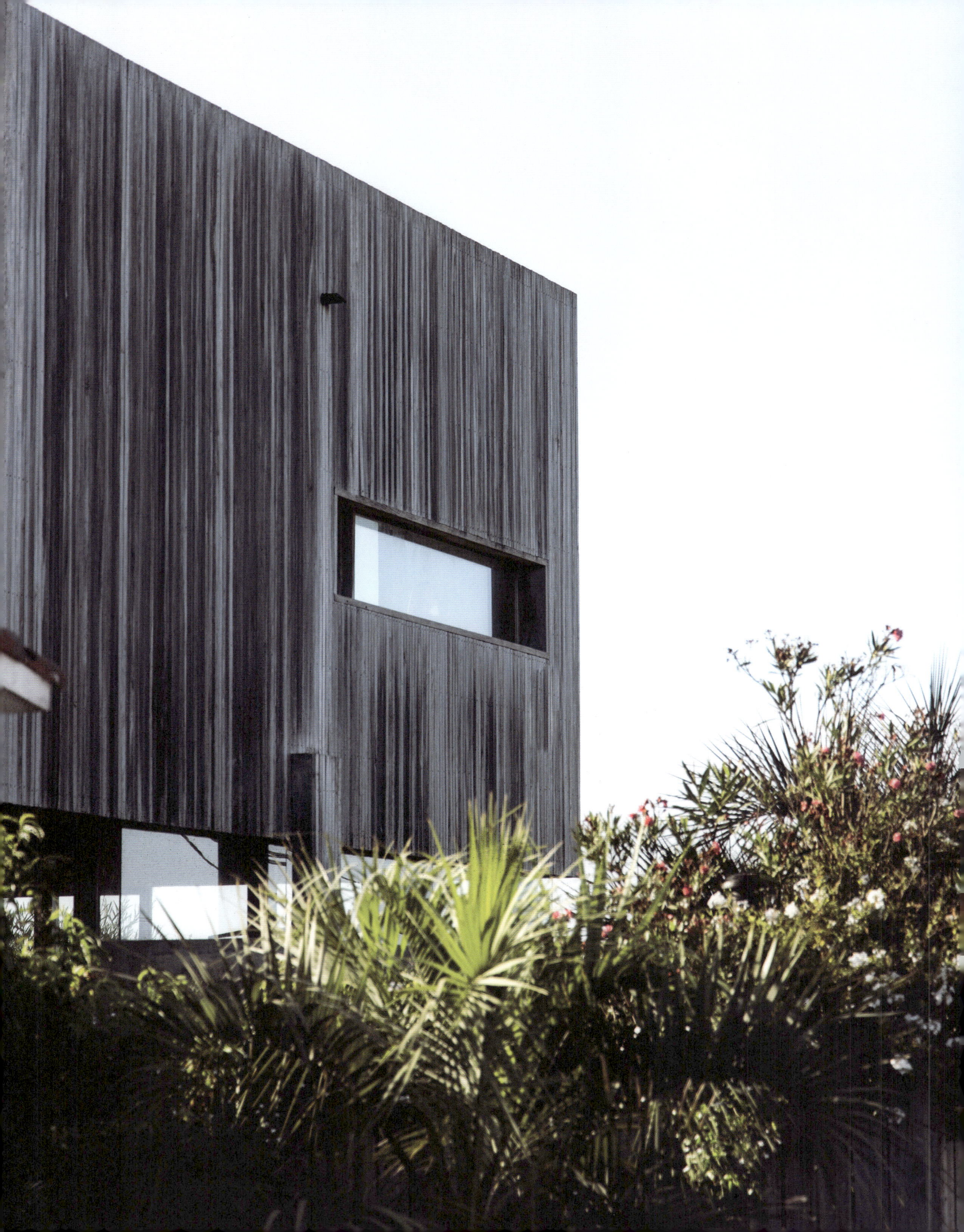

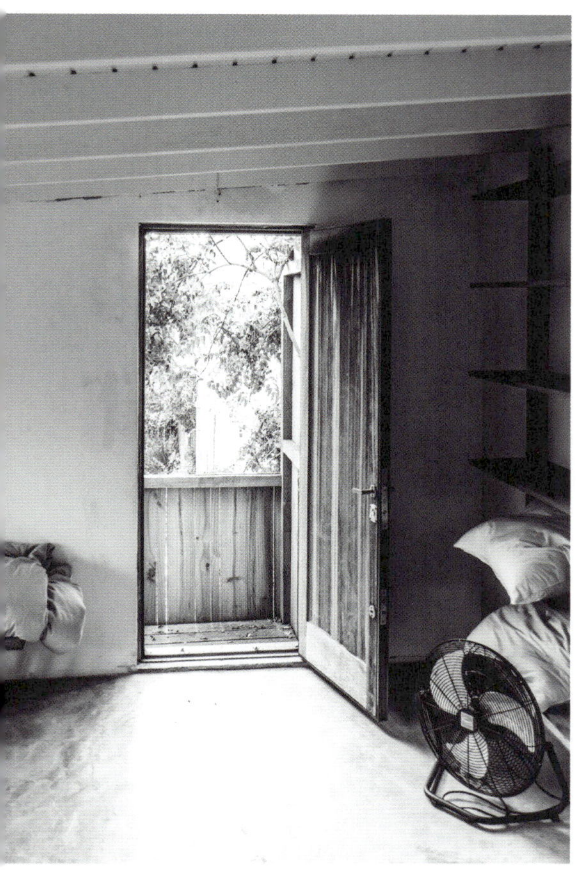

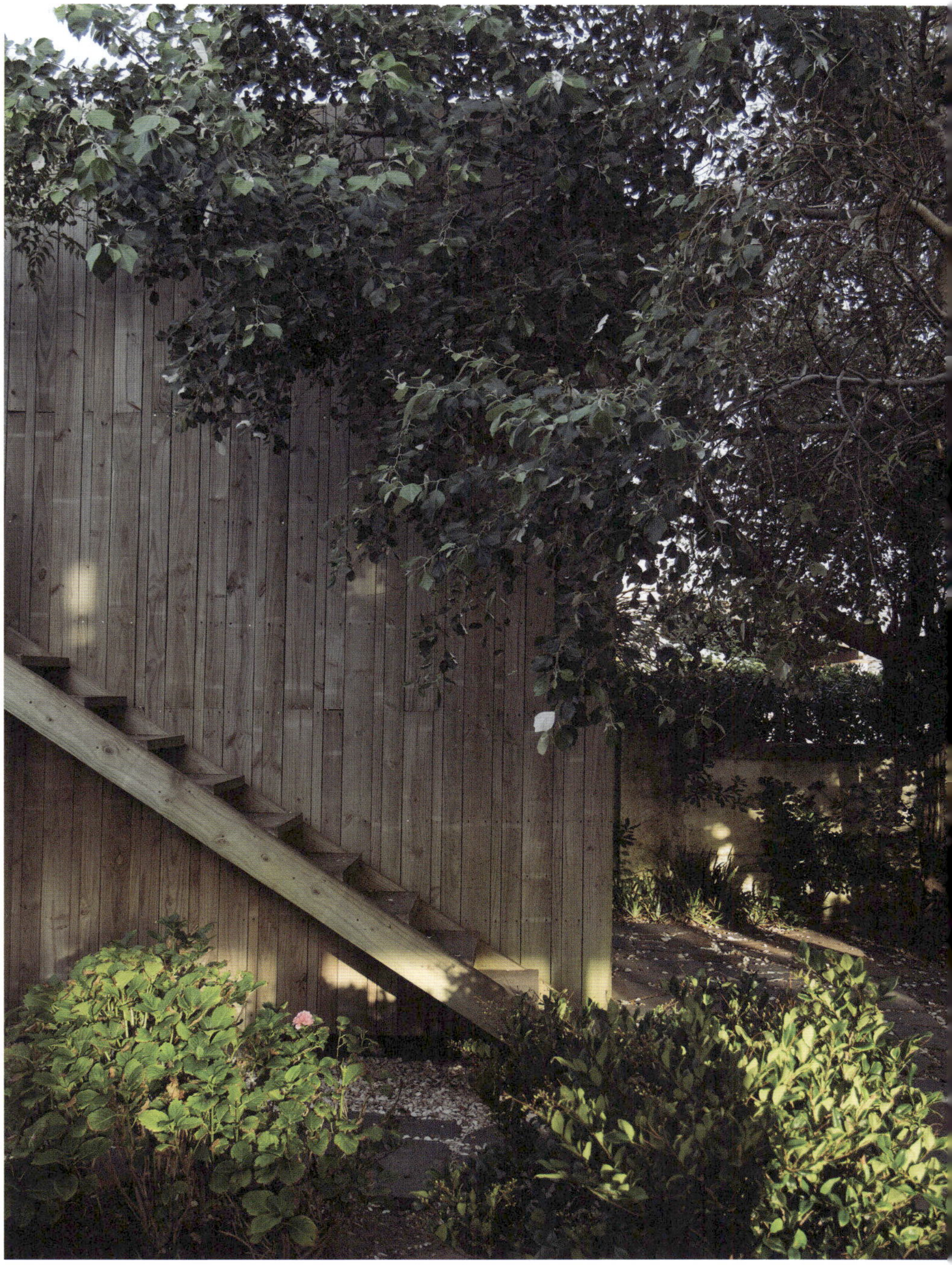

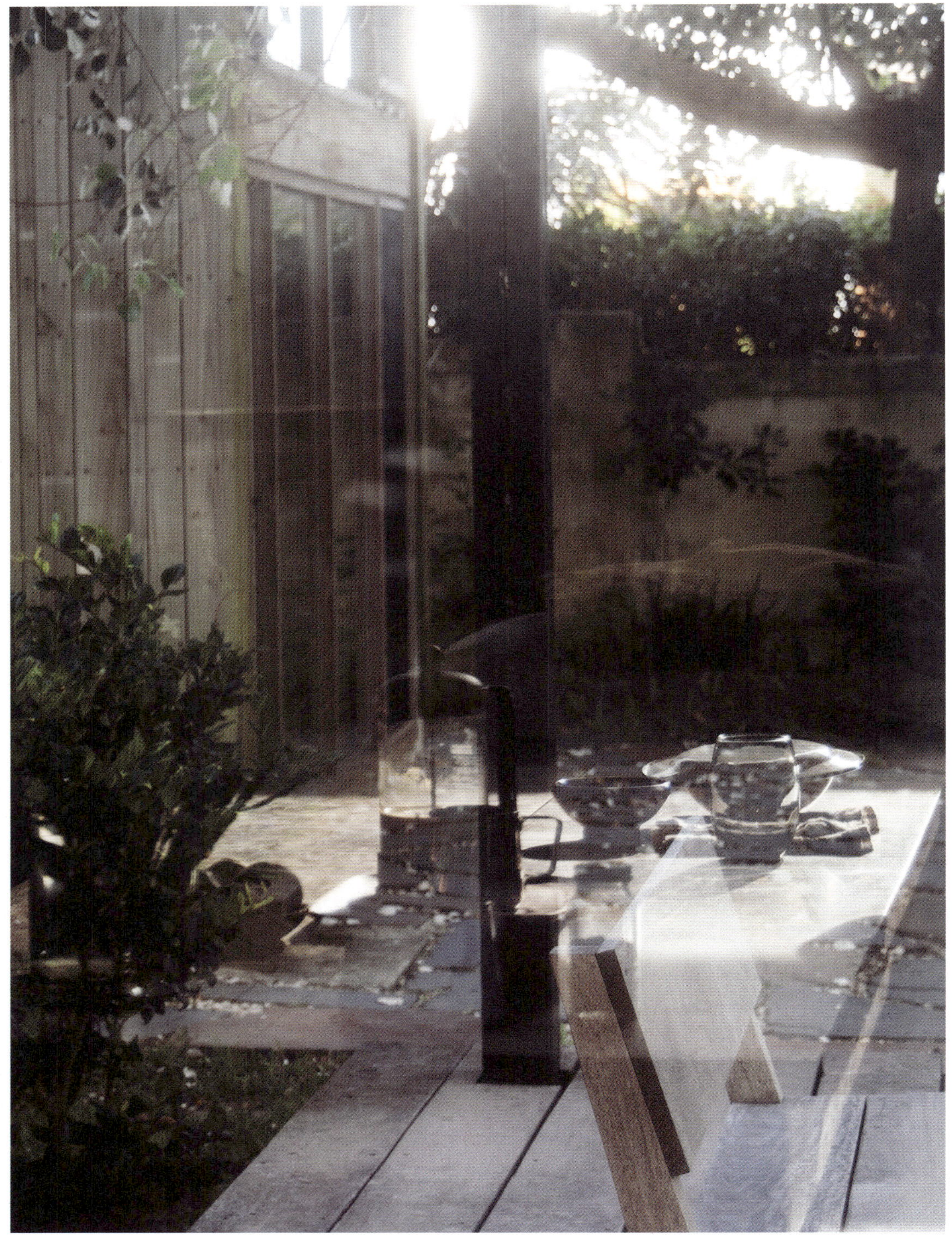

Simplicity meets elegance and hospitality in this dwelling, with the ground-floor kitchen and dining room wrapped by weathered wood walls and large expanses of glass making up the heart of this home. This is where the architect could be found most often, cooking up a storm for friends and family who gathered around the large table. He and his second wife Mercedes, along with their blended family of four children, loved a crowded house. He designed their holiday home with this in mind, building a two-storey guesthouse with two bedrooms and bathrooms in the garden.

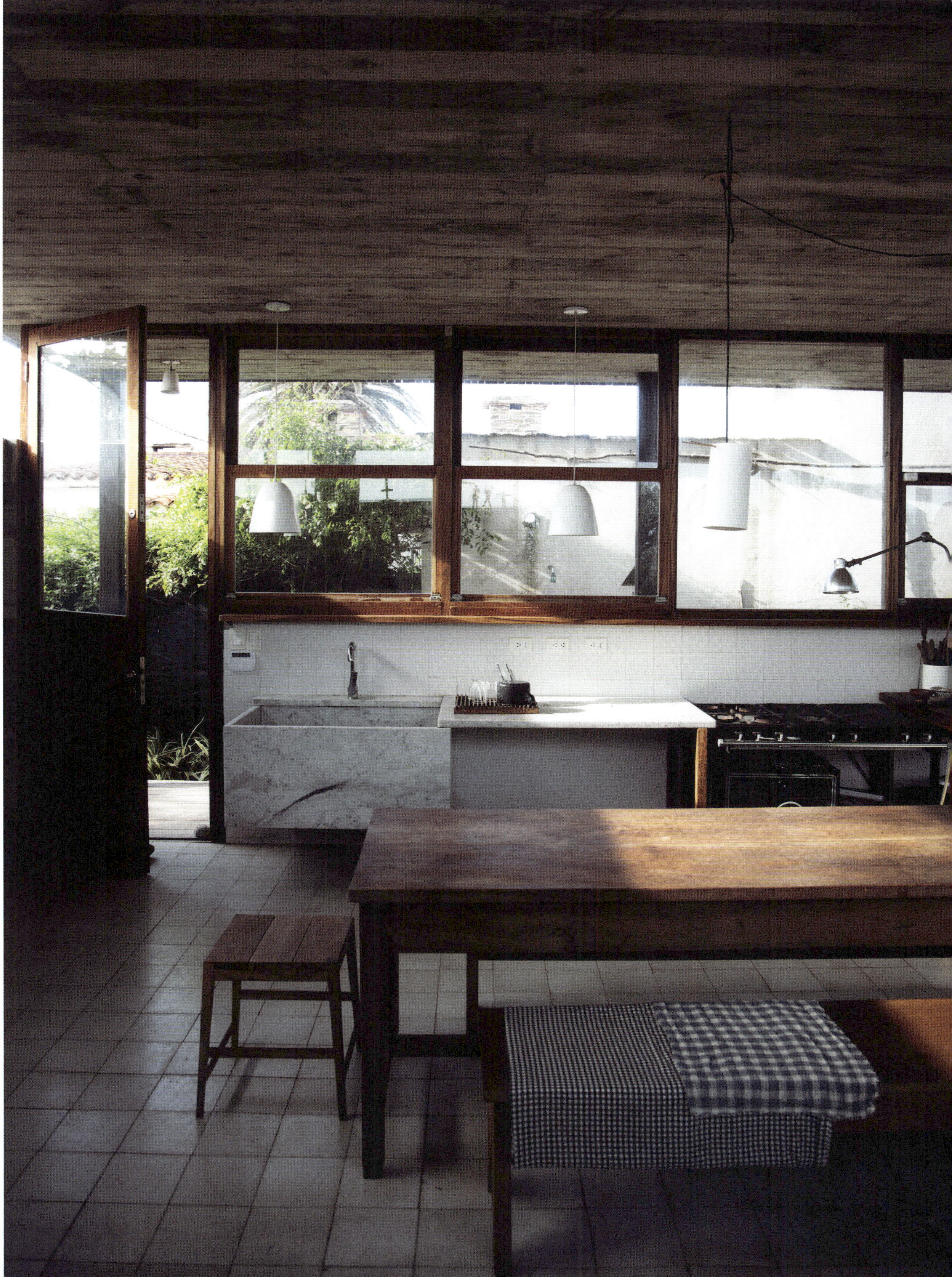

The home's greatest strength lies in its modesty: it knows its place in relation to the force of nature. The upper-level walls that are visible from the street are covered in slender wood panels that weather with time under the influence of the elements, blending in with their surroundings. Inside, the architect opted for board-marked concrete walls, floors and ceilings that are textured with the imprint of timber boards. These materials and the architecture as a whole deepen the senses, allowing you to fully experience the magic of the environment in which it stands.

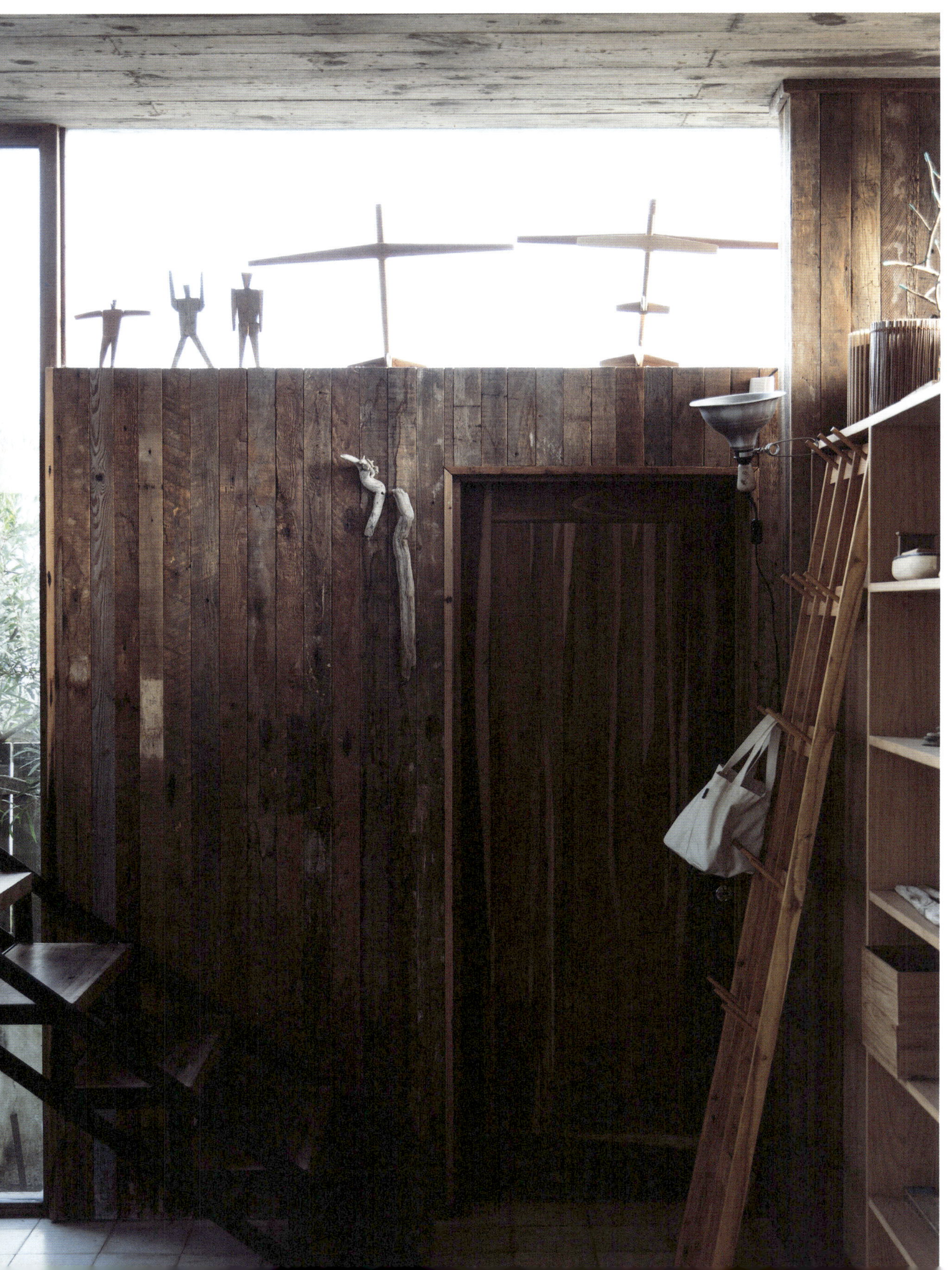

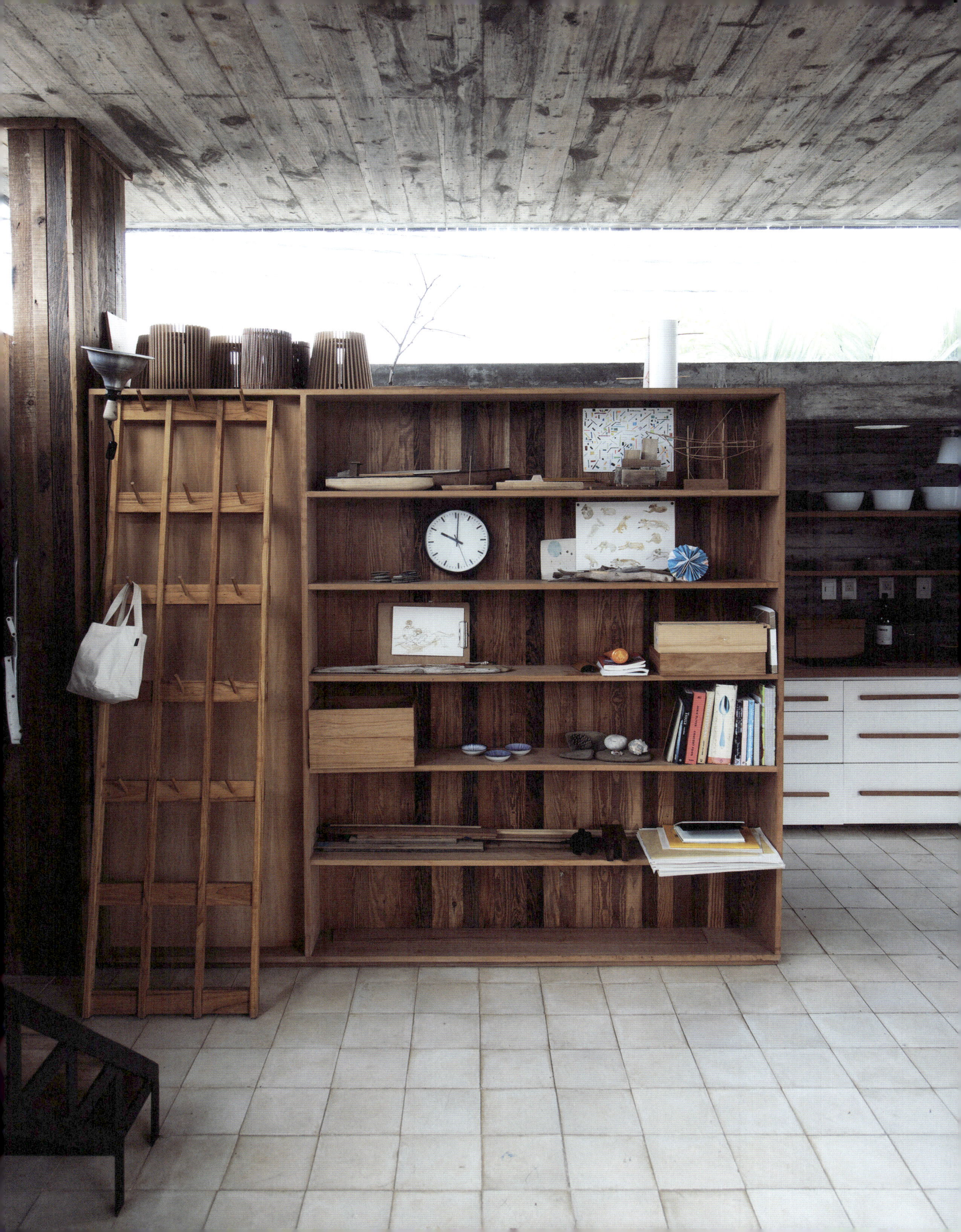

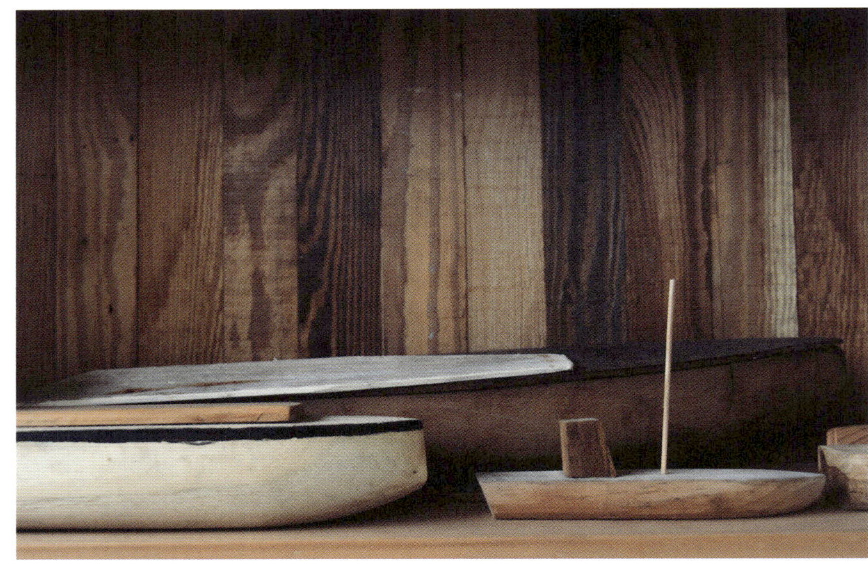

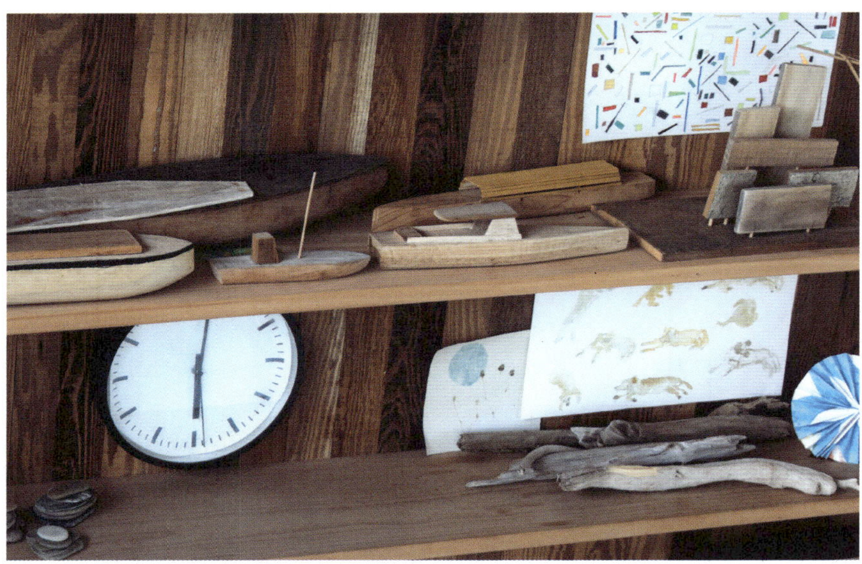

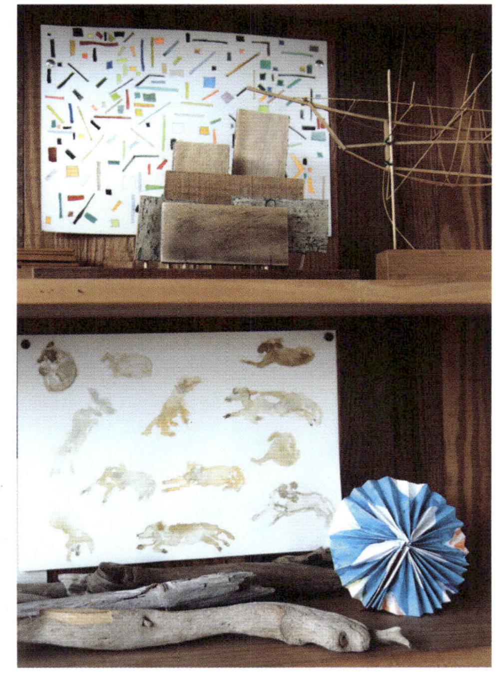

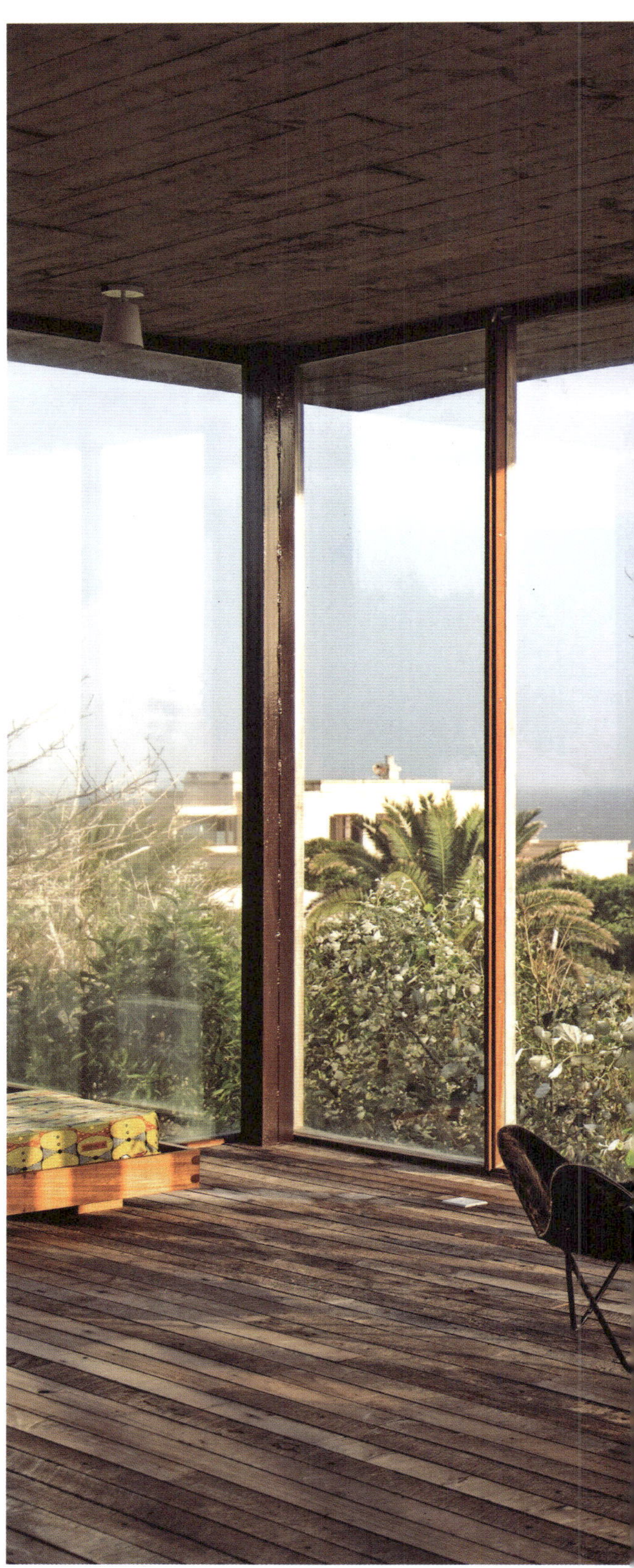

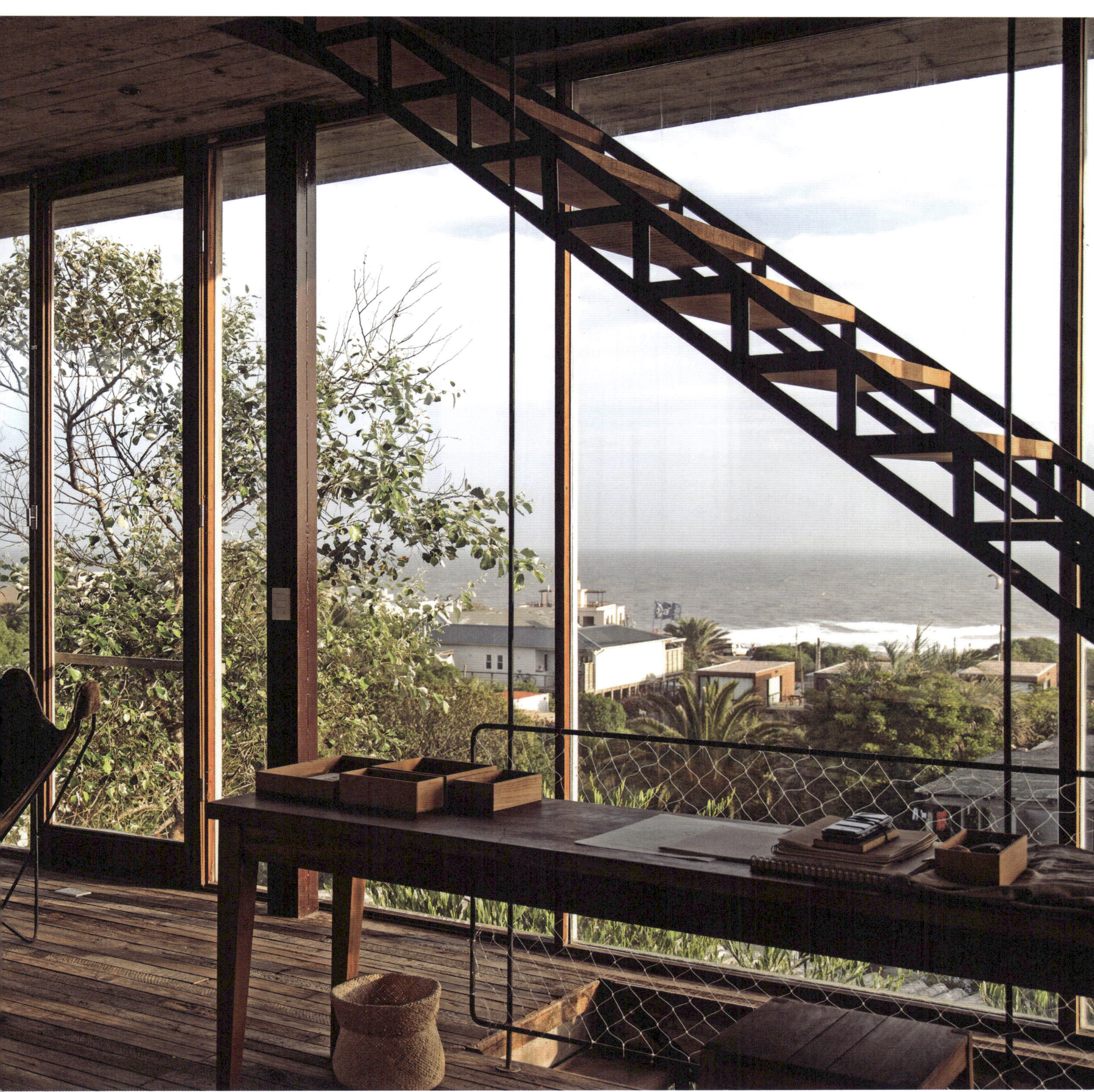

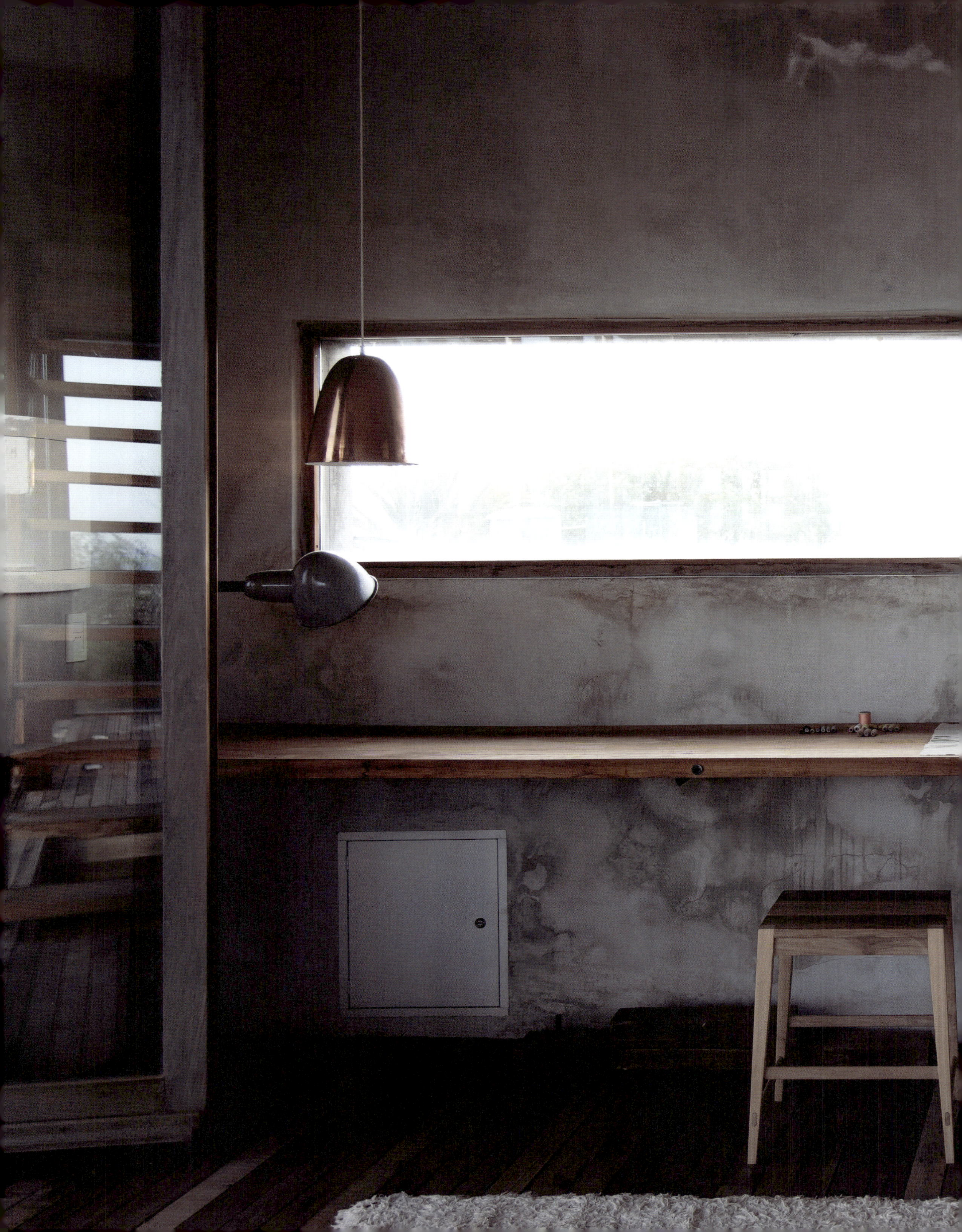

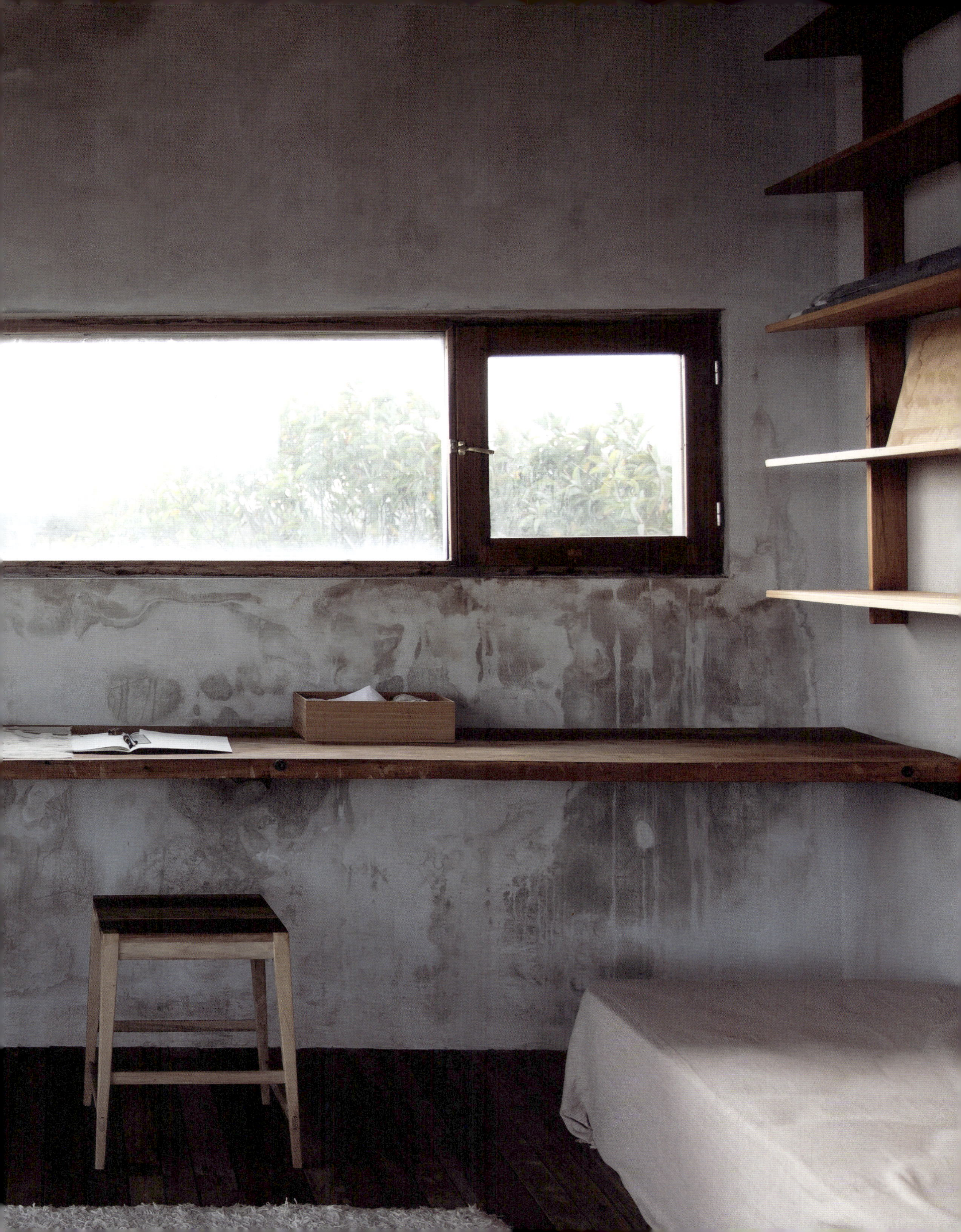

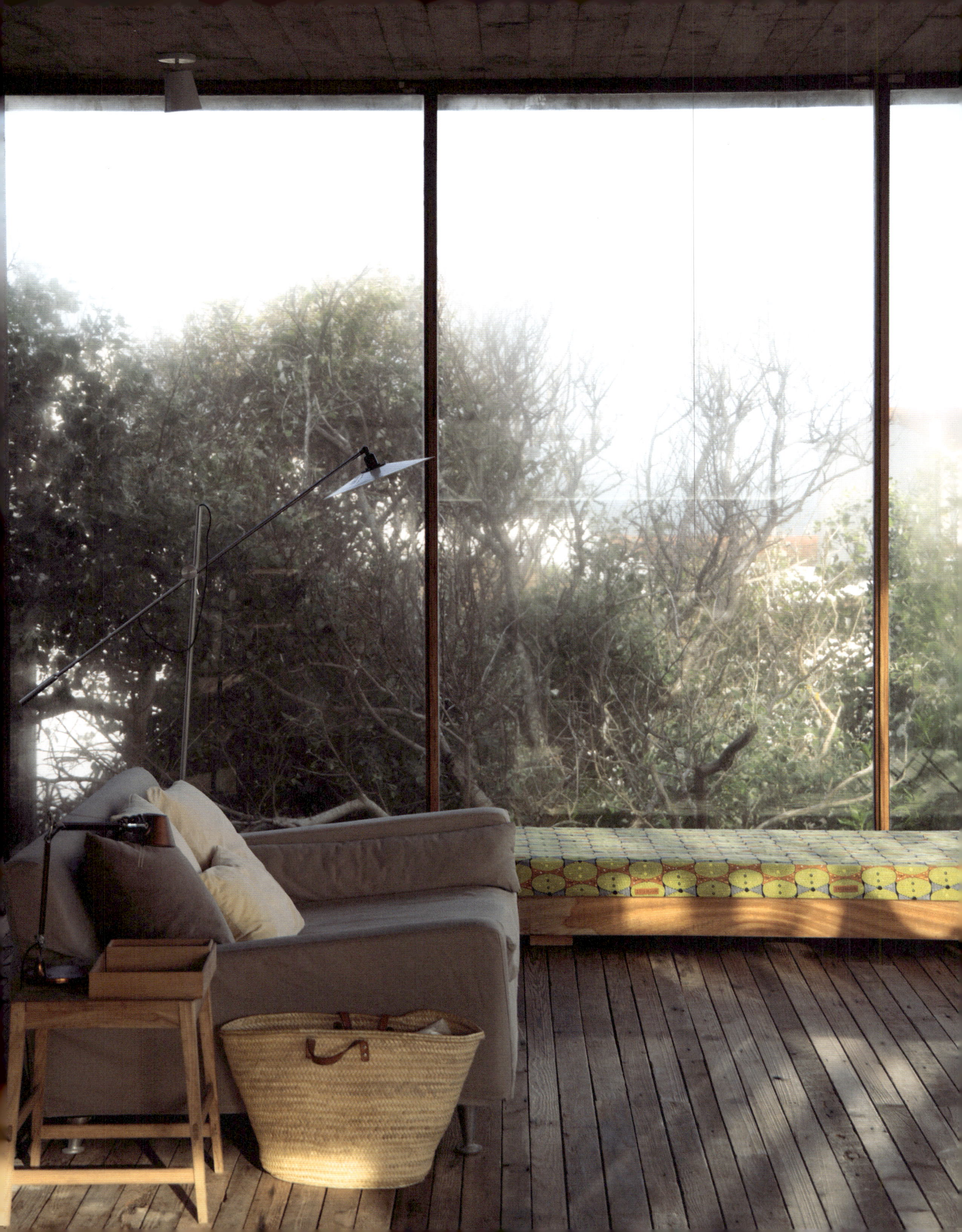

The guesthouse and the main house both look out onto the garden and the impressive canopy of the old Álamo tree, which was already there before the house was built. But the most sweeping views can be found on the first floor of the private home, an elevated wood-clad box on top of the kitchen. This is also where the living room is located, its main attraction being the ever-changing views at sunset of La Pedrera's skyline. The master bedroom offers more striking views of the ocean: the beauty of the unspoilt natural surroundings is quite literally everywhere you look.

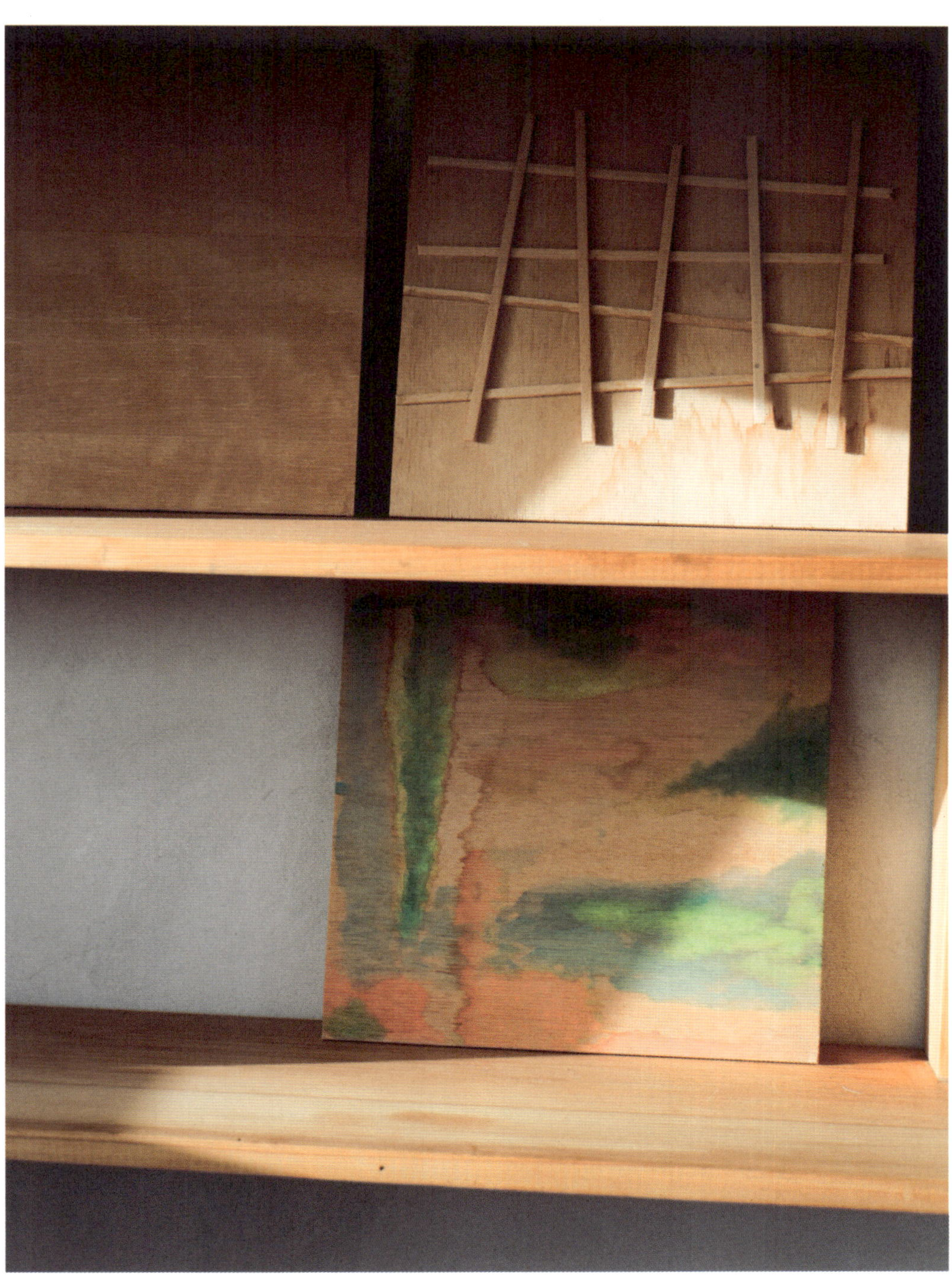

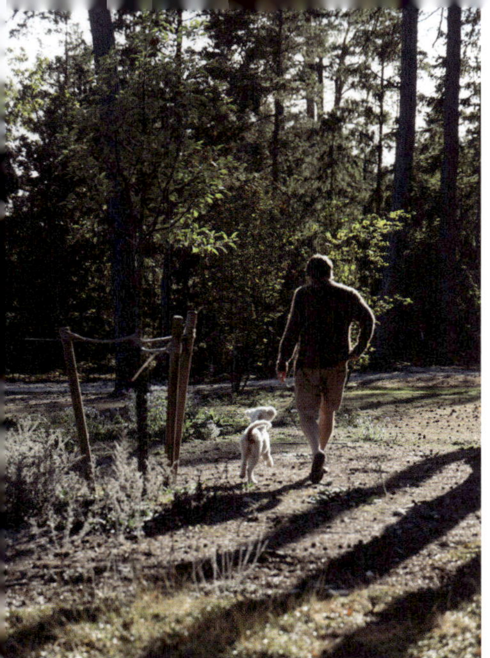

The island of Gotland is located in the Baltic Sea, off the eastern coast of Sweden. This is the kind of place that gets under your skin. The minute you set foot on the island you understand what inspired Ingmar Bergman when he first visited the island and decided to stay. "I had found my landscape, my real home," he said. The same happened to Dutch couple Maurice Dekkers and Benthe Forrer about twenty years ago as they drove off the ferry to Gotland in their vintage Mercedes camper van, with their young daughters Bibi and Moos and their big Bernese dog Hummer in tow.

Ljugarn
Sweden

GOTLAND

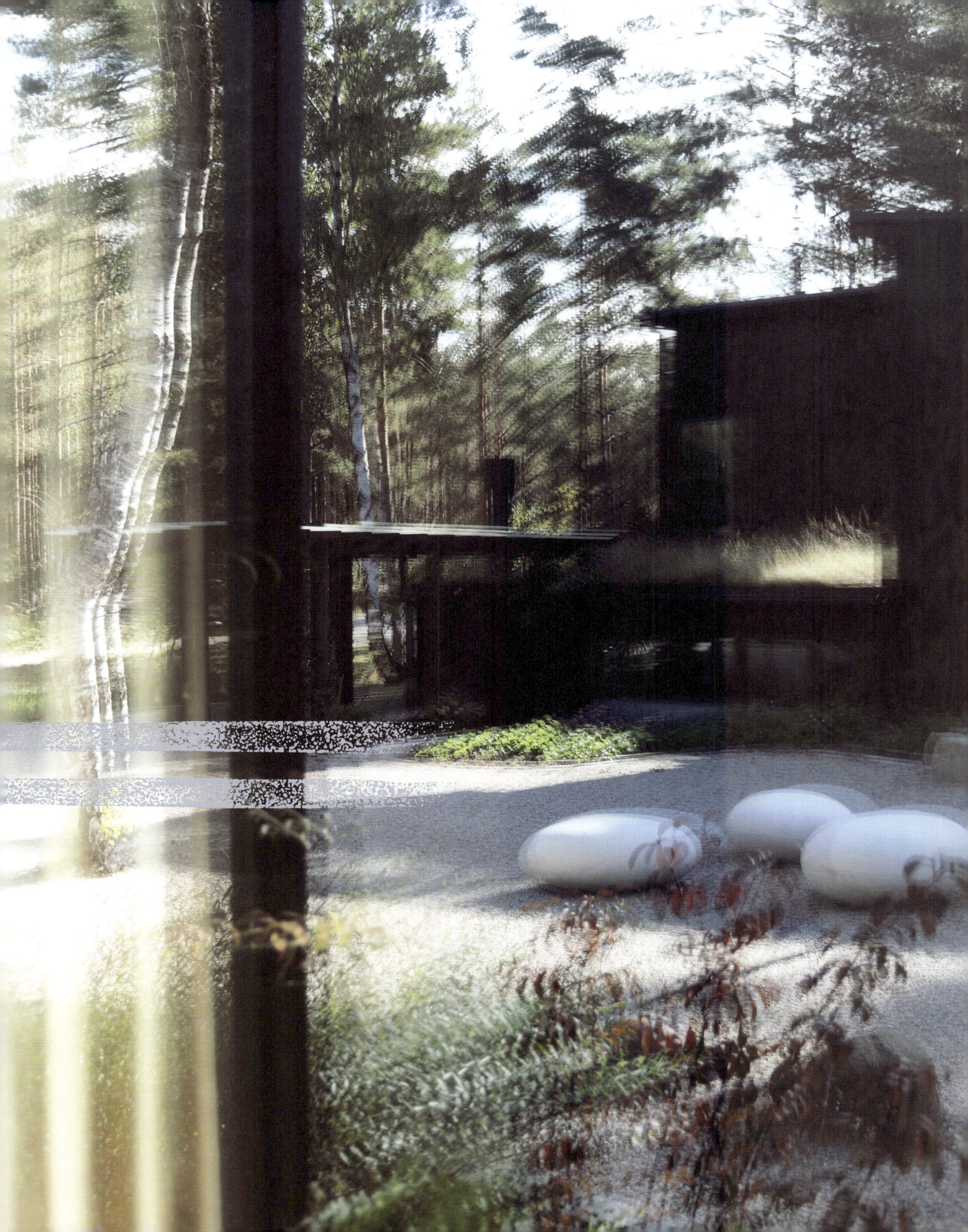

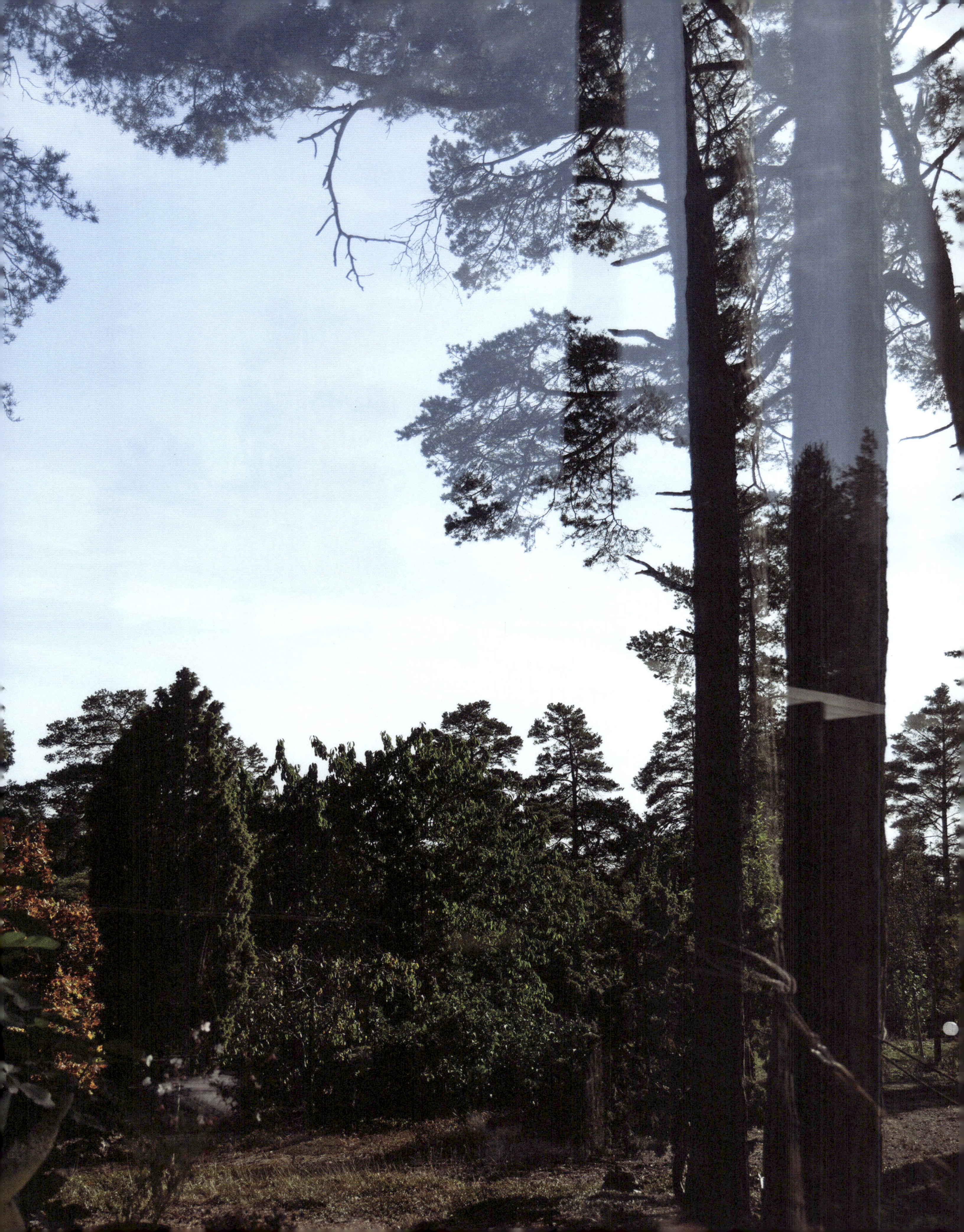

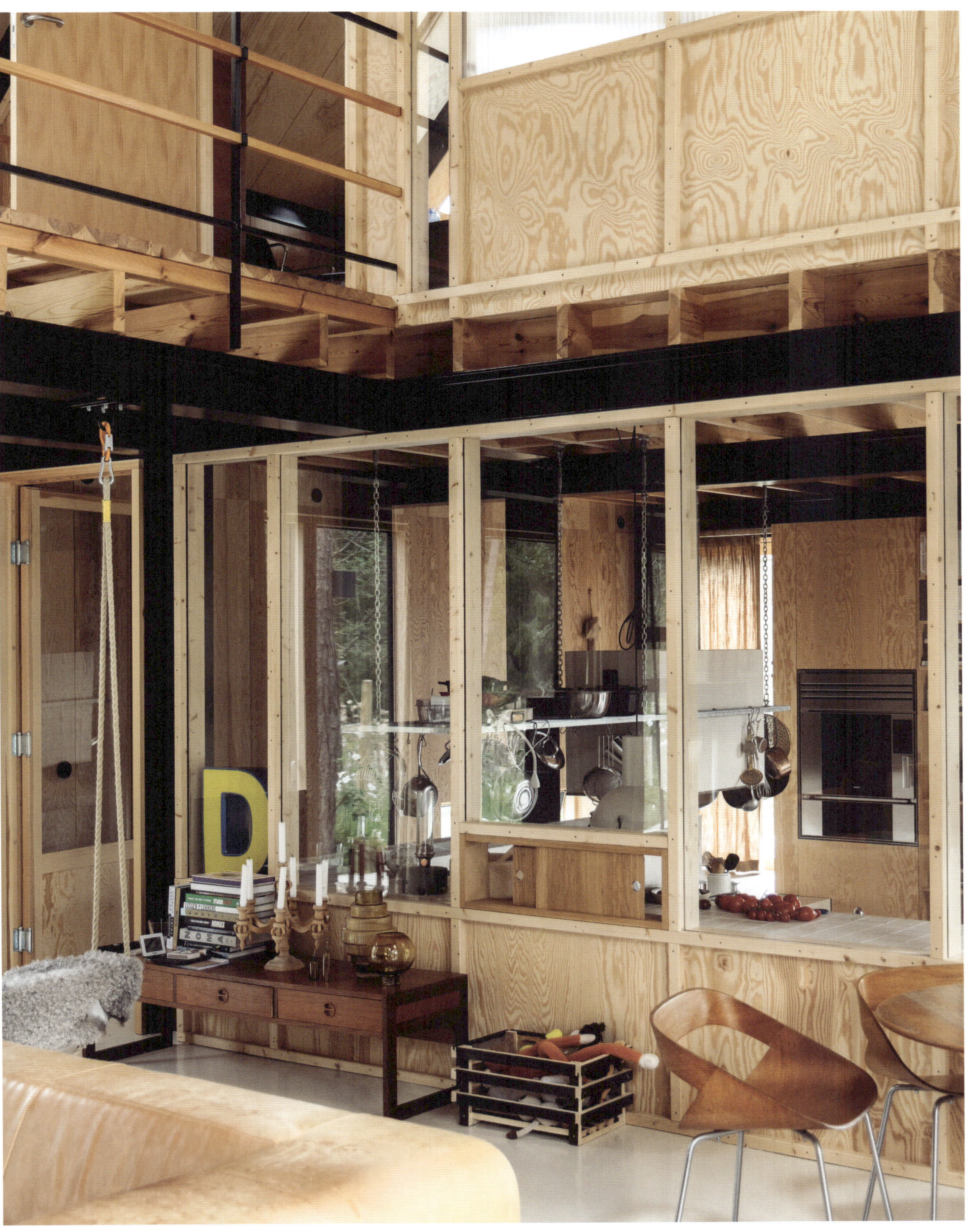

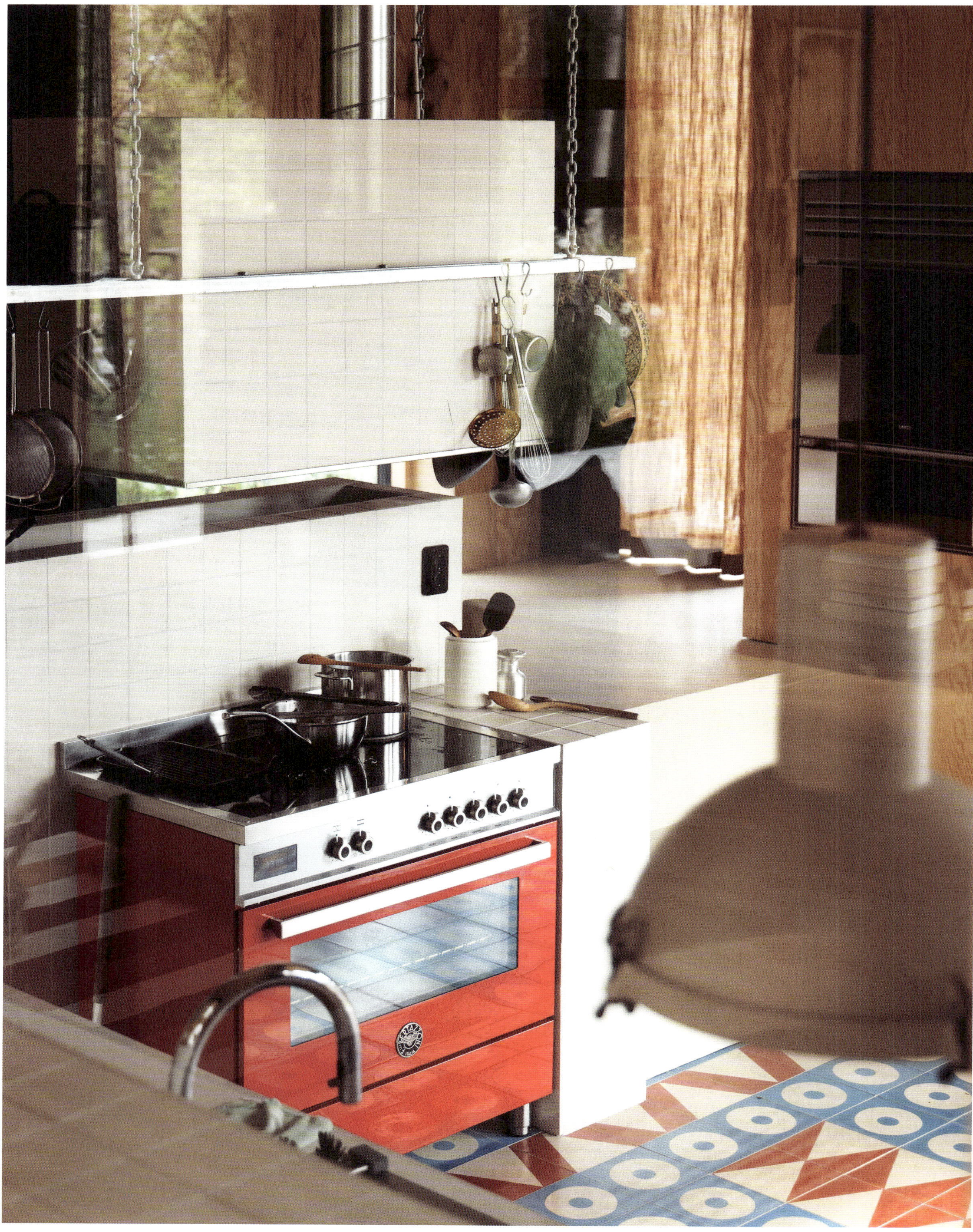

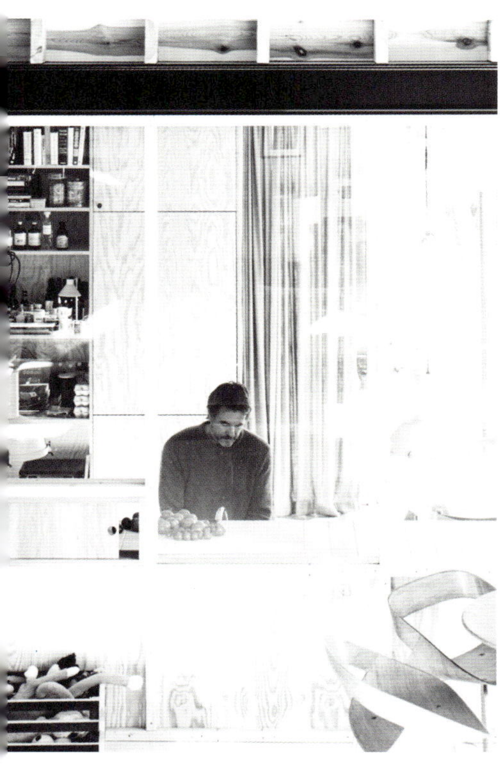

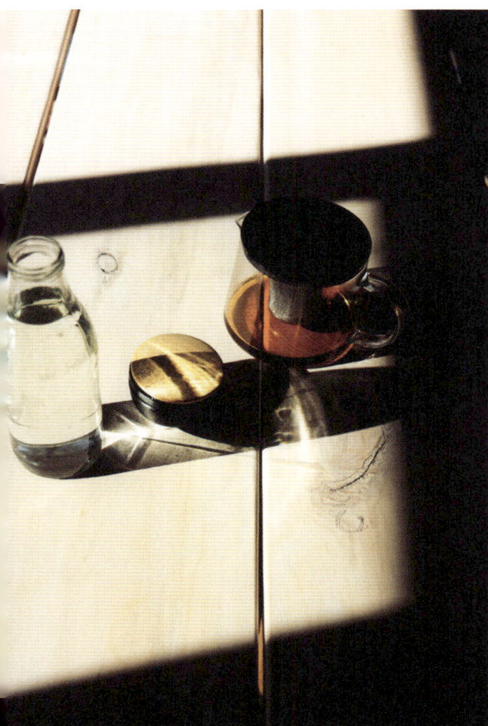

Maurice and Benthe were living and working in the Netherlands at the time in the film and TV industry. When they finally got the chance to buy an acre of land on Gotland in 2014, they did not hesitate for a second. The location was simply perfect: on a hill with the forest at the rear, right on the beach and facing the Baltic Sea, close to Ljugarn, the island's oldest seaside retreat. This village with its old typical Swedish wooden houses covers a three-kilometre strip, between sandy beaches and the impressive rocky outcrops that seem to rise out of the sea.

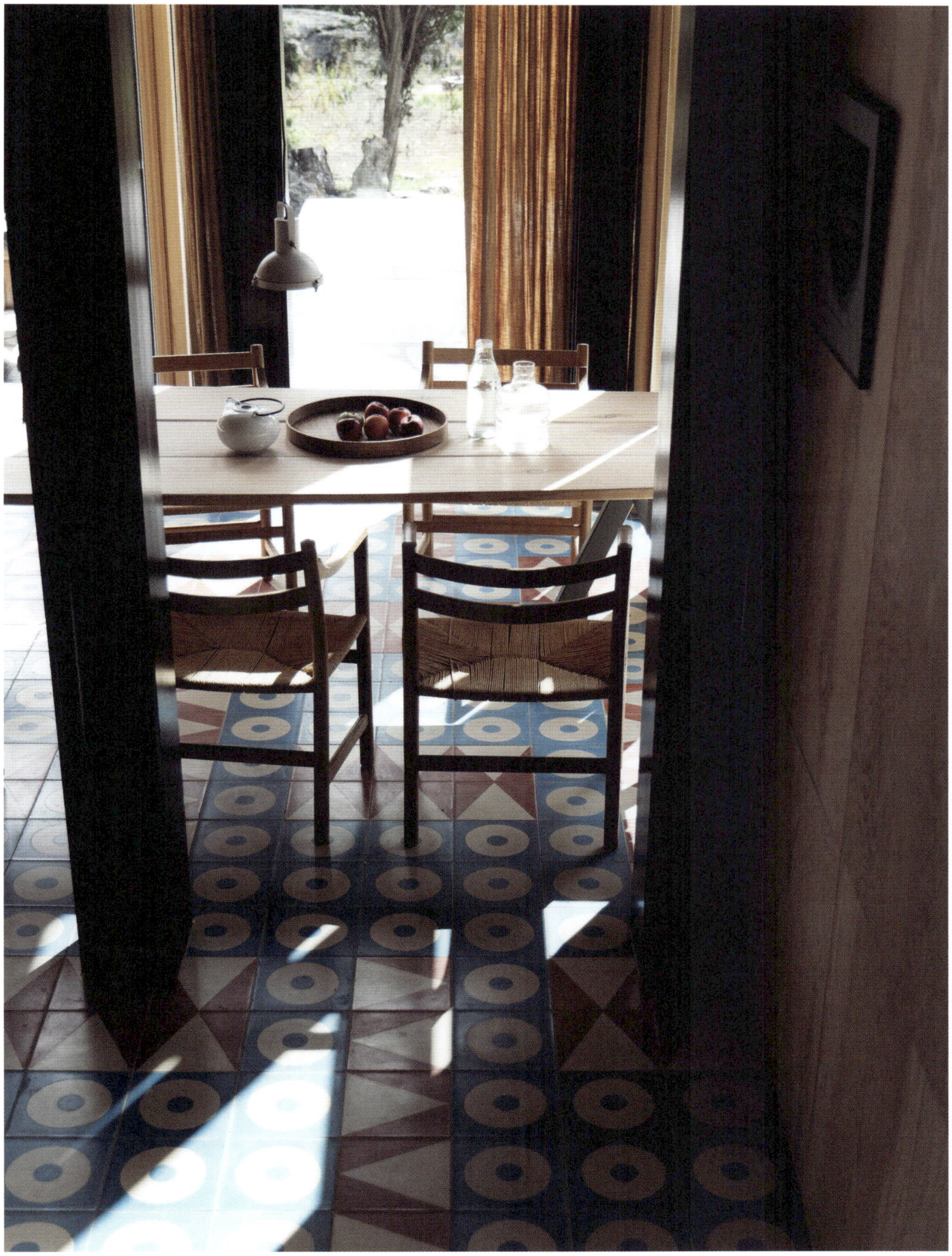

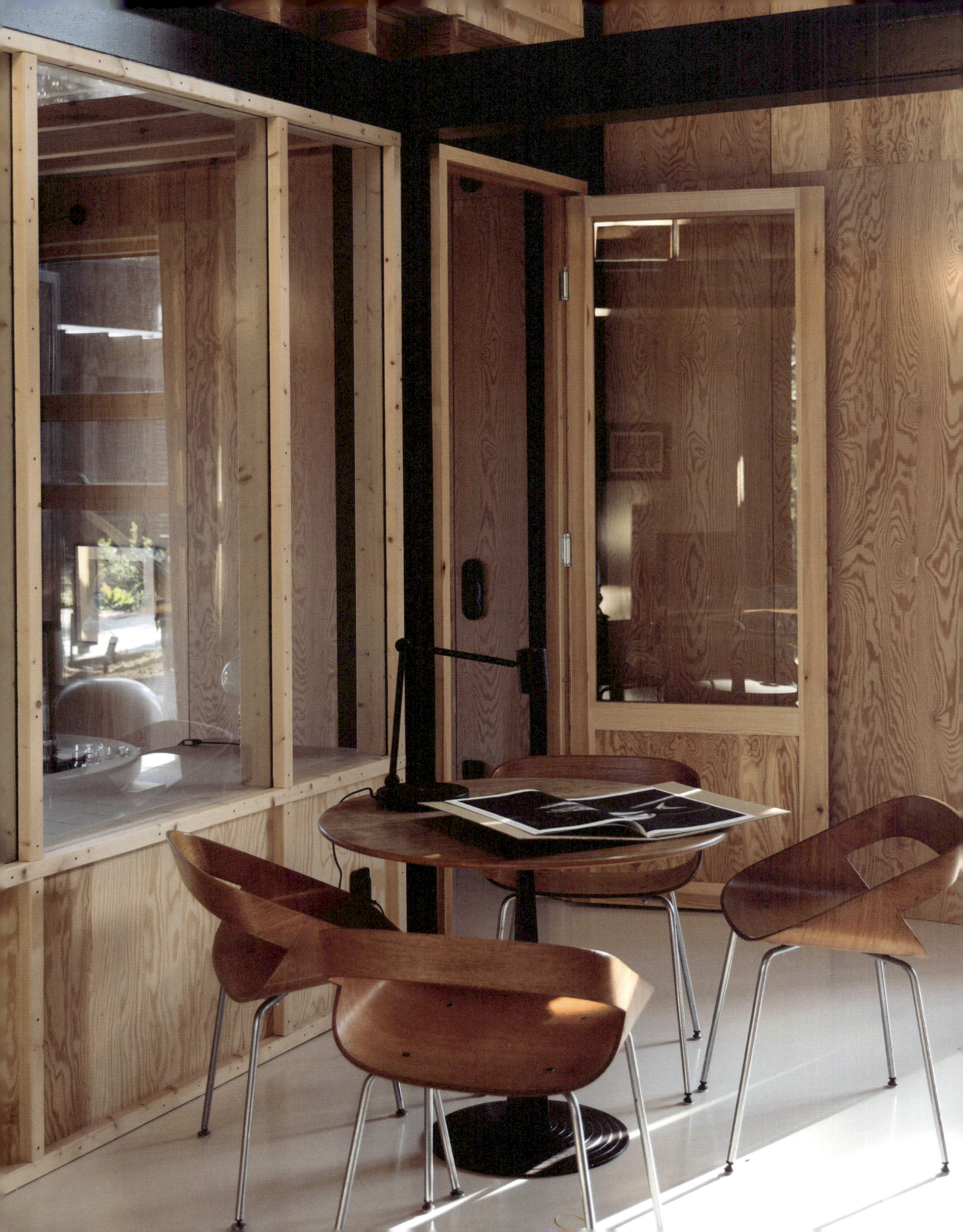

While Gotland may feel remote, Benthe and Maurice – and their dog – love it there. More than an escape from reality, it feels like they have created a new reality for themselves, like they used to do as film directors. Their house is surrounded by the sound of the sea and the wildlife, and that's it. While some people might find this boring, to Benthe and Maurice this 'nothingness' is inspiring.

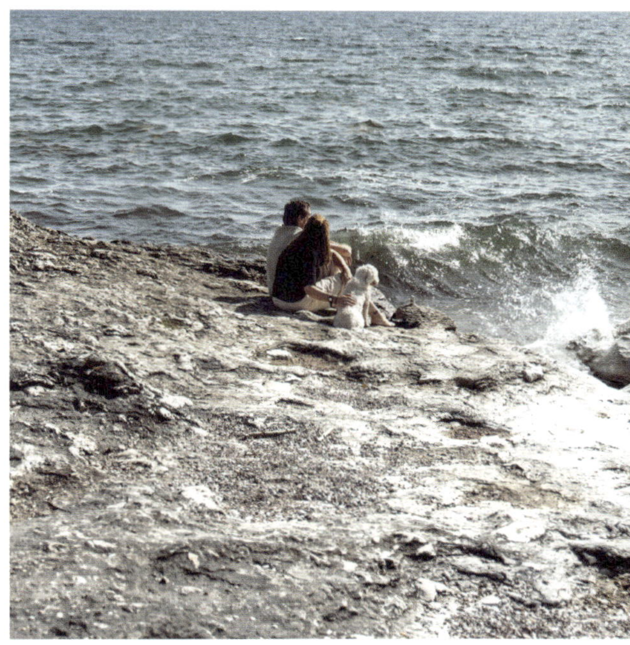

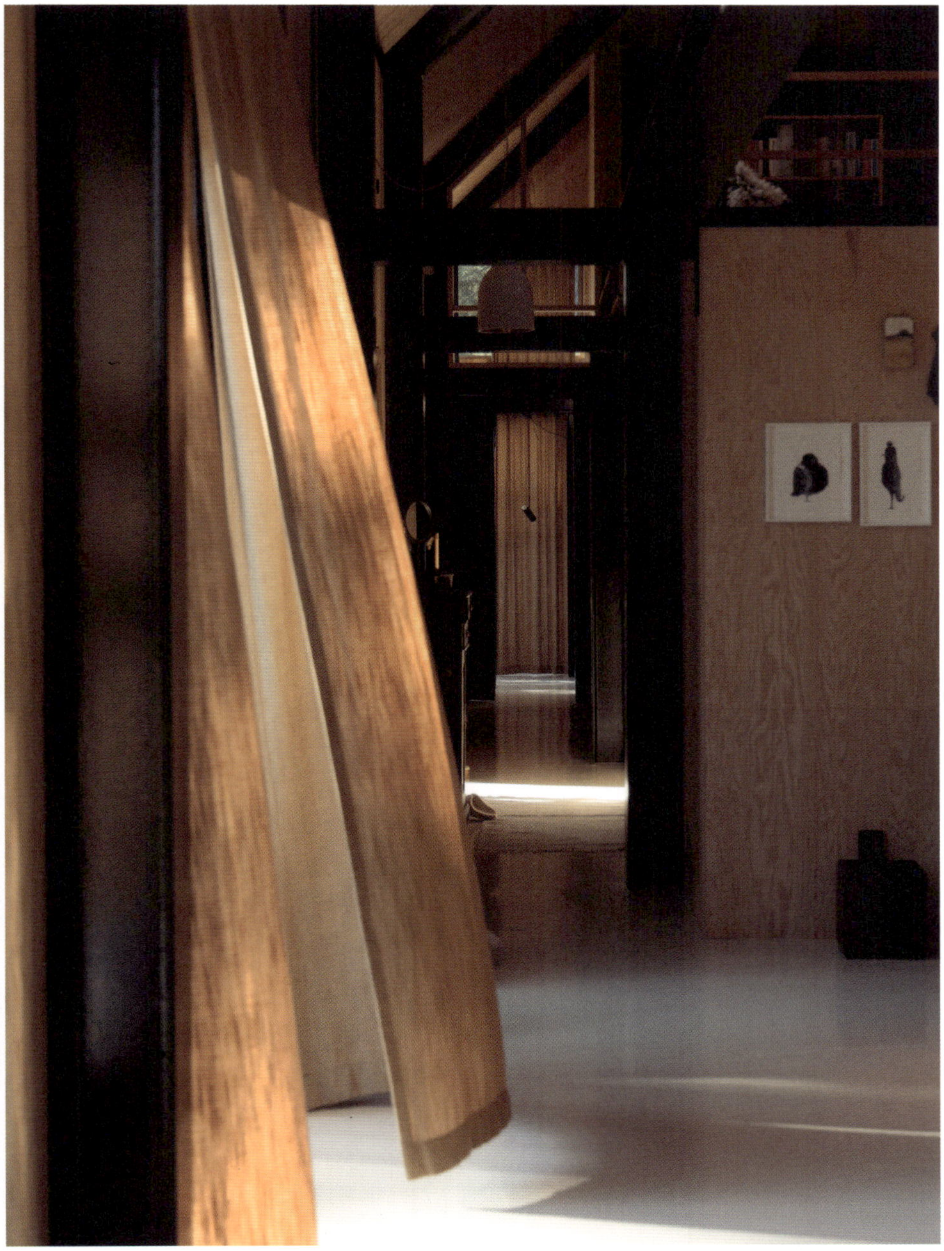

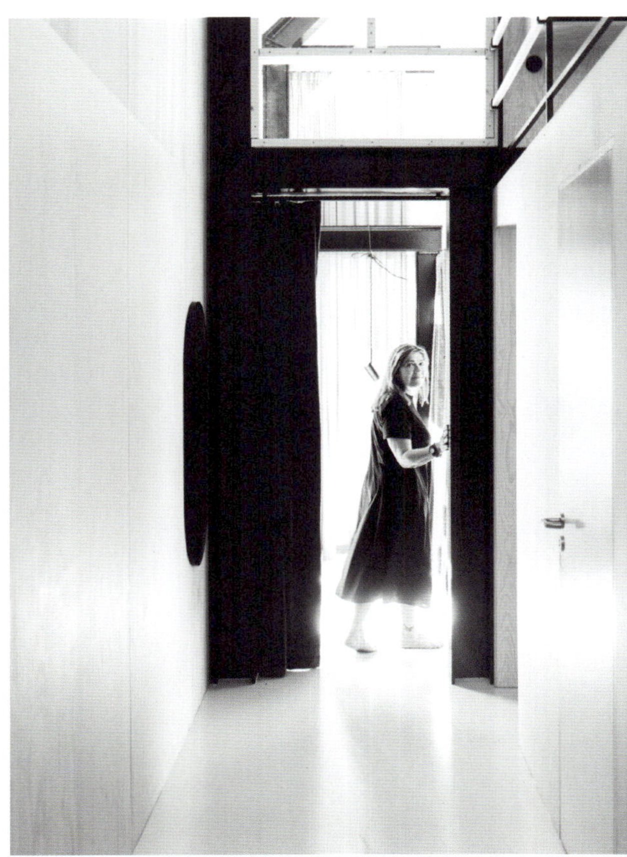

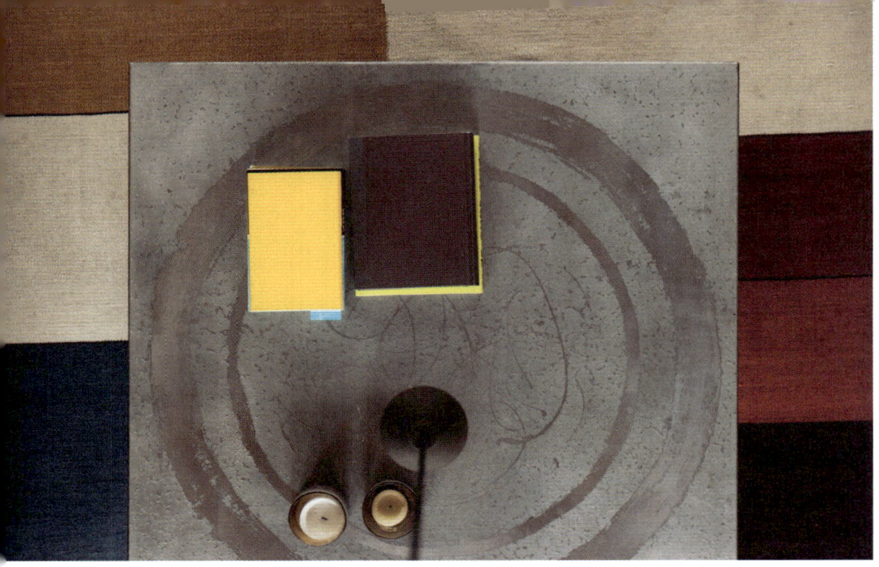

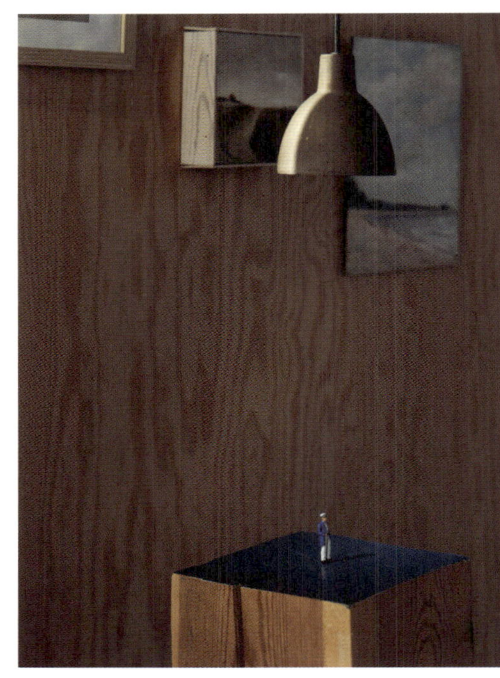

When they decided to build a new house on their beloved spot near the sea, Benthe and Maurice knew that they wanted it to blend in with the surroundings. They wanted an archetypal, simple and transparent home. Strong enough to withstand a falling tree during a winter storm but with all the cosiness of a warm home. The result is reminiscent of a traditional Gotlandic barn with an open structure. The steel frame is visible, and the outside walls are clad with Gotland pine: nothing fancy, but well executed by local craftsmen. Unlike the what-you-see-is-what-get outside, the inside is quite un-Swedish, with its variegated colour palette. The furniture is a mix and match of old and new items that Maurice and Benthe inherited and collected. The art in the house is mainly by friends and the couple's daughters. Next to the main house, Benthe and Maurice built what they call 'the Sistershouse', which consists of two identical small wooden boxes with bedrooms, connected by a central in-ground kitchen-and-living space for their daughters and visiting friends.

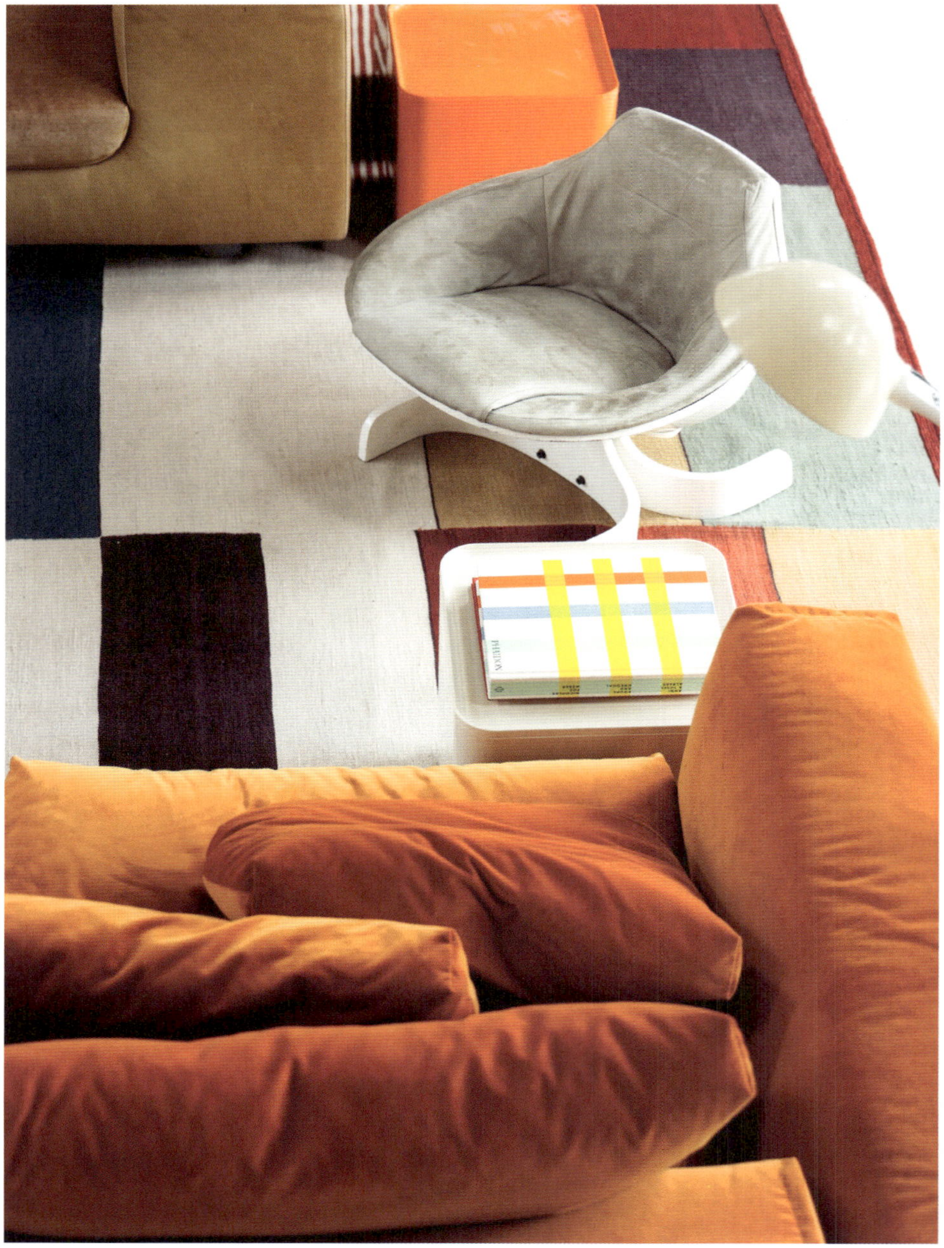

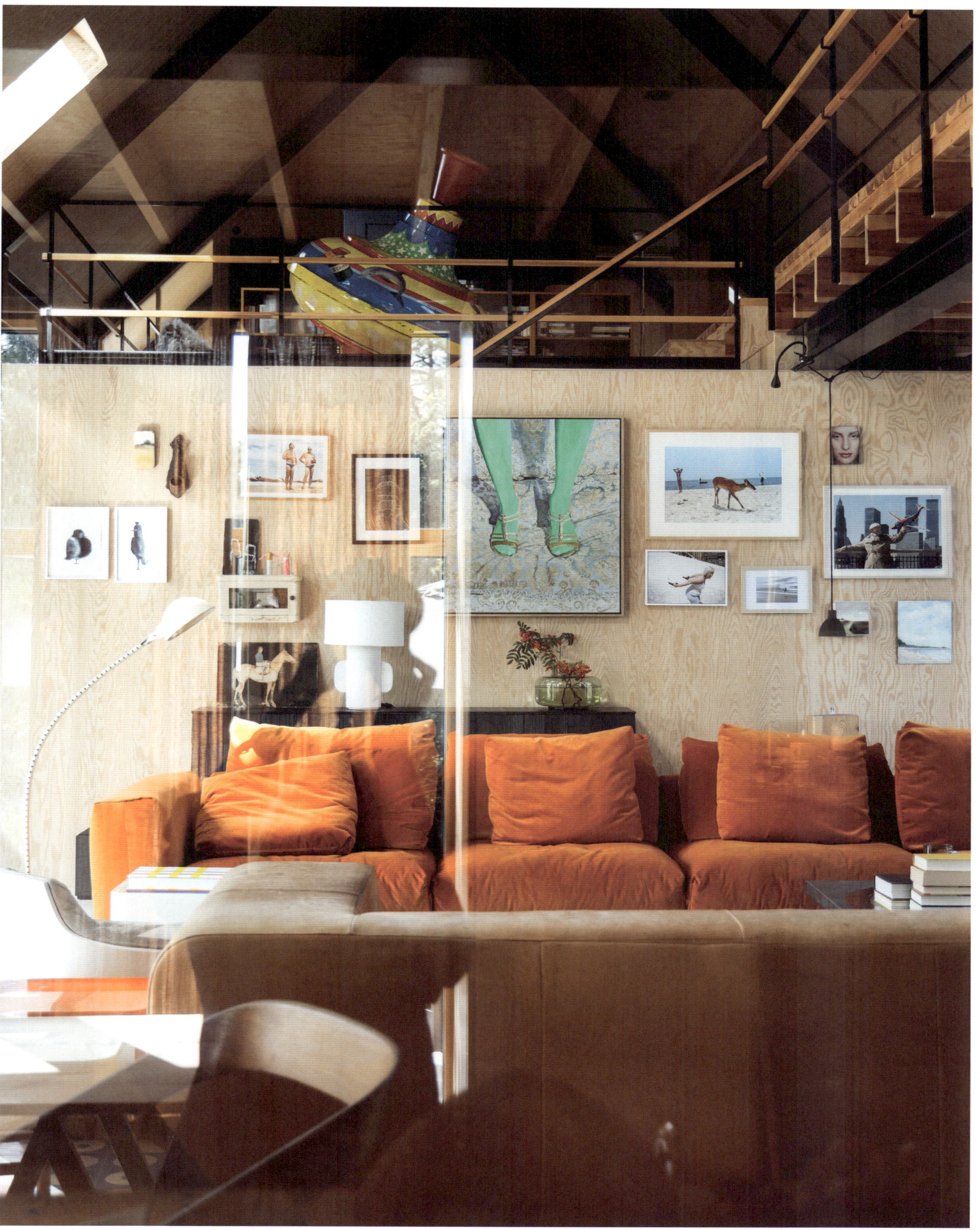

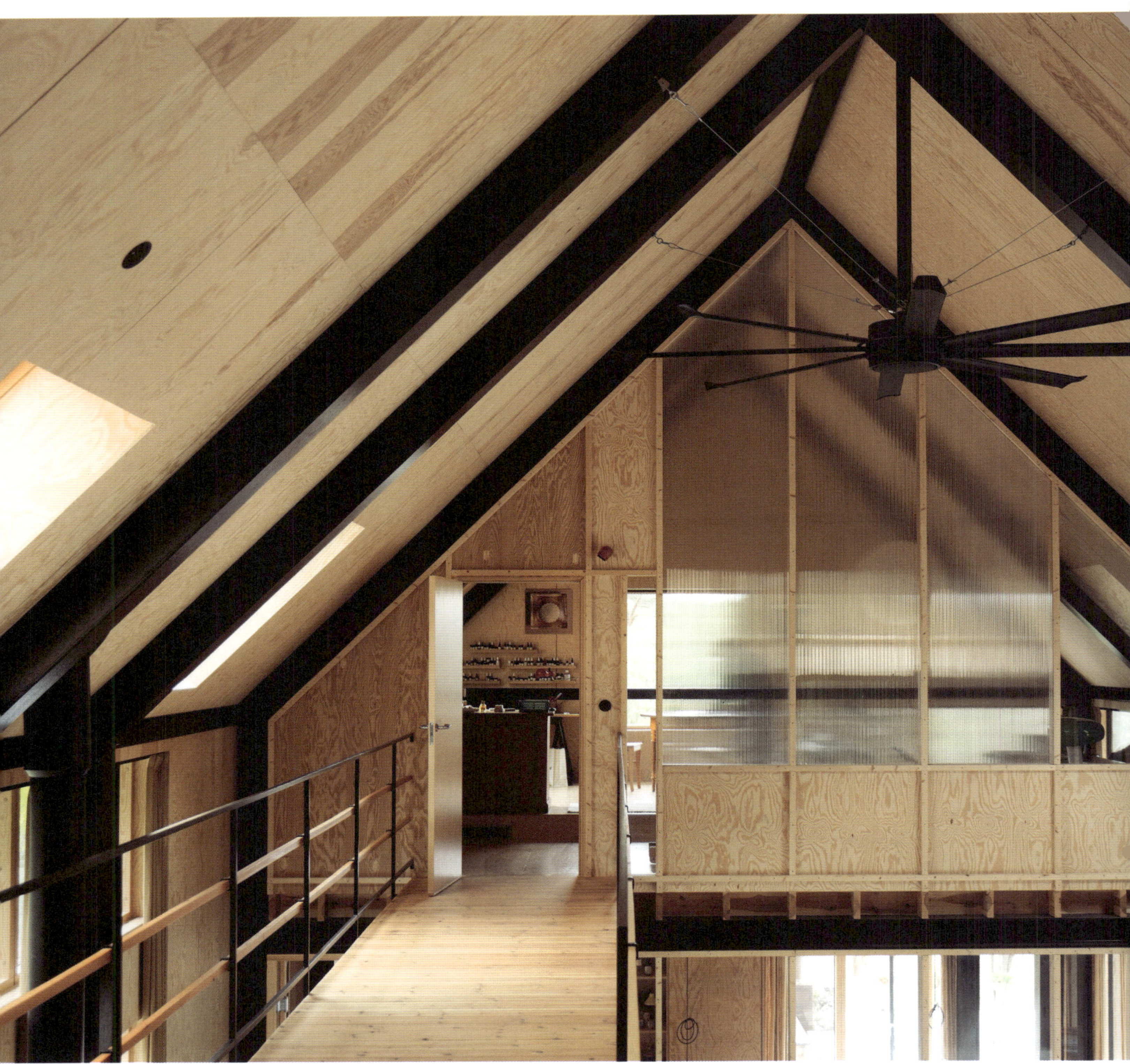

Benthe and Maurice's door is always open: they love it when family and friends undertake the journey to visit them. The house's architecture is open as well, with vast spaces inside and lots of glass offering expansive views. Being so close to nature and to the sea was the biggest inspiration for Benthe to become a perfumer: she created the LenaBlum perfume brand in her studio at her Gotland home, seeking to capture the scent of the island's nature in a bottle.

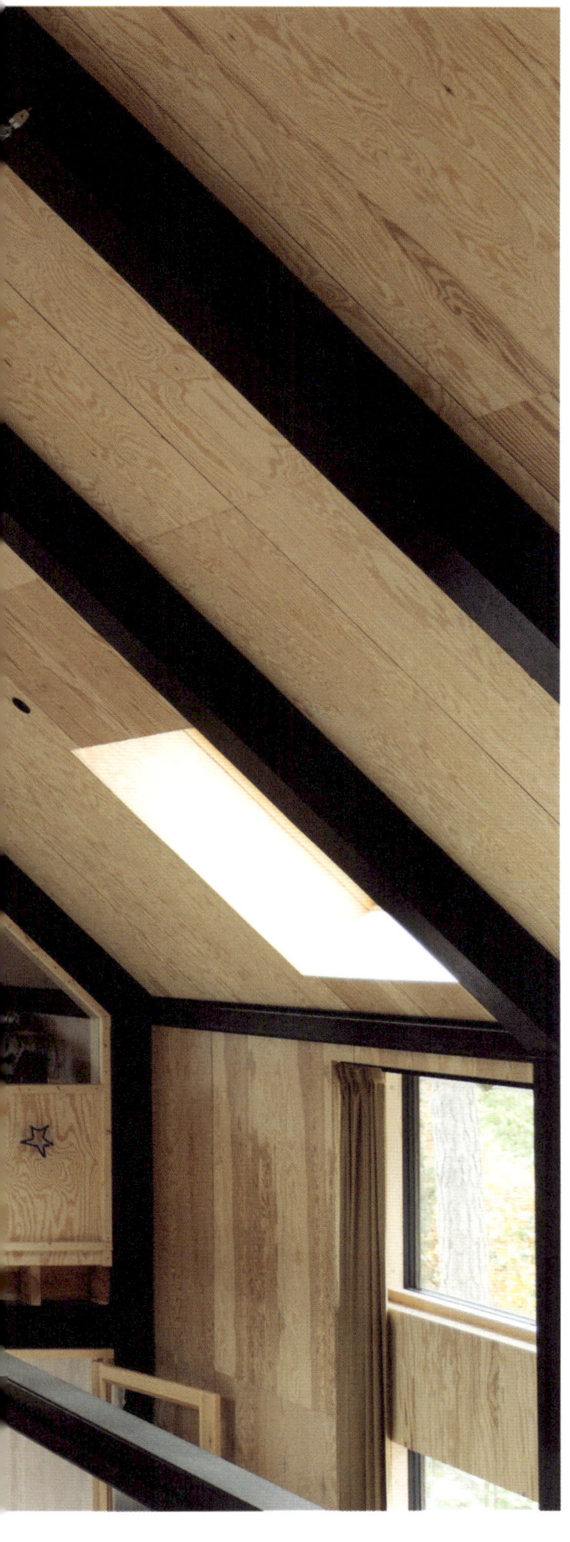

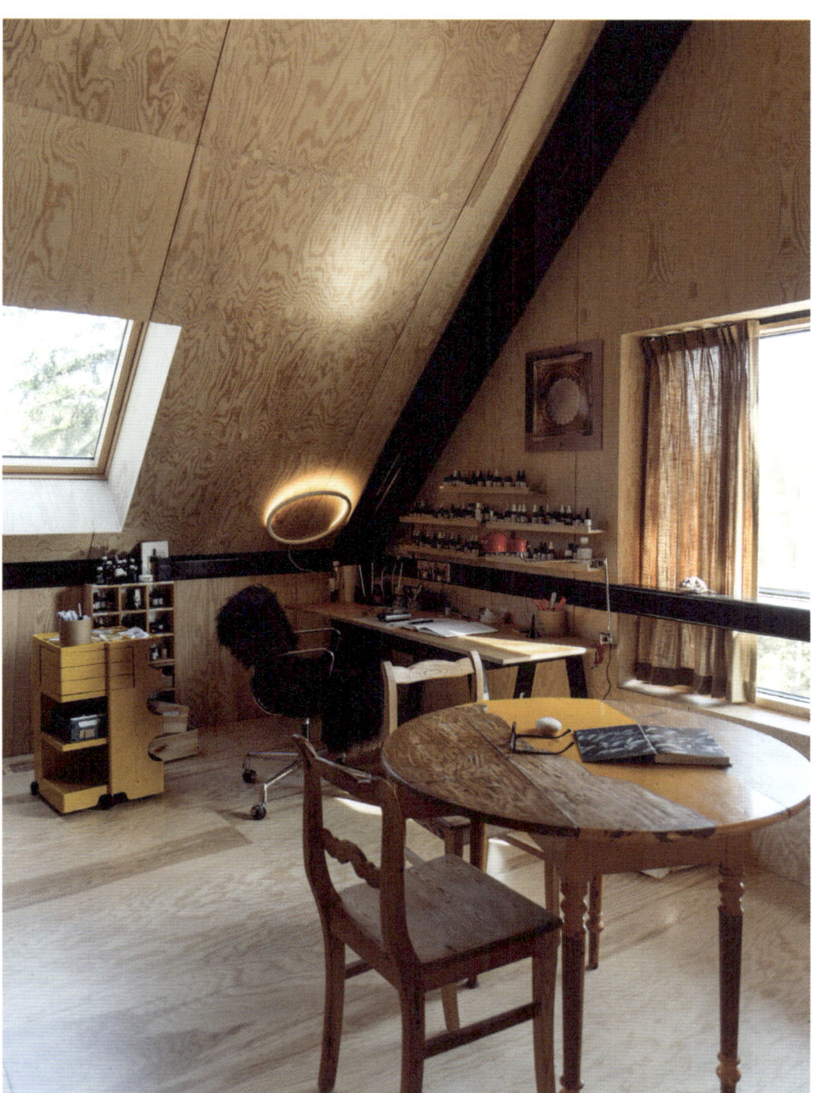

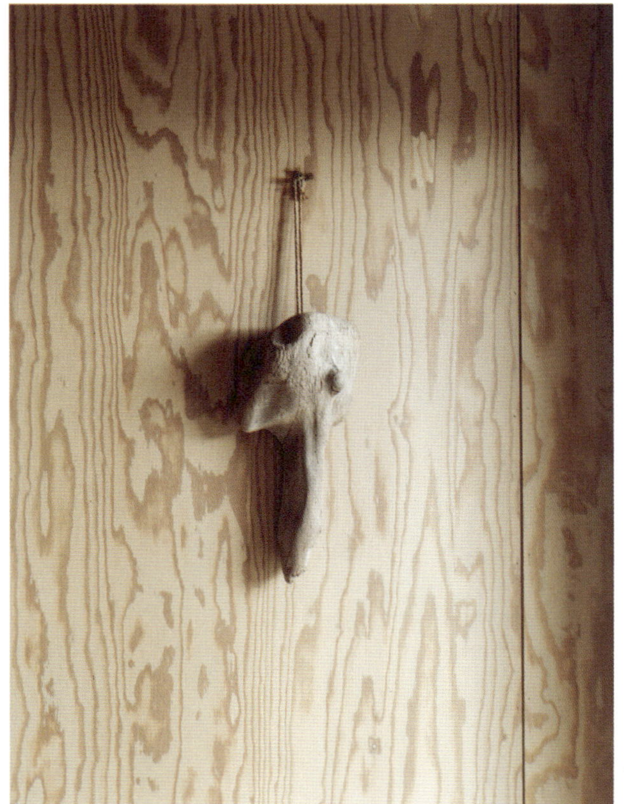

All ancient civilisations that originated in coastal regions attribute mythical powers to the sea. Since time immemorial, the waters and tides have shaped the lives of the people who have lived there, serving as a never-ending source of sagas and stories. The Vikings who once walked the rugged coastline of the island of Gotland liked to tell legends about dragons. Frank created Gotke, a baby dragon who came into the world from the sea, out of cloths and rags. Gotke feels at home among the enchanting rauks. These column-like coral rock formations near the waterfront were formed by the sea millions of years ago. In their presence, you become very aware of the power of nature and how everything in it constantly changes: the light, the colour of the water, the sound of the sea.

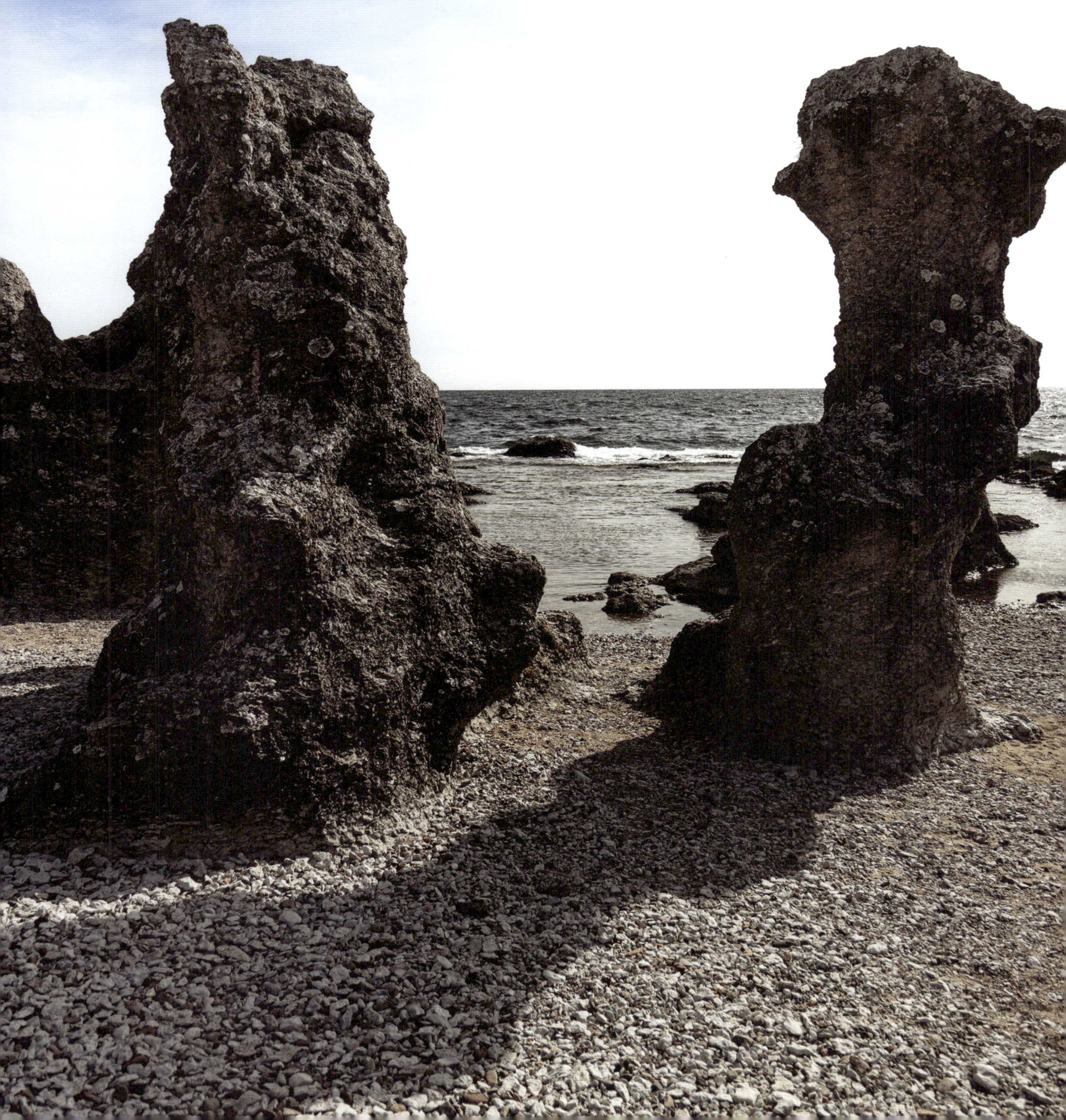

THE LEGEND OF GOTKE

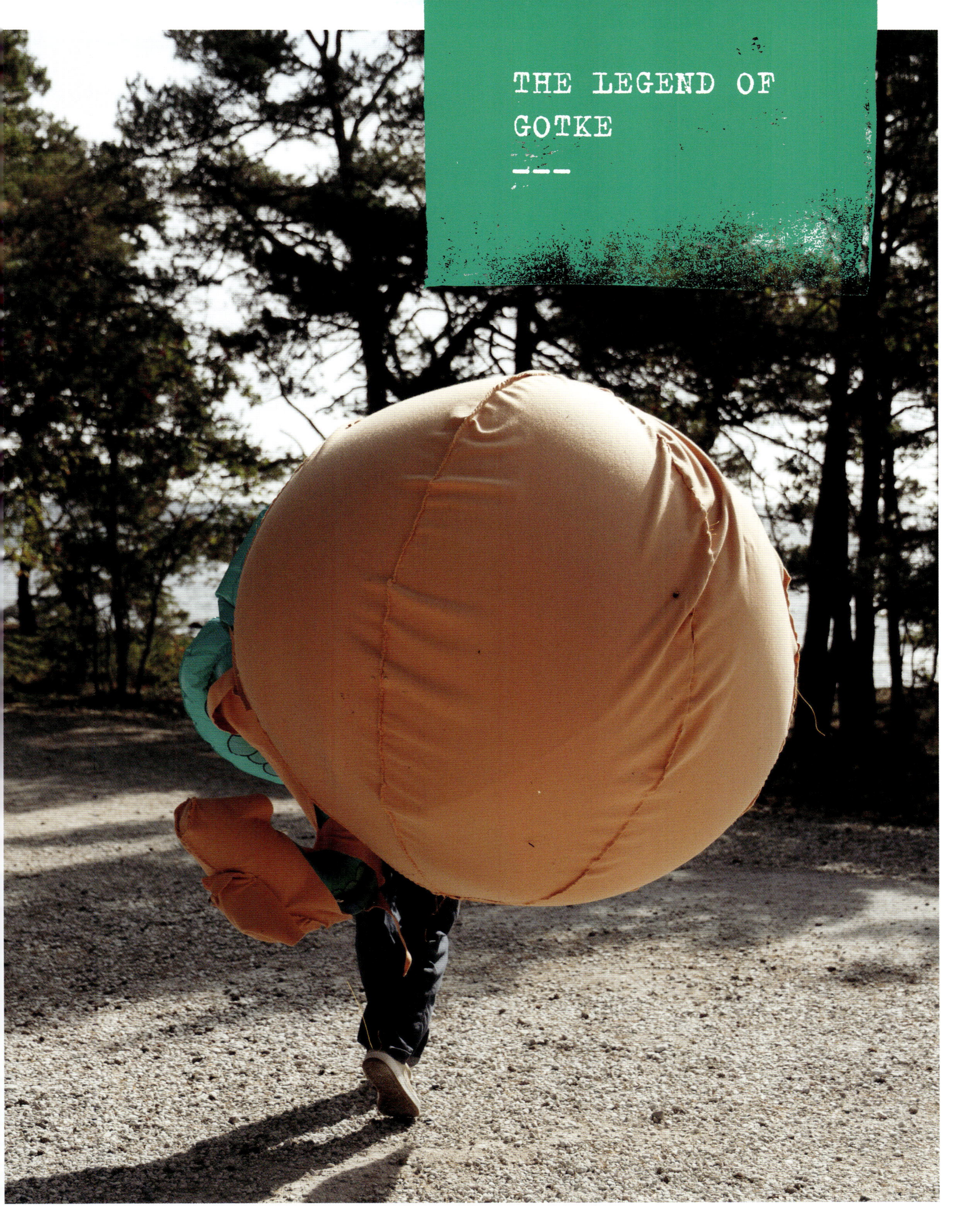

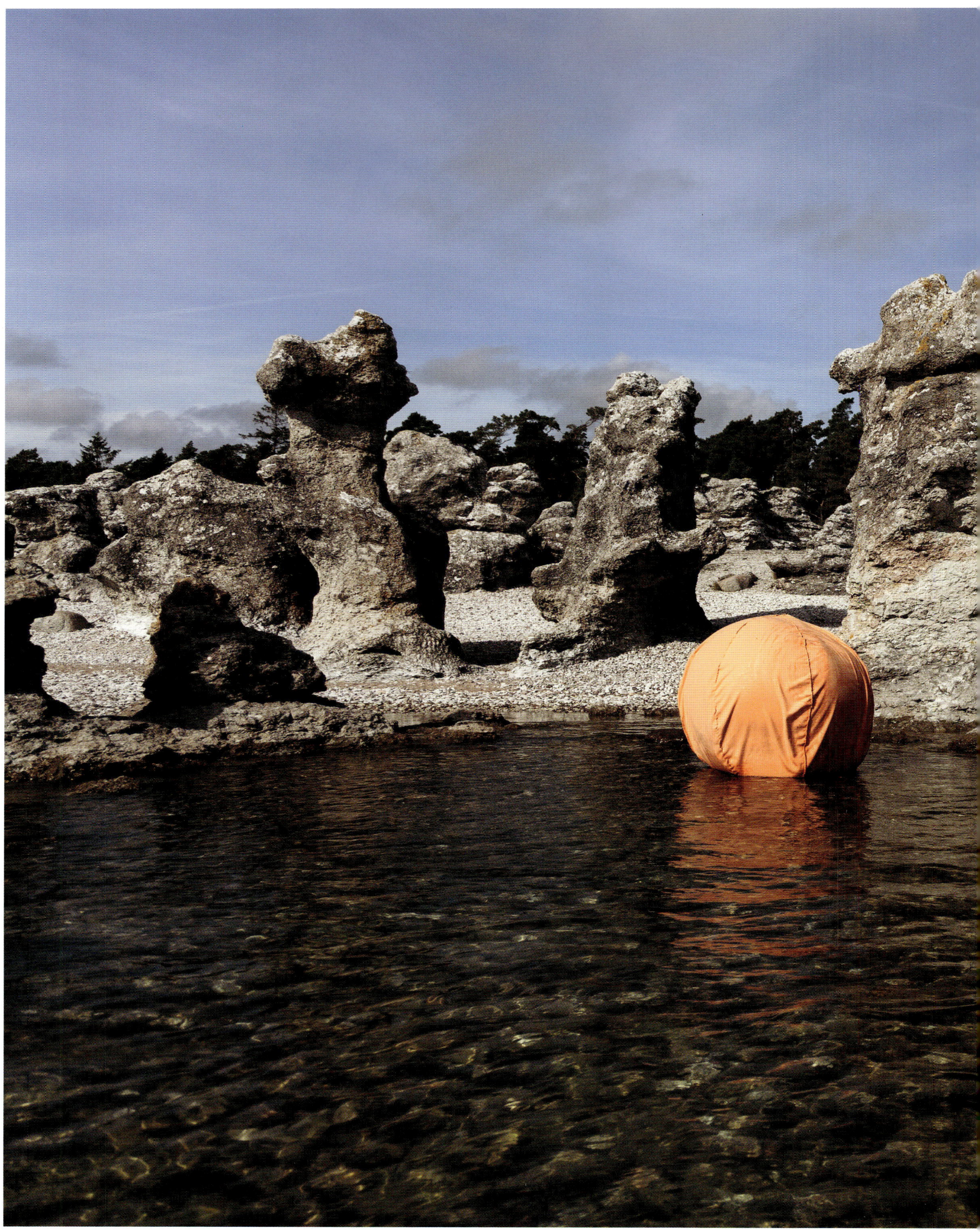

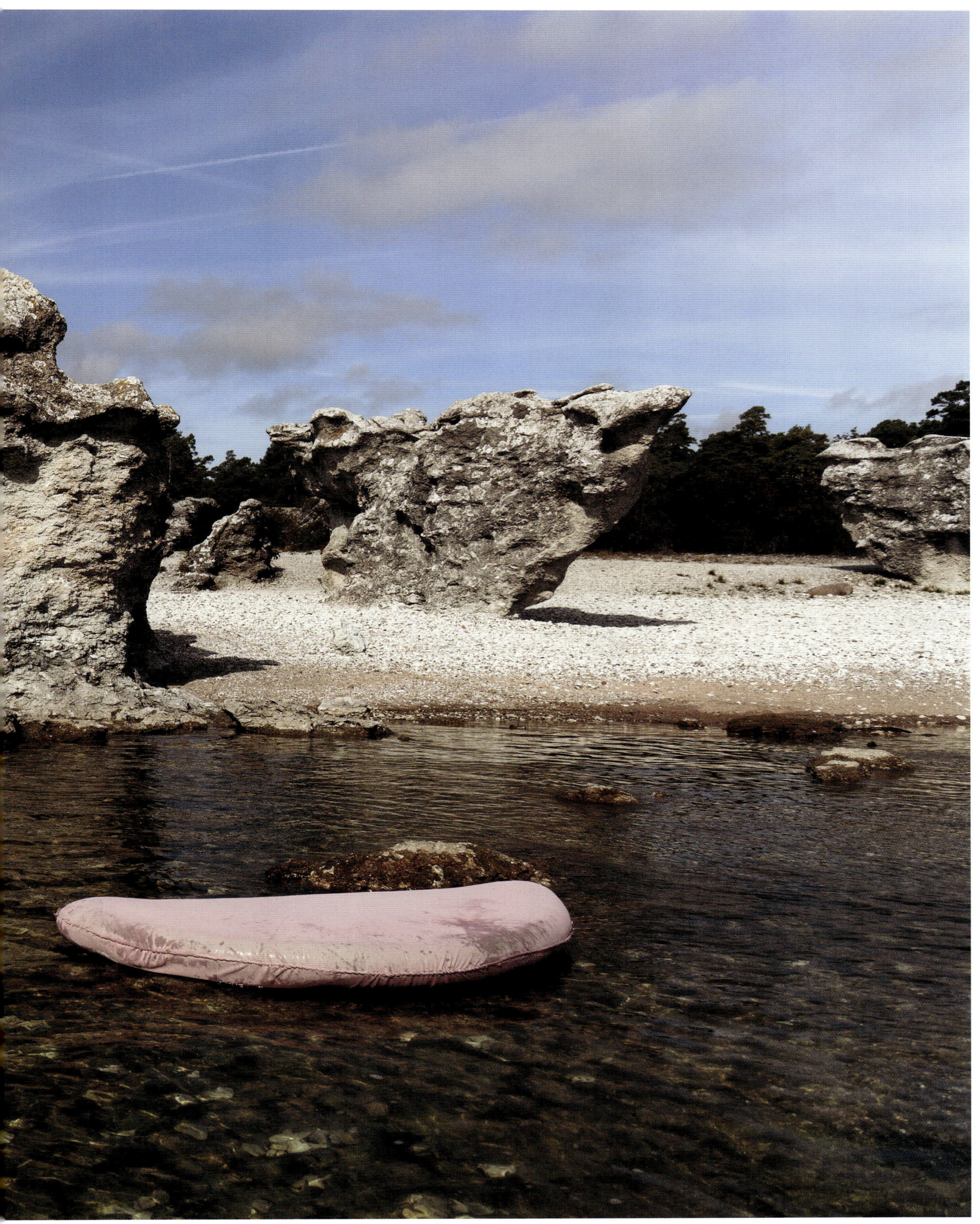

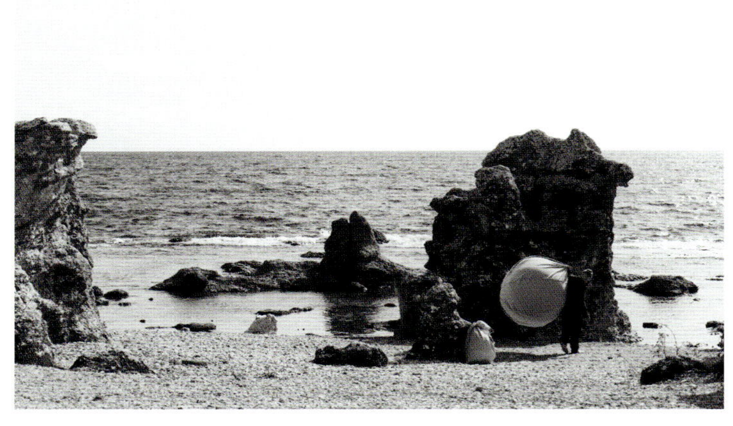

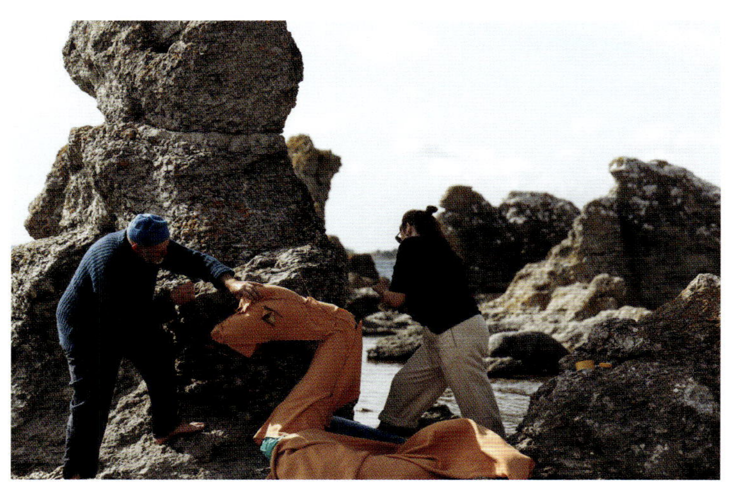

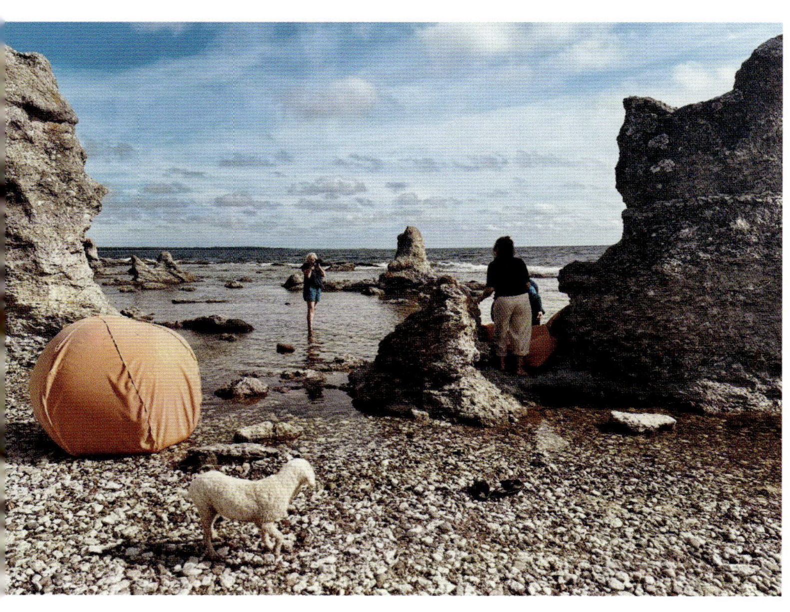

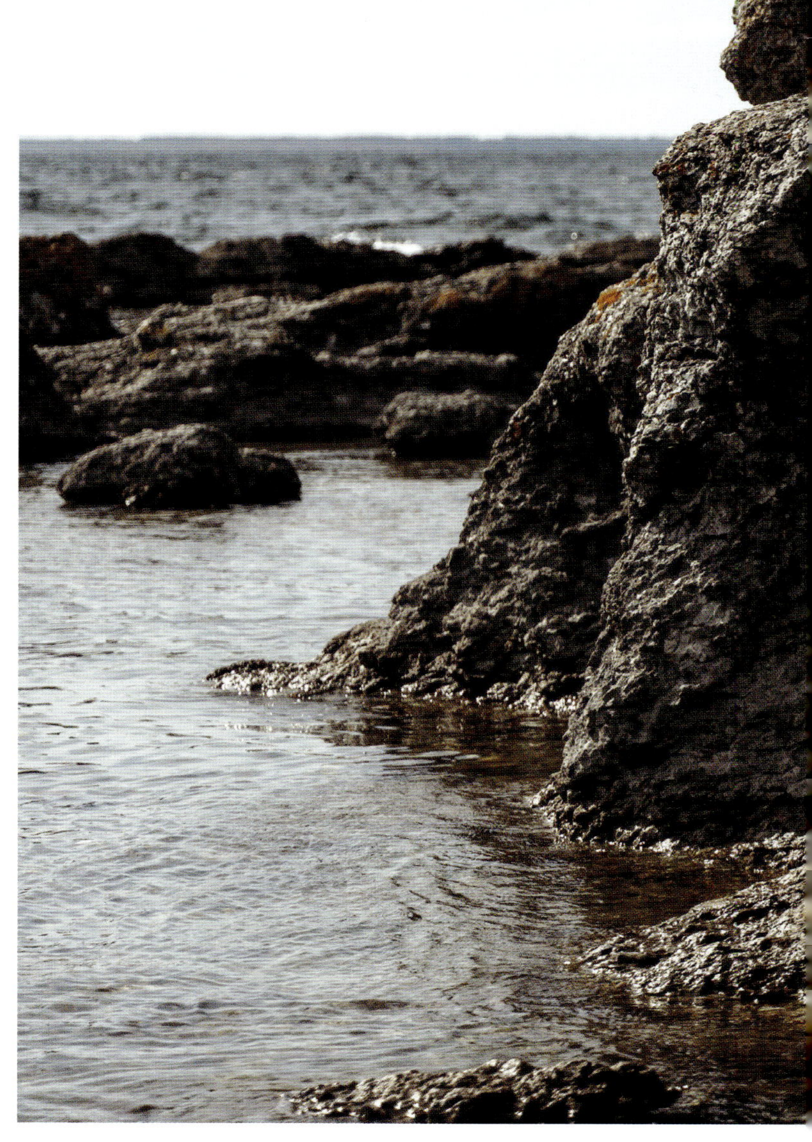

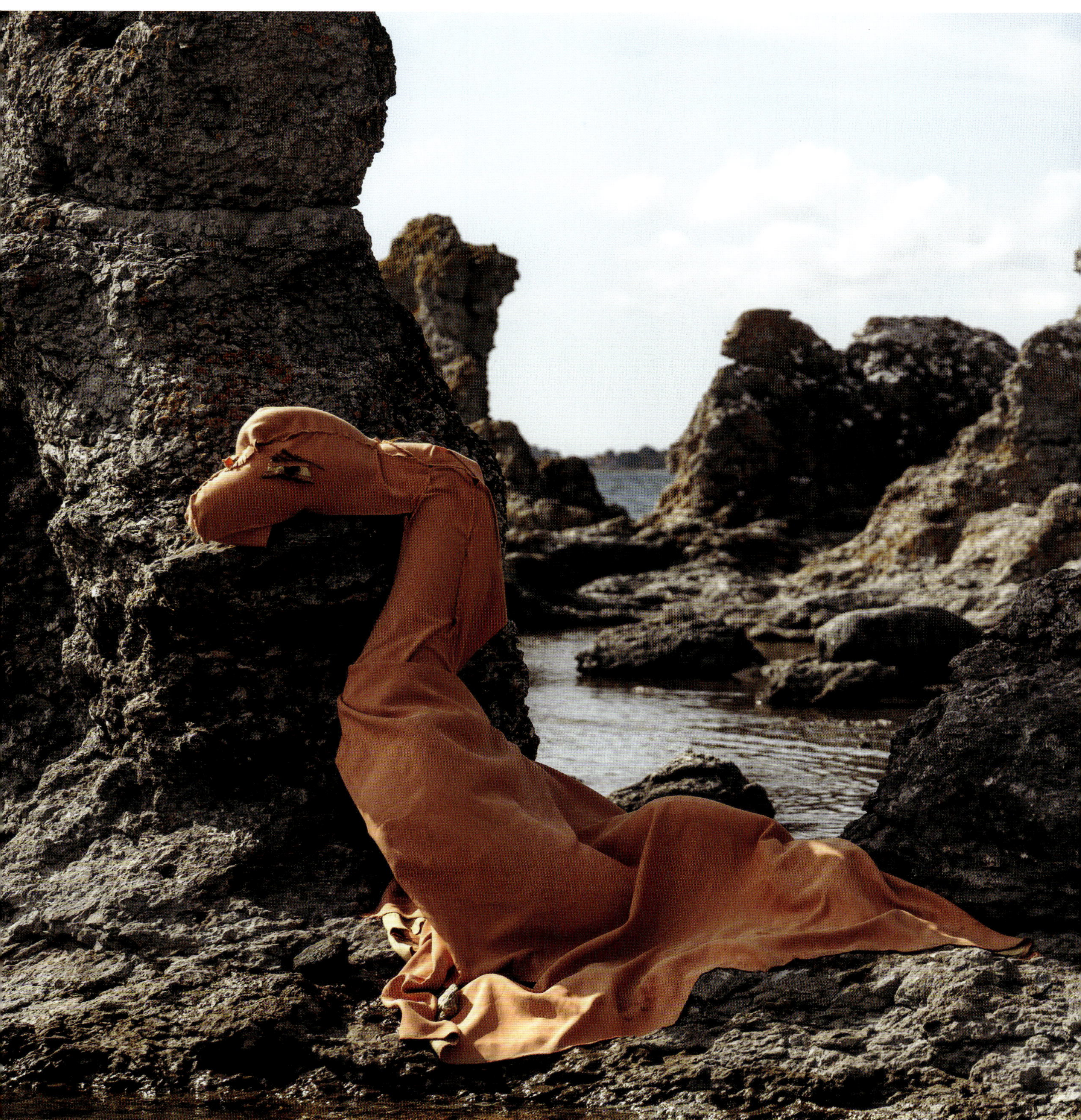

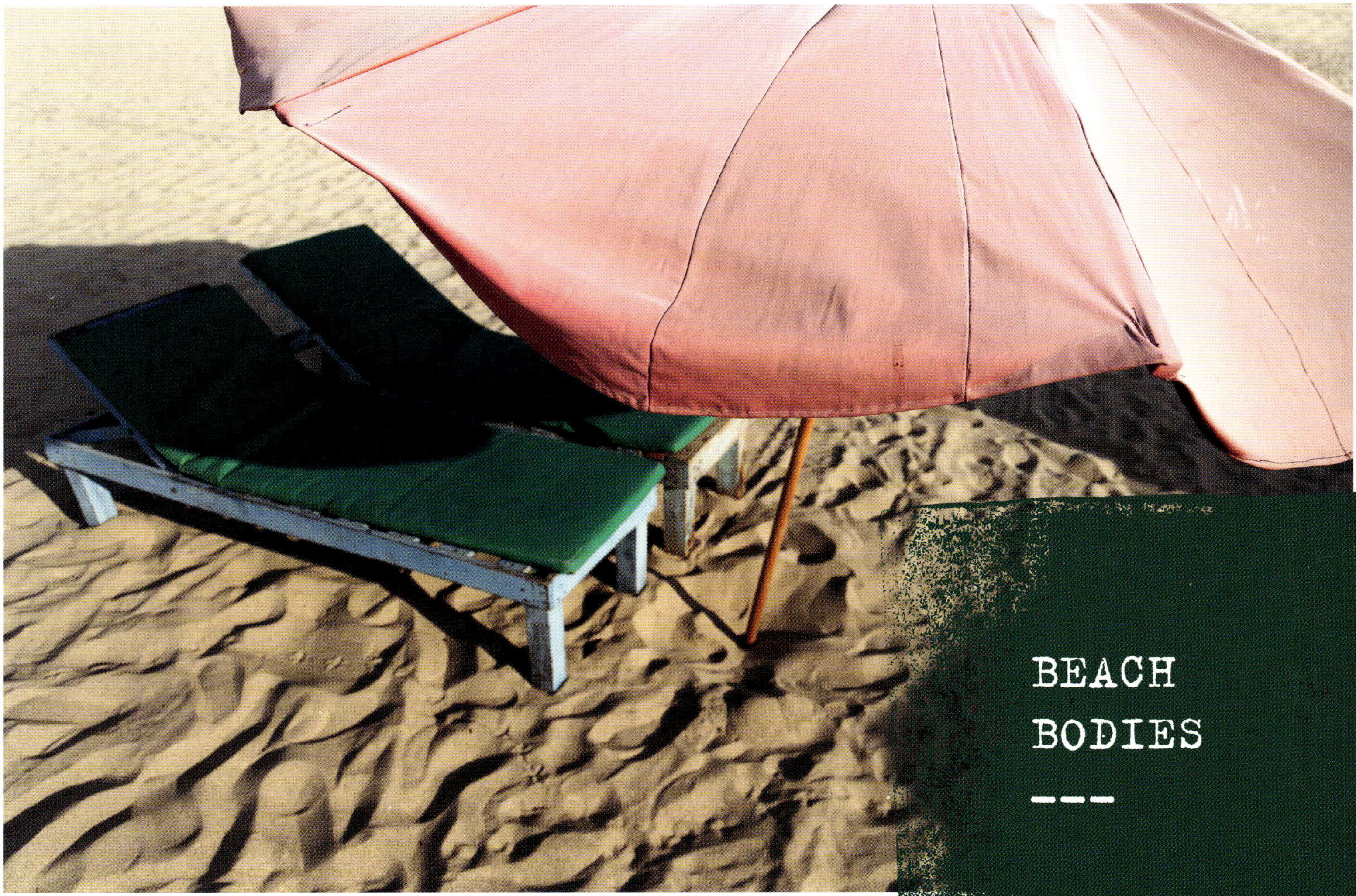

BEACH BODIES

These faceless 3D fabric figures journeyed all the way from the Netherlands to one of Mexico's stunning beaches, to do little more than lounge in the sun, soaking up rays, and perhaps even risking a sunburn. It's the kind of carefree vacation that feels perfect when you're young and naive what a delightful time that was.

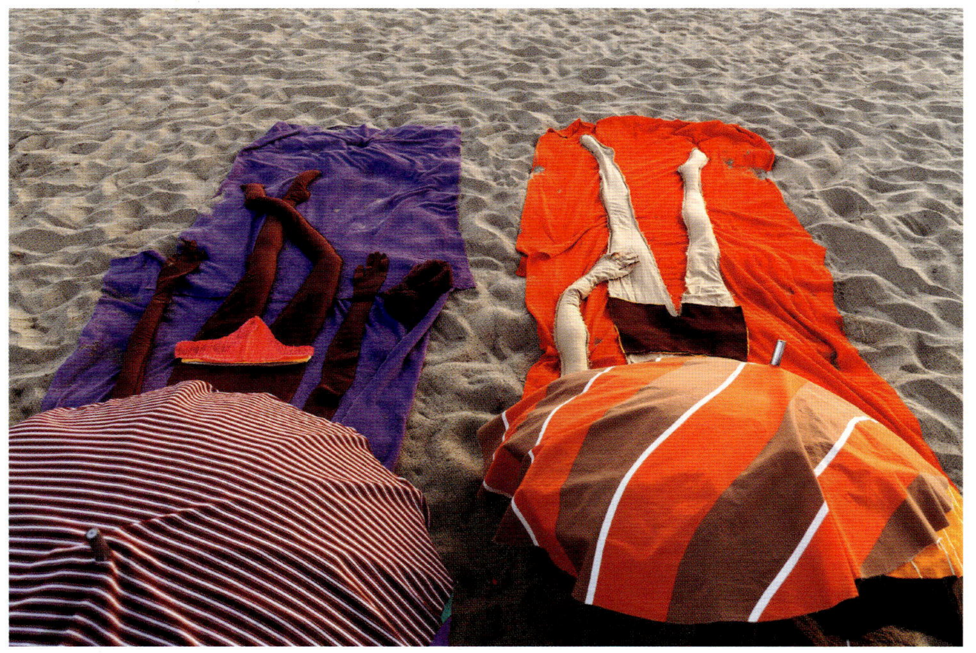

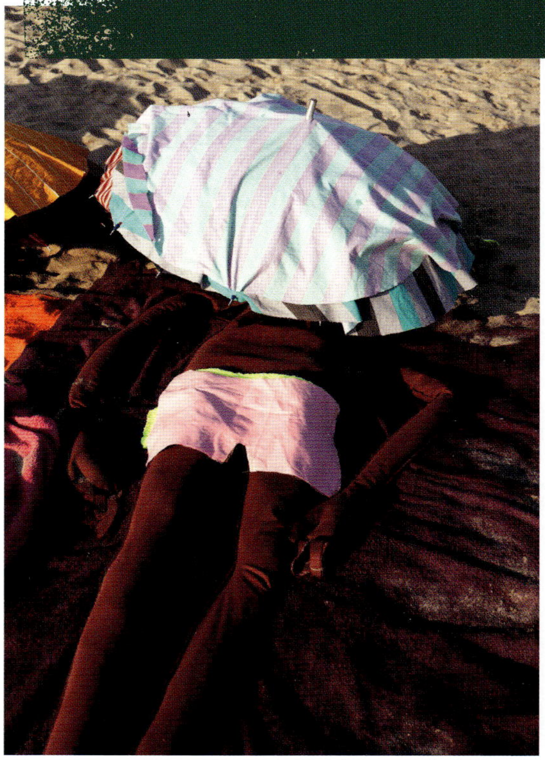

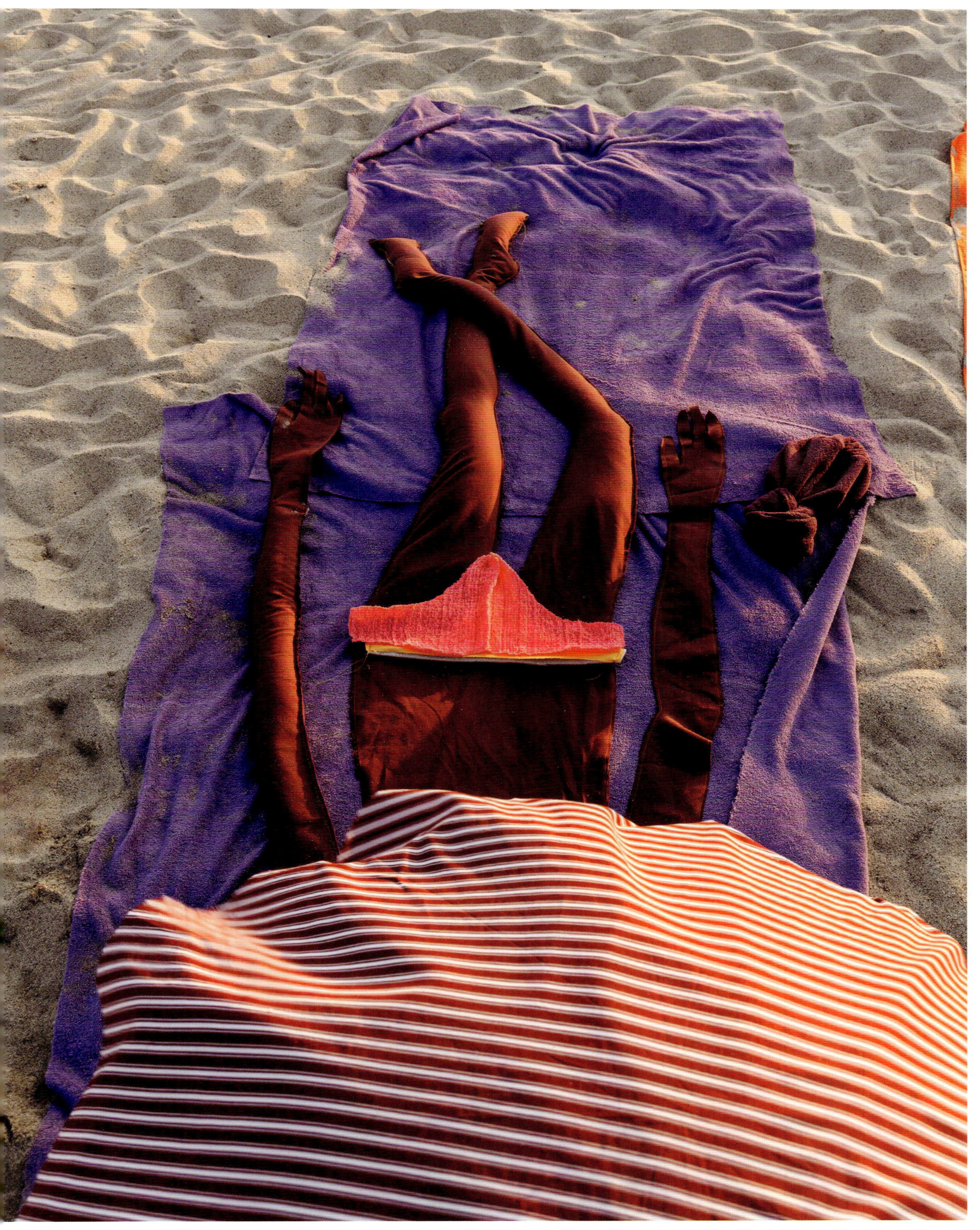

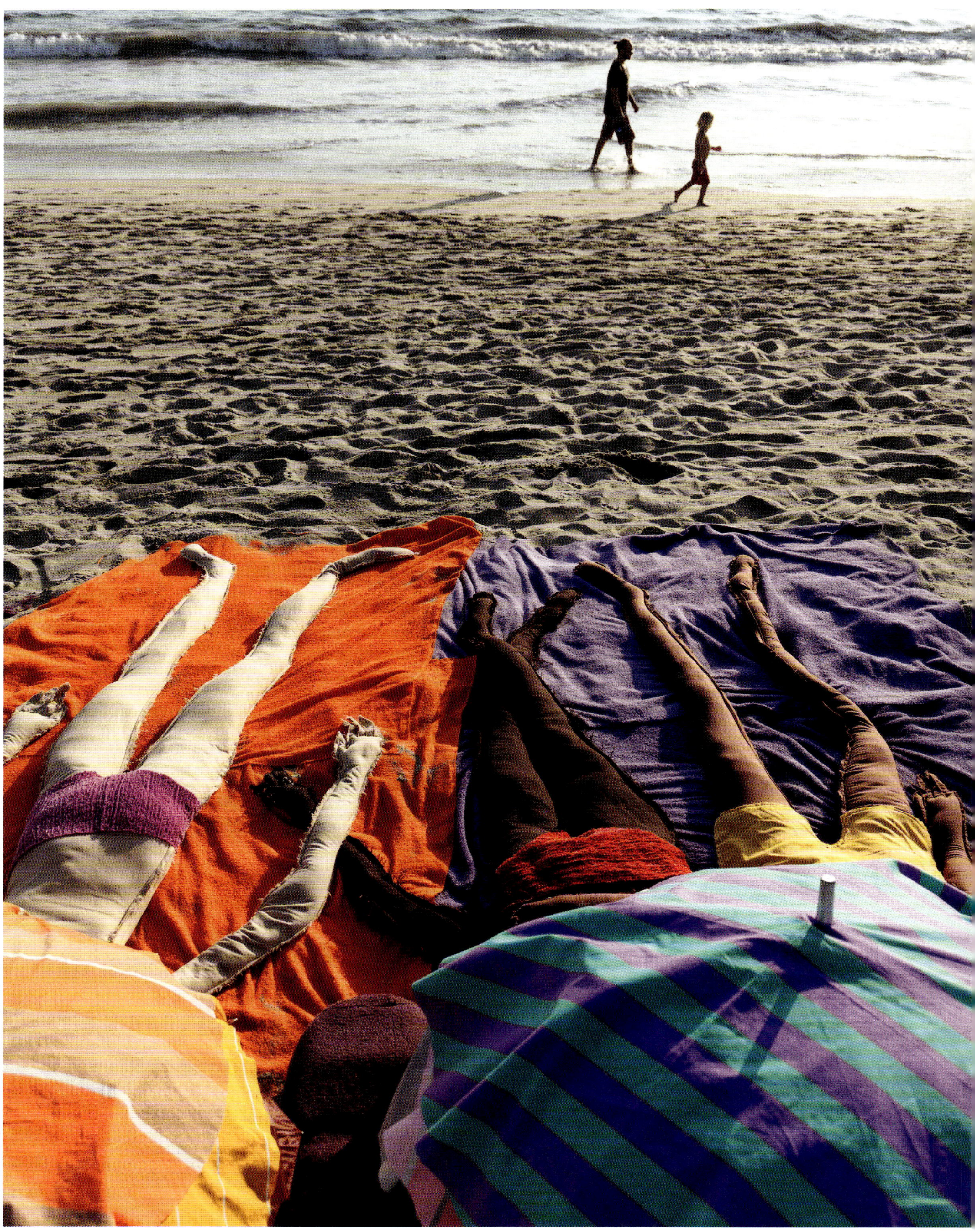

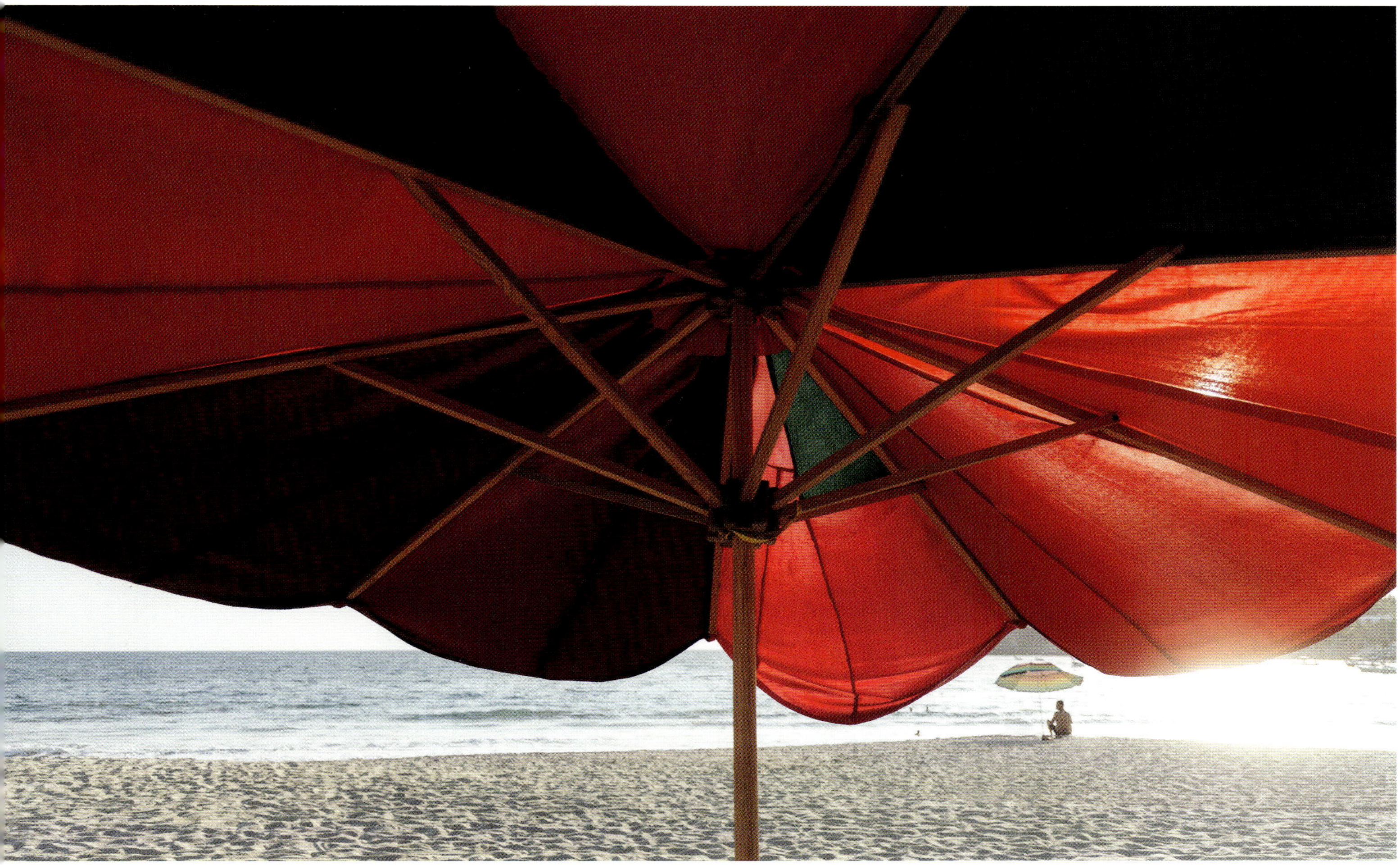

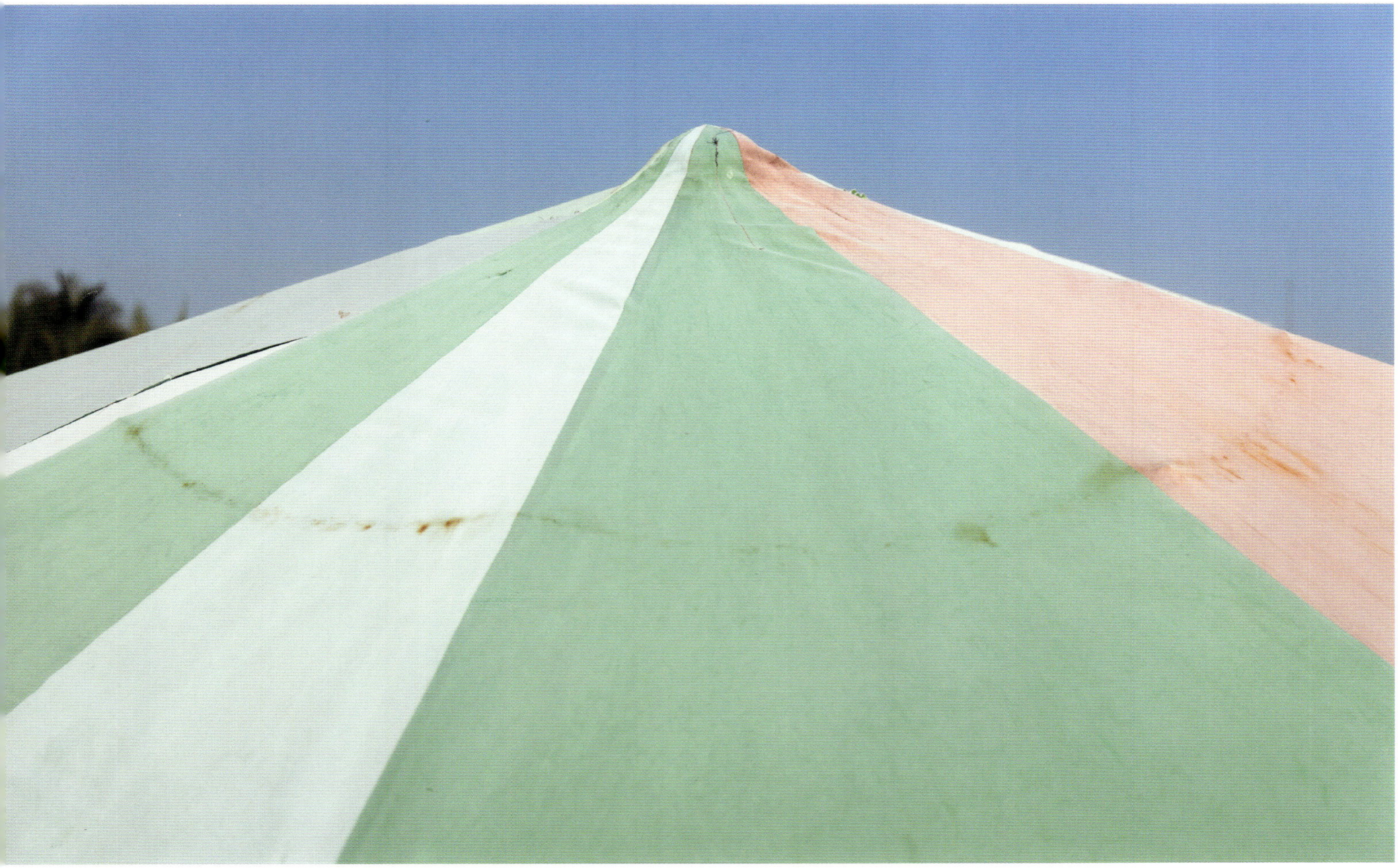

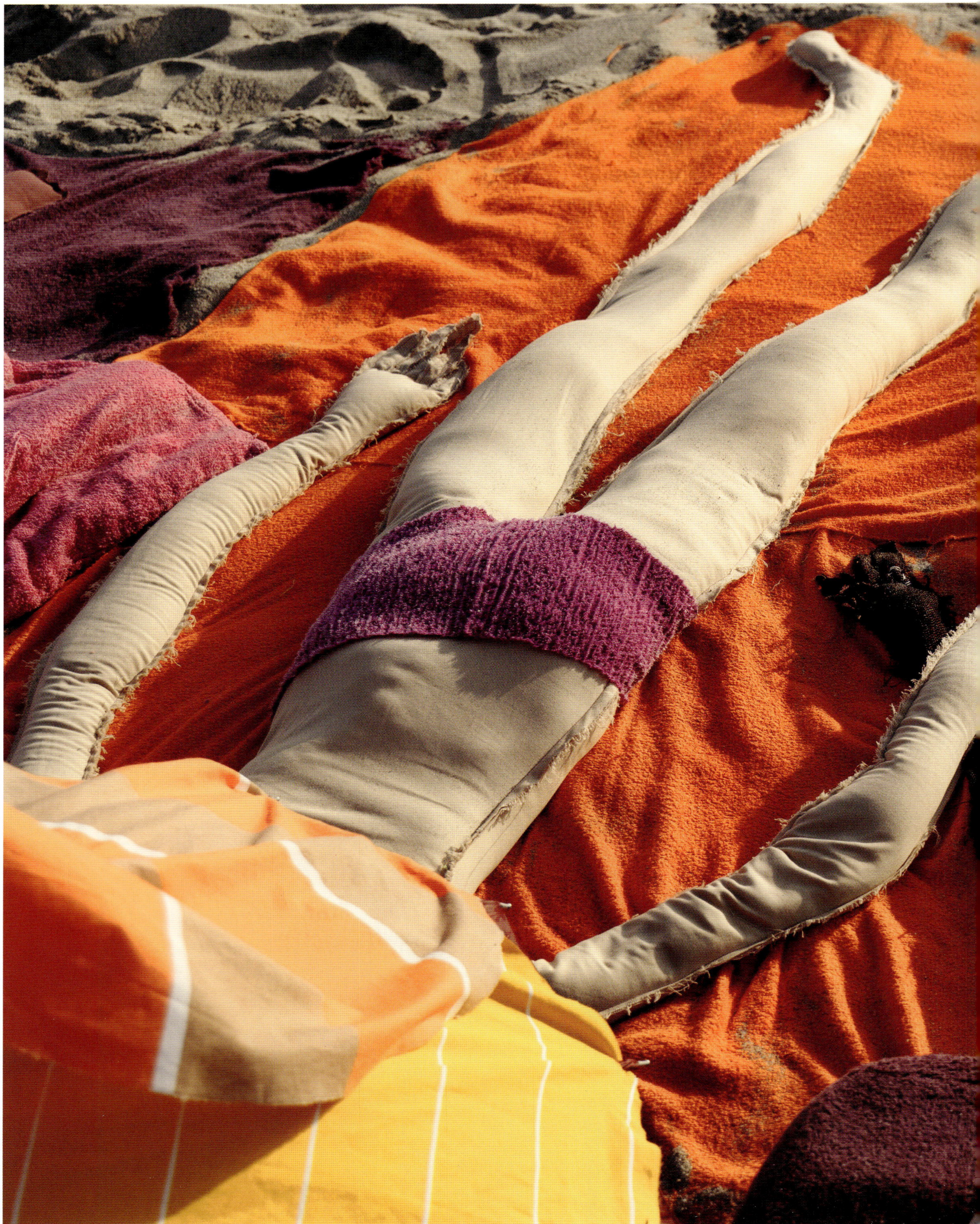

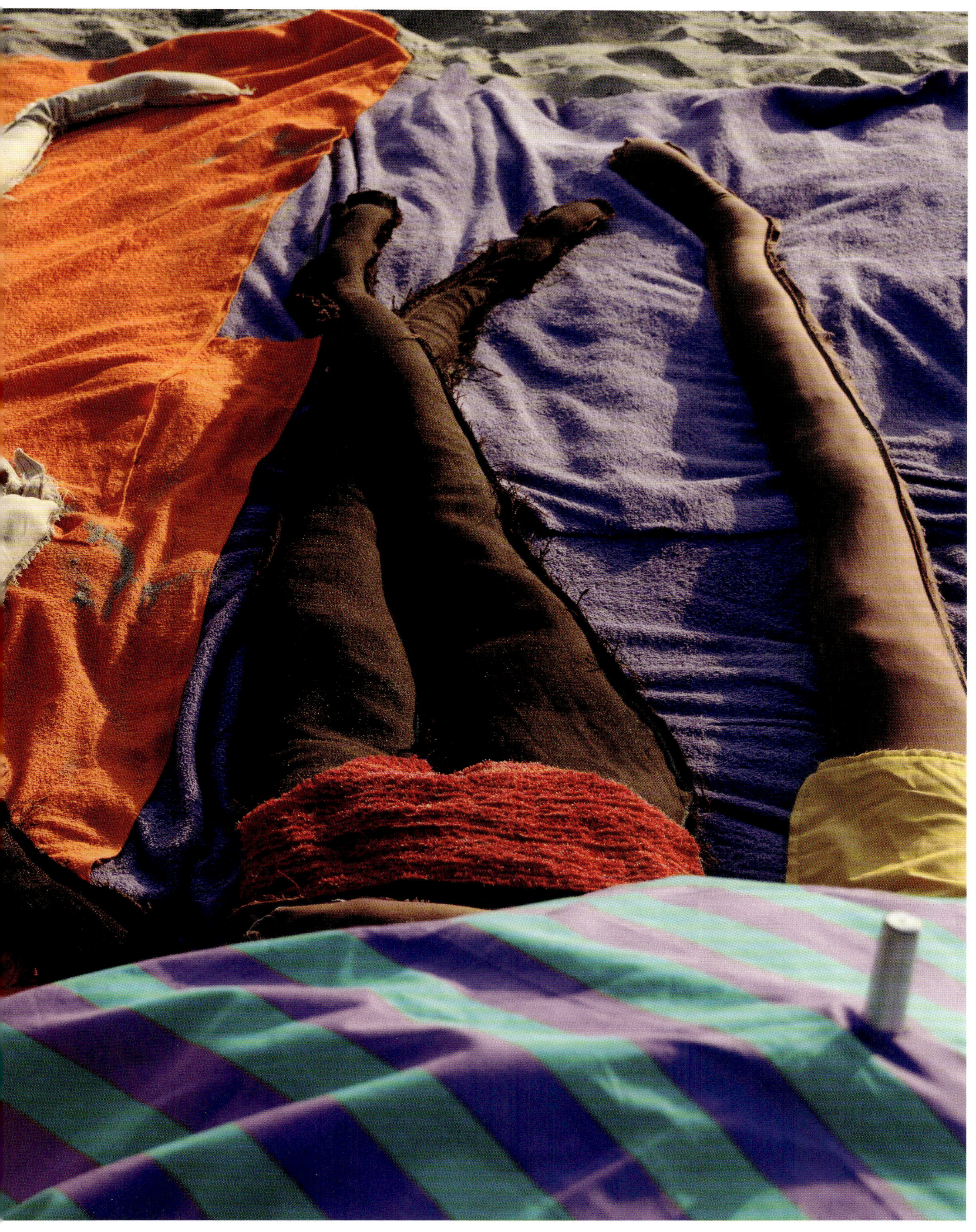

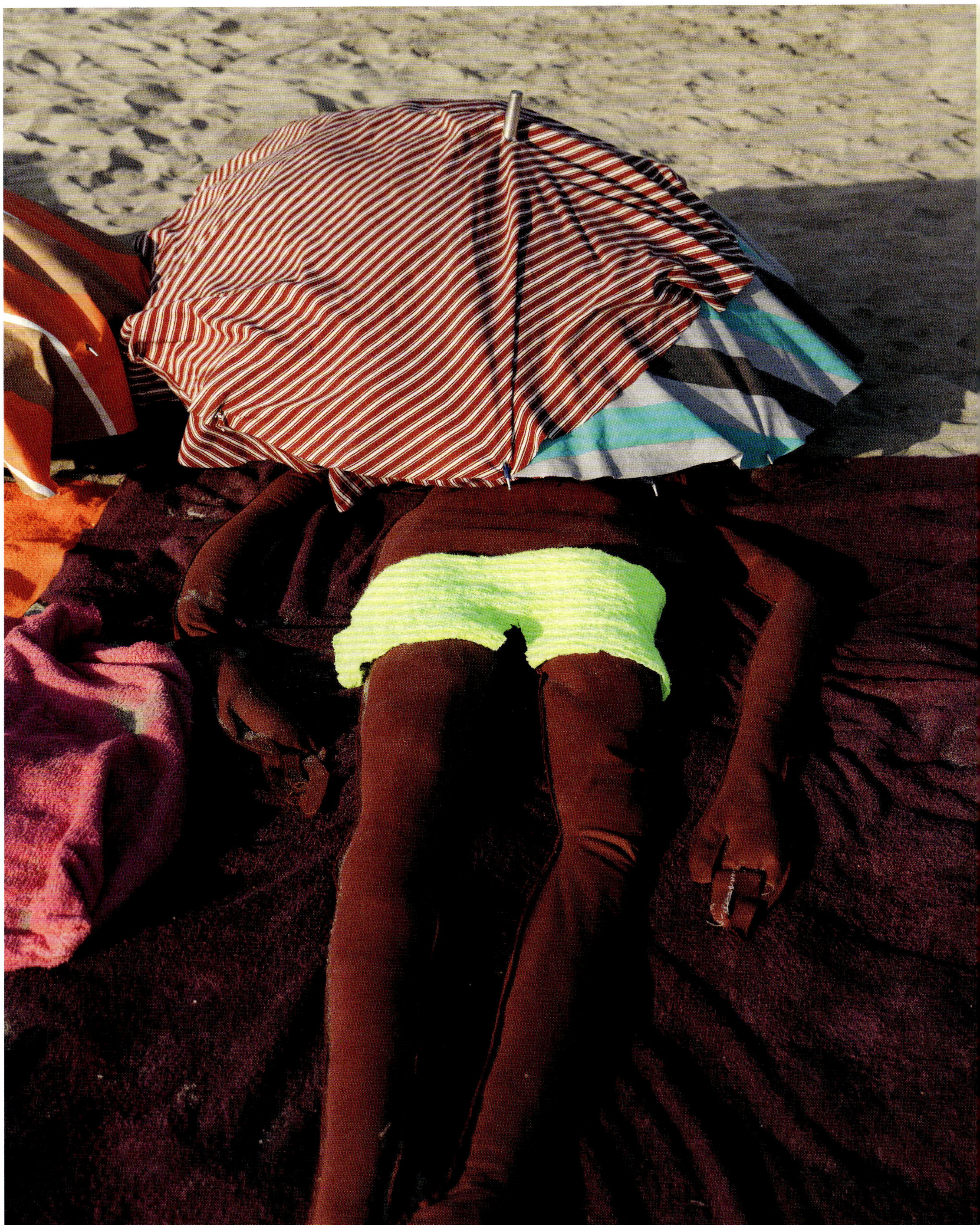

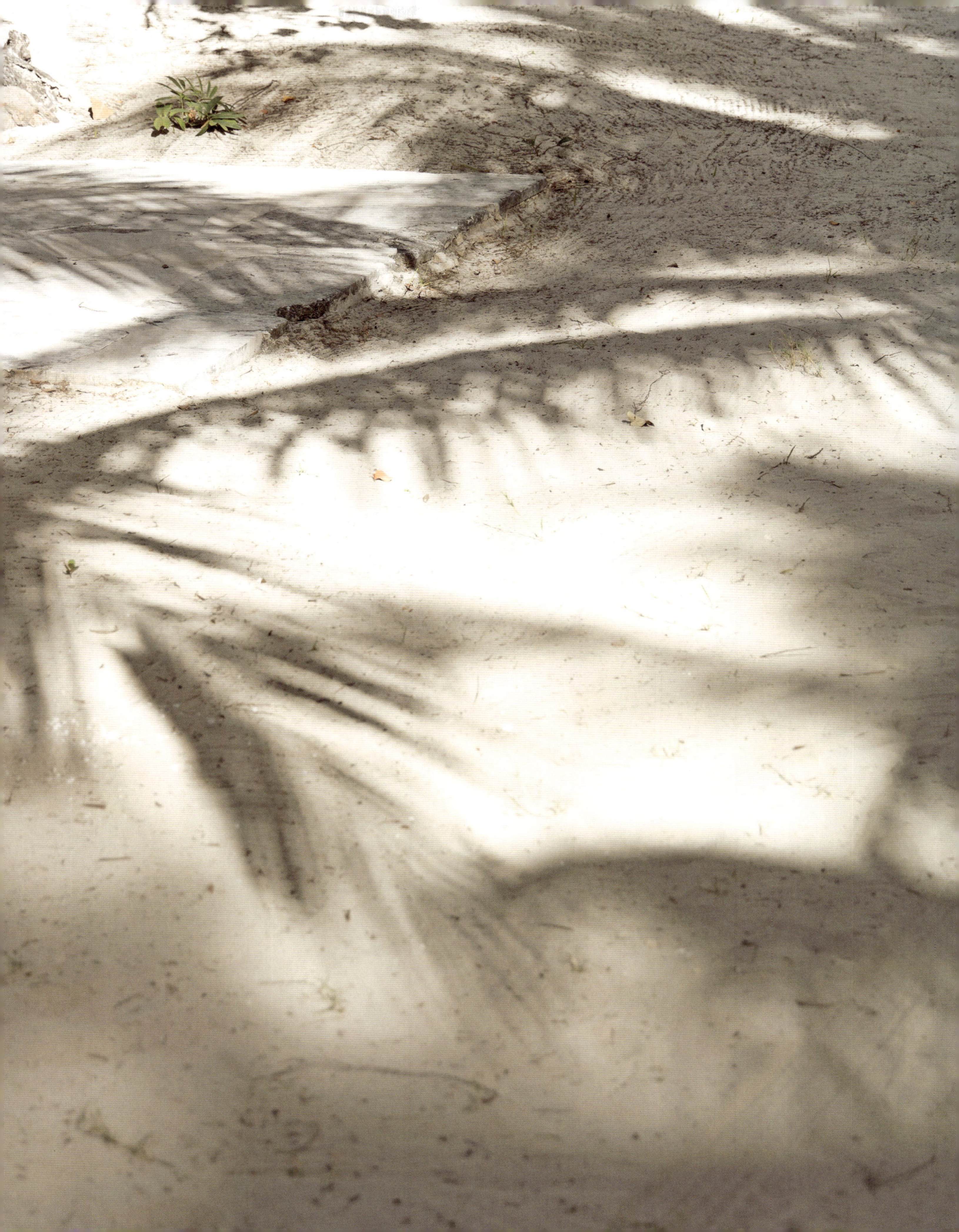

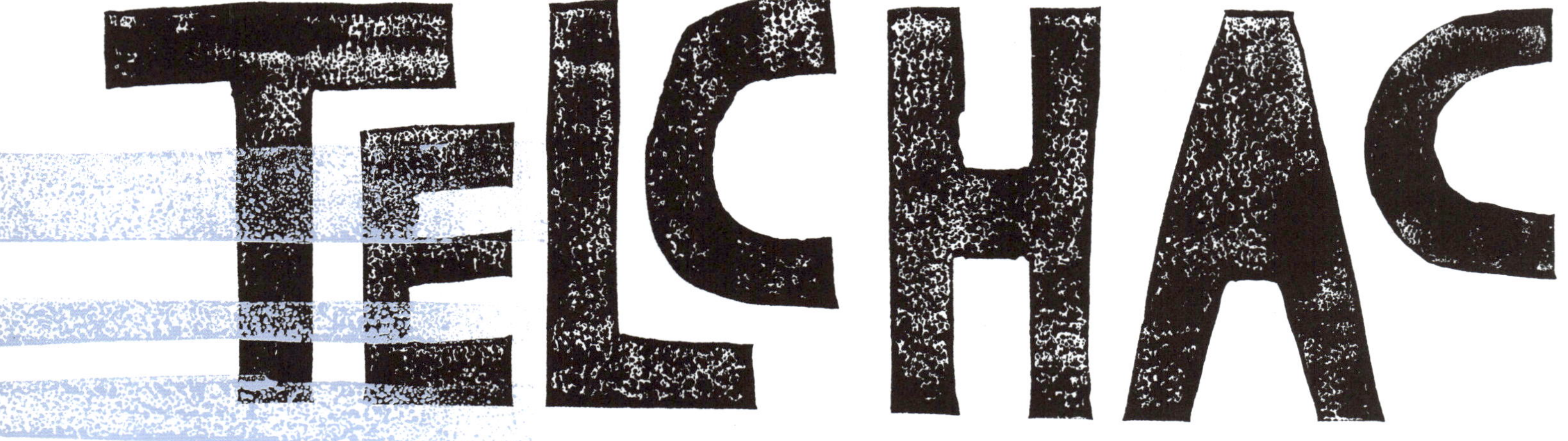

TELCHAC

Yucatán
Mexico

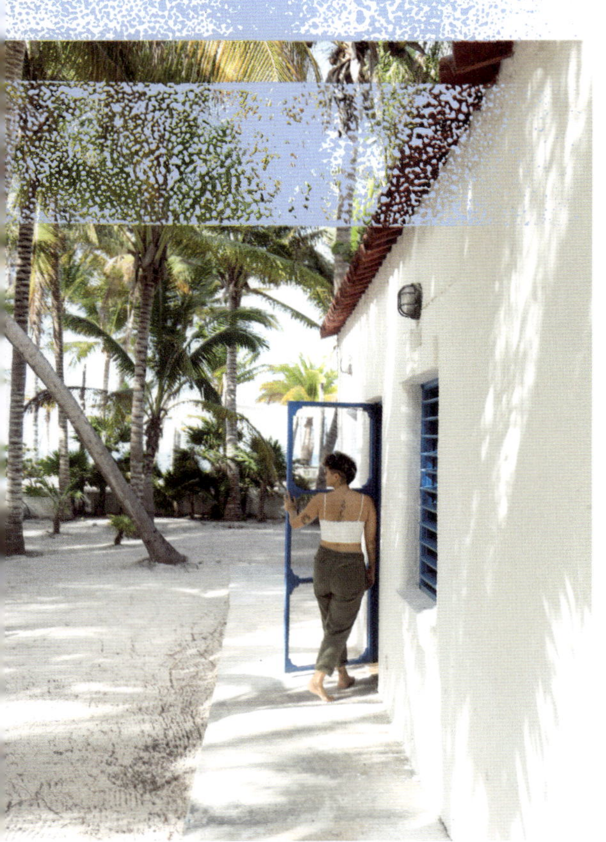

The harbour of Telchac Puerto on the Gulf of Mexico played a fascinating role in the history and Mayan culture of the Yucatán peninsula. It once was the main port for exports of henequen, a type of agave plant grown by the Mayas in Yucatán for its leaf fibre (sisal) from which all kinds of objects can be made, such as rope, baskets, bags, hammocks, and rugs. Henequen production peaked between about 1876 and 1919, bringing great wealth to the region. Bales of this 'green gold' were shipped to the US and Europe in large quantities from ports like Telchac until the invention of plastic signalled the industry's demise.

From one day to the next, the beautiful beachfront warehouses in Telchac Puerto, where the henequen was stored, became deserted as all trading activities ceased. Today, one of them is 'Miramar', Luna Patrón Le Doux's beach villa. This enchanting property has been in her father's family for several generations. It was renovated piecemeal, and the structure was modified where necessary to transform it into a home while retaining the building's historical essence.

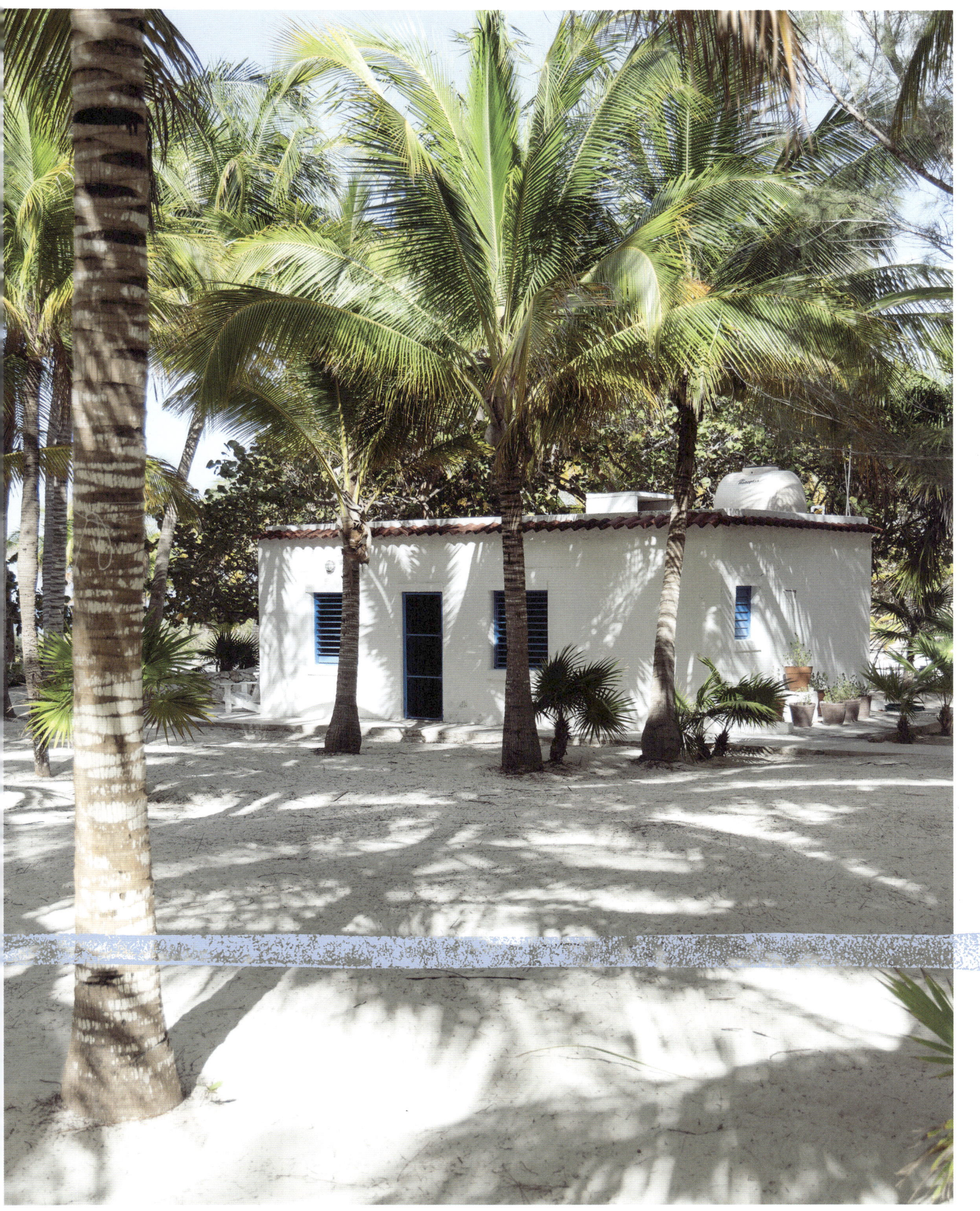

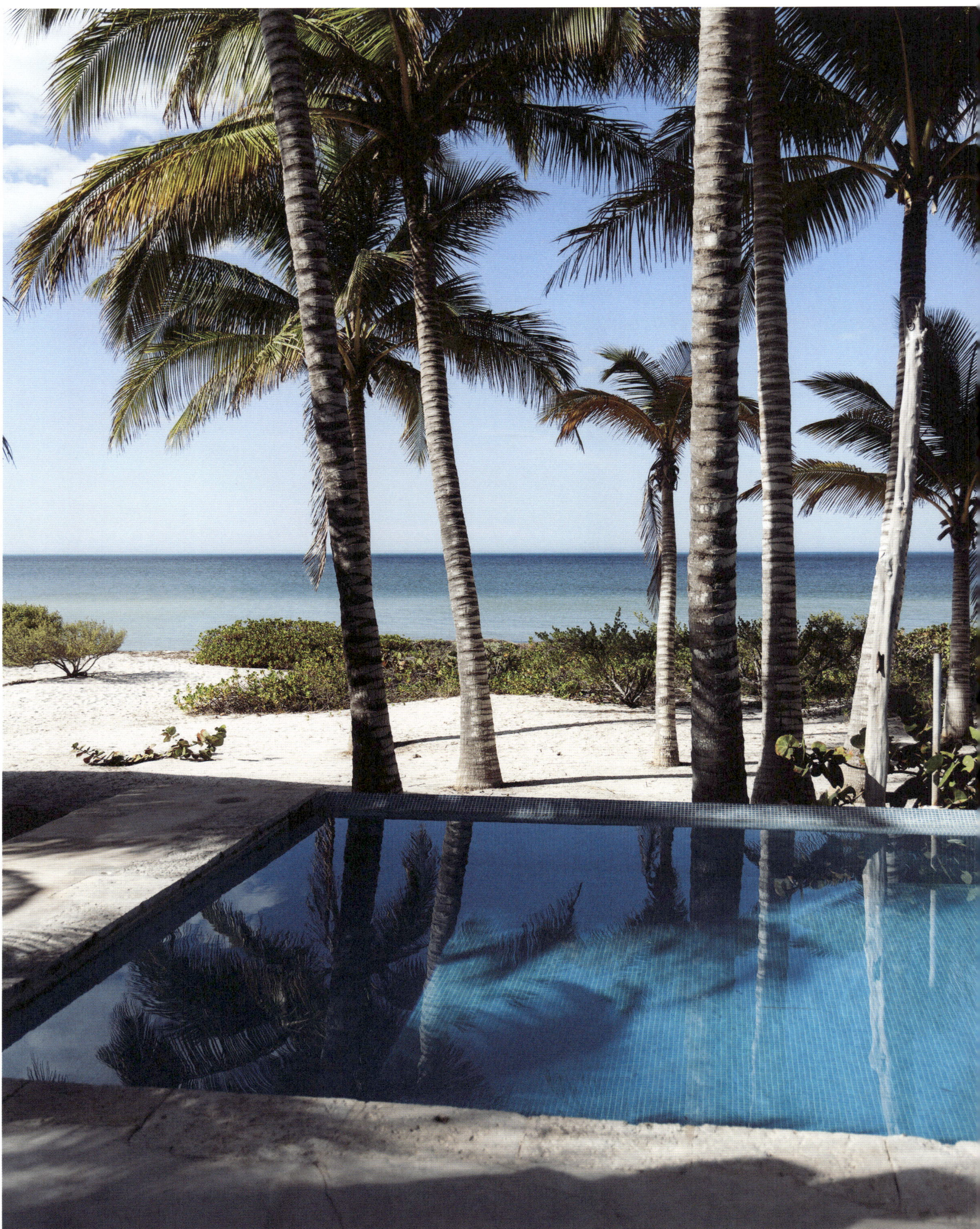

Miramar is a true paradise, not only because of its history but also, and probably more so, because of its location: right on the beach, surrounded by palm trees. To Luna, the calmness and peace of the surroundings are what makes Miramar so magical. She cherishes a story that her father used to tell her: as a boy, he and his brothers and cousins used to spend their weekends cleaning up the area around Miramar, especially the beach, at a time when it was covered with cypress leaves. One night, a storm passed through, and the following morning, the sand was completely clean and white. "That was nature working its magic," Luna's father said.

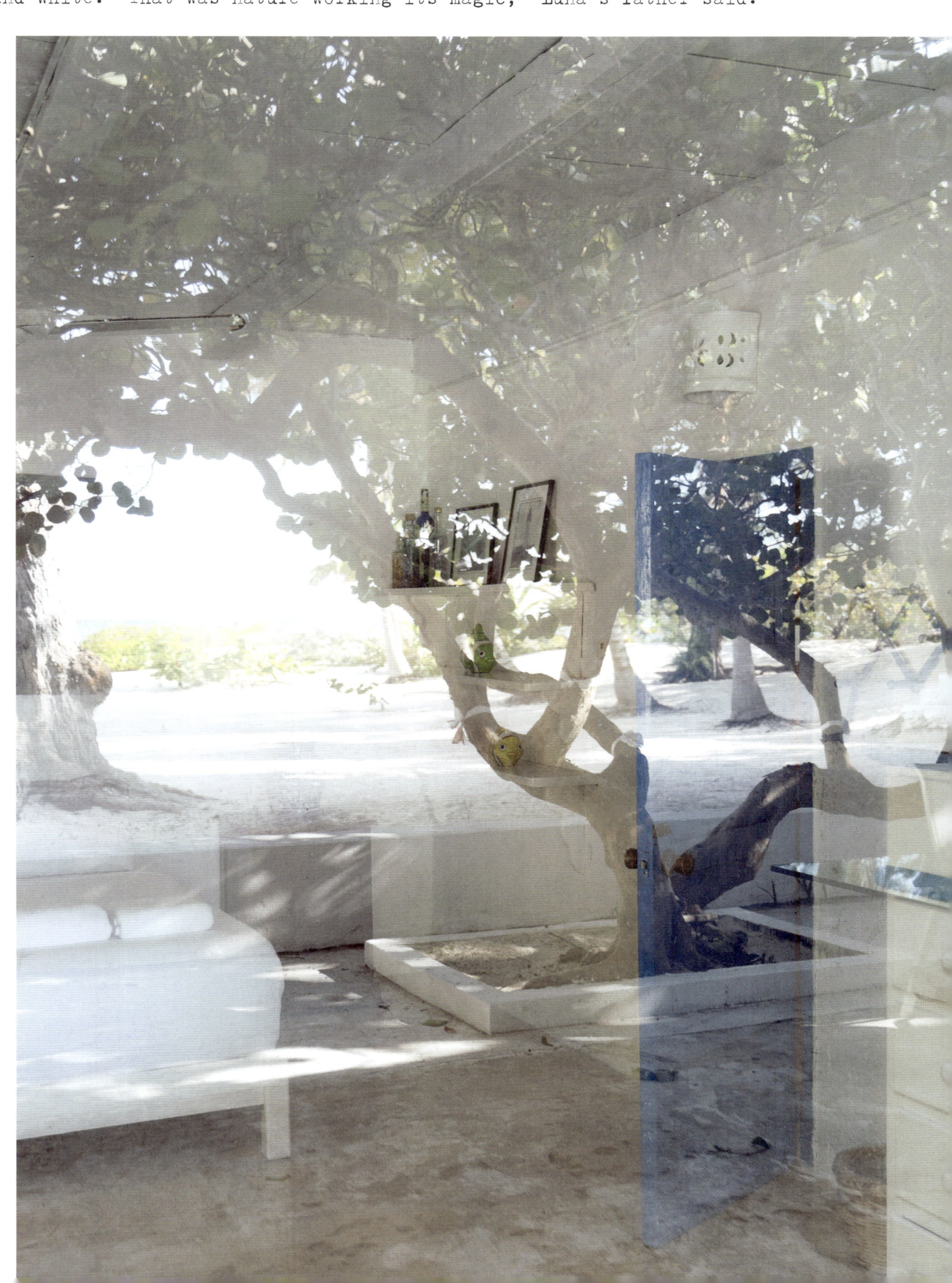

You feel that connection to the primal power of the sea inside the house. The interior is reminiscent of a large sailboat, thanks to the many wooden elements, bright blue and red colour accents, model ship hulls on the walls and a large shell collection. Luna's parents were keen mariners, sometimes spending days at sea on their sailboat. That is also what makes Miramar such a personal place and a safe haven for all those who dock there.

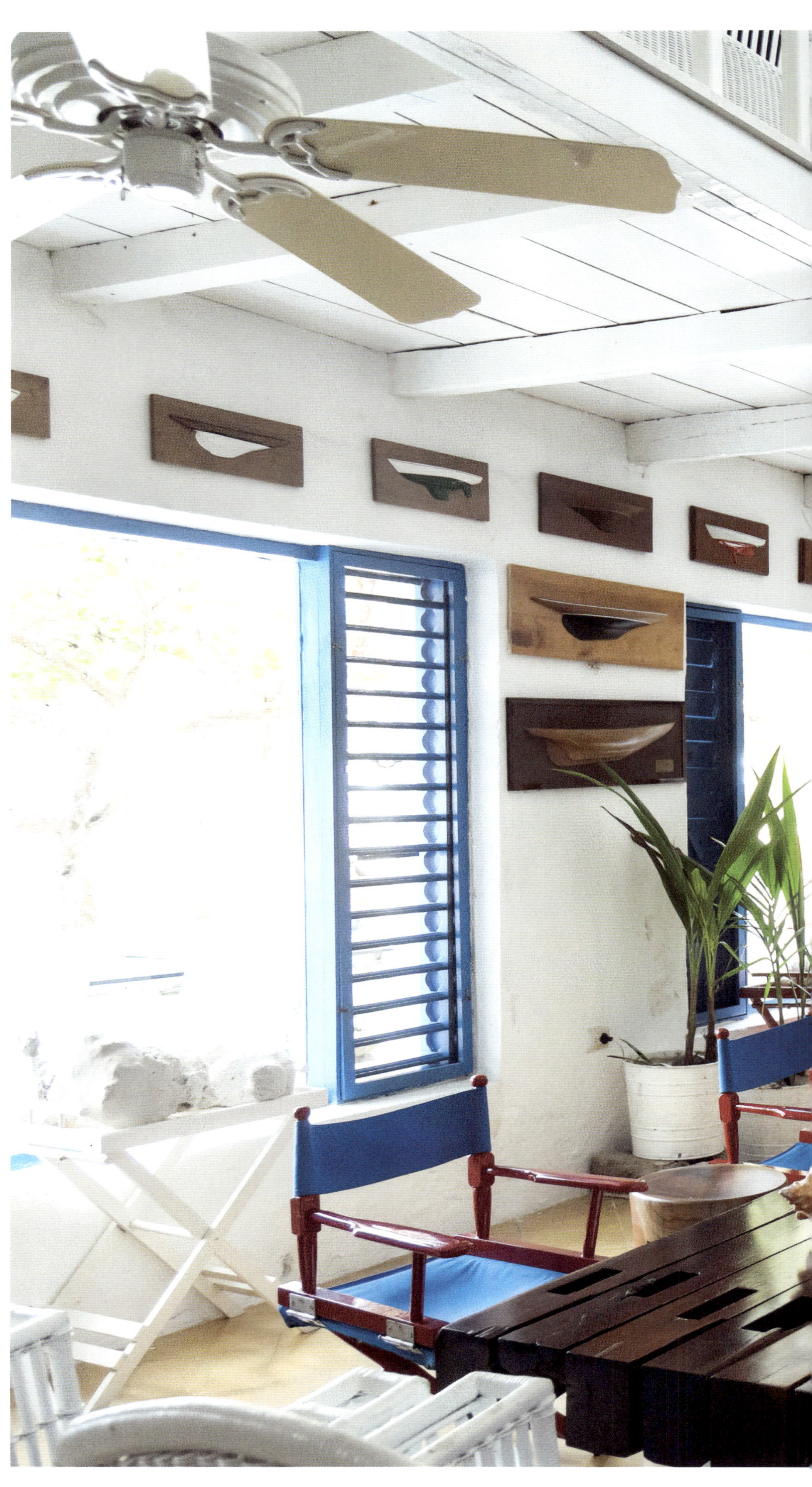

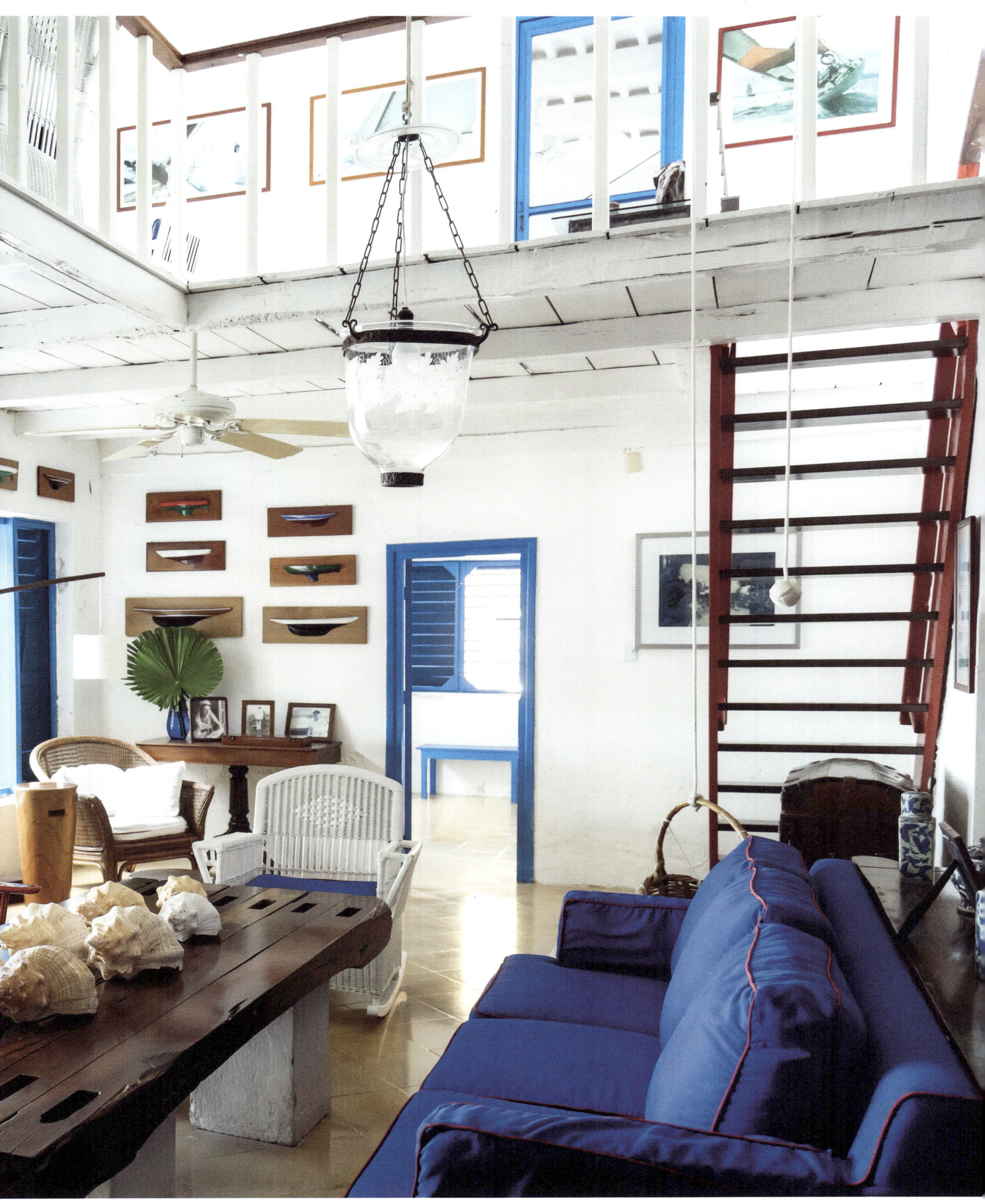

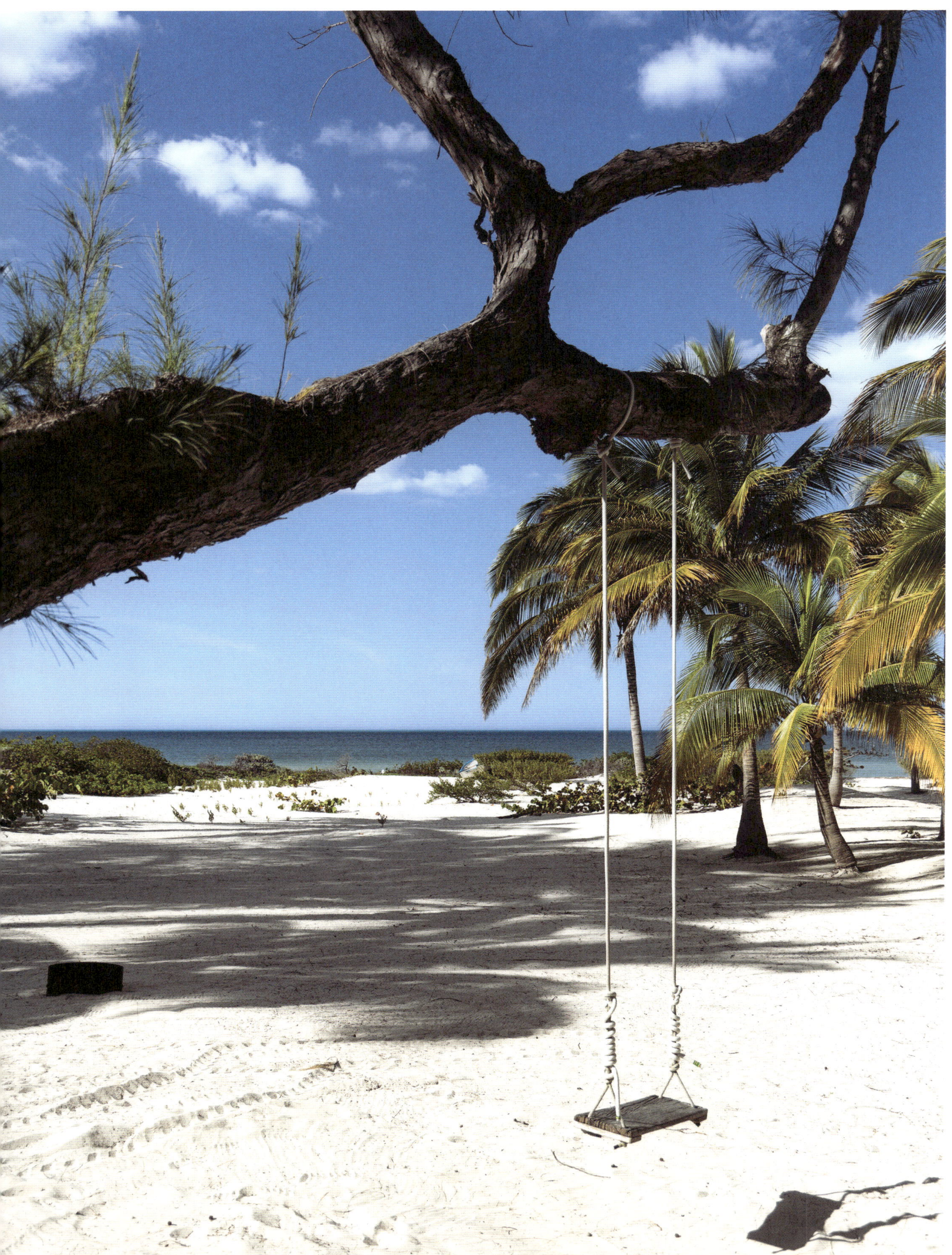

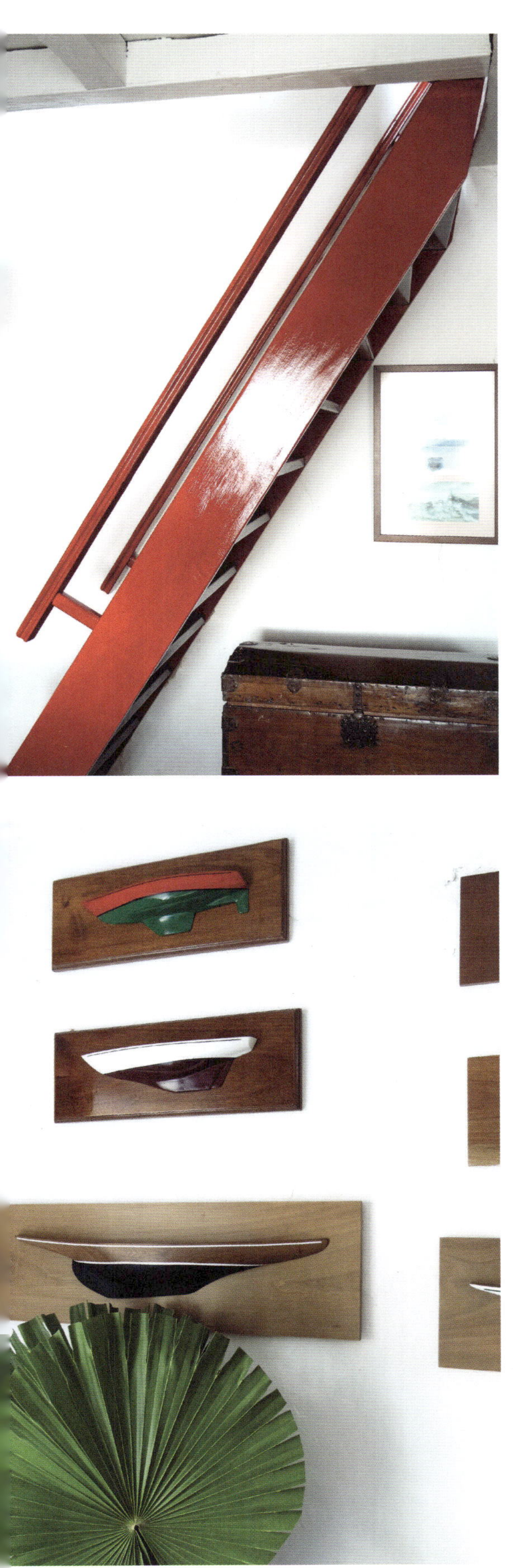

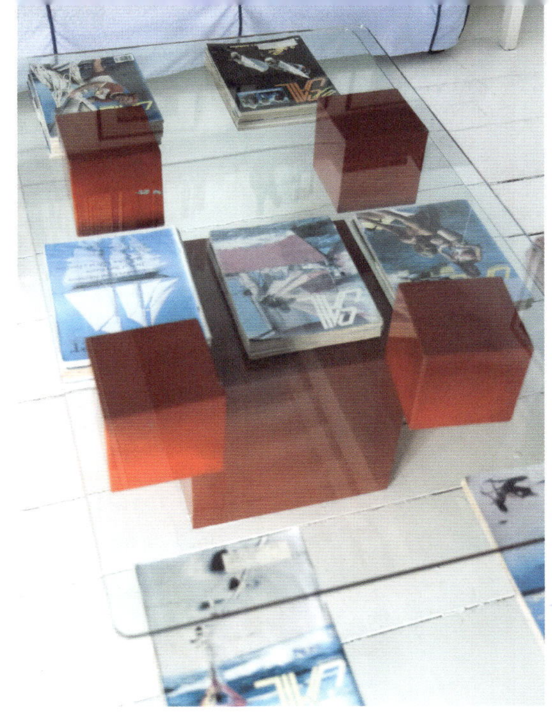

The family makes every effort to keep the nature around Miramar as unspoilt as possible. Luna's father planted coconut palms to protect the dunes, which are a vital habitat for thousands of sea turtles that are found only in the Gulf of Mexico. Every year, between July and September, they come ashore at Telchac to lay their eggs.

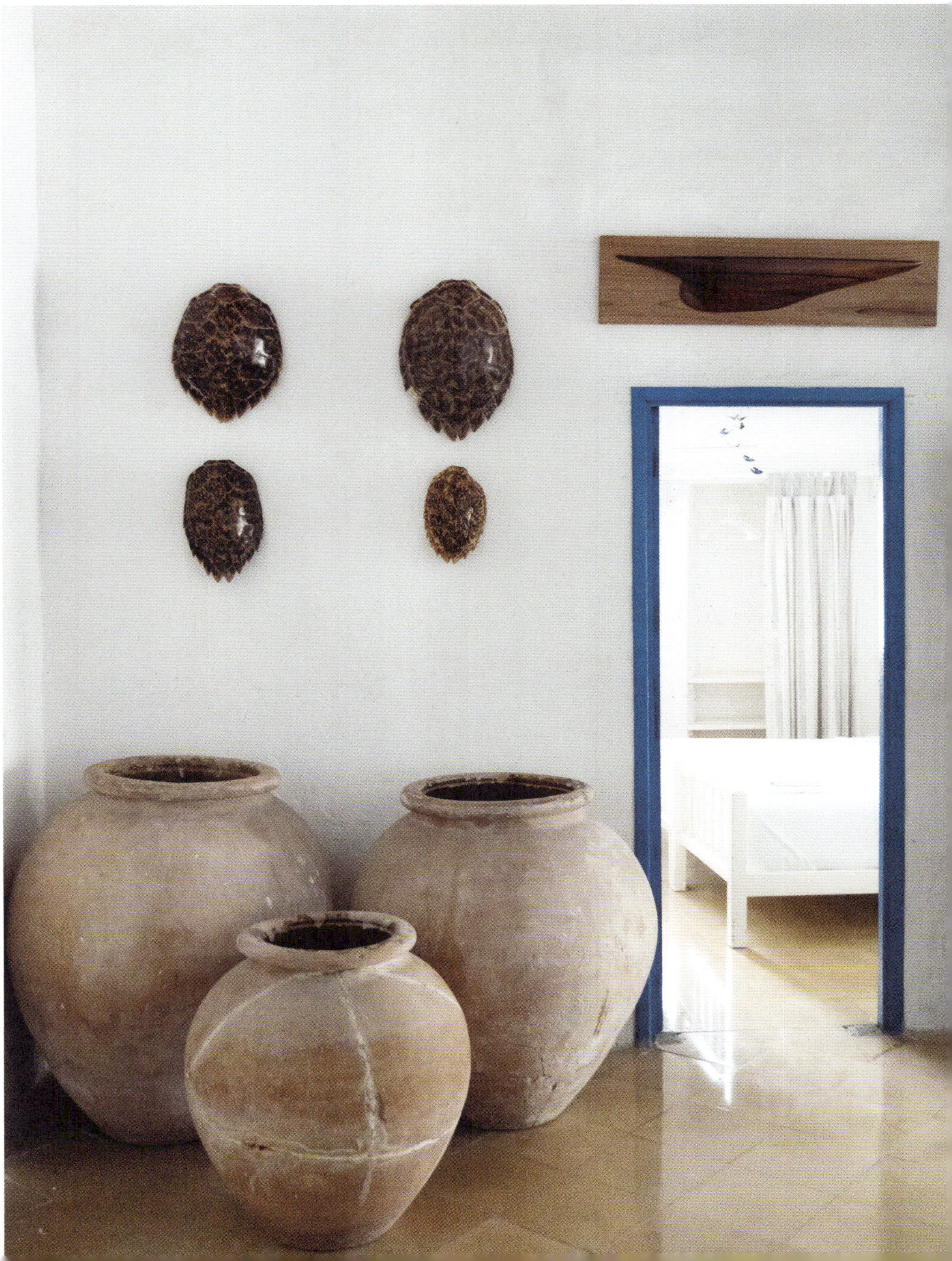

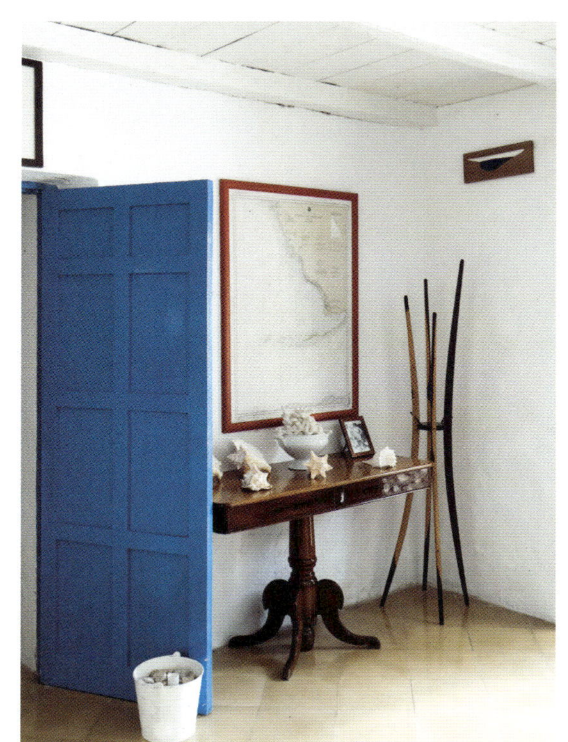
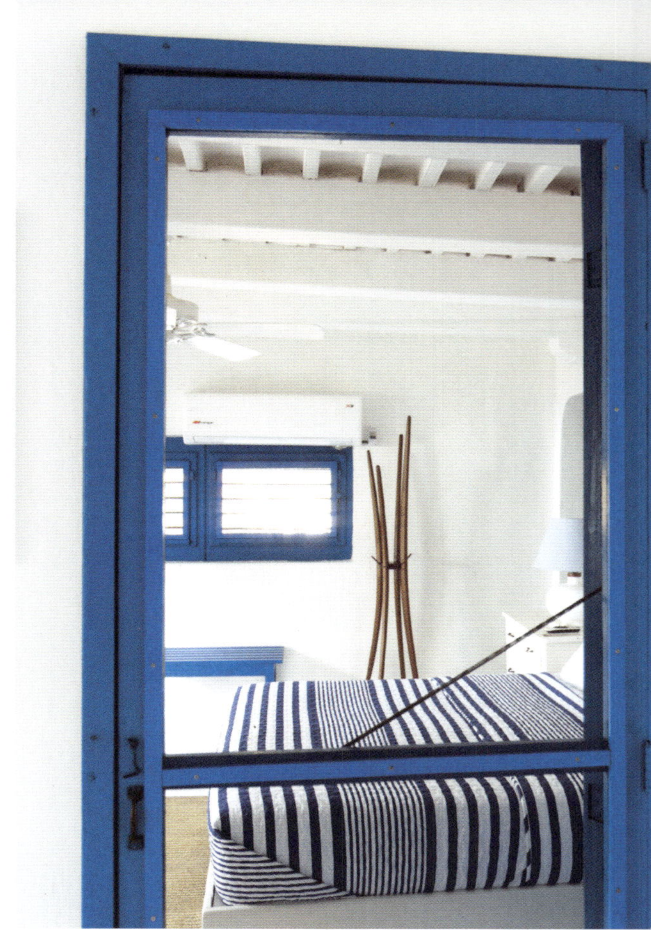
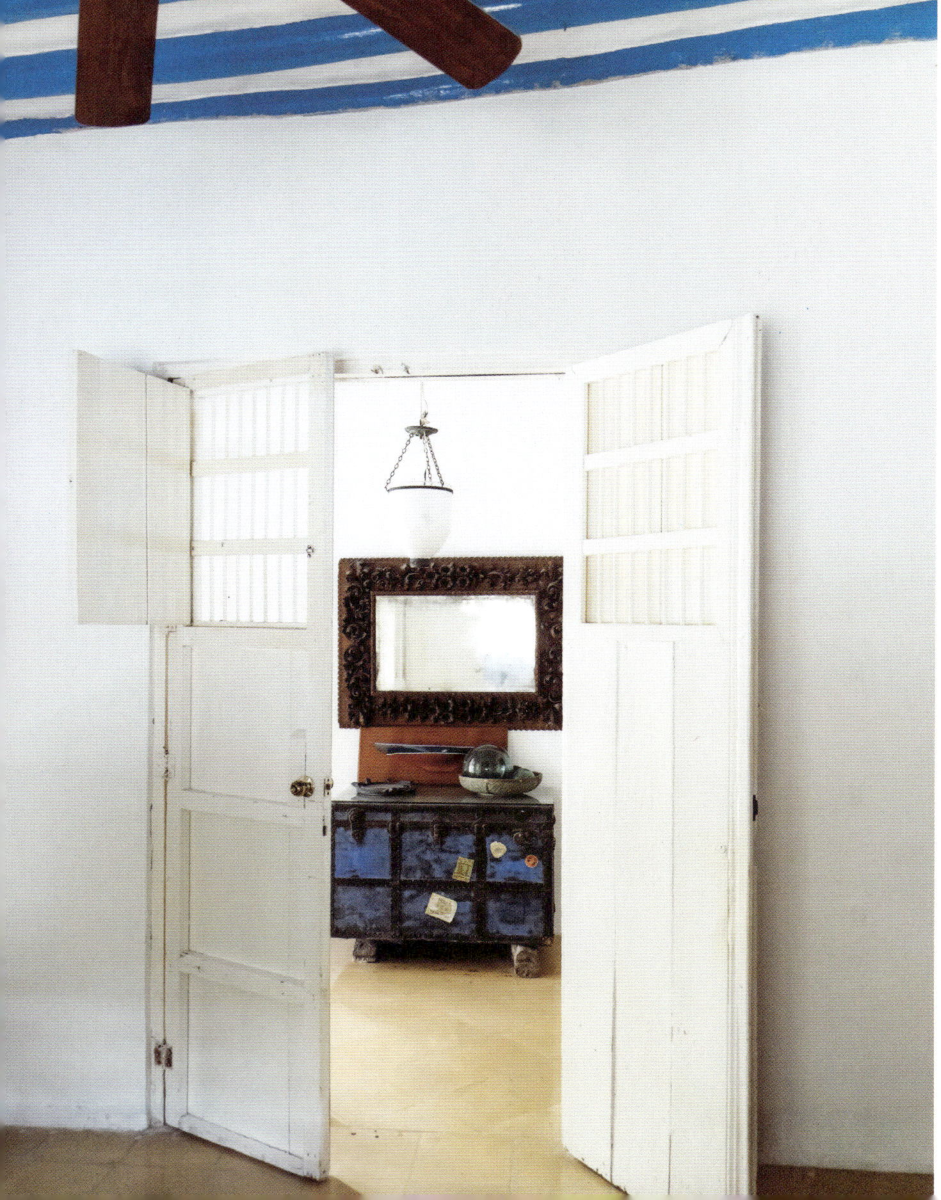
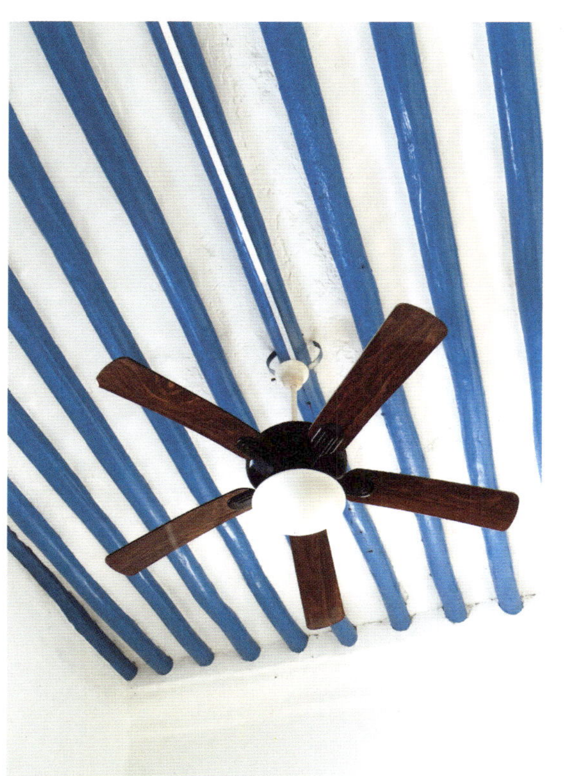

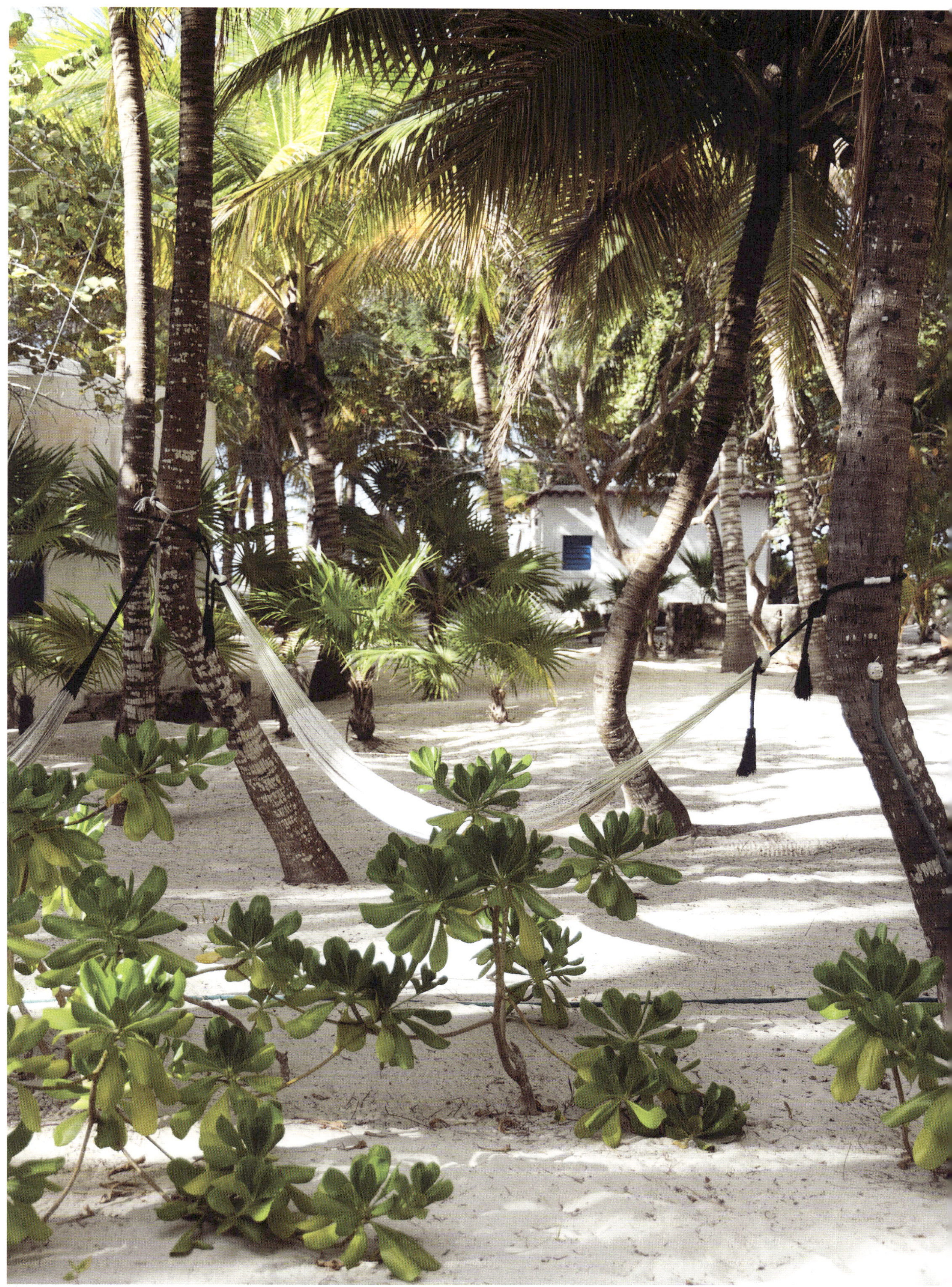

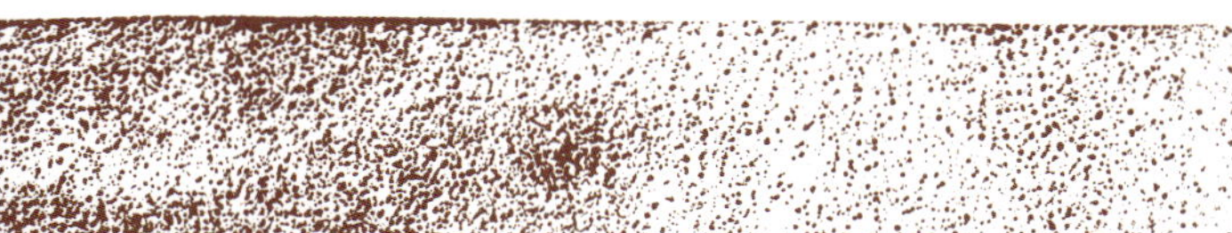

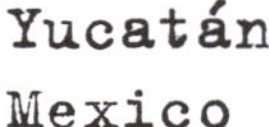

The Gulf of Mexico
is separated from the Caribbean Sea by the Mexican peninsula of Yucatán. A stunning and unique region, it is known for its blend of centuries-old Maya ruins and miles and miles of white sandy beaches. Because this strip of land is bookended by water on all three sides, the sea is everywhere you look - in the air, in the way the light shifts throughout the day - even if you venture deeper inland.

SANTA ELENA

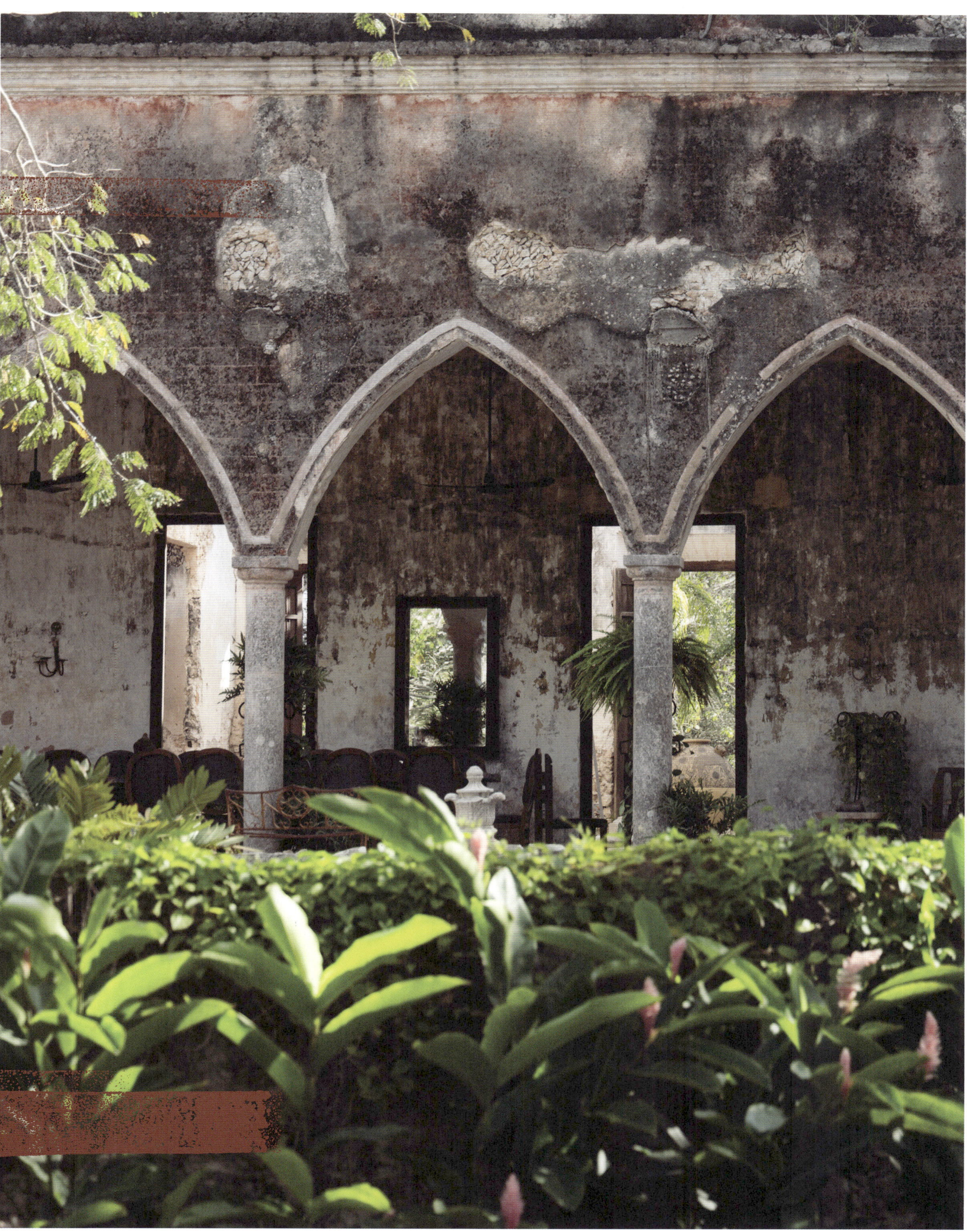

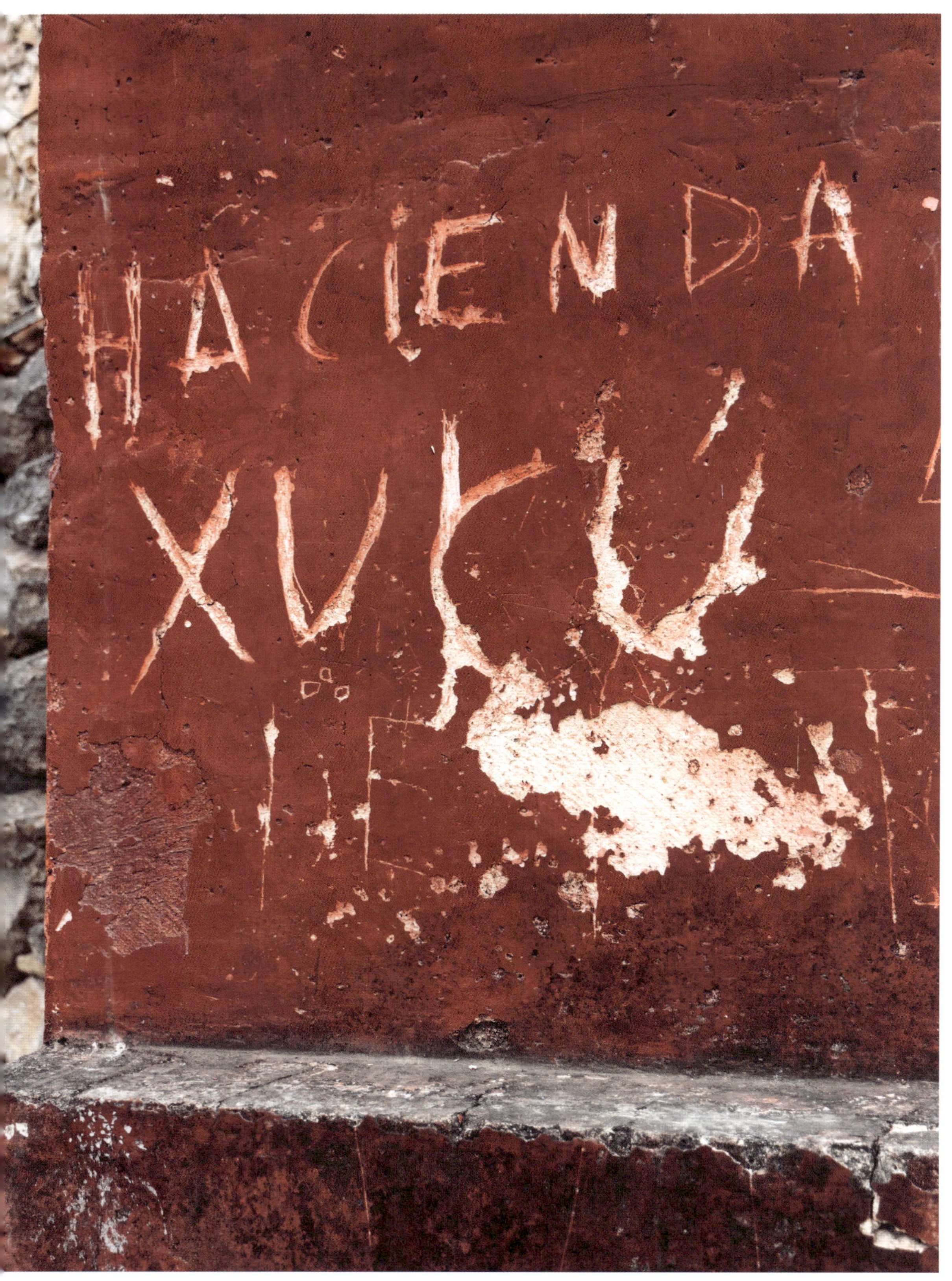
HACIENDA

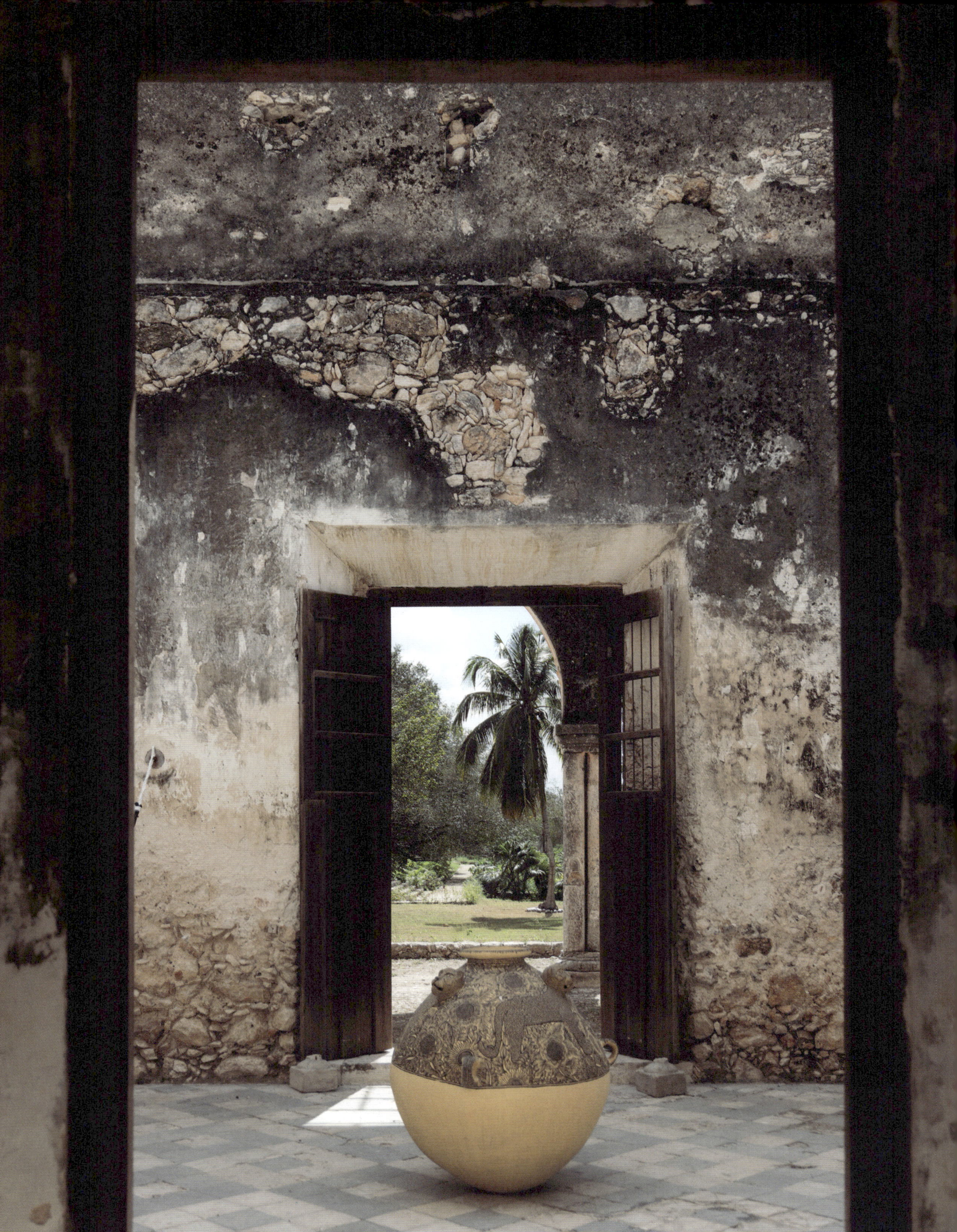

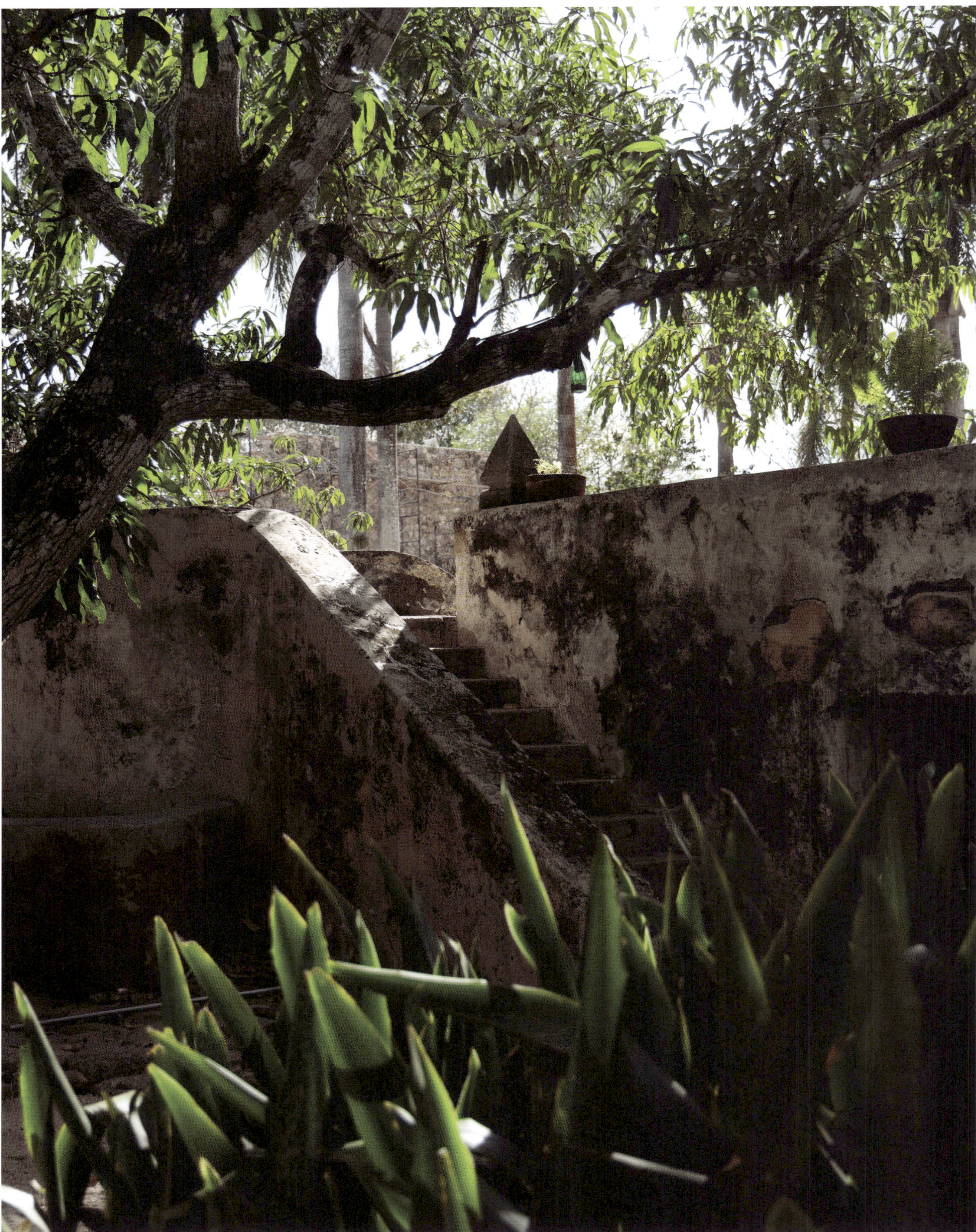

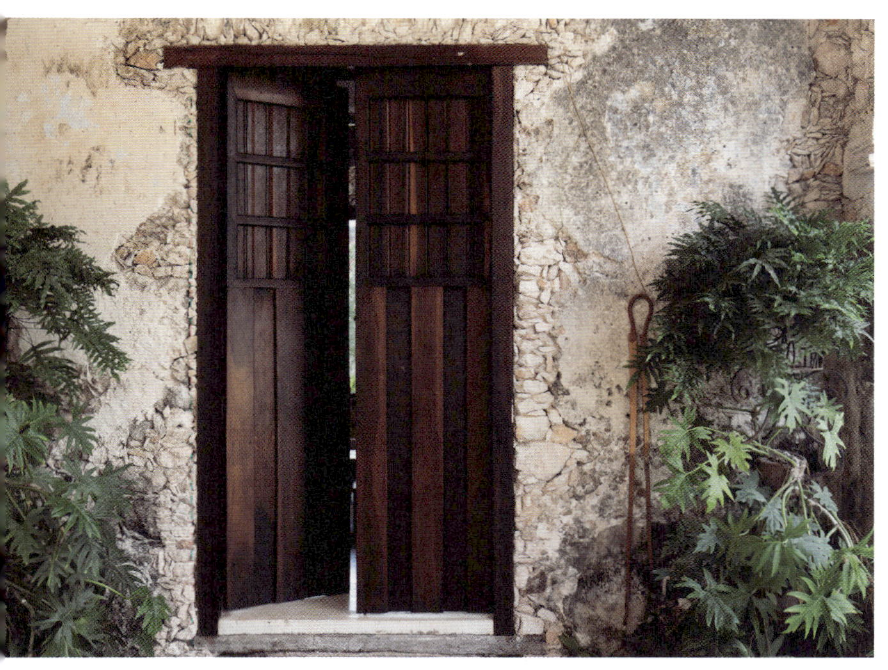

To the south of Yucatán's cultural capital Mérida, tucked away within the confines of the sprawling jungle near the village of Santa Elena, sits Xucu, a historic estate with a hacienda in its heart. This genuinely enchanting building dates from around 1880, when it was built as a henequen farm, becoming part of the 'green gold' boom that drove Yucatán's economy. Following the decline of the henequen market, the haçienda was repurposed for livestock production until the 1970s, after which it fell into a state of severe disrepair. When the current owner acquired the property in the early 2000s, it was overrun by the jungle and weakened by the region's extreme climate.

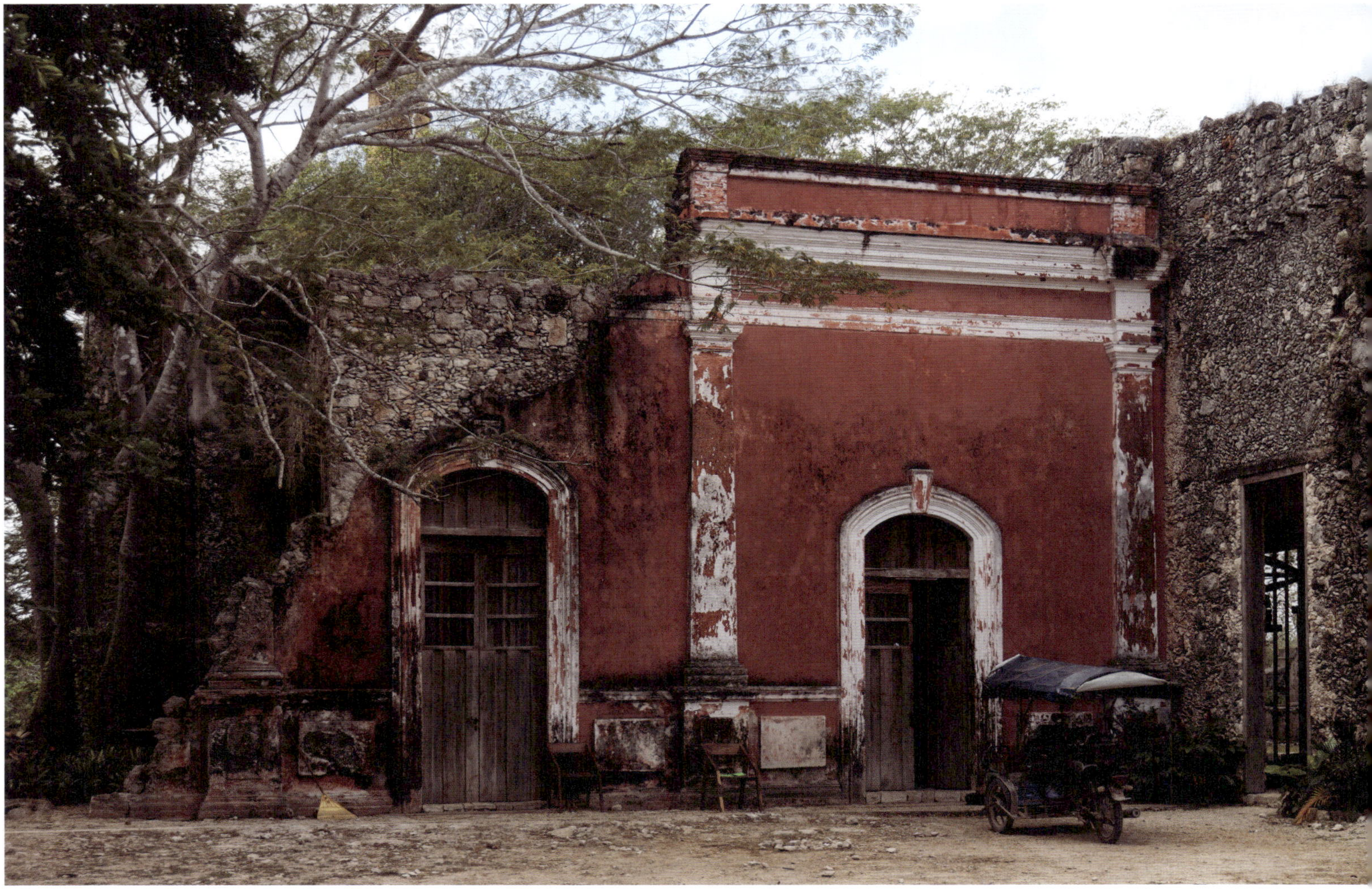

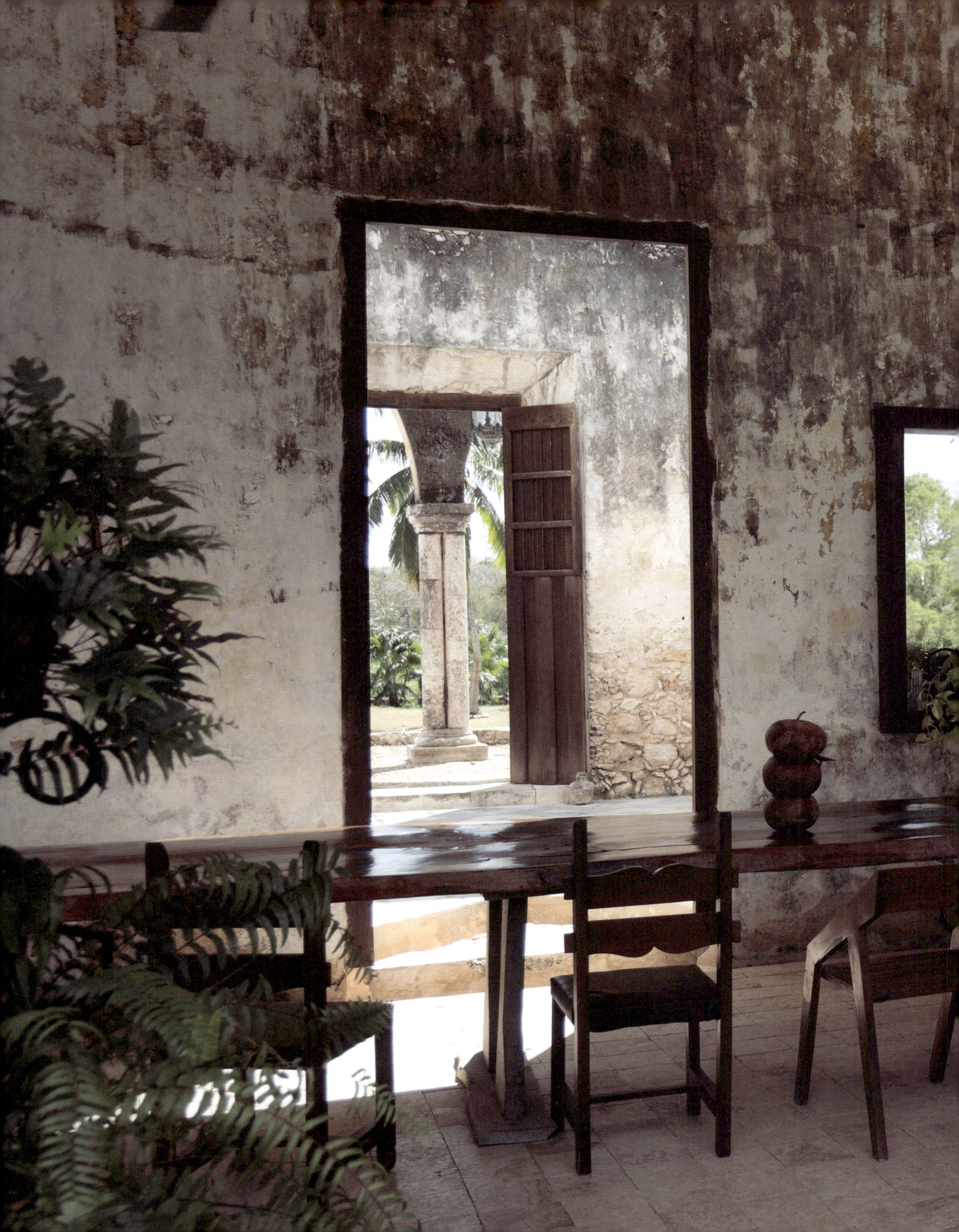

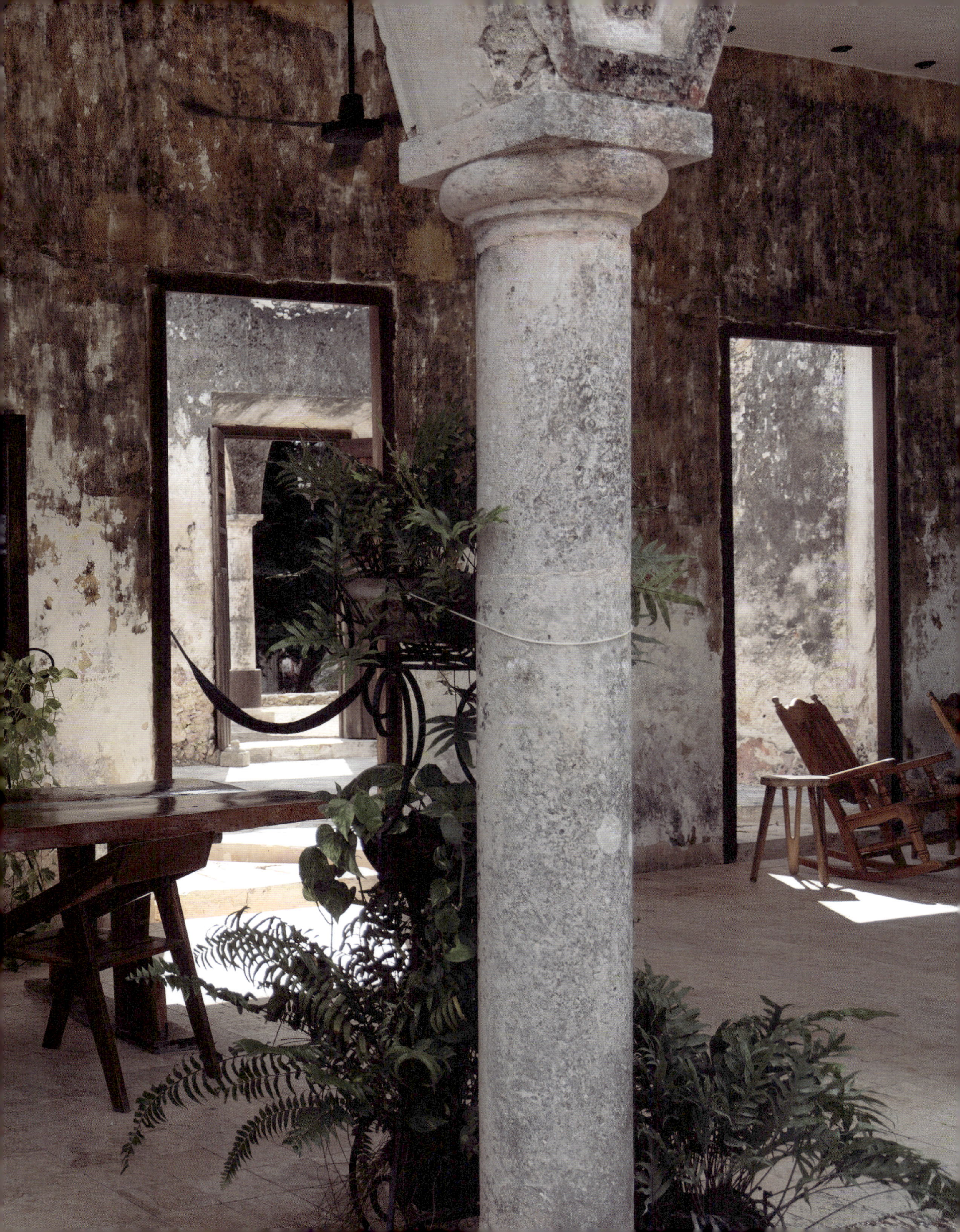

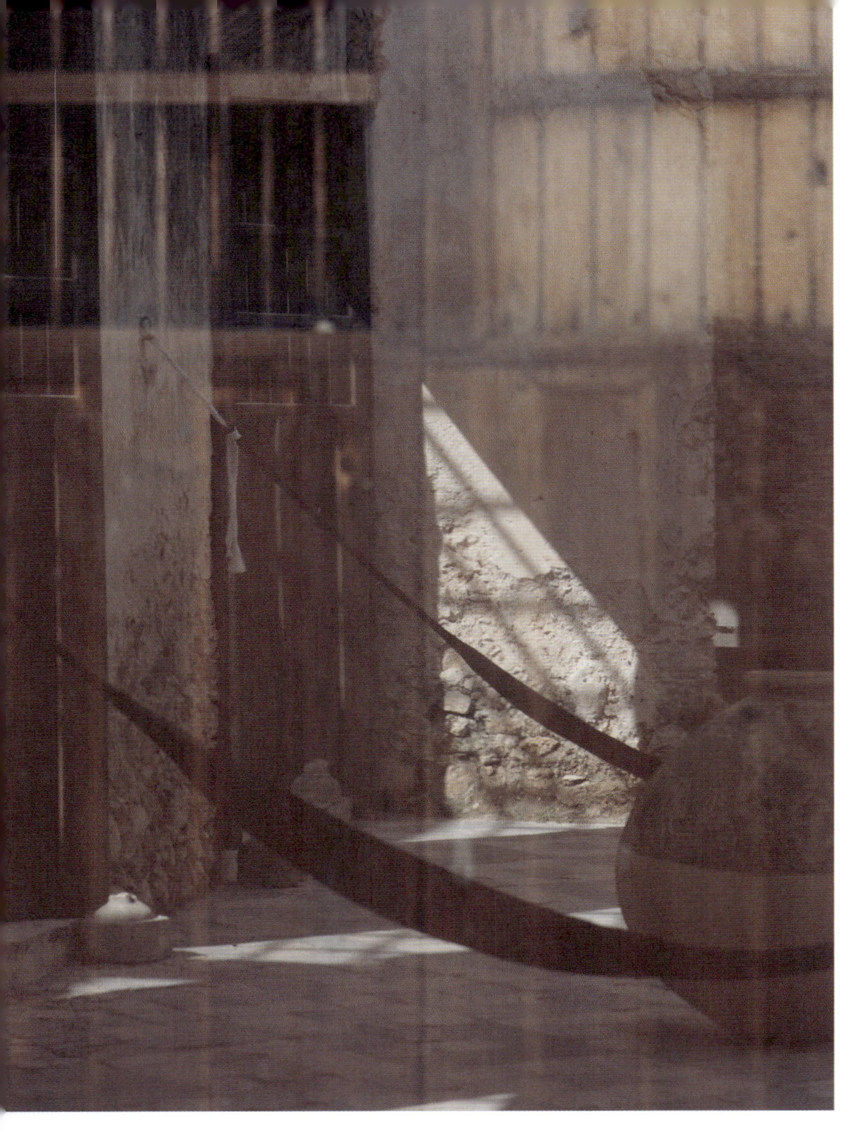

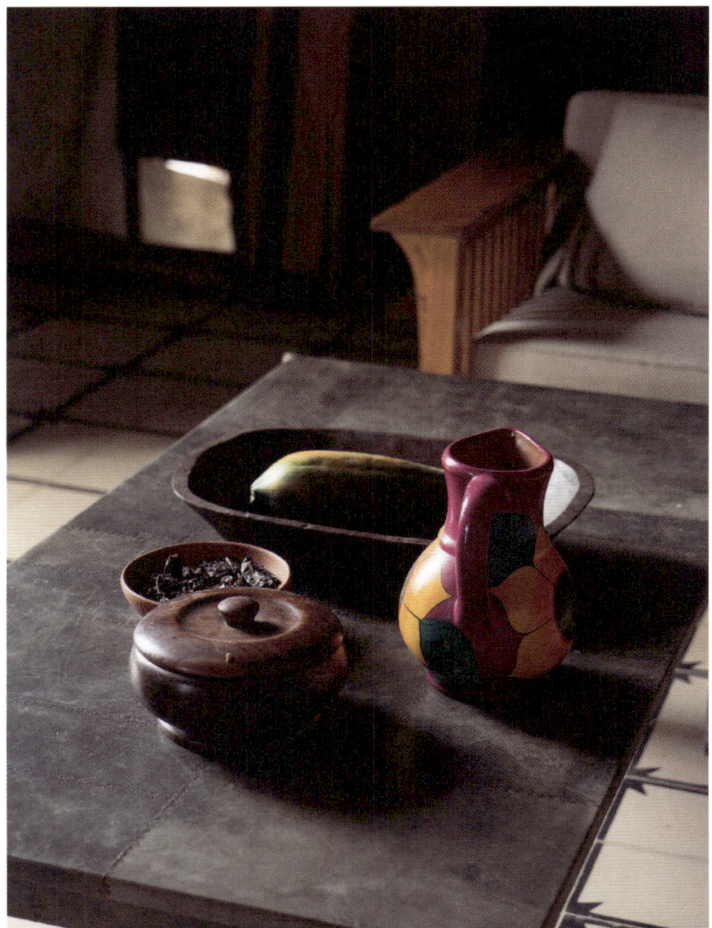

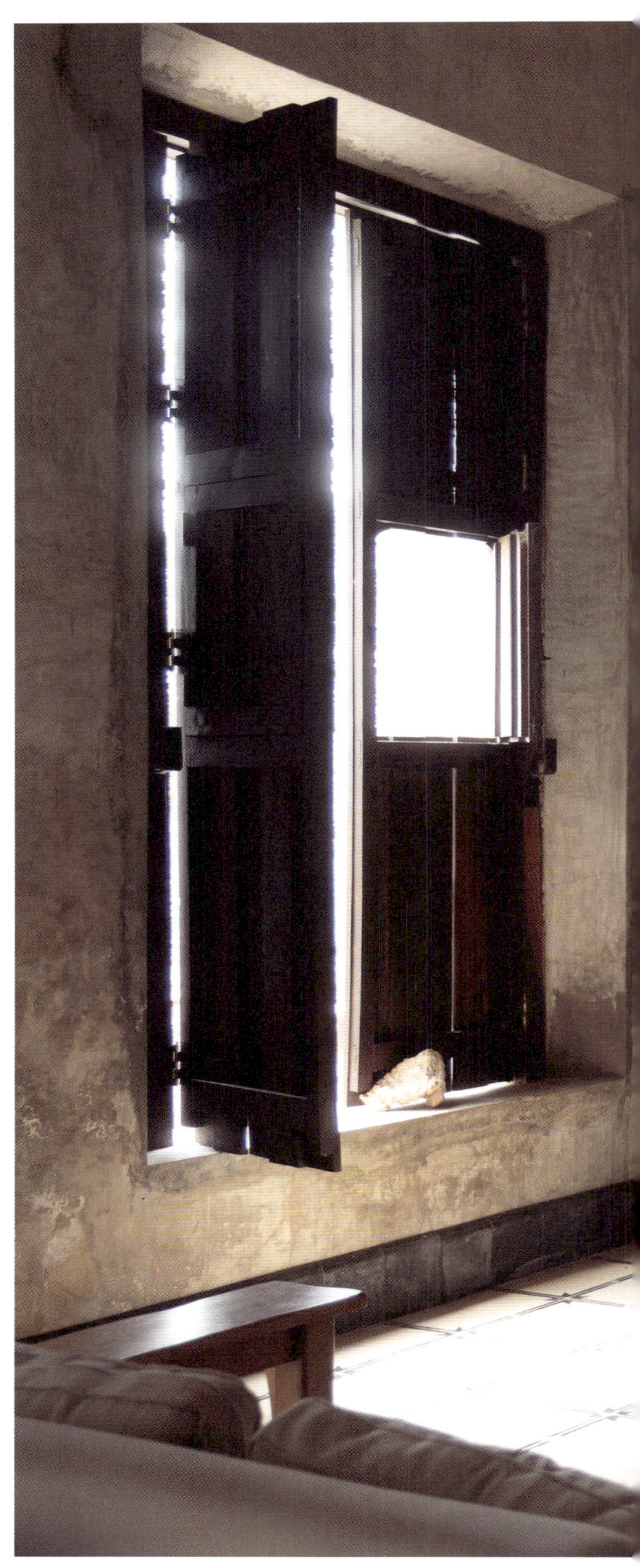

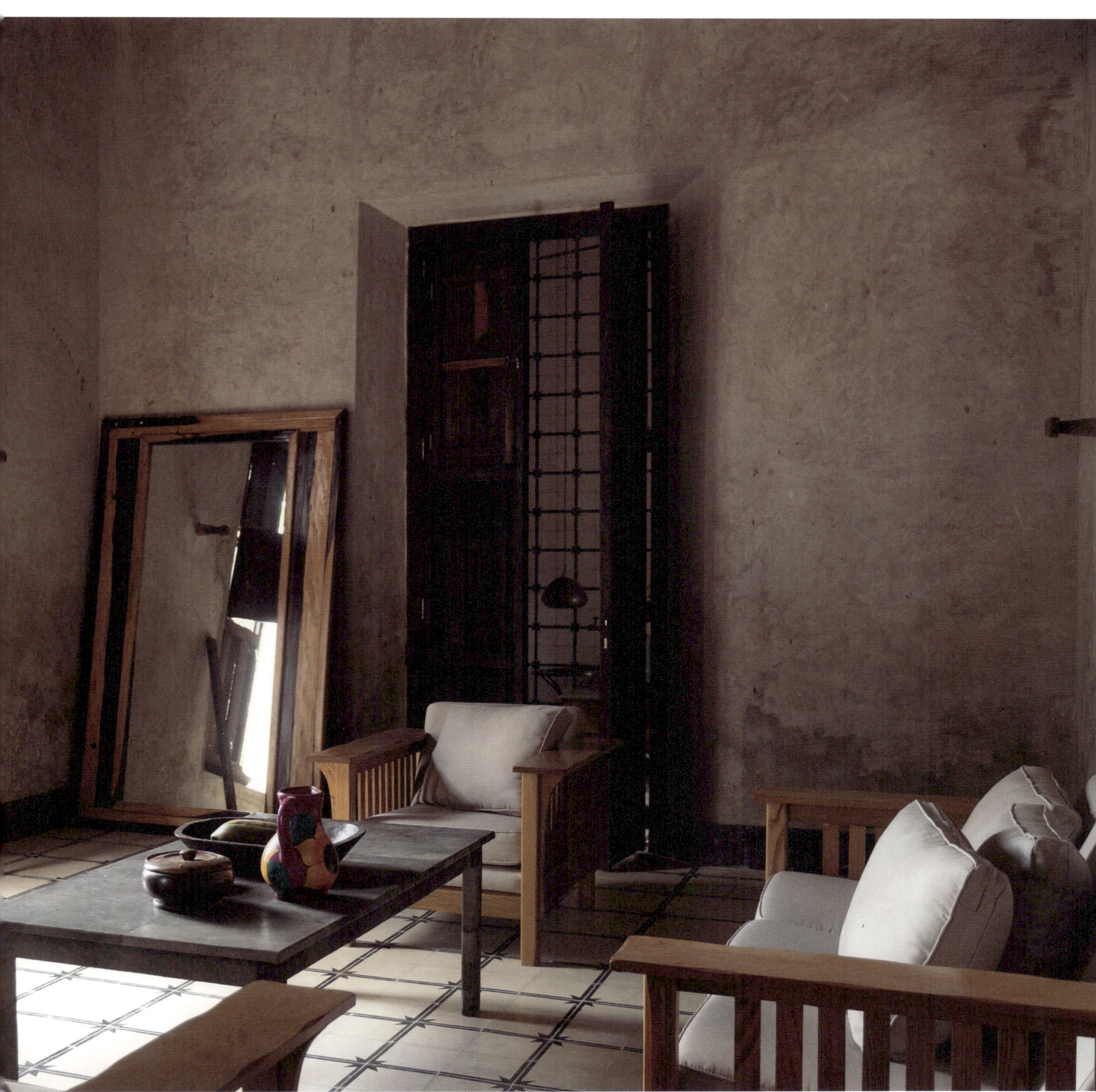

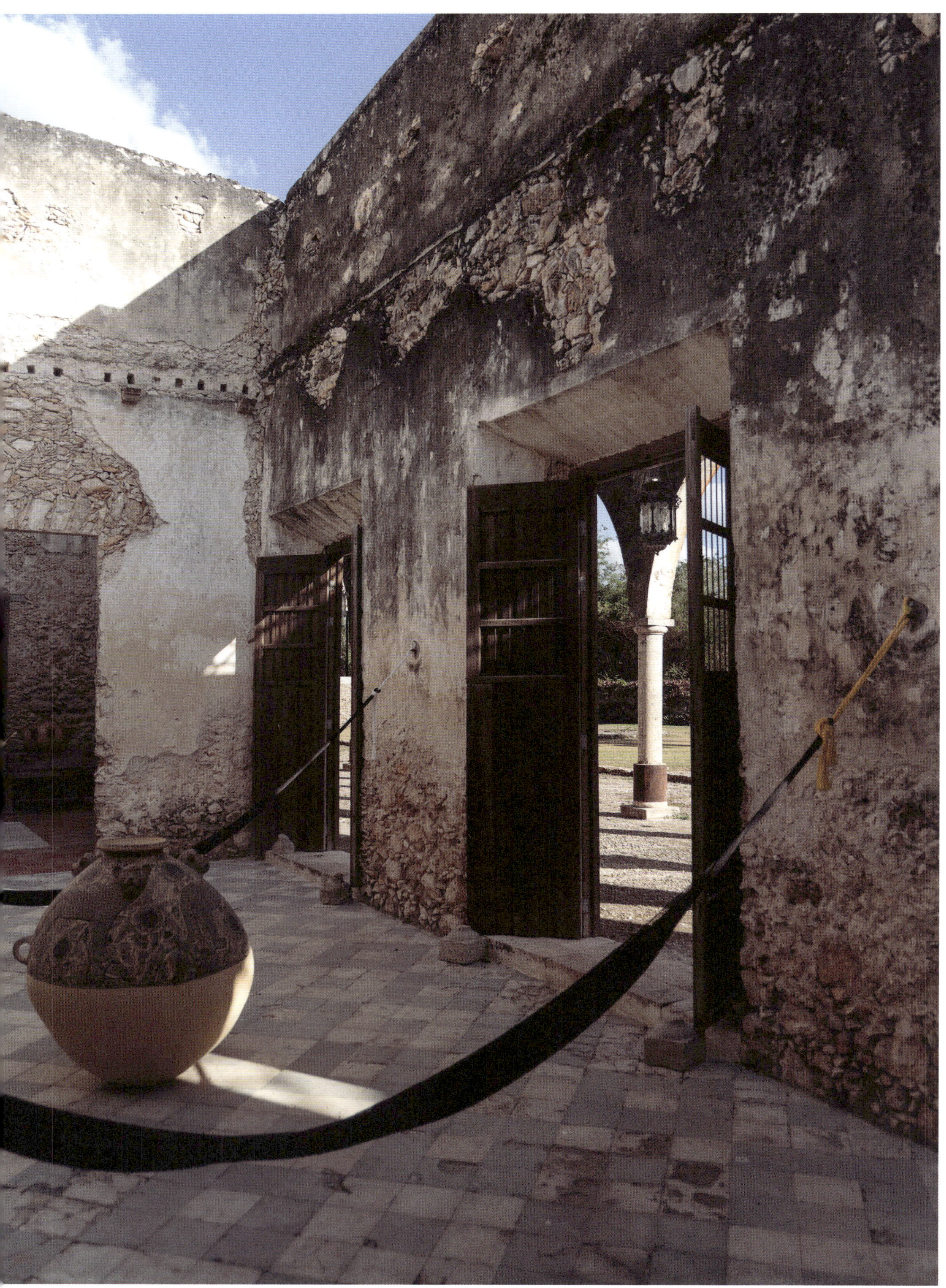

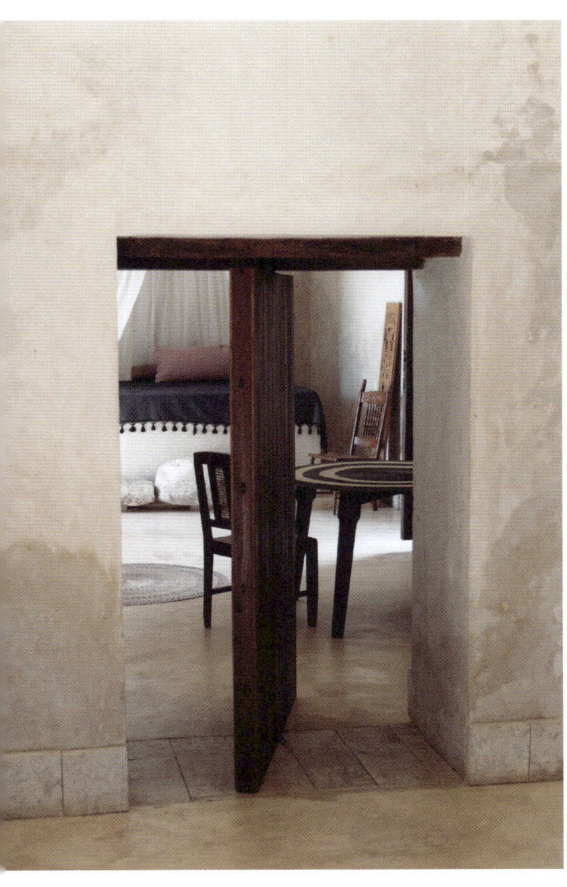

The project's sheer magnitude may have seemed overwhelming at the time, but today, the hacienda has been restored to its former glory, and a renewed sense of life and beauty has been added to its rich history. Emmanuel Picault of the Mexico City-based architecture studio Chic by Accident managed to incorporate all necessary modern comforts and functionalities in subtle ways while preserving the ruins and retaining the essence of the hacienda's story.

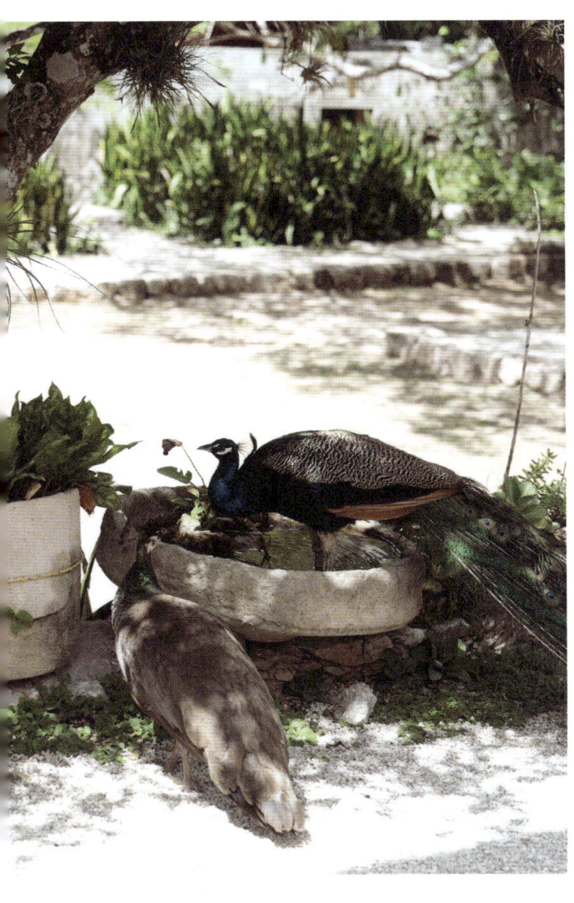

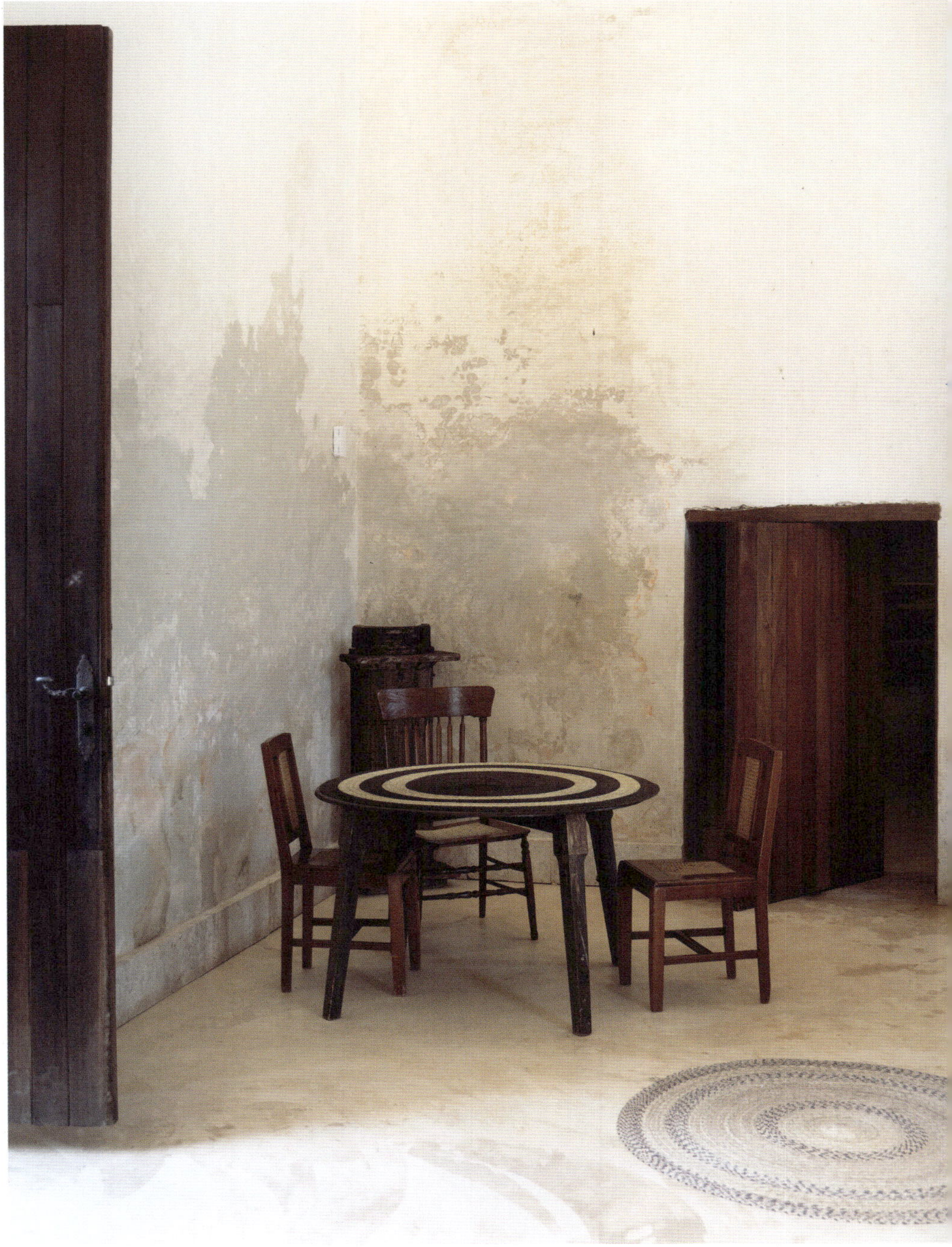

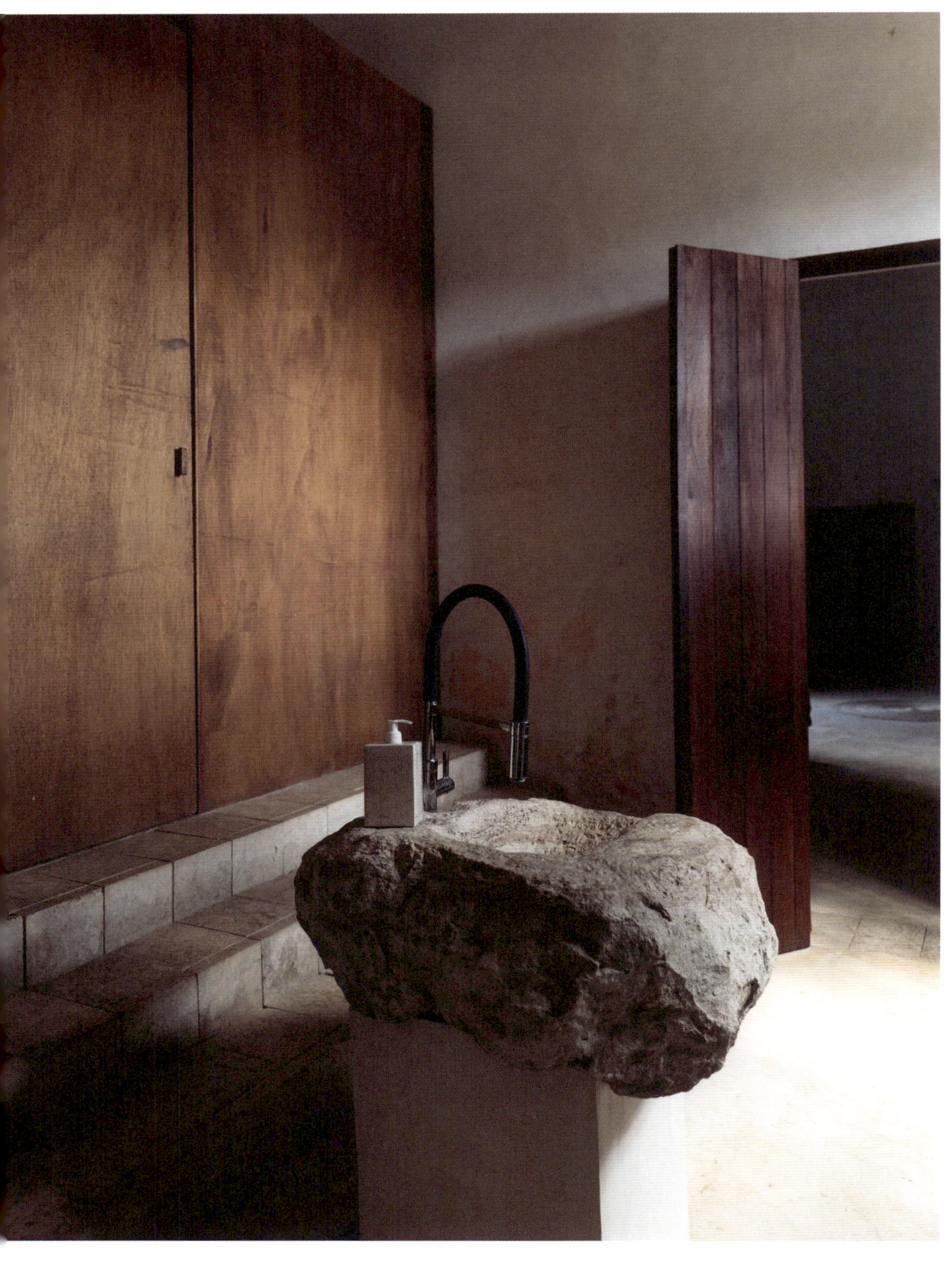

The decoration was guided by the same principle as the architecture: to create a living space that meets today's standards of comfort and feels modern while simultaneously retaining its poetic past. Emmanuel intuitively chose to work with local materials and artisans, drawing on Yucatán's rich craft traditions. The furniture he picked out is often raw, simple, and textural, complementing the aged walls and weathered structures. Some of the objects blend seamlessly into the environment, whereas others make a bold, contemporary statement.

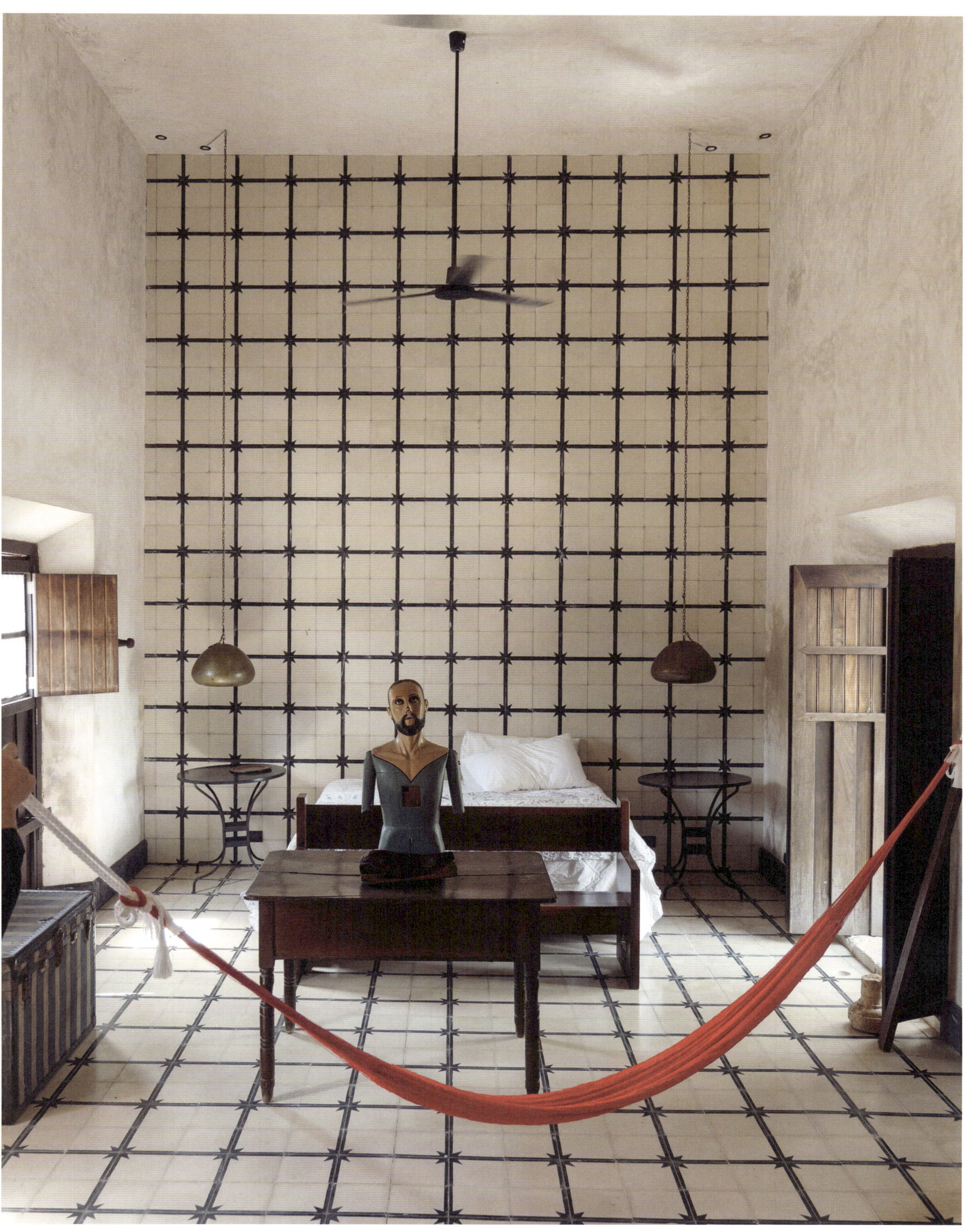

The hacienda's beauty stems from the contrasts throughout: between blending in and standing out, past and present, the untouched and the refined. This is echoed by the surrounding landscape, which is shaped by the wild and untamed force of the jungle as well as the serenity of the sea, reminding us of the never-ending ebb and flow of time.

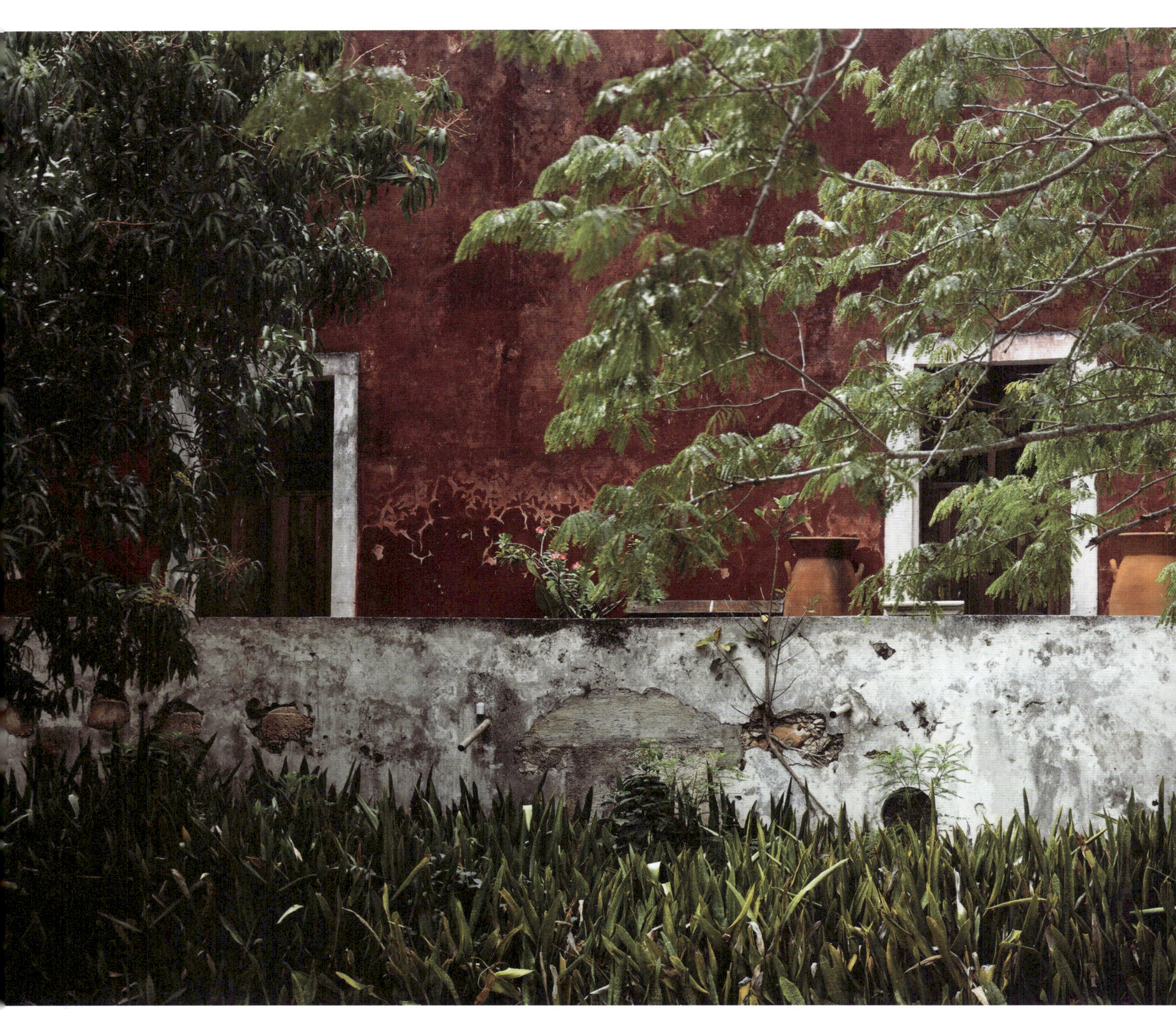

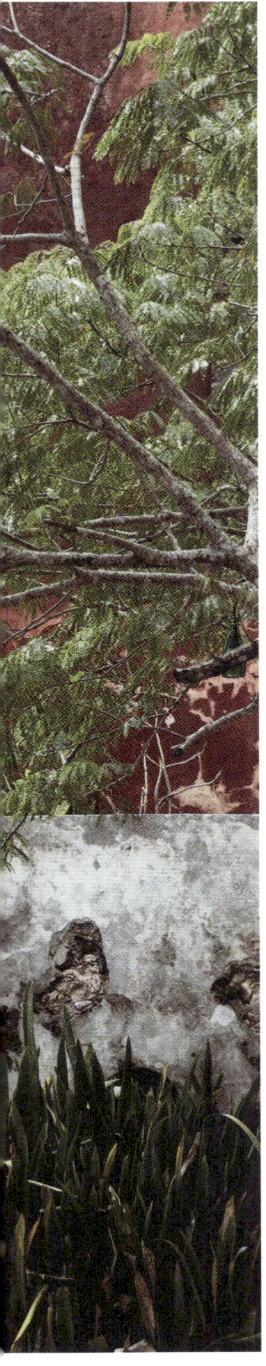

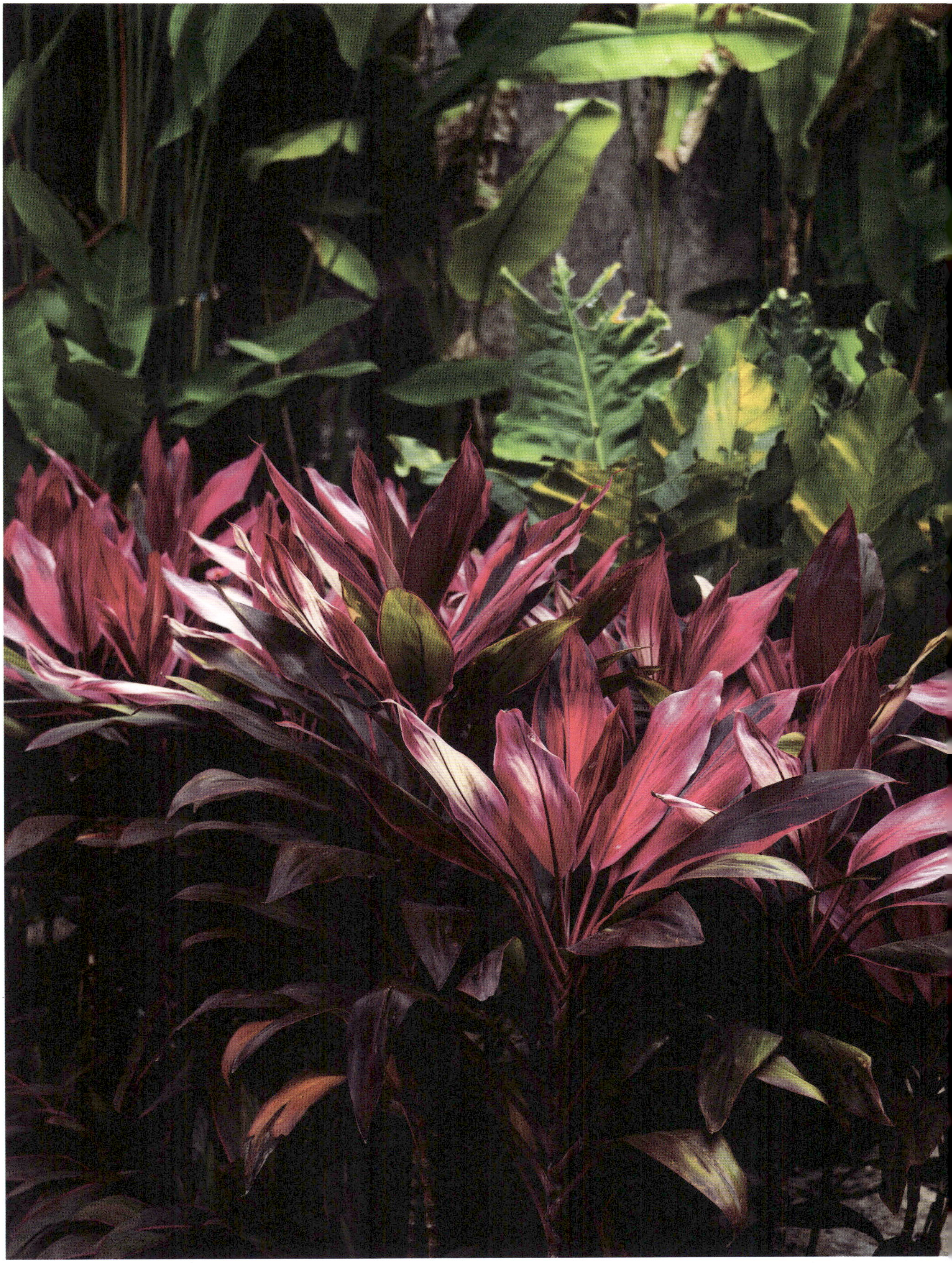

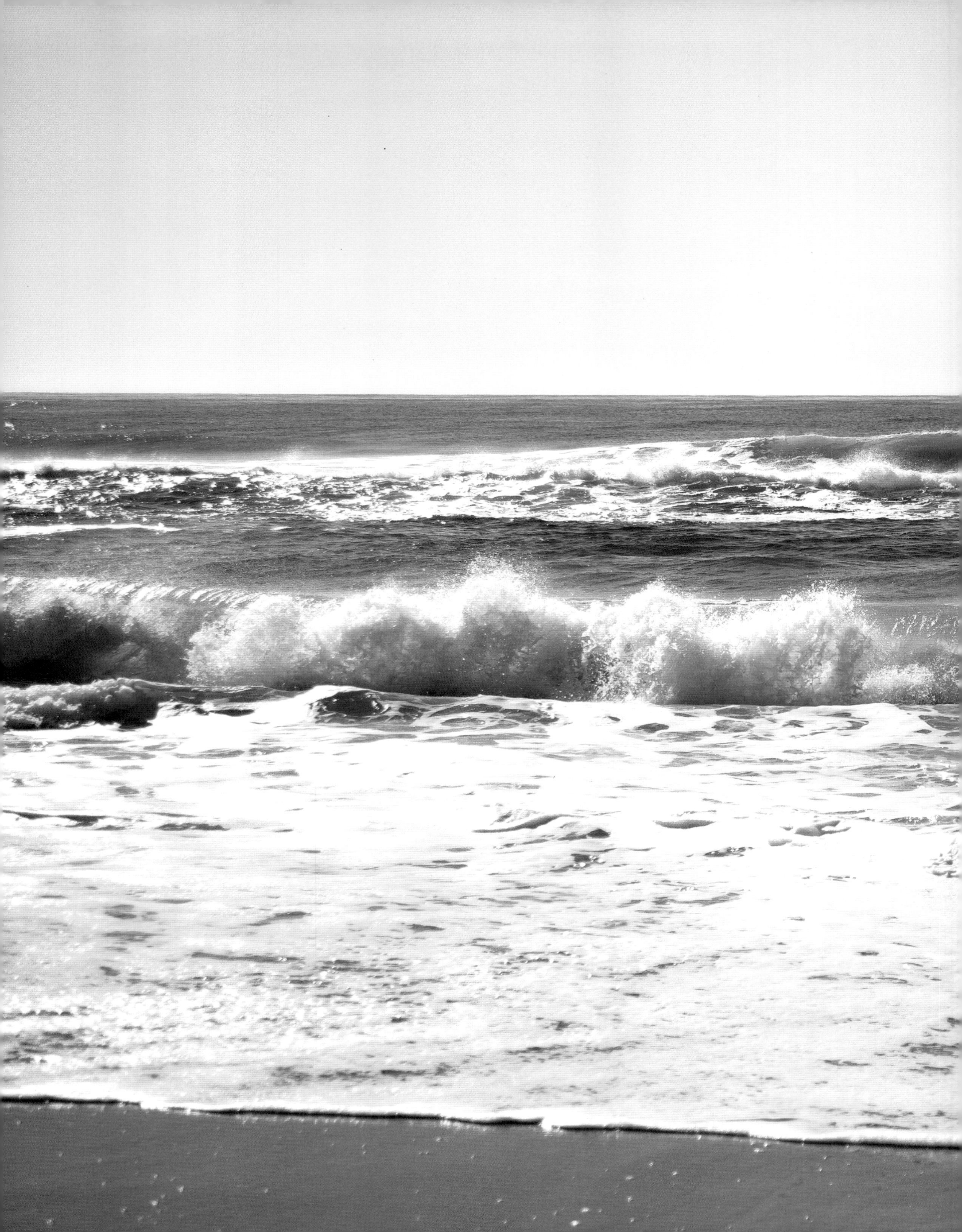

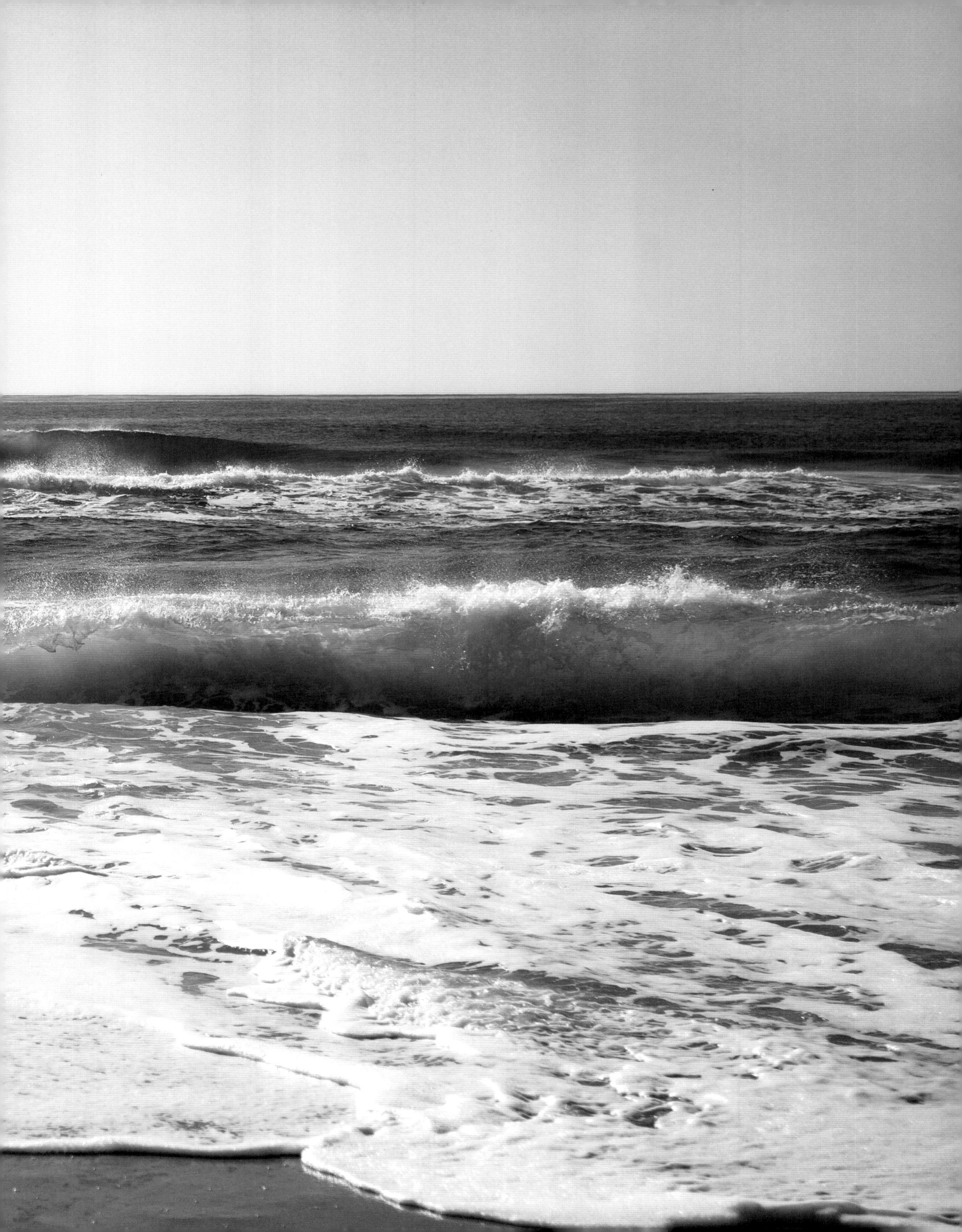

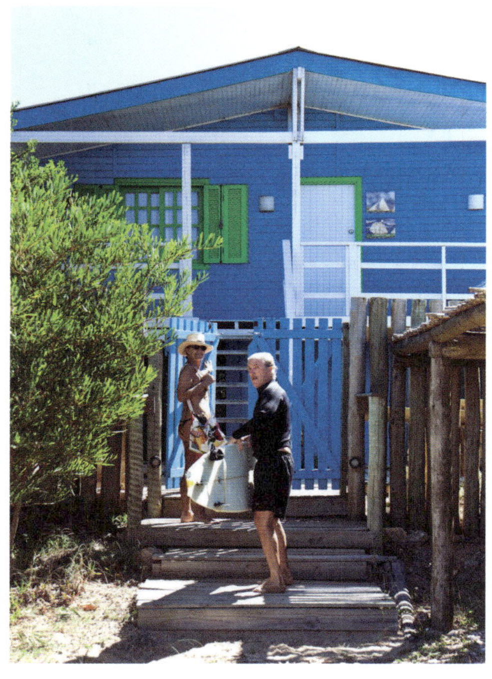

LA PEDRERA

Rocha
Uruguay

The most picturesque village on the Atlantic Coast
in the east of Uruguay has to be La Pedrera. One of the oldest seaside resorts in the country, it has managed to preserve the quaint spirit of a small town of the olden days. Here you don't need to hop into your car to grab a coffee or something delicious to eat. The atmosphere is laid back, and the locals know how to celebrate carnival. The town is divided in two by a rock hill: its main street ends in an elevated promenade, making it feel as if you are standing on the bow of a ship, with a striking view of the sweeping beach and the ocean. It is all the more enchanting in the evening when the sun disappears behind the horizon, and the moon rises.

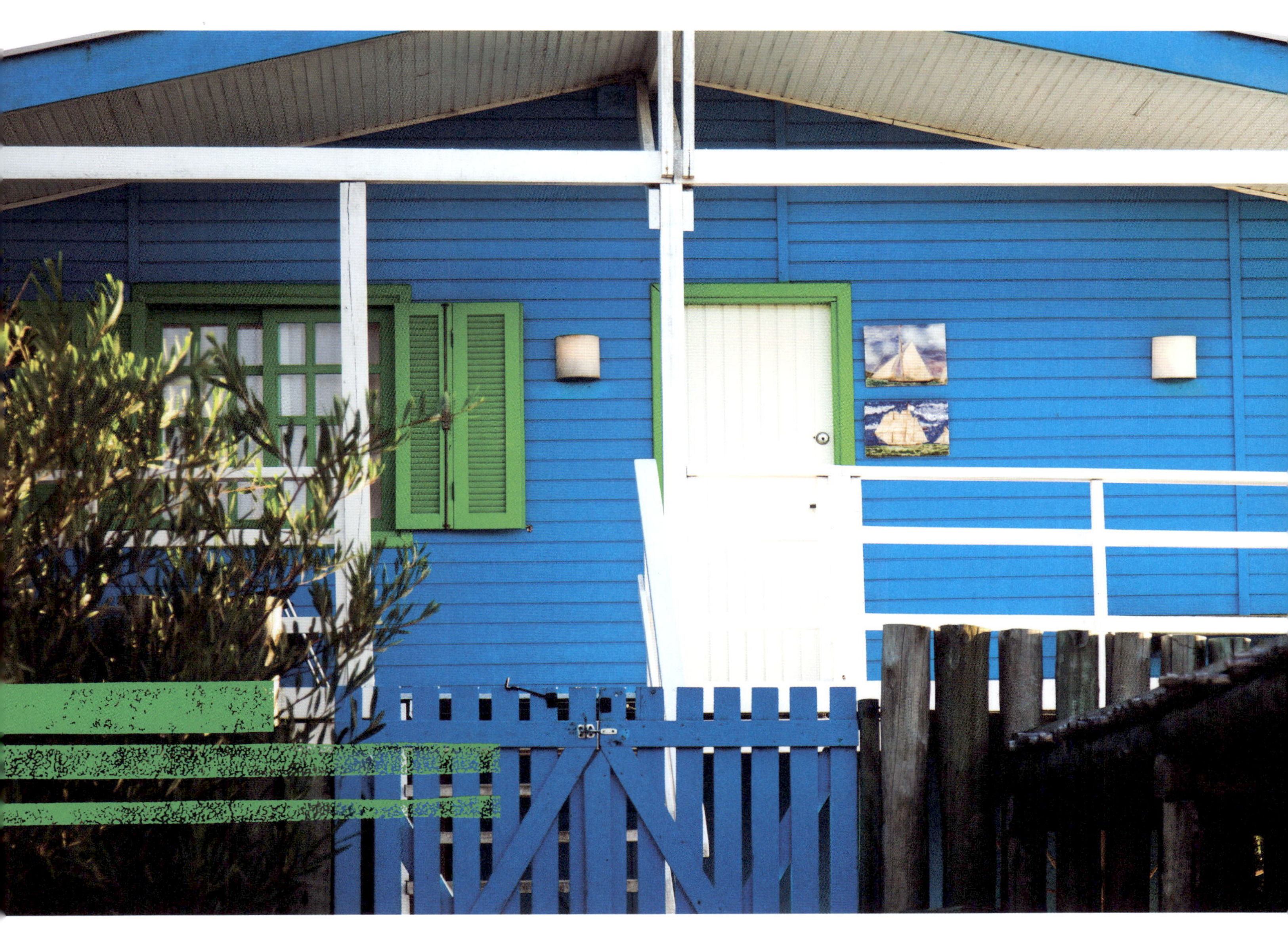

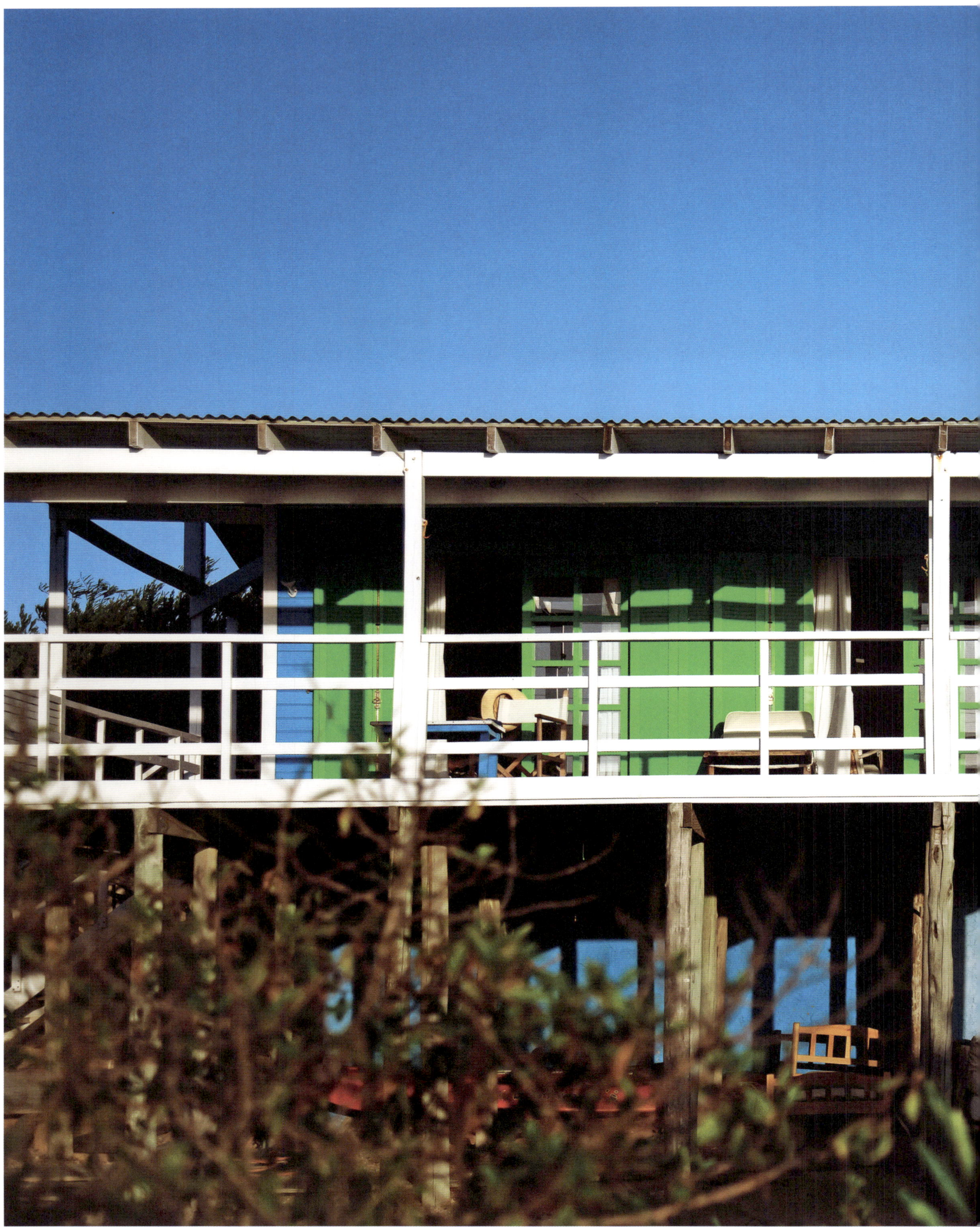

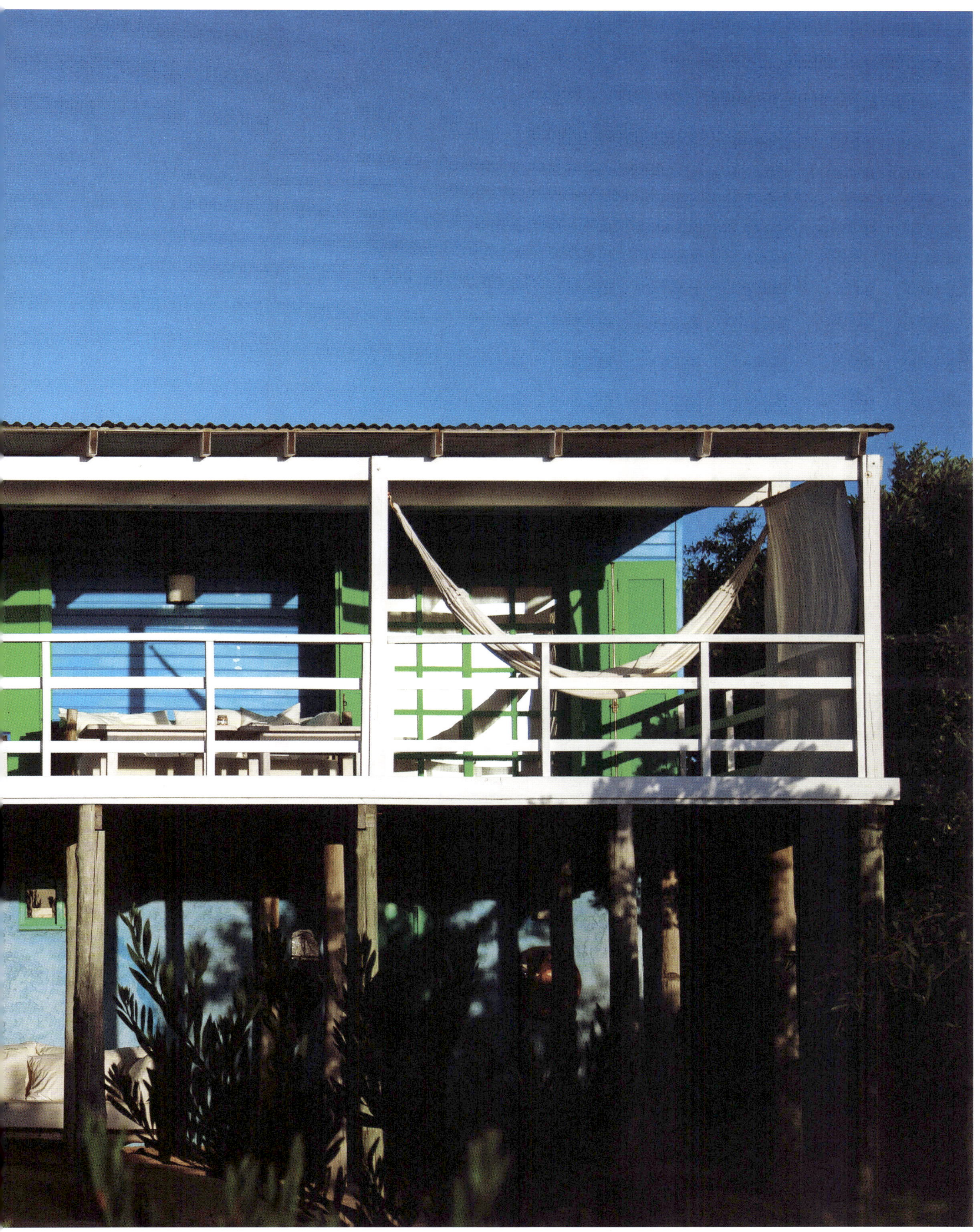

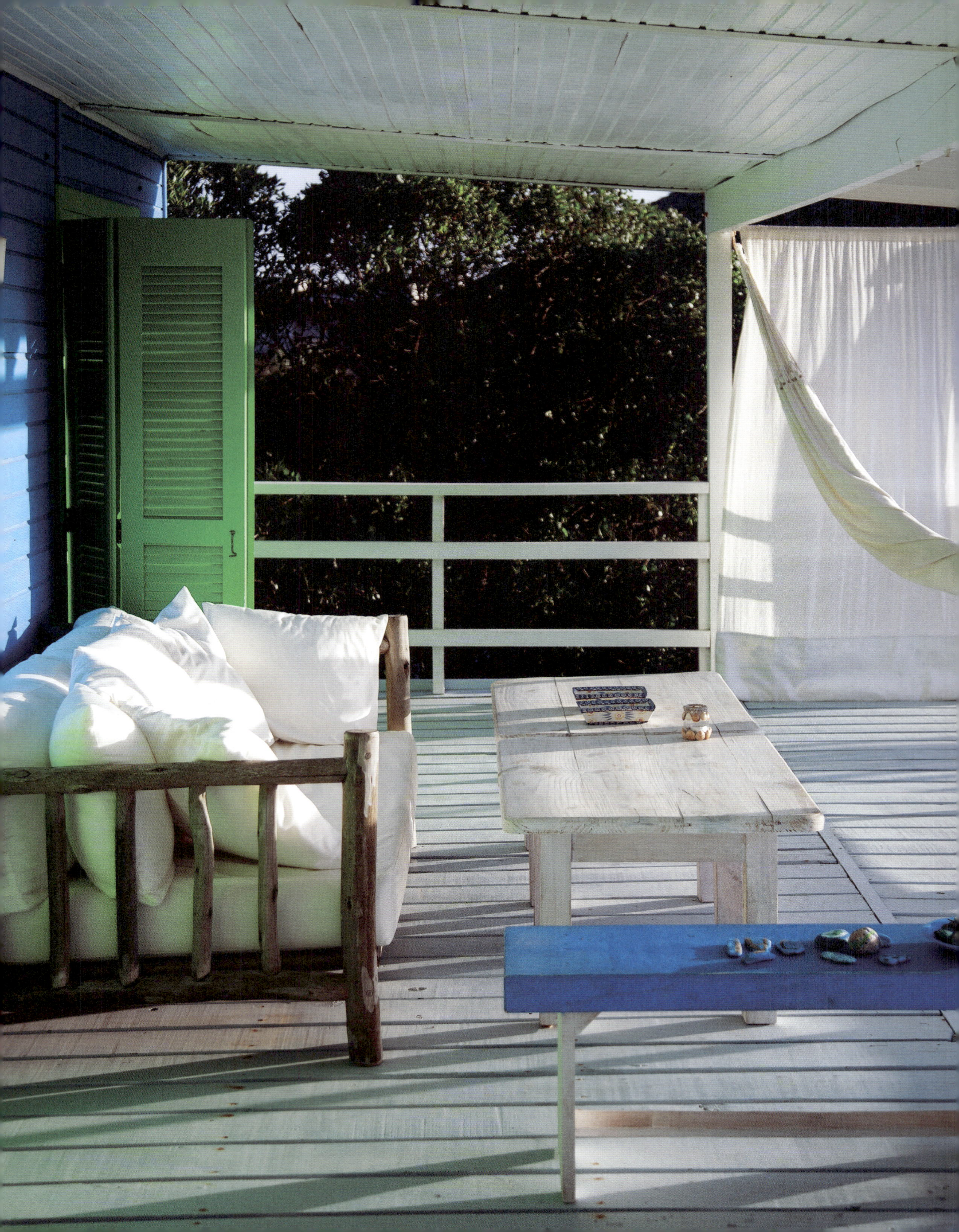

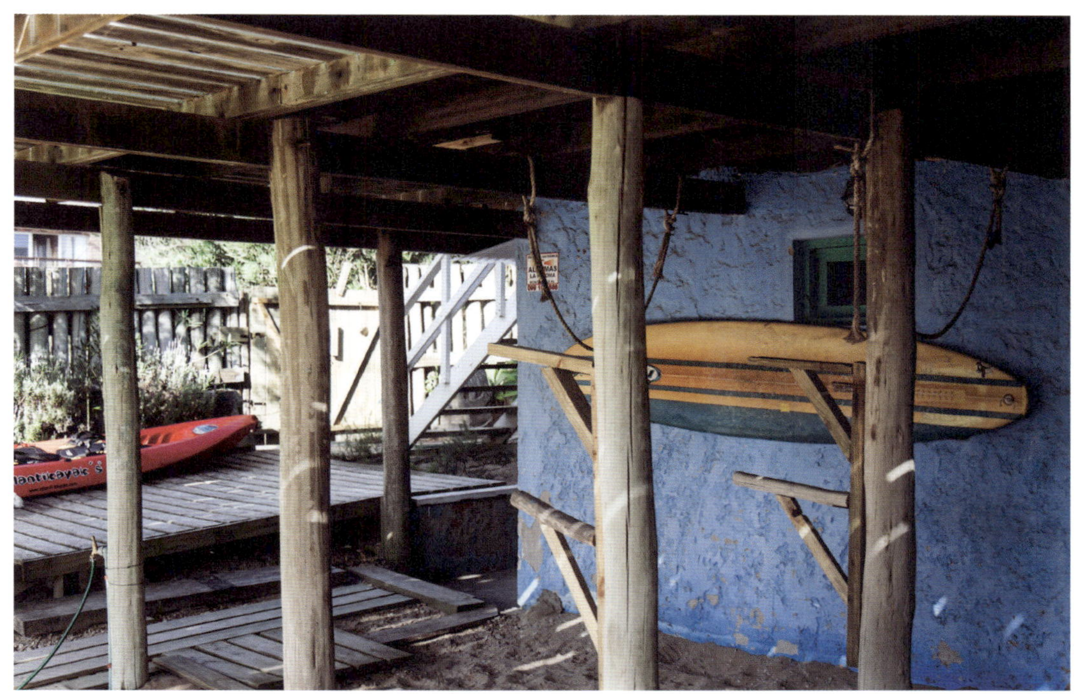

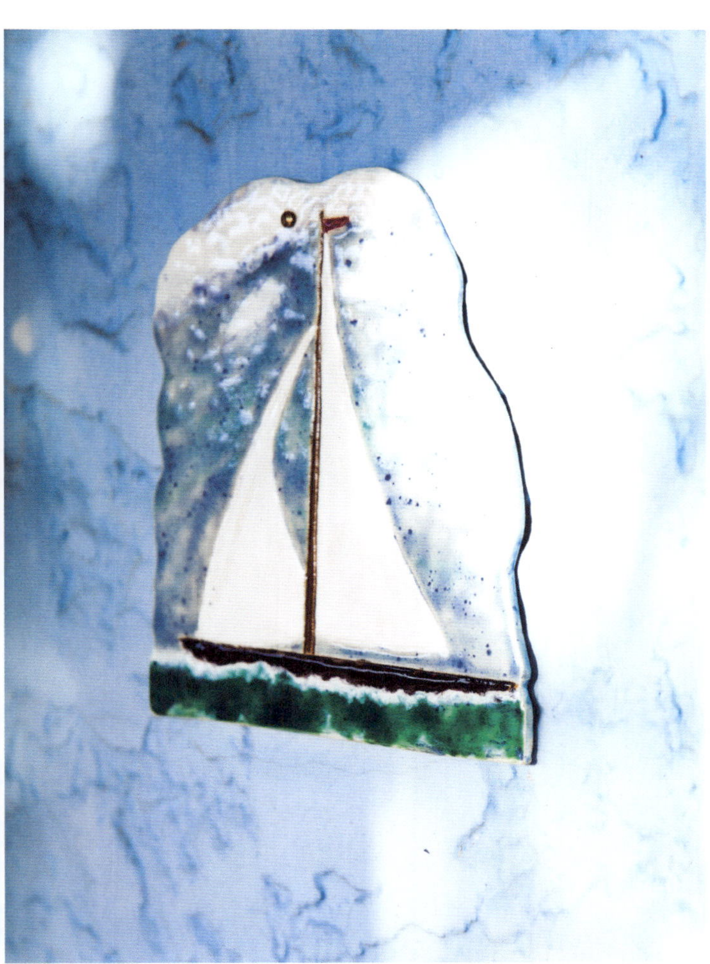

The first time Nora Borlasca and Silvestre Sivori spent the summer in La Pedrera, they fell in love with the town and its surroundings - including its great nature trails and surfing spots - but maybe even more so with this dreamy house they spotted on the beach: a French blue, white wooden cottage with green shutters, standing on stilts in a dune, with a great view of the ocean. They tried to rent it on several occasions, but the owner never agreed. A few years later, they found out by chance that it was for sale.

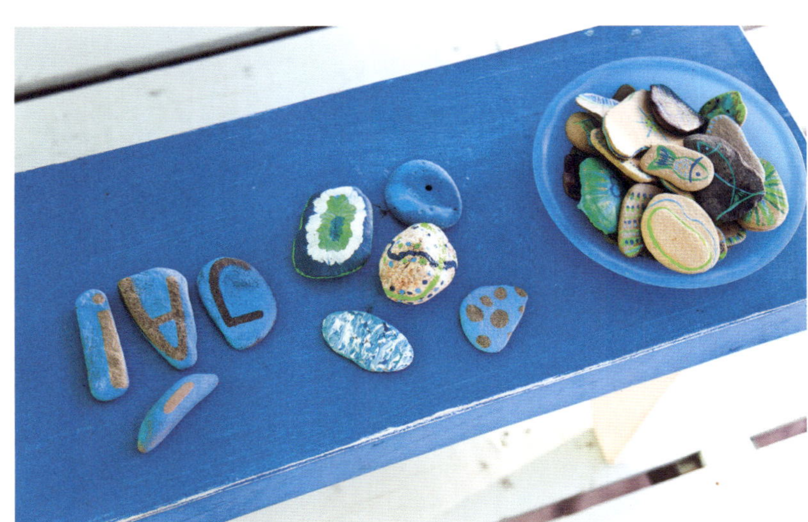

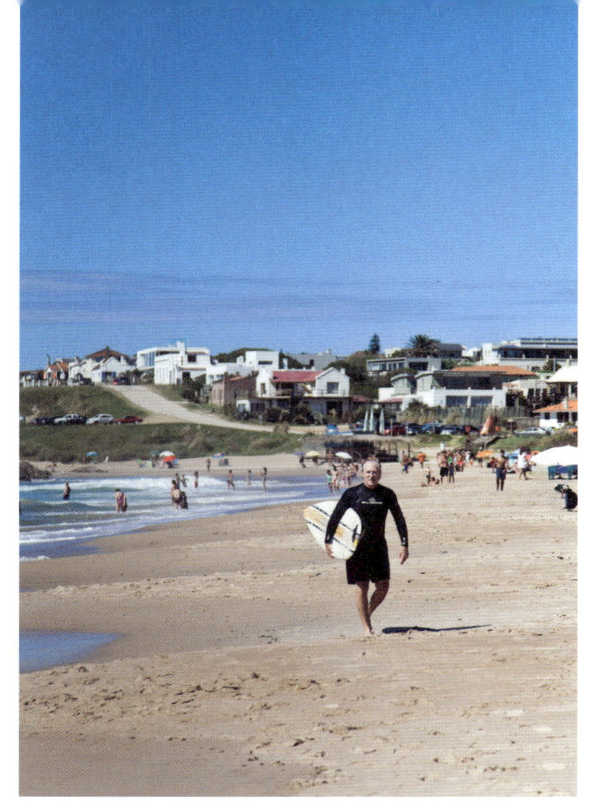

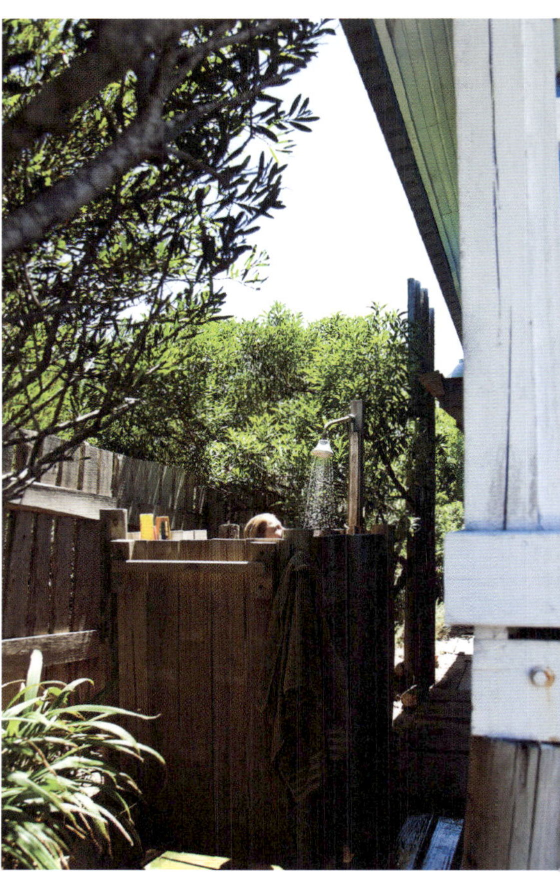

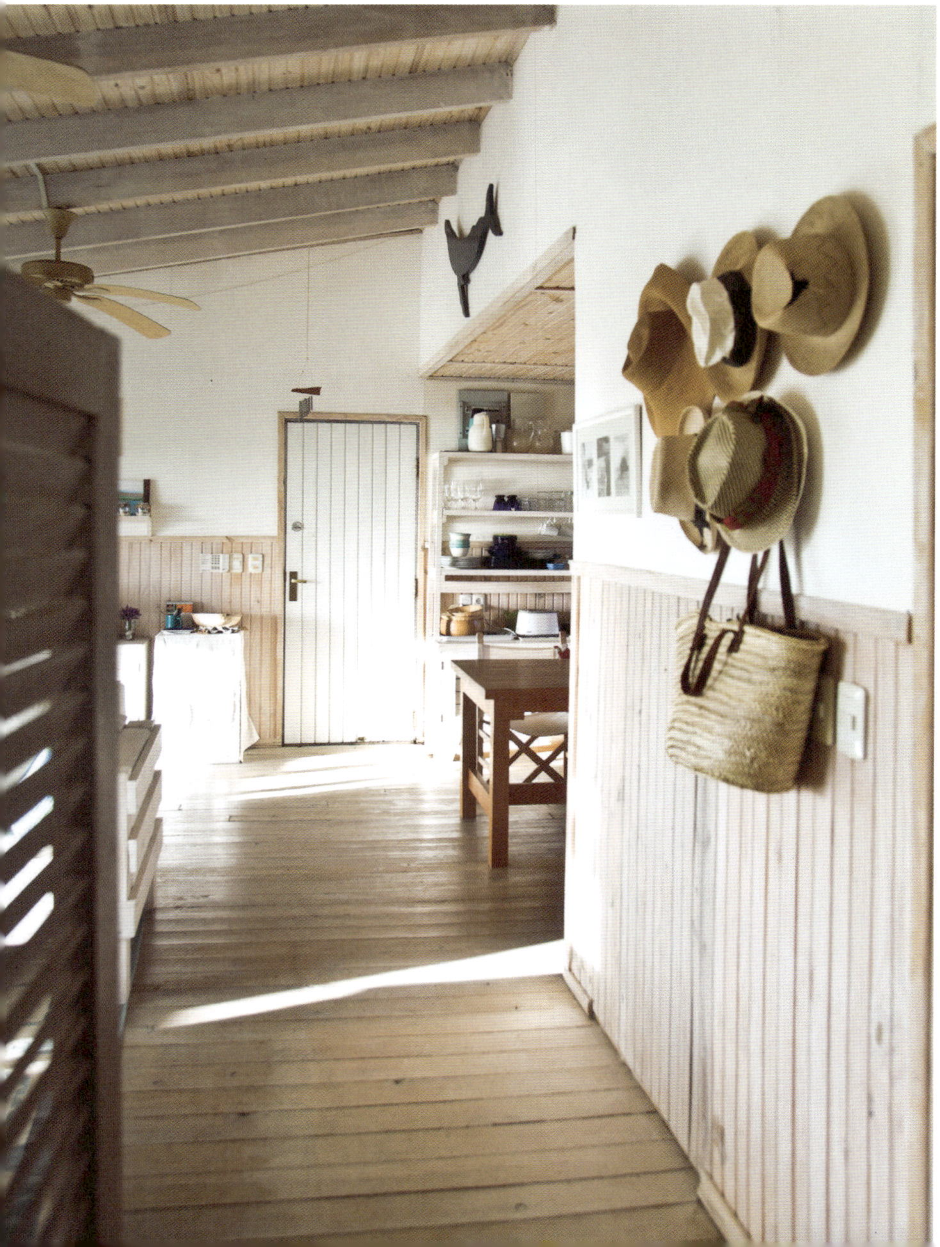

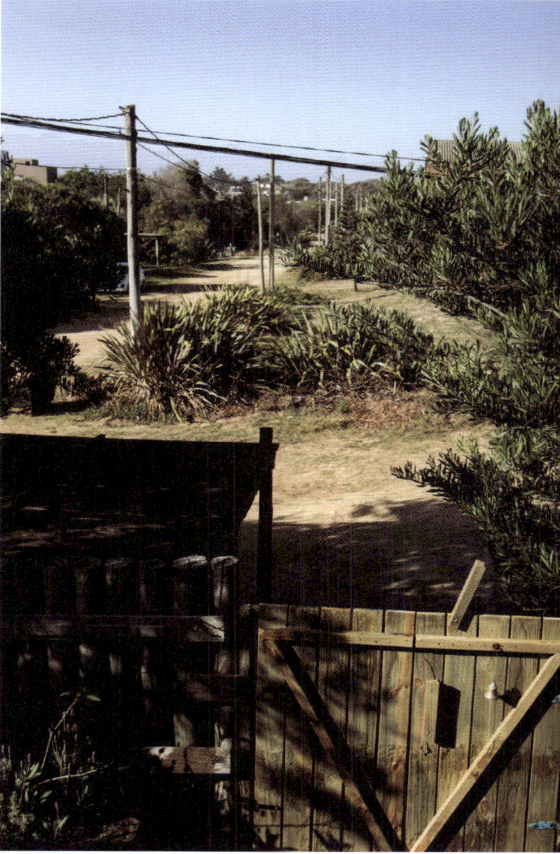

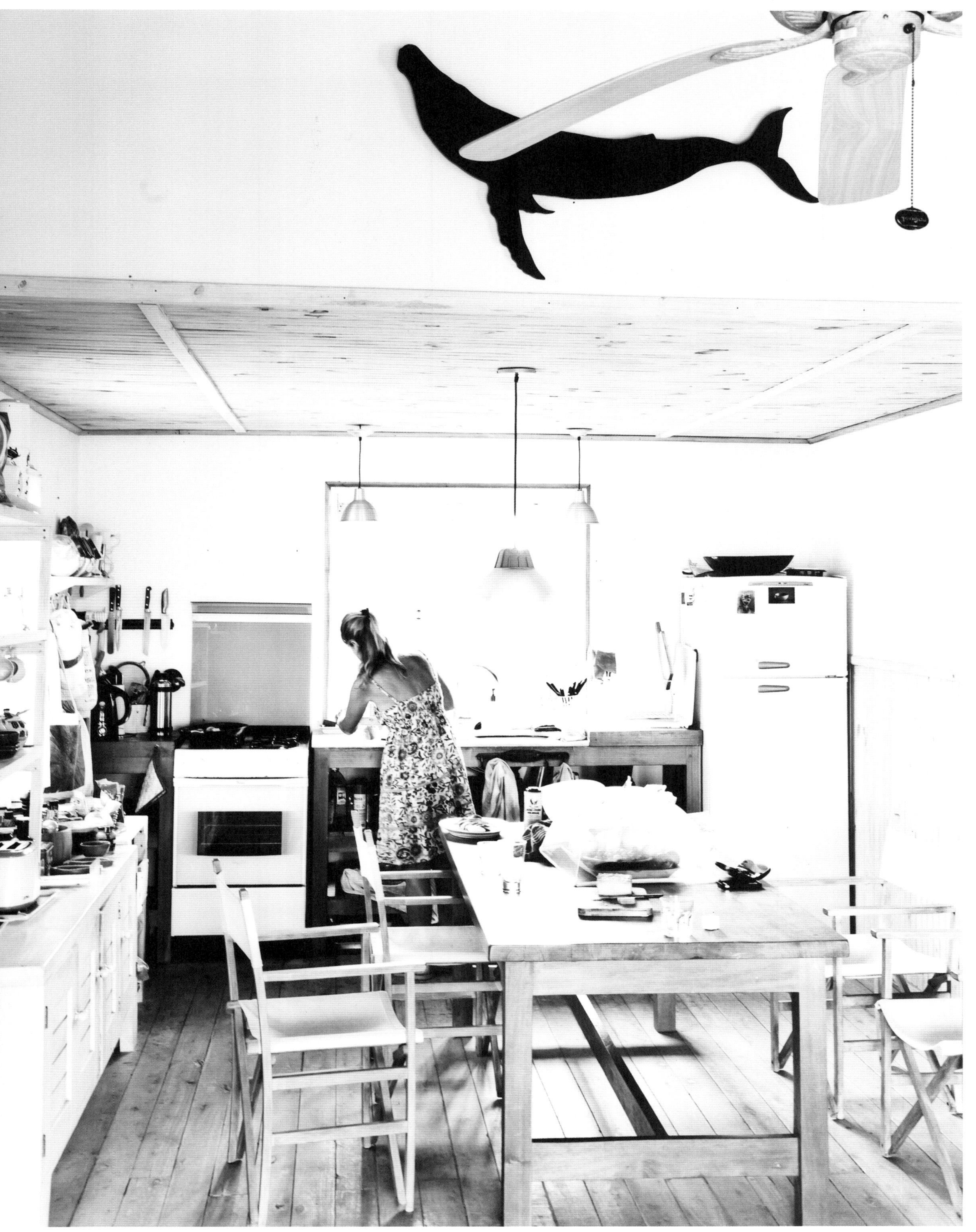

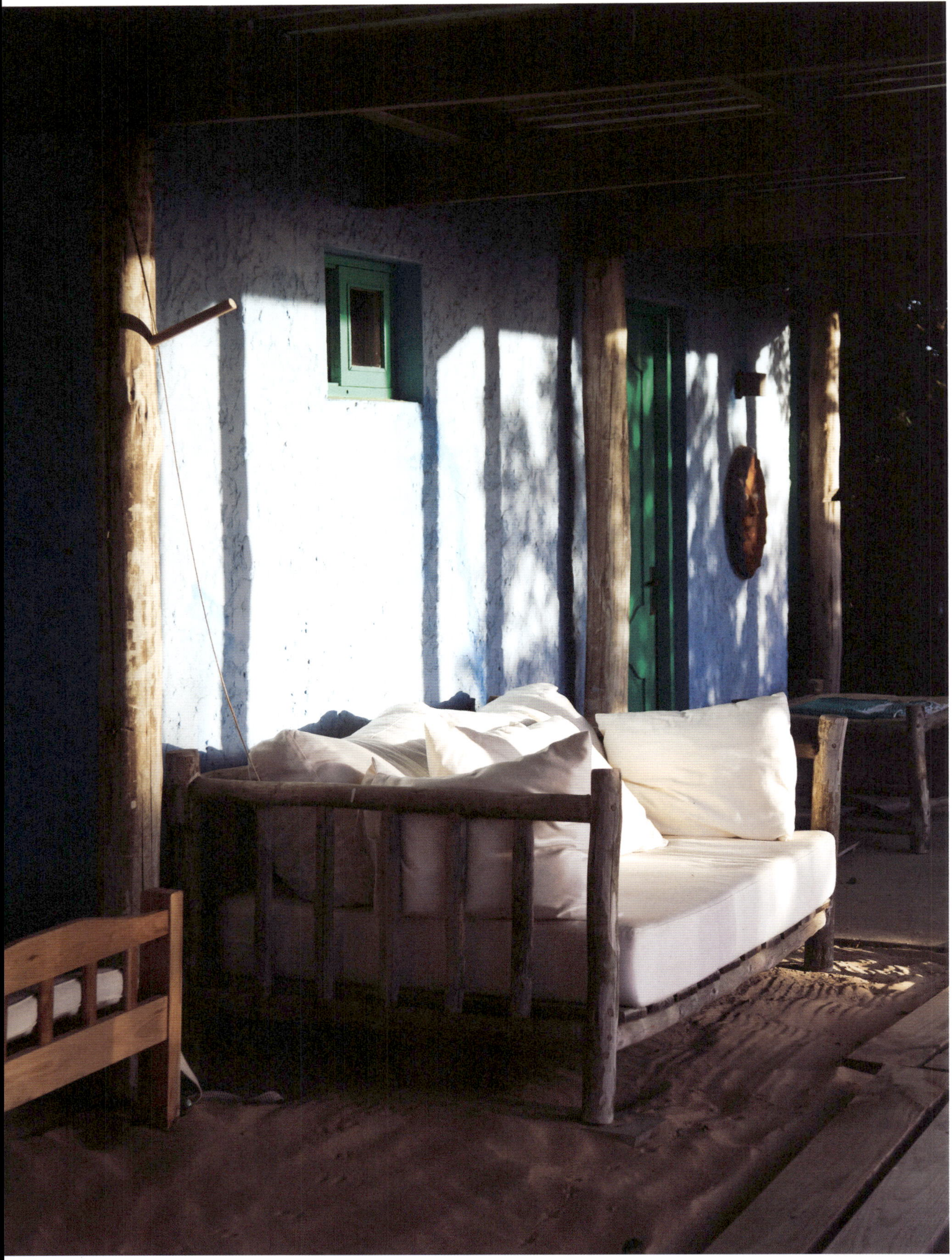

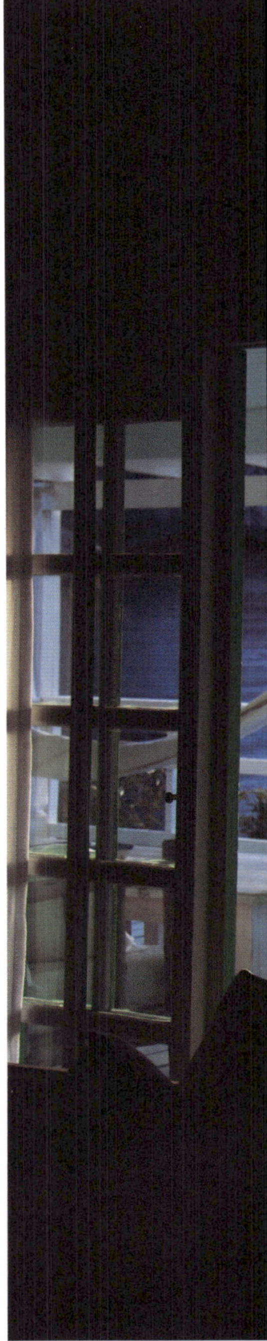

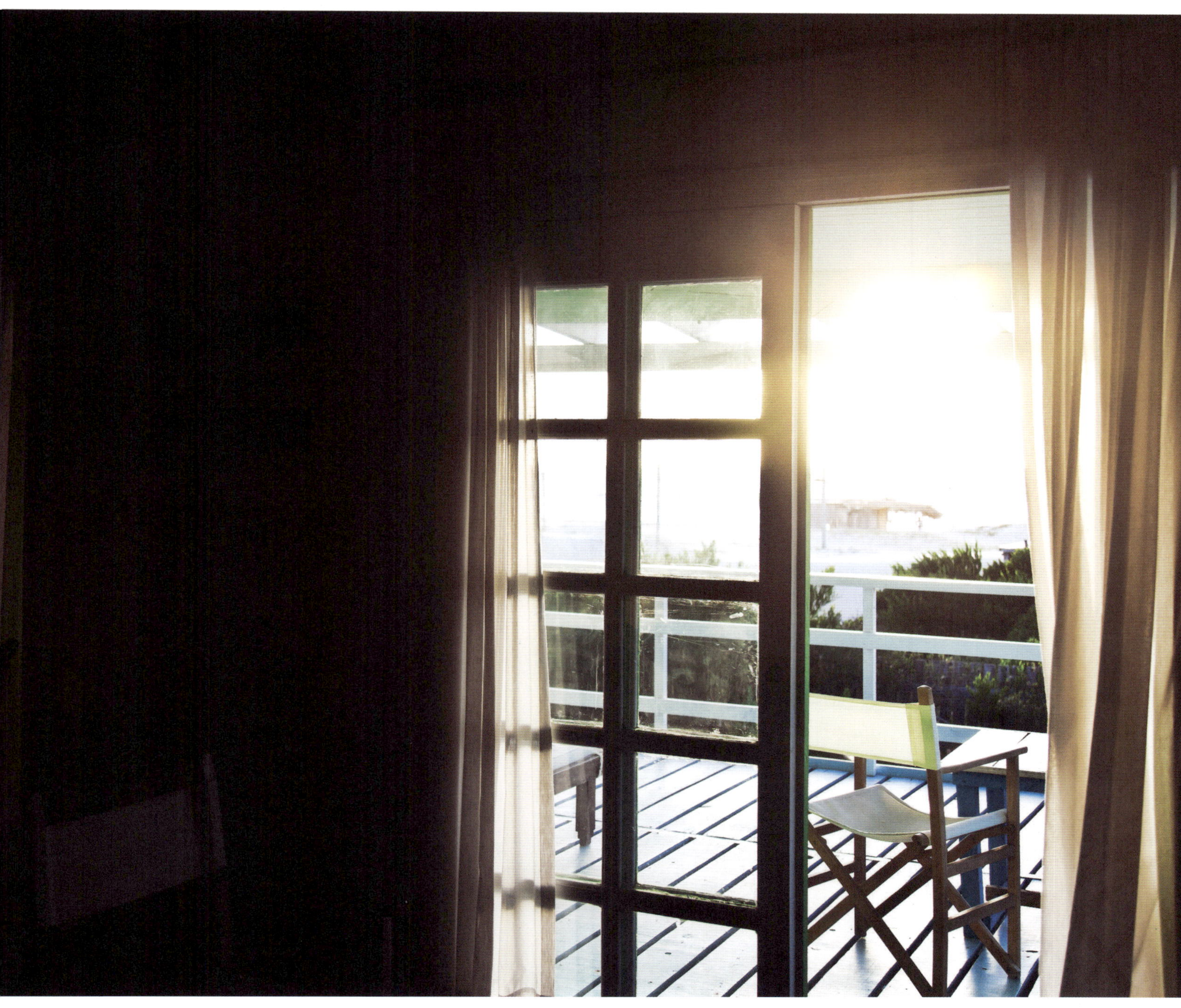

Nora and Silvestre bought their dream holiday home, preserving the structure and vibrant colours that had caught their eye initially. The only major transformation they made consisted of adding a large deck facing the sea. It turned out to be a great decision because this is where they spend most of the day. It's where they have breakfast, relax and catch up with friends and family over dinner or lunch. Most of the furniture on the deck and inside the house as well, is handmade by Silvestre, whose hobby is carpentry, and then painted by Nora.

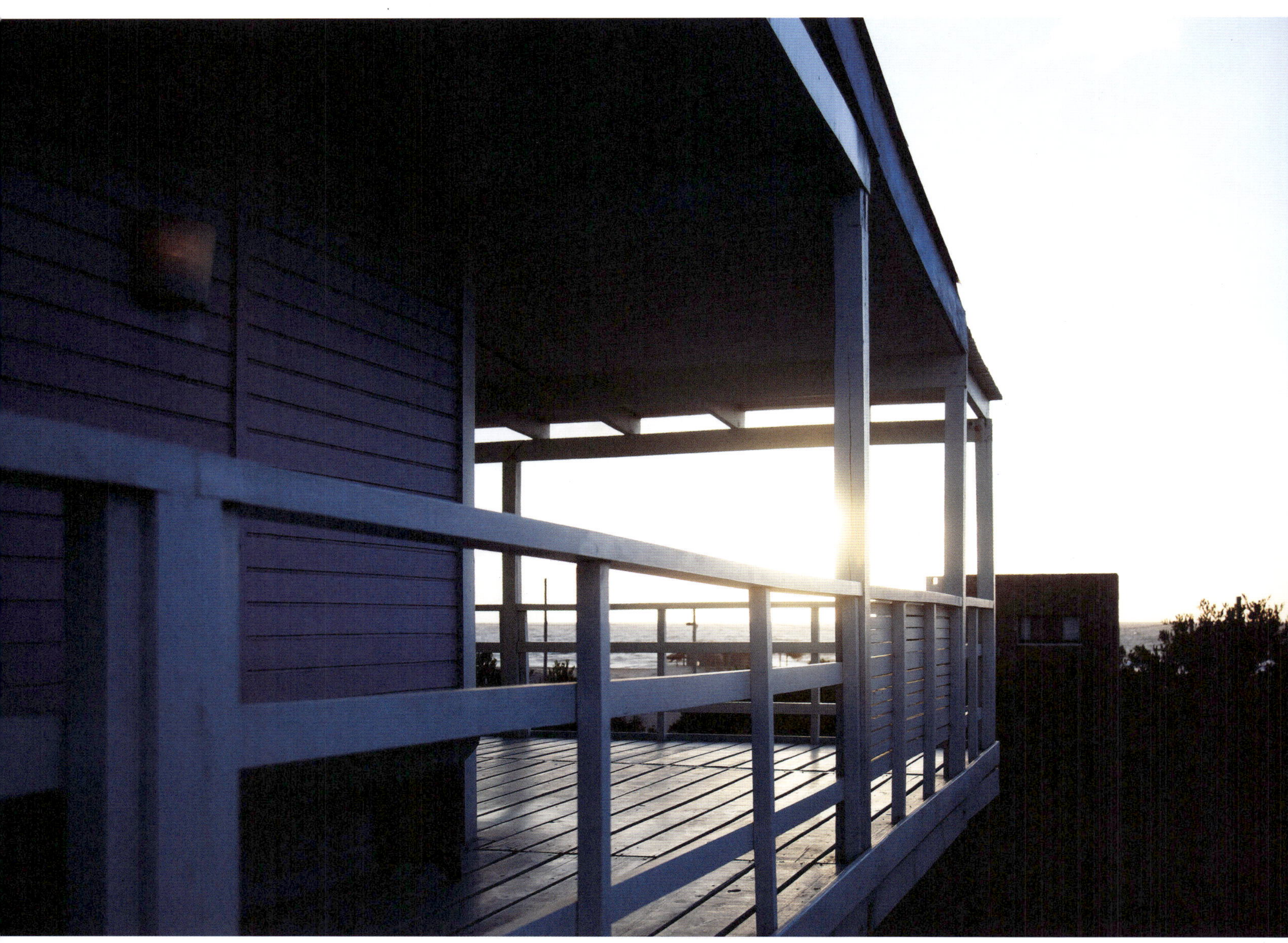

Nora and Silvestre live and work in Argentina, but as soon as the weather (and their schedules) permit, they head for their summer house. Life in La Pedrera is especially nice between October and April when the days are long, and you can live outside. Ideally, the day starts early with breakfast on the deck, followed by long walks along the beach, occasionally interrupted by a dip in the water. The sea glass, shells and fossils Nora finds on these walks are often so beautiful that she takes them home, finding a place for them on the wall or on a shelf.

Nora and Silvestre prefer to spend time in their summer home with friends and family. There is always someone visiting, so everyone ends up going for a swim, after which they enjoy a lazy, blissful lunch on the deck. Nora puts on a magnificent spread so everyone can pick and graze at their own leisure. When evening falls, they like to entertain their guests by the fire pit in the garden - a stretch of dune which they 'fenced off' with plants that can withstand the wind, sand and climate. The perfect setting for a barbecue or for quietly gazing at the stars by the crackling fire.

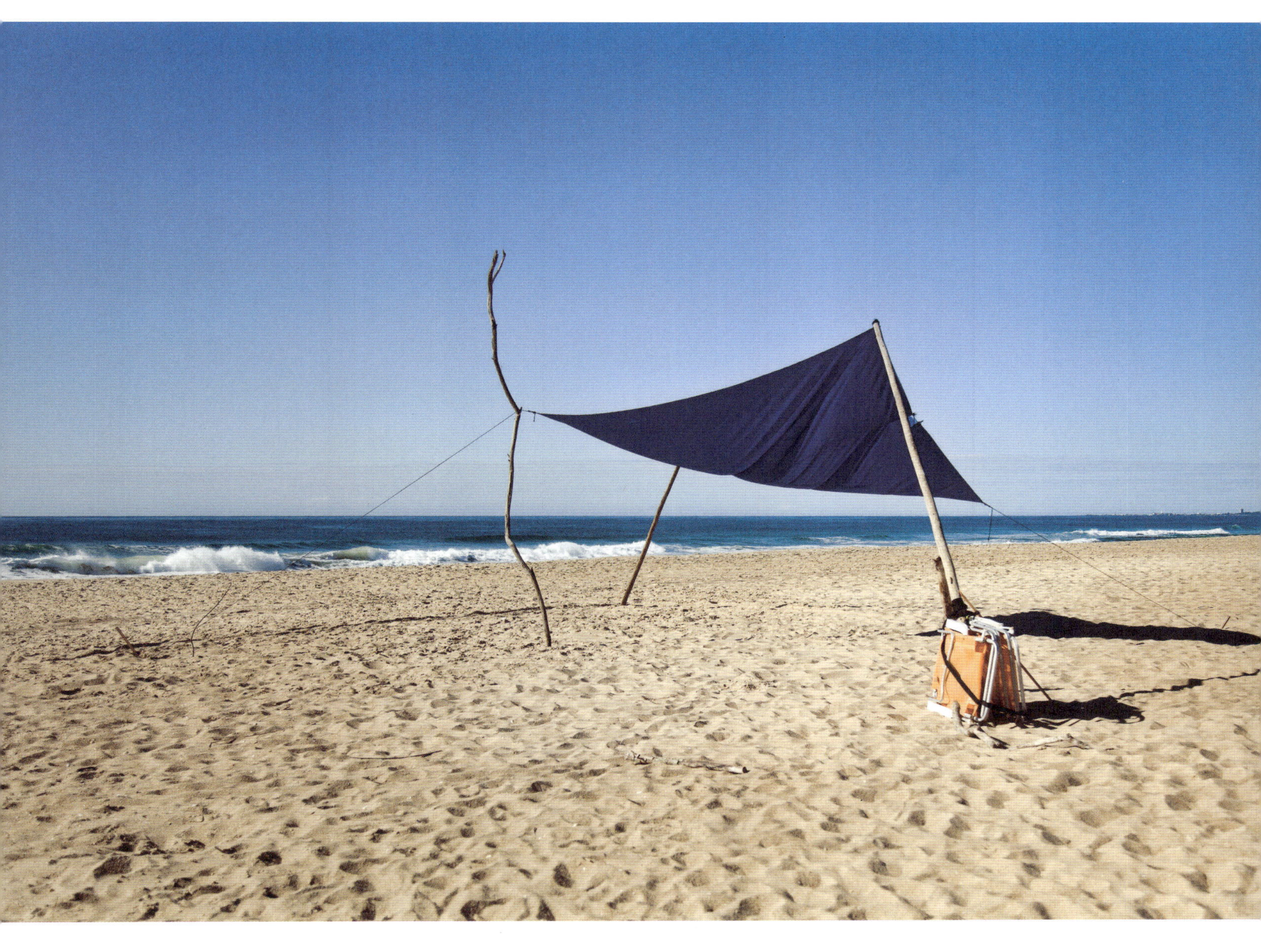

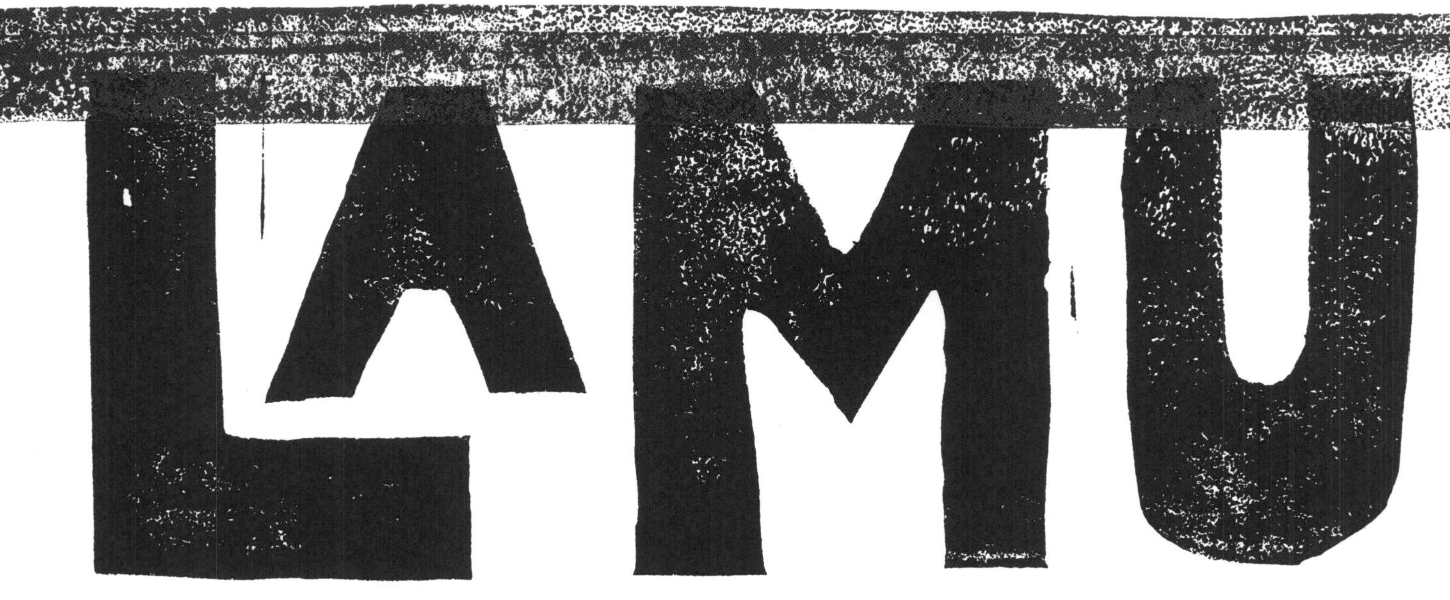

A fishing boat drifting on the Indian ocean,
off the spectacular pristine coast of Lamu Island: in a film about the life of Daniella Blattler, this would be a key scene. The photographer and creative entrepreneur, who originally hails from Switzerland, set foot on Lamu Island fifteen years ago, with a head full of dreams and a heart full of love. To cope with the grief of a breakup soon after, Daniella took to the water with her camera. Her intention was to document the lives of the traditional fishermen of Lamu Island, and that is how she ended up on Ali Omar's fishing boat.

Shela
Kenya

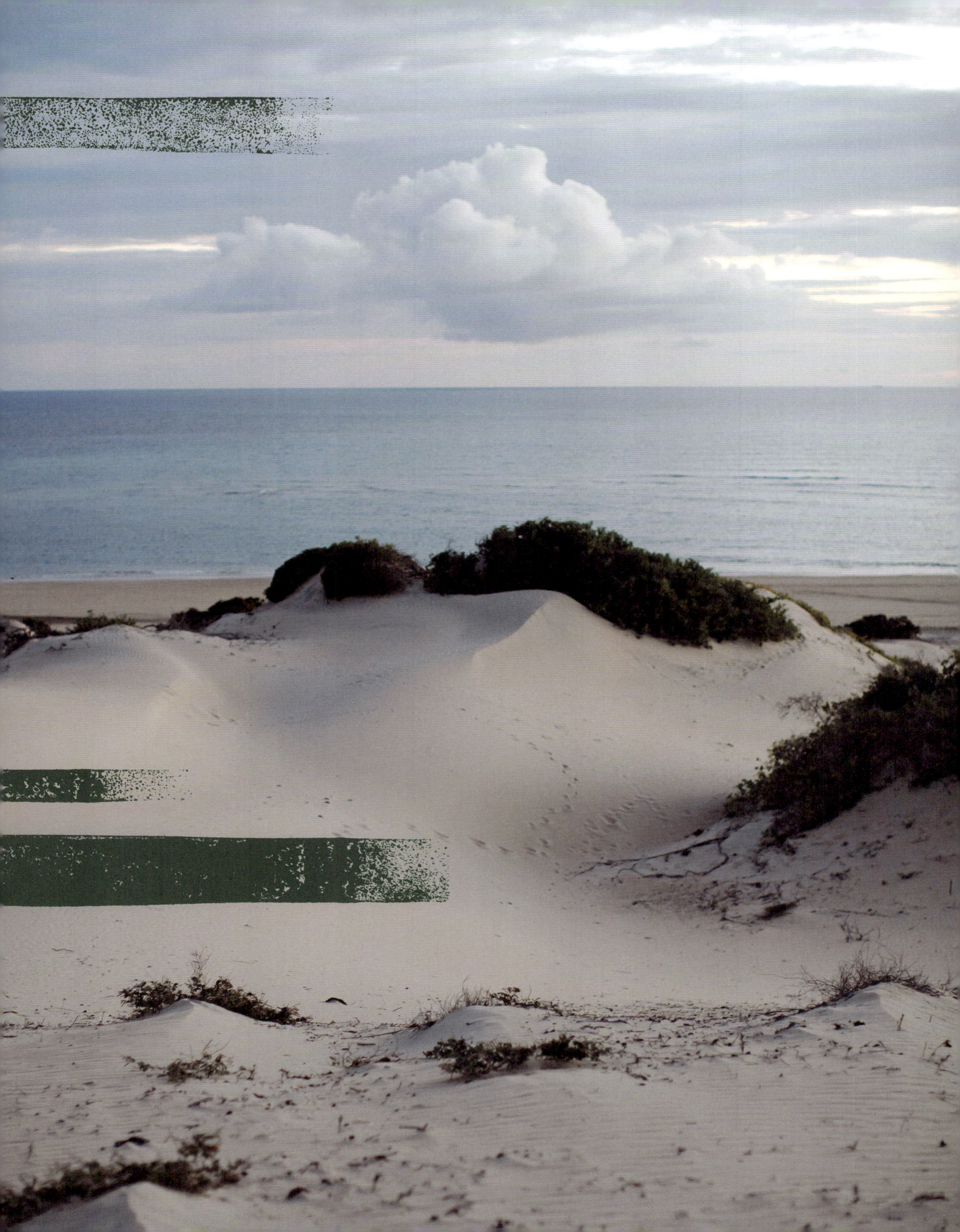

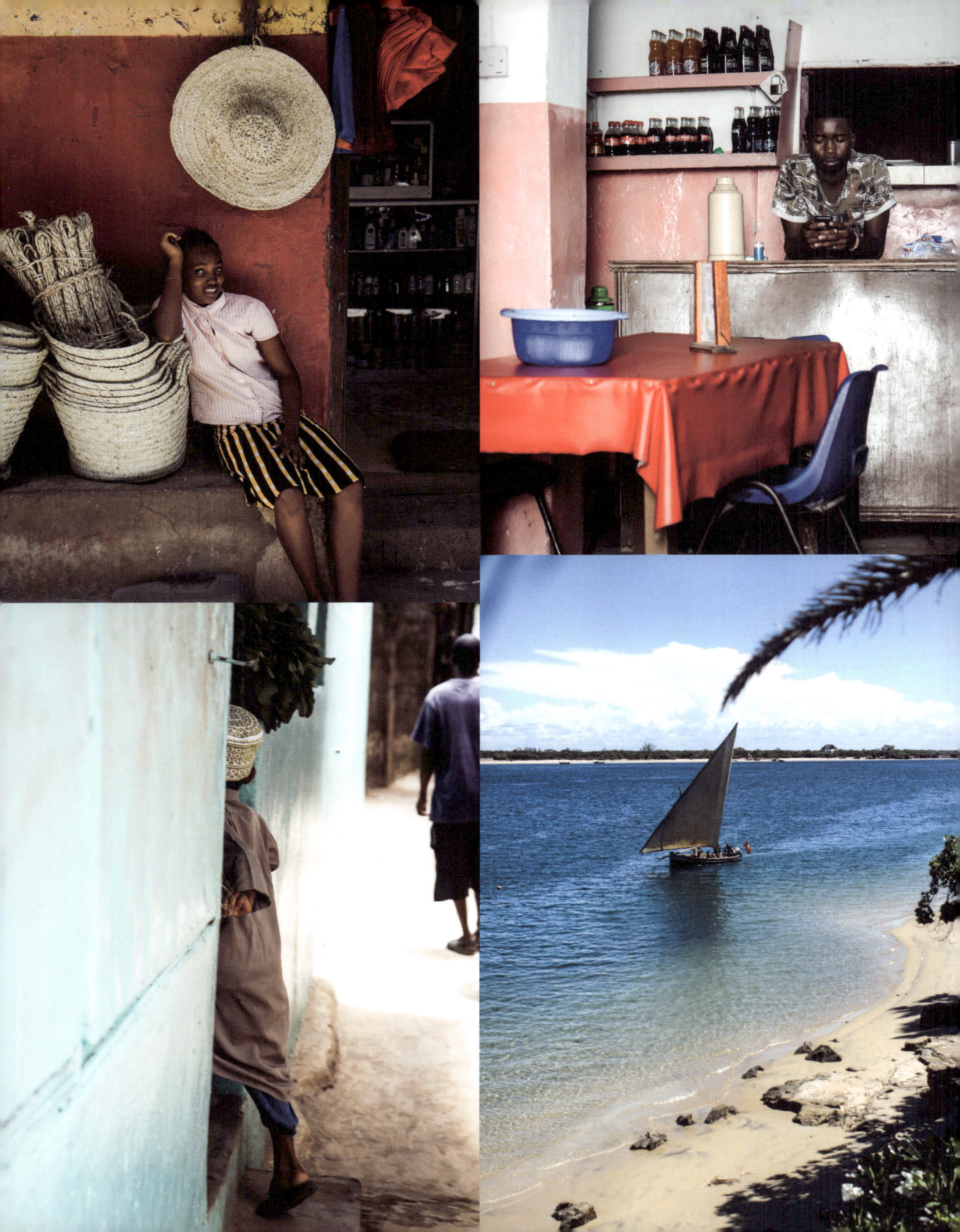

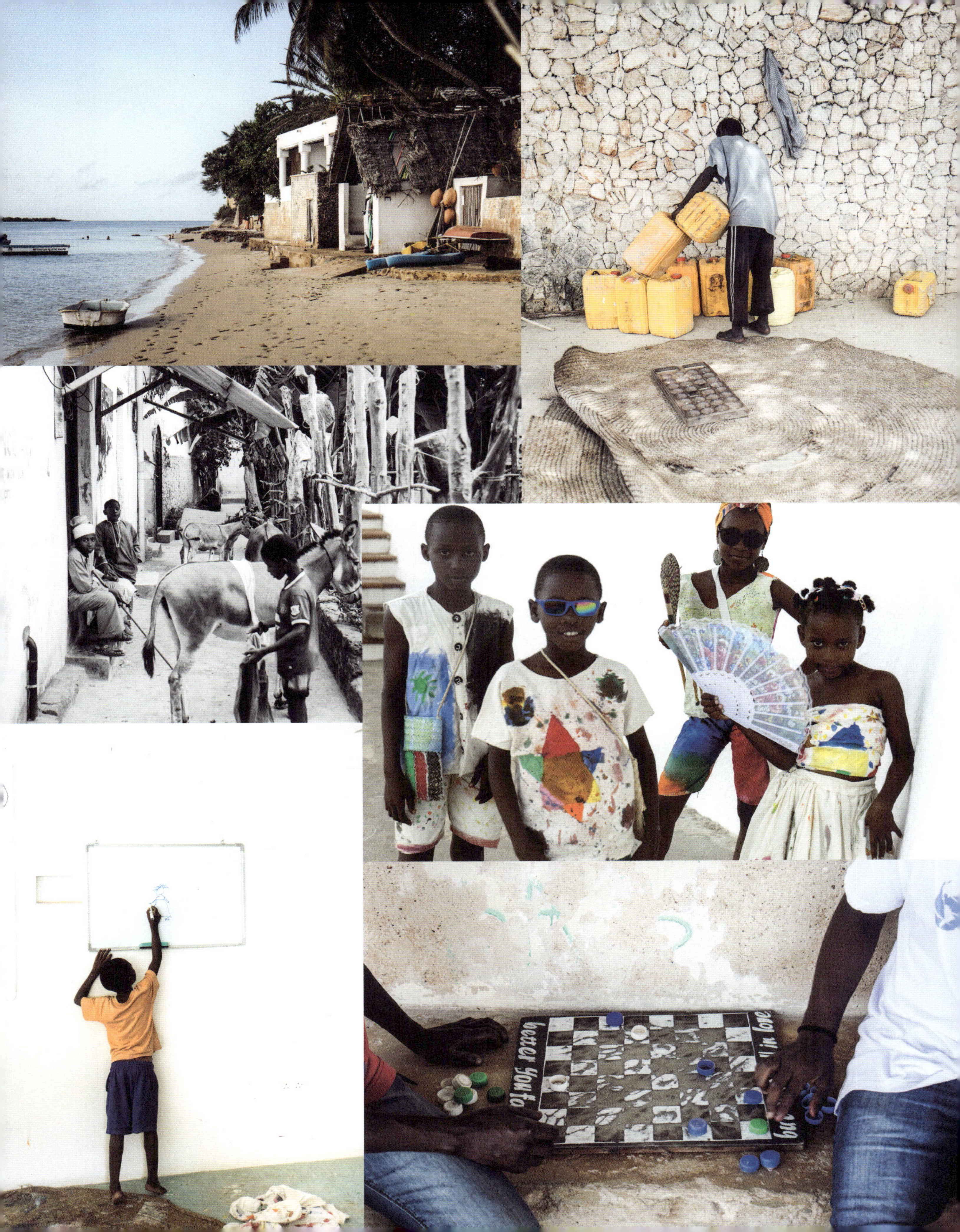

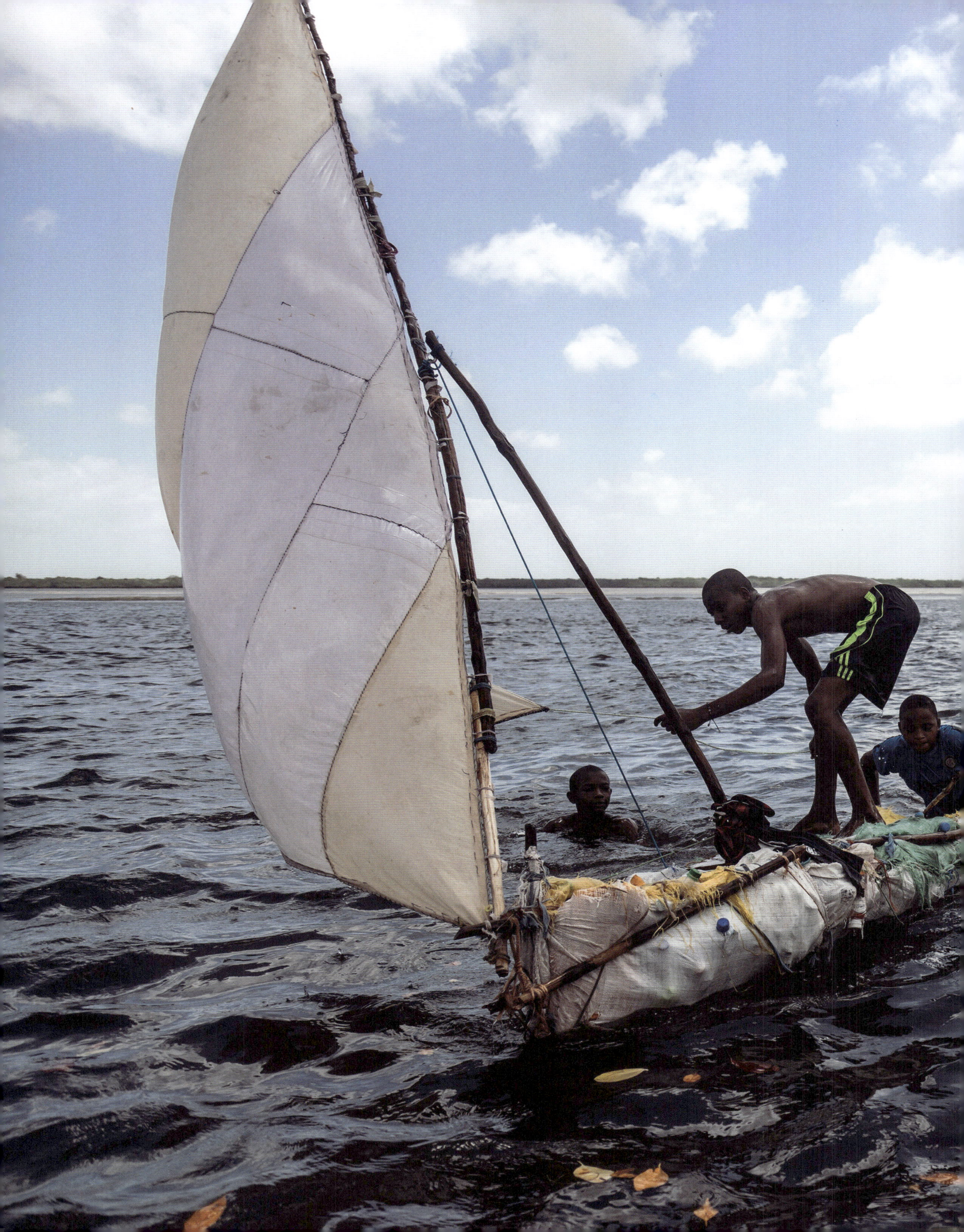

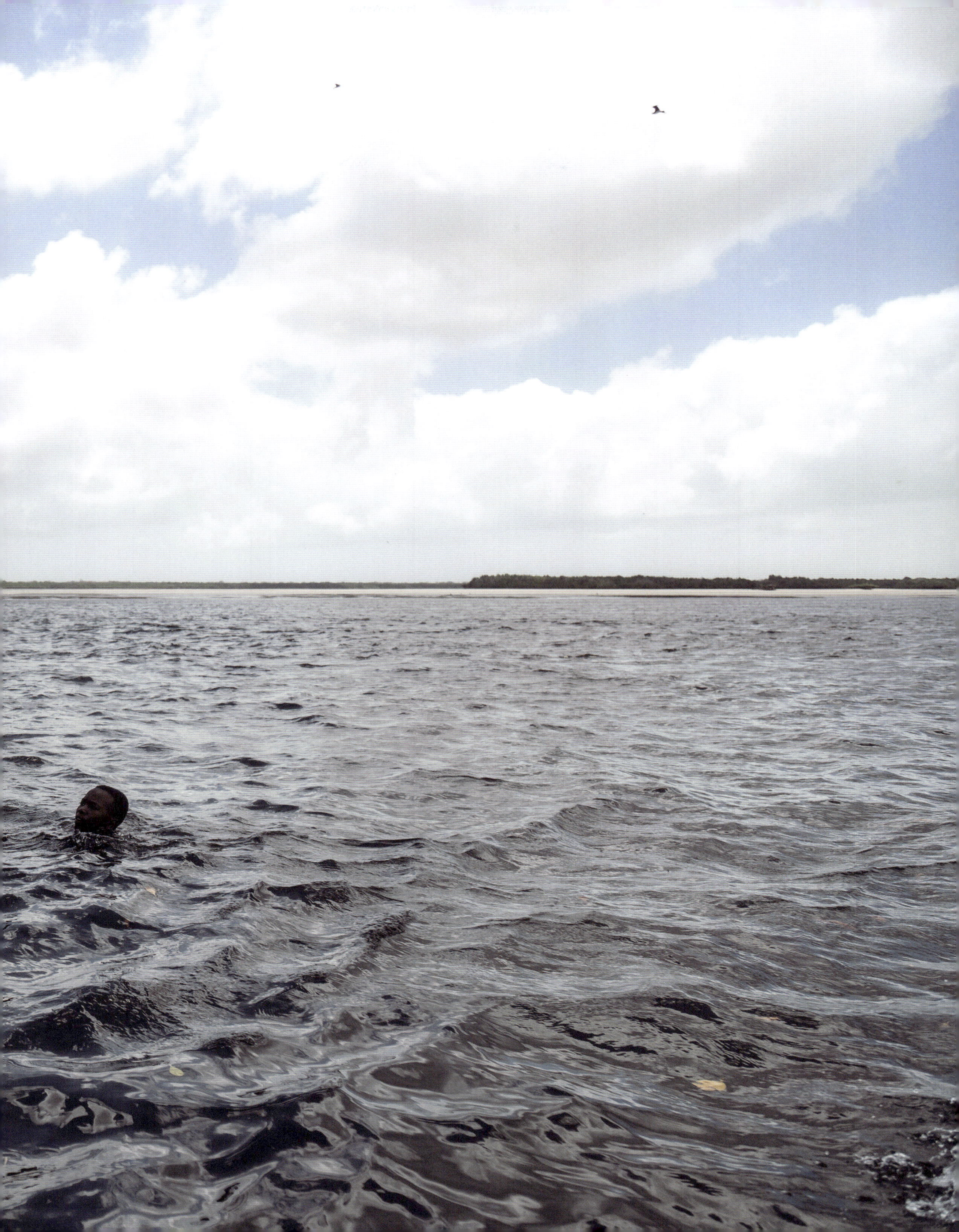

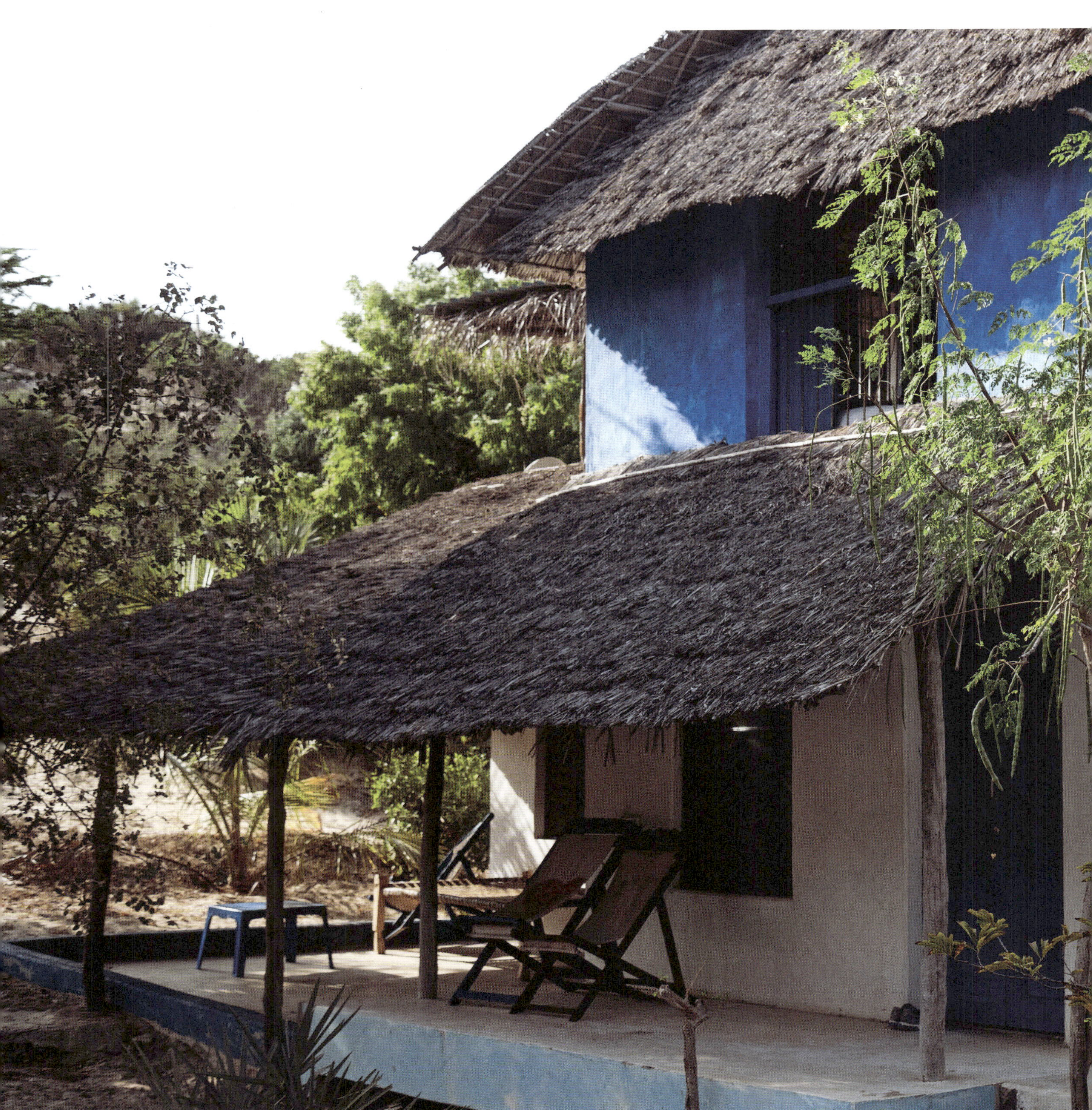

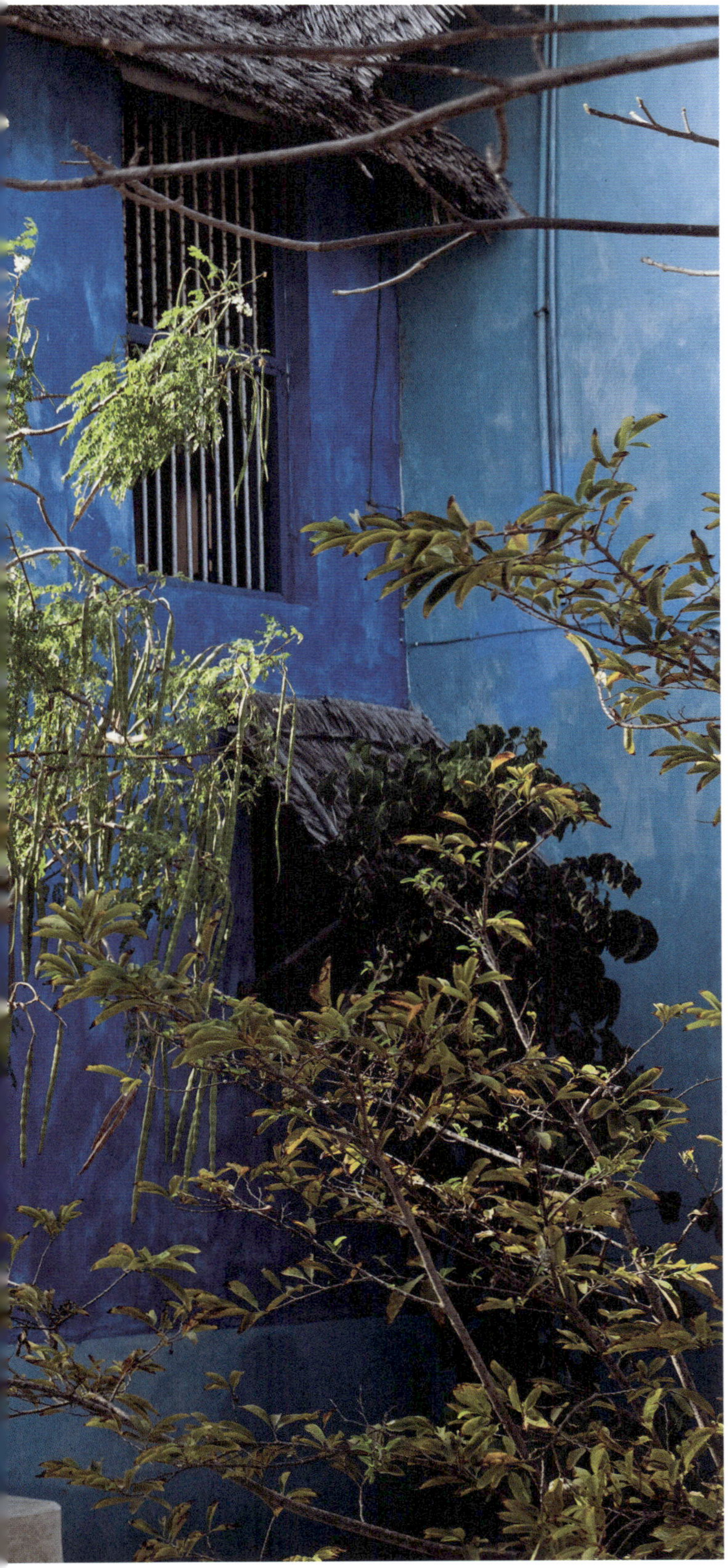

The two became firm friends, even though Daniella only knew a few phrases in Kiswahili, the language spoken on Lamu Island. Although she had no idea at the time, the seeds of her new life on Lamu Island were sown when she asked him whether she could take a closer look at the sail of his traditional 'dhow' boat – the sail is called 'tanga' in Kiswahili. After years of being exposed to the elements on the Indian Ocean, the sails turn a beautiful weathered brown, unlike anything you have ever seen. The colour and texture of these tangas intrigued and inspired Daniella, who saw them as works of art created by the wind, seawater and rain.

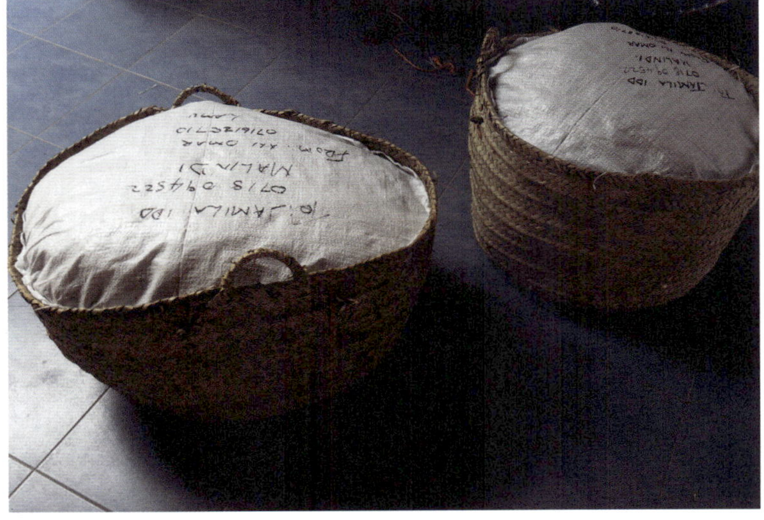

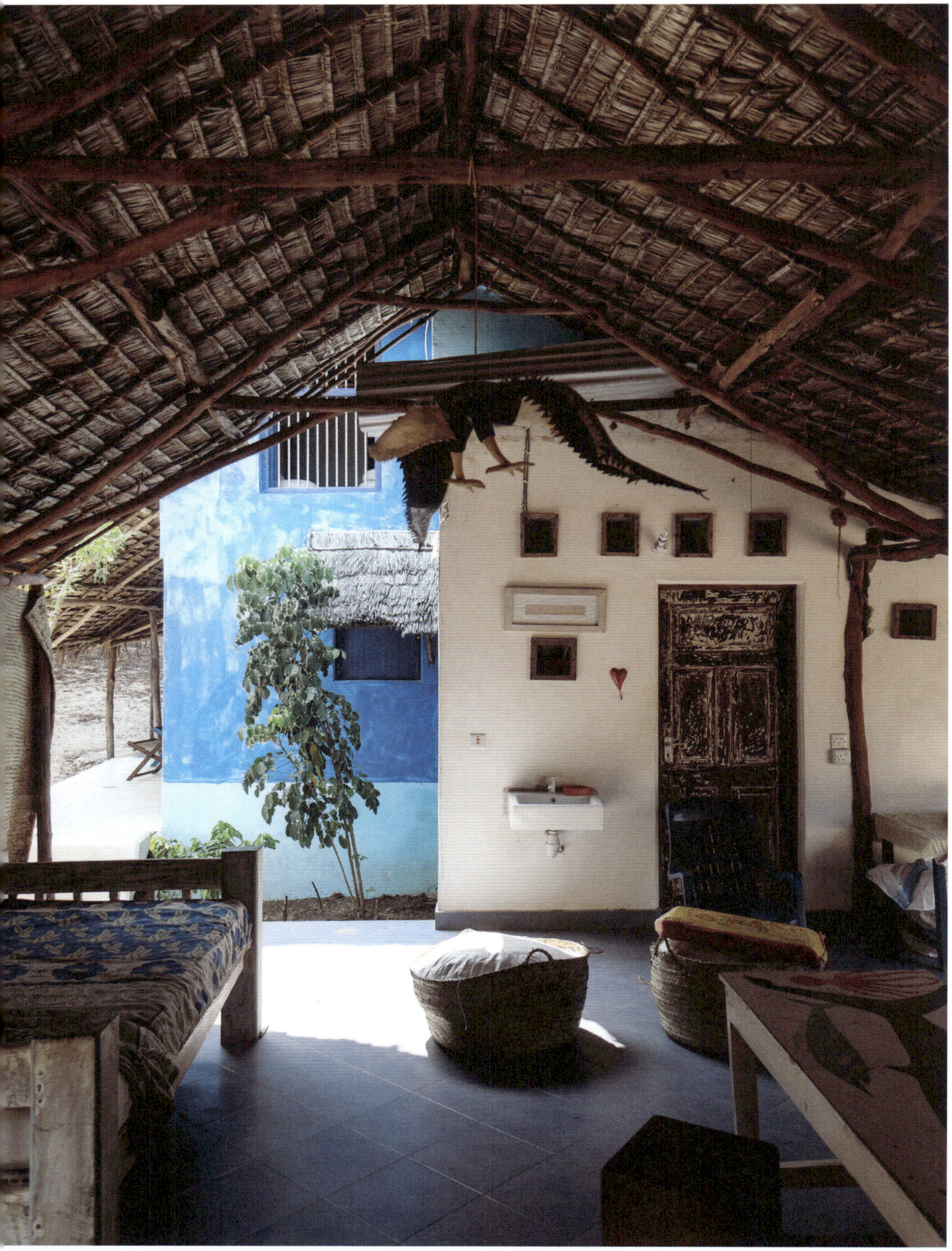

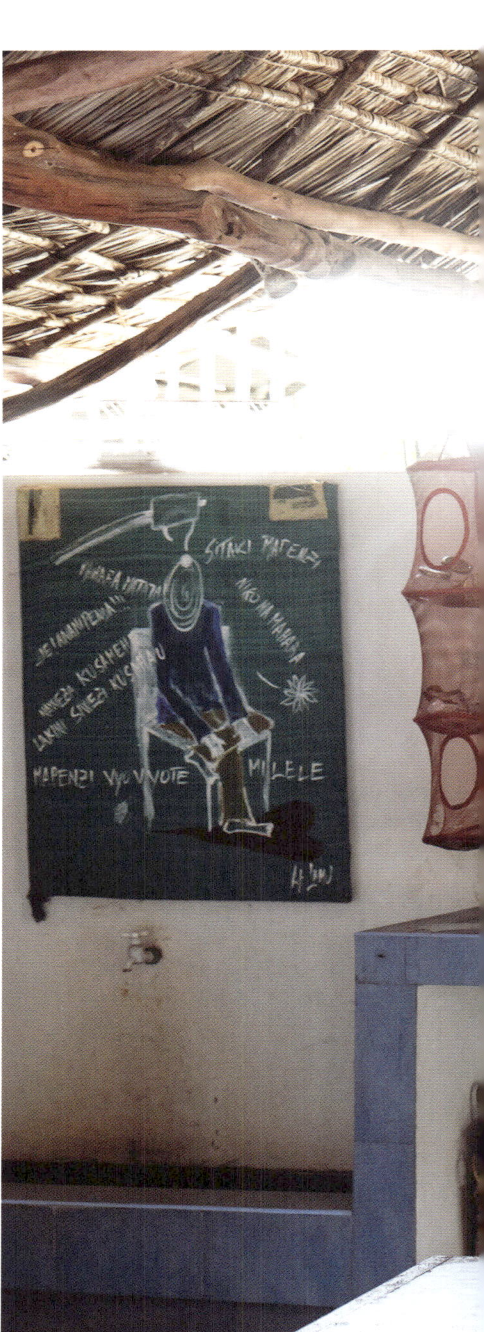
SITAKI MAPENZI
MILELE

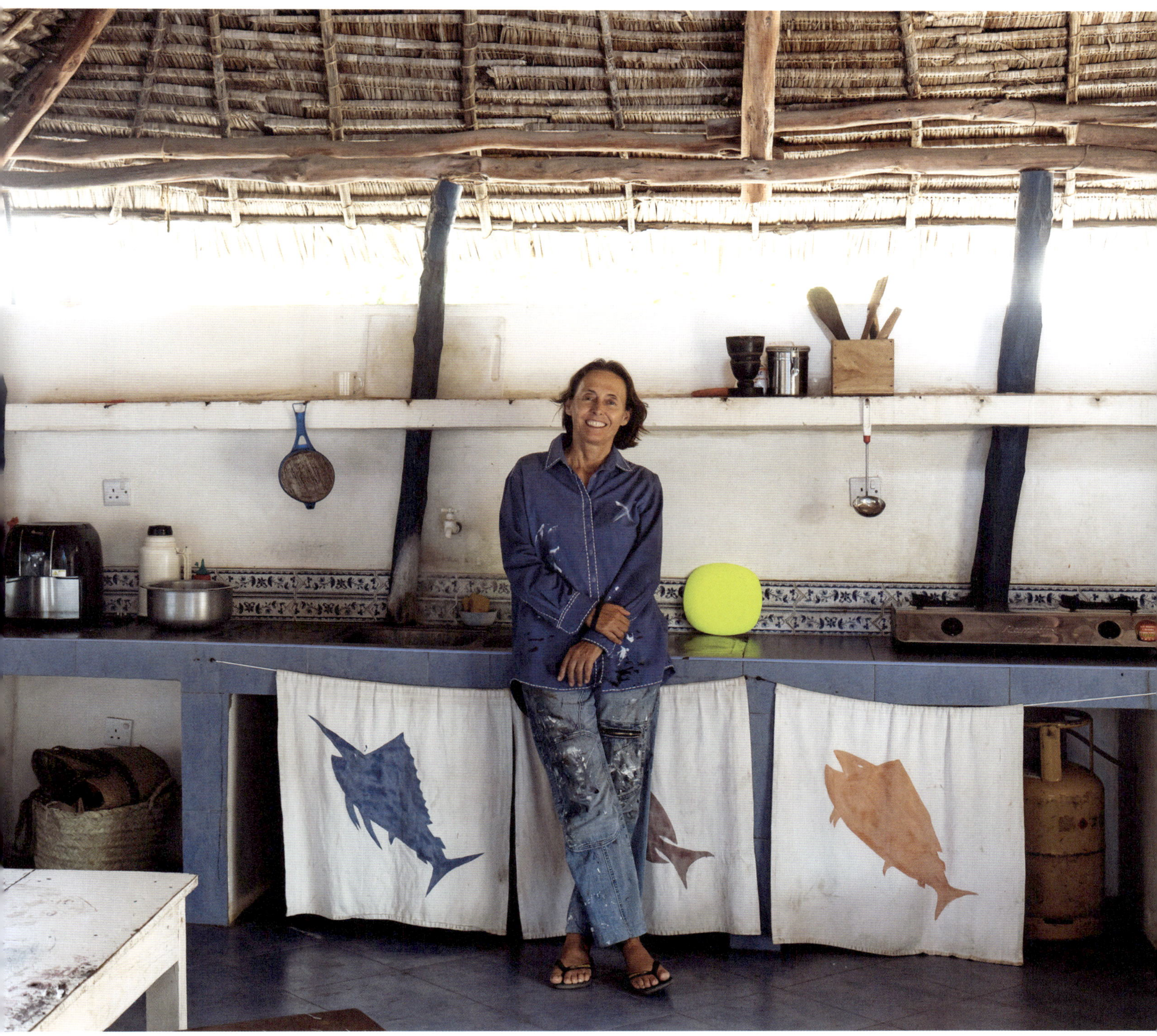

In time, Daniella and Ali began to decorate these beautiful sails: first with red broken hearts, later with colourful stars, donkeys, fish, elephants - a species that holds a special place in Daniella's heart - and much more. That is how Ali and Daniella's bag and interior decoration brand Ali Lamu came about. All items are hand-crafted with passion on the Kenyan Island, from where they are dispatched to retailers and fans around the world. Ali Lamu exists by virtue of the local community, whose traditions inspire each item, as well as for the community: Daniella's company offers the islanders work and an income, as well as playing a community-building role.

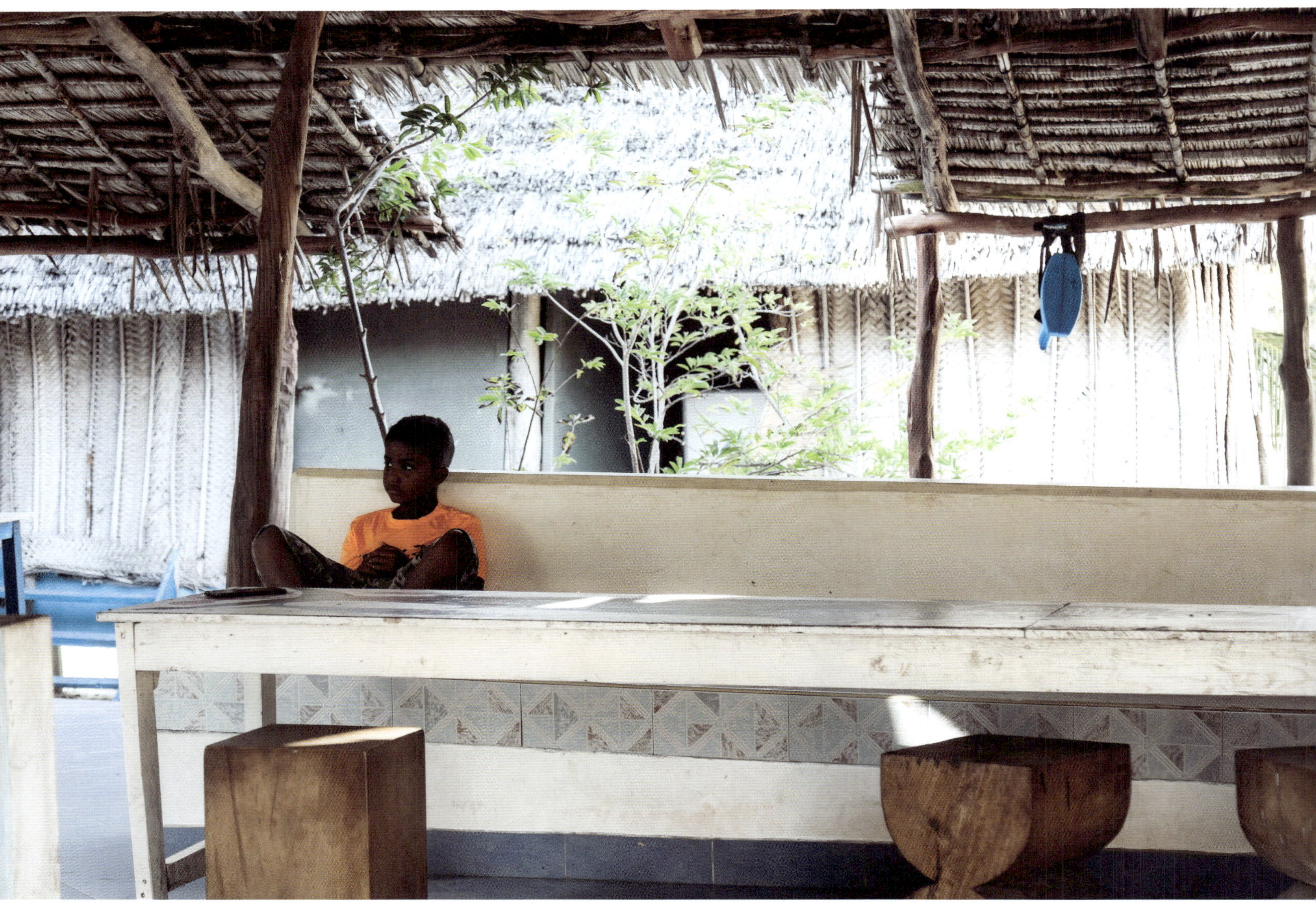

Like the Ali Lamu brand, Daniella's house, which is tucked away in the dunes, was the result of lots of love and hard work. She was able to buy this lovely plot with a small advance payment. It helped that the owner also trusted her. There, she and her Lamu framily set about slowly building their own little paradise by the ocean. Each Ali Lamu painting or piece that was sold meant a new step forward for the house: the wooden trusses, the whitewashed walls, the thatched roof...

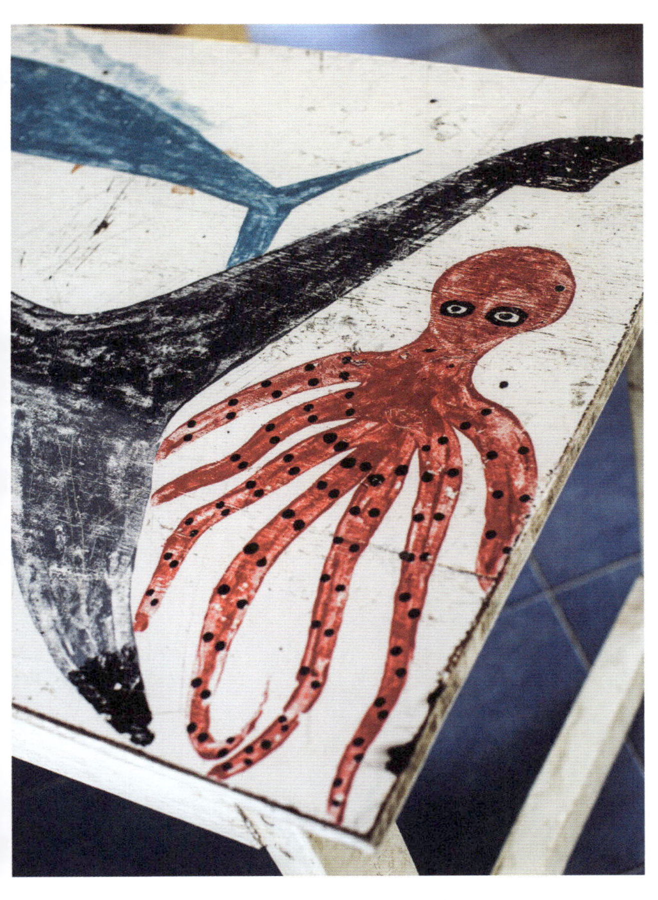

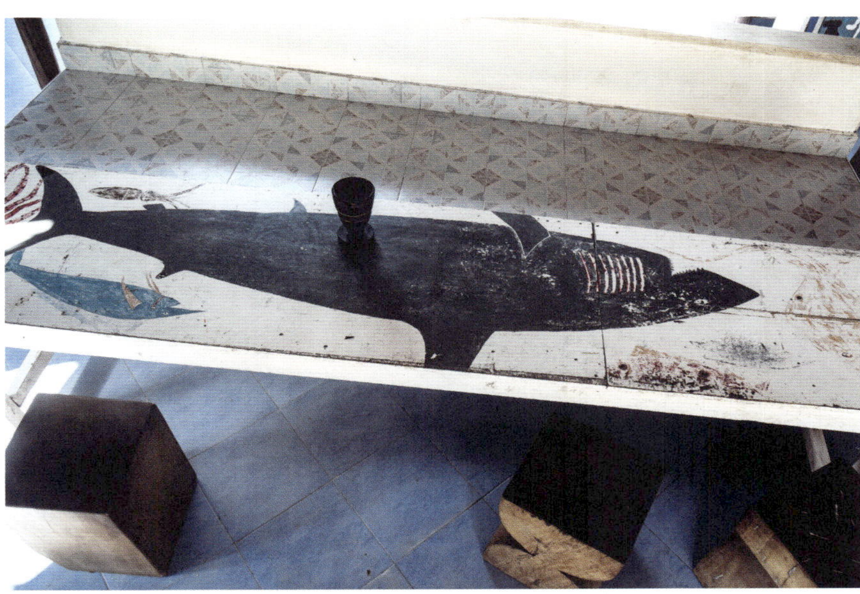

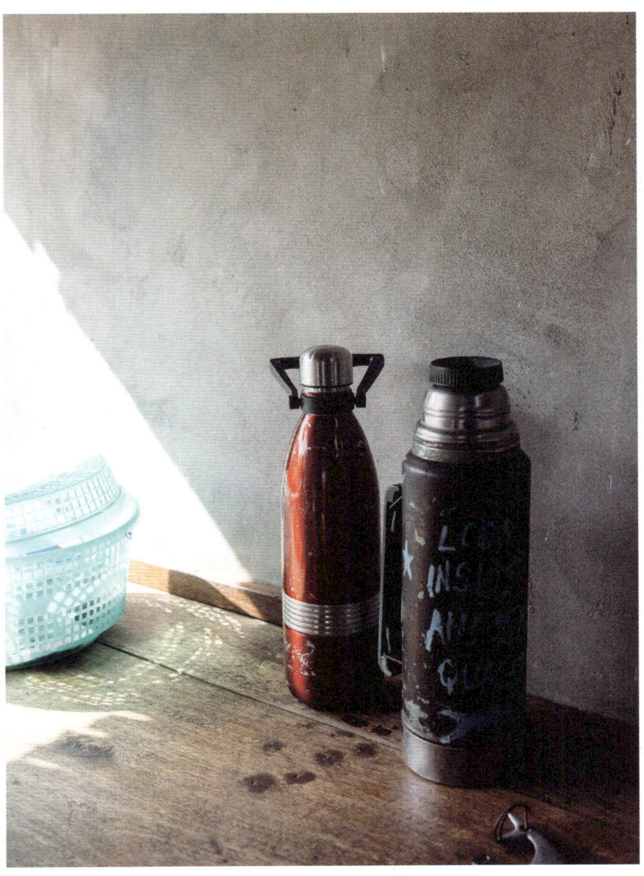

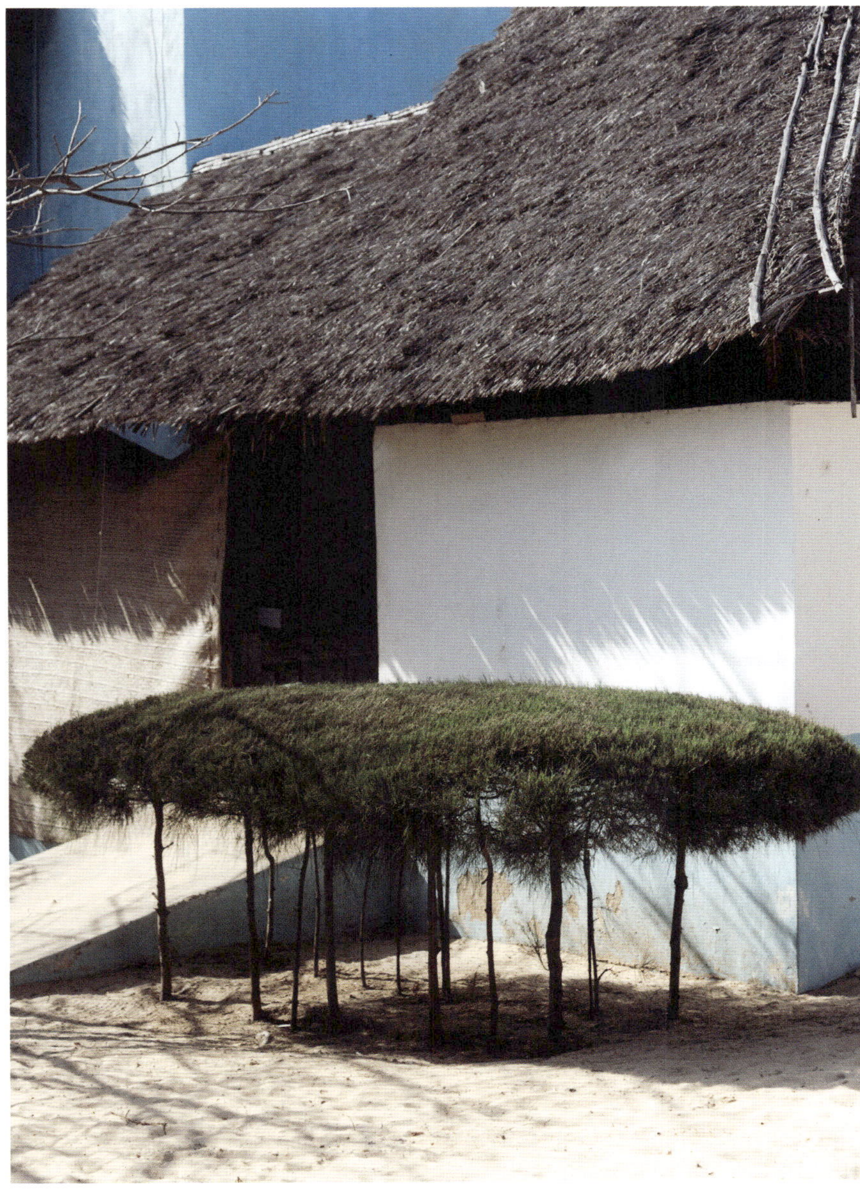

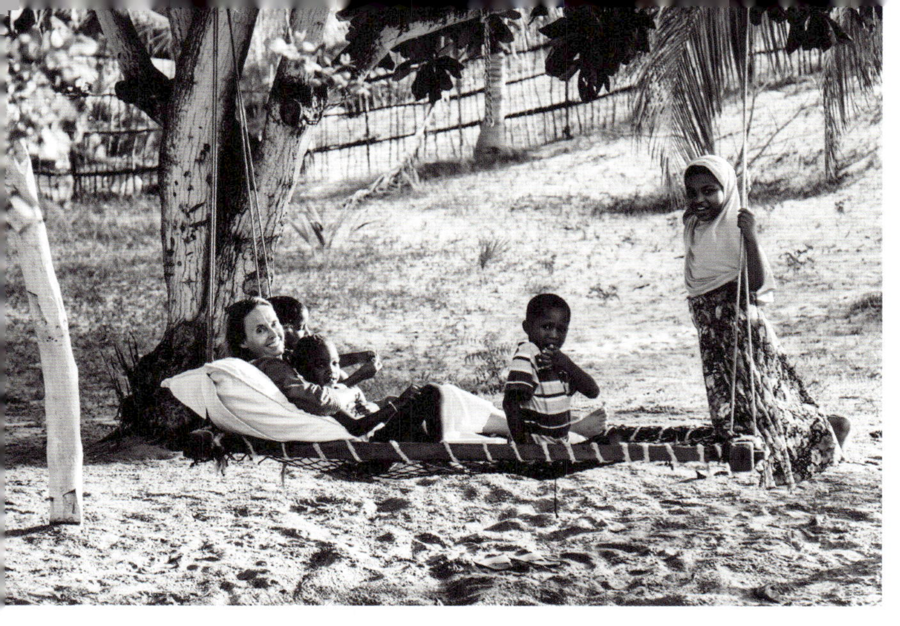

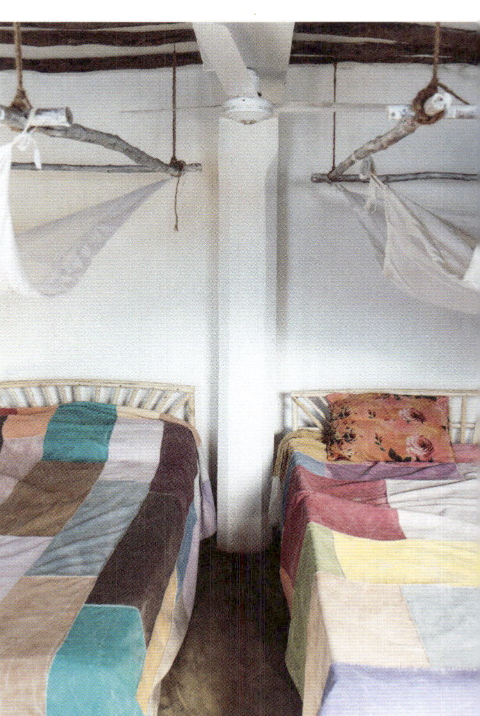

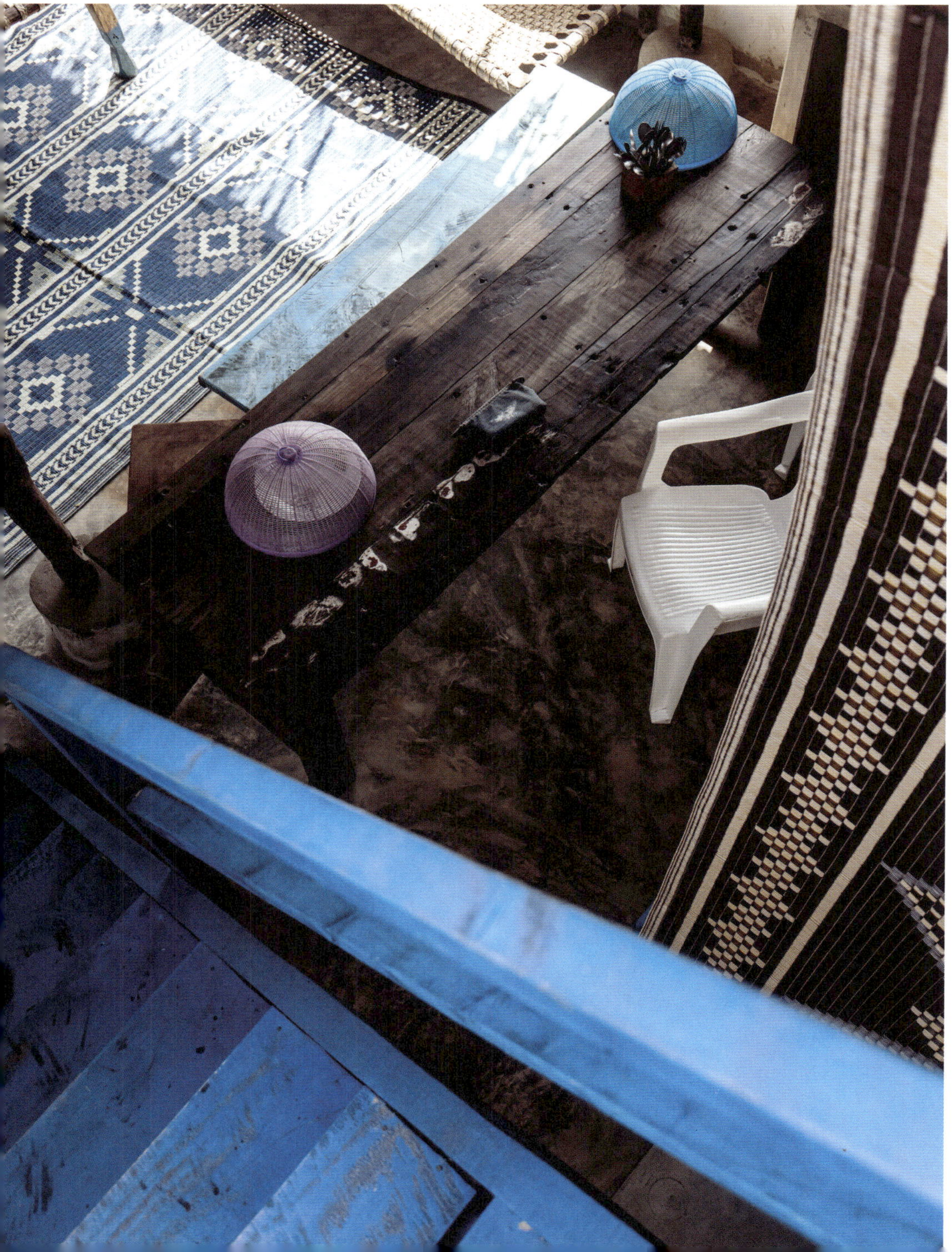

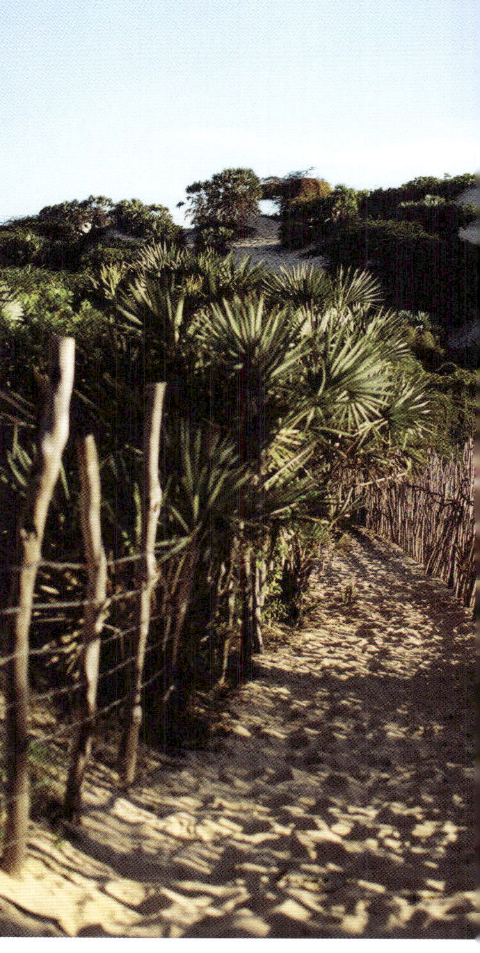

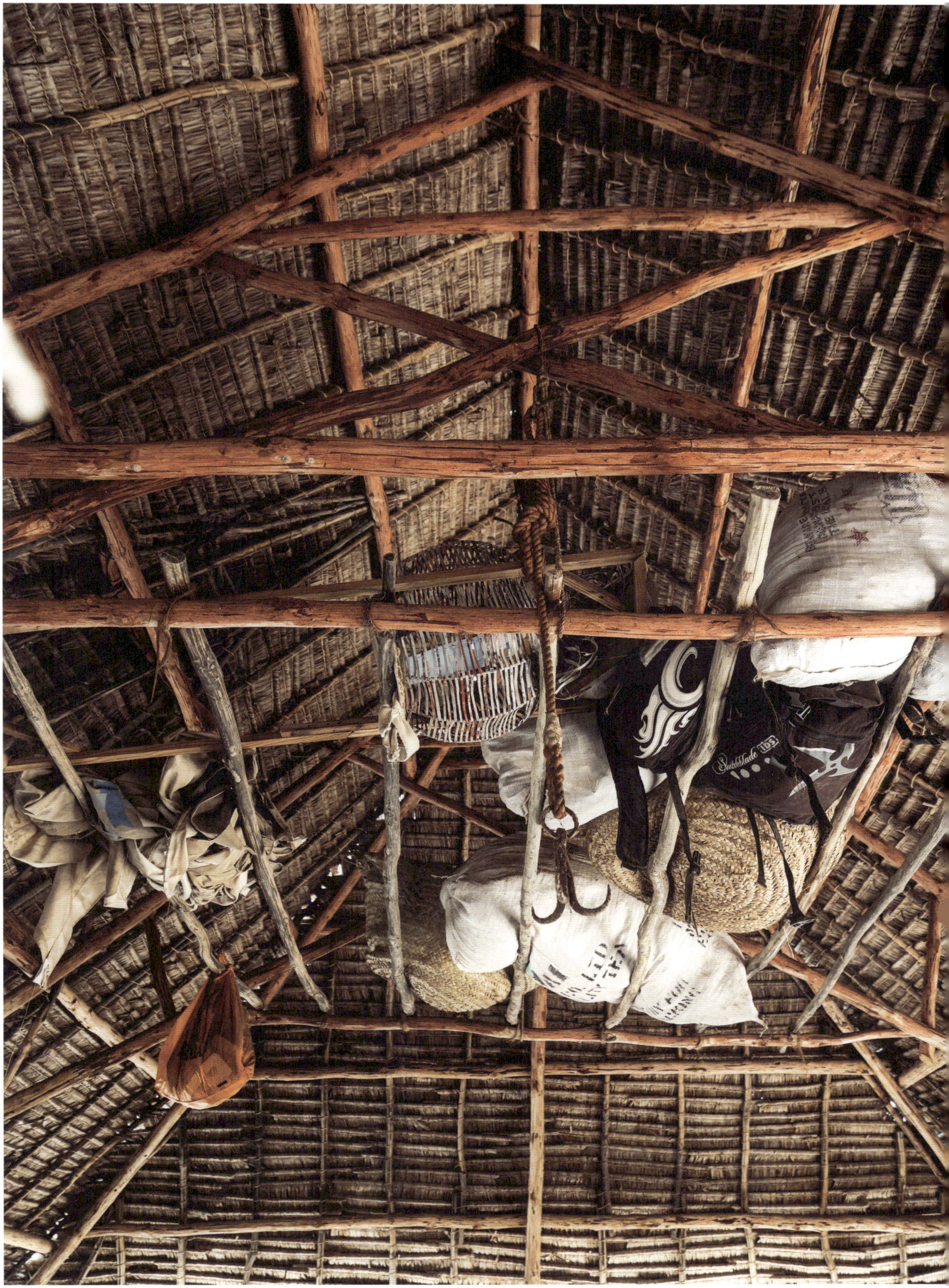

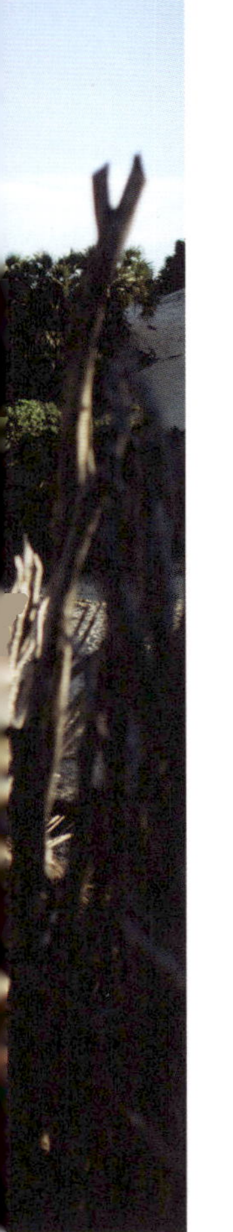

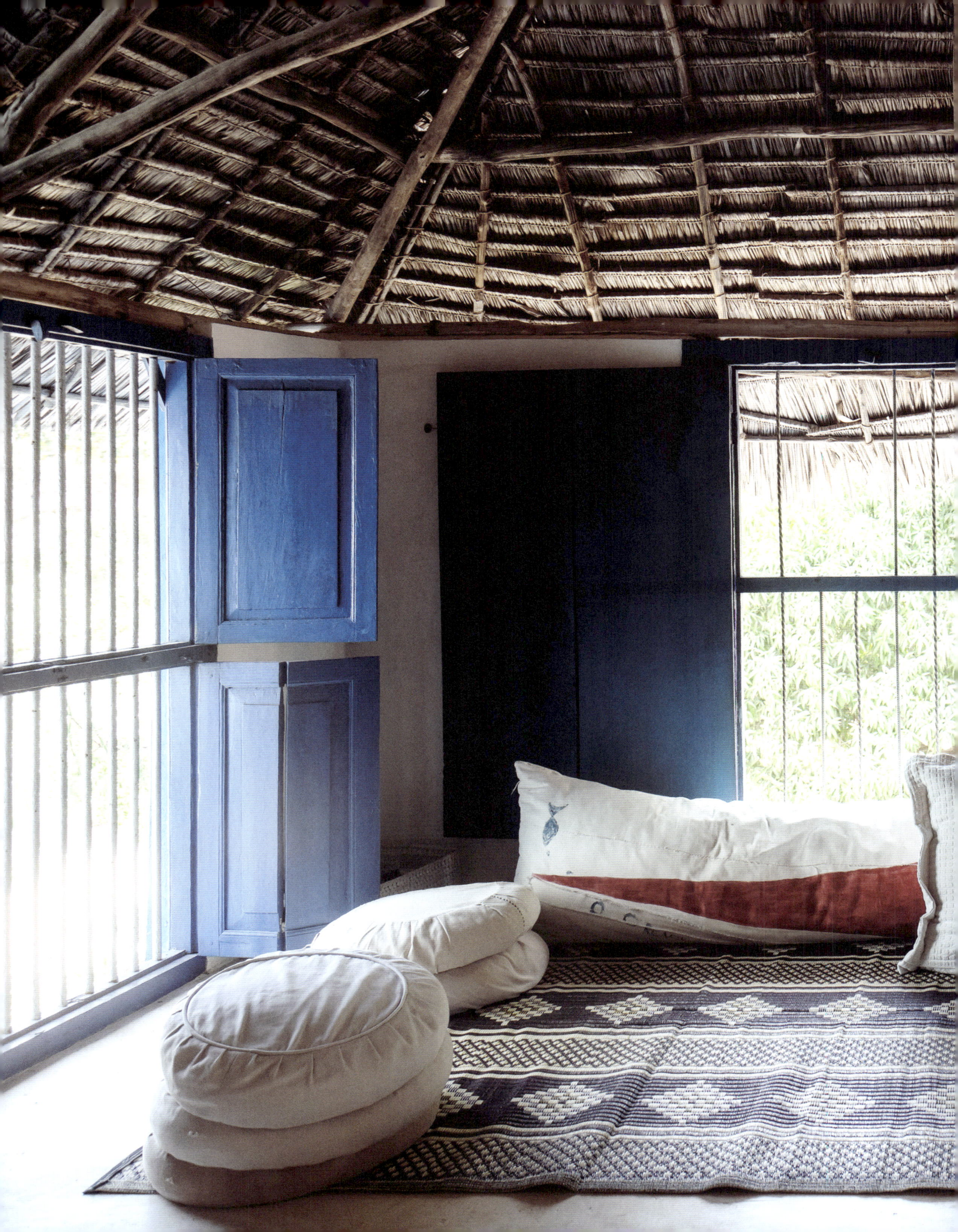

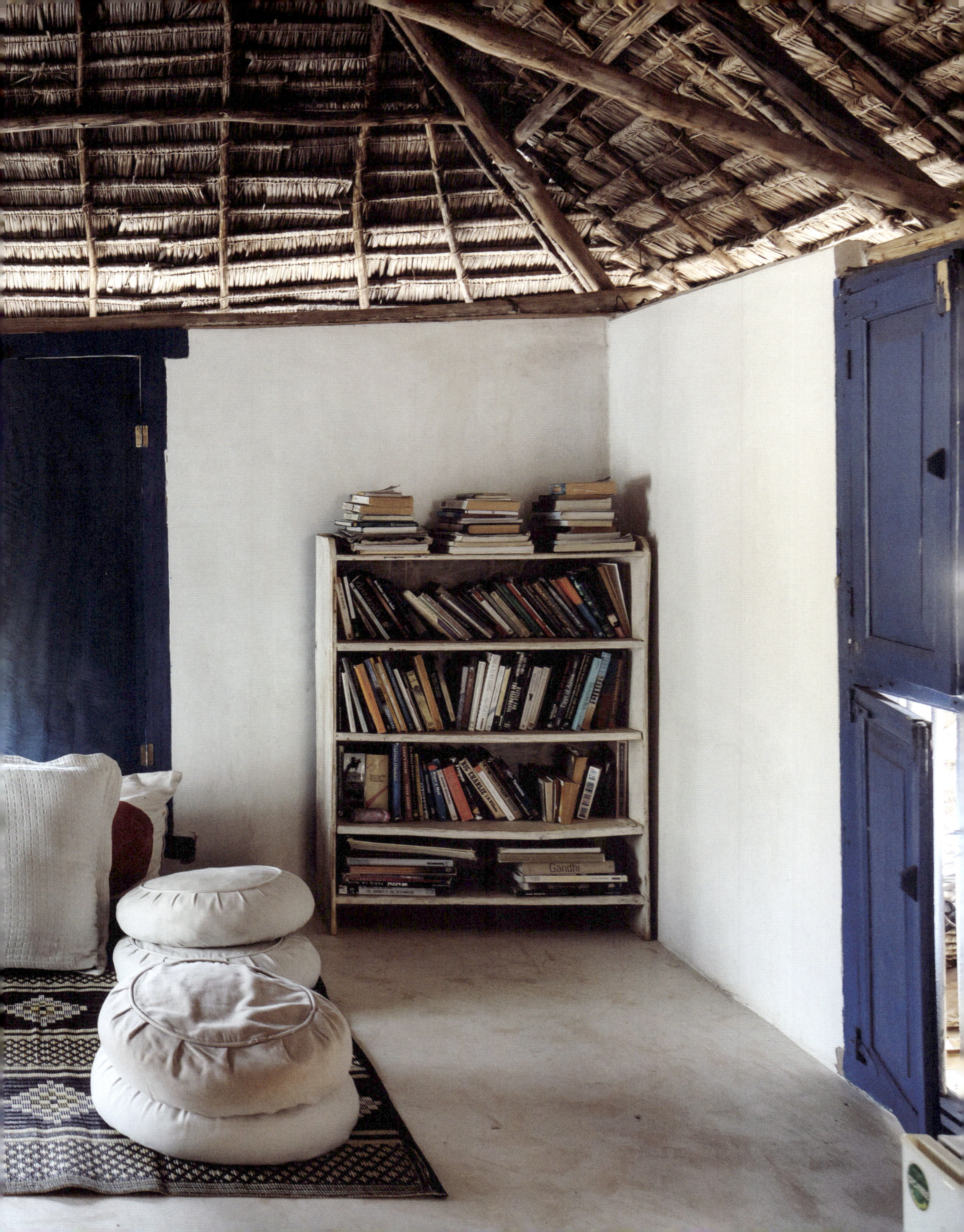
Gandhi

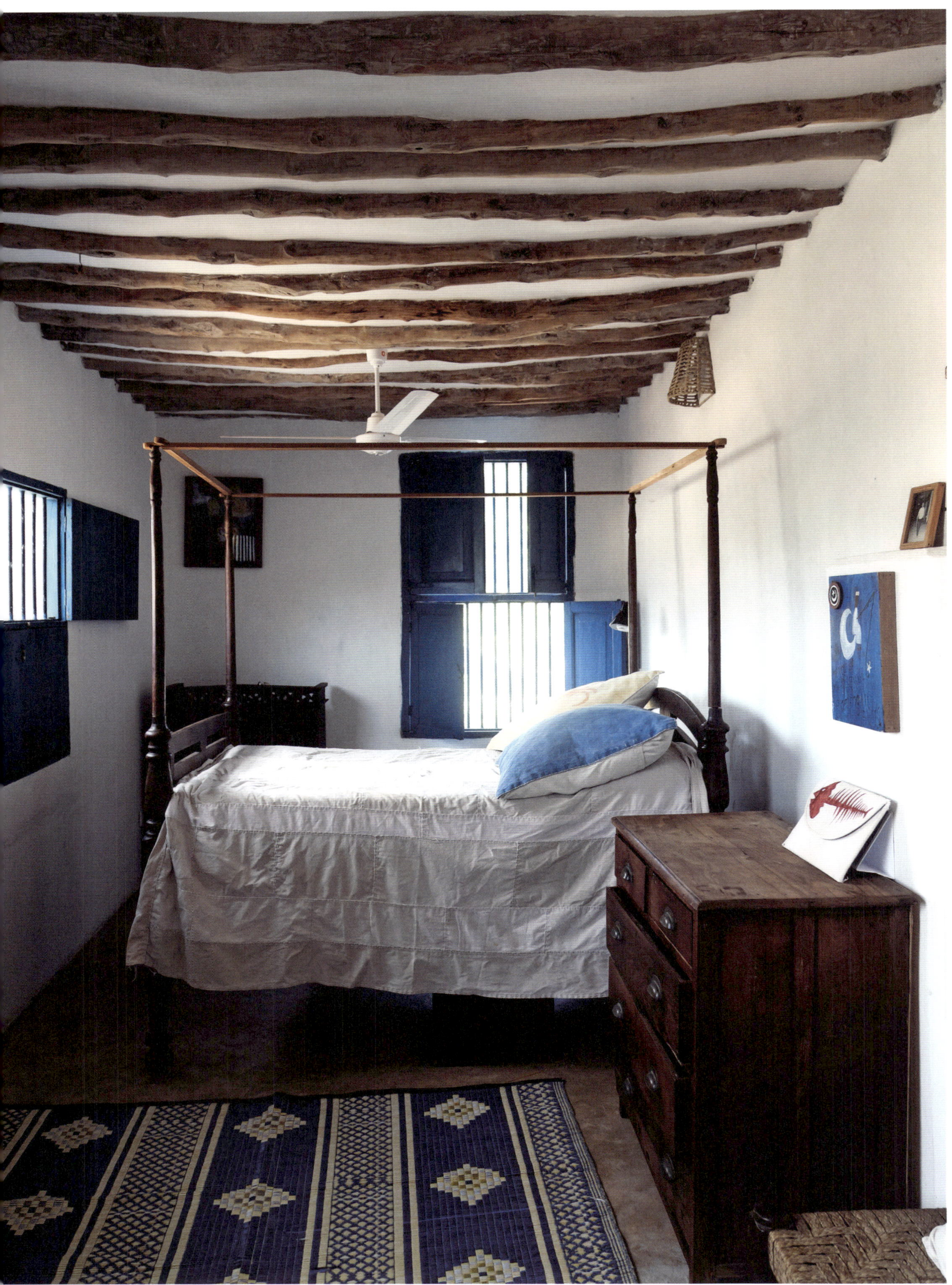

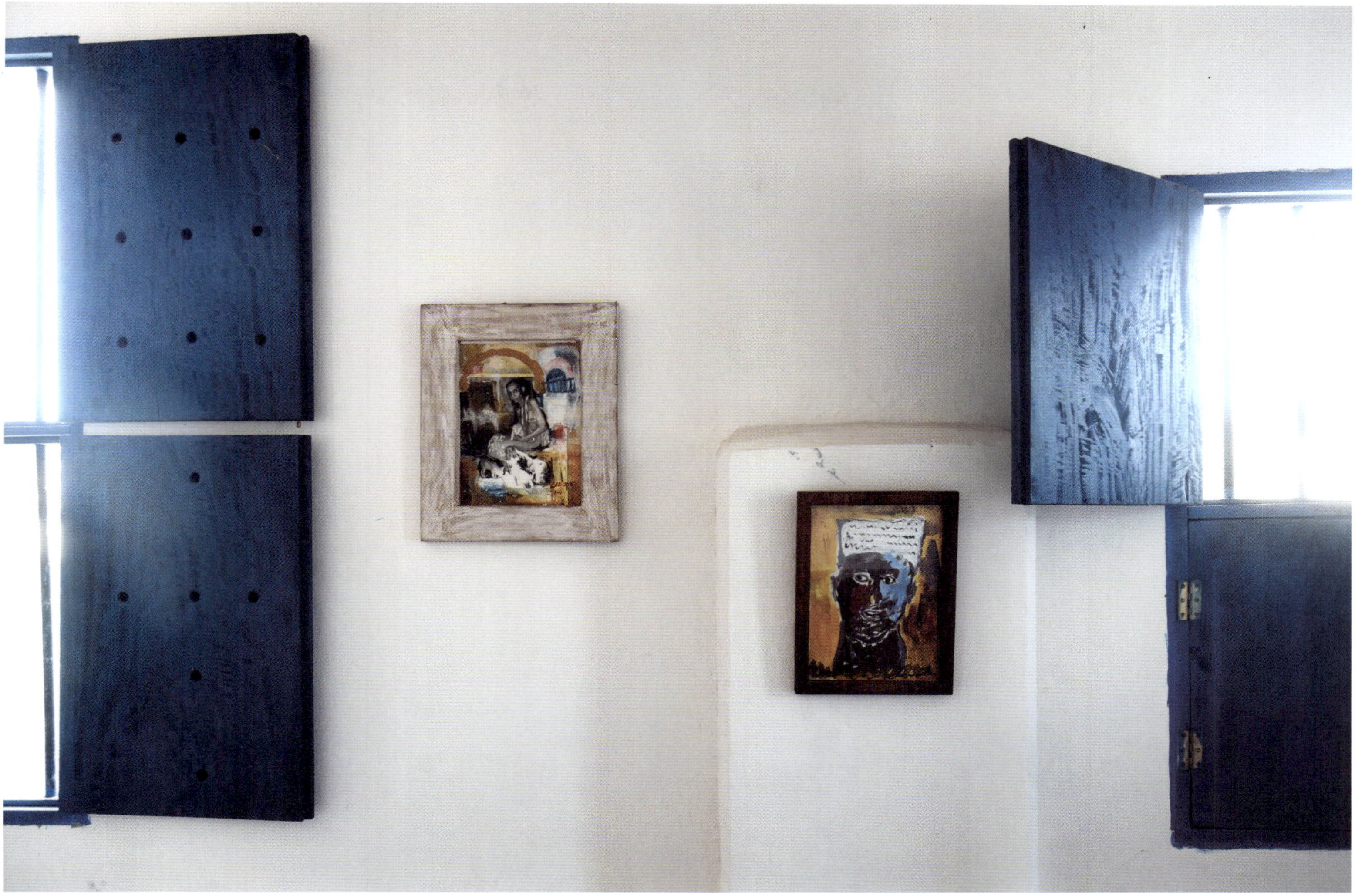

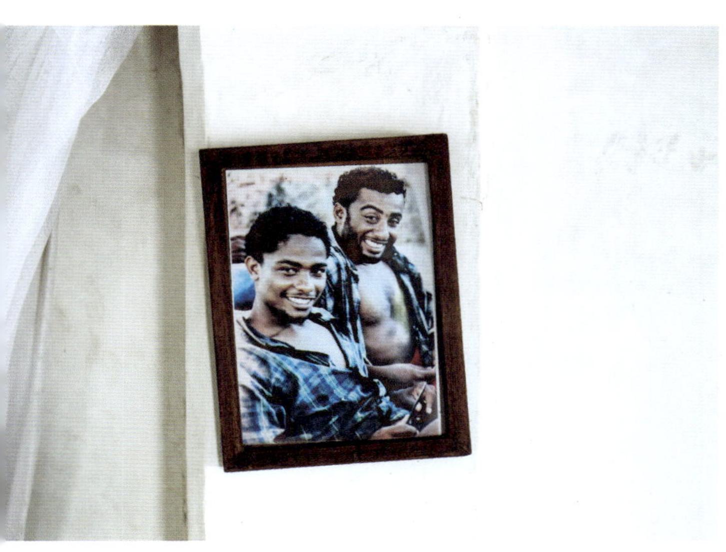

The woodwork was painted a bright blue, the walls sparsely decorated with personal photos and paintings, and rugs and cushions added a cosy touch. Daniella's passion for fabrics and colour and the people of Lamu Island is palpable throughout. The local children, including Ali Omar's, are always welcome and regularly drop in. Sometimes they pay a quick visit, sometimes they stay to live with Daniella for a while. For Daniella, they are all part of one big, recycled family, along with her five dogs and three donkeys.

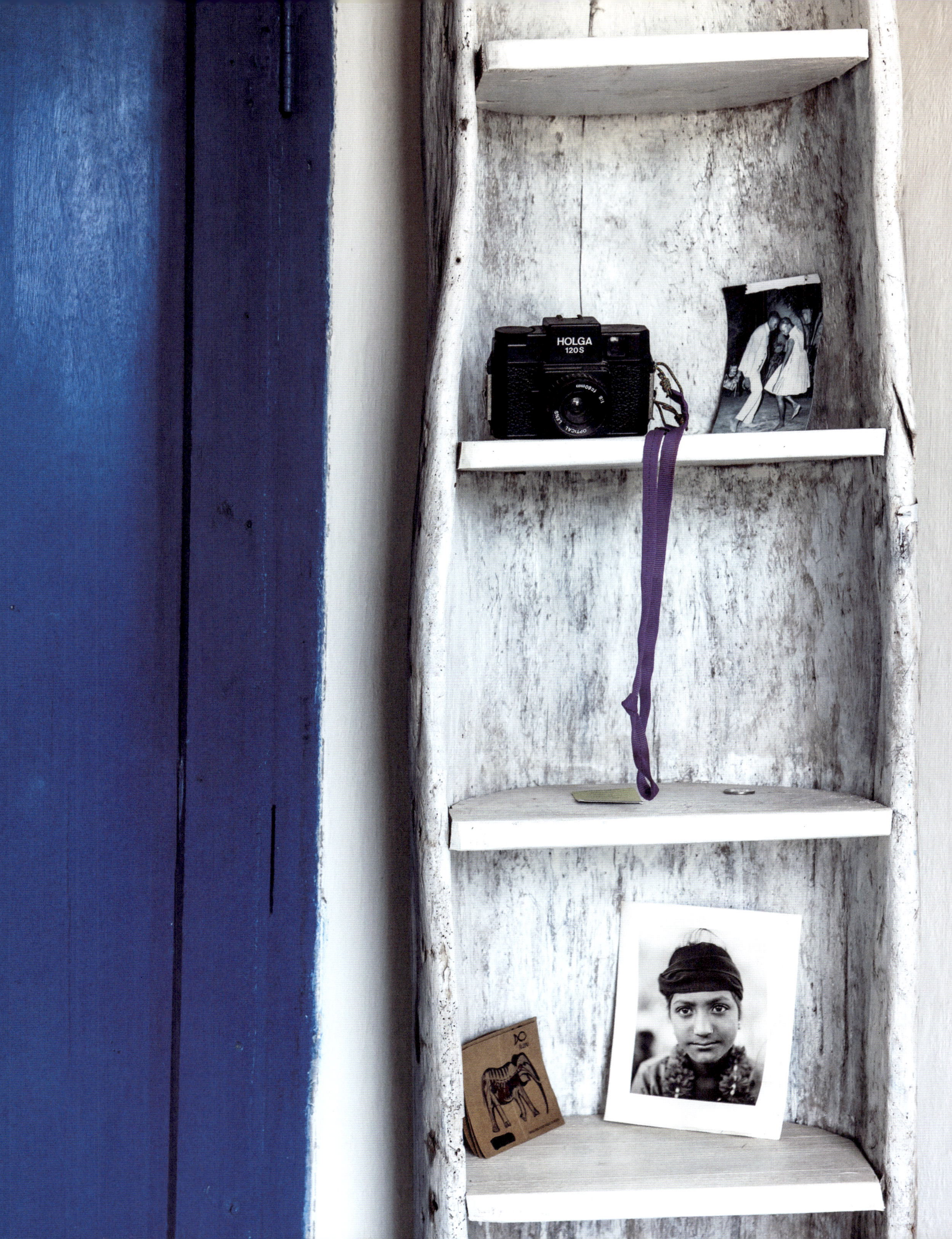
HOLGA
120S

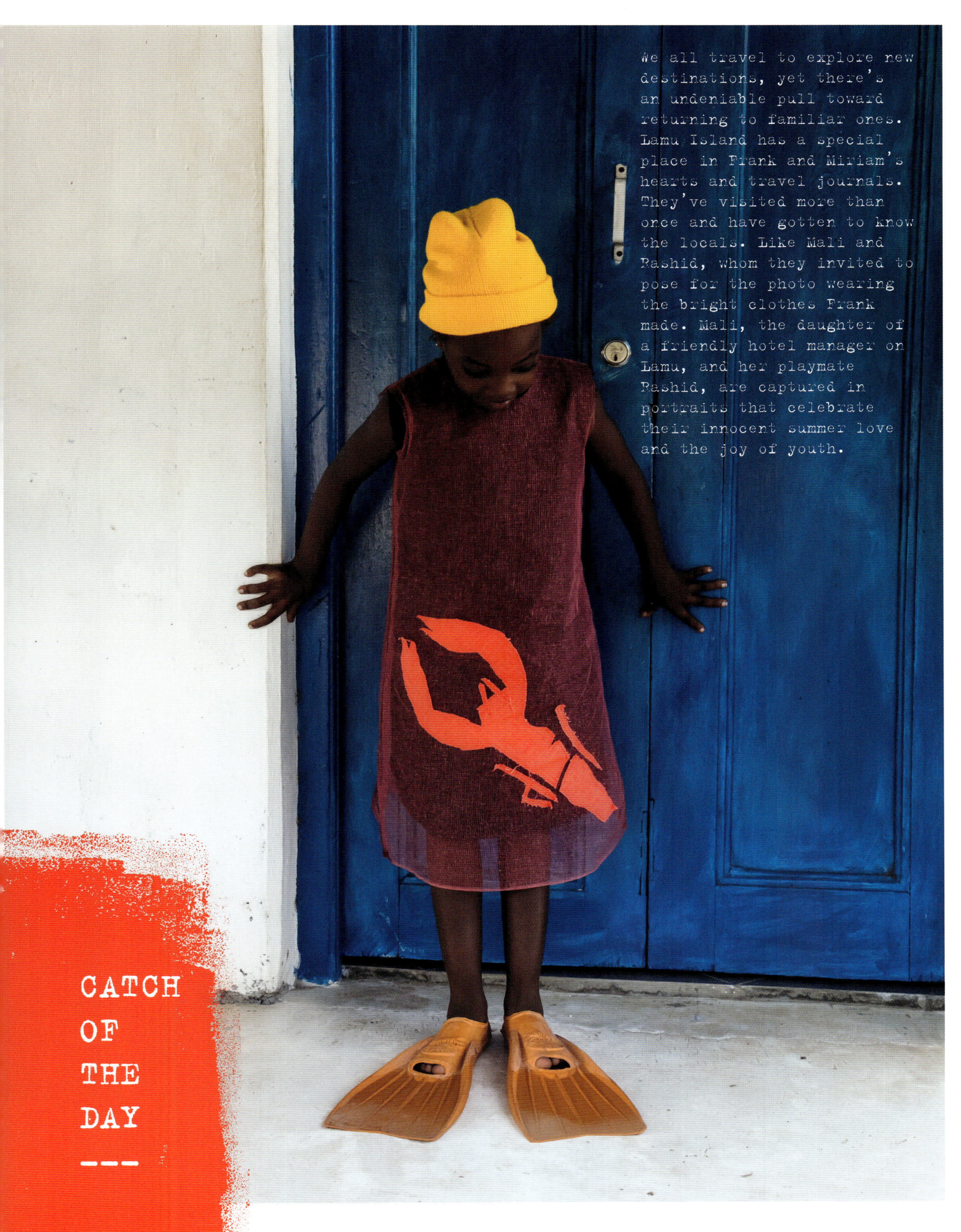

We all travel to explore new destinations, yet there's an undeniable pull toward returning to familiar ones. Lamu Island has a special place in Frank and Miriam's hearts and travel journals. They've visited more than once and have gotten to know the locals. Like Mali and Rashid, whom they invited to pose for the photo wearing the bright clothes Frank made. Mali, the daughter of a friendly hotel manager on Lamu, and her playmate Rashid, are captured in portraits that celebrate their innocent summer love and the joy of youth.

CATCH OF THE DAY

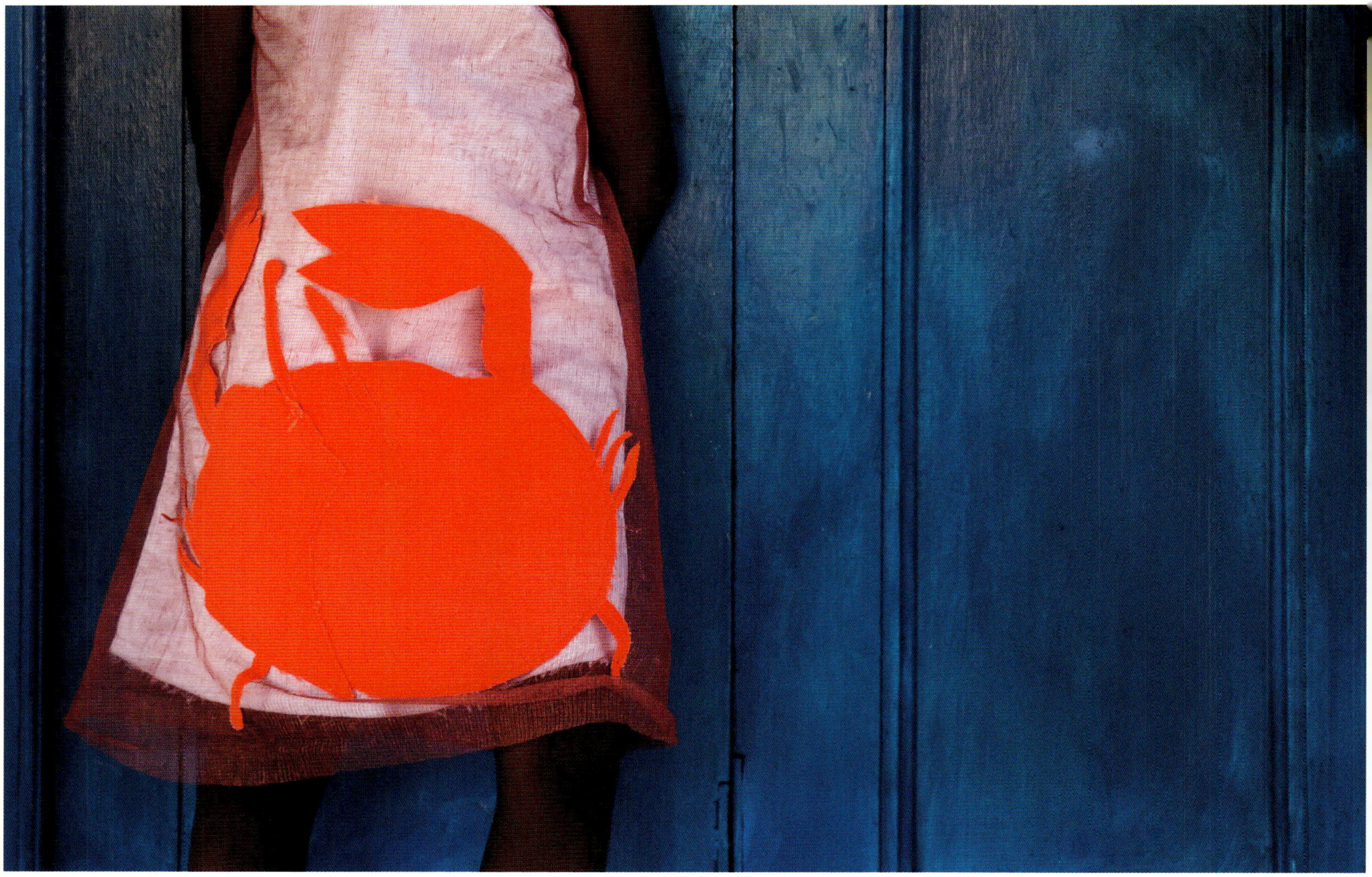

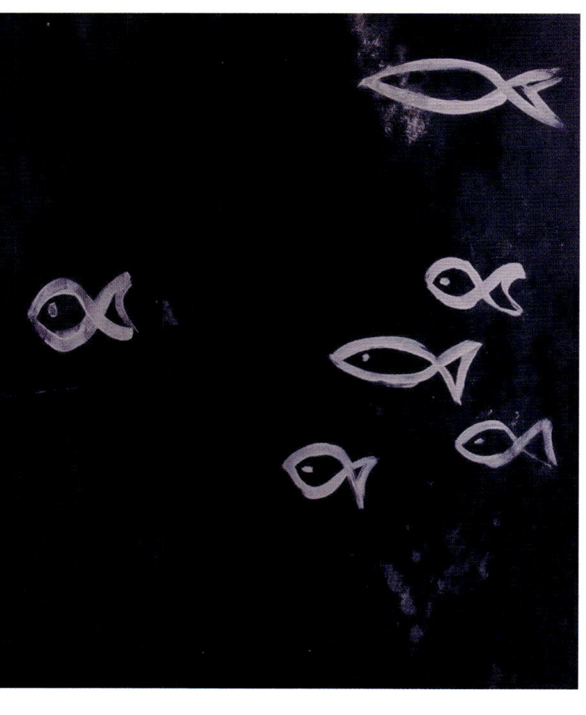

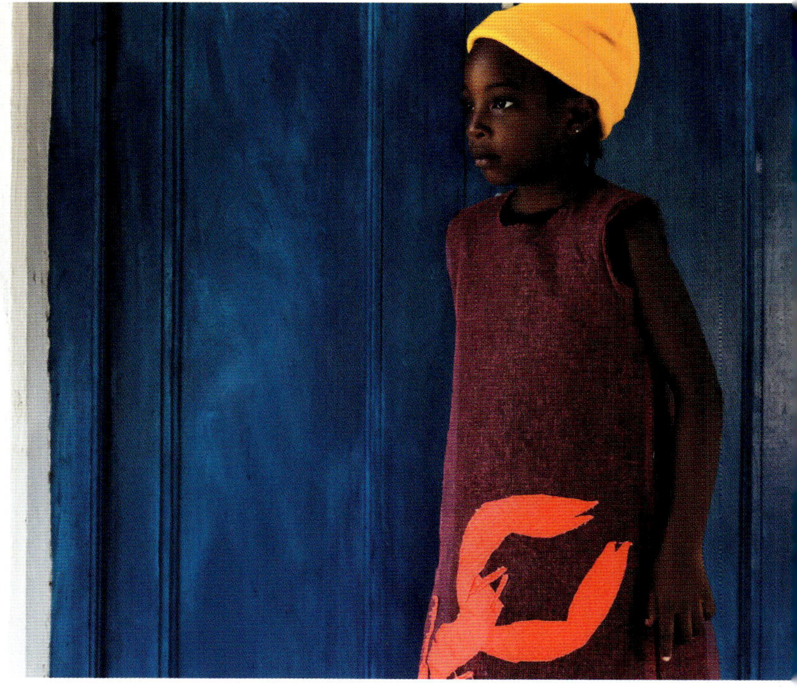

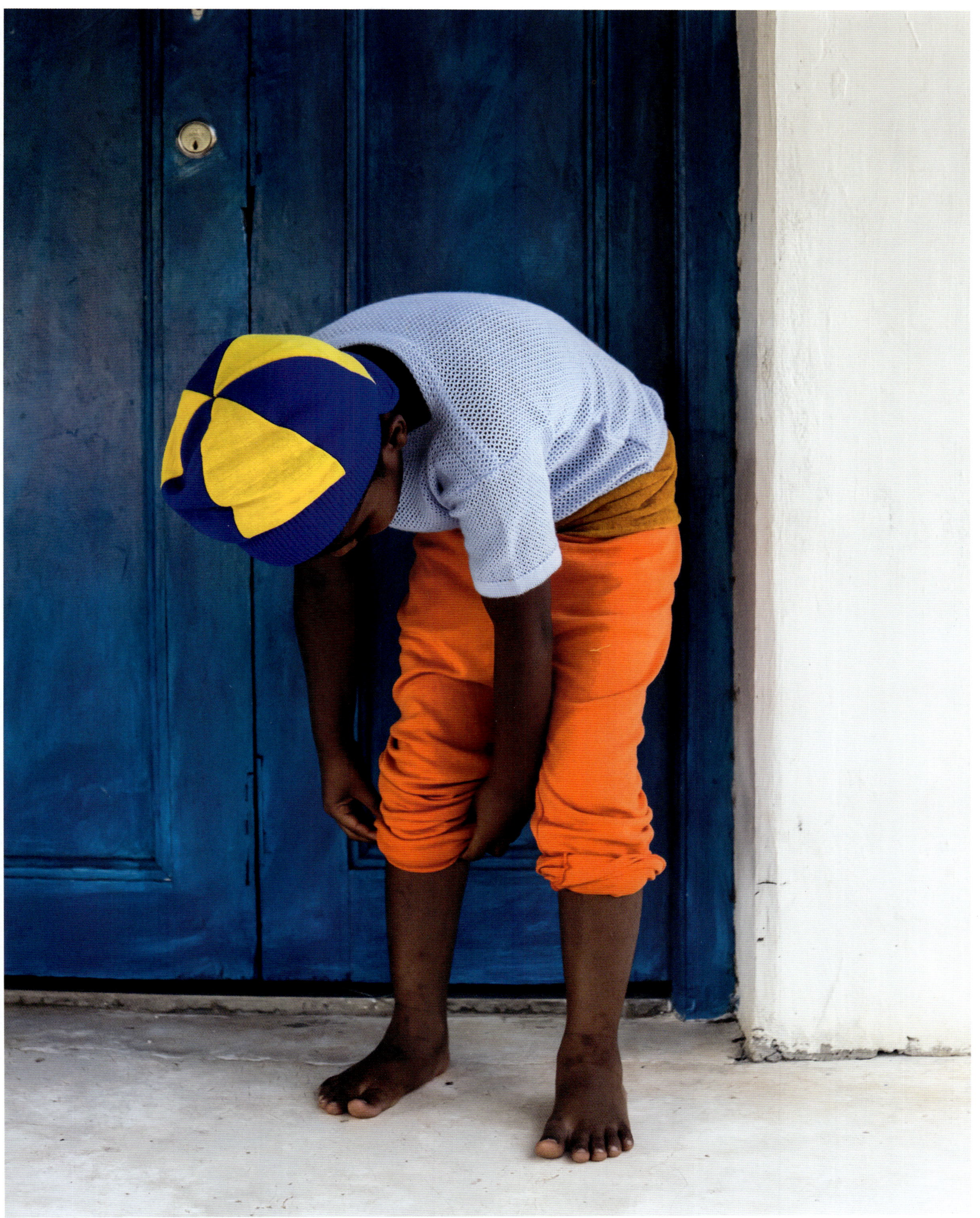

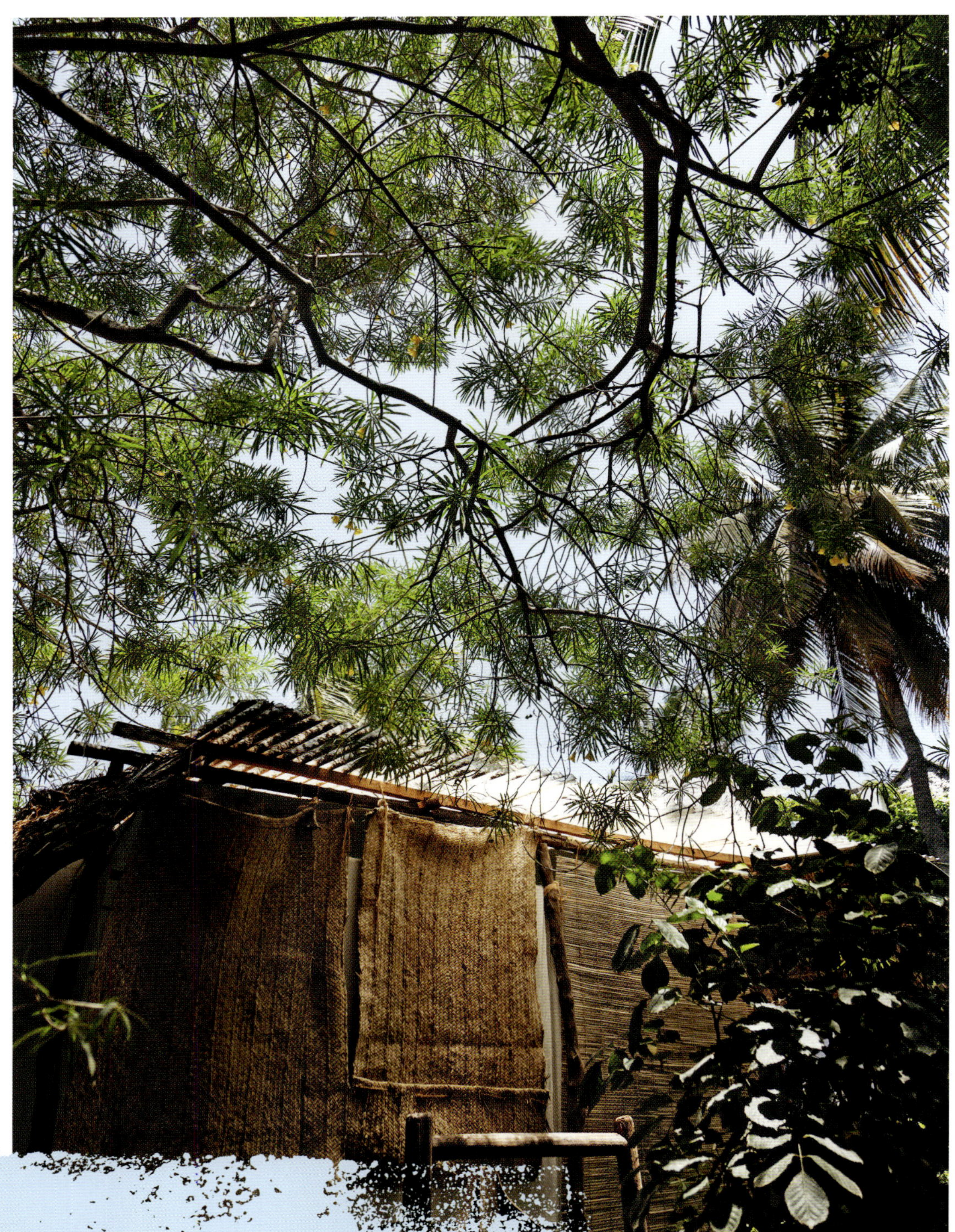

The natural beauty, the people, the sea, and the light, ... Lamu Island beckons you to stay, relax, and do little more than let inspiration find you. When Frank and Mirjam rented a house there, they were captivated by a small cottage on the property, which they adorned with textiles inspired by the island's light and colors. It's their tribute to the freedom and creativity they experience there.

THE COTTAGE NEXTDOOR

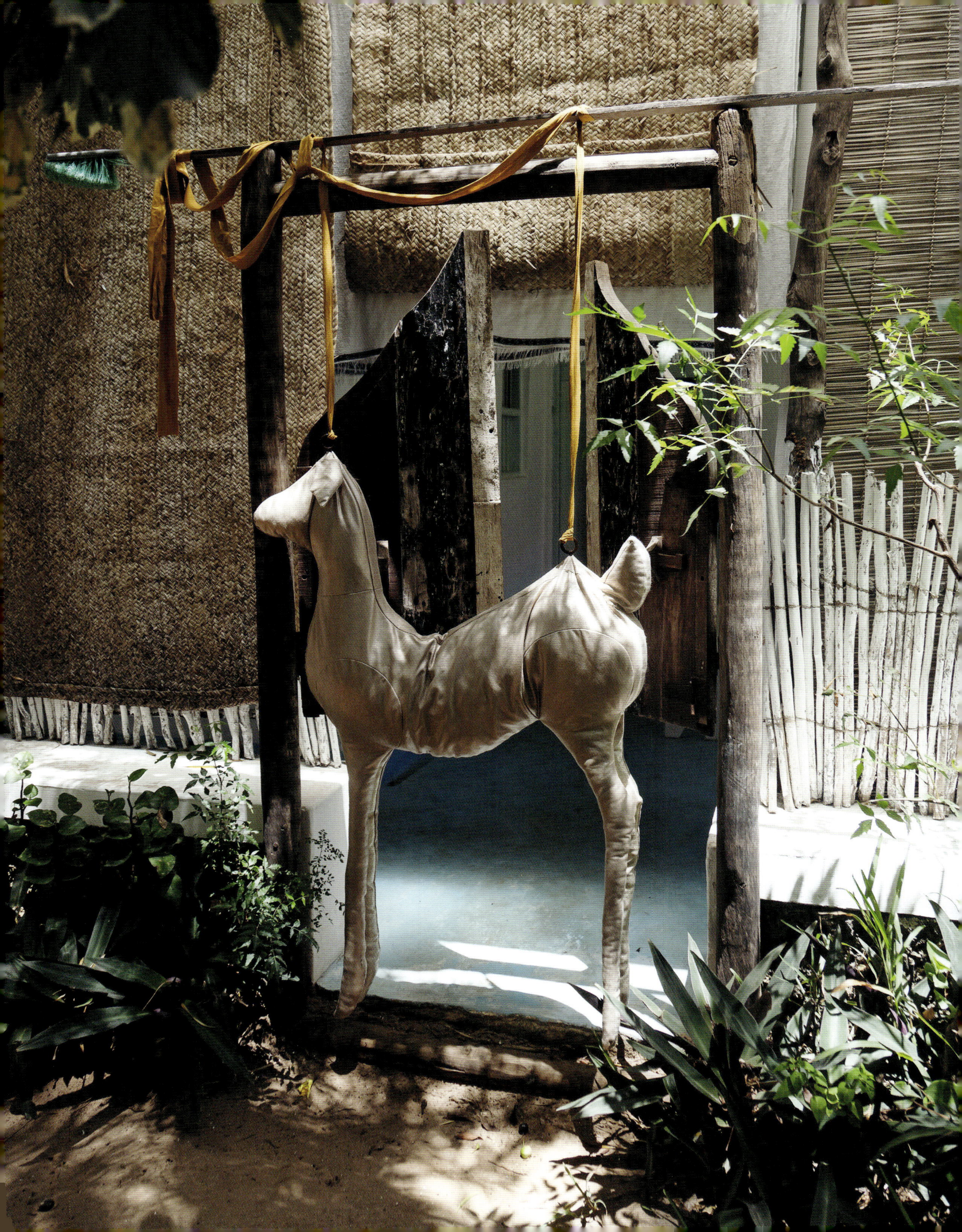

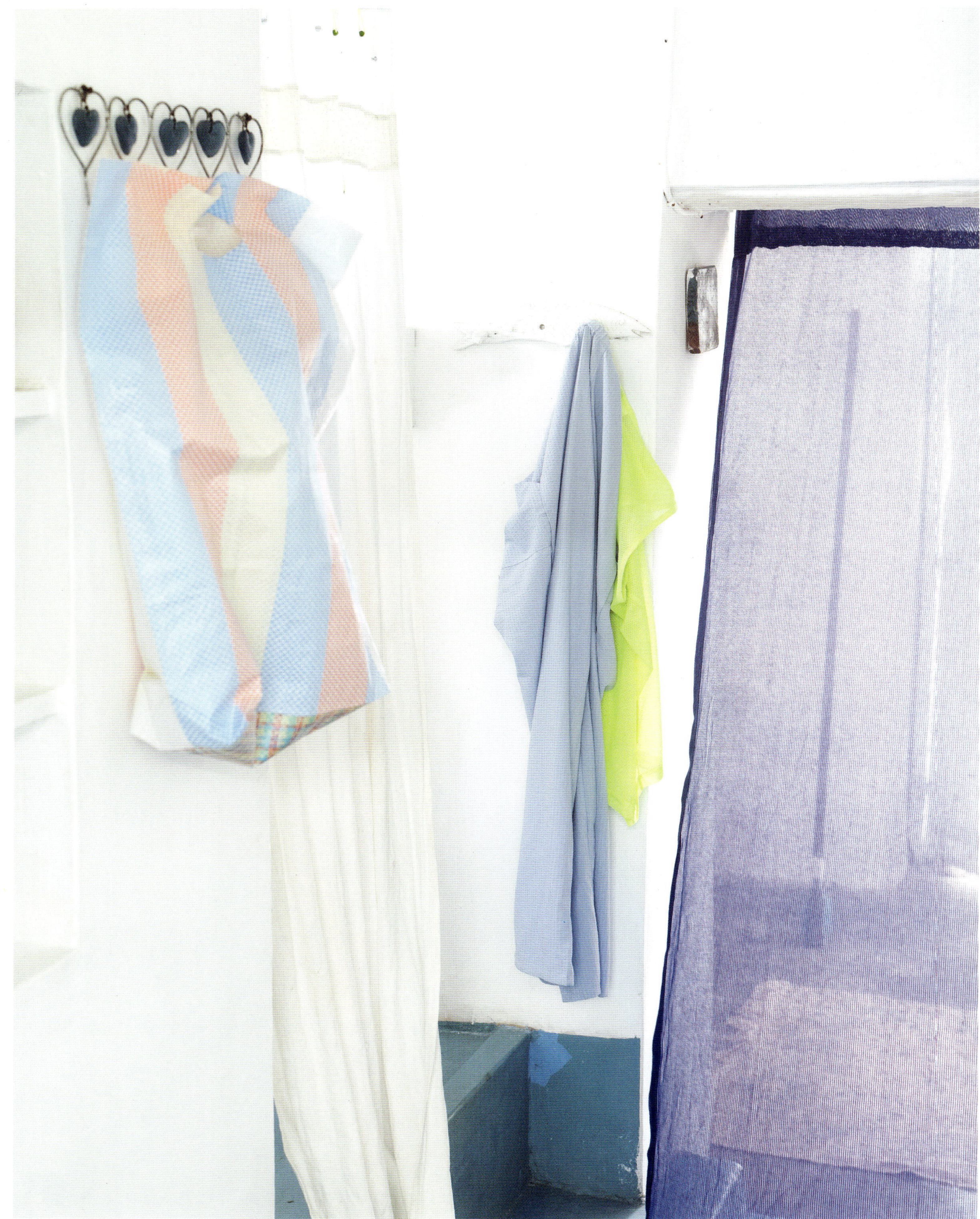

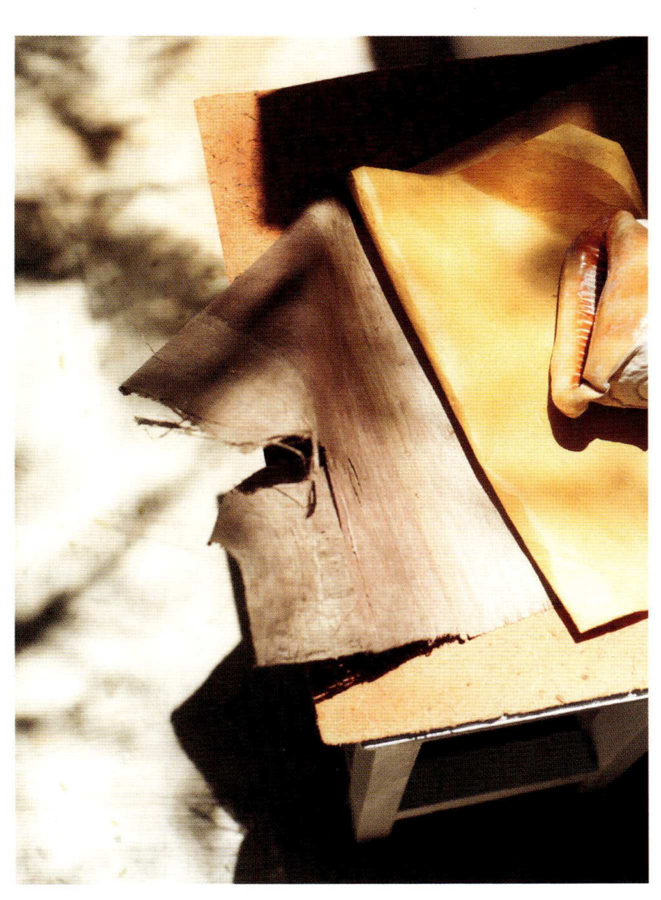

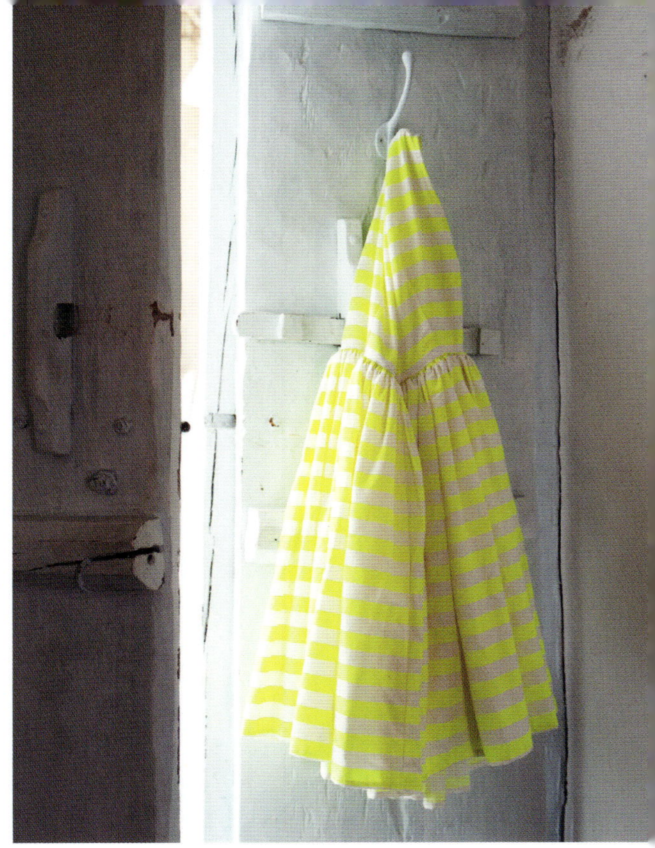

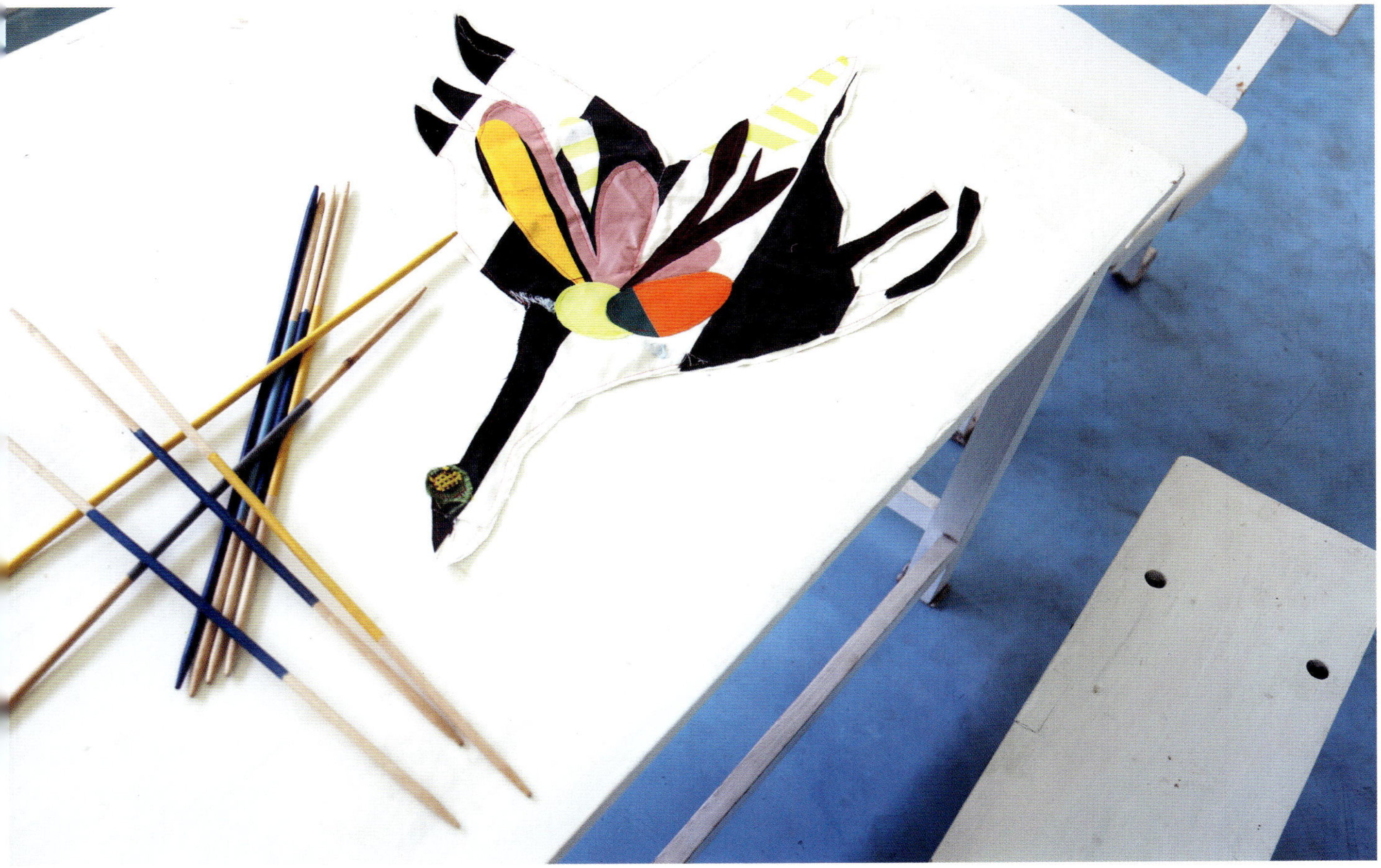

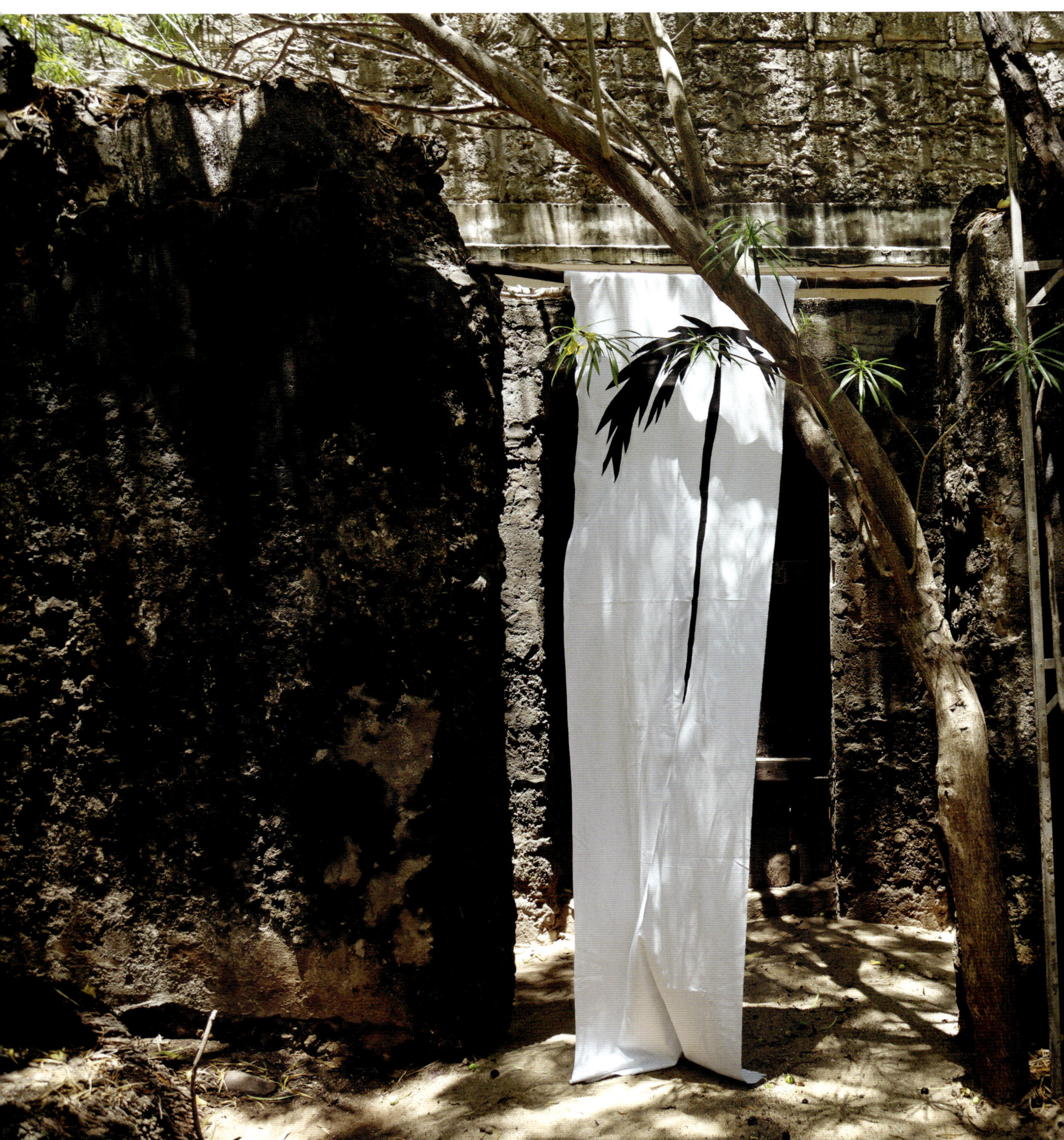

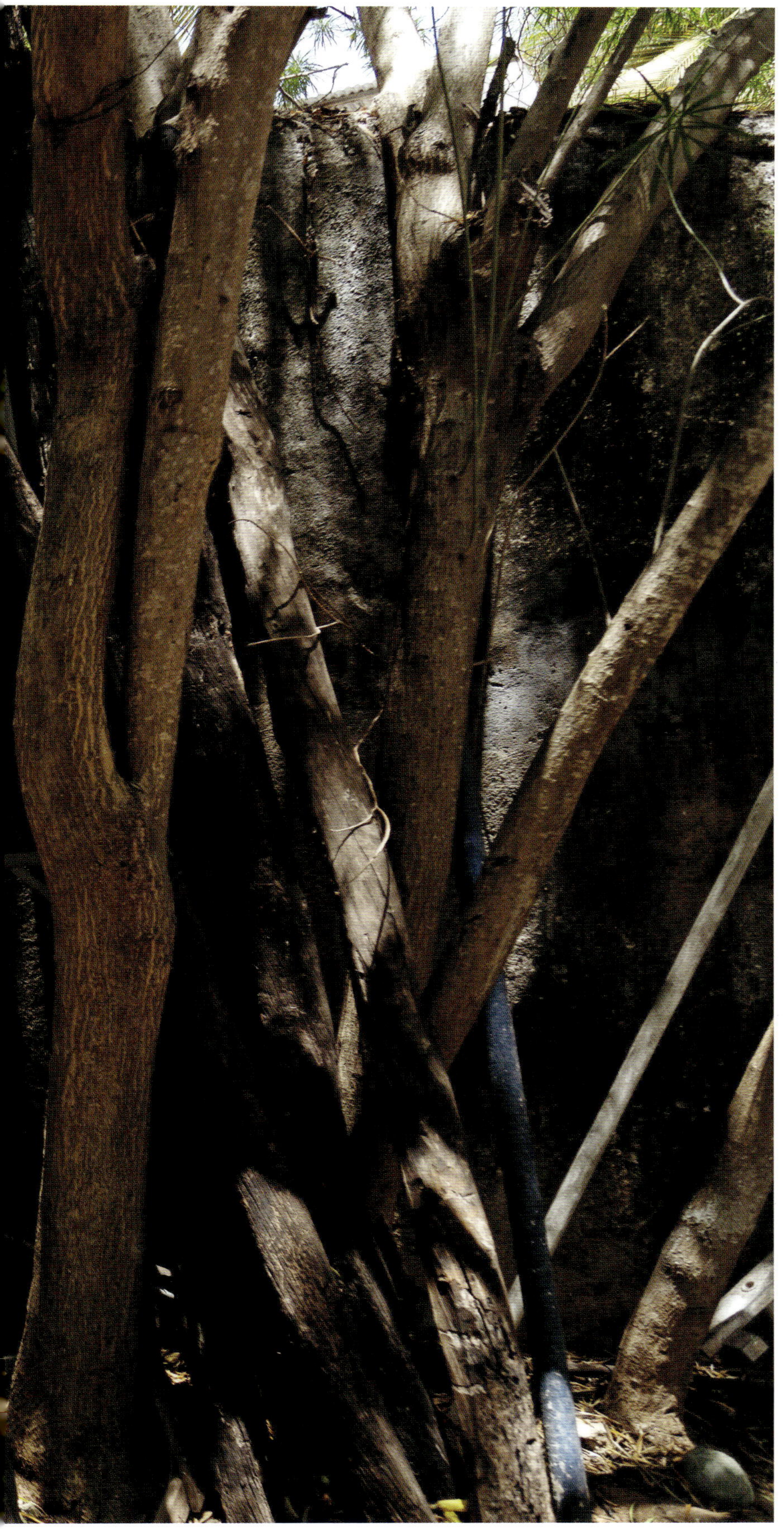

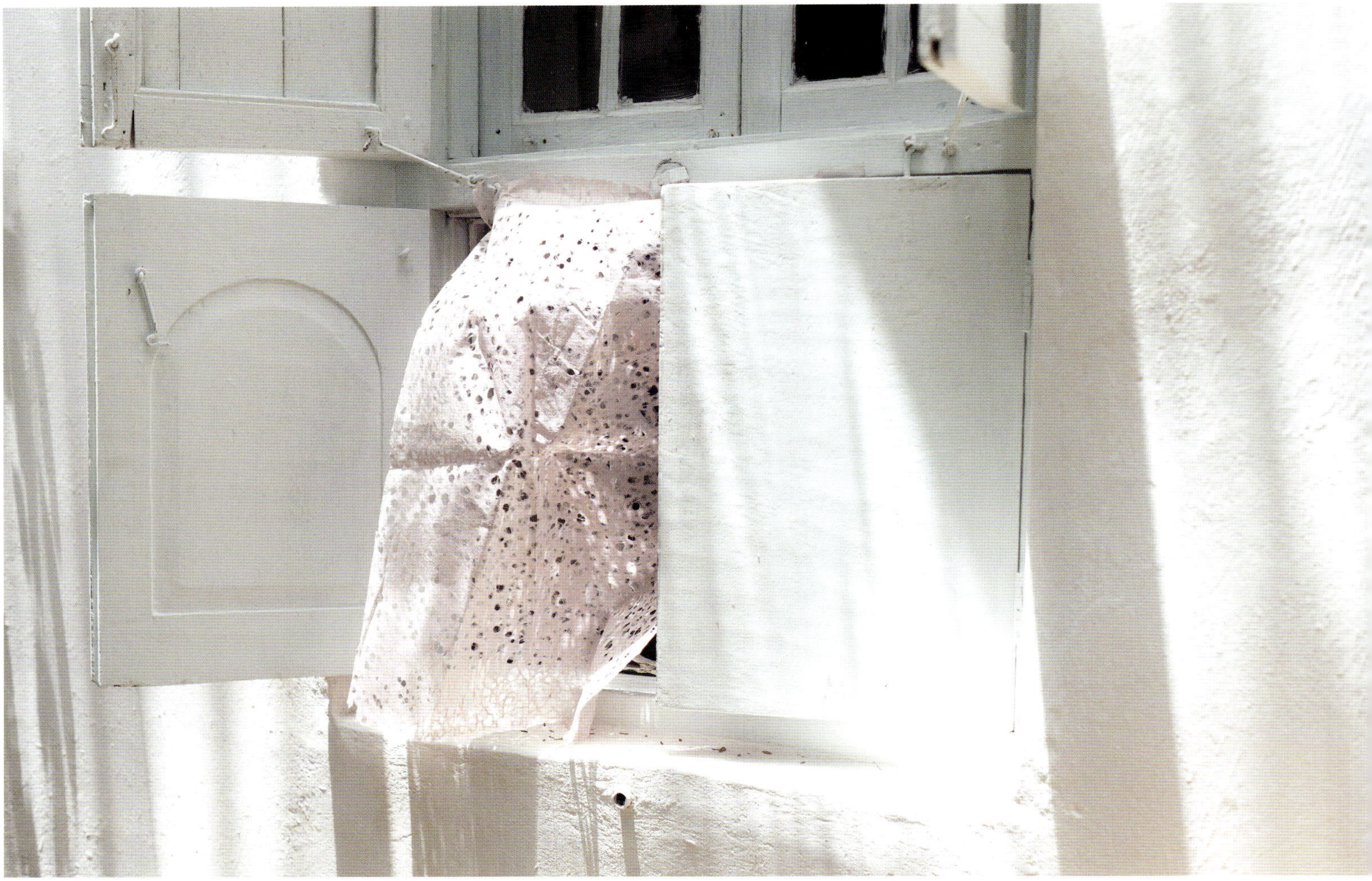

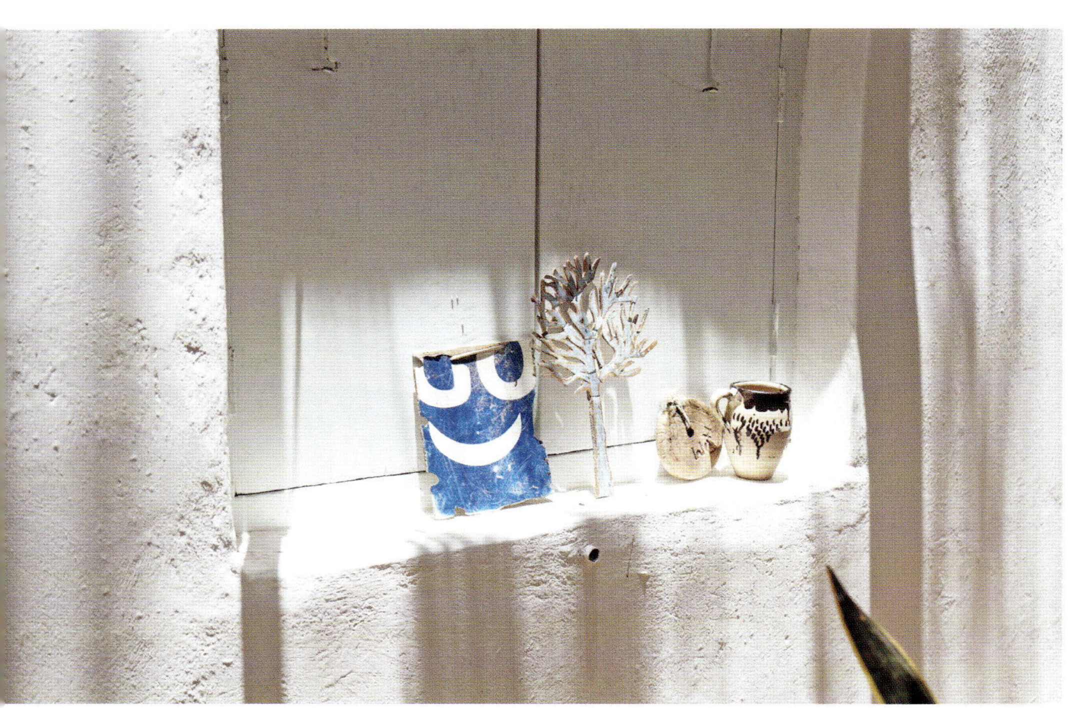

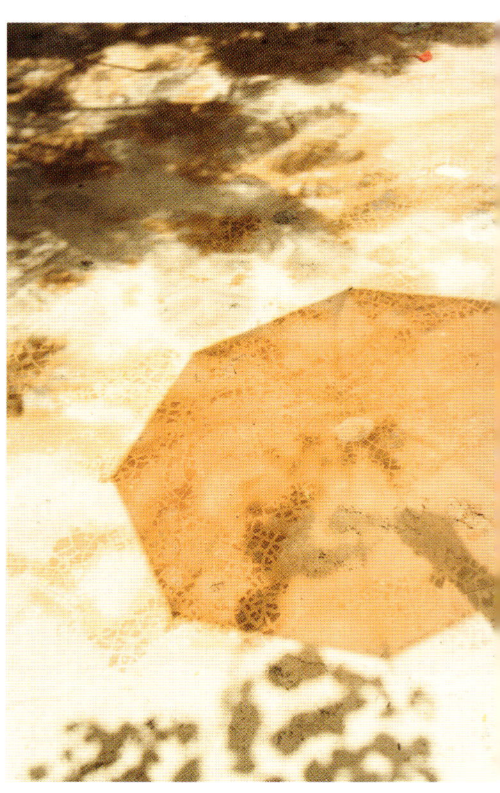

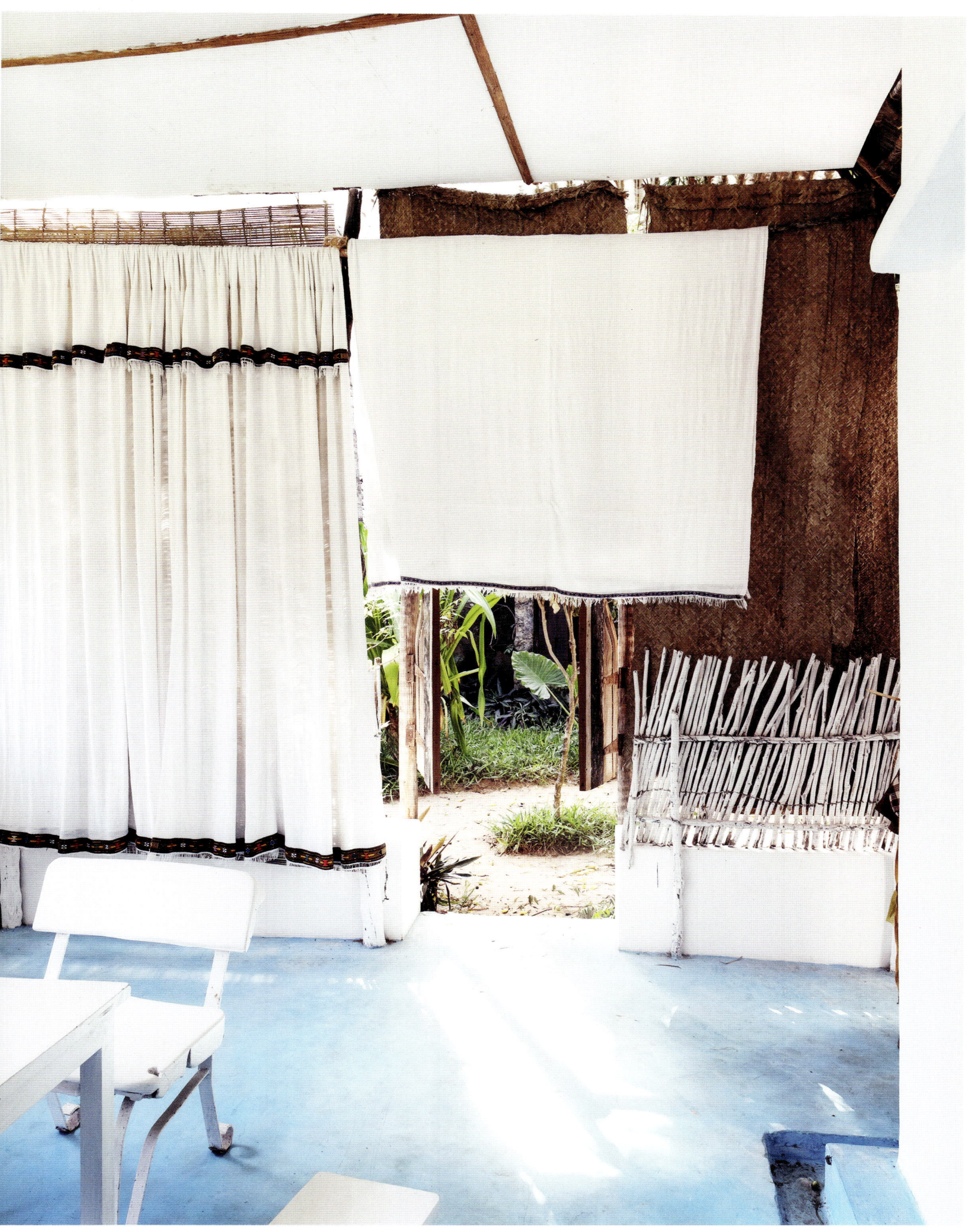

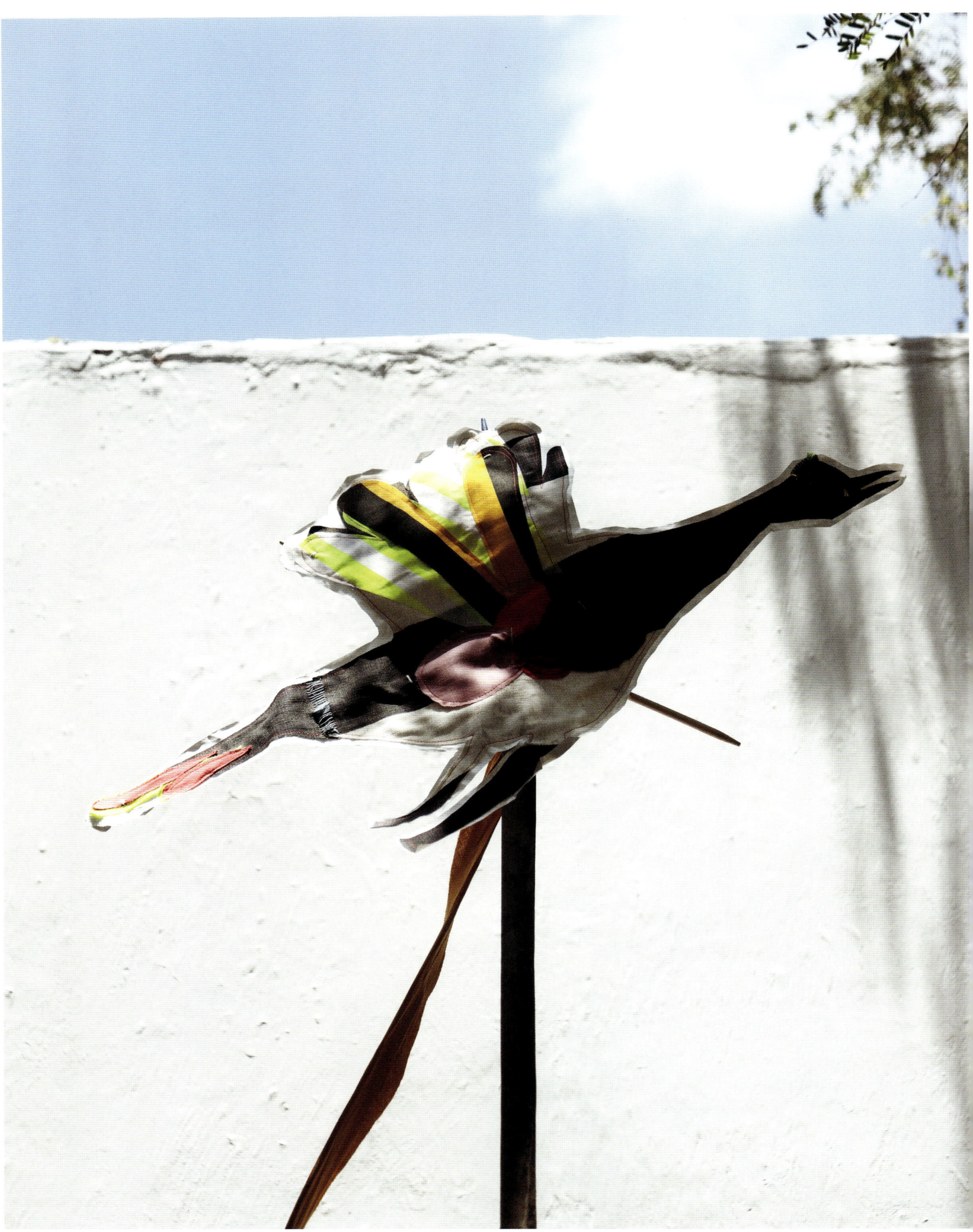

Amsterdam
The Netherlands

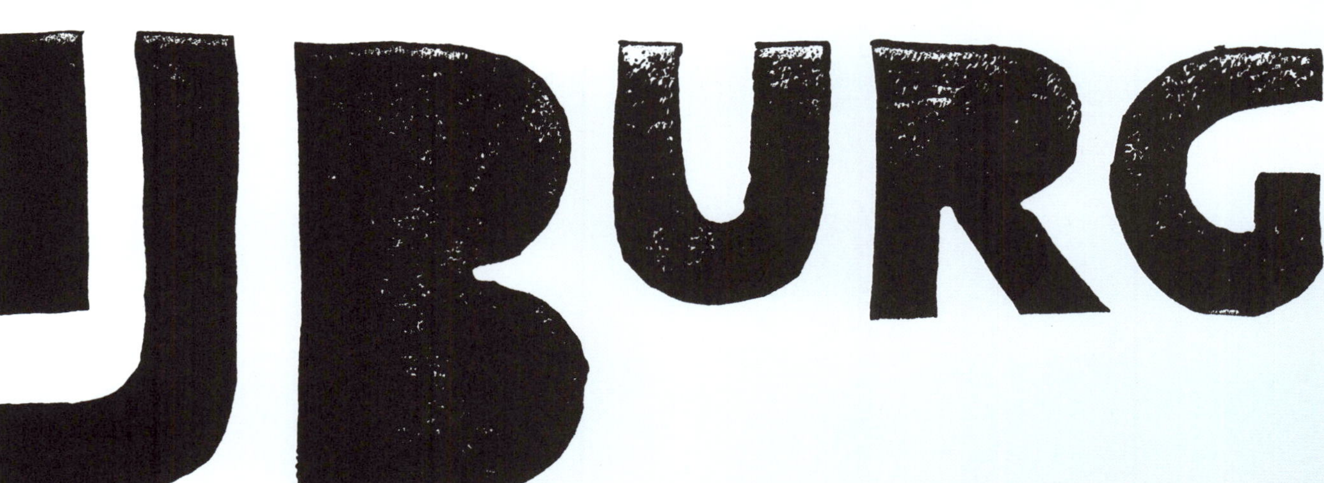

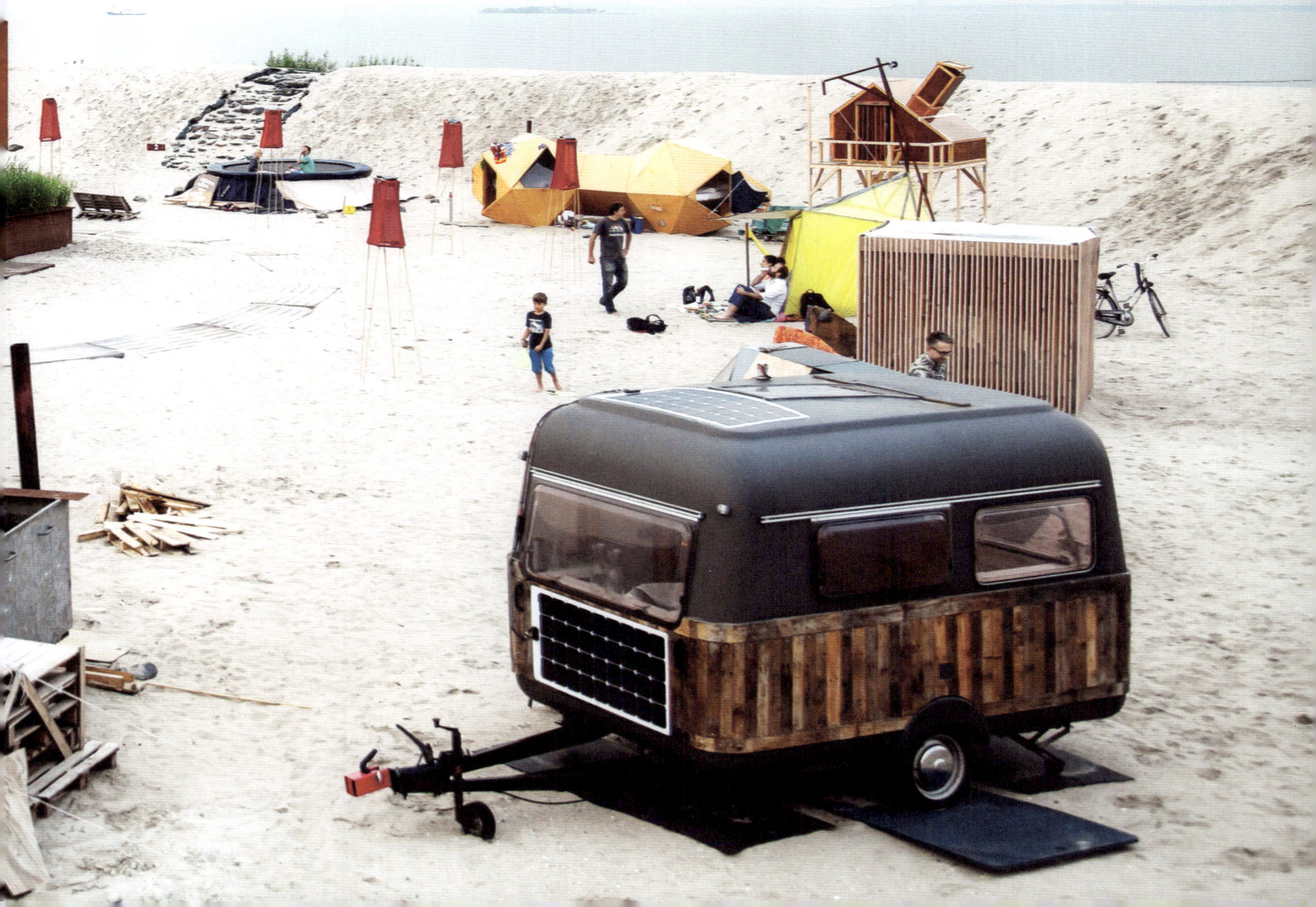

The Dutch shape their lives next to and on the water.
Amsterdam's IJburg district is a fine example: this urban development project is situated in the IJmeer where it's built on reclaimed artificial islands in the lake. As such, it provides lots of opportunities for creative entrepreneurs to experiment and turn wasteland into people-filled happening places. Add a waterfront location to this already exciting mix and you have all the ingredients for something new and captivating. This is what drew Annette van Driel and Francis Nijenhuis of the UrbanCampsite foundation to IJburg. They organise pop-up open-air exhibitions of artworks in surprising locations and found a perfect spot on IJburg's Centrumeiland when it was still an urban wasteland, on a sandy plain directly on the water.

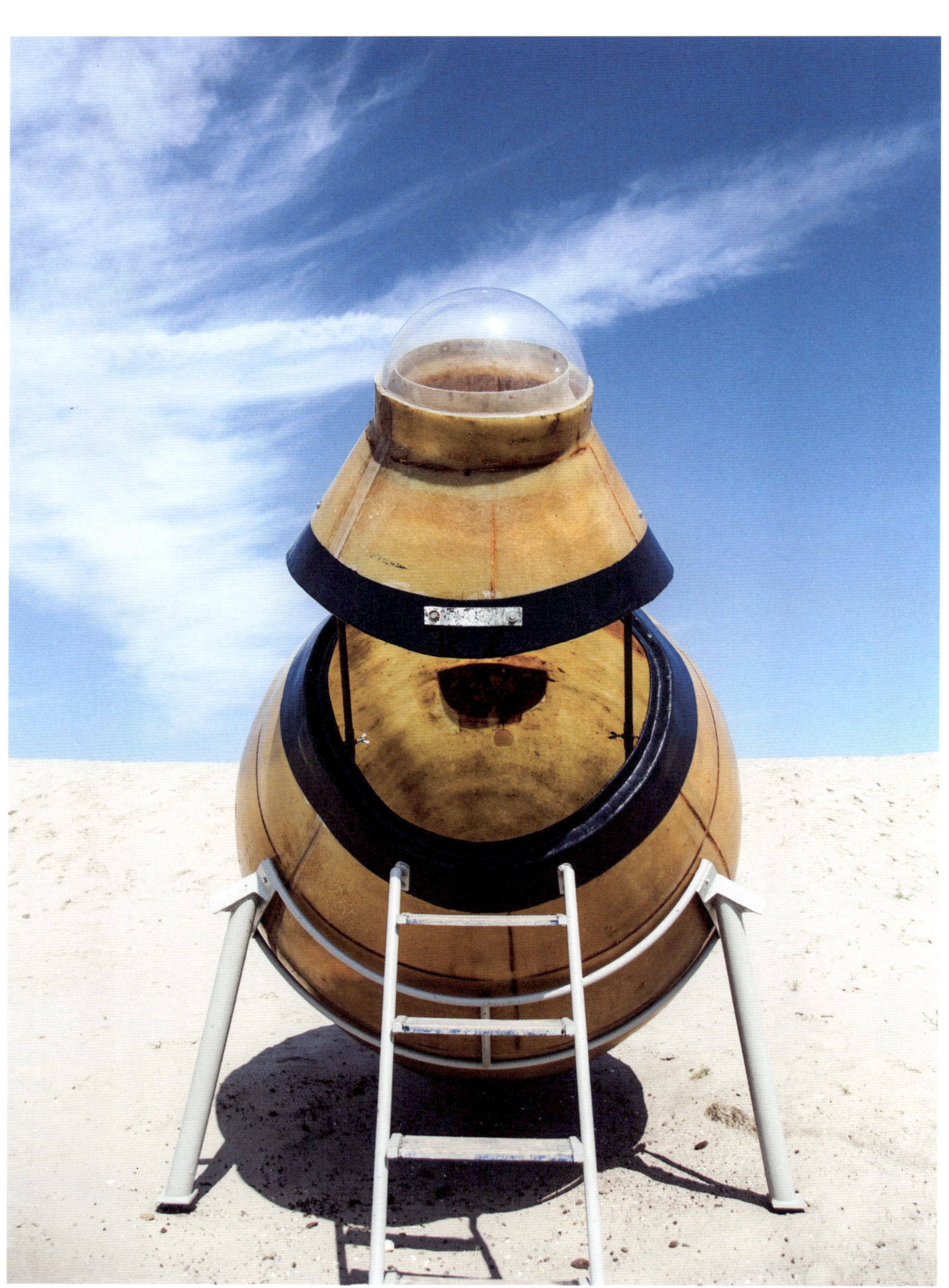

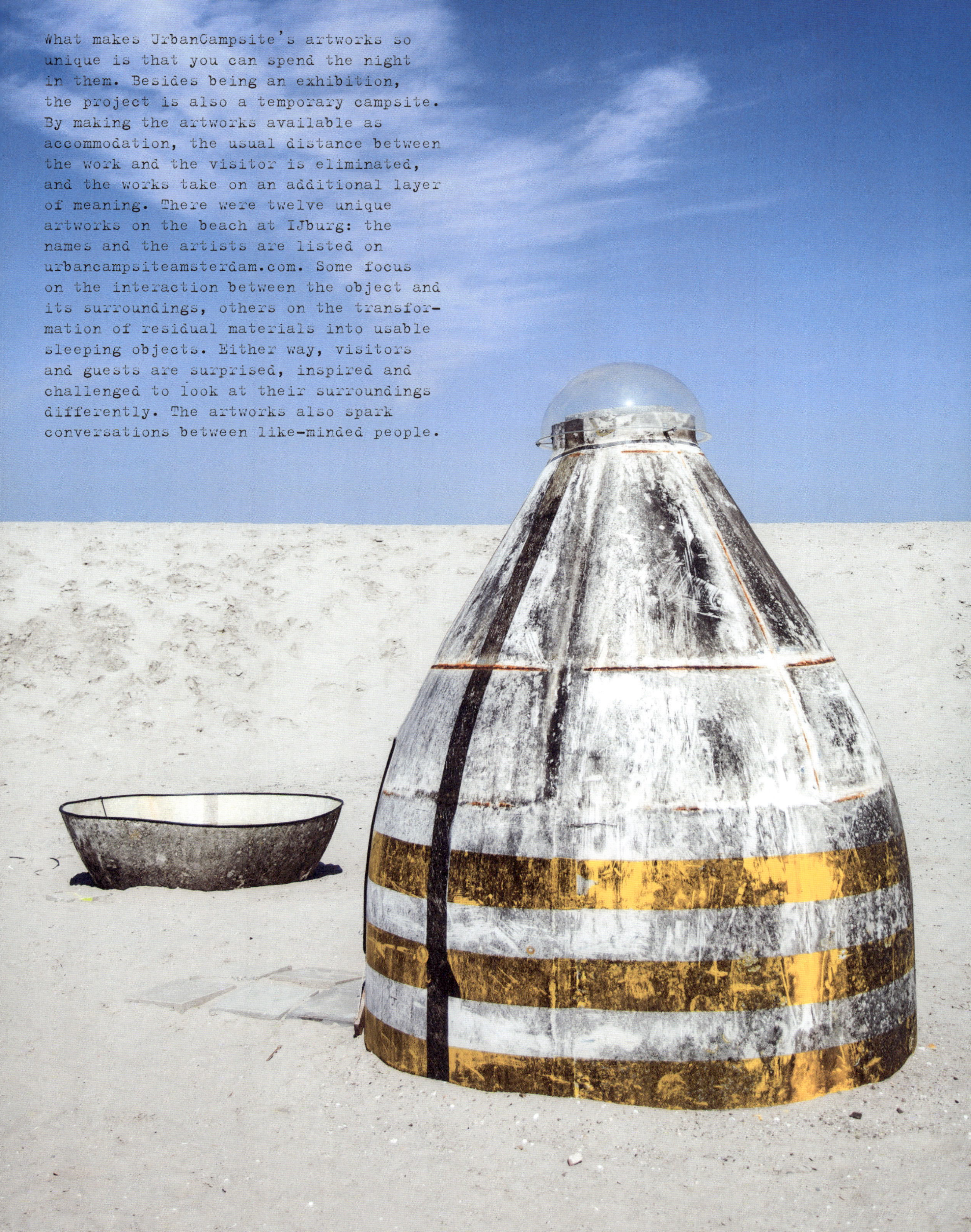

What makes UrbanCampsite's artworks so unique is that you can spend the night in them. Besides being an exhibition, the project is also a temporary campsite. By making the artworks available as accommodation, the usual distance between the work and the visitor is eliminated, and the works take on an additional layer of meaning. There were twelve unique artworks on the beach at IJburg: the names and the artists are listed on urbancampsiteamsterdam.com. Some focus on the interaction between the object and its surroundings, others on the transformation of residual materials into usable sleeping objects. Either way, visitors and guests are surprised, inspired and challenged to look at their surroundings differently. The artworks also spark conversations between like-minded people.

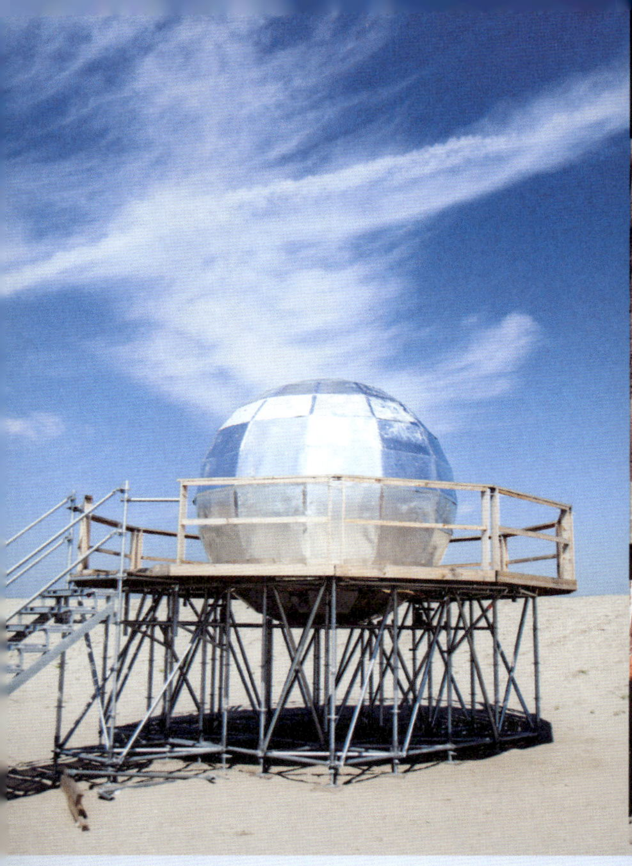

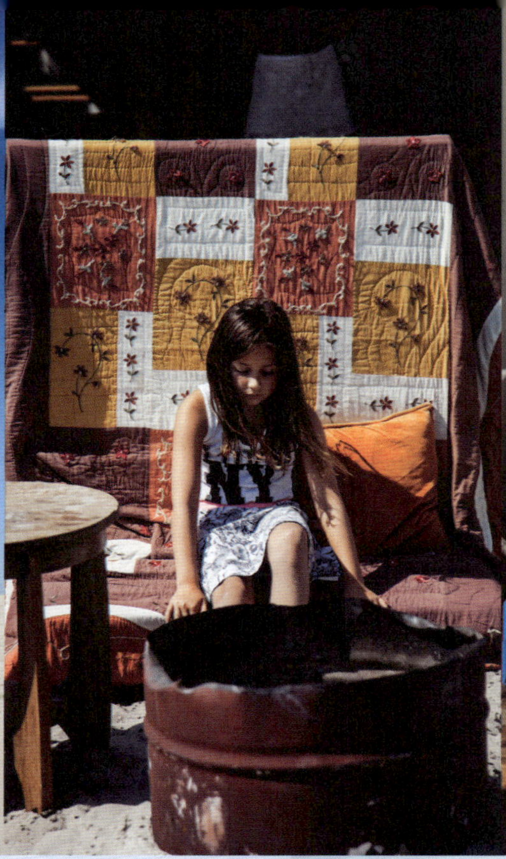

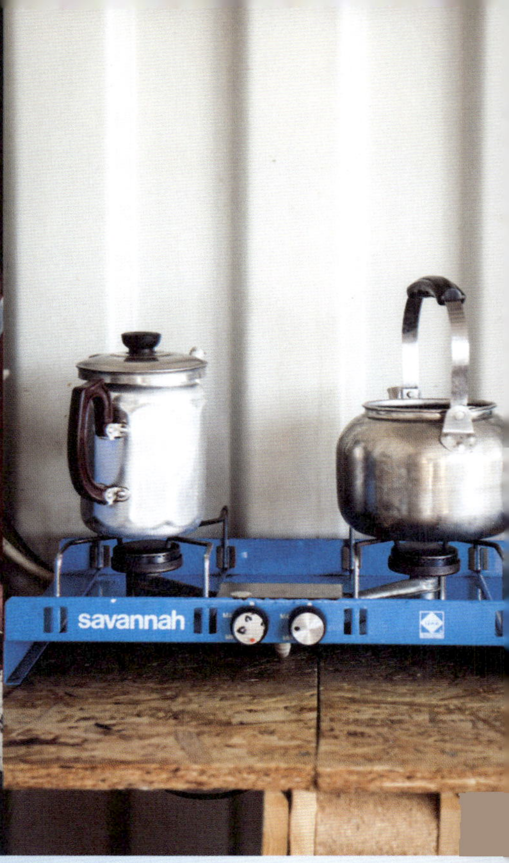

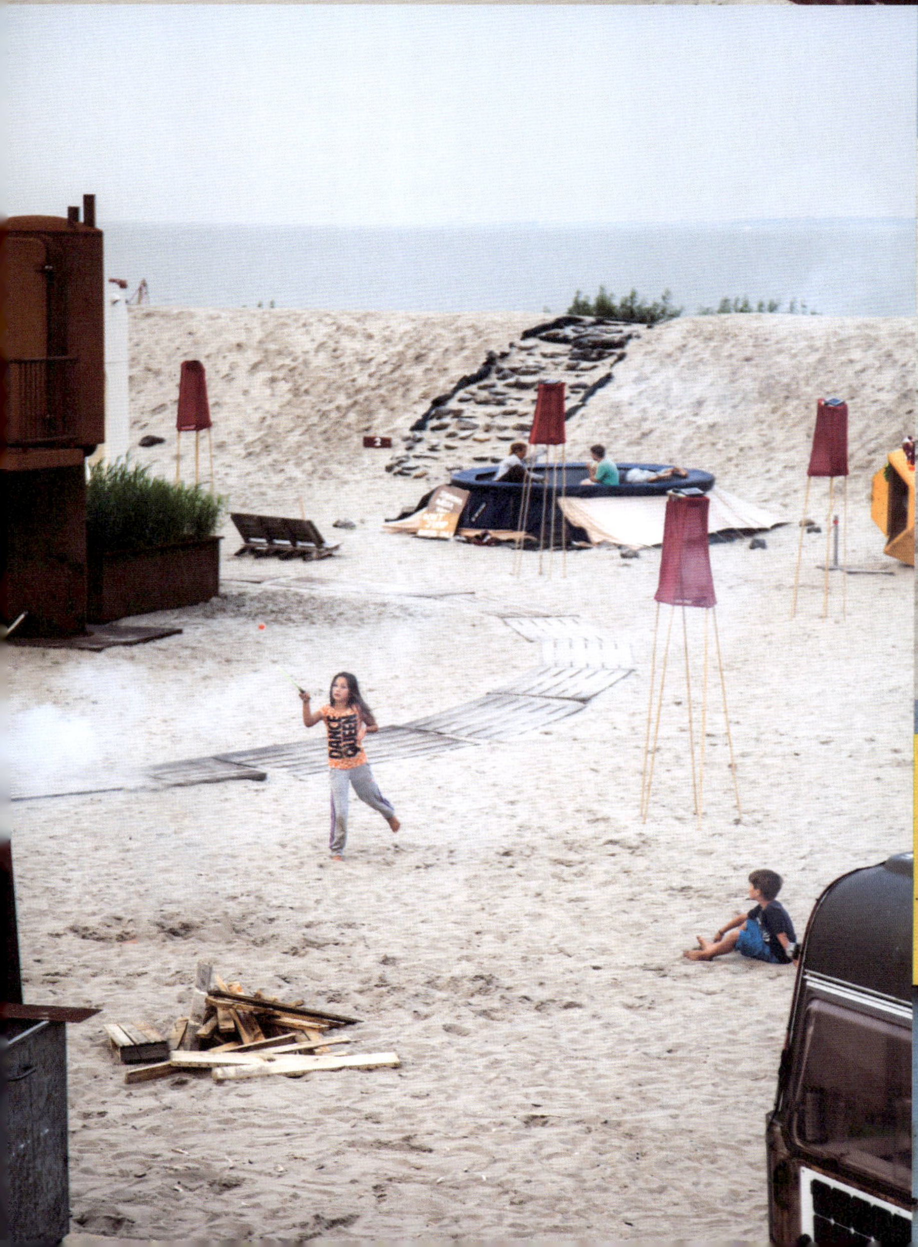

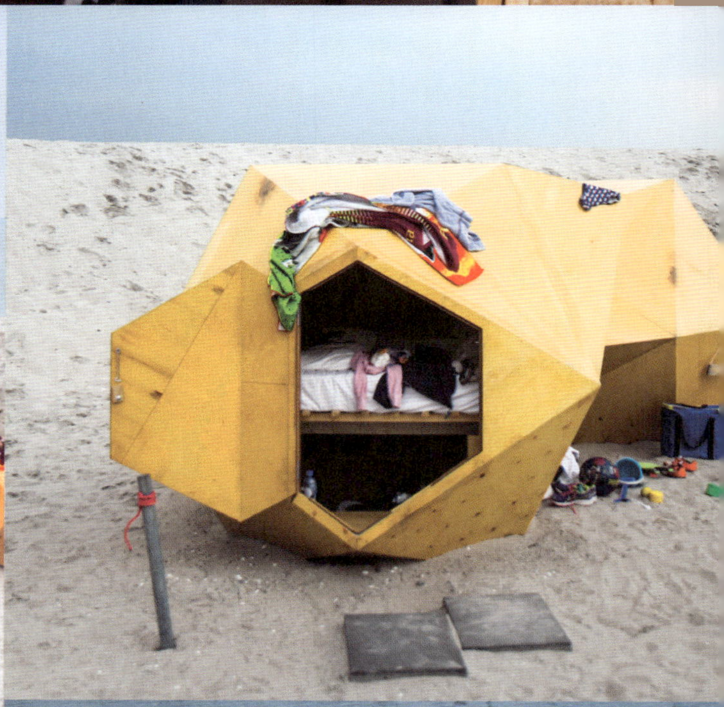

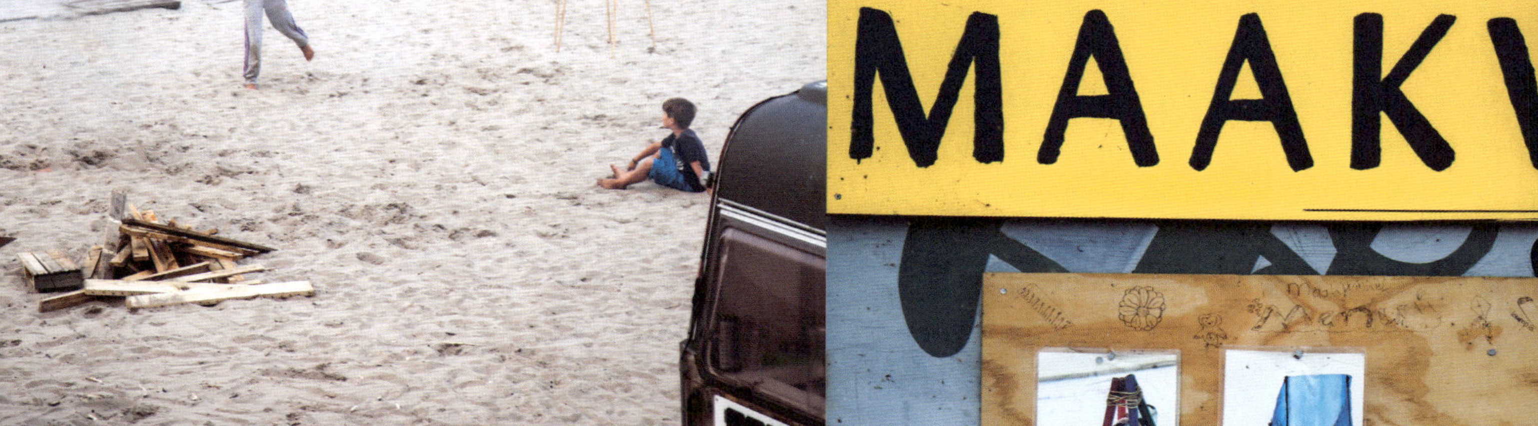
MAAK

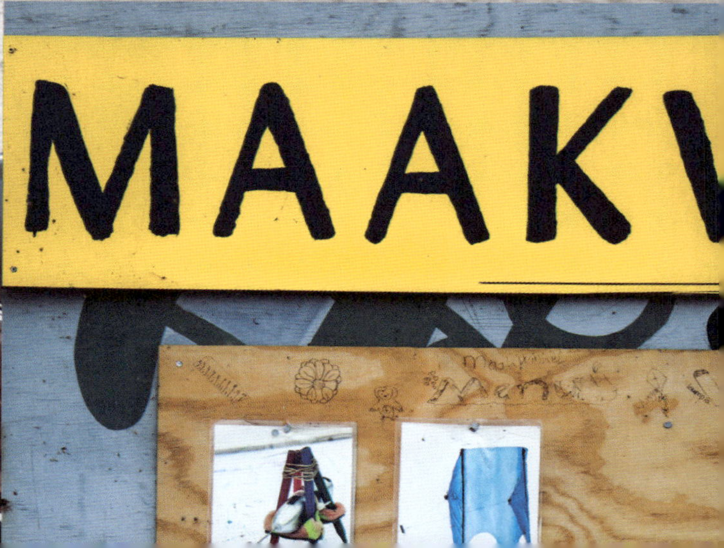

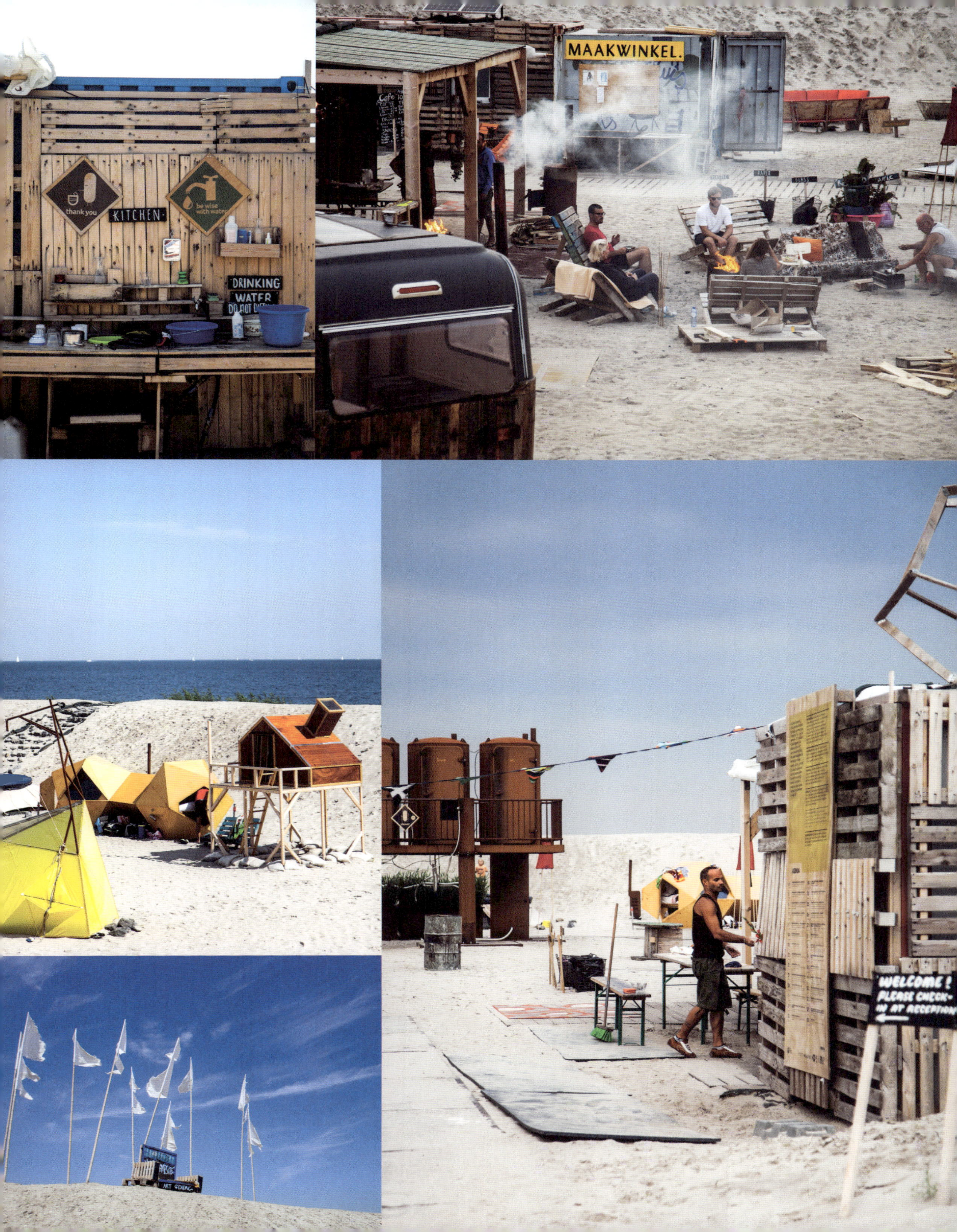

thank you
KITCHEN
be wise with water
DRINKING
WATER
MAAKWINKEL.
WELCOME!
PLEASE CHECK-
IN AT RECEPTION

The port of IJmuiden on the North Sea is a rugged industrial site with a vast complex of locks through which water from the North Sea Canal is ferried to the sea. In the generally very tidy Netherlands, this place feels like an anomaly. The dunes of IJmuiden are home to the bunkers of the Atlantikwall, and its beaches and quays are used by fishermen, sailors, and port workers. Here, living by the sea has all the raw beauty of yesteryear.

IJMUIDEN

Noord-Holland
The Netherlands

The port is a motley collection of buildings, which are used by industry and businesses. The sheds and factory workshops come in all kinds of styles and states of repair, with some houses scattered in between. Frank Visser has established his studio IJM in one of the waterfront buildings. A relatively narrow and very elongated construction, this former warehouse was used to fully unroll ship ropes for drying or repairs. Frank has the top two floors. Before his arrival, the building had stood empty for years. There was nothing there at all: no electricity, no running water, no toilet or kitchen even.

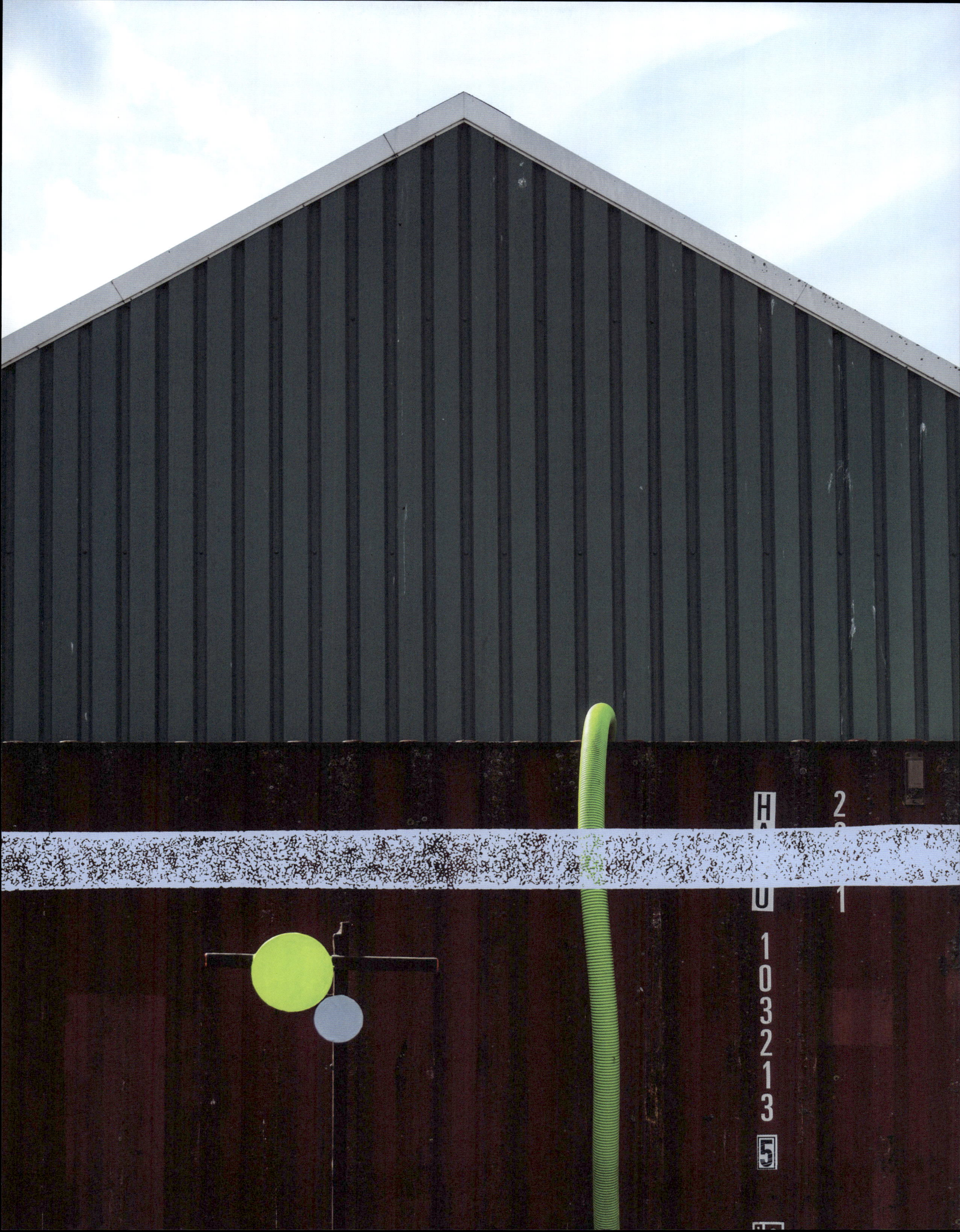
103213
5

Adding life and atmosphere to the abandoned harbour house proved quite challenging. But Frank saw lots of potential in the wooden floors, rough walls and ceilings with a hundred overhead beams. It was the way the light fell in that cinched the deal, however: the light is different in every part of the studio, surprising you every time and everywhere you look. This is mainly due to the house's proximity to the sea: when you are that close to the water, the colours and light seem much more vibrant, depending on the season and weather. Besides the light, the sounds you hear in and around the studio are also typical of the sea. Not the waves, but the screeching of the seagulls or the horn of the ferry that reminds you every day that it is five o'clock and it is ready for departure.

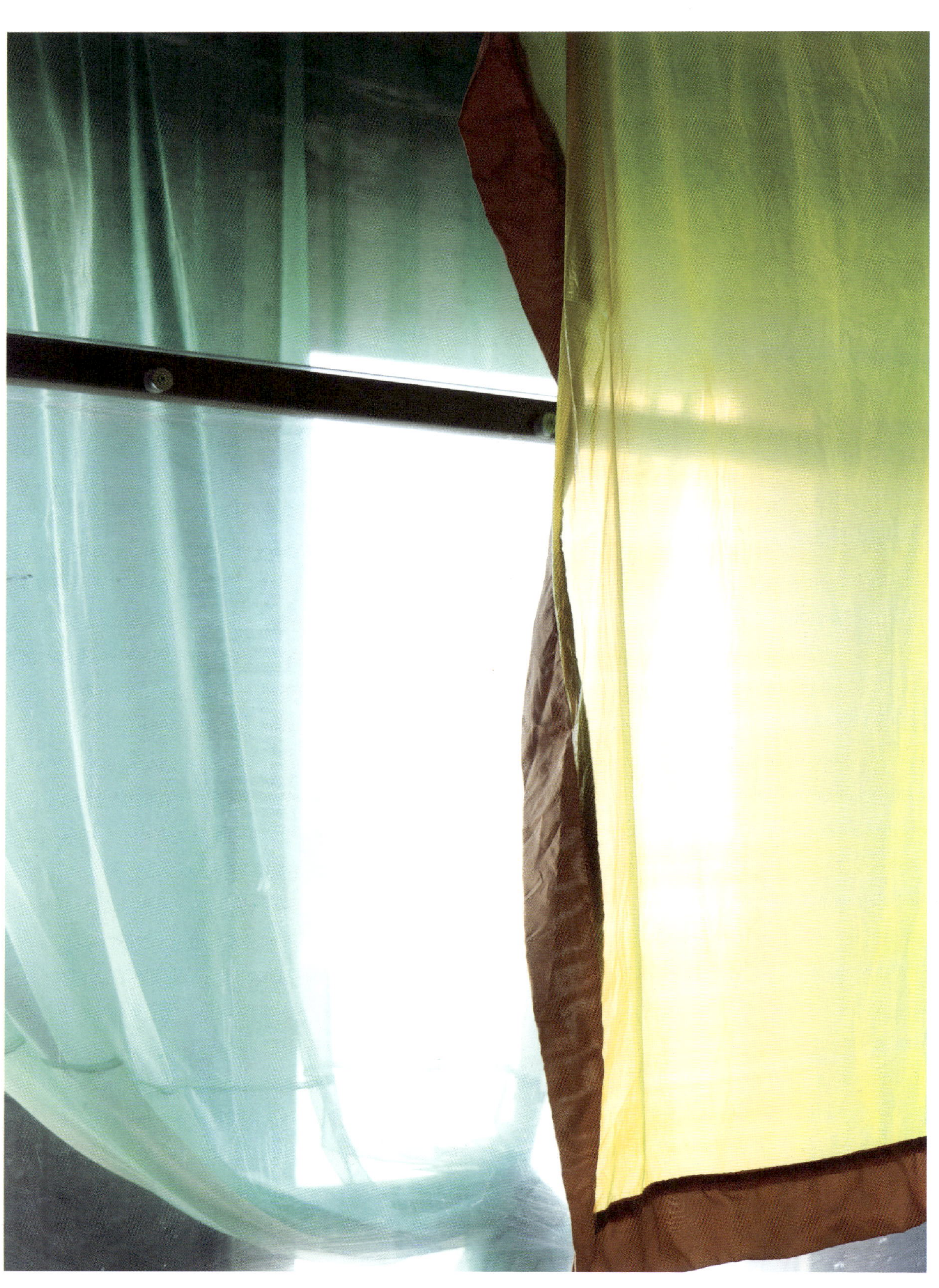

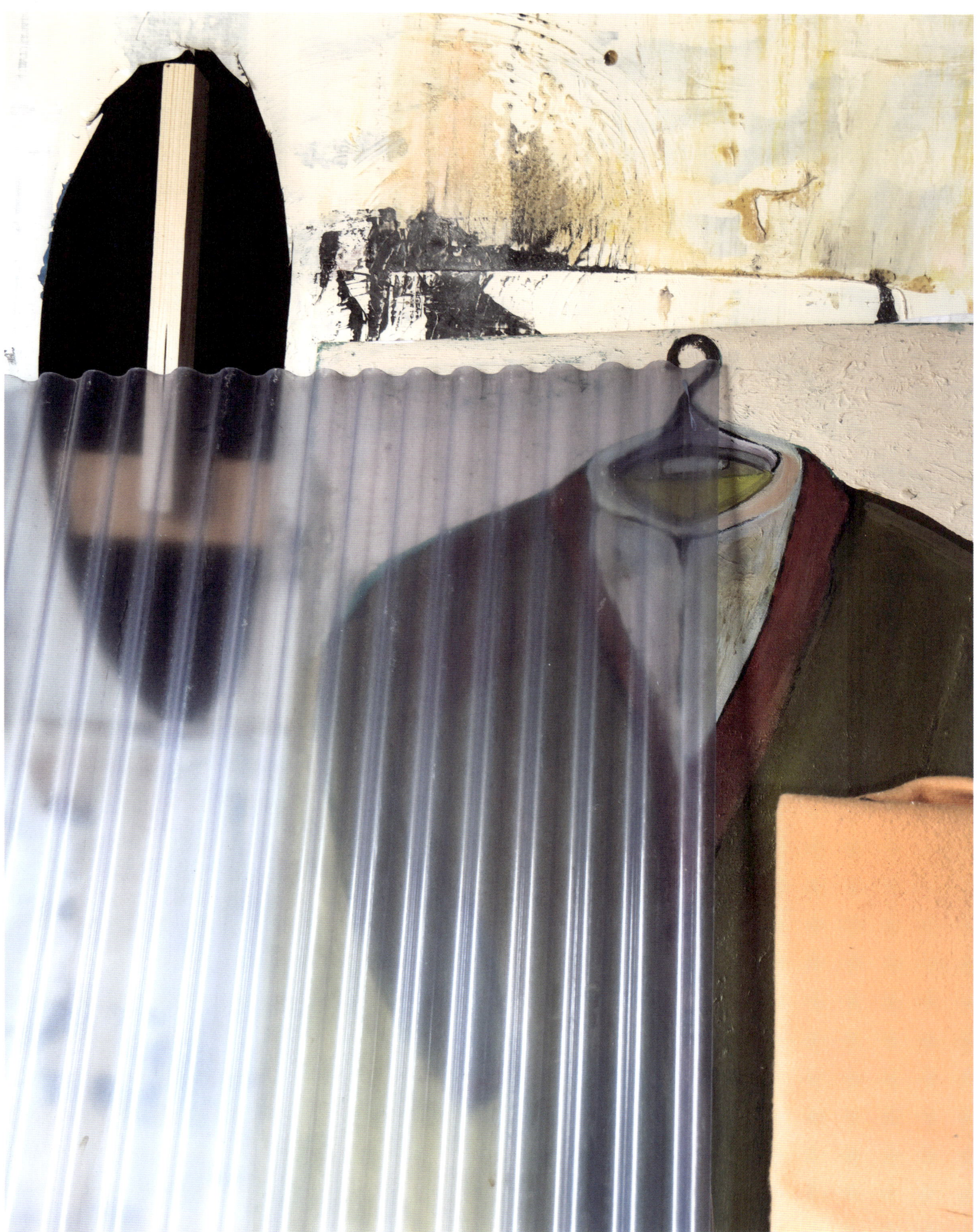

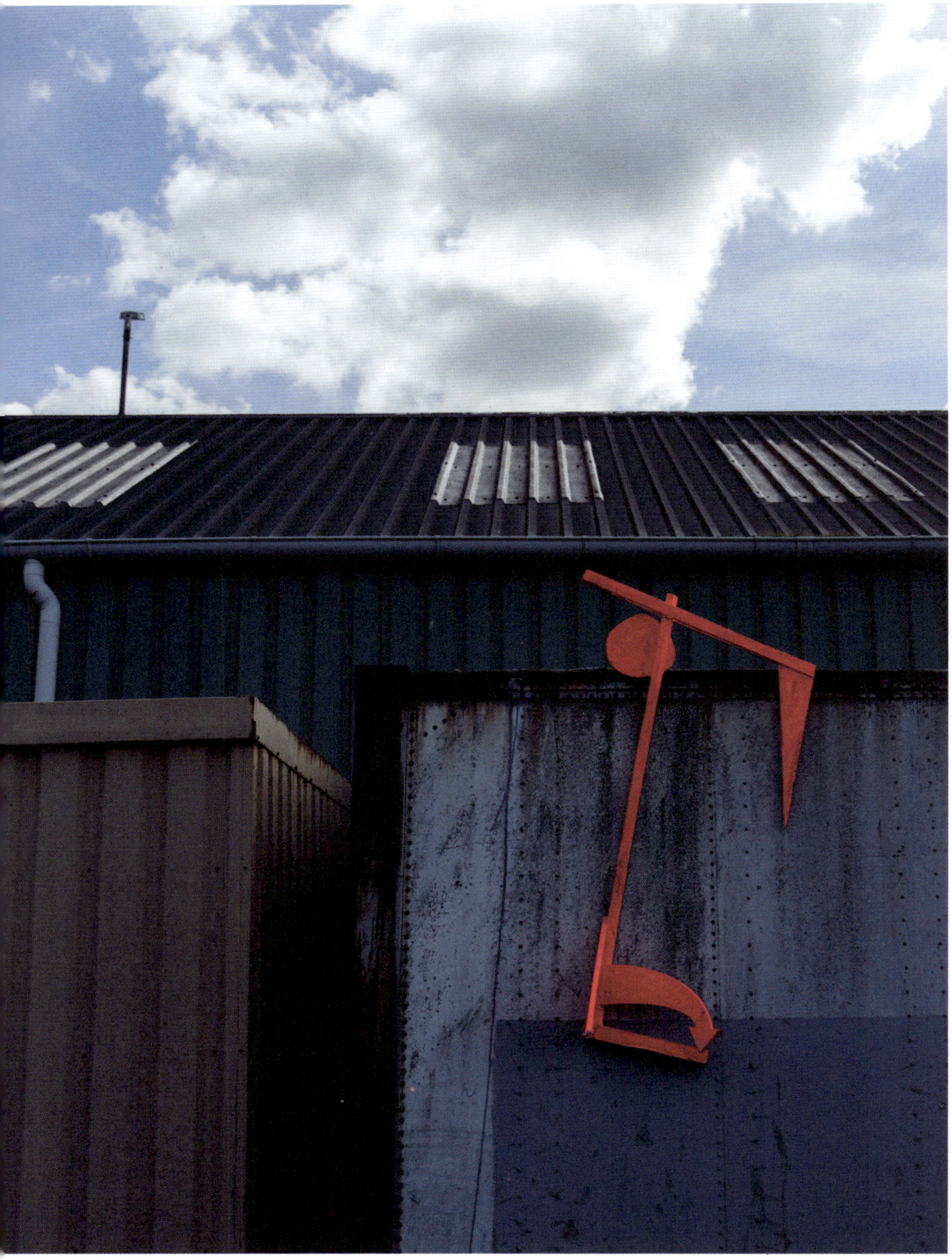

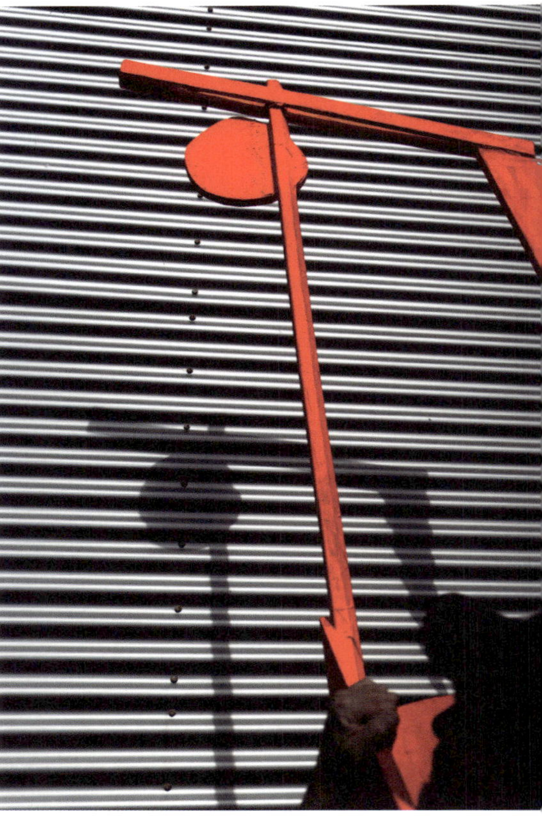

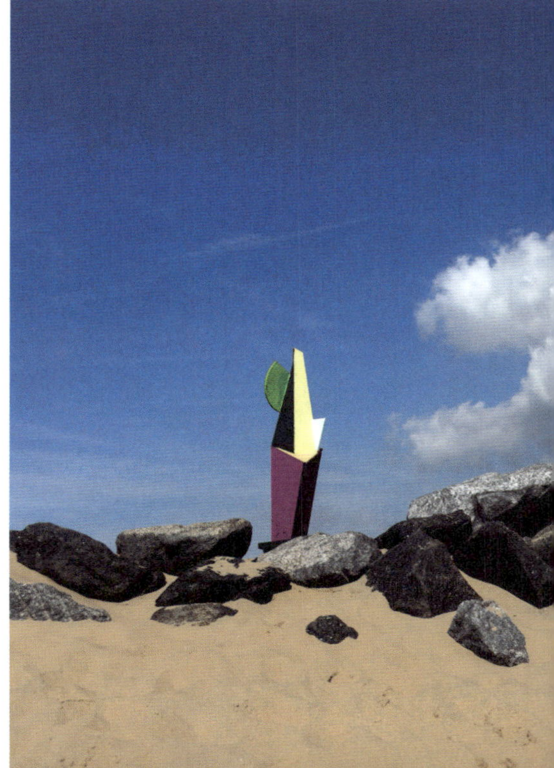

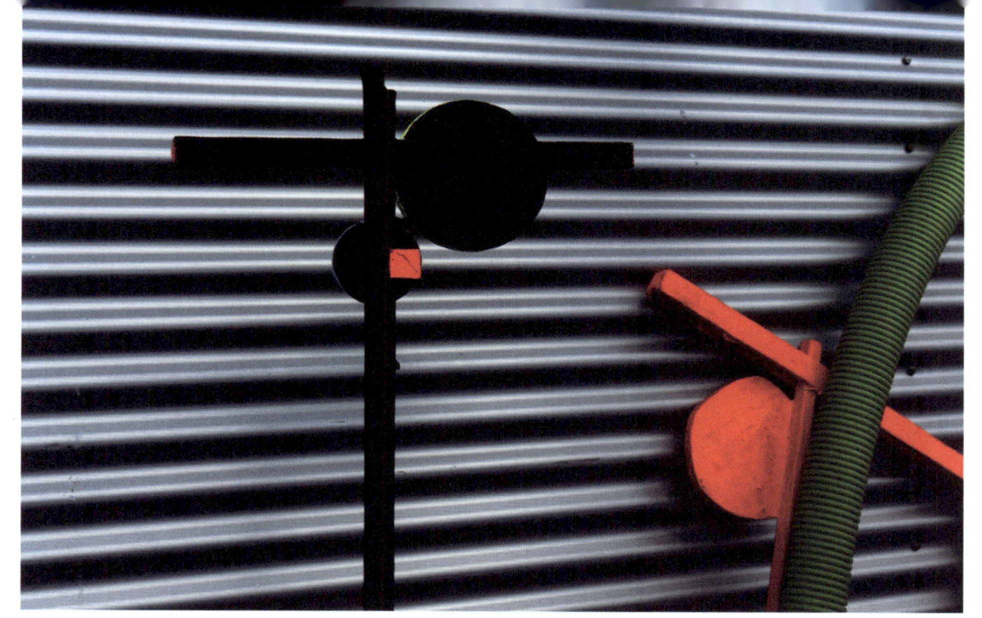

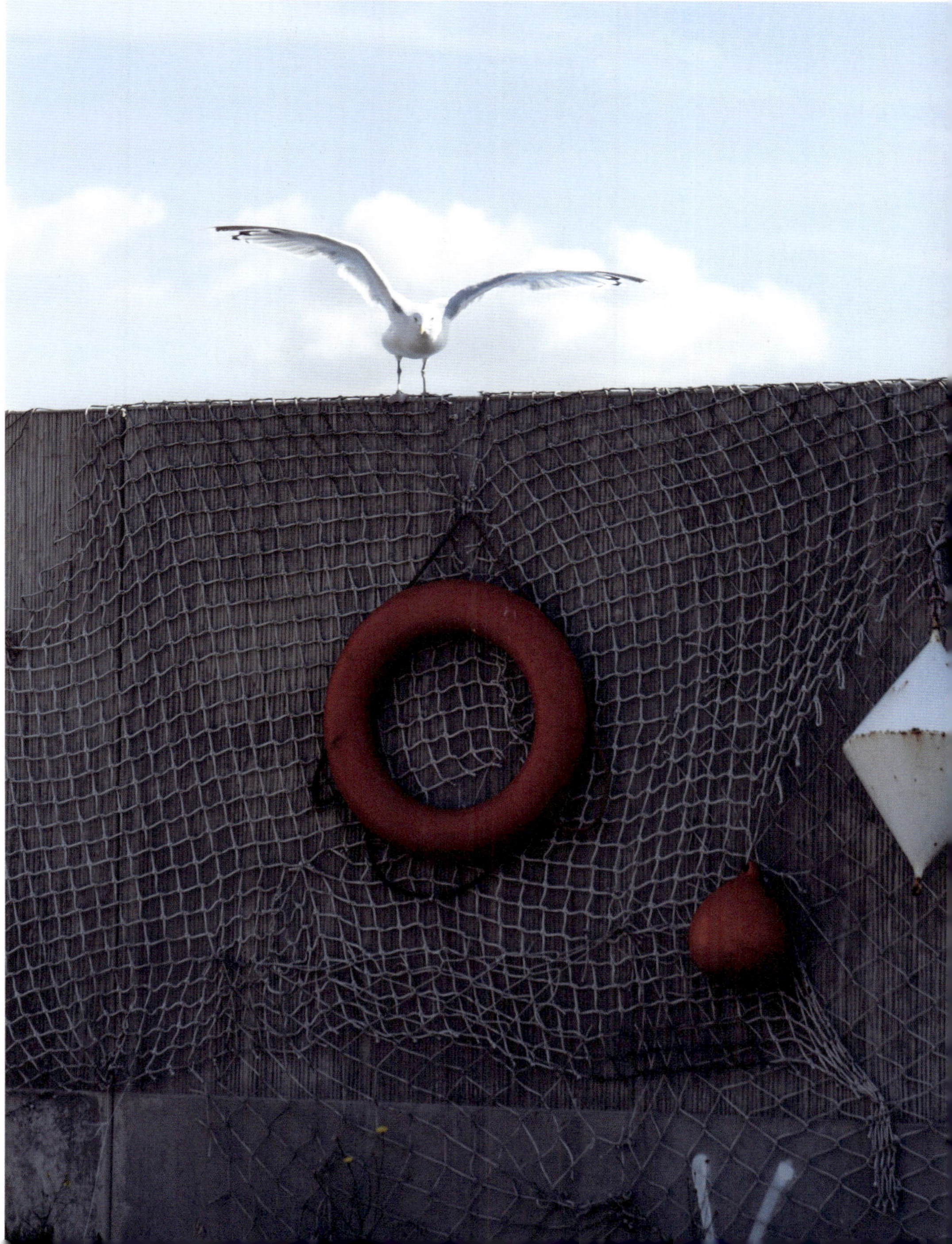

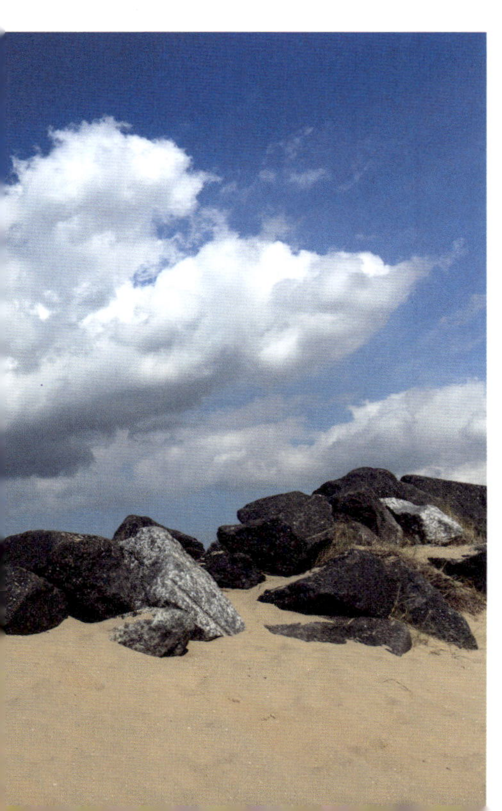

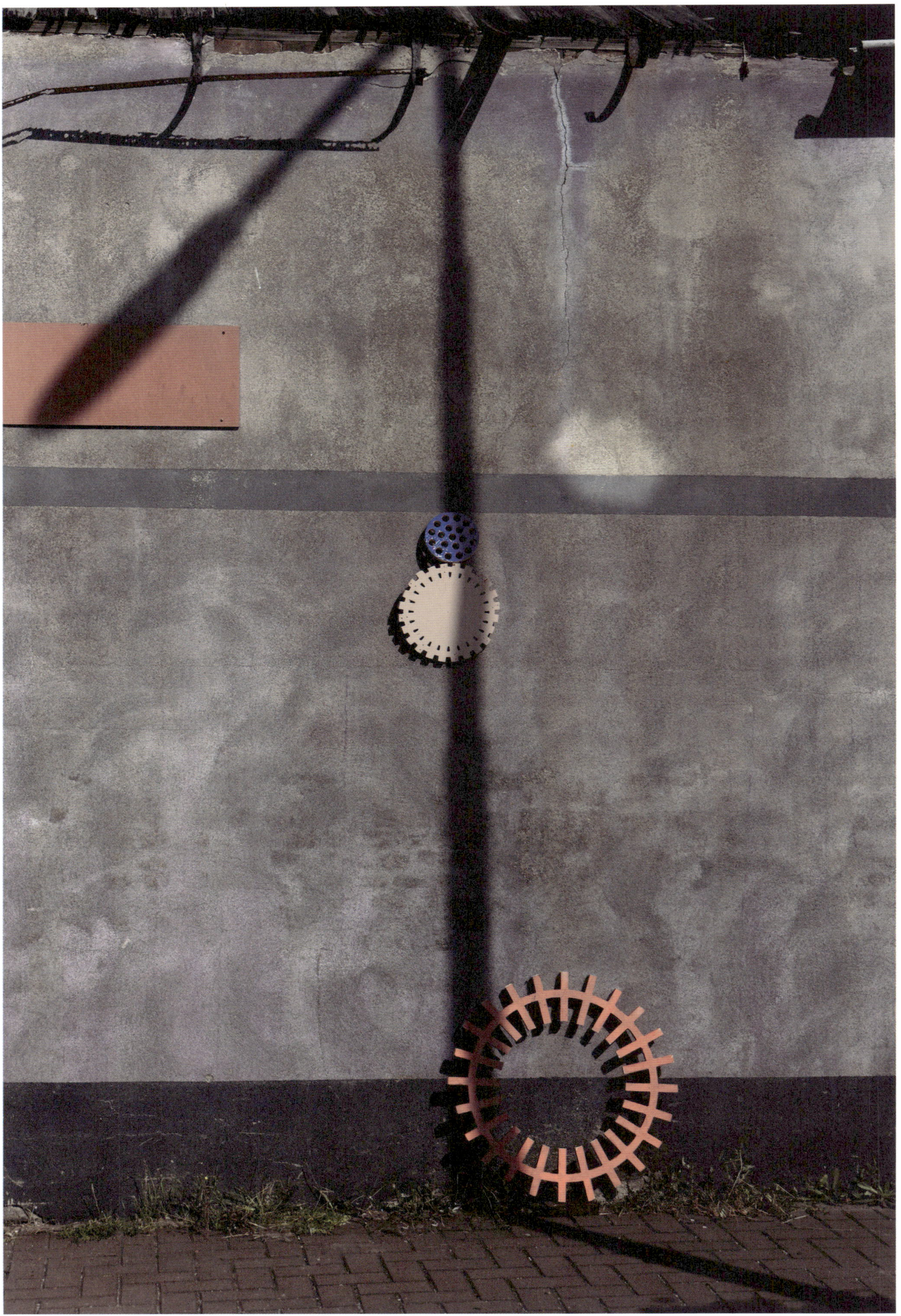

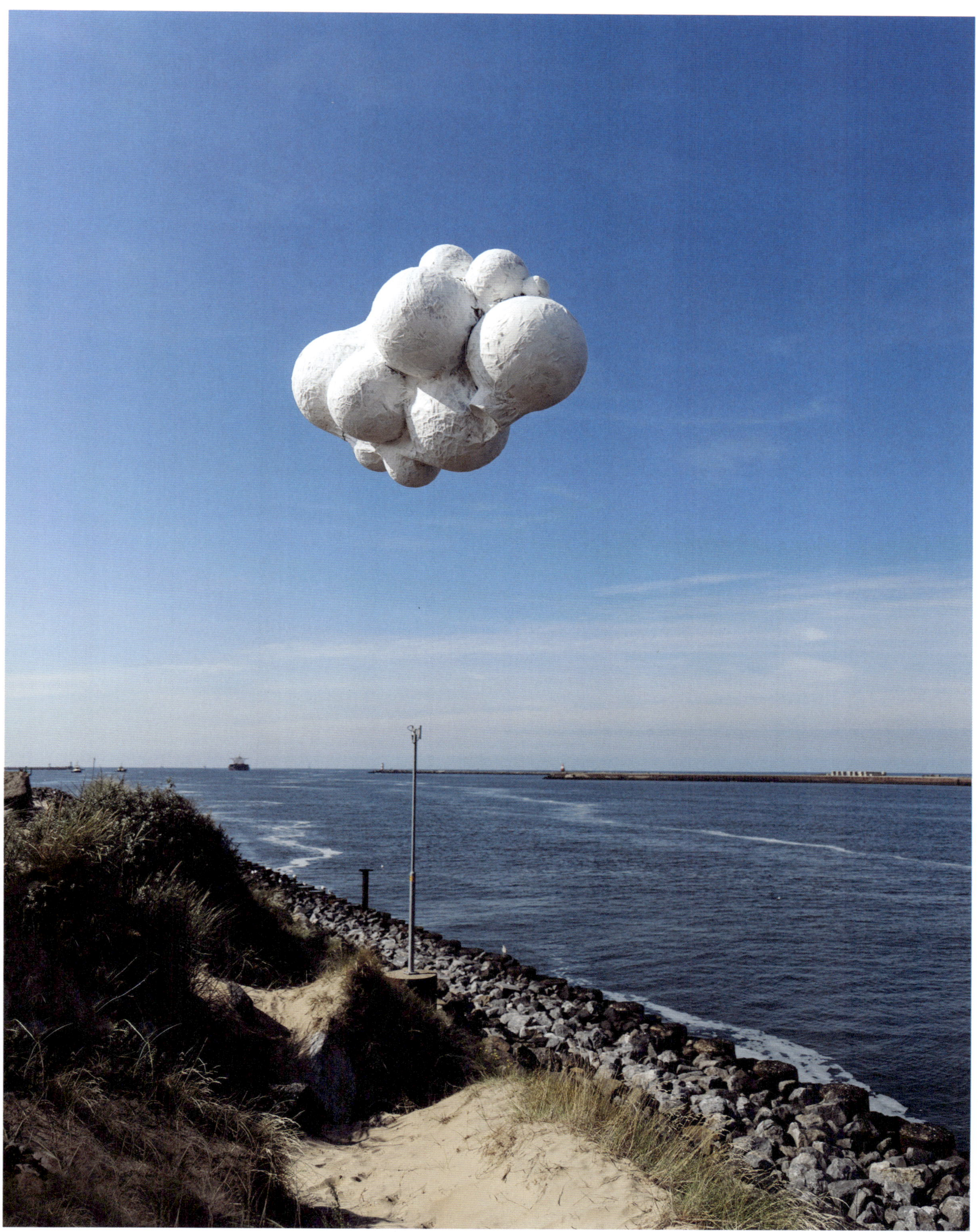

It took some getting used to at first, but now Frank feels that all the time he can spend in his studio in IJmuiden in such close proximity to the sea fills him with joy. As he drives onto the quay in the early morning light, the fishermen's cutters are at their moorings. You can just make out the large ferry that has just arrived from Newcastle as it enters the port. On warmer days, the big doors of the warehouse are invariably open, filling the studio with light and drawing in the sounds of the port even more than usual. Frank mostly works in his studio during the day, having lunch there with his team. But more often than not, he also likes to linger, sometimes working late into the evening. He had a kitchen put in so he can cook and eat with a view of the port at dusk.

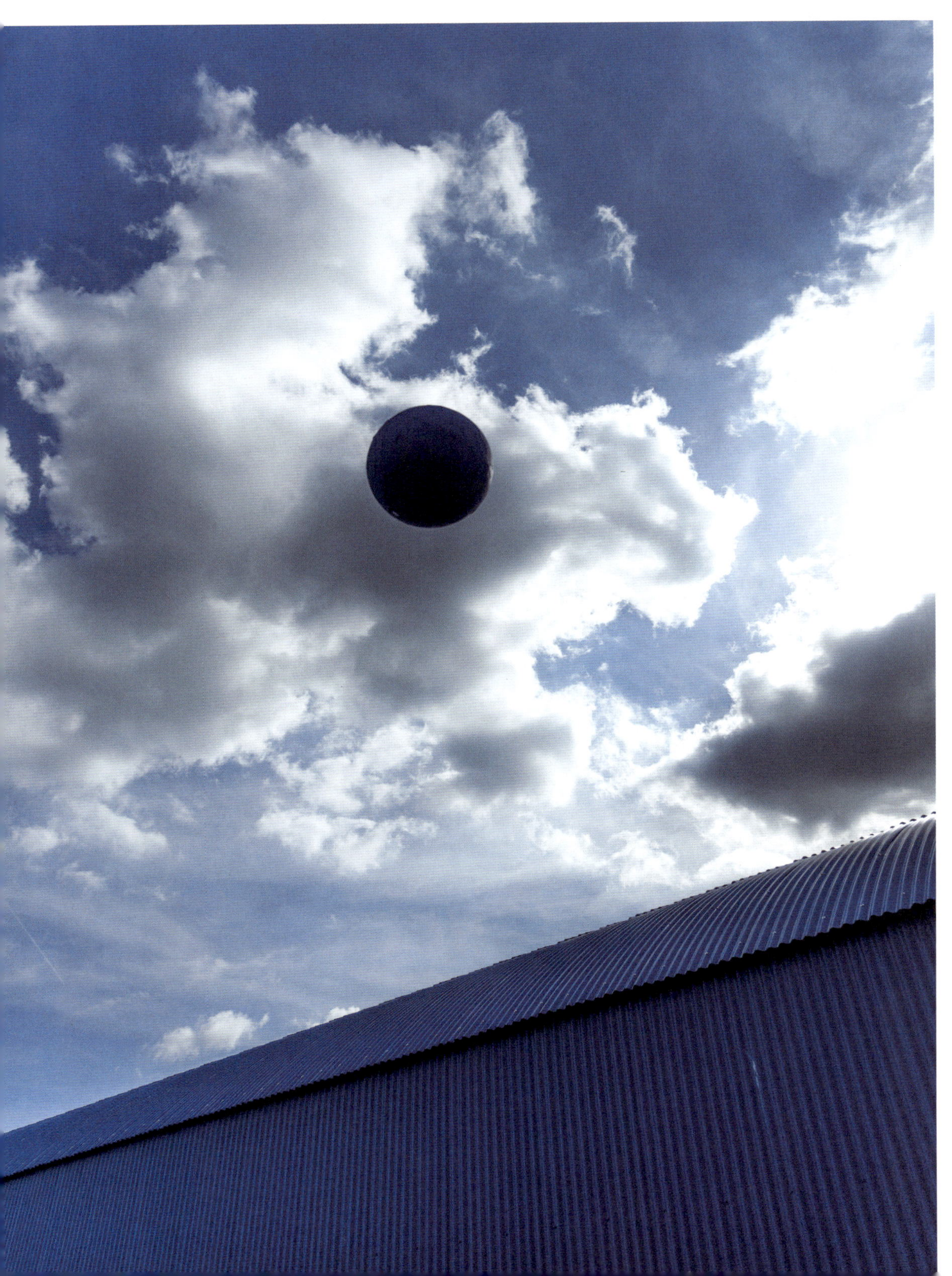

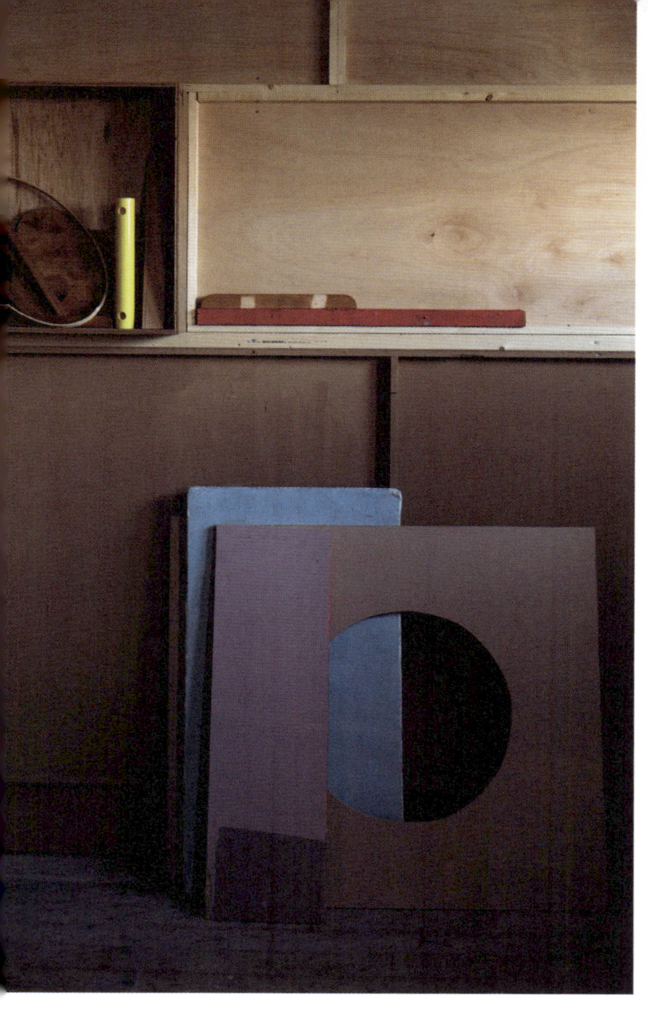

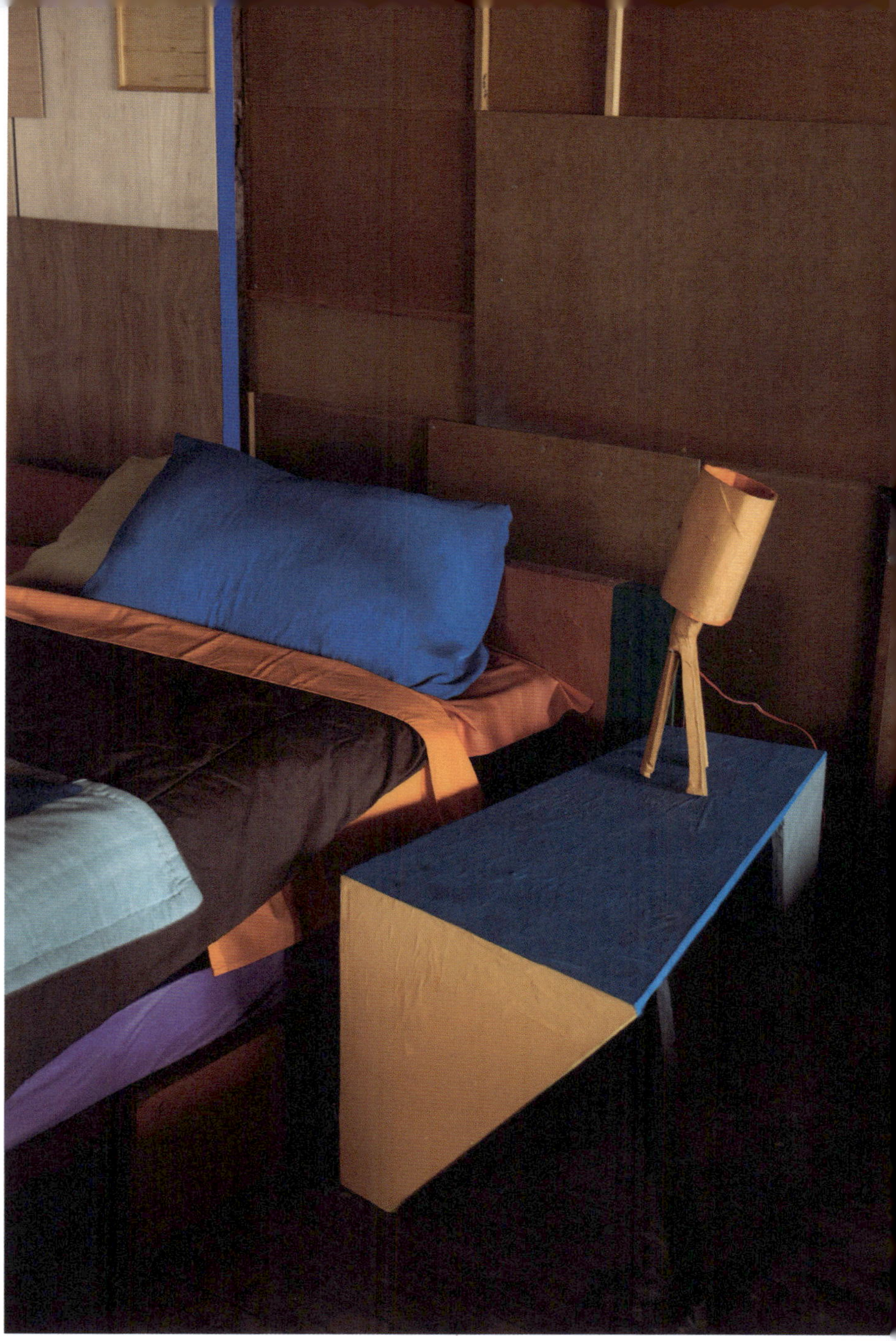

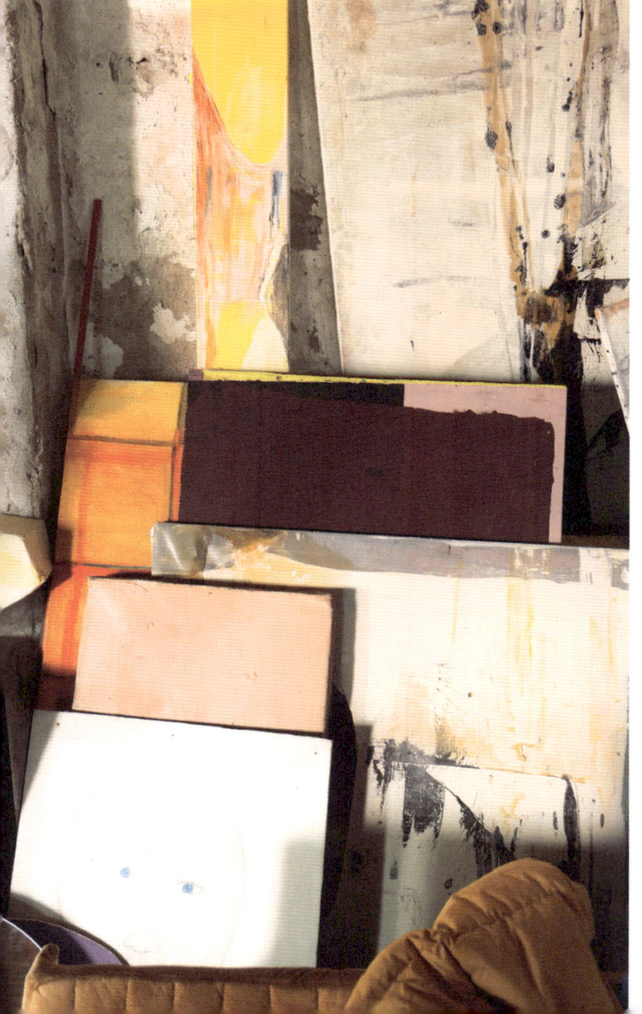

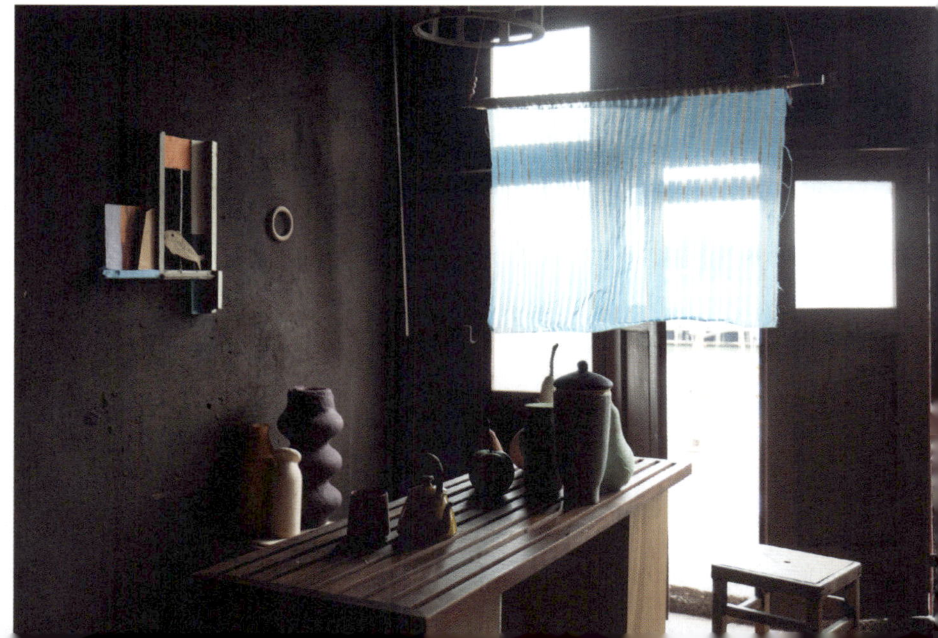

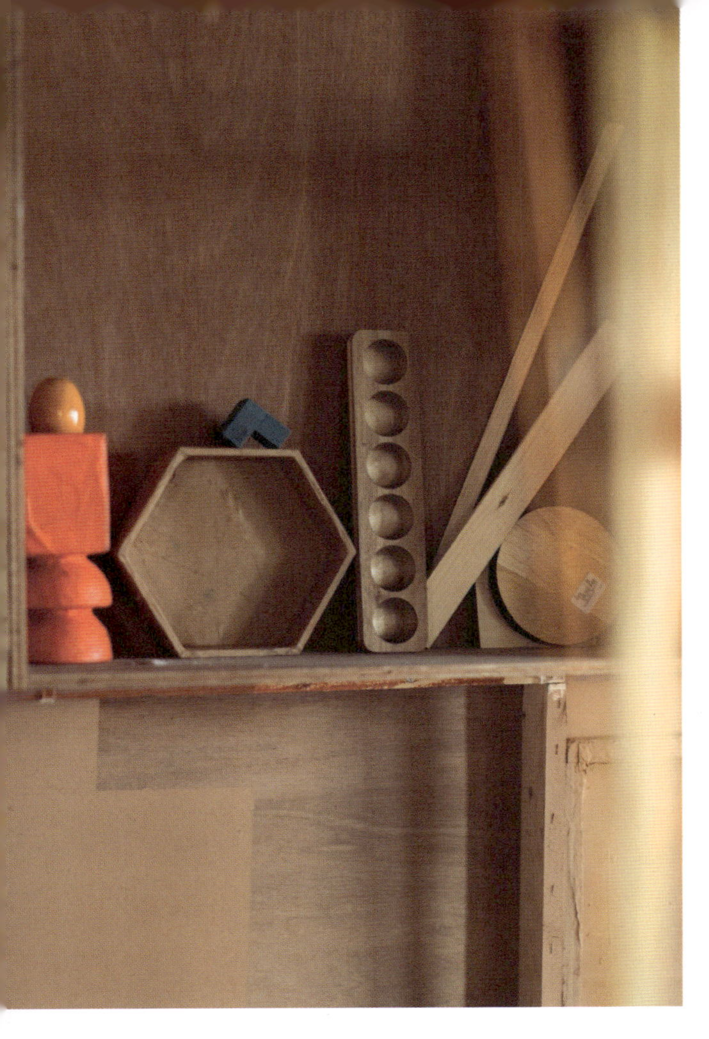
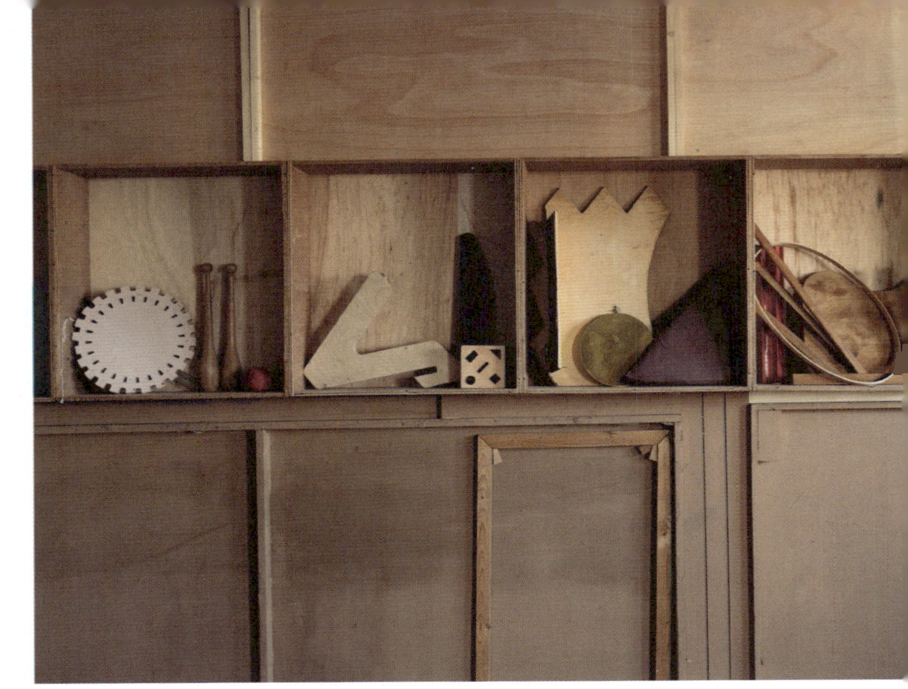
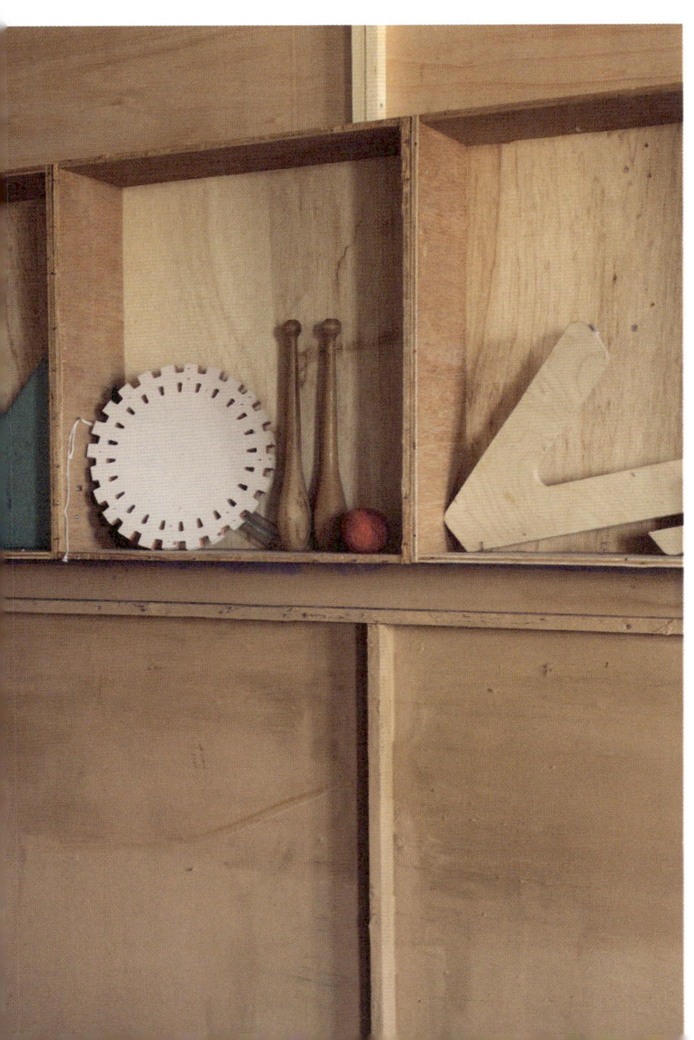
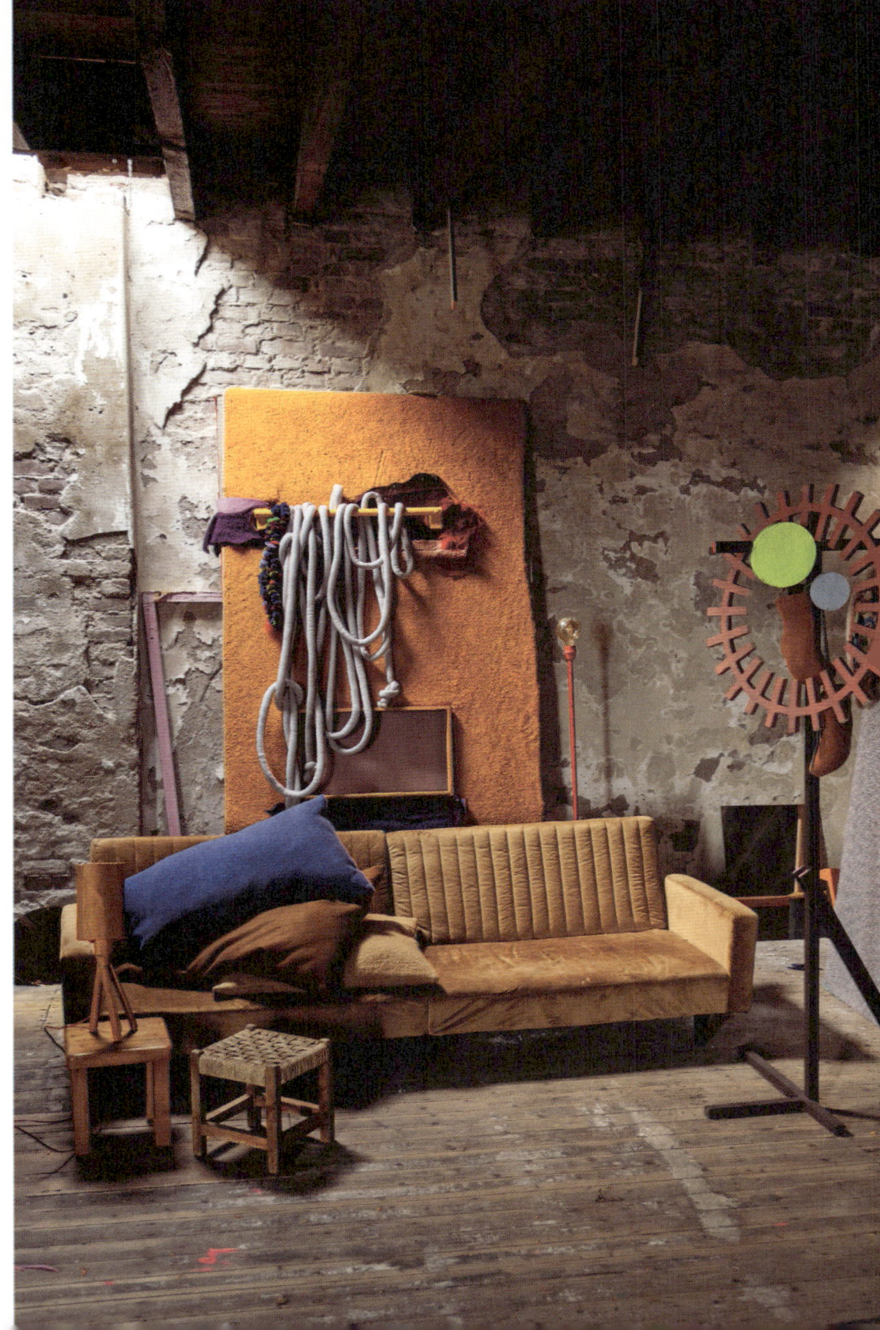

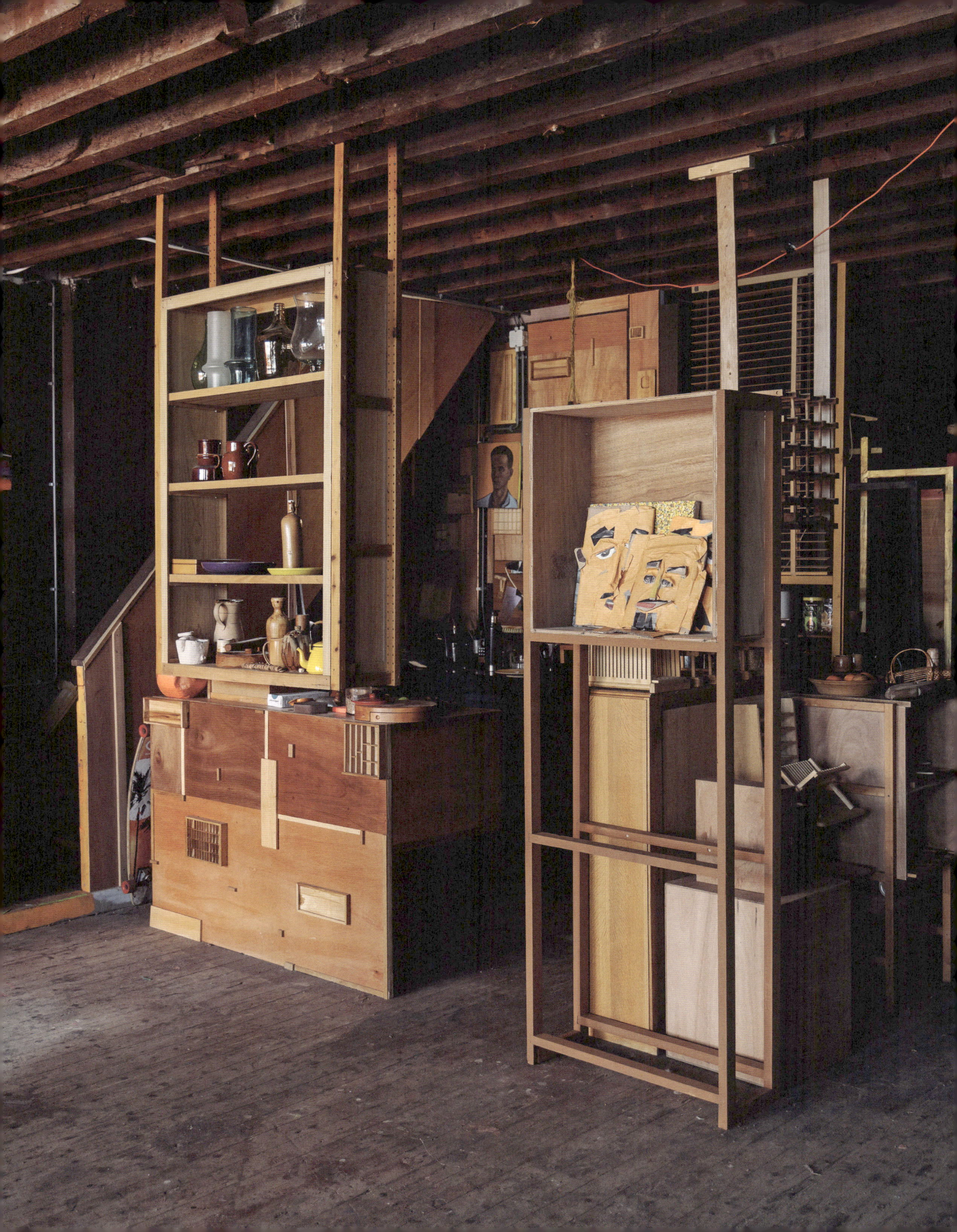

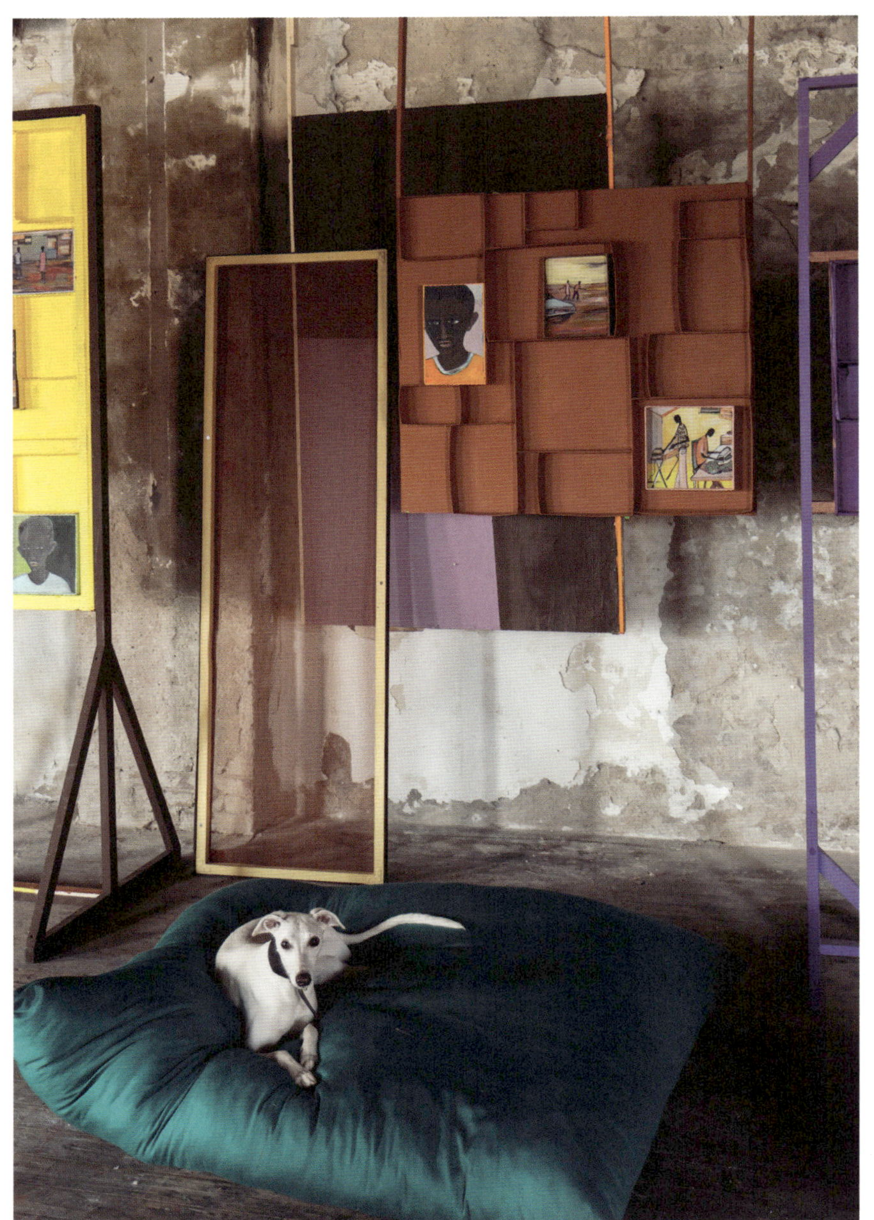

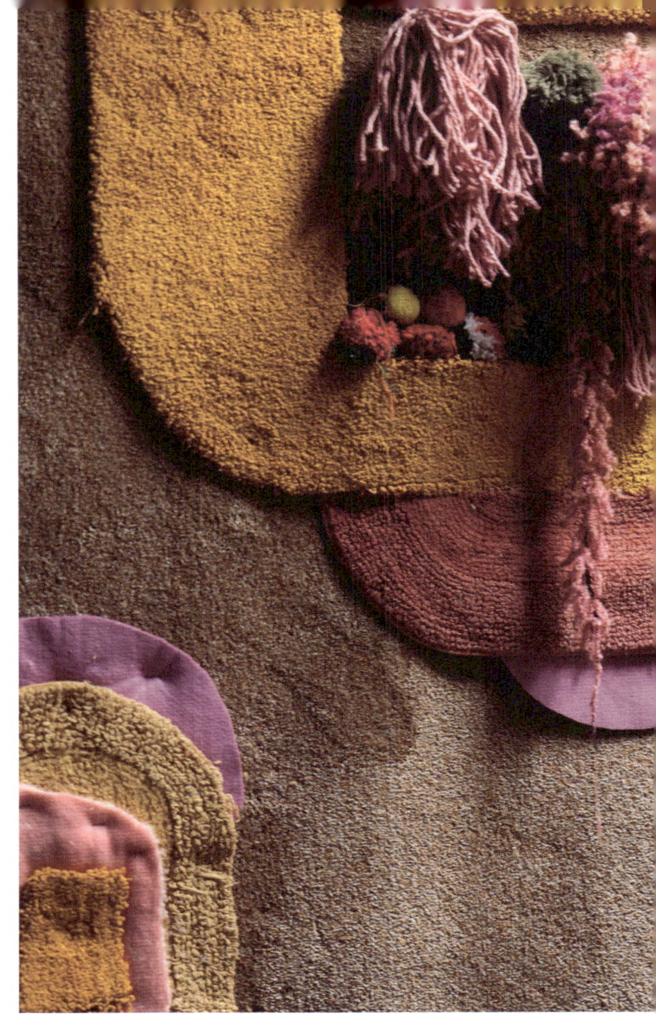

The unpolished port of IJmuiden is a source of inspiration for Frank. He continuously discovers new beautiful places among the many sheds and warehouses. And some places invite you to add something of your own. Frank likes to toss some objects from his studio into his car, setting off with his team to create structures or artful interventions. On the pier, they threw a big cloud into the air, a little like a goodbye and farewell and an ode to the vastness of the sea and the possibilities that await beyond the horizon.

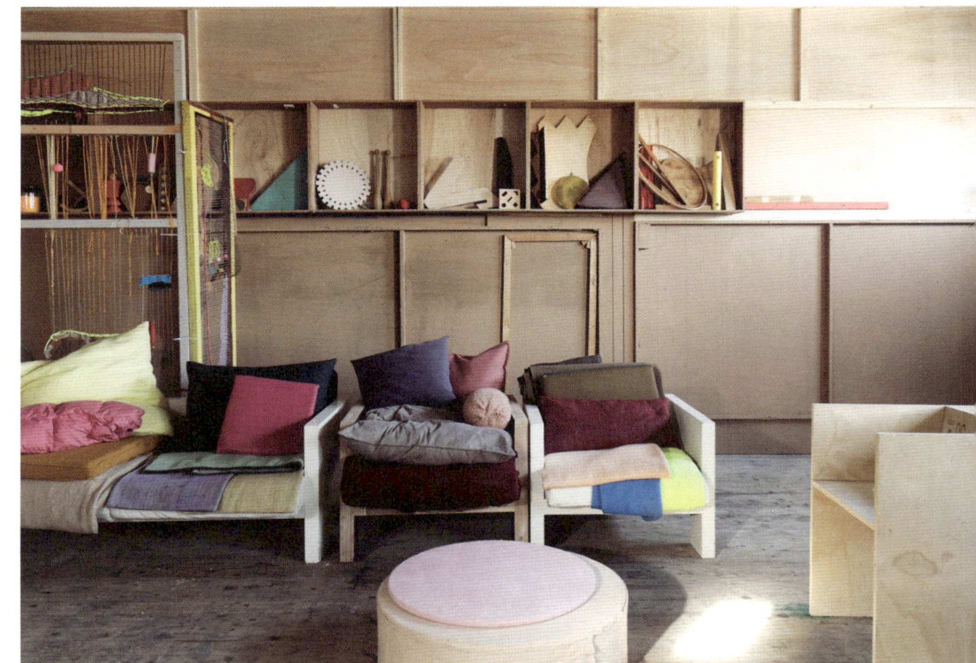

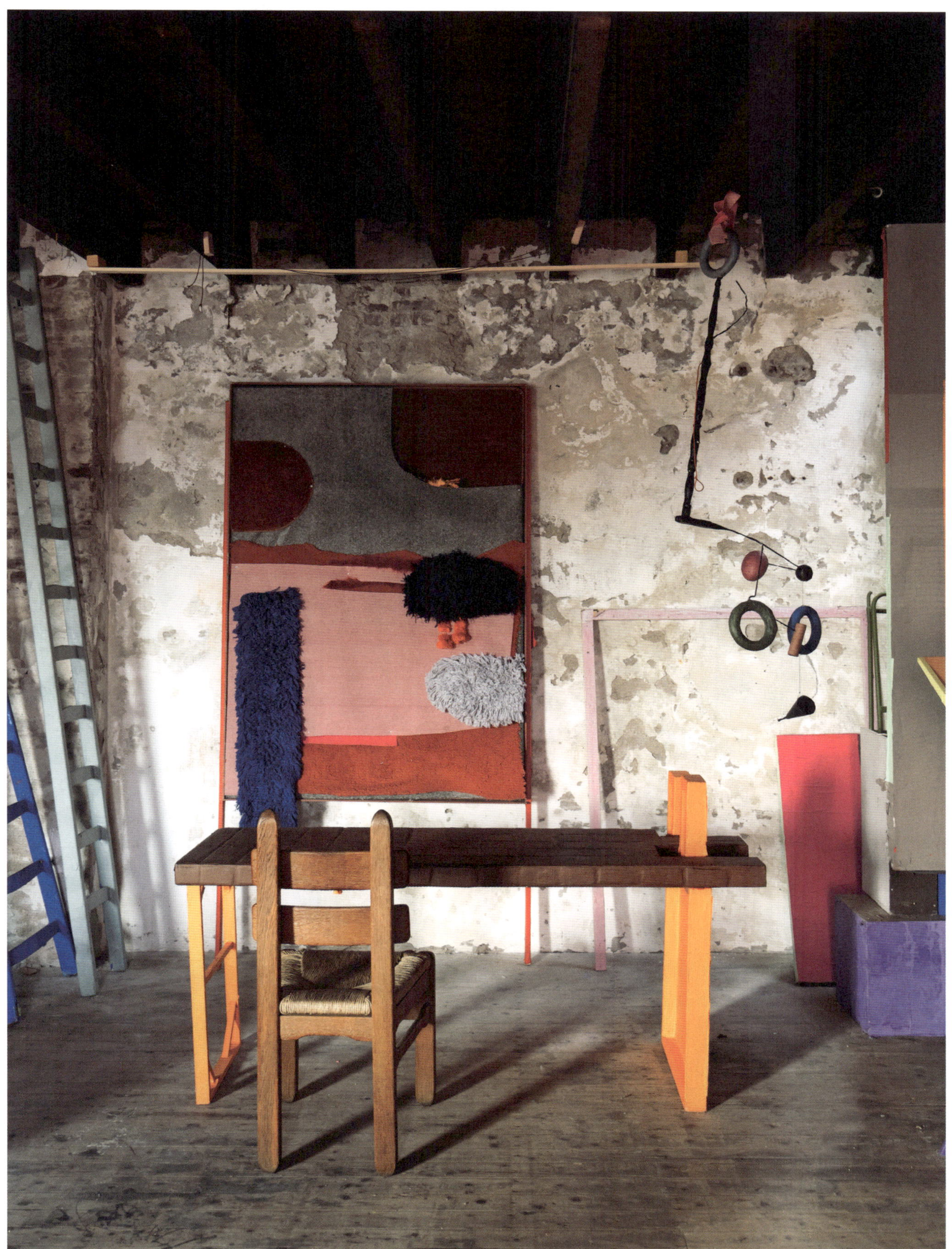

THANK YOU
We are deeply grateful to everyone who welcomed us into their homes for this book. Coordinating our itinerary with your schedules was sometimes a challenge, but we're so glad it always worked out. On a few occasions, we were even lucky enough to stay for a few days, which was a real privilege. Thank you for your hospitality, flexibility, and trust, as well as for the enthusiasm you showed from the moment we asked to photograph your home. We are very happy with the outcome and hope you are as well.

Special thanks to Adam who was such a big help with the 'dancing' sheets and the big kites in Ibiza.

Mirjam and Frank

BY THE SEA
Inspiring coastal houses and refuges

Photography
Mirjam Bleeker

Styling & Artwork
Frank Visser

Production
Mirjam Bleeker & Frank Visser

Graphic Design
Madeleine Wermenbol

Words
Hadewijch Ceulemans & Frank Visser

Translation & Editing
Sandy Logan

D/2024/12.005/17
ISBN 9789460583698
NUR 450, 454

www.lusterpublishing.com
info@lusterpublishing.com
@lusterbooks